small arms survey 2004

rights at risk

A Project
of the Graduate Institute
of International Studies,
Geneva

OXFORD
UNIVERSITY PRESS

Great Clarendon Street, Oxford OX2 6DP

Oxford University Press is a department of the University of Oxford.
It furthers the University's objective of excellence in research, scholarship,
and education by publishing worldwide in

Oxford New York

Auckland Bangkok Buenos Aires Cape Town Chennai
Dar es Salaam Delhi Hong Kong Istanbul Karachi Kolkata
Kuala Lumpur Madrid Melbourne Mexico City Mumbai Nairobi
São Paulo Shanghai Taipei Tokyo Toronto

Oxford is a registered trade mark of Oxford University Press
in the UK and in certain other countries

Published in the United States
by Oxford University Press Inc., New York

© Small Arms Survey, Graduate Institute of International Studies, Geneva 2004

The moral rights of the author have been asserted
Database right Oxford University Press (maker)

First published 2004

All rights reserved. No part of this publication may be reproduced,
stored in a retrieval system, or transmitted, in any form or by any means,
without the prior permission in writing of Oxford University Press,
or as expressly permitted by law, or under terms agreed with the appropriate
reprographics rights organization. Enquiries concerning reproduction
outside the scope of the above should be sent to the Rights Department,
Oxford University Press, at the address above

You must not circulate this book in any other binding or cover
and you must impose this same condition on any acquirer

British Library Cataloguing in Publication Data

Data available

Library of Congress Cataloguing-in-Publication Data

Data available

ISBN 0–19–927334–0

1 3 5 7 9 10 8 6 4 2

Typeset in Garamond Light
by Latitude
Printed in Great Britain
on acid-free paper
by Ashford Colour Press Limited
Gosport, Hamphire

FOREWORD

During my five years as United Nations High Commissioner for Human Rights, I spent much of my time meeting people who were terrorized by armed violence. In places such as the Balkans, Cambodia, Colombia, the Democratic Republic of Congo, and Sierra Leone, the proliferation of small arms threatens lives and puts fundamental human rights at risk.

The death and injury of millions of innocent civilians are not the only human rights consequences of small arms proliferation. In conflict-torn countries, governments dedicating limited resources to weapons of war are much less able to meet long-term commitments to education, health care, and housing—all of which constitute basic economic, social, and cultural rights.

The responsibility for controlling small arms proliferation and misuse lies with all exporting and importing countries. Yet many states are reluctant even to release their arms trade data, let alone confront the consequences of their transfers. This lack of transparency impedes a fuller understanding of the small arms trade.

An innovation in this year's *Small Arms Survey* is a new barometer designed to gauge national levels of arms trade transparency. This will prove a welcome tool for policy-makers and advocates who seek to monitor and confront non-compliant governments. As the Small Arms Trade Transparency Barometer indicates, most states have a long way to go in opening their small arms policies to public scrutiny.

Despite a growing awareness among some governments that small arms proliferation inhibits development and humanitarian efforts, the impact on human rights is often underestimated or overlooked. In fact, the UN *Programme of Action* makes no reference to this vital issue.

In tackling these problems, the Control Arms campaign—led by Amnesty International, Oxfam, and IANSA—depends on data and analysis provided by the Small Arms Survey project. Other stakeholders, both governmental and non-governmental, also look to the *Survey* for reliable and in-depth research on small arms production, stockpiling, transfers, impacts, and measures.

The annual *Small Arms Survey* remains an essential source of impartial and public information on the state of global small arms proliferation and misuse—including its human rights implications.

Mary Robinson
Former President of Ireland
Honorary President, Oxfam International
Executive Director, The Ethical Globalization Initiative
April 2004

Contents

About the Small Arms Survey vi
Notes to readers vi
Acknowledgements vii
Introduction 1

Chapter 1. Continuity and Change: Products and Producers
Introduction 7
The global small arms and light weapons industry: Annual update 9
Regional survey: Small arms production in Latin America 16
Popular military small arms and light weapons 26
Old technology, new applications: The RPG-7 and its derivatives 35
Conclusion 37

Chapter 2. From Chaos to Coherence? Global Firearm Stockpiles
Introduction 43
Iraq's abandoned arsenal 44
Latin America: Lethal stockpiles and weak states 50
Stockpile security: Who's minding the store? 54
Casual loss: Individual theft and disappearance 60
Registration and responsibility 66
Conclusion 71

Chapter 3. Big Issue, Big Problem? MANPADS
Introduction 77
Characteristics and technologies 78
MANPADS production 81
Stockpiles 83
Factors governing use 85
Transfers 87
Measures to control MANPADS 90
Prospects for controlling MANPADS 94

Chapter 4. Back to the Sources: International Small Arms Transfers
Introduction 99
The authorized global small arms trade: Annual update 100
Developments in transparency: Annual update 114
Small Arms Trade Transparency Barometer 117
Exporting small arms: A question of survival for producers? 118
Small arms transfers and human rights: Making the connection 125
Conclusion 134

Chapter 5. Targeting the Middlemen: Controlling Brokering Activities
Introduction 141
Making illicit brokering possible 142
Global and regional initiatives for the control of brokering activities 147
National regulations on brokering activities 151
Are national regulations effective? 162
Conclusion 166

Chapter 6. A Common Tool: Firearms, Violence, and Crime
Introduction 173

Mapping the problem: Global and regional patterns of small arms use in violence and crime	174
Beyond numbers: The role of small arms in violence and crime	180
Experiences and responses to small arms-related crime in African communities and other local settings	192
Conclusion	199

Chapter 7. Critical Triggers: Implementing International Standards for Police Firearm Use

Introduction	213
International standards	213
National regulation	215
States of emergency	220
Differentiated use of force	220
Selection and training	224
Community links	227
Firearm storage	229
Persons in custody or detention	230
Political manipulation	232
Corruption and criminality	233
Crowd control	233
Vulnerable persons	235
Oversight systems	237
Post-conflict police reform	240
Conclusion	241

Chapter 8. Under the Spotlight: Monitoring Implementation of Small Arms Measures

Introduction	249
The UN Conference process	250
UN arms embargoes	263
Conclusion	271

Chapter 9. Trouble in Paradise: Small Arms in the Pacific

Introduction	277
Lawful gun trade and stockpiles in the Pacific	280
The illicit trade: Gun smuggling, leakage, and crime	285
The human cost of firearm misuse in three Pacific communities	290
Disarmament Pacific style: Experiences in Bougainville and the Solomon Islands	296
Domestic and regional arms control legislation	300
Conclusion	304

Chapter 10. An Anomaly in Central Asia? Small Arms in Kyrgyzstan

Introduction	309
A troubled state in a volatile region	309
Legal small arms possession	312
Unregistered and illegal possession	314
Security perceptions	317
Cultural attitudes to guns	318
Gun availability	319
Black market	319
Production and trade in weapons	321
Trafficking	322
Conclusion	324

Index 328

ABOUT THE SMALL ARMS SURVEY

The Small Arms Survey is an independent research project located at the Graduate Institute of International Studies in Geneva, Switzerland. Established in 1999 with the generous financial support of the Swiss Federal Department of Foreign Affairs, it currently receives additional funding from Australia, Belgium, Canada, Denmark, Finland, France, the Netherlands, New Zealand, Norway, Sweden, and the United Kingdom.

The objectives of the Small Arms Survey are: to be the principal source of public information on all aspects of small arms; to serve as a resource centre for governments, policy-makers, researchers, and activists; to monitor national and international initiatives (governmental and non-governmental) on small arms; and to act as a clearing house for the sharing of information and the dissemination of best practices. The Survey also sponsors field research and information-gathering efforts, especially in affected states and regions. The project has an international staff with expertise in security studies, political science, law, economics, development studies, and sociology. It collaborates with a worldwide network of researchers, partner institutions, non-governmental organizations, and governments.

Notes to readers

Abbreviations: Topic-specific lists of abbreviations are placed at the end of each chapter.

Chapter cross-referencing: Chapter cross-references appear capitalized in brackets throughout the text. For example, in Chapter 3: 'In contrast to most other small arms and light weapons, the production of MANPADS is currently limited to a small number of manufacturers (PRODUCERS).'

Exchange rates: All monetary values are expressed in current US dollars (USD). When other currencies are additionally cited, unless otherwise indicated, they are converted to USD using the 365-day average exchange rate for the period 1 September 2002 to 31 August 2003.

Small Arms Survey: The plain text—Small Arms Survey—is used to indicate the overall project and its activities, while the italicized version—*Small Arms Survey*—refers to the publication itself. The *Survey,* appearing italicized, refers generally to past and future editions of the yearbook.

Web site: For more detailed information and current developments on small arms issues, readers are invited to visit our Web site at: http://www.smallarmssurvey.org

Small Arms Survey
Graduate Institute of International Studies
47, Avenue Blanc
1202 Geneva, Switzerland
Tel.: +41 22 908 57 77
Fax: +41 22 732 27 38
Email: smallarm@hei.unige.ch
Web site: www.smallarmssurvey.org

ACKNOWLEDGEMENTS

This is the fourth edition of the *Small Arms Survey* yearbook. It is a collective product of the staff of the Small Arms Survey project, based at the Graduate Institute of International Studies in Geneva, Switzerland. A large number of researchers in Geneva and elsewhere have contributed to this volume, and it has benefited from the input and advice of a number of government officials, activists, experts, and colleagues from around the world who form part of the ever-growing global small arms research community.

The principal chapter authors were assisted by a large number of in-house and external contributors who are mentioned by name in the relevant chapters.

In addition, detailed comments on the chapters were provided by: Rod Alley, Holger Anders, David Atwood, Sibylle Bauer, Eric Berman, Michael Brzoska, David Capie, Pablo Dreyfus, Adedeji Ebo, Barbara Frey, Tamar Gabelnick, Owen Greene, Suzette Grillot, Maria Haug, David Hemenway, Ernst Jan Hogendoorn, Alun Howard, Dave Kopel, Benjamin Lessing, Nicholas Marsh, Sarah Meek, Stephen Mihorean, Lisa Misol, the Norwegian Initiative on Small Arms Transfers (NISAT), Maxim Pyadushkin, Colin Roberts, Kizito Sabala, Elisabeth Sköns, Carlo Tombola, Pieter Wezeman, Siemon Wezeman, Brian Wood, and Herbert Wulf.

Peter Batchelor and Keith Krause were responsible for the overall planning and organization of this volume. Philip Alpers, Aaron Karp, Emile LeBrun, and David Mutimer provided valuable editorial inputs during the in-house review process. Tania Inowlocki managed the editing and production of the *Survey*; she and Michael James copy-edited the book. Vick Arnò and Nicoletta Forni of Latitude provided the layout and design; Estelle Jobson and Donald Strachan proofread the *Survey*; and Lisa Kenwright compiled the index.

Dominic Byatt and Claire Croft of Oxford University Press provided support and encouragement through the production of the *Survey*. Elli Kytömäki, Stéphanie Pézard, Ruxandra Stoicescu, and Pamina Firchow assisted with research. Delphine Zinner, Fridrich Štrba, and Carole Touraine provided administrative support.

The project also benefited from the support of personnel of the Graduate Institute of International Studies, in particular Andrew Clapham, Wilfred Gander, Jean-Michel Jacquet, Nicole Mouthon, Daniel Warner, and Simon Wermelinger.

We are extremely grateful to the Swiss Government for its generous financial and overall support of the Small Arms Survey project, in particular Heidi Grau, Thomas Greminger, Laurent Masmejean, Peter Maurer, and Marc Stritt. Financial support for the project was also provided by the Governments of Australia, Belgium, Canada, Denmark, Finland, France, the Netherlands, New Zealand, Norway, Sweden, and the United Kingdom. The project has also received financial support for various research projects from the Geneva International Academic Network (GIAN), the Organisation Internationale de la Francophonie, the United Nations Development Programme (UNDP), and the South Eastern Europe Clearinghouse for the Control of Small Arms and Light Weapons (SEESAC). The project further benefits from the assistance and support of a number of other governments and international agencies including the ICRC, UNDDA, UNIDIR, and WHO.

In Geneva, the project has received support and expert advice from: Damien Angelet, David Atwood, Prosper Bani, Cate Buchanan, Christophe Carle, Martin Griffiths, Randall Harbour, Maria Haug, Peter Herby, Yann Hwang, Kuniko Inoguchi, Judit Kiss, Patricia Lewis, Bennie Lombard, Harri Mäki-Reinikka, Patrick McCarthy, David Meddings, Ann Pollack, Daniël Prins, Rakesh Sood, Fred Tanner, Annika Thunborg, Peter Truswell, and Camilla Waszink.

Beyond Geneva, we also received support from a number of colleagues. In addition to those mentioned above, and in specific chapters, we would like to thank: Pete Abel, Péricles Gasparini Alves, Antonio Rangel Bandeira, Ilhan Berkol, Peter Croll, Wendy Cukier, Paul Eavis, Sami Faltas, Rubem César Fernandes, William Godnick, Björn Hagelin, João Honwana, Kate Joseph, Guy Lamb, Edward Laurance, Herbert Loret, Andrew Mack, Geraldine O'Callaghan, Atef Odibat, Yeshua Moser-Puangsuwan, Rebecca Peters, Robert Scharf, and Adrian Wilkinson.

Our sincere thanks to many other individuals (who remain unnamed) for their continuing support of the project. We also express our apologies to anyone whom we have forgotten to mention.

This edition also marks the departure of Peter Batchelor, one of the founders of the Small Arms Survey project. On behalf of the staff—Peter, thank you for your hard work and dedication over the past four years. You will be missed.

Keith Krause
Programme Director

Peter Batchelor
Project Director

Principal Chapter Authors

Introduction
Keith Krause
Chapter 1
Peter Batchelor and James Bevan
Chapter 2
Aaron Karp
Chapter 3
James Bevan
Chapter 4
Anna Khakee
Chapter 5
Silvia Cattaneo
Chapter 6
Nicolas Florquin and Christina Wille
Chapter 7
Brian Wood and Glenn McDonald
Chapter 8
Glenn McDonald
Chapter 9
Philip Alpers, Robert Muggah, and Conor Twyford
Chapter 10
Neil MacFarlane, Stina Torjesen, and Christina Wille

Small Arms Survey 2004

Editors
Peter Batchelor and Keith Krause
Editorial Consultants
Philip Alpers, Aaron Karp, and Emile LeBrun
Publication Editor
Tania Inowlocki
Layout and Design
Vick Arnò and Nicoletta Forni
Copy Editor
Michael James

A soldier stands behind bullet-riddled glass in Israel in June 2002.
(© AP Photo/Gadi Kabalo)

Introduction

The widespread proliferation and misuse of small arms threatens the realization of basic human rights and security in various ways. In the hands of repressive forces, small arms can serve to intimidate, threaten, and coerce whole communities, limit free movement, and prevent access to basic entitlements and services. Small arms are also routinely used to facilitate or commit human rights abuses, such as extrajudicial executions and torture.

In this edition of the *Small Arms Survey*, subtitled 'Rights at Risk', we examine the complicated relationship between small arms and human rights violations. Our interest in this theme parallels the engagement of major human rights actors with the issue, including Amnesty International, Human Rights Watch, and the United Nations Commission on Human Rights. In particular, in 2003 the UN appointed a Special Rapporteur to study the prevention of human rights violations committed with small arms and light weapons, while several NGOs launched the Control Arms campaign with a strong human rights orientation.

In identifying the linkages between the proliferation and misuse of small arms and the violation of human rights, we encounter a thorny conceptual problem. Guns are inert objects, which do not as such violate human rights. In this sense, there is some truth in the oft-repeated slogan of the US National Rifle Association that 'guns don't kill people, people kill people'. Guns do not by themselves breach anyone's rights, but people with guns can—and do—violate human rights on a regular basis, in a variety of ways and contexts. One must construct a complex causal (and sometimes legal) chain of reasoning to show how individuals who produce, hold, export, or use guns can be held responsible for the misuse of these weapons. Certainly this principle has been advanced in tort law. In the United States, various groups have attempted unsuccessfully to hold weapons manufacturers and dealers legally accountable for the misuse of weapons they have produced or sold, especially those used most prominently in crime (such as the so-called 'Saturday night specials').

Through this year's focus on the theme of small arms and human rights, we seek to untangle the many ways in which small arms and light weapons contribute to human rights violations—whether by facilitating such violations or, as some advocates of gun ownership would have it, by helping prevent them. In this edition of the *Small Arms Survey*, three different chapters address three distinct dimensions of the small arms–human rights nexus:

- the legal duty of all states to uphold the human rights of their citizens in situations involving the use of potentially lethal force by state agents;
- the legal responsibility of states to exercise necessary caution when transferring arms to others, especially where these may facilitate human rights abuses; and
- the growing conviction that states have a legal duty to protect their citizens from widespread crime and insecurity on their territory.

> Many states are failing to adhere to international policy standards governing the use of force and firearms.

Chapter 7 (Policing) takes up the first of these themes, which coincides with the classic legal understanding of human rights: the responsibility of states to uphold the human rights of their citizens. This chapter presents the international standards governing the use of force and firearms by law enforcement officials and looks at how these are reflected in national legislation and jurisprudence. While the chapter does not attempt a systematic evaluation of national implementation, its selection of practice from around the world reveals that a great many states are failing to adhere to relevant policing standards. This shortfall is less a result of limited resources than of insufficient political commitment—above all, a state's commitment to respecting the human rights of its citizens.

The second dimension is addressed in our annual chapter on small arms transfers (Chapter 4). As we noted last year in our chapter on norms, states have a legal duty to exercise necessary caution in transferring arms that could be used to violate human rights or commit other violations of international law. To what extent do states exercise sufficient oversight in practice? Given that small arms are more likely to be involved in human rights abuses than major conventional weapons (such as military aircraft or submarines), one would expect states to follow more restrictive policies in transferring small arms to countries where human rights violations are common. In reality, as the chapter documents, state practice in this area remains quite imperfect. While some countries with problematic human rights records do encounter difficulties in importing arms in the authorized market, these states are usually able to procure small arms from international sources without too much trouble.

The third approach zeroes in on an issue that has been indirectly linked to human rights, namely the role of firearms in violence and crime (Chapter 6). States, so the argument goes, have a duty to protect the fundamental rights and freedoms of their citizens where these are threatened by widespread firearm crime and insecurity. While the use of firearms by private citizens to threaten, injure, or kill other citizens is invariably treated as a crime, rather than a violation of human rights, it is increasingly recognized that states have a duty under human rights law to take reasonable measures to prevent and punish such violence. Moreover, the fact that states around the world treat individual firearm misuse as a serious crime is in accordance with our understanding that such conduct breaches the rules and norms underpinning law-governed societies.

Ongoing international efforts

International efforts to combat small arms proliferation and misuse continued in 2003. The First UN Biennial Meeting of States (BMS) was held in New York in July 2003 to examine states' implementation of the *Programme of Action*, negotiated at the 2001 UN Small Arms Conference. The First BMS showcased the wide range of activities many governments, international organizations, and NGOs have already undertaken, and helped foster a sense of gathering momentum on the small arms issue. Since then, the development of a international instrument on the marking and tracing of small arms has moved forward, as has a parallel process examining issues surrounding brokering.

At the same time, however, progress by some countries in meeting their commitments under the *Programme of Action* has lagged. A report by the Biting the Bullet Project and the International Action Network on Small Arms (IANSA) concludes that a large number of countries have not implemented many of the most basic measures outlined in the *Programme*. The obstacles to implementation include a lack of awareness, engagement, and institutional will. Increasing the involvement of inactive governments stands out as a particular challenge for NGOs in the months leading up to the next BMS in mid-2005.

INTRODUCTION

Chapter highlights

The *Small Arms Survey 2004* presents updated information on global small arms production, stockpiles, transfers, and international measures. Besides the policing and crime chapters introduced above, this edition also features chapters on man-portable air defence systems (MANPADS) and arms brokering as well as case studies on the Pacific and Kyrgyzstan.

Chapter 1 (Products and Producers): At least 1,249 companies in more than 90 countries are involved in some aspect of small arms and light weapons production—more firms but fewer countries than previously reported. The global small arms and light weapons market is relatively stable, although producers from countries including Australia, Brazil, Israel, Singapore, and South Africa are challenging established European and North American producers.

In a declining international small arms market, powerful forces are pushing for both change and continuity. The most notable change is the trend towards consolidation among major small arms producers. New designs of small arms and light weapons are also emerging, as armed forces in Europe and elsewhere begin major rearmament programmes. Continuity is demonstrated, above all, by the continuing reliance on weapons that have proven their worth over the decades, such as high-powered rifles, medium and heavy machine guns, and rocket-propelled grenade launchers (RPGs)—notwithstanding the appearance of new weapon designs.

Chapter 2 (Stockpiles): This year's chapter focuses on the management of small arms and light weapons. The collapse of Saddam Hussein's regime led to the single most significant small arms stockpile transfer the world has known. We estimate that Iraqi civilians may have gained control of 7 million–8 million small arms. Unless the international community takes aggressive steps to improve control of small arms stockpiles worldwide, many countries will remain vulnerable to similar disasters. The gradual leakage of weapons as a result of negligence and theft is an equally serious problem. At least one million firearms are stolen or lost annually around the world.

> At least one million firearms are stolen or lost annually around the world.

The most ambitious recent measure for the registration of civilian weapons came into force in Canada in 2003. Brazil also approved a major initiative to combat firearms proliferation and radically alter its national gun culture. Comparable initiatives are emerging elsewhere, for example in Thailand.

Chapter 3 (MANPADS): Man-portable air defence systems (MANPADS) are small, light missile-launching weapons designed to be fired by an individual against aircraft. It appears that about 15 producers manufacture MANPADS in at least as many countries. Production is no longer limited to established companies in the high-tech arms industry, as producing countries now include Egypt, North Korea, Pakistan, and Vietnam. Developing country demand for affordable anti-aircraft systems will be likely to ensure that many more orders are placed for MANPADS in the near future. Although some estimates put the number of MANPADS as high as 500,000, fewer than 100,000 complete units (missile and launcher) have probably been produced. This figure includes an unknown quantity of MANPADS in the hands of non-state groups, including terrorist organizations.

International efforts to control the proliferation of MANPADS have so far been limited, but there is growing momentum for strengthened controls. This may be one of the few cases in which the politicization of a small arms/light weapons issue serves to rein in proliferation—provided the international community continues to engage with this problem.

Chapter 4 (Transfers): The reluctance of many states to provide trade information constitutes a major impediment to the accurate measurement of small arms transfers. This year, we introduce a new tool to evaluate state transparency in this area: the Small Arms Trade Transparency Barometer. Based on national export reports and customs data, the Barometer finds that the most transparent states among the larger small arms exporters are the United States, Germany, and France, but even these countries fall well short of full transparency, however. The average score for larger exporters is 8.5 out of 20, which suggests that much needs to be done to improve transparency. Mexico, China, Israel, South Africa, and Bulgaria are at the bottom of the list.

International customs data indicate that the export value of small arms, parts, and ammunition was about USD 2.4 billion for 2001. The 2000 total, which did not include small arms parts, was estimated at USD 2.1 billion. The total authorized trade (documented and undocumented) is estimated at about USD 4 billion. The largest exporters by value are the United States, Italy, Belgium, Germany, the Russian Federation, Brazil, and China. Countries that are known to be medium producers of small arms, but about whose exports we know very little, include Iran, Pakistan, and Singapore.

Chapter 5 (Brokers): Brokers carry out a wide range of activities that are instrumental in diverting weapons from legal to illicit markets. A number of regulatory gaps allow brokers to act almost entirely without oversight in much of the world. Controls on legal and illicit brokering are strongly linked; unless states regulate the first, they will be unable to prevent the second.

In 2003, states focused on brokering to a greater degree than ever before. These initiatives took as their starting point the need to regulate brokering at the national level. Only 25 countries now explicitly regulate brokering. National measures, however, vary greatly, creating loopholes and allowing for the possibility of circumvention. Even in countries where necessary legislation is in place, the effective implementation of brokering controls is often difficult. Although essential, national regulation is not sufficient. The transnational nature of brokering activities makes international cooperation indispensable in this area.

Chapter 6 (Crime): This chapter tries to untangle the complex relationship between firearm availability and use and non-conflict-related violence. It stresses the prevalence of firearms in the perpetration of societal violence, given their widespread use in assaults, threats, robberies, sexual offences, and suicides, as well as in nearly 40 per cent of all homicides. A systematic analysis of available data allows us to confirm that at least 200,000 and possibly up to 270,000 persons are killed by firearms in non-conflict-related situations each year (including homicides, suicides, and unintentional shootings).

> At least 200,000 persons are killed by firearms in non-conflict-related situations each year.

Whether gun accessibility affects overall levels of violence is more difficult to determine. The lethality of guns increases the risk of injury and death, but responsible firearm ownership can also contribute to deterring crime. The impact of gun violence, however, is not limited to fatal and non-fatal firearm injuries. Many types of small arms-related crime—whether committed by individuals or the state—can threaten a community's physical, economic, social, political, and cultural security. Furthermore, gun violence can challenge a state's monopoly on the maintenance of law and order as communities seek alternative means of increasing their sense of security. These methods may include a reliance on private security companies, informal vigilante groups, and private gun ownership. While quantifying these impacts can be difficult, recent research suggests that the social costs of gun violence are substantially higher than those incurred through other forms of violence.

Chapter 7 (Policing): Policing is an essential test of a state's willingness to uphold the human rights of its citizens and respect the rule of law generally. Against the backdrop of relevant international standards, this chapter examines several critical issues associated with the use of force and firearms by police. These include training, equipment, and oversight systems. The chapter also examines instances where security and policing systems break down as a result of political manipulation, institutionalized corruption, and criminality.

The chapter's selection of national practice from various parts of the world, while not sufficient for a systematic assessment of national implementation worldwide, does demonstrate that a large number of countries are not adhering to international policing standards. Resources are obviously necessary for good policing, but the chapter stresses that political commitment is the key factor in determining whether national policing is firmly rooted in respect for human rights.

Chapter 8 (Monitoring): Reporting, monitoring, and verification appear essential to the success of ongoing efforts to tackle the small arms problem. This chapter looks at the contribution these processes make to the implementation of the UN *Programme of Action* and UN arms embargoes, as well as the important corresponding roles played by governments, international organizations, and NGOs.

In its review of the UN Conference process, the chapter concludes that the July 2003 Biennial Meeting of States was largely successful in generating significant information and analysis on national implementation of the *Programme*. Nevertheless, existing information about initiatives does not provide a complete picture of implementation, nor of implementation challenges and solutions. A section on UN arms embargoes describes recent attempts to strengthen verification efforts—especially through the use of investigative panels. Important as these are, however, such improvements remain vulnerable to weakening political will.

Chapter 9 (Pacific): Recent armed conflict, firearms proliferation, and weapons collection initiatives in the Pacific offer clear positive and negative lessons. The region is not afflicted with large-scale gun trafficking, yet the Pacific experience demonstrates how deeply even a small number of weapons can damage communities in such places as Fiji or the Solomon Islands. Safe storage is a particular concern as many of the guns that have fuelled armed violence in the Pacific leaked from legal owners.

Gun laws in the region are inconsistent, and although gun smuggling is currently rare, the Pacific will remain vulnerable to such activity as long as legislative loopholes remain unplugged. Although crude home-made guns are produced during times of scarcity and conflict, the chapter concludes that their relative importance is not great. Most of the recent efforts to mop up surplus or destabilizing weapons have brought positive results, and in the recently conflict-torn Solomon Islands and Bougainville, disarmament is now firmly linked to political reform, increased social stability, and economic development.

Chapter 10 (Kyrgyzstan): Despite Central Asia's reputation as an undifferentiated arc of instability, our study of Kyrgyzstan indicates that small arms possession, use, and proliferation is not a significant problem in the country. The study found no link between trafficking in small arms and trafficking in drugs and people. Small arms-related violence and casualties also appear limited.

The Kyrgyz government holds an estimated 50,000 weapons, with strict legislation regulating civilian possession. Of an estimated 15,000 registered hunting guns, 80 per cent are held in the area surrounding the capital Bishkek. Atypically, Kyrgyz state stockpiles outnumber civilian small arms, and more hunting guns are registered in urban areas than in the countryside. Illegal weapons possession is difficult to quantify, but several indicators suggest it is low. Although Kyrgyzstan does not produce small arms, ammunition production from Soviet days continues in Bishkek.

CONCLUSION

Our understanding of the human rights implications of small arms proliferation and misuse remains poor. But there are growing signs that the international community is taking the connection seriously. This year's focus on human rights derives from our mission to deepen the understanding of small arms proliferation as a multi-dimensional issue with complex linkages to a wide range of development, humanitarian, public health, and criminal justice concerns. By shedding light on these linkages, we hope to provide governments, analysts, and advocates with the tools needed to develop policies and programmes that address small arms proliferation and misuse in all their aspects.

US soldiers fire M-16 rifles in Indiana in March 2003. (© AP/Michael Conroy)

Continuity and Change:
PRODUCTS AND PRODUCERS

INTRODUCTION

In a declining international small arms market, there are powerful forces for change in the global industry. Among the most visible aspects is the trend towards consolidation of major companies. In December 2003 two of the best-known small arms producers, Germany's Heckler & Koch (H&K) and Santa Barbara Sistemas, the Spanish subsidiary of General Dynamics, initiated a joint venture, which will manufacture a variety of new types of small arms (*Jane's Defence Weekly*, 2003d). The venture is similar to many initiatives launched in recent years, involving such companies as Belgium's FN Herstal, France's Giat, Germany's Dynamit Nobel, Switzerland's RUAG, and Alliant Techsystems in the United States. These firms and their counterparts in other leading producing countries, such as those of the Russian Federation, are investing heavily in new small arms and light weapons (SALW), partly in response to rearmament and procurement programmes.

Alongside this trend of change is another of continuity. In recent US-led military operations in Afghanistan and Iraq, high-tech armies continue to confront combatants using older types of small arms and light weapons. The coalition forces themselves still rely greatly on small arms technology that has changed little in the past decades. These conflicts and many others around the world reveal unchanged demand for staple weapons, such as high-powered rifles, medium and heavy machine guns, and other veteran designs such as rocket-propelled grenade launchers (RPGs).

What do these two contradictory trends tell us of the state of global small arms and light weapons production? The key findings of this chapter are as follows:

- At least 1,249 companies in more than 90 countries are involved in some aspect of small arms and light weapons production.
- The global market for small arms and light weapons is relatively stable, although producers from countries such as Australia, Brazil, Israel, Singapore, and South Africa are challenging established European and US producers.
- New small arms and light weapons designs are appearing, as armed forces in Europe and elsewhere begin major rearmament programmes. This development will boost global production in coming years.
- At least ten countries in Latin America have the capacity to produce small arms, light weapons, and/or ammunition. Brazil is Latin America's largest and most diversified small arms producer.
- Small arms and light weapons technology is changing rapidly, but the oldest and cheapest weapons will continue to be the most widespread.

Reflecting the themes of continuity and change, this chapter provides an annual update of trends and patterns in the global small arms and light weapons industry. It offers a comprehensive update on two of the world's major producers—the Russian Federation and the United States—and a regional survey, which examines small arms and light weapons production in Latin America. The chapter also examines some of the main technological and product developments with respect to various categories of military-style small arms and light weapons. It focuses especially on the most popular and widely distributed of these, with a particular focus on RPGs.

What are the latest trends in the global small arms and light weapons industry? New information and research suggests that at least 1,249 companies worldwide are involved in some aspect of small arms and light weapons production. The latest available information suggests that there are slightly fewer countries with the capacity to produce small arms and light weapons than previously thought. In the Russian Federation and the United States, production of commercial firearms appears to be declining, but production of military-style small arms seems to be increasing. More than three million firearms were produced in the United States in 2001. The lowest level since 1992, this figure represents a considerable decline from the peak in 1994, when more than five million were produced. In recent years the Russian defence industry as a whole has experienced a significant increase in production, yet small arms and light weapons production decreased from around one million in 2001 to about 650,000 in 2002.

As part of a rotating series of regional surveys that included the Middle East in 2002 and Eastern and Central Europe in 2003, this edition of the *Small Arms Survey* explores small arms production in Latin America.

What are the most popular or common small arms? This chapter also focuses on the most widely distributed weapons among armed forces worldwide. Pistols and revolvers are the most numerous and widely dispersed of all small arms. Assault rifles are now the most numerous and effective infantry small arm. The international market for mortars is the most stable of all small arms and light weapons markets.

Among small arms and light weapons technology, old and cheap is often preferable. The RPG-7 rocket-propelled grenade launcher, now over 40 years old, is a prime example of the extent to which such weapons undergo considerable modification and enhancement over time. With an estimated nine million or more units produced, the RPG-7 is exceptionally cheap, easy to use, and destructive over a wide area. For these reasons it has become a weapon of choice for developing world armies and non-state actors alike. With no easy countermeasures to undermine its effectiveness, the RPG-7 and its later variants are likely to remain standard light weapons for years to come.

> **Producers from countries such as Australia, Brazil, China, Israel, Singapore, and South Africa are challenging established European and US producers.**

Box 1.1   Definition of small arms and light weapons

The *Small Arms Survey* uses the term 'small arms and light weapons' broadly to cover both military-style small arms and light weapons as well as commercial firearms (handguns and long guns). When possible, it follows the definition used in the United Nations' *Report of the Panel of Governmental Experts on Small Arms* (United Nations, 1997):

- *Small arms:* revolvers and self-loading pistols, rifles and carbines, assault rifles, sub-machine guns, and light machine guns.
- *Light weapons:* heavy machine guns, hand-held under-barrel and mounted grenade launchers, portable anti-tank and anti-aircraft guns, recoilless rifles, portable launchers of anti-tank and anti-aircraft missile systems, and mortars of less than 100mm calibre.

The *Survey* uses the terms 'firearm' and 'gun' to mean hand-held weapons that fire a projectile through a tube by explosive charge. The terms 'small arms' and 'light weapons' are used more comprehensively to refer to all hand-held, man-portable, explosively or chemically propelled or detonated devices. Unless the context dictates otherwise, no distinction is intended between commercial firearms (such as hunting rifles) and small arms and light weapons designed for military use (such as assault rifles). Government officials agreed to the UN definition through consensus. It was negotiated, in other words, to serve practical political goals that differ from the needs of research and analysis. While the UN definition is used in the *Survey* as a baseline, the analysis in this volume is broader, allowing consideration of weapons such as home-made (craft) firearms that might be overlooked using the UN definition. The term small arm is used in this chapter to refer both to small arms and light weapons, unless otherwise stated, whereas the term light weapon refers specifically to this category of weapons.

The material presented in this chapter is based on information obtained from open sources. These include official information, defence publications, the international press, corporate and non-governmental information services, defence exhibitions, and company promotional material, as well as research and analysis by small arms experts. These sources have been enriched by extensive field research and interviews in selected countries and regions.

THE GLOBAL SMALL ARMS AND LIGHT WEAPONS INDUSTRY: ANNUAL UPDATE

This section provides an update and new information on the state of the global small arms industry. It focuses on the distribution of production (i.e. the number of countries and companies that have the capacity to produce small arms, light weapons, or ammunition) and on general trends and patterns. In more detail, it reviews new information on small arms production in two of the world's major producers—the Russian Federation and the United States—and a number of smaller producers in a regional survey of Latin America.

Distribution

How many countries have the capacity to produce small arms? Is the number of countries growing? The *Small Arms Survey 2003* estimated that 98 countries have the capacity to produce small arms, light weapons, or ammunition (Small Arms Survey, 2003, p. 11). New information and research suggest that at least 92 countries worldwide have the capacity to produce small arms or ammunition (Omega Foundation, 2003).

This estimate of the global distribution of small arms-producing countries should be treated with caution, however. In some countries, a lack of reliable information, both official and unofficial, makes it difficult to ascertain whether any small arms or ammunition is currently being produced and, if so, whether regularly or only on an *ad hoc* basis. Some countries produce only components rather than finished products; in others, small arms production involves relatively marginal activities, such as loading or filling ammunition cartridges.

Figure 1.1   Number of known small arms-producing countries, by region, 2003

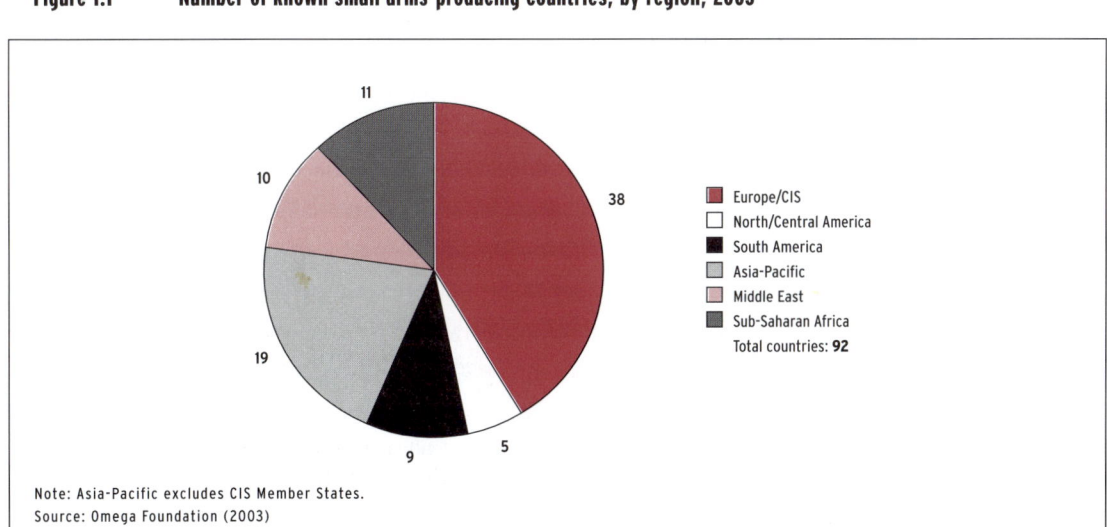

Note: Asia-Pacific excludes CIS Member States.
Source: Omega Foundation (2003)

Figure 1.2   Number of known small arms-producing companies, by region, 2003

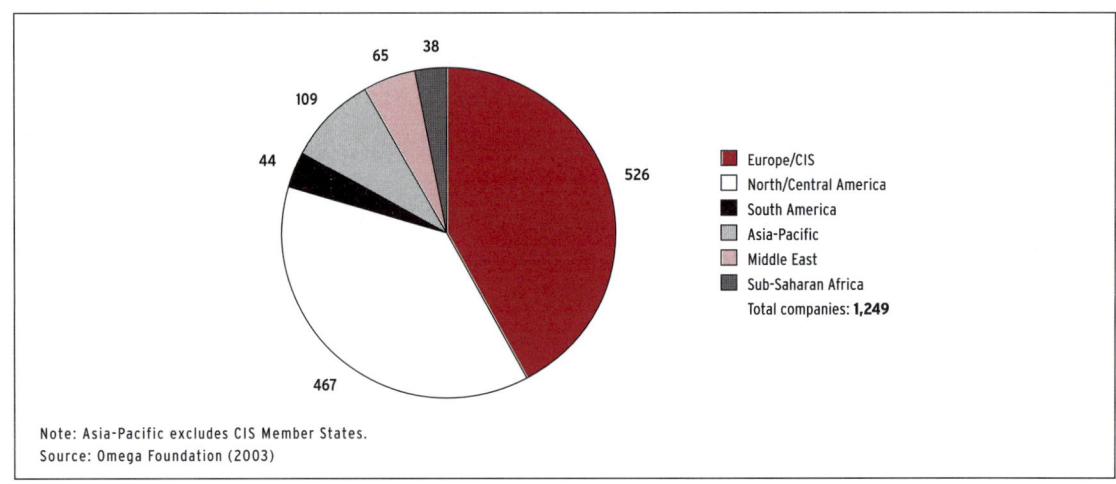

Note: Asia-Pacific excludes CIS Member States.
Source: Omega Foundation (2003)

The *Small Arms Survey 2003* estimated that 1,134 companies produce the world's small arms and ammunition (Small Arms Survey, 2003, p. 12). New information and research reveal that at least 1,249 such companies worldwide are involved in some aspect of small arms production (Omega Foundation, 2003). While this research includes both intermediate and end producers, it excludes low-rate craft production by highly specialized or improvised manufacturers.[1]

Nearly half of these companies (42 per cent) are located in Europe and the Commonwealth of Independant States (CIS) (see Figure 1.2). The United States remains the country with the largest number of producers. Smaller numbers of producers are found in Latin America, sub-Saharan Africa, the Middle East, and the Asia-Pacific region. Companies are extremely diverse, ranging from small family-owned businesses to subsidiaries or business units of large, multinational defence-industrial conglomerates and state-owned enterprises. Company sizes range from establishments with fewer than 10 to more than 1,000 employees—making reliable monitoring of at least smaller companies a difficult exercise.

Major producers: The United States and the Russian Federation

What are the trends in the world's three major small arms producers—China, the Russian Federation, and the United States? Our understanding is uneven and depends upon the degree of national transparency. There is still little detailed information about small arms production in China. In recent years, though, the amount of official and unofficial information about the value and volume of small arms production in the Russian Federation and the United States has increased. This development permits better analysis of production trends in the world's two largest small arms manufacturers.

Domestic production in both the United States and the Russian Federation exhibits contradictory trends, common to both. For each country, production of commercial firearms, by volume, appears to have declined in recent years. Together, the United States and the Russian Federation produced nearly four million commercial firearms in 2001. More recent information from both countries suggests that the figures for 2002 may be much lower (see Tables 1.2 and 1.5).

Production of military-style small arms, on the other hand, appears to be increasing, as a result of domestic demand as well as export sales. In 2002 the United States exported more than 50,000 military-style small arms (rifles, shotguns, and machine guns), more than double the number of the previous year. Two notable export increases were to South Korea and Kuwait, a possible function of international tensions in the past two years (Haug, 2003). In addition, the

PRODUCTS AND PRODUCERS

demands of the US-led invasions in Afghanistan and Iraq have led to significant increases in domestic procurement of certain types of weapons, such as the M-4 carbine (Colt's Manufacturing), M-16 rifle (FN Manufacturing, Colt's Manufacturing), and the M-107 sniper rifle (Barrett Firearms Manufacturing). Both the Russian Federation and the United States are likely to adopt new weapons in the near future. The United States is currently testing the new XM8 rifle (Galloway, 2004). Military restructuring in the Russian Federation may result in some of its troops adopting the Izhmash AN-94 assault rifle (*Jane's International Defence Review*, 2002).

The US small arms industry produces more than 3 million commercial firearms per year and employs about 16,000 people. The total value of small arms production, including ammunition, was USD 2.5 billion in 2001 (the latest year for which official figures are available) (US Census Bureau, 2003). In contrast, the Russian small arms industry produces 500,000–1 million commercial firearms per year, employs about 50,000 people, and had total sales of small arms of about USD 220 million in 2002 (CAST, 2003). Despite employing more than double the number of employees, the Russian small arms industry produces only ten per cent of the value of its US counterpart.

US production of commercial firearms, by volume, appears to have declined in recent years.

In 2004 the Israel Defence Ministry purchased 15,000 new Tavor assault rifles, developed by IMI to replace the US-made M-16 rifles.

In addition to major producers such as the United States and the Russian Federation, a number of medium-sized producers have emerged as major challengers to the world's most established producers for certain products in the past five years (Small Arms Survey, 2003, p. 14). These include Israel Military Industries (IMI) (Israel), Forjas Taurus (Brazil), Denel/Vektor (South Africa), Singapore Technologies Kinetics (Singapore), and ADI (Australia).

The United States

The United States remains the world's most important small arms-producing country. It has the largest number of companies producing small arms and ammunition, is a major exporter of small arms (TRANSFERS), and is estimated to have the world's largest domestic market for small arms.

There is still uncertainty about the total number of small arms manufacturers in the United States. According to an independent assessment by the Omega Foundation (2003), 443 companies in the United States are currently involved in the production of small arms and ammunition. The 1997 US Manufacturing Census lists 311 establishments (firms) that are involved in the production of small arms and small arms ammunition (US Census Bureau, 1999). The US Bureau of Alcohol, Tobacco, Firearms and Explosives listed more than 1,700 licensed firearm manufacturers in the United States (US ATF, 2003b). As we have no way of verifying the figures from the Economic Census or the ATF, we rely on the figures from the Omega Foundation (2003).

Recent trends suggest that the overall value and volume of firearm production in the United States continues to decline. Nevertheless, anecdotal reports indicate that specific US and foreign manufacturers have benefited from operations in Afghanistan and Iraq. Colt's Manufacturing, for example, the producer of the M-4 carbine and the M-16 assault rifle, won increased contracts from the US Armed Forces (Forecast International, 2004). Winchester Ammunition, the country's largest private manufacturer of small-calibre military ammunition, shared a USD 9.2 million US Army contract in December 2003 with Israel's IMI to meet increased US military ammunition demands for both training and combat (Galloway, 2004; *St. Louis Post-Dispatch*, 2004).

> US production of military-style small arms appears to be increasing as a result of domestic demand as well as export sales.

Box 1.2   Disclosure under threat: US arms transparency derailed?[2]

Soon to be suppressed? The semi-annual *Firearms Commerce in the United States*.

On 23 January 2004, President George W. Bush signed the Consolidated Appropriations Act (House Resolution 2673) into law. This act provides annual operating funds to several federal agencies, but it also threatens to end decades of public transparency regarding firearm commerce in the United States.

A healthy dose of public debate may have preceded the passage of this legislation, but a controversial amendment to the act went virtually unnoticed. The amendment restricts the operations of the Bureau of Alcohol, Tobacco, Firearms and Explosives (ATF) and prohibits the US federal government from preserving records of background checks on gun buyers, which critics feared could be used as a form of gun registration. Now records must be destroyed immediately, unless they reveal criminal intent. The provision also limits the ability of the ATF to monitor individual gun dealers.

The same measure appears to allow the Justice Department—which now runs the ATF—the authority to cease disseminating a series of long-established reports on US firearm issues. Reports include the annual *Firearms Manufacturing and Export Report* and *Firearms Commerce in the United States*.

These publications have provided data on firearm manufacturing, imports, and exports, putting the United States at the forefront of transparency on firearm issues. Given that the United States is the world's largest producer and exporter of firearms (TRANSFERS), this transparency has allowed observers to understand some fundamental trends in the global small arms market. The US reports have also encouraged some countries to open their firearm industries to public scrutiny, setting a precedent for openness that other governments are only now beginning to follow.

The newly passed Consolidated Appropriations Act may very well reverse the trend of growing transparency. Though designed to protect the privacy of individual gun owners and dealers, this policy may obstruct the disclosure of US gun industry figures, to the detriment of international small arms transparency.

Some commentators also suggest that figures for 2002 and 2003 will show increases in the domestic production of firearms in the Unites States. Such a trend might reflect post-11 September 2001 Homeland Security contracts, citizens' demands for self-protection, and a comeback in demand for recreational firearms. Actual figures will not be available, however, until 2004 and 2005 (Thurman, 2003).

Box 1.3   The XM-8: Limited innovation?

After relying on the M-16 and its descendants for almost 40 years, the US Army is finally expected to adopt a new standard infantry weapon. The basic XM-8 is intended to replace the US Army's current M-16. With similar performance to the M-16, the XM-8 should be 20 per cent lighter, thanks to the use of modern polymer and alloy technologies. The polymer reportedly can be coloured in virtually any standard military camouflage colour and the butt is adjustable to the person firing the weapon. The rifle will be produced in four configurations: a standard rifle; a short barrel and stock; a long-barrelled variety for trained marksmen; and a squad automatic rifle or light machine gun. Despite an innovative overall design, the XM-8 will fire the standard NATO 5.56mm ammunition employed in all NATO assault rifles.

Sources: *Jane's International Defence Review*, 2003a; 2003b

PRODUCTS AND PRODUCERS

In 2001, the latest year for which official figures are available, as shown in Table 1.1, the value of firearms production, including ammunition, was USD 2.51 billion in current prices. Total employment in 2001 fell slightly from the previous year, to 16,360 jobs (US Census Bureau, 2003).

Table 1.1 US production of small arms and ammunition, employment, and value of production, 1997-2001

Year	Employment	Value of production (USD in billions)*
1997	16,976	2.22
1998	16,761	2.26
1999	17,061	2.48
2000	17,037	2.39
2001	16,360	2.51
Average	**16,839**	**2.37**

Note: *Based on value of shipments (current USD).
Sources: US Census Bureau (2003); Thurman (2003)

More than three million firearms were produced in the United States in 2001 (US ATF, 2003b). A significant decline compared to the peak in 1994, when more than 5 million firearms were produced, this figure also represents the lowest level since 1992 and a steep drop since 2000 (Thurman, 2003). More than 1.41 million firearms were imported (up from one million in 2000) and more than 190,000 firearms (including military firearms) were exported in 2001 (US ATF, 2003b). Thus, the US domestic market consumed roughly 4.2 million firearms in 2001 (down from more than five million in 2000). The total size of the US domestic market has declined by four per cent between 1997 and 2001 (Thurman, 2003).[3]

As shown in Table 1.2, the volume of total firearms production in the United States declined by more than 20 per cent in 2000–01, after a decline of five per cent in 1999–2000. The decline in domestic production has been linked to various factors, most notably increased imports, a difficult domestic economic climate, and a very competitive domestic market (Thurman, 2003). While production of handguns and long guns—particularly pistols and shotguns—has declined to its lowest level since the early 1990s, however, categories such as machine guns have showed sustained increases since the late 1990s.

Table 1.2 US production and imports of firearms, 1998-2001

Production category	1998	1999	2000	2001
Pistols	960,365	995,446	962,901	623,070
Revolvers	324,390	335,784	318,960	320,143
Rifles	1,345,899	1,569,685	1583,042	1,284,554
Shotguns	1,036,520	1,106,995	898,442	679,813
Machine guns	32,866	22,490	47,400	56,367
Other*	25,151	55,114	62,465	46,833
Total	3,725,191	4,085,514	3,873,210	3,010,780
Total imports	**999,810**	**891,799**	**1,096,782**	**1,411,979**

Note: *Based on value of shipments (current USD).
Sources: US Census Bureau (2003); Thurman (2003)

The top five manufacturers of firearms in 2001, based on the number of items produced, were: Remington Arms Co. (565,586), Sturm, Ruger & Co. (513,597), Smith & Wesson (364,051), Marlin Firearms (258,383), and O. F. Mossberg & Sons

> More than three million firearms were produced in the United States in 2001, a significant decline since 1994, when more than five million were produced.

(182,091). This is a significant change since 2000, with Remington Arms Company replacing Sturm, Ruger & Co as the country's top manufacturer. These five companies accounted for more than 60 percent of total domestic production.

Ranked in terms of types of weapons produced, the list of top US manufacturers has changed somewhat as well (Table 1.3). Although the same firms dominated the American market from 1998 to 2001, their ranking varies from year to year. In 2001 Sturm, Ruger & Co. surpassed Smith & Wesson to become the largest producer of revolvers. Remington Arms replaced Sturm, Ruger & Co. as the leading maker of rifles (US ATF, 2003b).

Table 1.3 Top US producers of selected types of firearms, 2001

Type	Company	1998	1999	2000	2001
Pistols	Sturm, Ruger & Co.	161,058	213,876	233,598	112,847
Revolvers	Smith & Wesson	139,583	152,724	130,587	92,325
	Sturm, Ruger & Co.	-	-	-	150,844
Rifles	Sturm, Ruger & Co.	332,538	426,226	309,017	242,166
	Remington Arms Company	-	-	-	289,470
Shotguns	Remington Arms Company	336,527	364,354	355,178	276,116

Note: Figures are for number of items produced.

Sources: US ATF (2002, 2003a, 2003b); Thurman (2003); US Census Bureau (2003)

Thus, while the overall volume of firearm production in the United States has dropped, the decline has been most pronounced for the civilian market. Military procurement is likely to boost production of military small arms in the coming years, and there is some evidence to suggest civilian small arms production may also increase. If imports of foreign small arms remain competitive and recent production trends are considered, however, it is unlikely that overall US civilian production will increase significantly.

In 2001 US production of handguns and shotguns declined to its lowest level since the early 1990s.

The Russian Federation

Recent improvements in the quantity and quality of both official and unofficial data have helped to provide a more accurate picture of Russian small arms production (CAST, 2003; Pyadushkin, Haug, and Matveeva, 2003). The Russian defence industry, as a whole, has experienced a significant increase in production as a result of increased exports and restructuring efforts (SIPRI, 2003).

Table 1.4 Number of people employed by Russian small arms and light weapons producers, 2001-02

Company, location	2001	2002
JSC Izhmash, Izhevsk	3,673	3,554
Ishevsky Mekhanichesky Zavod (IMZ), Izhevsk	15,200	13,231
JSC Tulsky Oruzheiny Zavod (TOZ), Tula	7,000	7,000
Kovrov Mechanical Plant (KMP), Kovrov	3,000	3,000
OJSC V.A. Degtyaryov Plant, Kovrov	15,000	15,000
'Molot' Vyatskiye Polyany Machine Building Plant, Molot	7,430	7,430
Total	**51,303**	**49,215**

Sources: CAST (2003)

In 2002, the value of production of small arms and light weapons in the Russian Federation was estimated at USD 221.8 million (see Table 1.5). This figure was slightly higher than in 2001, when it was estimated at USD 167.9 million. Total employment in 2002 was slightly lower than in 2001 (see Table 1.4).

As reported in the *Small Arms Survey 2003*, the Russian government has formulated a new policy for the country's small arms and light weapons producers (Small Arms Survey, 2003, p. 19). The aim is to consolidate all Russian producers and developers of small arms and light weapons into two major government-owned holding companies: the Small Arms and Cartridges Corporation and the High-Precision Weapons Corporation (SIPRI, 2003; CAST, 2003; Pyadushkin, Haug, and Matveeva, 2003).

By late 2003, the formation of the Small Arms and Cartridges Corporation had still not been completed (CAST, 2003). JSC Izhmash was intended to become its core company. The holding company was to include IMZ, Molot, TOZ, and the Russian Federation's six ammunition plants (Nozdrachyov, 2002b; Small Arms Survey, 2003, p. 19).

A factory worker assembles part of an AK-47 assault rifle at the Izhmash plant in Izhevsk, the Russian Federation, in November 2002—55 years after the release of the inaugural Kalashnikov gun.

The formation of the High-Precision Weapons Corporation, planned for 2002, is also lagging behind schedule. The holding company was intended to bring together all manufacturers of light weapons, mainly man-portable air defence systems, and includes the Tula-based KBP Instrument Design Bureau, the Kovrov Mechanical Plant, the Degtyaryov Plant, and the Kolomna Machine-Building Design Bureau (MANPADS).

The main difficulty in setting up these holding companies has been the absence of a mechanism for integrating government-owned and private companies into one corporate entity. The government's plan of lumping together facilities on formal grounds has also tended to overlook the established production cooperation ties between individual facilities.

Table 1.5 Estimated value of SALW production in the Russian Federation* (USD millions in current prices)

Company	Products	2001	2002
JSC Izhmash	Kalashnikov assault rifles, Nikonov assault rifle, Bizon sub-machine gun, Dragunov sniper rifle.	13.8	13.2
IMZ	90% of the Russian Federation's short-barrelled arms, including the Yarygin (Pya) pistol.	57.7	52
TOZ	Konkurs anti-tank weapon, PPS pistol, 9mm AS carbine, VSS sniper rifle, AKS-74 SMG.	13.4	29.2
KMP	Kalashnikov machine guns, RPG-7 grenade launcher, anti-tank missiles, AEK-971 SMG, AEK-919K Kashtan machine pistol.	19.8	2.5
V.A. Degtyaryov Plant	Heavy machine guns, grenade launchers, anti-aircraft guns, anti-tank missiles, MANPADS.	42	108.5
Molot	Metis anti-tank weapon, automatic grenade launchers, Kalashnikov light machine guns.	21.2	16.4
Total		167.9	221.8

Note: * Including civilian firearms.

Sources: CAST (2003); *Eksport Vooruzheniy Journal* (2002); Kamakin (2003); Military News Agency (2000); Poroskov (2003); Tula (2003)

SMALL ARMS SURVEY 2004

The total value of all reported small arms and light weapons production in 2001 was USD 221.8 million, up 32 per cent from the year before (see Table 1.5). As shown in Table 1.6, at least 650,000 units of civilian firearms were produced in the Russian Federation in 2002, down from around one million in 2001 (Small Arms Survey, 2003, p. 20). Production figures for 2002 account for civilian production at Izhmash, IMZ, and Molot; no production information for that year is available from TOZ and TsKIOB SOO.

Table 1.6   Production of civilian firearms (units) in the Russian Federation by major manufacturers, 1999-2002

Company	1999	2000	2001	2002
JSC Izhmash	70,000	76,607	87,672	82,887
IMZ	630,000	570,000	800,000	560,000
Molot	26,651	21,979	12,755	12,802
TOZ	n/a	n/a	60,000	n/a
TsKIOB SOO	n/a	n/a	18,000	n/a
Total	**726,651**	**668,589**	**978,427**	**655,689**

Sources: CAST (2003)

A Russian saleswoman presents a display of Kalashnikov assault rifles at the Russian stand of the International Defence Exhibition in New Delhi in February 2004.

Domestic deliveries of small arms and light weapons may increase in 2004, when government spending on the procurement of new arms for the Russian armed forces is expected to grow by more than 50 per cent. For the first time in years, the government has announced that new types of small arms will be delivered to Russian troops (Safronov, 2003). The government has allocated about USD 33 million for the procurement of new small arms for the Defence Ministry, Ministry of Interior, and other Russian security agencies for 2004.

The Russian Federation's small arms industry is much more export-dependent than its US counterpart, largely because companies catering to the domestic market have often struggled to receive payment from government departments and have thus stagnated. This struggle to receive payment appears to be changing, as high oil revenues reduce Russian government debt burdens and facilitate renewed military procurement (*Jane's International Defence Review*, 2004a). The US and Russian small arms industries thus appear to display divergent trends. While the volume of production of US firms stagnates or declines as the domestic market shrinks or yields to imports, Russian exports appear to account for the industry's growth. The corresponding civilian market trends are not unrelated: Russian firms appear to have increased sales to the United States (TRANSFERS). Within their military small arms sectors, however, trends are more harmonious. Both countries are likely to expand production of at least some types of military small arms, as orders are placed for new weapons systems in the near future.

REGIONAL SURVEY: SMALL ARMS PRODUCTION IN LATIN AMERICA

To gain greater insight into global trends, this edition of the *Small Arms Survey* focuses on small arms production in Latin America, a region that illustrates the heterogeneity of the global small arms industry. While virtually every country in the region has some production capability, this capability ranges from very modest, state-run ammunition and

PRODUCTS AND PRODUCERS

small arms assembly plants, to large-scale, private production of a full range of small arms for export. In this section we present a survey of the region, by country, with case studies of the most important arms-producing companies.[4]

In contrast to the United States and the Russian Federation, there is little pressure to develop new military weapons in Latin America. Most of the region's armed forces use older licence-produced European, and in some cases Israeli, weapons. Exports to the United States appear to have experienced consistent growth over most of the past five years (see Table 1.8). The civilian and law enforcement markets appear to be staples of the region's largest companies, located in Argentina, Brazil, and Mexico. Predictably, major producers in Latin America are not immune to global trends towards industrial consolidation and joint ventures.

At least ten countries in Latin America have the capacity to produce small arms, light weapons, or ammunition. Generally speaking, we can divide the countries of the region into major producers, medium-sized or growing producers, and minor producers. The vast majority of countries in the region are minor producers, with most production limited to state-owned factories or arsenals, often controlled or run by the armed forces. These countries occasionally export ammunition or even small shipments of small arms, but production runs tend to be sporadic and the quality of products is low.

The only major producer in the region is Brazil, whose arms industry is highly developed and diversified. In 2002, it exported at least ten times as many small arms and ammunition as its closest regional competitor, Argentina. Brazil is the second-largest producer in the Western hemisphere after the United States. It is the third-largest supplier, by value, of small arms—mainly handguns—and ammunition to the US domestic market.

Medium-sized producers include Chile, Mexico, and Argentina, based on the quality and variety of small arms production and the presence of consistent exports. Of these, Argentina has the most diversified industry and has the longest history of arms production. Though its industry was hit hard by liberalization in the 1990s, it is showing signs of resurgence in the wake of currency devaluation. Mexico is not a major producer of firearms, but it has benefited from the North American Free Trade Agreement, becoming a major exporter of ammunition and parts to the United States, thanks to the *maquila regime*.[5] Chile's production is still limited to a single state-owned company, but its licensing agreements and joint venture with Brazil's Taurus make it an important regional producer.

> Most Latin American countries occasionally export ammunition or small arms, but production runs tend to be sporadic and the quality of products is low.

Map 1.1 Latin American countries producing small arms and light weapons

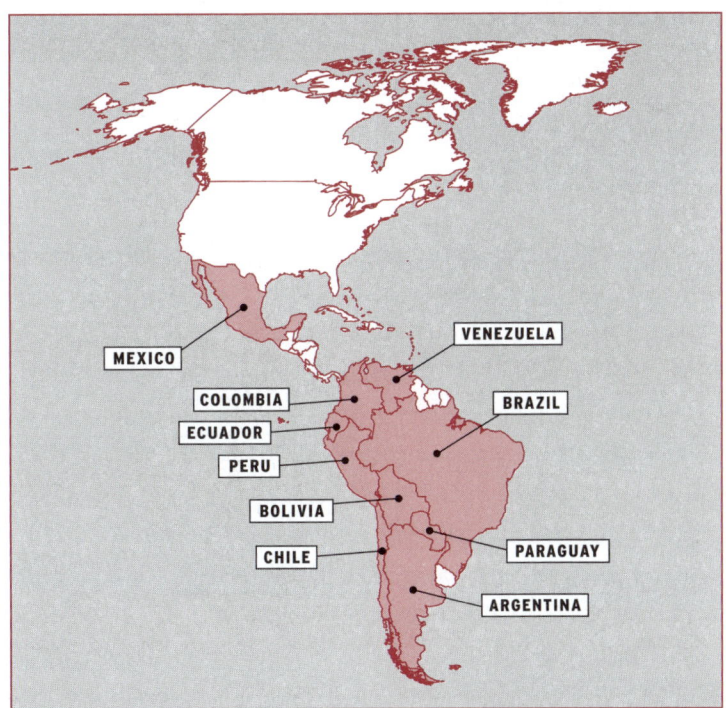

SMALL ARMS SURVEY 2004

Table 1.7   Production of small arms and light weapons and ammunition in Latin American countries*

Country	Military small arms and light weapons	Civilian small arms	Ammunition (military and/or civilian)	Significant exporter of small arms and light weapons
Argentina	X	X	X	X
Bolivia		X	X	
Brazil	X	X	X	X
Chile	X	X	X	X
Colombia	X	X	X	
Ecuador	X		X	
Mexico	X	X	X	X
Paraguay			X	
Peru	X	X	X	
Venezuela	X	X	X	
Total (known)	8	8	10	4

Note. * Assessment of current production capabilities based on both primary and secondary sources.

Sources: Dreyfus and Lessing (2003); Omega Foundation (2003); Forecast International (2003); Gander and Cutshaw (2003)

Table 1.8   Latin American exports* of SALW and ammunition to the United States, 1996-2002 (current USD millions)

Country (ranking in 2002)	1996	1997	1998	1999	2000	2001	2002	Total
Argentina (19)	1.75	2.56	2.26	3.72	4.08	5.16	5.72	25.25
Brazil (3)	31.88	30.96	28.00	36.57	40.69	35.62	56.76	260.46
Mexico (15)**	8.81	11.33	12.13	14.76	12.47	22.22	16.09	97.80
Total imports from Latin America	42.44	44.84	42.39	55.05	57.24	62.99	78.57	383.51

* By customs value.
** Includes parts and air and blank pellet precision rifles, which are not classified as small arms according to the 1997 UN definition.

Source: International Firearms Trade (2003)

Argentina

Argentina is one of the most important and long-established small arms producers in Latin America. Its small arms industry comprises private companies and a state-owned military–industrial complex. Both sectors prospered in the 1970s and 1980s under the umbrella of protectionist import-substitution policies. Having undergone a serious crisis in the 1990s (Small Arms Survey, 2001, p. 28), the industry today faces an uncertain future.

The opening of the economy and the US dollar–Argentine peso (ARS) parity regime under President Carlos Menem (1989–99) and President Fernando de la Rúa's neo-liberal policies (December 1999–December 2002) led to the closure or downsizing of several small arms companies. The reform of the country's small arms control legislation in 1994 created new prerequisites for the purchase and possession of .22 and .32 calibre handguns and hunting rifles, which especially affected producers of low-quality handguns. Of the more than 20 private Argentine firms that produced small arms in the early 1980s, only five have survived.

The state-owned Dirección General de Fabricaciones Militares (DGFM) has also undergone restructuring. The Ministry of the Economy intervened in DGFM in 1996, suspending all its state-to-state exports of military weapons, a policy that remains in effect to this day. DGFM has responded by reorienting its small arms production towards the civilian and police markets, emphasizing semi-automatic pistols and .22 rifles.

Since 2001, however, the industry has begun to recover. Three factors have contributed to its rejuvenation:

- Currency devaluation made exports internationally competitive, with a positive impact on the country's domestic industry as a whole, including the small arms sector.[6]
- The demand for small arms rose significantly in response to civil unrest after the December 2001 devaluation.[7]
- The government relaxed its policy on permits for small arms purchases and possession by civilians in 2002–03.[8]

These three factors led to increased sales by the well-established Argentine arms manufacturers. They also rescued a few small-scale, lower-quality producers that were on the verge of bankruptcy in the 1990s.

Although total production figures for small arms production in Argentina are not available, the evolution of exports provides an idea of the expansion of the industry since 2000. Between 2000 and 2002, exports grew by more than 40 per cent.[9] The major component of small arms exports was pistols and revolvers. In 2002, Argentina was the 19th-largest supplier, by value, of small arms and ammunition to the United States, and the third-largest supplier from Latin America (after Brazil and Mexico). Total exports in 2002 were worth USD 5.7 million (USD 5.1 million in 2001) (International Firearms Trade, 2003).

Police fire tear gas during civil unrest in December 2001 in Buenos Aires, Argentina.

DGFM/Fray Luis Beltrán (FLB): Until the early 1990s, DGFM was a large military–industrial complex of 12 factories whose production was directly and indirectly linked to meeting Argentina's national defence requirements (Small Arms Survey, 2001, p. 29). By 2003, all but four plants had been either closed or privatized; only two of them produce small arms.

The production of small arms and light weapons was, until the beginning of the 1990s, concentrated in three factories.[10] These were the Portable Military Arms Plant (FMAP) Domingo Matheu (small arms), the Fábrica Militar ammunition plant FLB (small arms and ammunition), and the Fábrica Militar Río Tercero (FMRT) (light weapons).[11]

In the late 1990s, FMAP Domingo Matheu was closed and merged with FLB. The production of small arms continues at FLB, together with the production of hand grenades and small arms ammunition. The plant currently produces small arms for civilian use and for the military, police, and security forces (gendarmerie and coast guard), as well as ammunition and hand grenades.

In 2000, FLB's prospects were extremely poor. The company was in the process of being dismantled and there were no prospects or plans for the remaining plants (Small Arms Survey, 2001, p. 29). The USD–ARS parity also made foreign handguns and ammunition, especially those from Brazil, a much cheaper and more attractive option for federal and provincial police and security forces, once a captive DGFM market of more than 150,000 personnel.

The demand for small arms in Argentina rose significantly in response to the general civil unrest after the December 2001 currency devaluation.

By early 2003 the situation had changed. The plant had set production records for the manufacture of .22 ammunition cartridges, mostly for export to Brazil, Paraguay, and the United States. There were plans for the launch of new pistol models and for recovering police and public security markets.[12] And although there were no changes in legislation regarding defence production, soon after President Néstor Kirchner took office in May 2003, he urged expansion of the state military–industrial complex as a development tool for the country (Braslavsky, 2003).

FLB's principal products for the civilian market include 9mm pistols and a .22 carbine. At present, the plant has the capacity to produce 20,000 pistols and 2,000 carbines per year. Although it has the licences to produce FN-FAL assault rifles and FMK-3 sub-machine guns, it is not currently doing so. The company now has 211 employees, down from 249 in 2000. Exports of products for both the civilian and military markets have increased in the wake of the devaluation, but no detailed information is currently available on the value, volume, or destination of exports.

The most important private sector small arms producers in Argentina include Bersa S.A., Lasserre S.A., F&L SRL, Azor, and FANAC, whose activities are briefly described below.

Bersa S.A.[13] had consolidated its position as the leading Argentine private producer of pistols for the civilian market by the 1980s, by which time it had also begun exporting. In 1990, Bersa began producing 9mm and .380 pistols, which were well received by both domestic and foreign markets (especially the United States). In 1994, however, a change in US legislation limited the number of rounds semi-automatic weapons could hold in their magazines, and Bersa's Thunder 9 model pistols were excluded from the US market. Nonetheless, the company adapted very quickly, changing the features of its weapons and launching a number of new models in order to recover its former markets.

With the devaluation of the ARS in 2002, Bersa expanded its position in the international market. The company was responsible for nearly 70 per cent of Argentine exports of pistols and revolvers in 2003 (through April) and 77 per cent in 2002.[14] Production is heavily influenced by, and responsive to, 'gun fashion' and market preferences. The company launched a .40 model in 2000, .40 and 9mm compact models in 2001, and .45 ('fashionable' again) models in 2002. In 2002 Bersa's exports were worth USD 3.5 million , compared to USD 3.6 million in 2001. The United States accounted for 80–90 per cent of the company's exports.

> In 2002, the US accounted for 80–90 per cent of Bersa's exports.

By late 2002, Bersa was producing 20 different models of pistols in six different calibres. The majority of its production is exported, mostly to the United States. The company employs 70 people and produces an average of 40,000 pistols per year. Besides the civilian market, Bersa is an important supplier to the Argentine Armed Forces and Security Forces, as well as some provincial police, to whom it sells about 10,000 pistols a year (Casciotti, 2004). With new machinery acquired in 2002, Bersa expects to expand its production by 20 per cent in the coming years.

Lasserre S.A. (also known as Rexio) is a mid-sized company that concentrates its production on revolvers and shotguns. It produces 26 models of revolver in three different calibres as well as six models of shotgun. The company survived the crisis of the 1990s and has consolidated its position as a leading domestic producer of revolvers. Exports totalled USD 136,725 in 2002 (significantly down from USD 446,366 in 2001).[15] The main external markets for its products are other Latin American countries and the United States.

F&L SRL is a small company that produces low-cost, low-price revolvers. It manufactures six models in three different calibres. The company reactivated its production after the 2002 devaluation. The principal destinations for exports are neighbouring Latin American countries. The value of exports in 2002 was in the range of USD 200,000–300,000.[16]

Azor and *FANAC* are two small companies that produce low-cost, low-priced revolvers. FANAC produces Forastero revolvers and shotguns, and reactivated its production after the devaluation of the ARS. Azor, which produces M99 model revolvers, was recently established.[17]

Bolivia

Bolivia has a small ammunition factory, the *Fábrica Boliviana de Municiones* (FBM). It produces various types of ammunition for the Bolivian armed forces (Forecast International, 2004). FBM is administered by the Armed Forces Corporation for National Development, known as COFADENA, which is linked to the Ministry of Defence. The factory reportedly also engages in limited production of shotguns for the civilian market.

Brazil

Brazil is one of the world's most important small arms producers (Small Arms Survey, 2003). It is by far Latin America's largest producer of small arms and military equipment. Its small arms industry is made up of both state-owned and private companies which have, in recent years, expanded into foreign markets, signed licensed production and joint venture agreements, and created foreign subsidiaries (Small Arms Survey, 2001, p. 30).

According to Brazilian government statistics, total sales of civilian small arms and related ammunition and parts in 2001 (the latest year for which data is available) were worth USD 100.3 million. The vast majority of this production was exported (TRANSFERS).

Like many countries in the region, Brazil's arms industry dates back to the country's independence and government efforts to supply its own armed forces. By the 1950s numerous private firms were producing handguns, hunting rifles, and shotguns for the domestic market, including the local Beretta subsidiary. Yet it was the staunchly protectionist economic policies of Brazil's military dictatorship (1964–85) that laid the foundations for the diversified, export-oriented industry that exists today. In 1974, the military government implemented the Military Equipment Export Policy (Política Nacional de Exportação de Material de Emprego Militar), a series of incentives for private and state-owned producers to export arms; in 1975, the armed forces reorganized their arms factories into a single company, Imbel; and throughout the decade, cooperation between military research institutes, industrial organizations, and the Brazilian Development Bank (BNDES) led to the development and consolidation of new arms-producing companies. In 1980, BNDES also provided capital funds for the repurchase by Brazilians of controlling shares in the Companhia Brasileira de Cartuchos (CBC), Brazil's only small arms ammunition producer (Purcena, 2003).

In the 1980s, Brazil's defence industry boomed as it exported heavy military equipment to the Middle East during the Iran–Iraq war. By the 1990s, Brazil was well established as a mid-sized global player in the international arms market, and in the two years that encompassed the Gulf War (1991–92), Brazil exported more than USD 300 million in small arms and ammunition, much of it to Saudi Arabia and other countries in the region.[18] The following years registered a tapering off of exports—due in part to the pegging of Brazil's currency to the USD in 1994—but the subsequent devaluation of the Brazilian real from 1998 onward has led to a resurgence of exports. In 2002, exports nearly doubled, reaching USD 156 million.

The 1990s were also a time of consolidation. Today Brazil's small arms industry is concentrated in three large producers: Taurus, CBC, and Imbel. Though only Imbel is state-owned, CBC and Taurus both maintain intimate contacts with the Brazilian military; the result is a great deal of company influence over both domestic and foreign policy. The industry also has its own lobby group, which is publicly active in opposing domestic arms control legislation.

> Brazil is the second-largest small arms producer in the Americas after the US.

> Brazil's total sales of civilian small arms and related ammunition and parts in 2001 were worth USD 100.3 million.

Imbel (Indústria de Material Bélico do Brasil), established in 1974, is a state-owned company with ties to the Brazilian Ministry of Defence and specifically the Brazilian army. In addition to a wide range of heavy conventional weapons, the company also produces various small arms and light weapons. It manufactures FN-FAL assault rifles under licence for military use, as well as a line of pistol models based on the Colt .45 for military and police use. It also produces .38 calibre handguns for civilian sales (Imbel, 2004). Imbel has a joint venture with Royal Ordnance of the UK and Schahin Participações Ltda. of Brazil to distribute Imbel small arms and ammunition worldwide (South America Ordnance, 2004). Its small arms are especially popular among security forces across Latin America.

Forjas Taurus is Brazil's leading producer and exporter of handguns. In 2002, Taurus had sales of USD 43.9 million, making it one of the most successful Latin American small arms companies.[19] It currently manufactures 24 models of revolver and 14 pistol models. Most of these are based on Beretta models, since Taurus purchased Beretta's Brazilian subsidiary in 1980 (Taurus, 2004). The Taurus name has become internationally recognized, particularly in the United States, where it has a major market presence. In Miami, Taurus has a factory that assembles arms especially for the US market. It also has a joint venture to produce guns in Chile. In 1997, Taurus purchased the patents, designs, and production rights for Amadeo Rossi handguns, making it the only Brazilian private supplier of pistols and revolvers for Brazil's domestic civilian market.[20]

> **Taurus is Brazil's leading producer and exporter of handguns and one of the most successful Latin American small arms companies.**

Companhia Brasileira de Cartuchos is the largest Brazilian producer of small arms ammunition. In addition to a wide range of ammunition for handguns and long guns, CBC produces 18 models of shotgun and four models of rifle (CBC, 2004). In 2002, CBC had total sales of USD 41.2 million, of which 34 per cent were from exports, 29 per cent from the Brazilian civilian market, and 37 per cent from the Brazilian police and military. Nearly 90 per cent of sales are from ammunition.[21]

Amadeo Rossi produces various shotguns and rifles, having sold its handgun business to Forjas Taurus in 1997. The company suffered a loss of USD 14 million in 2001, the last year for which data is available. In 2000, the company had total sales of USD 5.4 million and employed 1,354 people. Rossi exports 77 per cent of its production and 50 per cent of production is sold through Braztech Inc., its US distributor.[22]

Five other Brazilian producers also manufacture some small arms and light weapons or ammunition. These include: *E. R. Amantino & Cia.* (hunting shotguns); *Companhia de Explosivos Valparaiba* (hand grenades and rifle grenade launcher adapters); *Mekanika* and *Bilbao*, both involved in producing Uru Model II 9mm sub-machine guns (Gander and Cutshaw, 2003); *Hyrdroar S.A.*[23] (mortars and portable rocket launchers); and *FN Herstal* of Belgium, which has a local subsidiary plant producing FN MAG light machine gun parts for export to Belgium (Amantino, 2004; Forecast International, 2003b).[24]

Chile [25]

Chile has a well-established domestic defence industry (Small Arms Survey, 2001, p. 30); however, there is virtually no domestic production of small arms for the civilian market in Chile. Domestic civilian demand for small arms is met almost entirely by imports, with products sold in authorized private gun shops. There is no private production of small arms in Chile, although one private company, *Metalnor* (*Industria Metalurgica del Norte Ltda.*), produces two types of hand grenade (Gander and Cutshaw, 2001, pp. 560–61).

Domestic production of small arms is concentrated in one state-owned company: *Fábricas y Maestranzas del Ejército* (FAMAE). Administered by the army, the firm primarily supplies the Chilean Armed Forces with arms and equipment. FAMAE has various divisions, including an Arms Division (specializing in the production of small arms); and an Ammunitions Division (specializing in the production of ammunition for small arms, light weapons, and major conventional weapons).

PRODUCTS AND PRODUCERS

FAMAE has a staff of 134 working in its small arms plant, which produces about 5,000 arms per year at prices ranging from USD 500 to USD 900. Exports (which are not constant) represent about 15–20 per cent of the company's sales.

FAMAE's development was indirectly spurred by the Kennedy Amendment, passed by the US Congress in 1974 to prohibit US arms sales and security assistance to Chile (Dreyfus, 2000; USAID, 2004).[26] In 1984 FAMAE obtained a licence from SIG Arms AG of Switzerland (now Swiss Arms AG) to produce rifles. Production began in 1991 and continued until 2003 with the SG 540 series assault rifles, which are slowly replacing the old Swiss SG 510 in service with the Chilean Army. Production is now concentrating on newer models as part of an ongoing process of shifting all Chilean Armed Forces rifles from 7.62mm to 5.56mm calibre.[27]

Most of FAMAE's exports consist of versions of its SAF sub-machine gun based on the SG 540 rifle. Serial production began in 1993. This indigenous sub-machine gun has had a lot of success as a weapon for police forces and special military forces and has been sold to the National Police of Paraguay, the Police of the Province of Buenos Aires (Argentina), the National Police of El Salvador, the National Police of Panama, and the Portuguese Gendarmerie (FAMAE, 2002). In 2000, FAMAE entered into a strategic alliance with Forjas Taurus of Brazil to produce a version of the SAF sub-machine gun for the military police forces (uniformed security police) of the 27 states of Brazil, some 385,000 personnel in all (IISS, 2002).

Domestic production of small arms in Chile is concentrated in one state-owned company: FAMAE.

Colombia

Colombia's constitution of 1991 establishes a state monopoly on the production and commerce in small arms and light weapons. Private producers, retailers, importers, and exporters are not permitted. Small arms production in Colombia is legally monopolized by *Industria Militar* (INDUMIL), operated by the Ministry of Defence.

INDUMIL's main function is to supply Colombia's Armed Forces and the National Police. Civilian customers are a secondary market, with private security companies accounting for most of the civilian purchases. In addition to being a manufacturer, INDUMIL is also the only authorized firearms and ammunition importer in the country. There are no legal private gunsmiths in Colombia. Commercial small arms can only be purchased from INDUMIL's main commercial office in Bogotá and from its 30 retail offices located throughout the country. Besides its own revolvers and shotguns, the company also supplies the civilian market with imported small arms. As of July 2003, INDUMIL had a permanent staff of around 1,000.

The *General José María Córdova Small Arms and Ammunition Plant* is Colombia's main firearms and ammunition production facility. Until Germany stopped small arms exports to Colombia in response to allegations of human rights violations by military and security forces, the official standard assault rifle was the H&K G-3.[28] Today the plant produces the Israeli Galil assault rifle, which was adopted in 1994 as the standard rifle of the Armed Forces and the National Police. To date, INDUMIL has manufactured some 37,500 Galil rifles to replace the old G-3s (which, according to authorities at INDUMIL, were destroyed after being taken out of service) and outfit newly created units. The company also manufactures hand grenades and mortar bombs.

INDUMIL monopolizes small arms production in Colombia.

INDUMIL produces various weapons for the civilian market and private security markets, including revolvers made under licence from the Spanish company Llama Gabilondo. The terms of the contract specify that the production of revolvers is now autonomous—i.e. INDUMIL may modify the original models and export them. INDUMIL produces 7,000 to 8,000 revolvers per year. As Colombia does not import revolvers, there is a captive market for this product. The company also produces various types of shotgun and a range of ammunition for both the military and civilian markets.

SMALL ARMS SURVEY 2004

> **Box 1.4   Illicit production: FARC workshops and the underground war industry**[29]
>
> Illicit, small-scale craft production of small arms, especially rudimentary single-shot weapons, is common in many parts of Latin America. The situation in Colombia is quite different. A large-scale, illicit underground arms industry is run largely by one particular insurgent group, the FARC (Fuerzas Armadas Revolucionarias de Colombia). The FARC's underground arms industry was established during the 1990s as a result of various factors, including a history of illicit craft production in Colombia and corruption among some INDUMIL workers. Today its products include sub-machine guns, mortars, and hand grenades manufactured using industrial machinery.
>
> Illicit production for the FARC is organized into two main areas of manufacture: arms for urban militias and arms for rural FARC units. The arms for urban militias (mostly craft-made firearms for kidnapping, self-defence, and assassination) are produced in *talleres de armamento popular* (TAPs, popular arms workshops). TAPs first began operating in the late 1990s and are small enough to be installed in basements, homes, garages, and the like. Each workshop typically has 5–6 workers, supervised by a co-opted military officer or INDUMIL technician who earns a salary from the FARC. The most common weapons produced by the TAPs are single-shot, single-barrel shotguns or *changones* (derived from the English word 'shotgun'). The TAPs also produce copies of the Ingram 9mm machine gun, the preferred weapon for assassinations. The prices of these TAP-made Ingrams range from USD 70 to USD 140, compared to USD 1,400 for an original Ingram on the legal market. TAPs have also recently begun production of semi-automatic pistols based on Beretta models.
>
> The arms for rural FARC units are produced in *talleres de frente de guerra* (TFGs, front-line workshops). The most common weapons are combat support light weapons such as mortars, ammunition for mortars, and hand grenades. Most of the material needed for these weapons is stolen from the oil industry. Machinery is imported through front companies. Mortars and hand grenades produced by the TFGs are copied from standard Colombian military weapons. Technical advice is provided by active or retired INDUMIL technicians. Most of the TFGs started to operate in the mid-1990s, and serial production of mortar bombs is now carried out using sand mould technology.

Ecuador

Ecuador is not a significant producer of small arms. A factory in Santa Barbara, run by the armed forces, produces small arms ammunition for internal use, recharges shotgun cartridges, and at times has turned out PAME-90 sub-machine guns. The production runs have never been large, and the (official) destination of such weapons has always been internal use by the armed forces or the police, though it is possible that ammunition has been sold to civilians. There is no record of official exports of these weapons.

Ecuador has significant craft production of *cartucheras*, usually single-shot pistols. These are inexpensive weapons of low quality and rustic appearance, made in small workshops without advanced industrial equipment. These workshops may be clandestine or legal. There are currently 96 of these manufacturers registered with the Army's Department of Arms Control.[30] Though not produced on an industrial scale, *cartucheras* are extremely common in Ecuador.[31] They are widely available on the illicit market at prices accessible to the average Ecuadorean (USD 40–50) and are seen as a kind of 'people's gun', while imported handguns are bought by the middle class and wealthy individuals.

Mexico

Mexico has long produced various types of small arms, but has not developed a large or diversified defence industrial base. It remains a fairly significant small arms parts and ammunition producer in the Latin American context.[32] All domestic small arms production is tightly controlled by the state, and it is almost impossible for any new private company to begin manufacturing, importing, exporting, or selling small arms and light weapons. Existing private companies, including Productos Mendoza, Industrias Ruiz Cabañas, and Industrias Tecnos, are only authorized to produce small arms parts and .22 rifles exclusively for export.

The only company manufacturing military-style small arms is the state-owned *Dirección General de Fábricas de la Defensa Nacional* (DGFDN), which produces largely for the Mexican armed forces. The factory has around 1,000 employees and makes about 5,000 small arms per year. Since the late 1970s, DGFDN has produced H&K G-3 rifles. Its current products also include pistols and MP-5 sub-machine guns, all produced under licence from H&K of Germany. There are no reported exports by DGFDN. The company also produces mortars, hand grenades, and various calibres of ammunition for military small arms.

Productos Mendoza is one of the few private companies in Mexico allowed to produce a 'lethal' weapon—a sub-machine gun, the HM-3S 9mm Parabellum—which is in use by Mexican police and security forces. The company employs 350 workers, makes an average of 100,000 weapons per year, and exports nearly 50 per cent of its production.

Industrias Ruiz Cabañas is a medium-sized private company producing .22 rifles exclusively for the export market.[33] The company's total sales are about USD 2.5 million, of which 30 per cent are exported, mainly to the United States. It has recently moved to larger premises and is looking for a strategic partner in Europe.

Mexico's main producer of small arms ammunition is a private company, *Industrias Tecnos* (Tecnos, 2004). In the United States, the main destination of Tecnos products, the company's wholly owned distributor, Centurion Ordnances, markets the company's products under the trademark 'Golden Eagle'.

Paraguay

Paraguay has a limited domestic capability to produce small arms ammunition. Under the direction of the Ministry of Defence, Paraguay Military Industries manufactures small arms ammunition at the Piribebuy facility, originally set up with assistance from Belgium in the mid-1980s. It has the capacity to produce significantly more ammunition than the country's domestic requirement, and an agreement has been reached to provide small arms ammunition to Chile (Forecast International, 2002).

Peru

Peru has a modest state-owned small arms industry aimed primarily at satisfying domestic military and police needs. There are no private small arms producers in Peru, although there is widespread, clandestine, small-scale craft production, principally of shotguns and hunting rifles.

The Peruvian armed forces control two small arms and ammunition factories. The *Servicio Industrial de la Marina* (SIMA) operates the *Centro de Fabricación de Armas* (SIMA–CEFAR), located at the Callao Naval Base, near Lima. Renamed *SIMA Electronica* in 1996, this factory is the only one capable of producing small arms on an industrial scale in Peru. Its main product line has been a family of 9mm sub-machine guns (Hogg and Weeks, 2000). In addition to a range of 12-gauge shotguns for the civilian market, the factory has also produced Barracuda revolvers under licence from Colt's Manufacturing (United States) and FN Herstal (Belgium) made replacement parts for Argentine-made FMK-3 and FAL assault rifles, and assembled Browning HP-35 semi-automatic pistols (RENAR, 2002).

CEFAR produces 12-gauge shotguns in three model variants, as well as 9mm pistols and the MPG 79 sub-machine gun.[34] Production is often intermittent and deliveries include weapons not currently in production, such as the MPG-84.[35]

The *Fábrica de Armas y Municiones del Ejército* (FAME), owned by the Peruvian Army, produced a range of ammunition for internal use and some export markets until it was deactivated in the mid-1990s. Reports differ as to the current status of FAME, though the factory seems to be intact and may have been reactivated to fulfil one or more orders (Olive, 1999).

Venezuela

Compared to major regional producers such as Brazil and Argentina, Venezuela is not an important producer of small arms. The only relevant company is the state-owned and -administered *Compañia Anónima de Industrias Militares* (CAVIM), established in 1975. CAVIM has four divisions, each with its own facilities and personnel. The metal-mechanical division, which includes the small arms and ammunition branch, is based in the city of Maracay, in Aragua province. With a staff of 50, this facility assembles small arms from imported and locally produced parts, under contract to a variety of foreign producers, including the Belgian firm FN Herstal, Taurus of Brazil, and SIG of Switzerland. The company has assembled pistols and automatic rifles for the military market, and pistols for the civilian market.[36]

In 1997, CAVIM entered into a three-year agreement to assemble SIG-Sauer P226 9mm pistols, with the intention of replacing the old FN HP 9mm of the Armed Forces. The agreement was unilaterally rescinded by SIG in 1999 and production was discontinued following a series of disagreements. In 2002, CAVIM signed a strategic alliance with Glock (Austria) for the assembly of 9mm and .40 pistols.[37] CAVIM manufactures ammunition, producing about 50 million rounds per year. As a result Venezuela is largely self-sufficient in small arms ammunition (Forecast International, 2002). The main markets for these products are the domestic civilian market, national police and military forces, and Caribbean and Central American countries (CAVIM, 2004).

Three minor private companies produce small arms and ammunition: *Cartuchos Victoria S.A.* (ammunition); *Comercial Vasco–Venezolana* (ammunition and shotguns); and *Industrias Armaiola* (shotguns). None of these companies holds a significant share of the domestic market, which is basically dominated by imports and, particularly in the case of law enforcement and armed forces small arms and ammunition, by CAVIM.

Summary: Small arms production in Latin America

This regional survey of Latin America illustrates the diversity of production among a group of countries with a combined population of 457 million. Far from representing any uniform regional approach, Latin America's firms range from state-owned monopolies to large and small private companies. Some countries are dominated by a single national producer, while others are home to innumerable small-scale manufacturers. Some aggressively pursue industrial strategies and export opportunities, while others have very small domestic production and rely almost entirely on imports.

> The different trajectories of Latin American small arms producers will diverge even more in the years to come.

Among the most important factors tying the region together is dependence on foreign designs, whether formally licensed or informally copied. With the important exceptions of major exporters led by Argentina, Chile, Mexico, and above all Brazil, its small arms producers tend to be niche manufacturers, serving captive local markets.

These countries share a particular commitment to establish and maintain a national small arms production capability, even when it seems uneconomic and impractical. Beyond widely shared origins in nationalized industries run by the armed forces and a common technological foundation, the small arms and ammunition makers of Latin America have little in common. Their different trajectories—the result of specific economic circumstances, legal environments, domestic markets, and export ambitions—will diverge even more in the years to come.

POPULAR MILITARY SMALL ARMS AND LIGHT WEAPONS

What are the most popular or common small arms? *The Small Arms Survey 2001* compiled a list of some of the world's largest producers and best-known small arms, updated here in Table 1.9. This section focuses on the weapons most widely distributed among armed forces worldwide (STOCKPILES). Characterized by advanced materials (i.e. composites) as well as lighter ammunition, greater rates of fire, and increased lethality, the recent emergence of new designs of weapons is driven by major rearmament programmes in a number of countries, including China, France, the Russian Federation, Spain, and the United States (*Jane's Defence Weekly* 2003a, 2003b, 2003c; NTI, 2004; VIC, 2000).

Table 1.9 Major producers of SALW by weapon type, company, and country of manufacture

Weapon type	Producer company (country)
Sidearms	Beretta (Italy) FN Herstal (Belgium) Glock (Austria) Heckler & Koch (Germany) Smith & Wesson (United States)
Assault rifles (including carbines)	Colt's Manufacturing (United States) FN Herstal (Belgium) Heckler & Koch (Germany) Izhmash (Russian Federation) Norinco (China)
Sniper/anti-materiel rifles	Accuracy International (UK) Barrett (United States) Heckler & Koch (Germany) Izhmash (Russian Federation)
Sub-machine guns	Heckler & Koch (Germany) IMI (Israel) Izhmash (Russian Federation) KBP (Russian Federation) Norinco (China)
Machine guns	FN Herstal (Belgium) General Dynamics (United States) Heckler & Koch (Germany) IMI (Israel) Norinco (China)
Small arms ammunition	FN Herstal (Belgium) Nammo (Finland/Norway/Sweden) RUAG Ammotec (Germany/Switzerland/Sweden) Sellier & Bellot (Czech Republic) Winchester Olin (United States /Belgium)
Grenade launchers	General Dynamics (United States) Heckler & Koch (Germany) KBP (Russian Federation) Norinco (China) Singapore Technologies Kinetics (Singapore)
Anti-tank guided weapons	Euromissile (France) Norinco (China) Raytheon–Lockheed Martin (United States)

Note: Recoilless guns and mortars are not included.

Source: Gander (2003); Gander and Cutshaw (2003)

Sidearms (pistols and revolvers)

Pistols and revolvers are the most widely dispersed and numerous of small arms. By their very nature, being easily concealed, easy to handle, and inherently attractive to many, the main types vary from region to region and even within each armed forces establishment. The FN Herstal 9mm Browning High Power and its predecessors were first produced in 1935, and the pistol is in service in nearly 70 countries. The Tokarev and Makarov pistols, both originally produced in the Russian Federation, are in service in more than 30 countries. No new military-specific pistol designs have appeared for years, other than in the Russian Federation, where production is limited by a lack of funding.

The most common sidearms in military use are listed in Table 1.10. Few revolvers—handguns with ammunition stored in a rotating magazine—remain in military service. These are now largely confined to military police and similar organizations. Automatic pistols are now regarded as reliable, take up less space, and can carry more rounds (15 to 20 on some models) for immediate use. Revolvers remain in some military and paramilitary hands, however, due to the large numbers manufactured by commercial producers.

> Pistols and revolvers are the most widely dispersed and numerous of all firearms.

The global military market for pistols is relatively stable. For many years it has been dominated by established European producers such as Beretta (Italy), FN Herstal (Belgium), Glock (Austria), H&K (Germany), and SIG-Sauer (Switzerland/Germany). A number of firms, including IMI (Israel), Norinco (China), and Taurus (Brazil), are challenging these established European producers (Forecast International, 2004).

Unlike other areas of the military small arms market, sidearms have a significant parallel in civilian use as personal defence weapons. The distinctly personal nature of the sidearm tends to engender consumer loyalty in military procurement circles, often trumping technical innovation.

Assault rifles

Assault rifles (also known as automatic rifles) are the most numerous and effective type of infantry weapon. Few innovations have emerged over the last years, the category being dominated by the Kalashnikov series, both in 7.62x39mm and 5.45x39mm. These rifles may be encountered almost anywhere—they are manufactured in a number of countries and are in service in nearly 80 countries (see Table 1.10). It is estimated that between 70 and 100 million of these weapons have been produced since 1947. They are rugged, durable, easy to operate, and effective, even when maintenance is lacking.

Other common assault rifles include the US M-16 and its derivatives, the H&K G-3 series, and the Austrian Steyr AUG. The M-16, which has been produced since 1962, and is in service in more than 60 countries, is still produced in Canada and the United States. It has also been produced under licence in South Korea, the Philippines, and Singapore (Gander and Cutshaw, 2003). The FN-FAL is becoming obsolete because of its 7.62mm full-power cartridge, and it is rarely deployed on a large scale, other than in India. Many other types continue in service to suit national preferences and local manufacturing facilities. Although new models continue to appear, the market is saturated. Even promising designs such as the FN Herstal 5.56mm F2000 have yet to attract any orders, while Singapore's 5.56mm SAR-21 or the resurrected Croatian 5.56mm APSA-95 are unlikely to do any better.

> Assault rifles are the most numerous and effective type of infantry weapon.

The most common types of assault rifle in military use include the following:

- 7.62mm AK-47 and AKM series (Russian Federation)
- 5.56mm M-16 series (United States)
- 7.62mm H&K G-3 (Germany)
- 7.62mm FN-FAL (Belgium)

A recent trend is that 5.45 and 5.56mm calibres, designed for ranges up to 400m, are increasingly being considered as underpowered. Recent operations by the US Army and Marines in Afghanistan and Iraq have demonstrated that infantry engagements increasingly take place at much longer ranges. At such ranges small bullets not only lack destructive power, but they can also be highly vulnerable to adverse environmental conditions such as side-winds, vegetation, and extreme temperatures. In both Iraq and Afghanistan, such factors induced US forces to deploy at least 500 modified 7.62mm M-14 rifles—a rifle originally selected by the US Army in 1957 and largely decommissioned by the late 1960s (*Jane's International Defence Review*, 2002).

A number of nations are in the process of 'rearming' as part of their military modernization. This may give a temporary lift to the assault rifle market, including development of new models. The market cannot support the current scope of activity for long, however. Market conditions will probably force more corporate consolidation among major producers, particularly in Europe and the United States. European producers such as FN Herstal (Belgium) and H&K (Germany) dominate the assault rifle market, but other companies outside Europe such as IMI (Israel), Norinco (China), and Singapore Technologies Kinetics (Singapore) are emerging as important producers (Forecast International, 2004). The primary impetus for design and innovation tends to come from European producers such as H&K (Germany) and Izhmash (Russian Federation).

> As many countries 'rearm', the assault rifle market may be in store for a temporary boost.

Rifles

The term rifle is applicable to bolt-action and semi-automatic models. *Bolt-action rifles* are increasingly rare, in national service only among the most impoverished armed forces or low-grade militia units. Otherwise they are kept exclusively for ceremonial use and as costly special weapons for sniping, trained marksmanship, and similar applications.

The most important development in this field, other than the gradual proliferation of the large calibre anti-matériel rifles, is the re-emergence of the trained marksman. Marksmen are trained to get the best results from their rifles yet remain an integral part of any infantry formation, whereas the more specialized snipers usually operate in small teams away from the usual command structures. Trained marksmen are employed to knock out enemy weapon teams or similar targets at distances of up to 800m—greater ranges than assault rifles can effectively engage—and are typically deployed one to a platoon and under platoon command. Specialized ammunition such as the 0.338 Lapua Magnum provides accuracy at extended ranges, while the 7.62x54R round, dating from 1895, is still highly regarded by many Eastern European forces.

The most common specialist rifles in military use include the following:

- 7.62mm SVD Dragunov (Russian Federation)
- 0.338 Accuracy International AWM (United Kingdom)
- 7.62mm M-40A1 (United States)

The *carbine* is a short-barrelled variant of a standard rifle. With the changeover to smaller calibre ammunition, usually 5.56mm or 5.45mm, it is possible to create shorter-barrelled assault rifles with greater firepower and combat ranges than the sub-machine gun, yet in a relatively compact weapon. In general, the use of these short weapons is a feature of special forces or non-commissioned officers (NCOs) and officers, due to ease of handling and carrying. It is noticeable, however, that the US Army has been using the M-4 Carbine increasingly with front-line units in its operations in Afghanistan and Iraq. The main reason is ease of use without loss of effectiveness at close combat ranges.

The most common carbines in military use include the following:

- 5.45mm AKS-74U (Russian Federation)
- 5.56mm Colt's M-4 Carbine (United States)
- 5.56mm H&K G-36K (Germany)

SMALL ARMS SURVEY 2004

Each family of assault rifles includes a carbine variant, and assault rifles are now marketed as but one component of a range of mechanically similar weapons. A complete range now includes the assault rifle itself, a heavy barrelled squad fire-support model intended to deliver supporting fire to about 600m, and the short-barrelled carbine. Some ranges also include an ultra-short-barrelled carbine for special forces. The assault rifle still remains the main component within the range in sales terms.

Anti-matériel rifles are specialist weapons intended for use against high value military assets such as helicopters (while on the ground), radar, and communication installations. They are not normally anti-personnel weapons. The intention is to place a destructive heavy bullet with calibres of 12.7 (.50), 14.5 or even 20mm into a target at stand-off ranges of 2,000m or more. They are usually long and heavy bolt-action rifles (some are semi-automatic) with powerful optical sights. Their users have to be specially trained in their deployment and use, especially regarding target selection. They are therefore largely confined to special operations forces and are not normally part of the infantry's general inventory. The market for anti-matériel rifles is dominated by Barrett Firearms (United States) but numerous other manufacturers also produce large-calibre rifles, so that the market is fast being saturated in sales terms.

The most common types of anti-matériel rifles in military use include the following:

- 12.7mm Barrett Model 82 (United States)
- 12.7mm Accuracy International AW50 (United Kingdom)
- 12.7mm V-94 (Russian Federation)

The South African PMP NTW 14.5/20mm rifle in this category (it can have barrels for either 14.5x114mm or 20mm cannon ammunition) has been sold outside its home nation. Well over 300 examples of these rifles have been sold to India for deployment along the Kashmir borders. Sales of anti-matériel rifles on this scale are rare, most production batches being ordered and delivered in tens (at the most).

An Indian army soldier aims an anti-matériel rifle as a fellow soldier holds a stand-alone multi-shot grenade launcher in New Delhi in October 2003.

Sub-machine guns

Sub-machine guns are small, light automatic weapons that fire pistol-calibre ammunition to short ranges—rarely more than 50m. They are now widely regarded as obsolete as a standard infantry weapon, largely because of their short combat ranges and lack of bullet power compared to carbines. Yet they continue in service with many regular, police, and special forces. In 2003 the Israeli military phased out the Uzi sub-machine gun, declaring that it was 'antiquated'. While revered for its hardiness and ease of operation—it is estimated that more than 1.5 million were produced—the Uzi is also inefficient and inaccurate, even at medium range. The Uzi was taken out of front-line units of the Israeli military two decades ago, but was still issued to some elite units, and soldiers carrying heavy gear who required a light weapon for self-defence (Keyser, 2003).

Although partly replaced by the carbine, the sub-machine gun can still deliver a high rate of fire. It is for this reason that designs such as the Uzi are increasingly popular within criminal organizations. The category also finds many applications with special forces. No innovations are anticipated in this weapon category, other than the growing use of armour-piercing ammunition to counter body armour.

The most common types of sub-machine gun in military use include the following:

- 9mm H&K MP5 (Germany)
- 9mm IMI Uzi (Israel)
- 9mm Ingram Model 10 and 11 (United States)
- 9mm Spectre M4 (Italy)

European producers now dominate the global sub-machine gun market—most significantly designs from Beretta (Italy) and H&K (Germany). While these weapons are now regarded as having limited utility, their mystique in popular culture continues to drive their popularity worldwide. Outside of Europe other important producers include IMI (Israel), ADI (Australia), and Norinco (China). Compact, intermediate-calibre assault rifles are gradually eclipsing sub-machine guns in military use (Forecast International, 2004).

Compact, intermediate-calibre assault rifles are gradually eclipsing sub-machine guns in military use.

Light machine guns

Light machine guns fall into two categories: squad fire support weapons and general-purpose machine guns (GPMG).

Squad fire support weapons are intended to provide supporting fire for an infantry squad of 9–12 soldiers. Operational ranges rarely exceed 600m. Few really new models have appeared of late, other than the H&K 5.56mm MP-43, which has yet to attract firm orders. The market leader is the FN Herstal 5.56mm Minimi, procured by the US Army under the designation M-249. The Minimi continues to be sold in significant numbers, one of the latest customers being the British Army (the initial order was for more than 600 weapons). The most common types of squad fire support weapons in military use include the following:

- 5.56mm FN Herstal Minimi (Belgium)
- 7.62mm RPD (Russian Federation)
- 5.45mm/7.62mm RPK-74 (Russian Federation)

The market for light machine guns is stable and dominated by established European producers and designs. European firms continue to dominate all three market segments (squad fire support, general-purpose, and heavy) of the machine gun market. FN Herstal's MAG general-purpose machine gun and the Minimi light machine gun are fast becoming the international standards in their respective market segments (Forecast International, 2004).

The production of GPMGs has changed little recently. The FN Herstal MAG, which is in service in more than 70 countries, and was first produced in 1955, also remains in production in Argentina, Egypt, India, the United Kingdom, and the United States. Other stalwarts, such as the RPD and the RPK, both originally produced in the Russian Federation, continue to serve on, increasingly as tripod-mounted weapons to provide fire support at platoon and company level. The most common types of GPMG in military use are listed in Table 1.10.

European firms continue to dominate all three segments of the machine gun market.

Heavy machine guns

Heavy machine guns have calibres of 12.7mm and upwards (see Table 1.10). They are intended as heavy fire support or air defence weapons, up to ranges as high as 2,000m. All weapons in this category are solidly built, have evolved little, and have a considerable lifespan. For instance, the 12.7mm M2, first mass-produced in 1933, and in service in more than 80 countries, remains an important weapon within the US inventory even though it is no longer manufactured there. It remains in production in the UK (Manroy) and Belgium (FN Herstal).

SMALL ARMS SURVEY 2004

Machine guns with calibres of 12.7mm and upwards, intended as heavy fire support or air defence weapons, have evolved little over the years.

The Browning M2HB remains the foremost weapon in the heavy machine gun market, though aggressive marketing by a number of other producers, including Denel (South Africa), IMI (Israel), Norinco (China), and Singapore Technologies Kinetics (Singapore), is keeping the otherwise stable market active (Forecast International, 2004). The DShK-38 is widely deployed—in nearly 50 countries—but has been out of production within the Russian Federation for decades, although it is still produced in China, Egypt, Iran, Pakistan, and Romania. There have been few innovations in this category, the only new example to appear for many years being the Russian 12.7mm Kord, an update of the NSV.

The most common types of heavy machine guns in military use include the following:

- 12.7mm M2HB (United States)
- 12.7mm NSV (Russian Federation)
- 12.7mm DShK-38 (Russian Federation)

Grenade launchers

There are two main categories of grenade launcher, single-shot rifle-mounted examples and pedestal-mounted automatic examples, although a limited number of stand-alone launchers are also available. Among *rifle-mounted grenade launchers*, low velocity 40mm grenades predominate while the heavier, automatic pedestal-mounted models fire high-velocity 20–40mm grenades to a greater range. Although many examples of the rifle-mounted types have been introduced, the market is dominated by the single-shot 40mm M203 (United States) and the 40mm GP-25, originally manufactured in the Russian Federation by Tula Ordnance and KBP, and produced under licence by several other states.

Among *pedestal-mounted automatic grenade launchers,* two tendencies can be detected. One is a move to develop models that weigh no more than a GPMG while continuing to deliver the required fire rates and ranges of their heavier counterparts. Two main models have emerged, the 40mm SLWAGL (Singapore) and a lightweight 35mm grenade launcher from Norinco (China). Technopol (Slovak Republic) has tentatively marketed its 30mm RAG-30, while the 30mm AGS-30 (Russian Federation) has yet to appear in significant numbers. The second tendency is for more countries to produce their own weapons. The list of manufacturing countries now includes China, Germany, Pakistan, Poland, Romania, the Russian Federation, Serbia, Singapore, the Slovak Republic, South Africa, Spain, and the United States. In many of these countries the products are scarcely past the prototype stage, but more can be expected (Gander, 2003).

A US soldier loads grenades into a US-made 40mm MK19 automatic grenade launcher south-west of Baghdad in January 2004.

The most common automatic grenade launchers in military use include the following:

- 40mm MK-19 (United States)
- 30mm AGS-17 (Russian Federation)

PRODUCTS AND PRODUCERS

Portable anti-tank and anti-aircraft weapons

Man-portable anti-tank and anti-aircraft guns have been largely replaced by anti-tank guided weapons (ATGW) and MANPADS. No new types of the former have appeared in years. Of those still in existence, air defence weapons are the more numerous of the two, most of them being some variant of the 14.5mm KPV heavy machine gun. These remain available from Bulgaria, China, North Korea, and Romania but are increasingly becoming ineffectual against any but the slowest and lowest-flying aircraft targets.

One partial exception to the decline in anti-tank guns remains the Swedish Saab Bofors Dynamics 84mm Carl Gustaf shoulder-fired recoilless rifle. Constant development and ammunition improvements have kept this highly portable system attractive to many who require an anti-tank gun system that can also be deployed in a more general infantry fire support role.

The market for ATGWs and MANPADS, however, is a growth area in the international arms industry, with a number of new designs recently accepted by some of the world's major armed forces (MANPADS). The Javelin ATGW is a case in point. Selected by the British Army in 2003, it has also been supplied to Australia, Jordan, Lithuania, New Zealand, and Taiwan (Army Technology, 2004).

Recoilless guns

The recoilless gun survives mainly by being able to deliver relatively heavy direct-fire projectiles from lightweight barrels and carriages. These guns have numerous drawbacks, such as an excessive firing blast, but remain favoured by many armies as their relatively light weight makes them very useful weapons, especially with airborne forces. Numerous models remain available for potential purchasers but few innovations have appeared recently. The 106mm M-40 series (United States), which is in service in more than 60 countries, is still licence-produced, or copied, in China, India, Iran, Pakistan, South Korea, and Spain. It remains the recoilless gun most likely to be encountered, the leading competitor being the 73mm SPG-9, produced by KBP in the Russian Federation and licence-produced in Bulgaria and Romania.

Mortars

The main trends in mortar production concern extending the range to which they can be used, and moving away from established medium-calibres (81mm or 82mm) down to 60mm. Through the use of longer barrels and streamlined projectiles, it becomes possible to deliver 60mm bombs to ranges of more than 6,000m without the weight penalties imposed by the 81mm and 82mm models.

There is no one leading producer or model of mortar. Virtually every country that wishes to do so manufactures its own local design, the result being that no two countries seem to field identical weapons. The United States does not currently produce mortars, but it uses mortars purchased from BAe (UK) and Soltam (Israel).

The international market for mortars is the most stable of all small arms and light weapons markets, and is dominated by European designs from producers such as TDA Armements SAS (France), Patria Vammas (Finland), and BAe Systems (UK). Other important producers include Denel (SA), Norinco (China), Singapore Technologies Kinetics Ltd. (Singapore), and Soltam Systems Ltd. (Israel). Even with the most important manufacturers, production runs are generally low, rarely reaching more than a few hundred per year. Mortar ammunition sales are more buoyant and are usually domestically manufactured.

An exception to this market stability is the new 98mm mortar calibre. This mortar was introduced to avoid the reporting thresholds of 100mm calibre stipulated in international disarmament treaties (excluding the UN Register of

> There is no leading producer or model of mortar. Virtually every nation is capable of manufacturing its own local design.

Conventional Arms, which includes mortars over 75mm). To date only two countries, Poland and the Slovak Republic, have produced 98mm mortars.

Table 1.10 Selection of the most popular military small arms and light weapons, by category +

Type and model	Calibre	Designed in	Country of manufacture (selected)**	Countries in service	First mass-produced
Pistol					
Browning Hi-Power	9x19mm	Belgium	Argentina, Belgium, Bulgaria, China, Hungary, India, Indonesia, Israel, Nigeria	68	1935
Tokarev	7.62x25mm	Russian Federation	China, CIS, Hungary, former Yugoslavia	35	1930
Makarov	9x17mm	Russian Federation	Bulgaria, CIS, China, Russian Federation	30	1952
Assault Rifle*					
Kalashnikov AK series	7.62x39mm	Russian Federation	Albania, Bulgaria, China, CIS, Egypt, Finland, Hungary, Kazakhstan, Iraq, North Korea, Poland, Romania	78	1947
FN-FAL	7.62x51mm	Belgium	Argentina, Australia, Brazil, Belgium, Canada, India, Mexico, South Africa, UK, USA, Venezuela	74	1955
Armalite M-16 series	5.56x45mm	United States	Canada, South Korea, Philippines, Singapore, USA	60	1962
Light machine gun					
FN-MAG	7.62x51mm	Belgium	Argentina, Belgium, Egypt, India, UK, USA	77	1955
RPD	7.62x39mm	Russian Federation	China, CIS, Egypt, North Korea	42	1962
RPK	7.62x54mm	Russian Federation	China, Kazakhstan, Poland, Romania, Serbia and Montenegro	35	1964
Heavy machine gun					
Browning M2	12.7x99mm	United States	Belgium, UK, USA	84	1933
DShK-38/46	12.7x107mm	Russian Federation	China, Iran, Pakistan, Romania, CIS	48	1938
NSV	12.7x107mm	Russian Federation	Bulgaria, India, Kazakhstan, Poland, CIS, Ukraine, former Yugoslavia	24	1980
Anti-tank weapon (guided and unguided)					
RPG-7 Rocket-propelled grenade launcher	40mm	Russian Federation	Bulgaria, China, Egypt, Georgia, Iraq, Pakistan, Romania, Russian Federation, Poland, Slovak Republic	63	1962
M-40 Recoilless rifle	106mm	United States	Austria, China, India, Iran, South Korea, Pakistan, Spain, USA	63	1953
Aerospatiale/Matra Milan	125mm	International	France, Germany, India	31	1973
M20 Rocket launcher	89mm	United States	Brazil	41	1950

Notes: + Based on number of countries that weapon is in service
   *Includes light support weapons and heavy barrelled assault rifles.
   **Italics signify current production. Weapons listed include derivatives, both licensed and unlicensed.
Sources: Small Arms Survey (2001); Gander and Cutshaw (2003)

PRODUCTS AND PRODUCERS

Numerous older models of weapons are currently in service around the world (see Table 1.10), but a number of them have been, or may be, upgraded to suit the demands of the modern user. Among these are the Saab Bofors Carl Gustaf recoilless rifle and the Kalashnikov series of assault rifles, carbines, and sub-machine guns. The RPG-7 is a prime example of the extent to which such weapons undergo considerable modification over time.

OLD TECHNOLOGY, NEW APPLICATIONS: THE RPG-7 AND ITS DERIVATIVES

Rocket-propelled grenade launchers have been produced in many countries, but the most widespread and recognizable variant is the Soviet designed *Raketniy Protivotankoviy Granatomet* (RPG) series. RPG-7s are probably the most common light anti-armour and general support weapon in service worldwide. Having been produced for more than 40 years, RPG-7s have seen service across the globe, from Angola to Zimbabwe, on the streets of Belfast and Baghdad. It has been estimated that nine million RPG-7s have been produced in various guises, although this figure may be an underestimate (Gander and Cutshaw, 2003). The RPG-7, which entered service in the Russian Army in 1962, and its subsequent variants, are produced by at least 12 companies in more than nine countries. Ammunition is produced by at least 17 companies in more than 14 countries. Craft production of parts of the weapon and warhead is widespread.

Developed from the US M1 'Bazooka'—the original light anti-tank weapon of WWII—the RPG-1 was initially manufactured in the 1940s. The design was upgraded to the RPG-2 when the Soviet army captured the blueprints of the German Panzerfaust reloadable anti-tank weapon from Hugo Schneider AG, of Leipzig, in 1945. The German design gave the RPG its distinctive shape—a narrow tube to house the solid-fuel rocket motor and a bulbous protruding 85mm warhead packed with 2.5kg of high explosive. The same basic format was kept when the Soviet army adopted the RPG-7 in the early 1960s.

The weapon was designed to be cheaply mass-produced. Its rudimentary design, pressed steel components, and reusable launcher ensure that the weapon stays in service for long periods of time. The RPG-7 can be upgraded with a variety of warheads, optical equipment, and other modifications to match the requirements of different services and combat conditions. The Russian Federation's *Kovrov Mechanical Plant* offers a modernization service for existing RPG-7s. Services on offer include upgrading sights, adding bi-pods, and making modifications to enable the use of more modern ammunition.

A Taliban fighter carries an RPG-7 rocket-propelled grenade launcher and two rocket-propelled grenades.

Despite its intended role against tanks, the standard RPG is ineffective against modern armour. RPGs have, however, been devastatingly effective against 'soft' unarmoured vehicles and personnel. A normal RPG-7 grenade can penetrate 40–50mm of protective armour, making less-armoured vehicles, such as Jeeps, trucks, and aircraft, particularly vulnerable. Both of the US Blackhawk helicopters destroyed in Somalia in October 1993 were brought down with RPGs (Bowden, 2000). In Iraq RPGs have been used in attacks against coalition forces in non-armoured vehicles. Indeed, the impact of RPGs has prompted countries such as Namibia, the Russian Federation, and South Africa to develop specialized tactics for dealing with RPG-armed combatants.

Table 1.11 Producers of RPG-7 variants, derivatives, and ammunition

Country	Producer	Designation	Ammunition	Newly developed ammunition
Bulgaria	Arsenal	RPG-7V, RPG-7VM1, RPG-7VM2		
China	NORINCO	Type 69, Type 69-1	4x Anti-tank, 1x Air-bursting Anti-personnel, 1x Multipurpose, 1x Illuminating warheads	Air-bursting anti-personnel warhead, thermobaric warhead
	Vazov Engineering Plant	–	GTB-7G warhead	Thermobaric warhead
Egypt	Saqr	Saqr PG-7	Saqr Cobra warhead	–
Iran	Armament Industries Group	Saghegh	Nafez HEAT warhead	–
Iraq	Al-Nassira	RPG-7	Unknown	–
Israel*	Israel Military Industries	Unknown designation	Standard warhead	–
Pakistan	Pakistan Machine Tool Factory Ltd.	Chinese Type 69 variant		–
	Pakistan Ordinance Factories	RPG-7	HEAT warhead	
Poland	Unknown	RPG-7V	PG-7VM warhead	–
Poland/Germany	Dezamet/ Dynamit Nobel	–	Panzerfaust warhead	Under consideration
Romania	Romarm SA	AG-7S, AG-7DS	PG 7VM HEAT warhead, incendiary warhead	–
Russian Federation	Bazalt State Research and Production Enterprise	RPG-7V	PG-7VL, PG-7VR, OG-7V, TBG-7V warheads	Thermobaric warhead
	Kovrov Mechanical Plant JSC	RPG-7	Various warheads	–
	FKN GkNIPAS	–	PG-7VYA, MRAR warheads	Upgraded multipurpose warhead and anti-helicopter/anti-personnel warhead
Slovak Republic	Kon_trukta Defence	Unknown designation	PG-7M 110 anti-tank warhead	–
Switzerland/Bulgaria	RUAG Munition/ Vazovski Mashinostroitelni Zavod	–	VPG-7MEP warhead	High penetration warhead
Thailand	The Thai Arms Company	RPG-7	Unknown designation	–

Note: * Limited, possibly discontinued.

Sources: Forecast International (2002); Foss (2004); Foundation Hemus (2003); Gander (2001, 2003); Israeli Special Forces Homepage (2003); Pengelley (2002); Shields (1996); South-Asian Defence News (2003)

The RPG is a particular danger to unprotected personnel. Effective to a range of 300m, the weapon's standard anti-tank round explodes with a lethal burst of shrapnel to a radius of four metres (Grau, 1998). In recent years, more specialized ammunition has been developed. Available ammunition ranges from standard high-explosive anti-tank, or HEAT, warheads, to 'tandem' warheads, which feature a twin explosion to defeat reactive armour. Bulgarian producers are developing more specialized thermobaric rounds for urban warfare, a formula that hitherto was limited to larger conventional weapons—particularly in Chechnya. Developed by the *Vazov Engineering Plant* of Sopot, the contents of the 93mm-diameter thermobaric warhead are scattered in an aerosol form on impact and then ignited to create a rapidly formed, high-pressure blast wave, equivalent to that produced by the detonation of 2kg of TNT. The warhead was reportedly on offer for export in 2001 (Gander, 2001). The Russian Federation's Bazalt has also developed a thermobaric warhead, whose explosive power reportedly can be compared to a 120mm artillery shell or mortar bomb (Bazalt, 2001).

The existing weapon's relatively low cost—a new unit price of around USD 1,500 and old weapons for as little as USD 10—make it attractive to developing world armies and non-state actors alike (Forecast International, 2002; Brown, 2002). The RPG-7's relatively small size and its light loaded weight (8–13kg) also makes it the ideal weapon for guerrilla

> The RPG-7 series is probably the most common light anti-armour and general support weapon in service worldwide.

warfare, especially in built-up areas. A case in point is Iraq, where more than 15 per cent of US soldiers killed in the seven months between 21 March and 21 October 2003 died in RPG-related incidents. The vast majority of these deaths—22 out of 23—occurred since major hostilities were declared over on 1 May 2003 (Bevan, 2004). Recent developments, such as Romania's *ROMARM SA's* air-portable variant, the AG-7DS, which can be divided into two halves for ease of carrying, arguably make the weapon yet more desirable for future guerrilla usage. The sheer number of countries in which the weapon is in service is a key factor explaining why these weapons often end up in the hands of non-state actors, particularly since many of these countries have not been able to guarantee the security of state arsenals in times of war (STOCKPILES).

The RPG-7 is currently in service with at least 27 countries' national forces (Gander and Cutshaw, 2003). It is also used by a large number of non-state groups, such as Hezbollah and the Liberation Tigers of Tamil Eelam (Jain Commission, 1997). A number of countries manufacture variants of the RPG-7 (see Table 1.11). Many modifications have been instituted over the 40 years it has been in service, and the demands for new capabilities at a low cost suggest this trend will continue. With no easy countermeasures to undermine its effectiveness, the RPG-7 and its later variants are likely to remain a standard light weapon for years to come.

CONCLUSION

The global small arms industry continues to experience both continuity and change. Continuity in terms of the enduring popularity of certain types of weapons—from the Browning Hi-Power 9mm pistol to the RPG-7 grenade launcher. Various established European and US producers—including H&K (Germany), FN Herstal (Belgium), Izhmash (Russian Federation), and Colt's Manufacturing (United States)—continue to dominate many categories and sub-categories of the global small arms and light weapons market. The primary impetus for design and innovation is concentrated in many of these established producers.

Change has come in the form of new designs and products, and in challenges to established manufacturers from smaller producers. Despite a high degree of stability in many of the categories of the small arms market, in recent years a number of new designs have begun to appear, driven by rearmament programmes in many countries (e.g. France and Spain), and by major procurement efforts (e.g. the United States) in others. Many of these new designs have incorporated advanced materials (e.g. composites), and have aimed to produce weapons with greater rates of fire and increased lethality.

Despite the dominance of established European and US producers, a number of firms in Australia (ADI), Brazil (Taurus), Singapore (Singapore Technologies Kinetics), and South Africa (Denel/Vektor) have started to challenge the established producers in some of the various categories and sub-categories of the global small arms market. The success of these new producers, together with other factors, has continued the drive towards consolidation in the European small arms industry, as witnessed by the recent collaborative ventures between RUAG (Switzerland) and Dynamit Nobel (Germany), between H&K (Germany) and Santa Barbara (Spain), and between Giat (France) and FN Herstal (Belgium). The recent experience of Latin America's small arms producers, and the growing exports of companies in Brazil, Argentina, and Mexico, are testament to the ongoing changes in the global small arms industry, and how countries such as Brazil are able to increasingly dominate their 'regional market'.

An important and under-researched issue is the distinction between the commercial small arms market (firearms produced for recreational activities such as sport and hunting) and the military small arms market. On the basis of existing, albeit limited, information, it appears that the global commercial small arms market might be experiencing a significant decline in demand, as reflected in lower production volumes among the major commercial producers in the United States (e.g. Sturm, Ruger & Co.), the Russian Federation (e.g. IMZ), and elsewhere. But whether companies in other countries are filling the production vacuum is not clear. On the military side, some national rearmament programmes and the US-led military operations in Afghanistan and Iraq have contributed to the emergence of a number of new designs and products. These developments also appear to have had a positive impact on the volume of production of military-style small arms and light weapons, particularly among US and other producers (e.g. FN Herstal of Belgium) that have long-term contracts with the US armed forces.

1. LIST OF ABBREVIATIONS

ARS	Argentine peso
ATF	US Bureau of Alcohol, Tobacco, Firearms and Explosives
ATGW	Anti-tank guided weapon
BNDES	Banco Nacional de Desenvolvimento Econômico e Social (Brazil)
CAVIM	Compañia Anónima de Industrias Militares (Venezuela)
CBC	Companhia Brasileira de Cartuchos (Brazil)
CIS	Commonwealth of Independent States
DGFDN	Dirección General de Fábricas de la Defensa Nacional (Mexico)
DGFM	Dirección General de Fabricaciones Militares (Argentina)
FAMAE	Fábricas y Maestranzas del Ejército (Chile)
FAME	Fábrica de Armas y Municiones del Ejército (Peru)
FARC	Fuerzas Armadas Revolucionarias de Colombia
FBM	Fábrica Boliviana de Municiones (Bolivia)
FLB	Fray Luis Beltrán (Argentina)
FMAP	Fábrica Militar de Armas Portátiles (Argentina)
FMRT	Fábrica Militar Río Tercero (Argentina)
GPMG	General-purpose machine gun
H&K	Heckler & Koch
IMI	Israel Military Industries
INDEC	National Institute of Statistics and Census (Argentina)
INDUMIL	Industria Militar (Colombia)
MANPADS	Man-portable air defence system
NCO	Non-commissioned officer
RPG	Rocket-propelled grenade launcher
SALW	Small arms and light weapons
SIMA	Servicio Industrial de la Marina (Peru)
SIMA–CEFAR	SIMA Centro de Fabricación de Armas (Peru)
SMG	Sub-machine gun
TAP	Popular arms workshop (taller de armamento popular)
TFG	Front-line workshop (taller de frente de guerra)
USD	US dollar

PRODUCTS AND PRODUCERS

1. ENDNOTES

1. Small arms are often produced in divisions, subsidiaries, or plants that are part of larger companies. Thus the total number of end producers is likely to be much lower than the total number of producers involved in some aspect of small arms production, including intermediate producers (Omega Foundation, 2002; 2003).
2. Personal communication with Garen Wintemute and Karen Rand.
3. The total number of weapons available to the US domestic market is equal to domestic production, minus exports, plus imports.
4. Information in this section on small arms production in Latin America is largely based on Dreyfus and Lessing (2003).
5. Under the *maquila regime*, a Mexican company is allowed to temporarily import the following goods into Mexico on a duty-free basis: machinery, equipment, materials, parts and components, and other items needed for the assembly or manufacture of finished goods for subsequent export.
6. Interview with the Director of Production of DGFM, Buenos Aires, April 2003.
7. Interview with the former Director of Operations of the National Arms Register (RENAR), Buenos Aires, April 2003.
8. Interview with the former Director of Operations of RENAR, Buenos Aires, April 2003.
9. Information from INDEC (2003). These figures exclude exports of parts for small arms and may exclude state-to-state exports of military small arms.
10. Information in this section obtained from Lt. Col. Jorge Ricardo Guido, Director of the Military Factory Fray Luis Beltrán, May 2003.
11. Production of mortars and other light weapons at the FMRT is currently suspended.
12. Interview with the Director of Production of DGFM, Buenos Aires, April 2003.
13. Information for this company analysis comes from a presentation given by Benso Bonadimani, president of Bersa, during the 'Firearms Industry and the United Nations Action Programme 2001 Conference', organized by the UN Centre for Peace, Disarmament and Development in Latin America and the Caribbean and the Government of Panama, Panama, 13–15 November 2002. See UN-LiREC (2002).
14. Percentage calculated from official customs information obtained via Urunet (2004).
15. Official customs information obtained via Urunet (2004). Information from company brochures.
16. Official customs information obtained via Urunet (2004). For more information, see F&L (2004).
17. For company information about FANAC, see FANAC (2004).
18. SECEX; see also Fernandes *et al.* (2001).
19. Ibid.
20. Company information for Forjas Taurus filed with the Securities and Exchange Commission of Brazil (Comissão de Valores Mobiliários, CVM). All information taken from Annual Reports (Informações Anuais, IAN) and Standard Financial Reports (Demonstrações Financeiras Padronizadas, DFP). See CVM Brazil (2004).
21. Company information for CBC filed with the CVM of Brazil. See note above.
22. Company information for Rossi filed with the CVM of Brazil. See note above.
23. Gander and Cutshaw (2003) and interview with the owner of the gunsmith company Gun Tec, Rio de Janeiro, December 2003.
24. Interview with the owner of Gun Tec, Rio de Janeiro, December 2003.
25. Unless otherwise noted, information for this section was gathered in an interview with employees of FAMAE, August 2003.
26. The subsequent International Security Assistance and Arms Export Control Act of 1976 prohibits transfers more generally to any country that 'engages in a consistent pattern of gross violations of internationally recognized human rights', except under extraordinary circumstances (USAID, 2004).
27. Interview with an employee of FAMAE, August 2003.
28. Interview with Graciela Uribe de Lozano, retired official from the Colombian Ministry of Foreign Affairs, August 2003.
29. Unless otherwise noted, this section is based on information presented by Colombian law enforcement officers during a conference entitled 'The Firearms Industry and the United Nations Action Programme 2001 Conference' (UN-LiREC, 2002).
30. Interview with Col. Luis Cruz, Director, Departamento de Control de Armas, Comando Conjunto de las Fuerzas Armadas Ecuatorianas, 8 July 2003.
31. The Department of Arms Control does not collect data on the total output of these legal craft firearms producers, but such data theoretically exists in their applications for permit renewals.
32. Unless otherwise noted, information for this section comes from an interview with a company official of Industrias Ruiz Cabañas S.A. de C.V., Alpuyeca, Xochitepec, Mexico, February 2003.
33. Interview wih Ruiz Cabañas.
34. Interview with Danny Rios Guitierrez, Superintendente Comercial de SIMA–CEFAR, 20 July 2003.
35. Ibid.
36. Interview with CAVIM official, Caracas, July 2003.
37. Interview with Marcos Tarre Briceño, president of the NGO Venezuela Segura and expert in public security issues, Caracas, July 2003; interview with Javier Mayorca, journalist in charge of the military and security section at the Caracas newspaper *El Nacional*, Caracas, July 2003.

1. BIBLIOGRAPHY

Aleksandrova, Lyudmila. 2002. 'Budet sozdana korporatsiya strelkovogo oruzhiya.' *Udmurtskaya Pravda* (Izhevsk). 5 November.
Altayskaya Pravda. 2003. Interview with Barnaul Instrument-Building Plant general director Viktor Yashin. Cited in 'S veroy v budushchee.' 28 July.
Amantino. 2004. Company Web site. <http://www.eramantino.com.br/>
Army Technology. 2004. 'Javelin Anti-Armour Missile, USA.' <http://www.army-technology.com/projects/javelin/>
Astkhov, Dmitry and Ekaterina Safarova. 2003. 'SOK sdaet patrony.' *Kommersant*. 18 September.
Aviatsia i Vremya. 2002. 'Kosmos i oruzhiye Rossii.' 6 March.
Bazalt. 2001. *RPG-7V Grenade Launcher: 40th Anniversary*. Moscow: State Research and Production Enterprise Bazalt. <http://www.bazalt.ru/articles/rpgbirthday_e.html>
Bevan, James. 2004. *Analysis of US Casualties in Iraq*. Background Paper. Geneva: Small Arms Survey.
BICC (Bonn International Center for Conversion). 2003. *BICC Conversion Survey 2003: Global Disarmament, Demilitarization and Demobilization*. Baden-Baden: Nomos Verlagsgesellschaft.

Bowden, Mark. 2000. *Blackhawk Down*. London: Corgi.
Braslavsky, Guido. 2003. *Resignación y escepticismo de los militares*. Clarin Periodismo en Internet. Vol. 7: 2655. 9 July. <http://old.clarin.com/diario/2003/07/09/p-00603.htm>
Brown, John. 2002. Spokesman for the Defence Science and Technology Laboratory, UK Ministry of Defence. Cited in *New Age Electric Armour Tough Enough to Face Modern Threats*. Salisbury: Defence Science and Technology Laboratory. 8 June. <www.defesanet.com.br>
Casciotti, Gino. 2004. 'Bersa Thunder: Pistola Bersa Thunder .22.' Montevideo: Gino Casciotti, Reparación y Restauración de Armas y Cuchillos. <http://www.ginocasciottiarmero.exactpages.com/pagina_nueva_8.htm>
CAST (Centre for Analysis of Strategies and Technologies). 2003. *Small Arms Production in the Russian Federation*. Background paper. Geneva: Small Arms Survey.
—. 2001. 'The Indian contract of the Instrument Building Design Bureau.' Comment. 16 February.
CAVIM. 2004. Company Web site. Maracay: Compañia Anónima de Industrias Militares. <http://www.cavim.com.ve/>
CBC. 2004. Online catalogue. Rio de Janeiro: Companhia Brasileira de Cartuchos. <http://www.cbc.com.br/catalogo/index.htm>
CVM Brazil. 2004. Institutional Web site. Rio be Janeiro: Securities and Exchange Commission of Brazil (Comissão de Valores Mobiliários). <http://www.cvm.gov.br/ingl/indexing.asp>
Dreyfus, Pablo. 2000. *Small Arms Producers in the Southern Cone Countries of Latin America*. Background paper. Geneva: Small Arms Survey.
—. and Benjamin Lessing. 2003. *Production and Exports of Small Arms and Light Weapons and Ammunition in South America and Mexico*. Background paper. Geneva: Small Arms Survey.
Eksport Vooruzheniy Journal. 2002. 'Ratings of Russian Defence Companies in 1999–2001.' Moscow: CAST. No. 3.
FAMAE. 2002. 'Defensa: Description.' Santiago: Fábricas y Maestranzas del Ejército. <http://www.defensa.cl/paginas/public/industria/4_empresas_estado/3famae.pdf>
—. 2004. Company Web site. Santiago: Fábricas y Maestranzas del Ejército. <http://www.famae.cl/>
FANAC. 2004. Company Web site. Lanus: Fabricación Nacional, armas civiles de Nicolás Colasanto e hijos. <http://www.cazayarmas.com.ar/FANAC/fanacav.htm>
F&L. 2004. Company Web site. Buenos Aires: F&L Fábrica de Armas. <http://www.fyl.com.ar/home1.htm>
Fernandes, Rubem César, Marcos de Barros Lisboa, and Ramon Stubert Aymore. 2001. As Exportações Brasileiras de Armas Leves 1989–2000. Rio de Janeiro: ISER. November. <http://www.iser.org.br/portug/segpub_texto_rubem.pdf>
Foundation Hemus. 2003. *Bulgarian Defence Industry Products Catalogue*. <http://www.hemusbg.org/>
Forecast International. 2002. *Ordnance and Munitions Forecast*. Newtown, Connecticut: Forecast International/DMS. September.
—. 2003. *Ordnance and Munitions Forecast*. Newtown, Connecticut: Forecast International/DMS. September.
—. 2004. *Ordnance and Munitions Forecast*. Newtown, Connecticut: Forecast International/DMS. January.
—. 2003a. *Military Small Arms (United States)*. Newtown, Connecticut: Forecast International/DMS. January.
—. 2003b. *Sub-machine Guns (International)*. Newtown, Connecticut: Forecast International/DMS. January.
Foss, Christopher. 2004. 'China Puts Thermobaric Weapons on the Market.' *Jane's Defence Weekly*. Coulsdon: Jane's Information Group. 4 February.
Galloway, Joseph. 2004. 'Army Running Short on Small Arms Ammunition.' Washington, DC: Knight Ridder/Tribune News Service. 10 January.
Gander, Terry. 2001. 'Thermobaric Warhead for RPG-7.' *Jane's Land Forces*. 5 January. <http://www.janes.com/defence/land_forces/news/jidr/jidr010104_2_n.shtml>
—. 2003. *Small Arms and Light Weapons*. Background paper. Geneva: Small Arms Survey.
—. and Charles Cutshaw. 2001. *Jane's Infantry Weapons 2001–2002*. Coulsdon: Jane's Information Group.
—. 2003. *Jane's Infantry Weapons 2003–2004*. Coulsdon: Jane's Information Group.
Grau, Lester. 1998. 'The RPG on the Battlefields of Today and Tomorrow.' *Infantry Magazine*. May–August. Fort Benning: US Army, pp. 6–8.
Haug, Maria. 2003. *US Small Arms Exports in 2002*. Background paper. Geneva: Small Arms Survey.
Hogg, Ian and John Weeks. 2000. *Military Small Arms of the 20th Century*. Iola, Wisconsin: Krause Publications.
IISS. 2002. *The Military Balance 2002–2003*. London: The International Institute for Strategic Studies.
Imbel. 2004. Company Web site. Piquete: Indústria de Material Bélico do Brasil. <http://www.imbel.gov.br/ingles/i_imb_loca.asp>
INDEC. 2003. Argentine National Institute of Statistics. Buenos Aires: Instituto Nacional de Estadistica y Censos. <http://www.indec.gov.ar/>
Interfax. 2003. 'V blizhaishiye tri goda obyom proizvodstva zavoda im. Degtyaryova uvelichitsya do 10–11 mlrd. Rub.' 20 February.
International Firearms Trade. 2003. St. Johnsbury, Vermont: IFT. Vol. 2:7. 1 July.
Israeli Special Forces Homepage. 2003. *Rocket Propelled Grenade* 7. Isaveret.com. <http://www.isayeret.com/weapons/rockets/rpg/rpg7.htm>
Jain Commission. 1997. Interim report of the Jain Commission of Enquiry Headed by Justice M. C. Jain on the Assassination of Shri Rajiv Gandhi. Sriperumbudur. August. Art. 43:1.
Jane's Defence Weekly. 2003a. 'Russia announces 2003 allocations.' Coulsdon: Jane's Information Group. 24 January.
—. 2003b. 'Spain confirms USD 4.6bn procurement package.' Coulsdon: Jane's Information Group. 12 September.
—. 2003c. 'French Budget Continues Modernisation Process.' Coulsdon: Jane's Information Group. 26 September.
—. 2003d. 'Heckler & Koch, Santa Barbara set up arms venture.' Coulsdon: Jane's Information Group. 12 December.
Jane's International Defence Review. 2002. 'Infantry Weapons: The Way Ahead.' Coulsdon: Jane's Information Group. 1 July.
—. 2003a. 'XM8 Lightweight Assault Rifle.' Coulsdon: Jane's Information Group. 1 March.
—. 2003b. 'US M-16 Replacement Is Emerging.' Coulsdon: Jane's Information Group. 1 November.
—. 2004a. 'Reconstructing the Russian Military.' Coulsdon: Jane's Information Group. 1 March.
Kamakin, Andrei. 2003. 'Ya dam vam Parabellum.' *Itogi*. 3 June.
Keyser, Jason. 2003. 'Israeli Army Laying down Its Famed Uzi Weapons.' *Toronto Star* (Associated Press). 18 December.
Nozdrachyov, Alexander. 2002a. General director of Russian Agency for Conventional Armaments. Statement. 29 May.
—. 2002b. General Director of Russian Agency for Conventional Armaments. Statement. Quoted in Izhmash press release. 28 October. <www.izhmash.ru>
NTI. 2004. 'China's National Defense 2000.' Washington: Nuclear Threat Initiative. <http://www.nti.org/db/china/engdocs/wpnd2000.htm>

Olive, Ronaldo. 1999. 'Subguns from the Inca Land.' Harmony, Maine: *Small Arms Review*. Vol. 2:5. February.
Omega Foundation. 2002. *Global Survey of Small Arms and Light Weapons Companies*. Background paper. Geneva: Small Arms Survey.
—. 2003. *Global Survey of Small Arms and Light Weapons Companies*. Background paper. Geneva: Small Arms Survey.
Pengelley, Rupert. 2002. 'Swiss Warheads for AT-3, AT-4 and RPG-7.' *International Defence Review*. 16 December. Coulsdon: Jane's Information Group.
Purcena, Julio César. 2003. 'A indústria de Armas Pequenas e Munições e a Violência no Estado do Rio de Janeiro nos Últimos Vinte Anos. Graduate Essay (Economics). Rio de Janeiro: Faculdade Moraes Júnior. November, pp. 11–15.
Poroskov, Nikolai. 2003. 'Proshchaniye s Makarovym.' *Vremya Novostei*. 7 July.
Pyadushkin, Maxim, Maria Haug, and Anna Matveeva. 2003. *Beyond the Kalashnikov: Small Arms Production, Exports, and Stockpiles in the Russian Federation*. Occasional Paper. Geneva: Small Arms Survey. August.
RENAR. 2002. 'Fábricas de Explosivos, Armas y Municiones en América Latina: una visión actual sobre los principales establecimientos estatales de producción para la Defensa. Registro Nacional de Armas.' Buenos Aires: Ministry of Defense of Argentina. <http://www.renar.gov.ar/cursos/expertos/notaa/fabricas.asp>
Safronov, Ivan. 2003. 'Mikhail Kasyanov vypolnil zakaz Minoborony.' *Kommersant*. 14 August.
Shields, John. 1996. *Military Industries in the Islamic Republic of Iran: An Assessment of the Defense Industries Organization (DIO)*. Monterey: Center for Nonproliferation Studies. May.
SIPRI (Stockholm International Peace Research Institute). 2003. *SIPRI Yearbook 2003: Armaments, Disarmament and International Security*. Oxford: Oxford University Press.
Small Arms Survey. 2001. *Small Arms Survey 2001: Profiling the Problem*. Oxford: Oxford University Press.
—. 2002. *Small Arms Survey 2002: Counting the Human Cost*. Oxford: Oxford University Press.
—. 2003. *Small Arms Survey 2003: Development Denied*. Oxford: Oxford University Press.
South America Ordnance. 2004. Venture Web site. Juiz de For a: Imbel, British Aerospace, Schahin. <http://www.southamerica.com.br/eng/princ.html>
South-Asian Defence News. 2003. 'Pakistan Ready for Joint Ventures in Defence Industry.' PakistaniDefence.com. January. <http://www.pakistanidefence.com/news/MonthlyNewsArchive/2003/Jan2003.htm>
St. Louis Post-Dispatch. 2004. 'Army deal could add jobs at Olin plant: $9.2 million for ammunition.' St. Louis. 16 February.
Taurus. 2004. Company Web site. Porto Alegre: Forjas Taurus S.A. <http://www.taurus.com.br/index.php>
Tecnos. 2004. Aguila Ammunition. Helotes, Texas: Centurion Ordnance. <http://www.aguilaammo.com/aguila.htm>
Thurman, Russ. 2003. 'Firearm Production: Special Report to the Industry.' San Diego: Shootingindustry.com. <http://www.shootingindustry.com/02pages/SpecRep1.html>
Tula. 2003. 'Traditsii okrylyayut I obyazyvayut.' 5 March.
United Nations (UN). 1997. Report of the Panel of Governmental Experts on Small Arms. A/52/298. 27 August.
UN-LiREC. 2002. 'The Firearms Industry and the United Nations Action Programme 2001.' Conference organized by the UN Centre for Peace, Disarmament and Development in Latin America and the Caribbean (UN-LiREC) and the Government of Panama. Panama, 13-15 November.
USAID. 2004. 'History of USAID Democracy and Governance Activities. Washington, DC: The United States Agency for International Development.' <http://www.usaid.gov/democracy/office/history.html>
United States. 1999. ATF (Bureau of Alcohol, Tobacco, Firearms and Explosives). *Annual Firearms Manufacturing and Export Report 1997*. Washington, DC: Department of the Treasury.
—. 2000. *Annual Firearms Manufacturing and Export Report 1998*. Washington, DC: Department of the Treasury.
—. 2001. *Annual Firearms Manufacturing and Export Report 1999*. Washington, DC: Department of the Treasury.
—. 2002. *Annual Firearms Manufacturing and Export Report 2000*. Washington, DC: Department of the Treasury.
—. 2003a. *Annual Firearms Manufacturing and Export Report 2001*. Washington, DC: Department of the Treasury.
—. 2003b. *Firearms Commerce in the United States 2001/2002*. Washington, DC: Department of the Treasury.
United States. Census Bureau. 1999. *1997 Economic Census: Manufacturing Industry Series*. EC97M-3329F. Washington, DC: Department of Commerce.
—. 2002. *Statistics for Industry Groups and Industries: 2000*. Washington, DC: Department of Commerce.
—. 2003. *Statistics for Industry Groups and Industries: 2001*. M01 (AS)-1. Washington, DC: Department of Commerce.
Urunet (Montevideo). 2004. 'Analisis de Comercio Exterior del Uruguay.' Commercial database. <http://www.urunet.com.uy/>
VIC. 2000. 'China's Defense Budget and Arms Procurement Priorities.' Virtual Information Centre. Hawaii: US Pacific Command. 12 December.

ACKNOWLEDGEMENTS

Other contributors

Philip Alpers, Michael Brzoska, Centre for Analysis of Strategies and Technologies (CAST), Pablo Dreyfus, Terry Gander, Lester Grau, Maria Haug, Aaron Karp, Emile LeBrun, Benjamin Lessing, David Mutimer, the Omega Foundation, Stéphanie Pézard, Elizabeth Sköns, and Ruxandra Stoicescu.

The gun as a symbol: An Iraqi woman holds a Kalashnikov automatic rifle during a pro-Saddam Hussein demonstration in Baghdad, in January 2003. (© AP/Hussein Malla)

From Chaos to Coherence?
GLOBAL FIREARM STOCKPILES

2

INTRODUCTION

Many of the most acute small arms problems of 2003 arose from the seemingly simple issue of stockpile management and control. In the most extraordinary case, the loss of control over millions of small arms and light weapons helped undermine the stability of an entire country. A similar phenomenon appeared elsewhere as armed forces were deployed to defend civilian airliners against weapons originally from their own inventories. Police faced much the same problem when pursuing criminals armed with former police guns. The situation is not very different for individuals, fearful of attackers bent on stealing guns originally acquired for self-defence.

Behind the shared irony was a serious and fundamental problem: How should the international community, governments, and individuals best manage the safety of their small arms and light weapons? This chapter examines recent trends in international and national efforts to control small arms and light weapons stockpiles. Like the vignettes above, it portrays a world without clear trends. Small arms lawlessness in some regions bears no relationship to strong reforms elsewhere. Everything, it seems, is happening at once.

This chapter's major findings include:

- In the wake of Saddam Hussein's defeat, the Iraqi people found themselves in possession of at least 7 million–8 million small arms, and probably more.
- Eleven Latin American countries examined here have roughly 45 million–80 million firearms. Their firearms stand out not for their numbers but for their lethal effects.
- At least one million firearms are stolen or lost annually worldwide.
- Firearms losses through negligence and theft range from enormous incidents involving armed forces to small-scale burglary from private homes.
- Small arms registration can be *active-universal,* requiring the participation of all gun owners, or *passive-partial,* involving only registration of newly bought guns.
- The most ambitious active-universal registration initiative in recent years came into full legal force in Canada in 2003.
- Brazil implemented a major reform package to combat firearms proliferation and radically alter the national gun culture.

Readers will notice that this chapter departs from the Stockpiles chapters in previous editions of this yearbook. In the 2004 edition it focuses less on the number and distribution of small arms and light weapons and more on their management. Instead of stressing who has what, it focuses on the problems of safely storing and keeping control of what they have. One could be excused for feeling that small arms violence shows the limits of efforts to exercise control over human affairs. As a partial corrective, the chapter stresses the enormous scope for better stockpile management.

SMALL ARMS SURVEY 2004

Iraq may be an extreme case of gun chaos, but it is special only in its scale and suddenness. The catastrophic loss of major arsenals has occurred elsewhere before. Unless aggressive steps are taken to ensure better control over small arms stockpiles, many countries will remain vulnerable to similar disasters. On a daily basis, however, the gradual loss of weapons from negligence and theft may be an even more serious problem.

In addition to its familiar task of detailing the global distribution of small arms and light weapons inventories, this chapter also looks at the management of firearm stockpiles. The importance of better managing inventories of MANPADS is stressed in the following chapter. Both cases highlight how better management depends fundamentally on owners, be they powerful states, weak governments, private firms, or individuals. By coincidence, the same year that saw an unprecedented collapse of government control in one country also saw the enactment of some of the furthest-reaching government reforms in other countries.

IRAQ'S ABANDONED ARSENAL

In 2003 Iraq became synonymous with gun-bred disaster. For a remotely similar case one must look back to the collapse of control over Albanian state arsenals in 1997. That event contributed to the escalation of fighting in neighbouring Kosovo and Macedonia. In Iraq, the lost arsenals were much larger and the effects may be as well.

Inspired by fear of weapons of mass destruction and fought largely with major conventional weaponry, the Iraq war created a situation little considered in pre-war rhetoric. Criminals, militias, guerrillas, and ordinary Iraqis armed with the smallest of weapons suddenly determined the prospects for peace and stability. For US-led coalition soldiers struggling to restore order, the greatest threat seemed to come from poorly understood groups of Ba'athist loyalists and militant Sunni Islamists. But for typical Iraqis it was the millions of firearms suddenly released into a chaotic social landscape—weapons in their own hands—which made life intolerable, even for those newly armed.

As the forces of Saddam Hussein collapsed in April 2003, little was left of his armies besides one of the largest military small arms inventories in the world. With a large proportion of these weapons already gone and much of the rest unguarded, the collapse precipitated what almost certainly was one of the largest and fastest transfers of small arms ever. Guns were littered among a tense population deprived of essential social institutions. The decision by Interim Administrator Paul Bremer in May 2003 to disband the Iraqi army and remove Ba'ath Party members from positions of authority further accelerated the transfer of weapons into civil society (Taheri, 2003).

The immediate result was unprecedented social disorder. The incidence of firearm homicides in Baghdad rose dramatically, including revenge attacks and more ordinary crime (Fleishman, 2003). The violence became a major barrier to the restoration of legitimate authority. In the long term, these events created an enormous pool of weaponry with the potential to spill uncontrollably through Iraqi society and across its borders. The effects are compounded by the geographic location of the country at the centre of the region. The consequences of the great Iraqi small arms abandonment may endanger stability in much of the Middle East for years to come.

From the beginning of the occupation, small arms and light weapons issues were a major preoccupation for US and other foreign forces. Highly publicized efforts to collect Iraqi small arms had limited success. This created an atmosphere of official and public scepticism about the prospects for control. Experience elsewhere, examined in several studies in previous editions of the *Small Arms Survey* (Small Arms Survey, 2002, ch. 7; 2003, ch. 8), leaves no doubt that controlling small arms proliferation will be an essential part of efforts to rebuild the country.

How many guns were released into public hands?

Although the Iraqi situation is especially acute, the problems of stockpile assessment are virtually identical to those in much of the rest of the world. The lack of a pre-war firearm registration system and the destruction of military records make it impossible to establish the exact number of small arms in Iraq. As shown in the subsequent section, for example, the situation is not very different in much of Latin America.

Previously developed to estimate the scale of national small arms inventories, formal estimating techniques can help establish a sense of the size of the problem that future Iraqi leaders will have to face (Small Arms Survey, 2001, pp. 80–81). They offer a tentative basis for the design of new Iraqi small arms policies as well as collection and disarmament initiatives. Until country surveys and smaller studies make stronger evaluations possible, this approach offers a useful guide to one of the most important unintended consequences of the Iraq war.

Even before combat officially began on 19/20 March 2003, there was little reliable information on the scale of small arms distribution in the country. The post-war gun situation created intense interest in establishing the scale of the problem. In the absence of reliable official data, early estimates were more evocative than analytical. They spoke more of the social impact of the problem than its physical dimensions.

This chapter works with reports and information that have become publicly available since then to establish what can be known in the murkiness of Iraqi small arms stockpiles. Its findings should be treated cautiously. They give a sense of scale rather than a precise total. Based on the information publicly available as of March 2004, it can be concluded with reasonable certainty that the Iraqi people currently control at least 7 million–8 million firearms. This estimate is conservative, reflecting the profound uncertainty permeating Iraqi society. The actual number of small arms in Iraq could be much higher, but there currently is no scientific basis for establishing the higher range of such an estimate.

At the conservative level established here, equal to 30 civilian firearms for every 100 people, the Iraqi people are highly but not exceptionally well-armed. If this estimate is correct, the country's public stockpile is higher than Canada or New Zealand with approximately 25 civilian firearms for every 100 residents, but lower than Finland where there are some 39 per 100 residents, or Uruguay where there appear to be roughly 25–46 civilian guns per 100 residents (Small Arms Survey, 2001, 2003). Where Iraq stands out most is not in the magnitude of its public stockpile so much as the suddenness with which it fell upon a fragile society.

The firearms of the pre-war Iraqi armed forces

While the former Iraqi regime did not make public the size of its official small arms inventory, its broad dimensions can be deduced with the use of orthodox multipliers. The country's armed forces reached their peak size around 1989 with approximately one million soldiers (IISS, 1989). If armed at the higher level typical of modern militaries, this force needed an average of at least 2.25 firearms—pistols, rifles, light and medium machine guns—for each soldier, sailor, and airman (Box 2.1). With roughly one million personnel in uniform at its peak, this created a basic operational requirement for approximately 2.25 million firearms.

Active-duty forces made up just part of Iraqi force planning. The basic national reserve was the People's Army, a paramilitary force estimated to number roughly 850,000 (IISS, 1989). Press reports generated by the Ba'ath Party in the

SMALL ARMS SURVEY 2004

weeks just before the invasion suggested that this and other militias were far more numerous, but this cannot be independently confirmed. Assuming the same multiplier—in this case a generous one—of 2.25 for each reserve soldier, and combining this figure with figures for the regular army, suggests that the combined active-duty and trained reserve forces probably controlled at least 4.2 million firearms. Many of these largely military weapons were abandoned, pilfered, looted, and sold to the Iraqi public after Saddam Hussein's defeat and disappearance around 9–11 April 2003.

In lieu of reliable data from the records of the pre-war Iraqi Ministry of Defence or its suppliers, it is hard to refine this estimate. The actual weapons total could be considerably higher. Just before the 2003 war began, for example, large numbers of weapons reportedly were distributed to Ba'athists and loyalist factions (Fisher, 2003). In addition to the firearms enumerated here, moreover, the Iraqi armed forces had vast inventories of other small arms and light weapons. These included hand grenades, mortars, heavy machine guns, MANPADS, and RPGs. Many or most were lost the same way as military firearms. Although these weapons are no less important, their quantities currently cannot be estimated. They have not been included here.

> *Iraq's civilian and military firearms stockpile is conservatively estimated at between 7 million and 8 million. It is likely to be considerably higher.*

Box 2.1 Arming militia-based armed forces: The example of Finland

The estimating procedures established by the *Small Arms Survey* in 2001 to gauge the likely dimensions of military firearms inventories were based on a handful of examples. The resulting military small arms multiplier was 2.25 firearms for every man or woman in uniform. The examples available then were regular, standing armed forces from the Cold War era. Although dated, the approach harbours an underlying truth; even though most countries have reduced their militaries since then, their old equipment remains somewhere, unless destroyed (Small Arms Survey, 2001, pp. 73-74).

In reality, not all countries are armed at the same level. Reserve forces, which can be very large, are especially distinctive. The differences are especially acute for countries that rely largely on militia-based formations. Data released from the Swiss Ministry of Defence offered unprecedented insights into one well-known militia-based national defence force (Small Arms Survey, 2002, pp. 78-79). In 2003 the Ministry of Defence of Finland offered new insights by providing detailed information about the firearms under its control as well.

In a letter to the Small Arms Survey dated 21 August 2003, the Ministry reported that the combined firearms of all the Finnish armed services amounted to approximately 531,000 weapons (see Table 2.1). These were allocated among a combined force of 27,000 active-duty personnel and some 435,000 reservists, for a combined ratio of 1.15 firearms for every uniformed officer, conscript, and reservist (IISS, 2003).

Although Finland depends on a militia-based defence force much like Switzerland, its weapons policies are quite different. Unlike Switzerland, Finnish military personnel are issued arms exclusively when on active duty or official exercises. At other times weapons are stored in locked depots, not at home. Each weapon is always in an individual's possession or responsibility. Retiring personnel are not allowed to keep their service weapons. Excess or obsolescent equipment is destroyed, sold, or donated.

Table 2.1 Finnish military firearms, August 2003

Type	Quantity
Self-loading pistols	8,000
Sniper rifles	4,500
Sub-machine guns	1,000
Assault rifles	510,000
Light machine guns	7,500
Total	531,000

Sources: Letter from Pauli Järvenpää, Director General, Finnish Ministry of Defence, Helsinki, 21 August 2003; figures from IISS (2003, p. 72).

> *Although Finland depends on a militia-based defence force much like Switzerland, its weapons policies are quite different.*

Well-armed under dictatorship: Pre-war Iraqi civilian ownership

To this total of at least 4.2 million firearms lost by the Iraqi military, privately owned firearms already in civilian hands before the war began must be added. The obvious assumption is that an authoritarian regime would tightly control public access to guns (Jackman, 2003). Surprisingly perhaps, compared with common assumptions about life under an authoritarian dictatorship, pre-war Iraq appears to have had relatively permissive ownership laws. Although gun ownership was not high by international standards, it was not unusually low either. Iraq reinforces the broader conclusion that gun policy is rarely straightforward, even in tightly controlled societies.

For politically loyal Sunnis, the Iraqi government reportedly made licences easily available. According to one report, the greatest barrier to civilian gun ownership before the war was the USD 150 licence fee (King, 2003). This entitled licence holders to buy as many weapons as they pleased from legally licensed dealers. Even before the war, it reportedly was normal for households, even in urban centres like Baghdad, to have several guns (Mite, 2003).

Other groups were able to acquire weaponry, but at greater effort and with varying success. Kurds were able to arm themselves extensively through well-organized smuggling and deals with corrupt officials. Iraqi Shi'ites were more isolated, but still appear to have acquired large numbers of firearms from illegal sources. Shi'ite ownership certainly became much more common after the end of Ba'athist rule. One report noted, 'Every household in (predominantly Shi'ite) Basra has two or three guns', including weapons from before as well as those taken after the collapse of Army resistance (*The Economist*, 2003). Another maintains that the average Basra household now has two to four guns (Jadwa, 2003).

Although exact data are not available, it appears that even under Saddam Hussein, public firearm ownership was commonplace, especially but certainly not exclusively among the Sunni minority. If officially oppressed Shi'ites were able to acquire guns relatively easily, the total number of firearms in the hands of Iraqi civilians compares to the situation in Lebanon and Jordan. In those countries, with historically similar per capita wealth and gun cultures, public ownership is estimated at roughly 15–25 guns per 100 people (Jackman, 2003).

Among a population of some 24 million Iraqis, the lower standard would equal a pre-war civilian arsenal (excluding the armed forces) of around 3.2 million firearms or more. Again, this figure should be used as a starting point for understanding a public weapon inventory that almost certainly was larger, even before the war. Iraq's combined civilian and military small arms stockpile can be conservatively estimated at between 7 million and 8 million firearms, with the potential to be considerably higher.

Unquenchable thirst? Rising supply and demand

A distinctive aspect of the Iraqi situation was the speed with which demand rose to meet supply. Although a cornucopia of weaponry fell into civilian hands, prices only collapsed very briefly and quickly recovered. Iraqi demand for firearms, in other words, quickly rose to meet supply. A well-armed society had remarkable ability to absorb a weapons windfall and keep looking for more. Despite the difficult social conditions of post-war Iraqi society, though, demand did not rise as fast as some press coverage might have implied. Prices at Iraqi markets appear to have stabilized at levels close to what they were before the war began on 19 March, generally USD 200–300 for an automatic rifle. Prices never reached the extremes seen in other regions in the midst of violent conflict, such as Kashmir or Palestine, where automatic weapons can trade for USD 2,000 to 3,000 or more (Small Arms Survey, 2002, pp. 66; 2003, pp. 90–91).

The prices quoted to foreign reporters are not uniformly consistent. But general trends emerge from a review of the many reports. News reports from various Iraqi cities and markets in the month before the invasion show that the price of an AK-47

Pre-war Iraq had surprisingly permissive ownership laws for an authoritarian dictatorship.

The Iraqi people controlled a pre-war civilian arsenal of around 3.2 million privately owned weapons.

SMALL ARMS SURVEY 2004

varied greatly, but stayed within the USD 150–300 range (Badkhen, 2003). During the worst disorder of March–April 2003, prices may have collapsed for a few weeks as military inventories flooded the market. According to one report, in Basra so many rifles appeared that they briefly became worthless (Jadwa, 2003). Prices appear to have dipped as resistance collapsed in Baghdad, falling to USD 25–150 in April and May, before returning to old levels a few weeks later (Glauber, 2003; Soriano, 2003).

After the temporary collapse of prices in April, there were no more reports from Iraq comparable to African clichés of guns for the price of a chicken. Most impressive perhaps, the flood of weapons created additional demand. Prices appear to have recovered quickly as these weapons were absorbed. Especially revealing about the priorities of Iraqi buyers, the steadiest prices appear to have been for second-hand pistols. These are easily concealed, making them often more desirable than automatic rifles for personal protection. According to one report, handgun prices remained steadier at about USD 150–400, depending on model and condition (Schaffer, 2003).

Unsecured weapons: A US Army soldier studies a gun found during a raid in Baghdad in November 2003.

Iraqi demand for firearms quickly rose to meet supply. So strong was public demand that imported small arms soon began flowing into Iraq.

Six months after the conquest of Baghdad, foreign reporters routinely noted Kalashnikov prices in the range of USD 200–300 (Murphy, 2003; Prothero, 2003). This suggests that the uncontrolled stock of ex-army weapons was gone, some of it destroyed by occupying Coalition forces, but most absorbed by the civilian market. So strong was Iraqi demand that, by the early summer, foreign small arms reportedly began to flow into Iraq, especially through Iran and Syria (Filipov, 2003). Subsequent reports maintain that this flow has continued, despite Coalition efforts to close the border (Hider, 2004). The strongest demand comes from the newly created militias of religious, regional, and political leaders. Their total membership in early 2004 was estimated at about 110,000 combatants (Kahwaji, 2004). Their requirements, though, are swamped by the huge public consumption.

The strength of public demand for guns reminds us of the limits of our knowledge of the situation in Iraq. Does unsatisfied public demand suggest that the collapse of the armed forces released fewer weapons than commonly assumed? Or might it imply that Iraqi demand is virtually limitless under current conditions of insecurity?

Re-establishing Iraqi security services

One of the most enigmatic aspects of Iraq's pre-war official small arms stockpile was the role of the police, intelligence services, and other internal security agencies. The most important key to estimating their weapons inventories—their manpower figures—is not known. Clearly, their arsenals were ransacked with the same thoroughness as elsewhere. Whether their weapons were pilfered by absconding staff or taken by ordinary looters, virtually nothing was left (Matthews, 2003). Given the absence of information on former levels of these stockpiles, however, they cannot be included in our estimate of total Iraqi stockpiles.

Ironically, re-establishing the police and the armed forces requires importing guns, since there no longer are state inventories to work with. The same phenomenon has been seen before in Afghanistan, the Balkans, Haiti, and Somalia. The new Iraqi police force initially planned to include roughly 85,000 sworn officers. Other security forces are to have a combined total of 50,000 troops (Cha, 2004). According to the former New York City police commissioner in charge of the project, 150,000 Glock-19 police pistols are being imported in 2003–4 (Filkins, 2003; Pruden, 2003). In addition, 50,000 AK-47s were purchased from Jordan, ordered by the US-led Coalition Provisional Authority to arm the newly created army, the Iraqi Civil Defence Corps (Matthews, 2003).

The problematic legacy of war: Unique in scale, not in type

Despite all the chaos and subsequent imports, the scale of the Iraqi arsenal is probably much the same; mostly it is its distribution that has changed. The collapse of civil authority created innumerable opportunities for a well-armed population to acquire even more weaponry. Previously oppressed Shi'ites, for example, acquired just as much equipment as did their erstwhile oppressors. In place of an exceptionally well-armed state, the world now must deal with a heavily-armed society.

An Iraqi police officer accepts Glock handguns from US soldiers in Tikrit in February 2004.

The pre-war civilian arsenal, estimated at a minimum of 3.2 million privately owned guns, was augmented by at least 4.2 million former military weapons. Hundreds of thousands of former police and intelligence service weapons should also be included, although their numbers still cannot be estimated. Nor is much known about the total number of light weapons such as RPG-7s. As noted above, additional quantities of foreign-supplied weapons continue to flow into the country as well.

In relative terms, the figure of at least 7 million–8 million firearms now in civilian hands is equal to at least 30 for every 100 residents. Although imprecise, this range leaves little doubt of how Iraqi society has been transformed. What used to be a typically armed Middle East society has become one of the more heavily armed places in the world. This public stockpile, so suddenly reinforced, is a major element in Iraq's social and political problems. It seems inevitable that significant quantities will haemorrhage into neighbouring countries as well.

US-led efforts to deal with the problem through post-conflict disarmament were too little, too late. Many small arms and light weapons, plus ammunition, were seized from government arsenals by Coalition troops during the occupation. But most of the country's stockpile had already fallen into private hands. Coalition arms seizures did little to keep the situation from deteriorating.

Less tangible results came through an aggressive disarmament programme aimed at Iraqi civilians. This appears to have caught few guns. It did more to get weapons off the streets. Critics have argued that such measures were unethical, hindering legitimate efforts at self-protection (Lott, 2003b). But, much like similar measures in other post-conflict environments such as Kosovo and Sierra Leone, they seem to have reduced crime and intimidation, even if there was little impact on total public ownership (AP, 2003c). This reaffirms the lessons about small arms problems previously learned from post-conflict situations as diverse as El Salvador and Sierra Leone. It strengthens the conclusion that events in Iraq are not of a unique type. What makes them stand out is their unique scale and suddenness.

> Small arms problems in Iraq are not of a unique type. What makes them stand out is their unique scale and suddenness.

LATIN AMERICA: LETHAL STOCKPILES AND WEAK STATES

What happened in Iraq was special in scale and suddenness, but in many respects it was typical of small arms problems today. Latin America and the Caribbean have gradually developed a firearm problem of even greater severity. The region loses between 73,000 and 90,000 victims killed by firearms annually. Of these, between 69,500 and 84,000 are homicides (CRIME). The level of firearm death, overwhelmingly from homicide, easily surpasses the fatalities of the 2003 Iraq war, which according to a prominent study cost between 11,000 and 15,000 Iraqi combatant and non-combatant deaths from all types of weapons (Conetta, 2003).

With an average of 16 firearm homicides per 100,000 residents for the entire region, the regional frequency of violent firearm use appears to be the highest in the world. Of the 33 countries of Latin America and the Caribbean, at least eight endure firearm homicide rates that kill more than 10 out of every 100,000 residents every year (CRIME). Several other regions are home to one or more countries affected by exceptional gun problems, such as South Africa and Albania. Latin America stands out as the only part of the world where so many such countries are packed together in a single region.

> With a combined population of 464 million people, the 11 Latin American countries examined here have a total of about 45 million–80 million firearms.

The firearm problems of Latin America have encouraged exceptional vision and activism, pushing the region to the forefront of international efforts to deal with small arms proliferation. It was a Latin American initiative (sponsored by Colombia) that first won United Nations support for the issue in 1993. The region is home to the most widely ratified international treaty to restrain illegal small arms transfers and has done more than any other to promote better policy among its governments. It also hosts a United Nations office in Lima, Peru, focusing on these issues, as well as scores of concerned NGOs.

Despite Latin America's leadership on these international issues, its domestic policies often leave much to be desired. The Latin American experience shows that it is not enough to focus on international or regional aspects of small arms issues. As recognized in the 2001 UN *Programme of Action,* effective policy-making must work at the national level. It is at just this level that Latin American responses typically are the weakest.

Latin America does not have an exceptional number of guns. This conclusion emerged from a series of country studies and extensive interviews by the Small Arms Survey and the Brazilian NGO Viva Rio. This review focused on 11 countries—the ten largest South American countries and Mexico. With a combined population of more than 464 million people, these 11 countries have a total stockpile of approximately 45 million–80 million firearms. This includes all the firearms of civilians and government institutions. The greatest source of ambiguity is poor knowledge of unregistered civilian gun ownership, which can only be estimated (see Table 2.2).

Table 2.2 Distribution of firearms in 11 Latin American countries, 2003

Country	Civilian registered	Total civilian unregistered	Armed forces firearms	Official police firearms
Argentina	2,597,122	(1,500,000–3,000,000)	*609,000*	*214,000*
Bolivia	–	85,000–340,000	*21,000–51,000*	*164,000*
Brazil	5,000,000	15,000,000–25,000,000	*3,000,000*	*565,000*
Chile	649,524	750,000–1,300,000	*480,000*	*36,000*
Colombia	670,000	3,500,000–9,500,000	(522,000)	(125,000)
Ecuador	39,537	(200,000)–500,000	*250,000*	*24,000*
Mexico	1,494,321	(2,000,000)–15,000,000	*1,000,000*	*425,000*
Paraguay	320,906	(400,000–700,000)	(135,000)	(34,000)
Peru	241,000	(250,000–750,000)	(638,000)	(110,000)
Uruguay	570,000	(300,000–1,000,000)	*80,000*	*30,000*
Venezuela	–	1,200,000–6,000,000	*250,000*	*112,000*
Total	**11,582,410**	**25,000,000–60,000,000**	**7,000,000**	**1,800,000**

Notes: Figures in normal type are official, those in brackets are estimates made by officials interviewed, and those in italics are Small Arms Survey–Viva Rio estimates. For Colombia, the small arms of insurgents and paramilitaries are included in civilian unregistered.

Sources: Country background papers by Small Arms Survey and Viva Rio, and Viva Rio interviews with government officials in 11 national capitals

Some trends correspond to common assumptions about social conditions. Other countries such as Bolivia, Ecuador, and Peru have much lower civilian ownership rates. In these three countries it is possible that official small arms outnumber those of civilians; the data are not accurate enough to be certain. Often overlooked Uruguay, on the other hand, may be one of the most heavily armed countries anywhere. The regional average is equal to approximately 8–16 civilian firearms for every 100 people (see Table 2.3). This is far behind the United States with approximately 83–96 guns for every 100 people. It is more comparable to Western Europe, home to an average of 17.4 guns for every 100 residents (Small Arms Survey, 2003, p. 64).

Table 2.3 Estimated total civilian firearms in 11 Latin American countries, 2003

Country	Population	Estimated civilian firearms (millions)	Firearms/100 people
Argentina	38,400,000	4.1–5.6	11–15
Bolivia	8,800,000	0.09–0.3	1–4
Brazil	178,500,000	20.0–30.0	11–17
Chile	15,800,000	1.4–2.0	9–12
Colombia	44,200,000	4.0–10.0	10–23
Ecuador	13,000,000	0.2–0.5	2–4
Mexico	103,500,000	3.5–16.5	4–17
Paraguay	5,900,000	0.7–1.0	12–17
Peru	27,200,000	0.5–1.0	2–4
Uruguay	3,400,000	0.9–1.6	25–46
Venezuela	25,700,000	1.2–6.0	5–23
Total	**464,400,000**	**36.0–74.0**	**8–16**

Note: Totals may not add up due to rounding.

Sources: Population from United Nations, Department of Economic and Social Affairs (2003); firearm data from Table 2.2

All the governments surveyed here require firearm licensing and registration. Even so, illegal ownership is the norm, a reflection of the weakness of most Latin American states. Altogether no more than 30–45 per cent of civilian guns appear to be registered (see Table 2.2). The rest are illegally held, constituting a large reservoir for crime and violence. This may help explain the exceptional lethality of the region's small arms, perhaps the most startling finding of this review. The dangers are worst in countries with the largest proportion of unregistered guns—notably Brazil, Colombia, Ecuador, Venezuela, and possibly Bolivia as well—although unreliable data inhibits strong correlations. The licensing system itself may exacerbate the problem, since regional laws typically allow licensees to carry a loaded weapon in public. Brazil has only just pioneered legislation rescinding this privilege.

Behind regional trends lie broad national differences. Public ownership is the greatest source of doubt about regional stockpiles. And problems with import data suggest that even seemingly reliable data should be used cautiously. The most ambiguous case is *Mexico*, where civilian gun ownership appears to be much higher than official figures, but how much higher is unclear. The Mexican Constitution says that the country's 103 million people have a right to own firearms (Mexico, 1968, 1:1, §10). Mexico's 1972 firearms law, however, has been interpreted to forbid much of the gun trade (Mexico, 1972). Most gun manufacturing is reserved to state arsenals (PRODUCERS). Legal gun shops have been closed and public ownership is legally limited to low-calibre weapons.

But international trade statistics open a window on a different Mexican reality. National import statistics reveal that Mexico received USD 7.9 million worth of firearms in 2000, the latest year available (Mexico, 2003). This is among the highest rate of importation for all of Latin America. Although Mexico does not report the number of small arms it imports, the quantities involved can be estimated using national trade statistics from other countries examined here. Among those Latin American countries that make complete data available—Argentina, Chile, Paraguay and Uruguay—the average wholesale value of the small arms they import was USD 89–168 each, depending on the country. At these values, Mexico's legal small arms imports would amount to 47,000–88,000 annually. If they are typical, such imports seem difficult to reconcile with the official figure of fewer than 1.5 million registered guns, especially when one recalls the major role of Mexico's own domestic firearm industry (Dreyfus and Karp, 2003). Nor does this include illegal smuggling through the United States. The evidence strongly supports the conclusion that there are many more guns in Mexico than official figures indicate.

Uruguay illustrates a much more permissive gun culture. With approximately 570,000 firearms registered among its population of 3.4 million, its confirmed rate of legal ownership almost certainly is much higher than Mexico's. Here as well, though, doubts surround official data. Uruguayan national data shows that the country imported 4,928 small arms in 2000, and imports dropped dramatically as the economy crashed, falling to just 762 guns imported in 2002 (Uruguay, 2003). Even at the higher rate, such small imports are difficult to reconcile with the level of legal ownership. Local authorities estimate that Uruguayans have an additional 300,000 to one million unregistered guns (Dreyfus and Karp, 2003). While Uruguayan law is less restrictive, the realities of ownership are only somewhat less mysterious. In both Mexico and Uruguay, as in most countries of Latin America, official data are far from conclusive. One of the greatest sources of regional ambiguity appears to be the weakness of the state itself.

What is most distinctive about Latin American and Caribbean firearms is not their absolute number but their impressive *lethality* (see Table 2.4). Although the region as a whole does not have an exceptionally highly level of firearm ownership, its firearms are used with remarkable deadliness. Stockpile 'lethality' here refers to the ratio of guns to gun homicides, the actual number of people killed with guns, or the likelihood that a typical firearm will be used to kill. It should not be confused with a quality inherent to a particular weapon, such as calibre or other indices of firepower.

GLOBAL FIREARM STOCKPILES

Table 2.4   The deadliest gun use: Stockpile lethality in nine Latin American countries
(with selected examples from elsewhere, ranked by highest gun lethality)

Country	Total civilian guns (millions)	Annual gun homicides	Gun homicides per 100,000 *people*	Guns per gun homicide	Gun homicides per 100,000 *guns*
Ecuador	0.2–0.5	1,321	10.16	150–380	260–660
Colombia	4.2–10.2	21,898	49.54	190–470	220–520
Venezuela	1.2–6.0	5,408	21.04	220–1,100	90–450
Brazil	20.0–30.0	25,603	14.35	780–1,170	85–128
Mexico	3.5.0–16.5.0	5,452	5.27	640–3,000	33–156
Argentina	4.1–5.6	942	2.45	4,350–5,940	17–23
Peru	0.5–1.0	161	0.59	3100–6,200	16–32
Uruguay	0.9–1.6	104	3.05	8,650–11,400	7–12
Chile	1.4–2.0	82	0.52	17,000–24,400	4.1–5.9
Jamaica	0.08–0.2	450	16.97	180–440	230–560
South Africa	4.5	13,572	30.17	330	302.0
United States	243.0–281.0	10,310	3.45	24,000–28,000	3.76–4.2
Canada	7.9	170	0.54	48,000	2.2
Germany	20.0–30.0	155	0.19	129,000–194,000	0.5–0.8

Note: The data in this figure come from different base years. While firearm statistics are for 2002–3, gun homicide data is from the most recent year available, usually 1998–2001, except for Jamaica, which is 1995. Bolivia and Paraguay were excluded for lack of specific firearms homicide data. Figures for guns/gun homicide and gun homicide/100,000 guns have been rounded to avoid false precision.

Sources: compiled from Table 2.1 and 2.2 above. Firearm homicide data from Chetty (2000); CRIME; UN (1998); UNODC (2003). Civilian stockpile data for other countries from Cross *et al.* (2003), GPC (2002), and Small Arms Survey (2002).

Not all countries in the region face egregious levels of criminal violence. Uruguay has the highest rate of public gun ownership in all of Latin America: at least 25 civilian guns per 100 inhabitants. It may be among the most heavily armed societies in the world if the higher estimate of 46 guns per 100 people is correct. In silent testimony to the stability of Uruguayan society, however, the country with the region's highest rate of gun ownership also has one of the lowest firearm homicide rates, at 3.05 per 100,000. This is about ten per cent lower than the rate in the United States. The lowest firearm homicide rates of all the countries surveyed here belong to Argentina, Chile (armed roughly at the regional average), and Peru (which has few firearms by international standards).

The situation is very different in Colombia, Ecuador, Venezuela, and Brazil (see Table 2.4). The high number of annual firearm homicides in these countries is well-known. Less commonly appreciated is the exceptional lethality of their small arms arsenals, the ratio of guns to gun homicides. The last two columns of Table 2.4 show the statistical likelihood that an average gun in these countries will be used to kill. They show that some guns are much more dangerous than others. The penultimate column shows, for each society, the ratio of guns to each gun homicide. In other words, how likely is it that any *individual gun* will be used to kill in an average year? The last column presents gun lethality in terms of homicides per 100,000 guns. This gives a sense of the comparative lethality of a country's *entire firearm stockpile*.

Because of uncertainty over the number of civilian firearms in all of the countries surveyed here, precise comparison is impossible. In Colombia, with a reputation as one of the most violent countries on the face of the planet, one out of every 190–470 guns can be expected to take a life every year. Put differently, the final column shows that, for every 100,000 Colombian firearms, an average of 220–520 people will die annually. In Ecuador the absolute number of gun homicides is much smaller, but so is the national firearm stockpile. As a result, Ecuadorian guns are a little deadlier than those in neighbouring Colombia.

> What is most distinctive about Latin American and Caribbean firearms is not their absolute number but their impressive lethality.

53

Other cases are equally troubling; the examples of Jamaica and South Africa are included in Table 2.4 to give a sense of other extremes, as are examples from more peaceful societies. The others show just how serious the situation is in much of Latin America. Brazil and Germany, for example, appear to have roughly the same number of civilian-owned guns. But Brazil's firearm homicide rate is 165 times higher, and its guns are at least 110 to 250 times more likely to be used to kill. Such comparisons leave no doubt about the importance of better small arms policy to the security, welfare, and well-being of the region.

STOCKPILE SECURITY: WHO'S MINDING THE STORE?

Sure it works: Demonstrating a pistol in a street gun market in Baghdad in May 2003.

© AP/Alexander Zemlianichenko

The Iraqi small arms problem, like the MANPADS problem described in Chapter 3, is a highly publicized example of a well-known phenomenon. Stockpile security is—or should be—a serious issue for all weapon owners. In Iraq it was stockpile security that failed completely. More typical problems are caused by less extreme breakdowns. Both government and private small arms owners face serious challenges in controlling their weapons inventories. Poor stockpile security contributes directly to illegal acquisition of small arms, providing a window through which legal guns enter the illicit circuit.

The scale of losses through negligence and theft can range from millions of small arms over a short space of time to a one-by-one trickle, but the effect can be much the same. Illegally acquired weaponry is especially dangerous, most likely to exacerbate criminal violence and armed conflict. Pilfered or stolen guns are rapidly transferred, feeding crime and conflict elsewhere.

The risks for governments

Because governments keep the largest arsenals, they also face some of the greatest risks of losing stockpile control. In the most extreme examples, entire national arsenals are looted. Something similar to the Iraqi case happened in 1997 when Albania lost some 643,000 small arms and light weapons (Small Arms Survey, 2002, p. 76). Much the same happened in Somalia in 1991–2, when the government of Siad Barre collapsed and government arsenals were pillaged of several hundred thousand weapons by warring clans.

Government institutions can be more than passive victims in the process of diversion. Wilful neglect and official complicity may occur as official policy or when the convictions of well-placed officials lead to direct support for particular groups. In one of the largest examples on record, in 1991–3 the Russian military allowed new republics and non-recognized factions in Armenia, Azerbaijan, and Georgia to take 260,000 small arms from key bases. Some were transferred under official bilateral documents, but others were informally transferred by Russian regional commanders, tacitly allowed to be taken, or stolen through bribery, extortion, or simple theft (Pyadushkin, 2003, p. 151). The movement of weaponry from poorly controlled military arsenals can directly influence the severity and outcome of armed conflict. In the Caucasus, it directly exacerbated the scale of the fighting and altered the politics of the region, encouraging organized crime and secession.

More common but still spectacular thefts tend to involve hundreds of weapons taken from government arsenals in raids by organized crime, terrorist cells, or rebel groups. For many insurgencies, raiding police stations or military facilities is a standard—but risky—way to acquire weaponry. A recent study of small arms in Southeast Asia provides numerous examples of such attacks. It shows that the armed forces of Indonesia, Malaysia, the Philippines, and Thailand routinely lose hundreds of small arms in such incidents (Capie, 2002). The catastrophic loss of hundreds, thousands, or even millions of weapons in a short space of time galvanizes international attention and assures a response, however inadequate it may be. But innumerable smaller incidents are much more typical. Over time, their cumulative impact may be no less dangerous.

Large institutions and the danger of small losses

It is the explosive loss of vast quantities of small arms belonging to the armed forces, police, and other government agencies that gets the most attention. But such events, although far from rare, remain exceptional. In most of the world, it is the steady trickle of ordinary losses that releases the most small arms over time. In most countries, governments own considerably fewer small arms than civil society does. Their losses appear to be smaller as well. But, as constitutionally established organizations responsible for public welfare, they have a special responsibility. Losing their small arms to criminals or rebels is a betrayal of the social contract that establishes their authority.

Smaller-scale pilfering from official stocks can be equally dangerous. It was poorly secured government weapons from arsenals in the Pacific that provided the arms used to overthrow the elected government in Fiji and ignite civil war in the Solomon Islands. In Fiji only a few dozen rifles and pistols were lost, but in fragile societies this is enough to undermine social order and political stability. In the Solomon Islands, more than 1,000 military and police rifles were stolen (PACIFIC). Russian authorities say that the Russian army lost 8,000 stolen weapons from 1995 to 2001 (Shashkov, 2002). Other sources maintain that loss rates are much higher and that Russian government agencies have reported a total of 150,000 lost firearms during the same time period (Gusev, 2003).

Because of their special responsibilities, governments face harsh criticism for losing control. In an extreme example, Saudi Arabian officials reportedly discovered after a raid on 6 May 2003 that al Qaeda terrorists had acquired rifles, explosives, and ammunition from the Saudi Arabian National Guard (Finn, 2003). When similar matériel was used in a successful attack in Riyadh killing 34 people one week later, the culpability of the Saudi government ceased to be a purely academic question.

An illustration of the sensitivity of the issue came directly from the Saudi Interior Minister, Prince Nayef bin Abdul Aziz. He strongly denied allegations that al Qaeda armed itself out of government arsenals. The Saudi National Guard, he explained, did not use AK-47s and Czech explosives of the sort found in the May 2003 raids (AFP, 2003a; Saudi Arabia, 2003). Other sources have noted that the National Guard has long been armed with exactly this kind of equipment in its inventories (Metz, 1993). Indeed, the Kingdom reportedly purchased a 'large consignment' of former Soviet firearms less than two years earlier (Kazakh Commercial Television, 2001).

While the loss of a gun always is serious, the cause may not be calculated or intrinsically evil. Forgetfulness may be more of a factor than conspiracy. Employees of government agencies lose small arms from time to time, just as

> Because governments keep the largest arsenals, they also face some of the greatest problems of losing stockpile control.

they lose cars, laptop computers, and other valuable items through negligence or theft. German officials, for example, report that about 1,000 government-owned firearms are lost or stolen this way every year (UN, 1998, p. 84). The situation there hardly seems exceptional.

An investigation by the US General Accounting Office released in 2003 found that 18 US government agencies reported losing 1,012 small arms between September 1998 and July 2002. Losses included weapons belonging to the Federal Bureau of Investigation, the Immigration and Naturalization Service, the Drug Enforcement Agency, the US Customs Service, and the National Parks Service. Fewer than 20 per cent were ever recovered (US, GAO, 2000; Seper, 2003). The armed services have similar problems. The US Army has acknowledged the loss of 223 weapons—mostly small arms and explosives—since 1991 (Freedberg and Humburg, 2003). In August 2003, for example, two grenade launchers went missing from a New York Army depot. Negligence, not theft, was the likely explanation (Lemire, 2003).

Losses of dozens or hundreds of arms every year are hardly surprising given the scale of some official inventories. If the loss is quickly noted, corrective action can be taken. In countries where security is poor, losses of equipment can be much worse and may not be discovered for months or years. The problem has directly fuelled instability and fighting in the Pacific (Alpers and Twyford, 2003; Capie, 2003). In some states in Southeast Asia, most notoriously in Cambodia, Indonesia, and the Philippines, poor storage practices and lack of personal responsibility facilitate routine theft (Capie, 2002, pp. 31, 42, 76, 105). The problem is not confined to weapons in storage. Governments simply may have no idea of the disposition of the guns they own. In Uganda, according to one report, the government lacks any central information about an arsenal of 1.2 million small arms (Potgieter, 2003). When substandard monitoring and irregular discipline make it possible, impoverished soldiers will be tempted to sell their weapons and report them lost or stolen.

In poorer countries, where a small arm is often the most valuable item in an individual's immediate control, illegal sale is a serious problem. Army installations throughout the developing world must deal with a continuous risk that weapons will be sold by their own troops. Individual crimes often are small. In Malaysia, for example, soldiers were charged in 2003 with selling two M-16 rifles, three HK-P9S pistols, and ammunition (Simon, 2003). There was nothing special about the charge, which reflected a small part of a continuous problem. In the Philippines, the armed forces also have acknowledged a serious problem with systematic theft and illegal sales from government inventories (Guerrero, 2003).

Greed or ideology can be a stronger force than security. The Israeli Defence Forces have not been immune to allegations of personnel taking arms and ammunition to sell to Palestinian militants who may use them to kill Israelis. In 2002, Israeli military police reported that 160 guns and 361 hand grenades were stolen (AP, 2003b). Some of these items reportedly made their way to Palestinian militants (AP, 2003a). The scale of economically motivated malfeasance can rise astronomically when government officials misuse their positions to become arms brokers. In Thailand, military officials coordinate imports of small arms, some of which are cycled through official inventories before being sold on the black market (Davis, 2003).

> For governments to lose their small arms to criminals or rebels is a betrayal of the social contract that establishes their authority.

The fate of old weapons

Government agencies also face special responsibilities for their weapons, responsibilities that go beyond those they physically control. After they have been retired or decommissioned and disposed of, small arms previously owned by public institutions are just like any others in the public domain. Once used to protect the public, they can subsequently be misused by their new owners. As cheaper, second-hand models, these discards are especially likely to find their way to unsavoury owners.

By law or expectation, public security organizations have a special obligation to manage their weapons stockpiles. Increasingly this applies not just to their current weapons inventories but to their cast-offs as well. The discovery of a former police pistol in the pocket of a thug might not be considered a special police issue. But the responsibility to protect public safety has been applied to exactly such situations. Police departments and even military establishments used to routinely sell their old small arms to the public for extra income. As concepts of official responsibility expand, however, this practice is being challenged, although it still continues in much of the world.

The catalyst for the largest series of police weapons trade-ins was an incident in Dade County, Florida, on 11 April 1986. Bank robbers with an assault rifle and high-calibre revolvers killed two FBI agents and wounded five (Anderson, 1996). In the wake of the tragedy, police forces in the United States and many other countries urgently switched from traditional revolvers to more powerful weapons, usually automatic pistols. To help finance the switch, manufacturers purchased the older police arms for resale.

After the FBI-Dade shoot-out, the Austrian firm Glock, for example, resold over 150,000 old police revolvers this way. Not all these guns stayed in responsible hands. As some began to turn up at crime scenes, police have been pressed to abandon the practice (Vobejda, Ottaway, and Cohen, 1999). Weak finances, though, make the practice hard to break. Trading-in old police guns to subsidize the acquisition of new ones remains normal practice in much of the world. In the US state of Missouri, for example, a former police Glock pistol was recovered from a crime scene in 2003. The gun had been traded-in only a few months before (Sloca, 2003a, 2003b).

Destroying old police and military firearms instead of reselling them often requires pressure and financial support from governing authorities. With extra assistance, the Royal Canadian Mounted Police were able to destroy more than 20,000 surplus revolvers, old guns that previously would have been sold to the public (Canada, 2003). This approach remains far from universal, though, and many police forces continue to find it hard to turn down trade-in subsidies. Australian police in Queensland, for example, sought to stretch their rearmament budget by trading 3,674 older revolvers for a discount on 8,600 new Glock pistols. Despite extensive debate, in 2003 it was learned that state authorities had allowed the deal to go ahead (Parnell, 2003; private communication with Philip Alpers, 2003).

Poor storage practices and the lack of personal responsibility facilitate pilfering and unexplained losses.

The catalyst for the largest police weapons trade-in was a fatal robbery in Florida in 1986.

Eliminating surplus government weapons

The solutions to institutional small arms losses vary. For current weapons inventories the key is secure storage with regular monitoring of stocks, and careful oversight and rigorous responsibility for weapons issued to individuals. For excess or obsolescent weapons, the best solution is almost always destruction.

The most publicized small arms destruction programmes focus on the weapons of individual private owners. In 2003 several initiatives were under way to collect and destroy unwanted civilian firearms. Most were relatively small and even the largest received little international attention. In Kenya 8,000 illicit small arms and light weapons confiscated by the police and army were destroyed in the previous year (*Nation,* 2003). A highly publicized amnesty and buy-back programme in the Australian state of Victoria in 2003 brought in 18,934 newly illegal handguns, surrendered by civilian owners to police for eventual destruction (Mickelburough, 2004).

In other regions, disarming civilians and ex-combatants is controversial and politically sensitive. In Angola, a debate on how to collect weapons in civilian hands in the aftermath of the war has continued inconclusively (APA, 2003). An effort to disarm 40,000 former combatants in Liberia collapsed in December 2003 and had to be suspended, not because of opposition, but apparently due to poor planning and under-funding (Carroll, 2003).

SMALL ARMS SURVEY 2004

After repeated failures, a new disarmament programme aimed at former militiamen was launched in Afghanistan in October 2003. A pilot scheme was inaugurated by President Hamid Karzai with some 1,000 former fighters in the relatively peaceful province of Kunduz. The Japanese government has pledged USD 200 million to extend the project over the entire country, covering 100,000 former militiamen during 2004–05 (Constable, 2003; Reuters, 2003a).

The most successful individual-oriented collection programme in 2003 almost certainly was in the Solomon Islands, where hundreds of small arms previously taken from government arsenals were recovered. Although there currently are no plans for these weapons to be destroyed, the stockpile will be securely stored (PACIFIC).

Although institutional destruction receives much less public attention, it is responsible for the biggest changes in global stockpiles. When Ambassador Kuniko Inoguchi opened the 2003 UN Biennial Small Arms Conference, noting that four million small arms had been destroyed in the last decade, she was mostly referring to elimination of institutional surpluses. Similarly, when US Assistant Secretary of State Lincoln Bloomfield told the same meeting that since 2001 US-supported programmes had destroyed more than 400,000 weapons and 44 million pieces of ammunition, he too referred mostly to destruction of institutional surpluses (Bloomfield, 2003).

The total scale of global small arms destruction, mostly eliminating obsolescent or unnecessary weapons, is difficult to assess. Examples of some of these undertakings are listed in Table 2.5. The table lists 12 countries with major institutional destruction projects responsible for the elimination of roughly 4.2 million small arms and light weapons. This is in addition to the destruction of over four million institutional and public firearms previously reported destroyed by the Small Arms Survey (2002, p. 74). In all, more than eight million small arms are known to have been destroyed during the last decade.

Many police forces still find it difficult to say no to trade-in subsidies.

Table 2.5   Institutional small arms destruction, selected examples

Country	Items	Quantity	Years	Supervision
Australia	Revolvers	3,674	2002	Queensland police
Bulgaria	SALW	77,050	2001-2002	Multilateral
Canada	Pistols	20,000	2003*	RCMP
China	Firearms	1,300,000	1999-2001	Police
France	Firearms	140,000	1998-2000	France
Germany	SALW	1,576,419	1990-2002	German army
Netherlands	Firearms	143,632	1994-96	Dutch army
Romania	SALW	195,510	2002-2003	Multilateral
Russia	SALW	470,000	2002	Russian army
Serbia	SALW	117,269	2001-2003	Multilateral
South Africa	Firearms	115,711	1999-2001	Police
Total (rounded)		**4,200,000**	**1994-2003**	

Note: * Date reported.

Sources: Australia: Parnell (2003); Bulgaria: Hirst (2002, pp. 5, 11); Canada: Canada (2003); China: Small Arms Survey (2003); France (2003, p. 10); Germany (2003, p. 59); the Netherlands: Wezeman and Wezeman (1996, p. 8); Romania: Barbulescu (2003); Russia: Itar-Tass, 8 July 2003; Serbia (2003, p. 5); South Africa (2003)

Many of these destruction programmes came at the end of a period of political change and cannot be repeated. Reductions in Europe were facilitated by the end of the Cold War. This brought an end to requirements for large standing armies and their reserve components. Destruction of small arms was a logical extension of the principles articulated in the 1993 Treaty on Conventional Forces in Europe, which led to the destruction of a large number of major weapon systems.

Box 2.2 Sri Lanka's post-war firearms

As the case of Iraq demonstrates, it is often after wars end that stockpile security becomes most acute. After combat ceases, weapons earlier distributed to secure victory suddenly exacerbate social instability and crime. In times of war, small arms are often doled out despite poor record-keeping. The recipients might include village militias, unofficial military units and paramilitaries, and political sympathizers. These groups are often unwilling to return the weapons later.

Sri Lanka is the latest in a long list of countries where war weapons assumed a new post-conflict importance. After more than two decades of fighting, the government and ethnic Tamil rebels agreed to a preliminary ceasefire on 22 February 2002. This led to a deal on 6 December 2002 granting a degree of autonomy to the country's Tamil minority (*Washington Post*, 2003). Despite numerous incidents and limited support from the country's majority Singhalese population, the arrangement has held so far (Izzadeen, 2003).

The peace appears to have contributed little to reducing the problem of weapons now flowing throughout Sri Lankan society. The sources of these weapons are numerous. Black markets started initially to serve the rebels soon expanded to satisfy ordinary civilians and organized criminals (Ashtakala, 2003). Over the years, tens of thousands of soldiers have deserted, often taking their weapons with them. Government agencies issued additional weapons to politically sensitive groups. Army commanders are also alleged to have held on to captured rebel arsenals for their own reasons (*TamilNet*, 2002).

As in other countries emerging from war, the end of fighting triggered a post-war crime wave. The incidence of crime reached unprecedented heights, with over 1,900 murders annually (Interpol, various years). Cognizant of the problem, the Sri Lankan Ministry of Interior authorized an amnesty for unlicensed weapons in December 2001. This flopped, yielding only a few shotguns, according to one source (Nonis and Wijewardena, 2002). Threats of harsh police action were ignored (Jayasinghe, 2002). Even some of the 225 members of parliament who received police handguns for their personal security refused to cooperate (*Deepika*, 2003; *EelamNation*, 2003).

Returning to normal? An unarmed Tamil Tiger soldier and companion cycle past a police station in Kilinochchi, Sri Lanka, in July 2002.

Exacerbating the small arms problem is the unwillingness of public officials to acknowledge its true dimensions. According to then Interior Minister John Amaratunga, the number of unauthorized firearms in circulation before the end of the war was around 20,000 (Subramanian, 2001). More recently, official sources have spoken of 45,000. To judge from wars elsewhere—such as those in Central America and Africa—the real total is likely to be much higher. Independent experts place the figure in the hundreds of thousands (Muggah, 2003). Using survey estimating techniques and accounting for civilian possession, it is likely that the actual number lies somewhere between almost 1 million and 2.4 million guns in Sri Lanka (see Table 2.6). This is far from the last word, but it may offer a more accurate sense of the dimensions of small arms availability in the country.

Although the country has achieved an uneasy peace, the long history of ethnic tension and distrust will take decades to heal. The legacy of uncontrolled small arms may be no easier to deal with. The first step will be to assess accurately the scale of the challenge facing policy-makers. Re-establishing order will take time, but if well-conceived and designed measures match the size of the problem, it undoubtedly will be achieved more quickly and more permanently.

Table 2.6 Approximate distribution of Sri Lankan small arms, 2004

Group	Group population	Small arms multiplier	Estimated small arms inventory*
Armed Forces	157,900	2.25	355,000
Home Guard	20,000	2.25	45,000
National Armed Reserve	15,000	2.25	34,000
Police (with Special Task Force)	28,000	1.2	34,000
Civilians	19,000,000	3-10/100	600,000-1,900,000 **
LTTE combatants	7,000	1.6	11,000
Total (rounded)			**1,000,000-2,400,000**

Notes: *Estimated inventories of each group are rounded to the nearest 1,000.
**Estimated by the Small Arms Survey.

Sources: The size of the armed forces and LTTE from IISS (2002, p. 135); the Home Guard, National Armed Reserve, and police from Blood (1990, ch. 5) and TamilNet (2003); the civilian multiplier is based on Small Arms Survey (2002, pp. 101-2)

In the Balkans it was only through combined pressure from several sources that governments agreed to destroy their weapons surpluses. Only with the end of the Yugoslav wars was destruction domestically acceptable. Successor states also became vulnerable to outside pressure as a result of their desire to join Western security and political institutions. Other European governments and institutions grew alarmed at black market transfers originating in the region. Similarly, South Africa was able to reduce its small arms inventories following the end of apartheid. The most uncertainty surrounds China, where large quantities of confiscated firearms were destroyed by police during a major Strike Hard campaign. The reliability of the Chinese figure is questionable (Small Arms Survey, 2003). While the other numbers in Figure 2.4 appear solid, inclusion of Chinese firearm destruction necessitates rounding the final total.

Contrary to general expectations, the pace of institutional small arms destruction has not slackened following the destruction of many of the largest surpluses. Germany continued destruction through 2003, when the Bundeswehr scrapped an additional 96,510 small arms, mostly G-3 automatic rifles (Musik, 2003). The most spectacular projects tend to occur in countries where enormous military stockpiles remain. With few exceptions, these are associated with the infantry-dominated military doctrine of the Soviet Union or Maoist People's War. Russia reportedly has plans to eliminate a further 1.2 million 'light weapons' (Poroskov, 2003). Ukraine also is in negotiations for a major destruction programme involving the elimination of 1.5 million small arms and light weapons (NATO, 2003). Bulgaria reportedly has another 500,000 unwanted AK-47s awaiting a decision on their fate (Talev, 2001).

There also appears to be a need for major destruction projects in Latin America. In much of Latin America the armed forces are believed to hoard obsolescent equipment. This habit leaves massive stockpiles of redundant small arms (Pablo Dreyfus, private communication). The systematic destruction of these stockpiles, to prevent them being illegally diverted or dumped on civilian markets, has yet to be addressed by regional governments.

CASUAL LOSS: INDIVIDUAL THEFT AND DISAPPEARANCE

Daring attacks on government armouries and smaller cases betraying the public trust get the most media attention. But it is small-scale burglary, mostly from private homes, that appears to account for the majority of stolen firearms. This is another aspect of the gradual transformation of global stockpiles through individual decisions. Illustrating the tyranny of small actions, these inconspicuous events probably do much more to shape the global distribution of small arms than the better-reported major transfers.

Stolen guns can present the greatest risk to society. Most of the world's small arms—especially the roughly 400 million guns in civilian hands—are rarely fired. Typical of this situation is Germany, where there are an estimated ten million gun owners (UN, 1998). Of these, only some 2.4 million belong to shooting clubs, which permits them to buy ammunition. Presumably most of the rest do very little shooting. For most of these guns, the moment of greatest danger to human life often comes when they are stolen.

Stolen firearms are widely acknowledged to be among the most likely to be used in violent crime. This conclusion is illustrated most clearly in *time-to-crime studies* on typical intervals between gun theft and use in crime in the United States (US, ATF, 2002). In countries with relatively effective registration systems, unregistered and stolen weapons can often amount to 90 per cent or more of all guns seized at crime scenes (Mouzos, 2000). They play a major role in black markets. Stolen firearms become a serious problem for other countries when they feed into the domestic illicit trade.

The flow of small arms smuggled piecemeal out of the United States, for example, is a serious issue in bilateral relations with the country's neighbours.

The most comprehensive analysis of international statistics on theft, in the 1998 UN Firearm Regulation Study, covered 28 countries. These were the only respondents who were both able and willing to report data on the problem. If these one-year reports are regarded as annual averages, they indicate that in these 28 countries an average of 103,000 privately owned guns are reported stolen or lost every year (UN, 1998). The data are too incomplete to serve as a basis for a global estimate. Major gun-owning countries left out include China, France, Germany, Italy, Mexico, Pakistan, and most of the United States. Nor are there any reports from the Middle East or most of Southeast Asia. Worse, there are serious problems with many of the UN study's individual reports. There are no standards for international reporting of theft data, which varies greatly in comprehensiveness.

The Canadian figure, for example, uses a year in which a statistical 'house cleaning' took place, apparently in reaction to forthcoming changes in the law. This inflated the theft and losses by including a large number of events from previous years (Wendy Cukier, private communication, 28 July 2003). The US figure is drawn from a special study. This referred exclusively to a small category of thefts, namely those against federally licensed firearms dealers over nine months. The Argentine figure referred exclusively to the federal capital district of Buenos Aires (UN, 1998).

> Stolen firearms are widely acknowledged to be among the most likely to be used in violent crime.

US gun theft

As is often the case in these issues, the most incisive lessons come from the United States. It almost certainly has the largest theft problem, if only because it has the most publicly owned guns. But understanding the scale of gun theft in the United States is not easy, because it has only limited firearms registration and no central agency responsible for collecting reports of gun theft. The small figure supplied to the UN in 1998, for example, referred exclusively to thefts from federally licensed US gun dealers during a nine-month period (UN, 1998, p. 85).

The importance of the problem and the limits of knowledge about it are illustrated in a systematic study of firearms theft in the United States undertaken by American criminologist Gary Kleck. To evaluate the scale of US gun theft, he relied on the annual US National Crime Victimization Survey. This large, government-sponsored survey of crime trends showed 341,000 incidents of gun theft per year between 1987 and 1992. This says nothing about the number of guns actually stolen in each incident. Since American gun owners, like gun owners in much of the world, typically have several guns, it is likely that more than one was taken in an average theft. Assuming that an average of roughly 1.5–5 guns are taken in each incident, Kleck concluded that the total number of guns stolen in the United States each year ranges from 570,000 to 1,820,000 (Kleck, 1997, p. 92). Not all analysts are satisfied with this estimate. Many are more comfortable with the conservative round figure of 500,000 (Jacobs, 2002, p. 109).

Although the uncertainties remain troublesome, the rate of US small arms theft appears exceptional as well, a direct consequence of the special size of its public stockpile. Kleck's original calculation shows that the chance of an average US gun being stolen could be as high as one in 150 annually. At the lowest calculated rate of theft, US citizens are victims of one gun theft annually for every 417 privately owned small arms. Even the lower rate of theft is higher than that of any other developed country for which data is available. Australia and Canada, discussed below, appear to come closest to having comparable problems with gun theft.

> The most comprehensive international statistics on theft appeared in the 1998 UN International Study on Firearms Regulation.

Theft elsewhere

Comparison with other countries is complicated by the lack of systematic data on stockpiles, theft, or loss. Even where reported theft rates are available, it is difficult to establish the actual rate, above all because of uncertainties surrounding unregistered guns. Victims of gun theft are presumably less inclined to report the theft of an unregistered—illegal—gun when this might invite their own prosecution. While most crime is under-reported, small arms theft appears to be severely affected. In some countries, moreover, stolen or illegally sold guns can simply be reported as lost or missing. Despite its seeming innocence, this category introduces even more questions about what is actually going on.

A handful of countries have released data on both total registrations and total small arms theft and loss. Although these are not enough for conclusive estimates of global gun theft, they offer a basis for evaluating its possible scale. Table 2.6 compares registered stockpiles and theft rates in a smaller group of countries for which both kinds of data are available. It shows that for these countries the average annual rate of reported small arms theft is about one for every 1,500 legally owned guns. The average rate for developed countries is somewhat lower (about 1/2,000) while the only two developing countries in the sample have a much higher average (about 1/360). None of these figures includes theft of unregistered guns, the largest pool in many of these countries.

The US theft figures are more comprehensive since they are based on public surveys rather than police reports. This may explain why they are higher than those of other developed countries. Canada appears to be more typical, with reports of theft or loss averaging 5,000 guns annually for 1997–2001, or one out of every 1,600 guns annually, according to official statistics (Hung, 2003). Other sources maintain that actual theft rates are much higher. According to Barry Breitkreuz, an average of 17,000 guns were stolen annually during the same period (*Sault Star*, 2003). Although the source of the higher figure is not clear, it would be equal to the theft of one out of every 460 Canadian guns, apparently including unregistered firearms.

Many of the difficulties inherent in theft and loss data are especially stark in Canada. Canadian theft and loss statistics appear to be an inverse ratio of the proportion of firearms registered: the more guns registered, the fewer reported stolen. This partially results from better home gun storage, a requirement of Canadian legal reforms. In Canada, moreover, there is a legal responsibility to report all stolen and missing firearms. These laws have the unintended consequence of making owners of unregistered guns more vulnerable to prosecution themselves. As a result the Canadian figures probably do not include a significant share of the unregistered guns stolen or missing (Hung, private communication, July 2003).

Is Canadian gun theft declining or is reporting down? This is a critical subject for future research. Officially reported gun losses declined 75 per cent from 1995 to 2001 (see Figure 2.1). Did gun losses really drop that much, or are Canadians more afraid to report them? Other forms of gun crime fell in Canada during this period as well, albeit less dramatically. For instance, homicides with guns fell from 212 to 151. Robbery fell slightly, from 30,273 incidents reported in 1995 to 27,414 in 2001. Neither of these clearly substantiates a drop in gun theft. The crime statistic that best supports a real decline in gun theft is armed robbery, a crime often committed with stolen guns. This fell from 6,692 reported incidents in 1995 to just 3,833 in 2001, a decline of 43 per cent.

Much of the problem with understanding gun theft and loss trends in Canada stems from the impact of firearms registration, which has been largely, but not completely, successful so far, as described below. In Australia, where registration has been about as effective, probably covering at least two-thirds of all firearms, the reported theft and loss rate is one for every 516 annually (Mouzos, 2002). According to Justice Minister Chris Ellison, stolen guns have replaced smuggling as the largest source of firearms used in Australian gun crime (ABC, 2003). The US theft rate, it appears, may not be so exceptional after all.

> **Estimates of the total number of guns stolen in the United States each year may range from 500,000 to 1,820,000.**

GLOBAL FIREARM STOCKPILES

High theft rates are also found in the two developing countries examined here—the Philippines and South Africa. In South Africa the rate of reported gun theft is especially dramatic, rising in parallel with the general crime rate through the 1990s before stabilizing at the end of the decade (see Figure 2.2). Currently the country has approximately 3.5 million registered private firearms (Chetty, 2000). At the most recently published theft and loss rates, the chance that any one of these guns would be reported lost was one in 160 every year.

Comparison of gun theft and loss in most countries is complicated by the lack of systematic data.

Table 2.7 Selected annual gun theft rates

Country	Year	Reported stolen	Legal ownership	Theft ratio
Australia	2001	4,195	2,165,170	1/520
Canada	2001	3,638	1,938,338	1/530
England and Wales	1996	3,002	1,793,712	1/600
Finland	1996	932	1,700,000	1/1,820
Norway	1996	339	990,000	1/2,920
Philippines	1996	1,234	706,148	1/570
South Africa	2001	23,000	3,500,000	1/150
Spain	1996	1,389	3,051,588	1/2,200
Sweden	1996	1,400	2,096,798	1/1,500
United States	1997	500,000	260,000,000	1/520
Average for all ten countries				1/1,080
Continental Europe				1/2110
Other Western countries				1/540
Developing countries				1/360

Note: The original data often does not indicate a base year. The figure for the United States refers to total estimated theft. Theft ratios are rounded.

Sources: Australia: Mouzos (2002); England and Wales: Criminal Statistics (2000); South Africa: Cross *et al*. (2003); United States: Kleck (1997). All other theft statistics from UN (1998). United States firearms statistics refer to all firearms theft, since virtually all US private firearms are legally owned. Legal ownership statistics from Small Arms Survey (2002, pp. 86, 980; 2003, pp. 64-5, 83).

Figure 2.1 Canadian firearms reported stolen or missing, 1994-2001

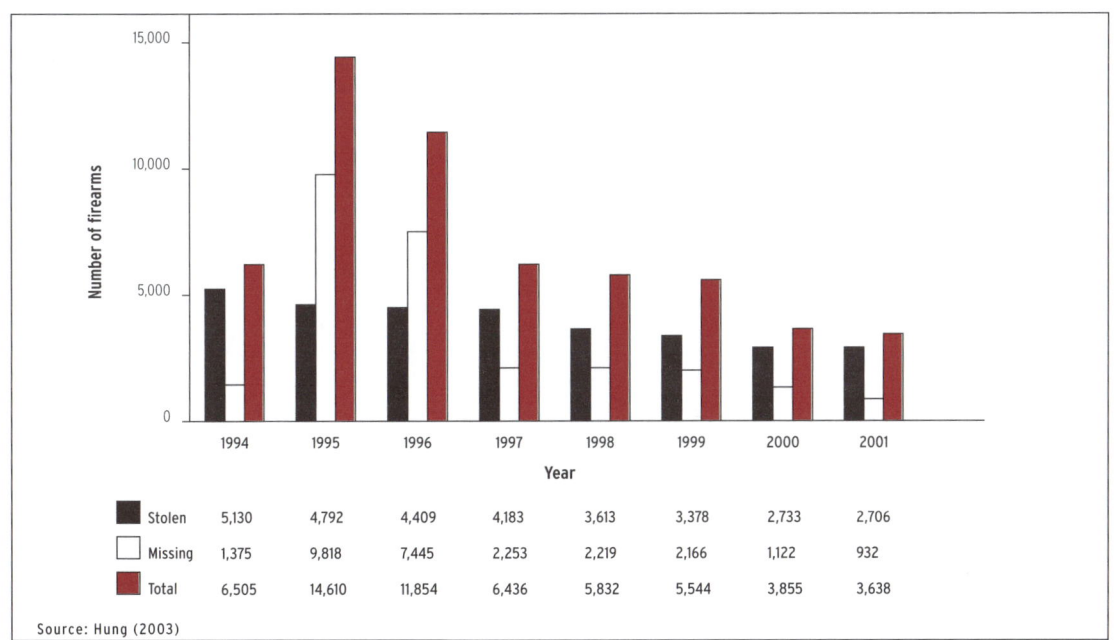

	1994	1995	1996	1997	1998	1999	2000	2001
Stolen	5,130	4,792	4,409	4,183	3,613	3,378	2,733	2,706
Missing	1,375	9,818	7,445	2,253	2,219	2,166	1,122	932
Total	6,505	14,610	11,854	6,436	5,832	5,544	3,855	3,638

Source: Hung (2003)

Figure 2.2   South African firearms reported stolen/missing and recovered, 1994–2002

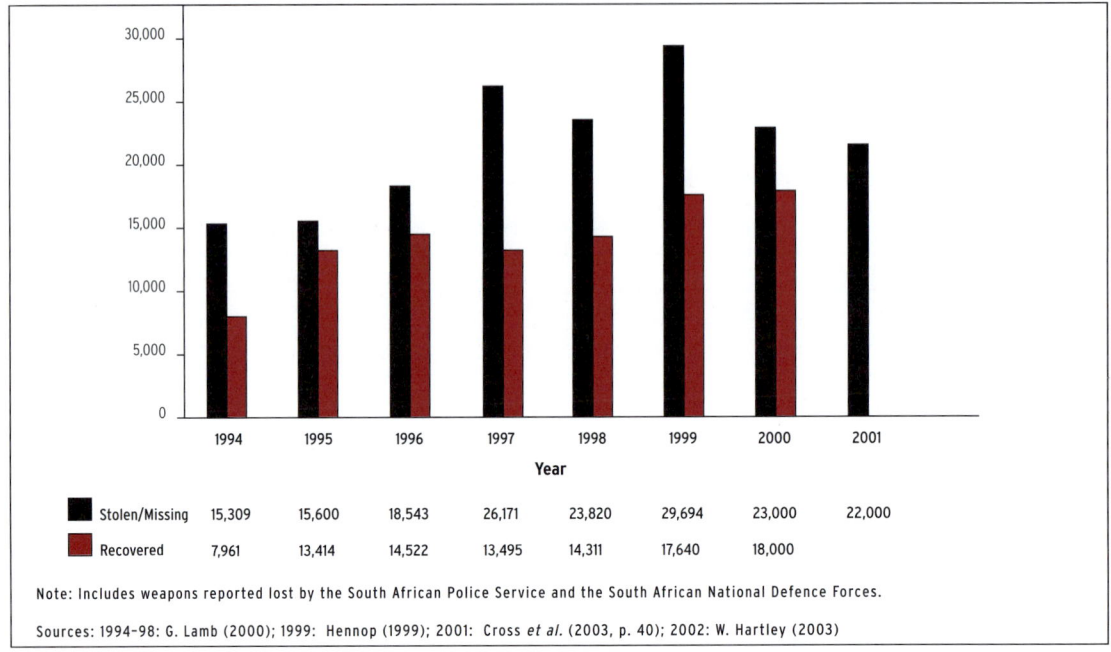

Note: Includes weapons reported lost by the South African Police Service and the South African National Defence Forces.
Sources: 1994–98: G. Lamb (2000); 1999: Hennop (1999); 2001: Cross et al. (2003, p. 40); 2002: W. Hartley (2003)

Estimating global firearms theft

Although the data examined here provides only a limited basis for assessment, a sense of global trends is emerging. The countries examined here fall into three broad categories: those with low rates of civilian gun theft such as the continental Europeans, with reported loss rates of one out of every 1,500–2,900 publicly owned guns; other Western countries with an average rate of reported theft of one of every 520 guns; and—most cautiously—developing countries with an average rate of one of every 360 legally owned firearms (see Table 2.6). All of these rates apply exclusively to legally owned firearms, a small proportion of civilian stockpiles in many countries.

> Total global gun theft and loss appear to be at least one million guns every year.

Determining even approximately how many small arms are stolen or go missing from the hundreds of millions of private owners around the world is not an easy task. If the average global rate approximates the continental European rate for legally owned guns of roughly one per 2,000, the total could be as low as 250,000 stolen or lost annually. This is just too optimistic, though, since even more probably are lost in the United States alone. In reality, global theft and loss rates are likely to be closer to that of other Western countries where it averages roughly one per 500 (see Table 2.6). At that rate, total global gun theft and loss from private owners appears to be at least one million guns every year. Better research is likely to show that it is actually much higher.

Solutions to casual losses

Gun ownership enthusiasts tend to argue that the solution to firearms theft and loss is stronger law enforcement. If there are fewer people willing to risk criminal behaviour, there should be less illegal demand for guns (Jacobs, 2002; Lott, 2003a). While laws focusing exclusively on gun crime undoubtedly help, there is no evidence to suggest that they are sufficient. Deliberate breaches of public trust and individual negligence suggest that training alone will not significantly reduce the scale of the problem either. Nor can educating owners have much effect on incidence of household burglary.

The key to stockpile management is combining measures to reduce illegal demand with programmes to reduce supply. This means making burglary less likely to succeed, negligence more likely to be discovered, and corruption more likely to be prosecuted. Increasingly aware of the scale and dangers of gun theft, governments are more willing to stress the issue (*Ghanaweb,* 2003). Lack of financing makes it impossible for many to establish the proper facilities that security requires, and secure storage is on the list of international small arms priorities for donor governments.

Assuring stockpile security: A gun-locking system made of solid steel and stress-tested to 4,000 pounds.

Even where financing is not available, there is much that government institutions can do. Money and secure storage facilities are important, but personal responsibility is even more consequential. The key to reducing theft and loss is promotion and reinforcement of a *culture of individual responsibility.* This appears to be the only way to minimize the risk of theft or loss from government stockpiles over time. It also is the best way to minimize the dangers of theft or loss of privately owned guns.

So long as there are few or no penalties for losing a gun, people will continue to lose them. When the men and women responsible for small arms security believe that their personal future depends on the safety of the weapons under their authority, they may be less likely to let those weapons disappear so easily. They are liable to be more vigilant, harder to bribe or intimidate. This leads to a short list of recommendations, preconditions for cultures of responsibility to emerge:

1. Specific individuals must be responsible for specific small arms.
2. Losses must be reported and investigated quickly.
3. Responsible individuals must be subject to serious disciplinary action for any loss.

By focusing exclusively on theft by street criminals, current practices in many countries fail to deal with equally important aspects of gun theft: supply and opportunity. By ensuring a ready supply of criminal firearms, negligence and corruption probably do as much to encourage theft and resale of official small arms as criminal demand. In light of the relatively permissive control cultures found in much of the world, more needs to be done to penalize not just the theft of small arms but also their loss.

These are problems that public policy and international assistance can help overcome. Creating cultures of responsibility involves the same kind of reforms as other practices of public safety, from mandatory seat-belt use to childproof medicine packaging. International support for safe storage facilities would help, as would campaigns to raise awareness. In many countries, regulatory and even legal reform may be necessary as well. Above all, theft and loss prevention requires new attitudes, treating firearm ownership not only as a right but also as a life-and-death responsibility.

The key to reducing theft and loss is the promotion and reinforcement of a culture of individual responsibility.

REGISTRATION AND RESPONSIBILITY

Better law enforcement to discourage crime is a crucial part of the solution to gun theft. To judge from the high theft rates in much of the world, though, individual owners need help too. Secure home storage facilities such as those already required in Australia, Canada, and Sweden are the most obvious way to make theft harder. Laws making individuals responsible for the fate of their guns also need careful evaluation.

A prominent result of international concern with the effects of small arms proliferation is greater interest in better firearm laws. This has taken two general forms: *reform* of existing laws to better address changing public priorities, and establishment of *new legal systems* regulating public firearm ownership.

Reform in the United States

The complicated and seemingly innumerable forms that small-scale legal reform can take are abundantly illustrated by the US gun control debate. Reform measures dominate the debate in the United States, where federal devolution and firearm rights make wholesale revision of ownership difficult. Even so, debate in the United States over firearm policy in 2003 reached a salience not witnessed for many years, an intensity almost certain to grow through 2004.

The impetus appears to come only partially from the 2004 presidential campaign, which has seen little discussion of an issue widely viewed as highly polarized. Instead, debate is dominated by a congeries of specific gun policy issues, often played exclusively on regional or local stages. With legal authority spread across 50 states, regulatory debate has been extremely diverse. Legislation often seems contradictory. For example, some states have restricted ownership rights by banning particular kinds of firearms (such as pistols that fire heavy—.50 calibre—machine gun bullets) or mandating that guns carry personalized identification technology (Winton, 2003). At the same time, other states are moving toward more permissive regulation. The most prominent innovations of 2003 were additional laws permitting ordinary adults to carry guns in public in states such as Michigan, Missouri, and Wisconsin.

In Washington, DC, some of the strongest interest in tighter gun control comes as an unintended side effect of the 'War on Terror'. Gun control is not explicitly mentioned in the US National Strategy for Combating Terrorism (White House, 2003). Tighter restrictions on gun ownership rights have emerged, instead, as an extension of US efforts to minimize terrorist threats. It was concern with prevention of terrorism that led President Bush to support extension of an emotionally charged law prohibiting sales of new semi-automatic assault weapons, although he has not lobbied aggressively for it. Passed as part of the 1994 Federal Crime Bill, the provision made it a federal crime for a private individual to possess or transfer a semi-automatic assault weapon manufactured after that date. Despite the presidential endorsement, the US Congress is sharply divided on extending the ban, scheduled to expire on 13 September 2004 (Lichtblau, 2003b). Instead, the Congress went along with a law to ban imitation guns (Baldor, 2003).

It would not be correct, though, to think that the War on Terror favours only gun control. It led to permission for US airline pilots to carry guns in the cockpit and mandated greater use of armed sky marshals. Both measures are strongly opposed in many other countries (Reuters, 2003b). Attorney General John Ashcroft strongly endorsed a proposal to immediately destroy records on background checks of gun buyers. Previously these were kept for 90 days. Many gun enthusiasts were afraid that the system could be used to undermine civil liberties and potentially evolve into a substitute for gun licensing and registration (*Washington Post*, 2004). Under the terms of the Consolidated (or Omnibus) Appropriations Bill passed by the Senate on 22 January 2003 and signed into law a few days later, federal records on *lawful* gun purchasers who are approved by the National Instant Check System must be destroyed within 24 hours (Kopel, 2004; PRODUCERS).

The greatest potential to add restrictions to US gun policy currently comes from state and federal courts, in which dozens of cities and interest groups are suing manufacturers and distributors for legal damages. These suits are intended to restrict and reduce sales by making manufacturers and merchants responsible for the use of their products. None of these suits has succeeded, but legal opinion seems to agree that this could change (Sebok, 2003). In response, Congress is debating legislation to prohibit such suits. Thirty-three US states already restrict such suits. After passing the House of Representatives in 2003, a bill to shelter the gun industry from negligence suits nationwide failed to reach debate in the Senate (Oliphant, 2003). But such measures have strong political support and seem likely to be enacted sooner or later (Holland, 2003).

> In Washington, some of the strongest interest in tightening gun control is an unintended side effect of the US 'War on Terror'.

Reform measures elsewhere

Reforms tightening existing gun laws and regulations are increasingly common elsewhere in the world. Where there is strong support, even modest reform processes can make significant contributions towards better stockpile control. In the *United Kingdom,* active-universal registration is long established. But devolution previously kept firearm registers at the local level. A new initiative sponsored by the Association of Chief Police Officers will lead to the establishment of a simple national database. Relying on nothing more than networking of existing local databases, this system is expected to become operational in August 2004 (Nash, 2003). Concerned with the rise of violent crime, the United Kingdom has increased the criminal penalties for gun crime and extended its gun prohibitions. Under the 2004 Anti-Social Behaviour Act, Britain banned a special form of air gun easily converted to fire live ammunition, as well as look-alike imitation guns (UK, Home Office, 2004).

Under the 2000 Firearms Control Act, *South Africa* is trying to limit handgun ownership and correct oversights like the one that left 200,000 firearms registered to deceased owners. Tighter restrictions on granting firearm licences are expected to make it harder for criminals to buy guns (Naidu, 2003; Schronen, 2003). In 2002 *Germany* tightened some of the requirements for a weapons licence (Small Arms Survey, 2003).

Not all reforms succeed at first try. In the *Philippines,* for example, an order by the Philippine National Police in January 2003 prohibiting the carrying of guns in public was overturned by the courts on procedural grounds (San Juan, 2003). A revised law went into effect in December 2003 and will stay in effect for six months, largely in an attempt to reduce criminal and political violence (Vargas, 2003).

New domestic legal regimes

Establishing new legal systems—with fundamentally different rules—for gun regulation is much more difficult and less common. Among the most sweeping measures of the 1990s were the ban on all handguns in the United Kingdom and Australia's ban on semi-automatic weapons and harmonization of state requirements for safe storage. Neither of these measures involved the active participation of more than a small proportion of gun owners. After a pause of several years, the momentum for radical change appears to be accelerating again. Among the most prominent themes to emerge are new national systems to license firearms owners and register their guns.

There are two types of new national firearms registration schemes. Each has distinctive problems of implementation and impact on gun issues:

- The more ambitious aims to register all guns in the country, including those purchased in the past. Such *active-universal registration* requires the participation of all gun owners, who must supply inventories of their collections. The approach promises relatively quick and far-reaching results, but requires the cooperation of gun owners.
- Less extensive cooperation is required by less ambitious systems of *passive-partial registration*. These stress registration only of newly bought guns. Typically this is done at the time of purchase. Passive systems are cheaper, easier, and less controversial, but take much longer to cover a substantial proportion of firearms—decades instead of years.

Firearms registration in Canada

New firearms registration schemes can be divided into two types: active-universal *and* passive-partial.

The most ambitious active-universal registration initiative in recent years came into full legal force on 1 January 2003. The Canadian reform, through its successes and shortcomings, is likely to influence other countries as they consider similar measures. In the long run it could do more to reshape the international climate for registration of personal weapons than any comparable measure has before.

In 1995 the Canadian Senate approved Bill C-68, the Firearms Act. This required all gun owners to be licensed and their guns registered. Previously the nation of 31 million had restricted ownership of handguns but allowed qualified buyers to acquire rifles and shotguns freely. A formal goal was 'to prevent people who are a danger to themselves or others from accessing firearms' (CFC, 2003a). Supporters also sought to prevent Canadian gun culture from evolving into something similar to that of the United States. The Firearms Act had strong public support (76 per cent) as recently as 2001 (Hartley and Mazzuca, 2001). Nevertheless, implementation has not been trouble-free and controversy has become acute.

A three-stage process of implementation began *first* with the creation of the Canadian Firearms Centre and the infrastructure for record-keeping and management. In 1998 the *second* stage began with mandatory licensing of all gun owners. When this task was completed in 2001, a total of 1.9 million owners had been licensed. This meant the system had won the participation of roughly 83 per cent of the country's estimated 2.3 million gun owners. The *third* stage of implementation involved registering guns. By July 2003, when the process was completed after several extensions, a total of 6.5 million firearms had been registered (CFC, 2003b). To judge from a public survey, this represented about 82 per cent of the estimated 7.9 million guns owned by the Canadian people (GPC, 2002).

After eight years of preparation, the new Canadian licensing and registration system is a reality. Gun crime appears to be down, including gun homicides and especially armed robbery. The latter fell to one-third the rate of a decade before, from 30.79 per 100,000 people in 1992 to 11.05 in 2002 (Hung, 2003). There also have been negative effects. Inadvertently, the law also may have erected barriers to reporting gun theft. Although the evidence is largely anecdotal, reports of seizures at the border suggest that smugglers are trying more aggressively to feed illegal demand with guns from the United States. This was mitigated by a 50 per cent increase in border seizures (Botchford, 2003). A curious side effect was the emergence of a rental market for illegal firearms in parts of Canada. Rarely seen outside developing countries, this is unambiguous evidence of a shortage of illegal weapons (Agrell, 2003).

Original estimates in 1994 claimed that the licensing and registration system would cost CAD 119 million (USD 90 million). All but CAD 2 million (USD 1.5 million) was to be recovered through fees. In December 2002, however, the Canadian Auditor General presented a report revealing that total expenses in the first seven years were CAD 688 million (USD 430.5 million) (see Table 2.8). The bill for the first ten years of operation is expected to top CAD 1 billion (USD 639 million) (Clark, 2002). These figures gave opponents their strongest argument against the system. The undertaking was tarred as a monument to waste, abuse, and inefficiency. Demands to stop the registry, previously dismissed as extremism, won greater support.

According to the Canadian government, costs rose for several reasons. The initial estimate referred exclusively to database development—the national web of computers and software at the heart of the system—and even this turned out to cost more than twice as much as expected. Implementation costs were also significant. Fees, intended to offset expenses, were waived in many cases to attract participation. Expenses are declining as the implementation phase ends, but running costs still are expected to average CAD 50 million–80 million annually (Naumetz, 2003).

Canadian planners appear to have underestimated the expense of establishing a new bureaucracy. The United States, by comparison, will spend over USD 1 billion to start a much smaller registry exclusively to check new buyers for criminal histories (Lichtblau, 2003a). The C-68 approach also faced disadvantages typical of universal registration schemes. It encountered resistance from gun advocates. This was exacerbated by regional politics as the system became a convenient tool for polarizing opinion. Paul Martin, the former Finance Minster and Liberal Party stalwart who replaced Jean Chrétien as Prime Minister on 12 December 2003, agreed to review the firearm system. Although he has refused to act precipitously, this could lead to changes.

In Canada, the most ambitious registration initiative in recent years registered a total of 6.5 million firearms as of July 2003.

Table 2.8   Canadian firearms licensing and registration costs, 1995–96 to 2001–02

Category	Cost in millions of CAD	Percentage
Programme administration	65.7	10
Communications		9
Advertising	29.3	
Outreach activities	15.0	
Training	8.7	
Database development	227.1	33
Programme delivery		48
Miramichi central processing site	59.5	
Royal Canadian Mounted Police registrar	64.0	
Form design and printing	40.6	
Opt-out jurisdictions*	28.5	
Provincial contributions	128.6	
Enforcement support	2.2	0.03
Total	**669.2**	**100**

Note: * When provincial governments refused to participate, their expenses were charged to the federal exchequer. The original source, cited below, gives total expenditures of CAD 688.3 million–699.2 million. The vagueness may arise from inclusion of unspecified budgetary items. Totals may not add up due to rounding.

Source: CFC (2002)

Who's next?

Brazil

In December 2003 Brazil became the first country since Canada to establish a major new gun control system. With roughly 26,000 firearm homicides annually, Brazil has one of the deadliest gun cultures in the world. Over the past decade the problem has inspired a national debate and a series of efforts to craft new legislation on firearms policy. Public dismay over firearm crime and the poor results of previous reform finally culminated in the radically visionary Disarmament Statute. Signed into law by President Luiz Inacio Lula da Silva on 22 December 2003, this is the most sweeping reform package enacted anywhere in memory. Unlike other measures enacted elsewhere—including ambitious reforms in Australia, Britain, and Canada—this statute seeks to fundamentally change an entire national gun culture.

Brazil established a new licensing and registration system in 1997. Ostensibly *active-universal* in conception, its effectiveness was undermined by poor enforcement and weak penalties. To address the numerous loopholes in this and other laws, the new reform package passed in 2003 emerged as a set of specific measures, each directed at a particular aspect of the nation's gun problems. It includes provisions to:

Small arms escalation: Brazilian federal police patrol a shanty town of Rio de Janeiro in May 2003.

- ban carrying firearms in public, with some exceptions. Illegally carrying a gun is punishable by jail. This empowers the police to get guns off the streets;
- raise the minimum age of legal possession to 25. This measure is addressed at the particular problem of gun crime among juveniles and young adults;
- authorize a national referendum in October 2005 on the proposal to ban sales of all firearms and ammunition;
- introduce criminal penalties for arms trafficking. This empowers the Brazilian government to act against illegal firearms imports, largely from Paraguay;
- eliminate the right of police and the armed forces personnel to purchase large numbers of guns. This right had been misused to promote illegal trafficking;
- criminalize random firing of guns; and
- subject the brokering of firearms sales to laws on arms transfers (Viva Rio, 2003b; VoA, 2003).

As this list shows, this is a reform package, not a completely new system. The cumulative effect, however, is unmistakable: it is intended to create a civic culture in which guns play less and less of a role. The statute as a whole has the support of about 63 per cent of Brazilians (Franklin, 2003). The most revolutionary and controversial part of the programme is the planned plebiscite to ban all gun sales. This could set an active-universal registration system in motion. This currently has strong public support—around 74–80 per cent according to different opinion polls—but its outlook remains uncertain (Bacoccina, 2003; Viva Rio, 2003a).

In December 2003 Brazil became the first country since Canada to establish a major new gun control system.

Another distinctive aspect of the Brazilian process is the role of foreign influence. Concerned about what it sees as a trend towards global gun control, the US-based National Rifle Association (NRA) made its first direct foray into the policy debates of another country. Charles Cunningham, Director of Federal Affairs at the Institute of Legislative Affairs, the NRA lobbying arm, visited Rio de Janeiro and São Paulo. He addressed meetings of industry and parliamentary opponents sponsored by Pró Legítima Defesa. The visit was arranged by the Brazilian and US chapters of the Society for the Defense of Tradition, Family and Property, a conservative Catholic political organization (McKenna,

2003; Pró Legítima Defesa, 2003). The indirect arrangement hints at the awkwardness of the NRA's first high-level foreign intervention. Although the opposition failed, it is likely to be a bigger force in the referendum.

The outlook for the new legislation is not clear. Implementation has long been a weakness of Brazilian legal reform. The 1997 reform, requiring registration of all firearms purchases, appears to have fallen into disuse. A temporary ban on all gun sales in Rio in 2000 also had little palpable effect. Not only is the new law dependent on enforcement, but parts like the referendum still have to be fully developed. Sustained public interest and official commitment will be essential to its success.

> The Disarmament Statute signed by Brazilian President da Silva seeks to fundamentally reform an entire national gun culture.

Thailand

Public anxiety over gun crime is the catalyst for political action in Thailand as well. The country also has emerged as the centre of the region's black market for firearms. Thai police estimate that there are approximately ten million guns—or which fewer than 40 per cent, or 3.87 million, are registered—in the hands of the nation's 60 million people (Ngamkham, 2003). Gun homicides, the highest reported in all of Asia at 33 per 100,000 annually in 2000, have become a major political issue (UNODC, 2003).

Following a major campaign against the drug trade and organized crime in 2003, Prime Minister Thaksin Shinawatra launched a personal appeal for dramatic change in firearms policy. In May 2003 he announced a one-month amnesty for criminals to turn in illegal guns (AFP, 2003b). In September the weapons collection programme was followed by presentation of a bill that gave owners of illegal guns 30 days to surrender them to police (*Bangkok Post*, 2003a). When the extended grace period finally ended in mid-December, more than 100,000 firearms had been surrendered. In its wake, police began a nationwide crackdown on illegal possession and illegal sales (*Bangkok Post*, 2003b).

A proposal by the Prime Minister to make the country gun-free in five to six years remains extremely controversial. Public opinion still appears to be highly malleable. One recent survey in Bangkok showed 78 per cent opposed (Ghosh, 2003). Another poll, however, showed 62 per cent of Thais supported the policy (Pattugalan, 2003, p. 6). Even so, the government has expressed its intention to persevere with the plan, beginning with a ban on all gun sales (Mahmood, 2003). With so much dependent on the leadership of Prime Minister Thaksin, the outlook for the proposal is obscure. Even if it fails, though, the plan seems likely to serve as a basis for other, less radical proposals in the near future.

> Thailand's Prime Minister Thaksin Shinawatra has proposed to make the country gun-free in five to six years.

CONCLUSION

There is nothing surprising in the twin trends emphasized in this chapter: the huge numbers of small arms lost from official control versus growing interest in better stockpile management in much of the world. The problem of post-conflict small arms reached a new apogee in Iraq. Small arms continue to be a serious social problem in Latin America. Both examples illustrate the worst side of a global problem. Even in regions and countries where the situation is much less severe, the links between deficient control and the need for public action are hard to miss.

Iraq may be one of the more extreme cases of gun chaos, but it is special exclusively in its scale and suddenness. The catastrophic loss of major arsenals has occurred elsewhere. Unless aggressive steps are taken to ensure better control over small arms stockpiles, many countries remain vulnerable to similar disasters. On a daily basis, the gradual loss of weapons from negligence and theft is even more serious, calling for better management by all owners, whether states or individuals.

SMALL ARMS SURVEY 2004

The experiences of 2003 confirm the importance of establishing effective regulation of global stockpiles. It was not the guns *per se* which contributed to the deadly environment of post-war Iraq, but the failure to maintain control over official stockpiles. The Iraqi small arms problem is an egregious version of the management problems responsible for the steady flow of weapons from public to criminal hands worldwide. In Iraq, a vital chance to prevent chaos was lost due to a lack of foresight and preparation. Better insight and preparation are no less necessary to reduce the risks of loss of control over official stockpiles elsewhere in the world.

Iraq and Latin America also illustrate fundamental problems and outlooks for civilian stockpile management. In both places, the huge numbers of unlicensed owners and unregistered guns are extreme examples of a global problem. While the Iraqi situation is much more dramatic, the civilian gun problems of Latin America are no less serious. Although reliable data is still lacking, the Latin American situation almost certainly remains more deadly. But because social order and a viable state are not in jeopardy in most of Latin America, the prospects for reform are infinitely healthier there. The Brazilian Disarmament Statute, although still untested, illustrates the enormous scope for reform throughout the region and much of the world.

2. BIBLIOGRAPHY

ABC (Australian Broadcasting Corporation). 2003. 'Minister blames theft for gun crime rise.' Australian Broadcasting Corporation. 29 December.
AFP (*Agence France Presse*). 2003a. 'Saudi Arabia Denies National Guardsmen Sold Arms to al-Qaeda.' 20 May.
—. 2003b. 'Thailand Offers Arms Amnesty to Preface Organised Crimes Crackdown.' 20 May.
Agrell, Siri. 2003. 'Cops Link Gun Rentals to Growth of Gangs.' *National Post* (Don Mills, Ontario). 25 August.
Alpers, Philip and Conor Twyford. 2003. *Small Arms in the Pacific*. Occasional Paper No. 8. Geneva: Small Arms Survey. March.
Anderson, W. French. 1996. *Forensic Analysis of the April 11, 1986, FBI Firefight*. Los Angeles: School of Medicine, University of Southern California.
AP (Associated Press). 2002. 'Mustafa Mashhour, 81, of Muslim Group in Egypt.' 17 November.
—. 2003a. 'Israelis Selling Stolen Army Guns to Palestinians: Report.' 22 January.
—. 2003b. 'Israeli Military Investigating Increasing Gun Theft.' 5 February.
—. 2003c. 'Iraqis Ordered to Disarm by Mid-June.' 5 June.
APA (Angola Press Agency). 2003. 'Home Minister Defends Disarming of Civilians.' 25 October.
Ashtakala, Tara. 2003. 'Huns and Guns: Small Arms in South Asia.' *IndoLink.Com*, 6 July.
Bacoccina, Denize. 2003. 'Brazil Seeks to Curb Gun Crime.' BBC, 23 July.
Badkhen, Anna. 2003. 'Gun Market Thrives on Dread.' *San Francisco Chronicle*. 26 March, W11.
Baldor, Lolita C. 2003. 'Plastic Weapon Ban is Small Victory in Difficult Times for Gun Control Advocates.' Associated Press. 10 December.
Bangkok Post. 2003a. 'PM: Hand in Your Firearms.' 5 October.
—. 2003b. 'Amnesty Nets Large Quantity of Weapons.' 16 December.
Barbulescu, Nineta. 2003. *Statement to the First Biennial Meeting of States to Consider the Implementation of the Programme of Action to Prevent, Combat and Eradicate the Illicit Trade in Small Arms and Light Weapons in All its Aspects*. New York. 8 July.
Blood, Peter. 1990. *Sri Lanka: A Country Study*. Washington, DC: US Government Printing Office.
Bloomfield, Lincoln P., Jr. 2003. *Implementation of the United Nations Program of Action for Small Arms and Light Weapons*. New York: US Department of State. 7 July.
Botchford, John. 2003. 'Group Says Canada Flooded by Illegal Guns.' *Edmonton Sun*. 5 January.
Canada. 2003. *Canadian Report on the Implementation of the United Nations Programme of Action to Prevent, Combat and Eradicate the Illicit Trade in Small Arms and Light Weapons in all its Aspects*. A/CONF.92/BMS2003/CRP.48 of 12 June.
Capie, David. 2002. *Small Arms Production and Transfers in Southeast Asia*. Canberra: Strategic and Defence Studies Centre, Australian National University.
—. 2003. *The Small Arms Challenge in the Pacific*. Wellington: Victoria University Press.
Carroll, Rory. 2003. 'Guns For Cash Offer Swamped.' *Guardian*. 17 December.
CFC (Canadian Firearms Centre). 2002. 'Canadian Firearms Centre summary of costs, 1995–96 to 2001–02'. News release. Toronto. 3 December.
—. 2003a, 'Canada's Gun Control Program: Keeping Firearms Out of the Wrong Hands.' Fact sheet. Toronto. 21 February.
—. 2003b, 'Firearms Registration Grace Period Successful—Solicitor General.' News release. Toronto. 4 July.

Cha, Ariana Eunjung. 2004. 'New Iraqi Forces Flaws Are Showing.' *Washington Post National Weekly Edition*. 5–11 January, p. 7.
Chetty, Robert, ed. 2000. *Firearm Use and Distribution in South Africa*. Pretoria: The National Crime Prevention Centre Firearm Programme.
Clark, Campbell. 2002. 'PM Tries To Deflect Blame For Gun Fiasco.' *Globe and Mail* (Toronto). 5 December.
Conetta, Carl. 2003. *The Wages of War: Iraqi Combatant and Noncombatant Fatalities in the 2003 Conflict*. Research monograph No. 8. Washington, DC: Project on Defense Alternatives. 20 October.
Constable, Pamela. 2003. 'Afghans Trade Guns For A Shot At a New Life.' *Washington Post*. 23 October, p. A1.
Criminal Statistics. 2000. *Criminal Statistics for England and Wales 1999*. London: Home Office. December.
Cross, Peter, *et al*. 2003. *Law of the Gun: An Audit of Firearms Control Legislation in the SADC Region*. London: Saferworld. June.
Davis, Anthony. 2003. 'Thailand Cracks Down on Illicit Arms Trade.' *Jane's Intelligence Review*. December, p. 3035.
Deepika (Trivandrum). 2003. 'Lanka to issue permits for arms to politicians.' 6 August.
Dreyfus, Pablo and Aaron Karp. 2003. 'Small Arms Stockpiles and Holdings in Mexico.' Unpublished background report. Geneva: Small Arms Survey.
Economist (London). 2003. 'Free For All.' US edition. 17 May.
EelamNation. 2003, 'Sri Lanka Security Forces Say Politicians Fail to Return Firearms.' 16 February. <http://english.eelamnation.com>.
Filipov, David. 2003. 'Arms Bazaar Offers Pick of Light Arms.' *Boston Globe*. 26 March, p. A23.
Filkins, Dexter. 2003. 'U.S. to send Iraqis to Site in Hungary for Police Course.' *New York Times*. 25 August, p. A1.
Finland. 2001. *Operational and Financial Plan for the Ministry of Defence's Segment of Administration in 2004–07* (White Paper). Helsinki: Defence Ministry. <http://www.defmin.fi/chapter_images/1134_ttsenglish.pdf>
Finn, Peter. 2003. 'Al Qaeda Arms Traced to Saudi National Guard.' *Washington Post*. 19 May, p. A1.
Fisher, Ian. 2003. 'Northern Iraq; A Diverse Band of Volunteers Sends a Warning to America.' *New York Times*. 5 February, p. A12.
Fleishman, Jeffrey. 2003. 'Baghdad's Packed Morgue Marks a City's Descent into Lawlessness.' *Washington Post*. 16 September.
Franklin, Jonathan. 2003. 'Soap Stars Join 50,000 in Rainy Rio to Demand Guns Crackdown.' *Guardian* (London). 15 September.
France. 2003. *Sur la mise en oeuvre du Programme d'Action des Nations Unies, sur la Lutte Contre le Commerce Illicite des Armes Légères et de Petit Calibre, sous tous ses Aspects, adopté lors de la Conference des Nations Unies a New-York, le 20 Juillet 2001*. New York. April.
Freedberg, Sydney P. and Connie Humburg. 2003. 'Wandering Weapons: America's Lax Arsenal.' *St Petersburg Times*. 11 May, p. A1.
Germany. 2003. *Letter dated 29 April 2003 from the Permanent Mission of the Federal Republic of Germany to the United Nations addressed to the Department for Disarmament Affairs on the Programme of Action to Prevent, Combat and Eradicate the Illicit Trade in Small Arms and Light Weapons in all its Aspects*. A/CONF.92/BMS2003/CRP.11 of 16 June.
Ghanaweb. 2003. 'Gov't Improves Physical Security of Armouries.' 26 June.
Ghosh, Nirmal. 2003. 'Thais Shoot Down Thaksin Proposal to Ban Guns.' *Straits Times* (Singapore). 17 September.
Glauber, Bill. 2003. 'High-Caliber Sales at Baghdad market.' *Chicago Tribune*. 23 April, p. 8.
GPC (GPC Research). 2002. *Fall 2001 Estimate of Firearms in Canada*. Ottawa: GPC. 20 August.
Guerrero, Friena P. 2003. 'AFP Admits Firearms Pilfered.' *Business World* (Manila). 1 August, p. 11.
Gusev, Anatoliy. 2003. 'Shahid Department Store.' *Izvestiya* (Moscow). 12 July (BBC translation).
Hartley, Thomas and Josephine Mazzuca. 2001. 'Seven out of Ten Canadians Support National Firearms Registry.' *The Gallup Poll* (Toronto). 27 November.
Hartley, Wyndham. 2003. 'Firearms Act Faces Court Challenge.' *Business Day* (Johannesburg). 8 October.
Hennop, Etienne. 1999. 'Illegal Firearms in South Africa: Tracking Sources.' *Nedbank ISS Crime Index*, Vol. 3, No. 2.
Hider, James. 2004. 'Iraqi Gun Runners "Too Professional" to be Caught Out.' *The Times* (London). 18 February.
Hirst, Chrissie. 2002. *Controlling Small Arms Proliferation: The View from Bulgaria*. London: Saferworld.
Holland, Jesse J. 2003. 'Gun Industry Nears Key Goal.' Associated Press. 10 October.
Hung, Kwing. 2003. *Firearms Statistics Tables*. Ottawa: Research and Statistics Division, Department of Justice, June.
IISS (International Institute for Strategic Studies). 1989. *The Military Balance 1989–1990*. London: Brassey's and the IISS.
—. 2002. *The Military Balance 2002–2003*. Oxford: Oxford University Press.
—. 2003. *The Military Balance 2003–2004*. Oxford. Oxford University Press.
Interpol. Various years. Interpol International Crime Statistics. <http://www.interpol.int/>
Itar-Tass. 2003. 'Russia Backs UN effort to Control Trade in Light and Small Weapons.' 8 July (BBC translation).
Izzadeen, Ameen. 2003. 'Sri Lanka Peace Process Under Threat?' *South Asia Intelligence Review*, Vol. 2, No. 2. 28 July.
Jackman, David. 2003. 'Approaching Small Arms Demand Work in the Middle East.' Unpublished manuscript. June.
Jacobs, James B. 2002. *Can Gun Control Work?* Oxford: Oxford University Press.
Jadwa, Ahmed. 2003. 'A Journey to Basra: Scenes of People and Places (2).' *Al Sharq al Awsat*, No. 9025. 14 August, p. 6. Translated by Jack Kalpakian.
Jayasinghe, Jayampathy. 2002. 'Police Tough on Violators.' *Sunday Observer* (Colombo). 6 January.
Kahwaji, Riad. 2004. 'Slow Rebuilding of Army Could Threaten Iraq's Future.' *Defense News*. 26 January, p. 4.
Kazakh Commercial Television. 2001. 'Saudi Arabia to Buy Weapons from Kazakh Plants.' 5 October (BBC Worldwide monitoring translation.)
King, Laura. 2003. 'Surrounded by Chaos in Iraq, Middle Class Takes Up Arms.' *Los Angeles Times*. 12 May.
Kleck, Gary. 1997. *Targeting Guns: Firearms and Their Control*. Hawthorne, New York: Aldine De Gruyter.
Kopel, Dave. 2004. 'Erasing a Clinton legacy: Rolling Back Antigun Regs.' *National Review*, 27 January.
Lamb, Guy. 2000. 'An Overview of Small Arms Production, Export, Ownership and Proliferation in South Africa.' Unpublished manuscript, 3 February.
Lemire, Jonathan. 2003. 'Grenade Launcher Loss Stirs Concern.' *New York Daily News*. 28 August.

Lichtblau, Eric. 2003a. 'Bush in Tight Spot with N.R.A. over Gun Legislation.' *New York Times*. 8 May.
—. 2003b. 'Bipartisan Agreement is Reached on Gun Bill.' *New York Times*. 26 September, p. A12.
Lott, John R., Jr. 2003a. *The Bias Against Guns*. Washington, DC: Regnery Publishing.
—. 2003b. 'Armed, and safer, Iraqis.' *New York Post*. 26 June.
Mahmood, Kazi. 2003. 'Thailand Plans Being Gun-free in Five Years.' *Islam Online*. 22 December. <http://www.islamonline.net>
Matthews, William. 2003. 'U.S. Officials Rap Rifle Buy for Iraqi Corps.' *Defense News*. 22 December.
McKenna, Thomas. 2003. *Crime Control Not Gun Control in Brazil*. The American Society for the Defense of Tradition, Family and Property (TPF). <http://www.tfp.org/what_we_do/index/nra_brazil.htm>
Metz, Helen Chapin. 1993. 'The Armed Forces: Saudi Arabian National Guard.' In *Saudi Arabia: A Country Guide*. Washington, DC: US Government Printing Office.
Mexico. 1968. Constitution of the United States of Mexico. Translated from Constitución Política de los Estados Unidos Mexicanos, Trigésima Quinta Edición, 1967, Editorial Porrua, S. A., México D. F. Washington, DC: Organisation of American States. <http://www.oas.org/juridico/MLA/en/mex/en_mex-int-text-const.pdf>
—. 1972. Ley Federal de Armas de Fuego y Explosivos (Federal Law of Firearms and Explosives). 11-I-1972. Mexico City: United States of Mexico.
—. 2003. Instituto Nacional de Estadística Geografía e Informática (INEGI, National Statistics, Geography and Information Institute) <http://www.inegi.gob.mx/inegi/default.asp>
Mickelburough, Peter. 2004. 'Buyback Scheme Nets 19,000 Handguns.' *Herald Sun* (Melbourne). 1 January.
Mite, Valentinas. 2003. 'Iraqis Prefer to Remain Armed.' *Asian Times.Com*. 11 June.
Mouzos, Jenny. 2000. *The Licensing and Registration Status of Firearms Used in Homicide*. Trends and Issues in Crime and Criminal Justice, Paper No. 151. Canberra: Australian Institute of Criminology. May.
—. 2002. *Firearms Theft in Australia*. Trends and Issues in Crime and Criminal Justice, Paper No. 230. Canberra: Australian Institute of Criminology. January.
Muggah, Robert 2003. 'Small Arms Control as a Peace Factor.' *Daily News* (Colombo). 11 October.
Murphy, Dan. 2003. 'Iraq Awash in Military Weapons.' *Christian Science Monitor*. 20 October.
Musik, Silke. 2003. 'German Armed Forces Reduce Stock.' *International Firearms Trade*. 1 December, p. 7.
Naidu, Edwin. 2003. 'One Man, One Gun, States New Law.' *Independent Newspapers* (South Africa). 28 September.
Nash, Emma. 2003. 'Work Starts on National Gun Register.' *Personal Computer World* (UK). 18 December.
Nation (Nairobi). 2003. '8,000 Illicit Firearms Are Destroyed in Crackdown.' 10 October.
NATO (North Atlantic Treaty Organization). 2003. 'Meeting of the NATO-Ukraine Commission in Defence Ministers Session.' Press Statement (Brussels). 2 December.
Naumetz, Tim. 2003. 'Liberals Beat Retreat on Gun Vote.' *CanWest News Service*. 18 February.
Ngamkham, Wassayos. 2003. 'Guns the "Weapons of Choice" in Murders.' *Bangkok Post*. 15 September.
Nonis, Anthony and Don Asoka Wijewardena. 2002. 'Firearms Amnesty Falls on Deaf Ears.' *Sunday Observer* (Colombo). 20 January.
Oliphant, Thomas. 2003. 'Power Grab by the Gun Lobby.' *Boston Globe*. 26 October.
Owen, Richard and Daniel McGrory. 2001. 'The Man to Really Fear.' *The Times* (London). 11 October.
Parnell, Sean. 2003. 'Effort to Save Money Means Police Guns Could be Turned on Themselves.' *Courier Mail* (Brisbane). 5 July, p. 32.
Pattugalan, Gina Rivas. 2003. *Two Years After: Implementation of the UN Programme of Action on Small Arms in the Asia-Pacific Region*. Geneva: Centre for Humanitarian Dialogue.
Poroskov, Nikolai. 2003. 'Army Gold.' *Vremya Novostei*. 13 May, p. 2 (BBC translation).
Potgieter, Jackie. 2003. 'Illegal Firearms Smuggled Into Kenya.' *Daily Standard* (Nairobi). 17 September.
Pró Legítima Defesa. 2003. <http://www.prolegitimadefesa.org.br/pldacao/20030819-conferencia/index.htm>
Prothero, P. Mitchell. 2003. 'Coalition Losing War for Iraqi Arms.' *United Press International*. 29 September.
Pruden, Todd. 2003. 'Army Reserve MPs Train Iraqi Police.' *US Army Reserve News*. 8 December.
Pyadushkin, Maxim. 2003. 'Arming the Caucasus: Moscow's Accidental Legacy.' In Anna Matveeve and Duncan Hiscock, eds. *The Caucasus: Armed and Divided*. London: Saferworld, ch. 8.
Reuters, 2003a. 'Afghan Leader Launches Disarmament Drive.' 24 October.
—. 2003b. 'Thai Air Needs No Guards on US Flights—PM.' 30 December.
San Juan, Joel R. 2003. 'Gun ban "Unconstitutional".' *Manila Times*. 6 October.
Saudi Arabia. 2003. 'No Substance to Report that Arms Captured Came from National Guard.' Press release. Washington, DC: Royal Embassy of Saudi Arabia. 21 May.
Sault Star (Sault Ste. Marie, Ontario). 2003. 'Bury the Gun Registry.' 26 September.
Schaffer, Michael Currie. 2003. 'A Glut of Gun Buyers.' *Philadelphia Inquirer*. 7 May, p. 1.
Schronen, Johan. 2003. 'Executors Face Arrest over Dead Men's Guns.' *Cape Argus* (Cape Town). 19 September.
Sebok, Anthony J. 2003. 'A Recent Ruling by Judge Weinstein Suggests that in the Future, Lawsuits against the Gun Industry May Succeed.' Find Law.Com. 18 August. <http://writ.news.findlaw.com/sebok/20030818.html>
Seper, Jerry. 2003. '800 U.S. Guns Issued To Officials Still Missing.' *Washington Times*. 1 July, p. 3.
Serbia. 2003. *Letter dated 19 May 2003 from the Permanent Mission of Serbia and Montenegro to the United Nations addressed to the Department for Disarmament Affairs on the Programme of Action to Prevent, Combat and Eradicate the Illicit Trade in Small Arms and Light Weapons in all its Aspects*. A/CONF.92/BMS2003/CRP.33 of 18 June.

Shashkov, Alexander. 2002. '8,000 Firearms Stolen from Army Stocks in 7 Years—Official.' Itar-Tass. 31 January.
Simon, Alina. 2003. 'Weapons Seized Were Stolen from Army Camp.' *New Straits Times* (Malaysia). 28 March, p. 10.
Sloca, Paul. 2003a. 'Gun Used in Plant Shooting Once Belonged to the Missouri State Highway Patrol.' Associated Press. 3 July.
—. 2003b. 'State Looks for Alternative to Trading Used Police Force Guns.' Associated Press. 18 September.
Small Arms Survey. 2001. *Small Arms Survey 2001: Profiling the Problem*. Oxford: Oxford University Press.
—. 2002. *Small Arms Survey 2002: Counting the Human Cost*. Oxford: Oxford University Press.
—. 2003. *Small Arms Survey 2003: Development Denied*. Oxford: Oxford University Press.
Soriano, Cesar G. 2003. 'All of Baghdad Keeps and Bears Arms.' *USA Today*. 13 May.
South Africa. 2003. *Statement to the First Biennial Meeting of States to Consider the Implementation of the Programme of Action to Prevent, Combat and Eradicate the Illicit Trade in Small Arms and Light Weapons in All its Aspects*. New York. 7 July.
Subramanian, Nirupama. 2001. 'Sri Lanka to Crack Down on Illegal Arms.' *The Hindu* (Madras). 17 December.
Talev, Illiya. 2001. 'Arms Business Conflicts Divulged its Scope.' *Kapital* (Sofia). 3 March (FBIS translation).
TamilNet. 2002. 'SLA Asked for EPDP Weapons over Journalist's Murder.' 11 November.
—. 2003. 'Fasting Sri Lankan' Soldiers Demand Fair Treatment.' 9 April.
Taheri, Amir. 2003. 'The Fires to Come.' *Newsweek International*. 31 December, p. 22.
UK (United Kingdom). Home Office. 2004. *Guide to the Anti-social Behaviour Act 2003*. London: Her Majesty's Stationery Office. 20 January.
UN (United Nations). 1998. *United Nations International Study on Firearms Regulation*. Vienna: United Nations.
—. 2003. *World Population Prospects: The 2002 Revision. Highlights*. Population Division of the Department of Economic and Social Affairs of the United Nations Secretariat. New York: United Nations.
UNCICP (UN Centre for International Crime Prevention). 2002. *Seventh United Nations Survey of Crime Trends, 1998–2000*. Vienna: UNCICP.
UNODC (UN Office on Drugs and Crime). 2003. *Surveys on Crime Trends and the Operations of Criminal Justice Systems*. Vienna: UNODC. <http://www.unodc.org/unodc/crime-_cicp_surveys.html>
Uruguay, 2003. Urunet <http://www.urunet.com.uy/>
US (United States). ATF (Bureau of Alcohol, Tobacco and Firearms). 2002. *Crime Gun Trace Reports (2000) National Report*. Washington, DC: ATF. July.
—. GAO (Government Accounting Office). 2003. *Firearms Controls*. GAO-03-688. Washington, DC: GAO. June.
Vargas, Anthony. 2003. 'PNP Vows to Strictly Enforce Gun Ban.' *Manila Times*. 15 December.
Viva Rio. 2003a. 'Brazilian Senate Approves Bill on Gun Carry Ban.' 25 July.
—. 2003b. 'Congress Bans Right to Carry Firearms in Brazil.' 24 October.
VoA (Voice of America). 2003. 'Brazil Moves Toward Increasing Gun Control.' 23 July.
Vobejda, Barbara, David B. Ottaway, and Sarah Cohen. 1999. 'Recycled D.C. Police Guns Tied to Crimes.' *Washington Post*. 12 November.
Washington Post. 2003. 'Tamil Rebels Set Off Explosion', 8 February, p. A22.
—. 2004. 'Misfires on the Hill.' 1 January.
Wezeman, Pieter D. and Siemon T. Wezeman. 1996. *Dutch Surplus Weapons*. Paper No. 5. Bonn: Bonn International Center for Conversion. July.
White House. 2003. *U.S. National Strategy for Combating Terrorism*. Washington, DC: White House. February.
Winton, Richard. 2003. 'Panel Oks Ban on Sale of .50 caliber guns.' *Los Angeles Times*. 28 May.

ACKNOWLEDGEMENTS

Other contributors
Philip Alpers, James Bevan, Wendy Cukier, Pablo Dreyfus, Emile LeBrun, and Ben Lessing.

A Boeing C-17 Globemaster III fires decoy flares in flight. The flares are designed to redirect missiles away from the aircraft if it comes under attack.
(© Boeing. Used under license)

Big Issue, Big Problem?
MANPADS

3

INTRODUCTION

In November 2002, an Israeli passenger aircraft, flying out of Mombasa, Kenya, came under fire from two surface-to-air missiles. Although the missiles missed their target, the event sent waves through the international media and launched another round of a long-standing debate—a debate since reinvigorated by strikes on civilian and military aircraft in Iraq. The weapon used was a Soviet designed SA-7, one of a variety of light weapons commonly called man-portable air defence systems, or MANPADS. MANPADS are small, light, missile-launching weapons designed to be fired by an operator on the ground against a target in the air.

MANPADS have been the focus of unprecedented media attention since 2002. A symptom of recent attacks, public alertness to the threat they pose to civilian aircraft is arguably greater than ever before. Much of this attention centres on the fear of terrorist attacks, although MANPADS have been, and still are, used primarily in war zones. Against a backdrop of often-conflicting reports, this chapter attempts to clarify some of the basic trends in MANPADS production, stockpiling, transfer, and use, and in the measures taken to control their proliferation. Many of the findings add to those already reported, while others cast doubt on prior claims and figures cited. The following are some of the chapter's key findings:

> MANPADS are small, light, missile-launching weapons designed to be fired by an operator on the ground against a target in the air.

- MANPADS are proliferating more widely and recent models are sophisticated enough to defeat many existing countermeasures.
- There are probably fewer than 100,000 complete systems in existence, but many older models may still be operational, contrary to some conservative shelf-life estimates.
- Not all states in possession of MANPADS police proliferation adequately, and the latest generation of MANPADS is proliferating at least as widely as older models.
- At least 13 non-state groups possess MANPADS. Some of these groups are considered terrorist organizations, although their ability to use MANPADS effectively may be in question.
- Much current speculation overplays the importance of MANPADS to date, but it has been key in prompting much-needed action from the international community.
- International measures to control proliferation are gaining support but are embryonic and late in coming.

This chapter is based on information obtained from open public sources. These include a number of MANPADS field manuals, which were obtained from the Internet. The chapter addresses the following questions:

- What are the trends in MANPADS production and transfer?
- What is the scale of global stockpiles of MANPADS and who is in possession of them?

- How easy is it for non-state groups to use MANPADS and are current fears justified?
- What initiatives are in operation to protect against MANPADS proliferation and use?

MANPADS have been in existence for nearly 40 years. Since the Cold War, the number of companies producing MANPADS has diminished, although in the last two decades the number of countries hosting their production has increased. Around 15 companies and consortia in more than 15 countries currently produce MANPADS. On the whole, production is confined to countries with well-developed defence industries, although some new cases indicate that this trend is unlikely to continue. MANPADS are in the arsenals of around 105 states. Many states that produce and stockpile MANPADS have poor records of stockpile security. Collapsed states, transfers to warring factions, and a lack of stockpile security are thought to be responsible for stockpiles in the hands of at least 13 non-state groups, some of which are considered terrorist. Whether all of these actors can use their MANPADS is questionable because of the training and maintenance needed to operate them, but knowledge is perhaps harder to police than the weapons themselves. Current speculation undoubtedly overestimates the number of MANPADS in existence, their longevity, and the ease with which they can be used. Yet proliferation, in terms of production and the number of states using MANPADS, in conjunction with increasingly sophisticated technology, suggests a significant potential problem. In truth, such exaggerated speculation has served a purpose, for it is, in no small part, responsible for a number of international initiatives, some more promising than others, that have been launched since 2002. MANPADS may thus be one of the few small arms and light weapons issues whose politicization has not followed a widespread loss of life and infrastructure, but only if the international community continues to act. MANPADS are a big issue with the potential to be a big problem.

CHARACTERISTICS AND TECHNOLOGIES

The technology involved in producing even the oldest models of MANPADS far surpasses the technology required to produce most types of small arms and light weapons. MANPADS offer an anti-aircraft capability that before their invention could be found either in less technologically advanced and often bulkier weapons such as light anti-aircraft guns or in far larger missile systems. They are by no means homogeneous, and some MANPADS are larger than others and mounted on substantial pedestals; however they can certainly be classified as light weapons, as the 2003 Wassenaar definition suggests:

a) surface-to-air missile systems designed to be man-portable and carried and fired by a single individual; and
b) other surface-to-air missile systems designed to be operated and fired by more than one individual acting as a crew and portable by several individuals (Wassenaar, 2003, §1.1).

Thus, factors of technology, not size, have often led to their placement alongside large conventional weapons in analyses of the national weapons inventories of states (IISS, 2003; SIPRI, 2003). Yet in practice they have not been included in major arms control initiatives, such as the Conventional Armed Forces in Europe (CFE) Treaty. Nor have they been prominent in the debate on small arms and light weapons—as is true of many light weapons. In short, their technology places them in the realms of major weapons systems, while their size defines them as light weapons. As a consequence they have, to date, occupied a grey area in between.

MANPADS

Another feature of the MANPADS debate in the media is that it is punctuated by inconsistency in reporting, in terms both of technological capability—particularly their shelf-life (see Box 3.1)—and of the names assigned to various systems. Lay persons are thus confronted with a plethora of designations, as Table 3.1 briefly illustrates.

Table 3.1   Selected Soviet/Russian MANPADS designations

US Dept. Defense	NATO	USSR/Russian	Manufacturer	Missile
SA-7	Grail	Strela-2	9K32	9M32
SA-16	Gimlet	Igla-1	9K310	9M313
SA-18	Grouse	Igla	9K38	9M39

Most MANPADS comprise a tube-like launcher, out of which is fired a rocket-propelled guided missile. These single-use missile tubes are fitted to a reloadable 'gripstock' (see Figure 3.1) or pedestal launcher. MANPADS also feature a battery to power the electronics of the weapon and often a coolant unit to cool the missile's sensors. Most missiles use either an infrared (IR) guidance system, which acquires a target by contrasting the heat signature from an aircraft's engine or exhaust tube with the temperature of the surrounding sky—so called fire-and-forget missiles—or a method of operator guidance, whereby the user's commands are conveyed to the missile via radio signal and, in recent years, along a laser beam.

Figure 3.1 Main elements of a MANPADS: Soviet SA-7b

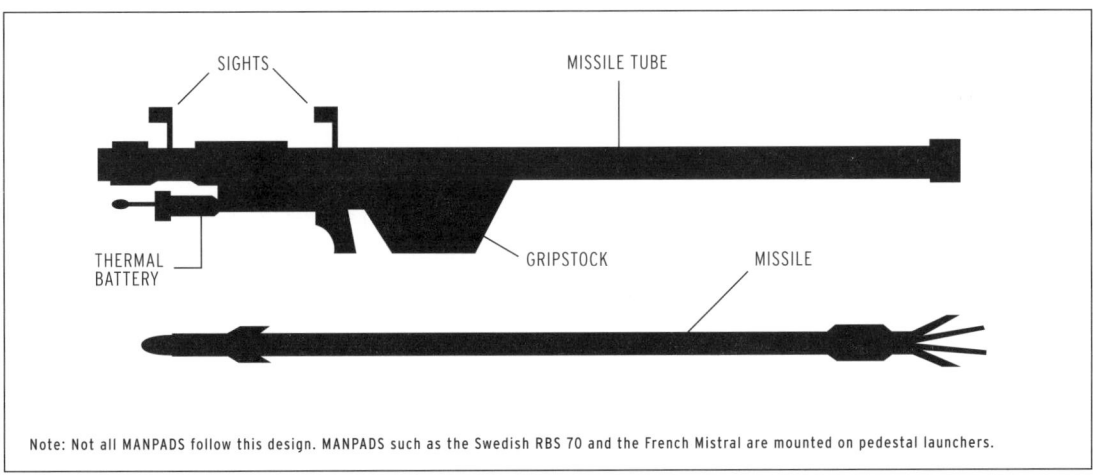

Note: Not all MANPADS follow this design. MANPADS such as the Swedish RBS 70 and the French Mistral are mounted on pedestal launchers.

The former method is more common and as this means of acquisition is 'passive'—that is, it does not rely on the launcher emitting energy (sending a signal to the missile)—such weapons are difficult to detect and greatly feared by aviators (*National Defense,* 2003). Nevertheless, in the hands of trained operators, the latter method may offer greater accuracy as the operator is able to guide the missile to its target, irrespective of countermeasures.

SMALL ARMS SURVEY 2004

Nicaraguan soldiers parade Russian-made SA-7 MANPADS during the celebration of the army's 24th anniversary in Managua in September 2003.

> MANPADS are becoming increasingly sophisticated.

MANPADS are becoming increasingly sophisticated. The latest models offer greater range, greater flexibility in launching against targets, more chance of hitting the target, and greater destructive effects upon doing so. First-generation MANPADS, such as the Soviet SA-7 and the US FIM-43 Redeye, relied on the passive IR guidance system. These weapons were somewhat limited because they had to be launched from behind an aircraft in order for their sensors to 'lock on' to the heat from its exhausts. They were also constrained by the range at which they could engage an aircraft—generally fewer than 5,000 metres. The latest MANPADS technology (see Table 3.2) has improved upon this, utilizing more sophisticated IR seekers that can target an aircraft head-on or direct the missile to strike the body of an aircraft rather than the exhaust alone. These later MANPADS are broadly classified as 'second generation' because their technology is better and their range exceeds that of their predecessors. Many now use a combination of energy seekers, operating on both the IR and ultraviolet (UV) spectrums. Others follow a laser beam with which the operator illuminates the target. These newer MANPADS can engage aircraft at ranges of up to 6,000 metres. The probability of destroying aircraft has also increased with proximity fuses, which detonate close to the target, thus eliminating the need for a direct hit. The combined results of these improvements are that MANPADS can now be operated from a greater number of positions, to greater ranges, and with a far greater chance of hitting crucial parts of the target, such as the fuselage or fuel tanks.

MANPADS PRODUCTION

In contrast to most other small arms and light weapons, the production of MANPADS is currently limited to a small number of manufacturers (PRODUCERS). This is a function both of barriers to production imposed by the technology involved and of measures taken by some states to limit the proliferation of MANPADS technology. Prospects for their long-term manufacture have been called into question by envisaged developments in kinetic energy weapons, but this is an extremely long-term view, and MANPADS are likely to remain in production for a number of years to come (Forecast International, 2003a), potentially by a greater number of companies.

At present, at least 15 companies and consortia produce MANPADS in more than 15 countries. The number of companies producing MANPADS has declined in recent decades because of an unprecedented number of company mergers and acquisitions following the end of the Cold War. Yet, while production was previously limited to the United States, the USSR and its satellites, Western Europe, and China, states such as Egypt, North Korea, and Pakistan have been producing copies of existing MANPADS since the 1980s. In the last decade states, including Singapore and Vietnam, have acquired government licences to produce Chinese and Russian systems. Thus, while the majority of states producing MANPADS have well-developed military industries, the case of Vietnam illustrates that states gaining either technology or manufacturing licences in the future—albeit for assembly rather than for complex manufacturing—may not possess such advanced military industries. The technology factor seems so far to have prevented more widespread production of MANPADS, because very few of the second tier of countries mentioned above have developed MANPADS themselves and, as a consequence, MANPADS-manufacturing states have a fair degree of control over the proliferation of production. Whether they exercise control is a matter of debate.

The vast majority of states that have recently begun producing MANPADS have acquired the technology from Russia or China. The production of US- and European-derived MANPADS appears to be confined to NATO counties and Switzerland, with the exception of the Swedish RBS, which is assembled in Pakistan (SIPRI, 2002). Western states at present appear to exercise tighter control over the flow of weapons and technology than some of their counterparts, for two reasons. First, MANPADS producers tend to be some of the biggest participants in the defence industry. The majority of these large firms are located in the West, and technological gains afforded by mergers or acquisitions are greatest with other Western companies rather than with relatively technology-poor developing country firms (Forecast International, 2003a). Second, the nature of the product has ensured that only select companies are allowed to receive Western technology by way of acquiring licences to produce. For example, in 1988 the United States awarded a licence to the Stinger Project Group (SPG), a consortium of seven states comprising Germany, the Netherlands, Belgium, Norway, Greece, Turkey, and Italy. The arrangement has permitted the manufacture of a preordained number of missiles and guarantees that Stingers are not to be sold to non-SPG countries (Redstone Arsenal, 2003; NISAT, 1999). For the most part, Western production technology is closely guarded. In the past decade, however, a number of countries have acquired licences to produce second-generation MANPADS. Pakistan now manufactures the Chinese QW-1 under the designation Anza 2 and has assembled the Swedish RBS-70 since 1988. Singapore and Vietnam have recently acquired licences to produce the Russian SA-16 (SIPRI, 2003; Pyadushkin, 2003). Future moves such as these will increase not only the number of potential suppliers of MANPADS but also the number of people with knowledge of MANPADS production technology.

There is some debate about the future utility of MANPADS for Western armies, but demand appears to ensure continued production for some time (Forecast International, 2003a). Conversely, the future utility of MANPADS is likely to be far higher for developing states' armed forces, which may value MANPADS as a relatively cheap alternative to larger anti-aircraft systems. Because ever more sophisticated designs have improved the capabilities of MANPADS, they are now arguably more attractive for any actor desiring the capability to destroy aircraft in the air. MANPADS are consequently a growth area at present in the international arms market (Gander, 2003). In the past 15 years or so, a number of companies have developed new systems or started production of existing designs. The Thales Air Defence Starstreak is a laser-guided

Table 3.2 MANPADS producers and basic specifications

Country	Designation	Producer	Guidance	Range*	Mass-produced since	Derivatives, copies, and licensed production		
						Country	Designation	Producer
China	HN-5	CPMIEC (exporter)	Passive IR homing	4,200m	–	Pakistan	Anza	AQ Khan Research Labs.
						N. Korea	HN-5	State factories
	QW-1 / QW-2	CPMIEC	Passive IR homing	6,000m	1994		Anza 2	AQ Khan Research Labs.
France	Mistral	Matra BAe Dynamics	Passive IR homing	6,000m	1988			
Japan	Type 91	Toshiba	IR and Image Matching	5,000m	1991			
Russia/CIS	SA-7	State Factories	Passive IR homing	4,200m	1968	China	HN-5	C.P.M.I.E.C.
						Egypt	Ayn as Saqr	Saqr
						Romania	CA-94M	R.E.I.G.
	SA-14	State Factories	Passive IR homing	5,500m	1978	Bulgaria	SA-14	V.M.Z.
	SA-18	KBM**	Passive IR homing	5,200m	1983			
	SA-16 Igla	KBM**	Passive IR homing	5,000m	1986	Bulgaria	Igla-1E	V.M.Z.
						N. Korea	Igla-1E	State factories
						Poland	Grom	OBR Skarzysko
						Singapore	Igla-1E	
						Vietnam	Igla-1E	
	SA-16 Igla-S	KBM**	Passive IR homing	5,000m	2001			
Sweden	RBS-70 / RBS-70 MKII	Saab Bofors	Laser Beam Riding	7,000m	1977	Pakistan	RBS-70	State factories
UK	Blowpipe	Short Brothers (now Thales)	Operator-guided	4,000m	1968			
	Javelin	Short Brothers	Laser Beam Riding	5,500m	1985			
	Starburst	Short Brothers	Laser Command Link	6,000m	1990			
	Starstreak	Short Brothers	Laser Beam Riding	7,000m	1993			
United States	FIM-43 Redeye	General Dynamics	Passive IR homing	5,500m	1967			
	FIM-92 Stinger	Raytheon***	Passive IR/ UV homing	5,000m	1981	Germany	Stinger	Stinger Project Group
						Switzerland	Stinger	Stinger Project Group

* Range given is the slant range: the 'line-of-sight' distance between two points, not at the same level, relative to a specific datum.
** Design and export: KBM; Missile and launcher production: V. A. Degtyaryov Plant; homing device production: LOMO.
*** Previously manufactured by General Dynamics.

Sources: Foss (2001); Richardson (2002, 2003); Karniol (1999); Army-Technology (2003); Pyadushkin (2003)

missile claimed to be almost impossible to jam, unlike jammable fire-and-forget SAMs such as the Stinger (Foss, 2003). Nevertheless, older designs, such as the SA-16, the Stinger, and the Mistral, still dominate the market. Matra BAe Dynamics' 15-year-old Mistral is expected to remain the market leader in the next decade, with a market share far in excess of its publicity in the media, in contrast to weapons such as the Stinger and SA-7 (Forecast International, 2003a).

STOCKPILES

Certain studies have reported that there are about 500,000 MANPADS in existence (BASIC, 2003; FAS, 2004; Kuhn, 2003). Table 3.3 indicates this estimate may be inflated because it appears to count missiles alone (see Figure 3.1). Single missiles are often included as separate items in accounting—the opposite of transfers information in which complete systems are more frequently reported than missiles. The number of entire weapons systems (launchers complete with missiles) will be much lower than these figures suggest. This is an important distinction because only entire systems can be used. Owing to the fact that figures are not available for a number of systems included in Table 3.3—notably China's HN-5—missile stockpiles are certainly well in excess of 500,000. Applying a ratio of five missiles per launcher—a conservative estimate based on deployment trends (US, Department of the Army, 1984)—suggests 100,000 complete systems in existence. Given that a number of missiles are produced for non-MANPADS systems, the true figure is probably a little lower—under 100,000.

There are about 100,000 complete MANPADS systems in existence.

Around 105 states stockpile MANPADS (IISS, 2003). Table 3.3 demonstrates that it may be the more sophisticated weapons that are the most widespread (in 93 countries, as opposed to 73 for the less sophisticated). A large number of older weapons are in the arsenals of states with poor records of stockpile security, particularly in the case of first-generation MANPADS, of which the SA-7 is the most prolific, accounting, for example, for 23 out of the 29 African states in possession of MANPADS (Forecast International, 2003b; IISS, 2003). Yet a number of second-generation MANPADS are also in widespread use, including the Russian SA-16, the US FIM-92 Stinger, and the French Mistral. All of these weapons appear in regions where conflict is widespread. Nonetheless, there appears to be a great disparity in MANPADS technology according to the industrial development of states, as noted above.

US Marines and Iraqi police officers discover dozens of boxes of Russian-made SA-16 MANPADS hidden in the garden of a Baghdad school in April 2003.

Worryingly, however, disparities in technology do not appear to correlate with problems of stockpile security. In truth, weapons lost from the world's weakest states may never go reported, but recent high-profile cases have implicated second-generation producers, such as Russia, in cases of stockpile leakage.

Many states that produce and stockpile MANPADS have poor records of stockpile security.

Table 3.3   MANPADS: Approximate number of missiles produced and in service, by country of origin and type*

Country	Designation	Total produced	Countries in service
1st generation			
China	HN-5	–	5
Russia	SA-7 (Strela 2M)	175,000**	59
US	FIM-43 Redeye	85,000	4
UK	Blowpipe	2,000**	7
Total known		**262,000+**	**75**
2nd generation			
France	Mistral	15,000	23
Japan	Type 91 and Type 92	3,000	1
Sweden	RBS-70 / RBS-70 MKII	18,000	12
China	QW-1 / QW-2	–	1
Russia	SA-18	11,000	7
	SA-16	30,000	20
UK	Javelin	16,000	6
	Starburst	10,000+	4
	Starstreak	9,000	1
US	FIM-92 Stinger***	84,000	18
Total known		**196,000+**	**93**

* Not all may be for shoulder-launch configuration
** Based on number of launchers multiplied by a reasonable estimate of 5 missiles per launcher.
*** Not all may be complete units

Note: A number of countries stockpile both 1st and 2nd generation MANPADS.
Sources: Total produced: Forecast International (2003b); Gething (1998); O'Halloran and Foss (2002); Zaloga (1989); Astronautix (2003a, 2003b).
Countries in service: IISS (2003). Thanks to Siemon Wezeman for much valued advice on the number of missiles per launcher.

MANPADS may be in the hands of more than 13 guerrilla and terrorist groups worldwide.

A number of other sources of MANPADS are of concern. The United States has long been troubled by the loss of Stingers in Afghanistan, and collapsed states appear to be one of the greatest potential sources of MANPADS proliferation. By December 2002, coalition forces in Afghanistan had retrieved a number of MANPADS of various types (Lapan, 2002; Bolkcom, Elias, and Feickert, 2003, p. 7). Iraq is also a recent case in point. If a MANPADS was indeed used in the November 2003 attack on a US helicopter in Iraq, then it is likely to have come from stockpiles of the former Iraqi army.

So too may the one that struck a civilian cargo plane in Baghdad the same month. Reflecting this possibility, coalition forces have been offering a USD 500 bounty for each system handed in (Bonner, 2003). Estimates vary greatly as to the number of MANPADS at large in Iraq, from 1,500 to 5,000, but numbers are perhaps not the most important aspect (Hordern, 2003). According to some accounts, MANPADS are in the hands of at least 13 non-state groups globally, although reported cases of their use are few (Hunter, 2001). Two crucial factors may dictate whether these weapons are likely to be used in the future: the knowledge needed to operate them and the continued functioning of the weapons themselves.

FACTORS GOVERNING USE

The proliferation of knowledge

The proliferation of MANPADS knowledge is at least as important an issue as the number of stockpiled weapons. The November 2002 Mombasa attack reportedly failed because the weapons were fired too close to their intended target (Kuhn, 2003). Launch sequences require extensive training, which is often not readily available outside of state armed forces. Although systems vary, the firer of an IR-guided MANPADS must first acquire the target; then activate the battery or battery/coolant unit, which powers the missile seeker; allow the IR sensor to lock on to the target and the missile gyro to start spinning; and only then launch the missile. The process can take more than ten seconds, and if it is rushed the missile will not lock onto the target (Gander, 2003). The process is similar for operator-guided missiles, although there is no seeker to cool. In both cases, the firer must be aware of the capabilities of the weapon and, in particular, the angles and minimum and maximum ranges at which it can be used. Countries employing MANPADS usually have a range of training devices and simulators which allow many simulated firings before an operator may ever use a MANPADS in combat (US, Department of the Army, 1984). These practices are not known to be available to non-state groups. If more trained operators become available, errors, such as may have happened in Mombasa, will be less likely to occur. The disbanding of the Iraqi army has undoubtedly meant a number of soldiers trained in the use of MANPADS are now unemployed and seeking an alternative career.

Another issue is the shelf-life of weapons. To date, this issue has centred on the Stinger in the United States, although it seems likely to become an issue of international concern. MANPADS contain sophisticated components, which may become damaged and inoperable with age, poor storage, or misuse. These components include the explosive warhead, guidance electronics, and the batteries used to power them. The proliferation of knowledge may certainly solve some of these problems, but operational life will continue to be governed by inbuilt characteristics. Yet the question remains: just how short is that life?

> The proliferation of MANPADS knowledge is at least as important an issue as the number of stockpiled weapons.

Shelf-life

There is some debate over the shelf-life of MANPADS, with a number of officials and specialists claiming that weapons such as the Afghan War-era Stingers are unlikely to function today due to material determinants, such as deterioration of the propellants, batteries, and coolant units. Nevertheless, there is some evidence that MANPADS may be more durable than has been speculated. MANPADS are designed for use in harsh environments. Their propellants and coolants are reported to be serviceable after nearly 30 years of storage (Kuhn, 2003). They are issued in protective cases—often featuring in-built environmental monitors, such as hygrometers—that are designed to protect them from the elements up until the last minutes before firing. British Blowpipe missiles recently found in Afghanistan were still stored in these cases (Gall, 2003). Storing MANPADS successfully and for an extended period of time may be less of a problem than has been previously thought. One related debate focuses on the extent to which battery power limits the operational lives of illicitly acquired MANPADS (see Box 3.1). The outcome of this debate will be determined by the longevity of the batteries and the ability to replace batteries should they fail. A battery is required for pre-flight operation and for spinning the gyros prior to launch (Blackman, 1985). If the battery ceases to function, the weapon cannot be used.

> The propellants and coolants used inside MANPADS are reportedly serviceable after nearly 30 years of storage.

> **Box 3.1 MANPADS batteries: A short shelf-life?**
>
> Most MANPADS feature a thermal battery, which differs from other types of batteries in that the electrolyte—which holds the electrical charge—exists as a non-conducting set, which is activated only on command. Once the battery is activated it has a life of just several minutes, and must be discarded and replaced immediately after use.
>
> This characteristic has two functions. On the one hand, it ensures that anyone using a MANPADS to engage successive targets must have a ready supply of batteries. This may be a significant problem for actors that have acquired a weapon through illicit channels. On the other hand, thermal batteries have a far greater shelf-life and durability than other batteries, raising concerns that systems in the hands of non-state actors may remain operational for long periods of time. US government reports have claimed that Stinger batteries have a 'shelf-life of at least ten years, with a reliability rate of 98 per cent to 99 per cent' (Kuperman, 2001). However, Eagle Picher, the maker of batteries for the Stinger missile system and supplier to US government agencies since 1982, claims: 'Established storage life is on the order of 20 years, and much longer periods are projected. Most external environments can be expected to have little or no effect on the unactivated battery. The battery is excellent for applications involving extended storage under uncertain conditions' (Eagle Picher, 2003). The precise storage life of a battery is impossible to determine and depends on environmental conditions, but if manufacturers are willing to claim a period of 20 years—and given that most military systems are 'over-engineered'—it is probable that a fair margin of error is built into this figure.
>
> With these functions in mind, anyone wanting to use a MANPADS must first know whether the system is operable. US Army *Stinger Team Operations Field Manual No. 44-18-1*, which is published on the Internet, provides the following detailed guidelines for determining whether the battery coolant unit (BCU) in the Stinger MANPADS is operational:
>
> ▶ Check the color of the heat-sensitive indicator. It should be pink. If not, discard the BCU.
> ▶ Check the holes over the burst disc diaphram. If the silver foil has been ruptured, discard the BCU.
> ▶ Check the BCU housing to insure that it is *not* cracked. If so, discard the BCU (US, Department of the Army, 1984).
>
> Whether this level of detailed information is available for other MANPADS is unclear, but SA-7s recovered in Afghanistan in 2003 reportedly were found with detailed instructions (Silverstein and Pasternak, 2003).
>
> If, on the other hand, the battery is found to be inoperative, the potential user is faced with two options: to locate another one, or to improvise a new power supply for the system. The first option may be facilitated by the fact that MANPADS are designed to be fired a number of times. For example, the Stinger is field-transported in a box including three to five BCUs—offering multiple firings with functional BCUs or increasing the likelihood of successful firing if one or more are damaged (US, Department of the Army, 2000). If another battery is unavailable, the user can attempt to adapt another power source to the weapon. This is not easy. One crucial feature of thermal batteries is that they are custom manufactured for acute voltage, start time, and configuration requirements—in short, batteries have to be tailored to the requirements of the weapon (*Molecular Expressions*, 2003). This is complicated further by the fact that most modern MANPADS, such as the Stinger, Mistral, SA-14, and SA-16, combine a battery and coolant unit in one, dictating the manufacture of a complex module.

It is probable that the 'Afghan' Stingers are nearing the end of their operational lives rather than non-functioning, as some authors have claimed. Whether other MANPADS will remain functional is unclear, but depends on whether their users have the means to repair or retrofit parts successfully. It is worth noting that the MANPADS fired in Mombasa were of 1978 vintage (United Nations, 2003c)—around seven years older than the 'Afghan' Stingers—and the miss was reportedly caused by user error rather than a technical fault (Kuhn, 2003).

TRANSFERS

The authorized transfer of MANPADS appears to be better documented than for most other transfers of small arms and light weapons. This is because transfers are politically sensitive and involve very large sums of money. However, this is not to say transfers are transparent—many states have MANPADS in their inventories and yet give no public documentation to explain from whom or how they acquired them. The illicit transfer of MANPADS is less clear, but its market dynamics appear distinct from the transfer of other small arms and light weapons.

The authorized transfer of MANPADS appears better documented than the majority of other categories of small arms and light weapons; the illicit transfer is less clear.

Authorized transfers

As Table 3.4 illustrates, recent, known authorized transfers for the most part feature second-generation MANPADS. The table is a snapshot of recent transfers and, while by no means exhaustive, demonstrates that the value of sales is higher than that of other types of small arms and light weapons, though the quantities involved are small. For example, the case of US exports of Stinger missiles to Greece, Italy, and the UK, at USD 89 million, is approximately the value of France's combined small arms exports and imports for 2000, while the Russian USD 48 million sale of SA-16s to Malaysia comprised only 40 launchers and 382 missiles (Small Arms Survey, 2003, p. 103; Malaysia, 2002). However, it is often difficult to establish just how many missiles are transferred in those cases reported, as data often refer only to complete weapons systems with an unspecified number of missiles. To complicate matters further, certain missiles, such as the Stinger and SA-16, can form part of major conventional weapons systems rather than MANPADS, as a USD 31 million sale of Stingers to Lithuania illustrates. This deal reportedly involved only eight missile launchers but, crucially, these were in multi-barrelled vehicle-launch format and consequently not MANPADS, although the missiles themselves may have been identical (*Jane's Defence Weekly*, 2002).

Table 3.4   Selected authorized transfers of MANPADS since 2001

Supplier (system)	Recipient(s)	Value (USD)	No. systems ordered	Year of delivery
Russia (SA-18)	India	32-50m	2,500	2001-2
Pakistan (Anza 1)	Malaysia	12.8m	100	2002
Russia (SA-16)	Malaysia	48m	70	2002
Russia (SA-16)	Vietnam	64m	48	2001-2*
Russia (SA-18)	Mexico	2.14m	50	2002
UK (Starstreak)	S. Africa	85m	-	2001-2
US (Stinger)	Greece, Italy, UK	89m	1007	2003-4

* Includes transfer of production licence.

Sources: SIPRI (2003); Foss (2003); Malaysia (2002); Brooke (2000)

While second-generation MANPADS make up the majority of declared transfers, a number of states produce MANPADS of a lower value. Lower-value MANPADS are likely to feature heavily in transfers between states with a poor record of transparency. The Soviet SA-7 is in service in the greatest number of countries (see Table 3.3), some of which are known for their lack of export transparency. These missiles may also feature prominently in re-export. A UN Panel of Experts report cites one possible source for the SA-7s used in the Mombasa attack of 2002 as an Eritrean government transfer to Somali faction leader Hussein Aideed in 1998, although by November 2003 the Eritrean government had yet to verify this information (United Nations, 2003c, § 129). Moreover, from 1982 to 1994 China is thought to have exported between 2,858 and 5,500 pieces of its SA-7 derivative, the HN-5, to states including Afghanistan, Cambodia, Myanmar, and North Korea (Byman and Cliff, 1999). These states are hardly transparent: none currently reports to UN Comtrade (UN Comtrade, 2003), and Cambodia at least is known to have 'lost' weapons from its national inventory in 2003 (Lyall, 2003; Agence France Presse, 2003), as may have North Korea (Karniol, 1999).

> Lower-value MANPADS are likely to feature heavily in transfers between states with a poor record of transparency.

Illicit transfers

The illicit transfer of MANPADS does not display the same market dynamics as that of the majority of small arms and light weapons, but their small size makes them as easy to conceal as their low-tech counterparts. Their illicit transfer is known to be widespread and governed by utility and cost, but the actual scale of trade is unclear, although transfers are probably confined to well-established non-state groups (Hunter, 2001).

The lightness and compact size of MANPADS make them highly portable on the battlefield, but this quality also makes them extremely easy to transfer illegally and discreetly within and between states. The Russian SA-7, for instance, weighs around 14kg (missile tube and launcher)—far less than most heavy machine guns—and is only 1.49m in length (O'Halloran and Foss, 2002). A weapon of this size fits easily into the boot of a car, into a golf bag, or within bundles of produce small enough to be carried on the back of a person or animal (Zeller, 2003). Perhaps because of this, most illicit transfers have become known only after a weapon has been used against an aircraft (Hunter, 2001). Of these, the implicated sources have been, directly, Central Africa, the Horn of Africa, and East Asia, and, indirectly, the United States, Russia, and China.

> Most illicit transfers become known only after a weapon has been used against an aircraft.

For many actors, MANPADS have little to no utility. They are ineffective tools for crime, coercion, or personal security. MANPADS are a specialist weapon; those that have been uncovered or intercepted appear either to have been safely stored for future use or sale, or to be en route to another location (*Moscow Times*, 2003, *Time Magazine*, 2003). One likely implication is that, as these weapons require considerable knowledge to operate, they are more likely to be requested for a specific purpose than transported to a conflict area in the hope of securing sales.

Many weapons, including FIM-92 Stingers in Afghanistan and Angola, are a legacy of the Cold War, but weapons are still finding their way from relatively peaceful states to conflict zones and have yet to be used. Of particular concern at present are those thought to be in the hands of groups loosely described as under the umbrella organization of al Qaeda.

Box 3.2 A tale of two missiles

The weapons used in the November 2002 Mombasa attack were Soviet-era SA-7s, reportedly produced at the VA Degtyarev Plant in Kovrov, Russia, in 1978 (Kuhn, 2003). While the launchers were produced in Russia, the missiles used were produced in Bulgaria in 1993 and sold as part of a larger consignment to Yemen in 1994. From Yemen, it is believed the missiles were smuggled either directly to Somalia, by a Mogadishu arms dealer in early 2003, or as part of three consignments from the Eritrean government to a Somali faction in 1998. In either case, the MANPADS then entered Kenyan territory by sea (United Nations, 2003c).

Other groups are also believed to have received weapons recently. Among these are the Revolutionary Armed Forces of Colombia (FARC), for which one potential source of weaponry is thought to be a drugs-for-arms pipeline extending between Russia and Colombia (Bolkcom, Elias, and Feickert, 2003, p. 9). Other recipients include

MANPADS

Lebanon's Hezbollah, which is thought to have received weapons from the Afghan mujahideen (Withington, 2003); the Palestinian Authority, thought to have received weapons transported in fishing vessels via Egypt (Hunter, 2001); and the Liberation Tigers of Tamil Eelam (LTTE), who were reported to have received SA-16 missiles diverted from a transfer from North Korea to Vietnam by black-market traders. The LTTE are further known to have acquired SA-7s and HN-5s in Cambodia (Karniol, 1999). Cambodia also appears to have been the origin of six MANPADS systems allegedly smuggled into Thailand in September 2003 (Lyall, 2003; Agence France-Presse, 2003). *Jane's Intelligence Review* outlines 13 non-state groups confirmed to be in possession of MANPADS, with a further 14 groups reported to possess them (Hunter, 2001).

The groups so far implicated in MANPADS transfers appear to be among the better-funded non-state organizations and have established international procurement and smuggling networks through which to acquire weapons.

The FARC, Hezbollah, and the LTTE are among the non-state groups believed to have received MANPADS.

Box 3.3 Blowback: The Stinger missile debate

Although MANPADS represent the most sophisticated of light weapons and are synonymous with modern military technology, significant international concern over their proliferation and misuse predates that of most other small arms and light weapons. In the mid-1980s, the United States Central Intelligence Agency, in conjunction with Pakistani Inter-Services Intelligence, played a key role in supplying and training the Afghan mujahideen with a variety of MANPADS to speed the defeat of the Soviet army. Foremost among these was the FIM-92 Stinger—then the very latest generation of MANPADS in service with the US army (Kuperman, 1999; Yousaf and Adkin, 2001).

'Blowback' is a US intelligence term used to describe an unexpectedly negative policy outcome. The Stinger debate encapsulates this phenomenon perfectly. It is estimated that, of the approximately 1,000 Stingers transferred, from 200 to 600 were never returned to the United States. Between 16 and 30 were transferred illicitly to Iran, and the rest apparently remain at large, although they may be unserviceable (Lumpe, 1994; Saleem, 2001). During the course of the 20-year debate, the focus of concern over Stinger proliferation has turned from the Soviet Union to the number of disparate terrorist groups linked to the Afghan mujahideen—a microcosm of changing US security concerns.

A guerrilla soldier aims a Stinger missile at passing aircraft near an isolated rebel base in Afghanistan's Safed Koh Mountains in 1988.

© Robert Nickelsberg/Liaison

Because the Stinger is claimed to have shot down around 250 Soviet aircraft in Afghanistan, it is synonymous with Western military might and concerns over its proliferation have long endured. Although the mujahideen were well trained in using Stingers, a somewhat condescending view prevails to the effect that, if the mujahideen could use them, any non-state group can do so, and this has helped fuel fears over terrorist acquisition of the weapon. Ease of use is probably overestimated, but is no guarantee of security in the future.

The Stinger debate indicates not only the long-term and negative legacies of transfer decisions but also that the spread of technology and training is as much an aspect of small arms control as the weapons themselves. It is no surprise that Stinger rhetoric has 'resurged' in much of the debate surrounding initiatives to control the proliferation of MANPADS post-11 September 2001.

MEASURES TO CONTROL MANPADS

Recent fuel for debate

In the years since 2001, concomitant events have demonstrated the threat from MANPADS in a number of different theatres, both civilian and military, and have created common ground among states that rarely cooperate on small arms control. These events have raised issues of the vulnerability of civilian aircraft and their military counterparts, the seemingly widespread proliferation of weapons—notably to non-state groups (including terrorists)—and the problems that occur when stockpiles are freed from state control. Given the long history of MANPADS transfers, this recent momentum is late in coming, but may spur the international community into action.

In May 2002, shortly before the failed attack in Mombasa, an SA-7 launcher was found near the Prince Sultan Airbase in Riyadh, Saudi Arabia. The weapon was later traced through its serial number to the same batch as that used in the attack in Mombasa (Creedy, 2003). To compound matters, in July 2003 at least eight SA-7 launchers were stolen from a naval arsenal in Bolshiye Izhory, near St Petersburg (*Moscow Times*, 2003), and, in August 2003, a British man was arrested and charged with attempting to sell up to 50 Russian 'Igla SA-18' shoulder-launched missiles to an FBI informant in the United States (*Time Magazine*, 2003). These cases demonstrated that MANPADS were not confined to state arsenals and were available on the international illicit arms market.

Another series of events has involved the use of MANPADS against the aircraft of major military powers. In Chechnya, MANPADS have brought down a number of Russian helicopters; in one incident, nine soldiers, including the deputy commander of the 58th Army, were killed (Agency WPS, 2003). More recently, coalition involvement in Iraq has further highlighted the threat of MANPADS. On 2 November 2003, a US helicopter was destroyed by what is widely believed to have been a MANPADS, with the loss of 20 lives—at that time the largest loss of life suffered by US forces in Iraq in a single attack (Schrader and Rubin, 2003). Later that month, an SA-14 missile struck a civilian cargo plane flying out of Baghdad, setting the wing on fire, although not preventing it from landing with the crew unharmed (Kirby, 2003; Daly, 2003; Wall and Hughes, 2003).

The threat to civilian airliners has the potential to affect the citizens of all states travelling on major air routes. This, and the fact that the armed forces of two of the world's largest and most influential states—the United States and Russia—have also recently been the targets of MANPADS on the battlefield, has widened debate in the past years and provides an opportunity for the establishment of effective future controls on the proliferation of MANPADS and their technology.

The defensive option: protection of the target

Civilian planes have been hit by MANPADS in an estimated 29–40 incidents between 1975 and 1992, with the total number of dead estimated at between 500 and 760 (Bayles, 2003; *National Defense*, 2003; Shaffer, 1993; Bolkcom, Elias, and Feickert, 2003). Many of these losses have occurred in war zones (*Aerospace America*, 2003). Nonetheless, since the 1978 and 1979 attacks on two Air Rhodesia planes, which killed scores of people, there have been relatively few attacks on civilian aircraft (*Time Magazine*, 2003). However, international concern has increased in recent years and progressively more actors, including politicians and the International Air Transport Association (IATA), are proposing action against MANPADS (*U.S. Newswire*, 2003; Fiorino, 2003).

IATA in particular is preparing a detailed study of MANPADS and the threat they pose to civilian aircraft. The association is also evaluating a diverse set of strategies designed to mitigate the danger of an attack.

US Senators Charles Schumer and Barbara Boxer and Representative Steve Israel hold a US-made FIM-43 Redeye MANPADS during a news conference in Washington, DC, in February 2003. Their proposed legislation would equip civilian aircraft with anti-missile protection devices similar to those currently used on military transport aircraft.

Following the Mombasa attack, Israel's El Al was the first airline to experiment with installing missile countermeasures on some of its aircraft (*BBC Monitoring International Reports,* 2003). The Israeli Ministry of Defence reportedly selected Elta Electronic Industries' decoy flare system for selected aircraft, at a cost of around USD 1 million per aircraft (Dror, 2003). A similar idea has been mooted in the United States, with congressional advocates, most notably Democratic Senator Barbara Boxer, promoting the idea of equipping the Civil Reserve Air Fleet (CRAF)—leased to fly troops and cargo in emergencies—with countermeasures (*Aviation Week,* 2003). Equipping the world's airline fleets with countermeasures will prove costly. The Chief Executive Officer of Australia's Qantas Airlines estimated it would cost the company AUD 442 million (more than USD 320 million) to install countermeasures on its fleet of 129 Boeing aircraft (Goodenough, 2003; Qantas, 2003). In response to congressional pressure, in January 2004 the US Department of Homeland Security commissioned three companies to explore ways of protecting civilian airliners against attack by adapting existing military technology. One or more of the companies may be invited to produce a system, although the process is expected to take up to 24 months, which means that no defences will be operational until at least 2006 (Waterman, 2004).

Even if airlines, and ultimately passengers, are willing to invest this amount in their security, the success of countermeasures is likely to depend on two factors: whether missile launches can be detected and, if so, whether the missiles can be diverted from their targets. In built-up areas, such as those surrounding international airports, background heat makes detecting a launch extremely difficult (Creedy, 2003). Should a launch be detected, the primary defence against MANPADS has so far been the ejection of flares designed to confuse the IR or UV targeting system of the missile when the flare passes through its field of view; newer methods include the use of IR transmitters—known as IR countermeasures (IRCMs)—to create fields of IR energy designed to confuse a missile's sensors (Bolkcom, Elias, and Feickert, 2003). The majority of the more cost-effective proposed countermeasures for civilian aircraft involve using flares or, at most, IR transmitters. These may be effective against first-generation MANPADS, but are impotent against second-generation operator-guided weapons. In this case, the only option is some form of energy emission—such as laser countermeasures—which are more effective than flares but may be much more expensive. For example, BAe has proposed a laser-jamming system for airliners, with an estimated cost, on the basis of a minimum of 1,000 units purchased, of USD 1 million (Laurenzo, 2003). A number of cheaper, more practical recommendations have recently been made. Perhaps the most important has been the idea of 'inerting' wing fuel tanks, which often ignite and make a MANPADS engine strike more effective, by replacing potentially explosive fumes in fuel tanks with nitrogen-enriched air (NASA, 2003). The hope is that, in large airliners with multiple engines, this measure would make aircraft better able to continue flying after a strike. Inerting fuel tanks would reportedly be more cost-effective, at an estimated USD 200,000 per aircraft, than active countermeasures, while also improving airline safety generally (*Air Safety Week,* 2003a). These measures notwithstanding, the case of the cargo plane struck in Baghdad stands as testament to the durability of large aircraft (*Air Safety Week,* 2003b).

> The success of countermeasures is likely to depend on two factors: whether missile launches can be detected and, if so, whether the missiles can be diverted from their targets.

The proactive option: Controlling proliferation

Despite the current focus on airline defences, other measures to control MANPADS have centred primarily on two initiatives: preventing the spread of weapons and retrieving weapons that have found their way into undesirable hands. Only since mid-2003 have international initiatives been launched to address both issues. Prior to this, the most notable initiatives were made by the United States, primarily in response to the Stinger debate in US politics and the press but arguably also because of recent military intervention and the threat posed to one of the United States' most powerful assets—its air force. The result is international interest in countering the threat of MANPADS, which has gathered momentum as states, or groups of states, have been made aware of the immediacy of the dangers posed to their interests.

Initially, in response to the loss of a number of Stingers in Afghanistan, the US government established bilateral regulations forcing recipients of US MANPADS to accept rigorous controls over any MANPADS that were purchased from the United States. Recipients were required to provide proof they had received the missiles and to submit to periodic inspections to verify their status. Furthermore, the Stinger Project Group (SPG) was set up to administer joint procurement of MANPADS for selected NATO countries. The Project established strict conditions whereby group members are permitted to export Stingers only to SPG countries (*Redstone Arsenal*, 2003).

Both of these US-led measures centred on reducing the potential for MANPADS technology to fall into the hands of potential enemies of the United States. However, given that the debate in which these measures originated was concerned primarily with non-state actors, there was always a fear that missiles already in the hands of such actors could be used against the West. Consequently, the first Bush administration set up a reward system to aid recovery of Stingers from the Afghan War. The fund at the disposal of the scheme was later increased in 1993, under the Clinton administration, to USD 55 million (Wright and Broder, 1993)—with offers of between USD 80,000 and 150,000 per missile reported in the early 1990s (Lumpkin, 2001; CNN, 1999). The programme was either still in existence or revived following the overthrow of the Taliban in 2001, possibly as part of the Office of Weapons Removal and Abatement (WRA, 2003; Burns and Turner, 2002). To date, it is not clear whether any Stinger missiles have been returned, but coalition forces have been very active in both Afghanistan and Iraq searching for MANPADS and other weapons.

Other members of the international community were slower to act on the subject of MANPADS, and initially did so only with US prompting. In 1998, one of the first international efforts to control MANPADS was launched under the direction of US Secretary of State, Madeleine Albright, when she stressed, before the UN Security Council, the need for an international agreement to impose tighter controls on the export of shoulder-fired missiles (Albright, 1998a, 1998b). Although initially unpromising, by December 2000 talks in the 33-state Wassenaar Arrangement led to participants agreeing that they would, in future, require end-user certification for all MANPADS exports and prohibit re-transfers to third parties without prior consent (Boucher, 2000). This initiative was furthered in December 2003 and, according to Kenneth Brill, US Ambassador to the UN's International Atomic Energy Agency, the tightening of controls was 'comprehensive', including stricter export reporting, closer controls over inventories, and technical developments to make the weapons more difficult to fire (Charbonneau, 2003).

In Chechnya, MANPADS have brought down a number of Russian helicopters.

In Russia, the threat from MANPADS has taken a different form, but has been no less influential on policy-making. Kremlin concern stems from the repeated use of SA-18s and similar weapons to down Russian aircraft in Chechnya (Myers, 2002). In November 2002, Defence Minister Sergey Ivanov urged the CIS and Baltic states to halt the flow of Igla (SA-16/18) missiles to the region (*BBC World Edition*, 2003). Initially there was strong disagreement on the proposal for mutual notification of transfers of former Soviet missiles, apparently due to commercial concerns. However, pressure from Moscow prevailed (*Associated Press Worldstream*, 2003; White House, 2003). In July 2003 Ukraine became the first to yield and an agreement by 11 CIS members—all except Turkmenistan—was completed a few months later (Bellaby, 2003; *Interfax,* 2003; Agency WPS, 2003). Russia has also faced pressure from both Israel and the United States. Israel has long feared MANPADS could end up in the hands of Lebanon's Hezbollah, and this prompted Moscow to terminate a deal which would have supplied Syria with Russian SA-18s (*Russia Reform Monitor,* 2002).

MANPADS are also a threat to a number of other Western countries. The danger to civilian airliners has been highlighted by the Mombasa attack and fears over terrorist threats to airliners in general. In June 2003, at the Organization for Security and Co-operation in Europe (OSCE) Annual Review Conference, the French delegation proposed using the OSCE Document on Small Arms and Light Weapons as a springboard for additional steps against the illicit trade in MANPADS (OSCE, 2003). That same month, the G8 countries expressed a determination to 'curb terrorist threats against mass transportation' and agreed to implement the following steps as part of an action plan to prevent the acquisition of MANPADS by terrorists:

- To provide assistance and technical expertise for the collection, secure stockpile management, and destruction of MANPADS surplus to national security requirements;
- To adopt strict national export controls on MANPADS and their essential components;
- To ensure strong national regulation of production, transfer, and brokering;
- To ban transfers of MANPADS to non-state end-users; MANPADS should only be exported to foreign governments or to agents authorized by a government;
- To exchange information on uncooperative countries and entities;
- To examine the feasibility of development for new MANPADS of specific technical performance or launch control features that preclude their unauthorized use;
- To encourage action in the International Civil Aviation Organization (ICAO) Aviation Security (AVSEC) Working Group on MANPADS (G8, 2003).

To date, most international measures have not dealt with weapons already beyond the control of state armed forces.

The Group also agreed to exchange information on national measures related to the implementation of the steps and to review the progress at the G8 summit in 2004.

The growing salience of the issue was confirmed by two international initiatives in late 2003. On the 21 October, an initiative at an Asia-Pacific Economic Cooperation (APEC) meeting in Bangkok, instigated in large part by the United States, resulted in a non-binding pledge to strengthen national controls on the production, export, and stockpiling of MANPADS. The move has brought China into the process; it is not a member of either the Wassenaar Arrangement or the G8 and yet is an important producer of MANPADS (*Arms Control Today,* 2003). A new international initiative then came to fruition on 8 December 2003, when the United Nations General Assembly approved a resolution expanding the Register of Conventional Arms which, while not shedding light on stockpiled MANPADS, should enhance transparency in future transfers (United Nations, 2003a; Wurst, 2003). MANPADS have been added to Category VII of the Register, entitled 'Missiles and Missile Launchers', as an exception to the fact that there is no specific category for surface-to-air missiles (United Nations, 2003b). To date, most international measures have not dealt with those weapons already beyond the control of state armed forces. In October 2003, in the run-up to the APEC meeting, Bangkok police held training seminars for around 5,000 taxi drivers, who were shown a missile system and what it looked like when stored in a golf bag (Zeller, 2003). The move followed reports that the Thai police were looking for six contraband MANPADS smuggled into Thailand from Cambodia (Lyall, 2003). Current international concern appears to be leading to better control over the export of MANPADS. With regards to missiles that are unaccounted for, the only available measures appear to be vigilance, recovery where possible, and perhaps some form of costly defence.

SMALL ARMS SURVEY 2004

PROSPECTS FOR CONTROLLING MANPADS

To date, MANPADS have been used infrequently in conflict situations and even less frequently against civilian targets. Factors that have controlled their proliferation and use include the small number of producers manufacturing and exporting them and the training needed to operate them. The impact of both factors seem set to fade; yet hope lies in gathering international initiatives to stop the proliferation of MANPADS. The current bout of media attention may have exaggerated the threat of MANPADS, but it has done much to raise international awareness of a threat with the potential to become more acute.

The total number of MANPADS producers is limited but has increased in the post-Cold War environment, as has the number of countries in which production occurs. Older MANPADS technology will probably become more widespread as technology diffuses, and so too may the knowledge required to maintain and operate MANPADS, as suggested by a number of developments. Advances in communications—especially on the Internet—allow detailed operating materials to be disseminated to a potentially worldwide readership. Even if efforts are made to control this, it must be assumed that the information is already in the hands of interested parties. Another factor is the availability of trained operators. Ex-mujahideen fighters from Afghanistan have long been feared for their training in the use of MANPADS, but there are a host of states that could potentially contribute skilled operators to the illicit market. As indicated above, MANPADS may not have as short a shelf-life as had been generally assumed. The sensible storage of weapons is certainly not beyond the capacity of most organized terrorist groups. It has long been known that many groups are technologically adept, and safely storing a MANPADS is probably not dissimilar in principle to storing a modern personal computer.

In principle, safely storing a MANPADS is not unlike storing a modern personal computer.

Against these trends, however, the international community appears to be in a position to institute some essential controls on the export of MANPADS. The fact that Russia and China have been party to discussions is an important step forward, but is no guarantee of action. Past experience seems to indicate that the likelihood of initiatives coming to fruition may depend, unfortunately, upon whether the threat of MANPADS continues to be confirmed in the form of actual attacks.

As for defensive measures against MANPADS, there is no single, adequate form of protection that can encompass all eventualities or is affordable to all parties concerned—as is the case with most small arms. It appears that civilian airliner defences may be adopted by the world's wealthier states but, unless measures are instituted now to prevent the latest generation of MANPADS eventually finding their way out of government stockpiles, such efforts to enhance security may be ineffective.

Security from MANPADS will be increased only if proliferation is checked and those states in possession of MANPADS can secure, or can be helped to secure, their own stockpiles. As for those MANPADS already on the illicit market, limiting the further transfer of knowledge and training through planned security sector reform appears the most sensible precaution. MANPADS remain a big issue with the potential to become a big problem.

3. LIST OF ABBREVIATIONS

APEC	Asia-Pacific Economic Cooperation
AVSEC	Aviation Security
BCU	Battery coolant unit
CFE	Conventional Armed Forces in Europe
CRAF	Civil Reserve Air Fleet
FARC	Revolutionary Armed Forces of Colombia
IATA	International Air Transport Association

ICAO	International Civil Aviation Organization
IR	Infrared
IRCMs	Infrared countermeasures
LTTE	Liberation Tigers of Tamil Eelam
MANPADS	Man-portable air defence system
OSCE	Organization for Security and Co-operation in Europe
SPG	Stinger Project Group
UV	Ultraviolet

3. BIBLIOGRAPHY

Aerospace America. 2003. 'MANPAD attacks on civilian aviation.' July, p. 5.

Agence France-Presse. 2003. 'APEC Leaders to Impose Controls on Shoulder-Launched Missiles.' Bangkok. 17 October.

Agency WPS. 2003. 'How to Stop Strella and Igla Missiles.' *What the Papers Say*. Translated by Arina Yevtikhova. Part A (Russia).

Air Safety Week. 2003a. 'Aviation Safety Issues Head "Most Wanted" List of Improvements.' Vol. 17, No.33. 25 August.

—. 2003b. 'The Vexing Problem of Protecting Airliners from Missiles.' Vol. 17, No. 46. 8 December.

Albright, Madeleine. 1998a. 'Secretary's Remarks to Stimson Center.' US Department of State, *USIS Washington File*. 10 June.

—. 1998b. 'Statement to the UN Security Council Ministerial on Africa.' Washington, DC: US Department of State. 24 September.

Arms Control Today. 2003. 'Asian and Pacific Leaders Pledge to Control Shoulder-Fired Missiles.' Vol. 33, p. 9. Washington, DC: Arms Control Association.

Army-Technology. 2003. *Mistral Air Defense Missile System, France*. <http://www.army-technology.com/projects/mistral/index.html#mistral5>

Astronautix. 2003a. 'Blowpipe.' *Encyclopaedia Astronautica*. <http://www.astronautix.com/lvs/blowpipe.htm>

—. 2003b. 'General Dynamics FIM-43 Redeye.' *Encyclopaedia Astronautica*. <http://www.astronautix.com/lvs/redeye.htm>

Associated Press Worldstream. 2003. 'Russian Defence Minister Calls for Controls on Shoulder-Fired Missiles.' Moscow. 8 June.

Aviation Week. 2003. 'Lawmakers Unveil "Interim" Plan for Airliner Countermeasures.' *AviationNow.com*. 1 October. <http://www.aviationnow.com/>

BASIC. 2003. 'EU and US Cooperate on Arms Export Controls in a Post-9/11 World: Session 3.' Discussion Paper: Man Portable Air Defense Systems. 23 January. <www.basicint.org/WT/armsexp/MANPADS.htm>

Bayles, Fred. 2003. 'Threat is "no longer theoretical".' *USA Today*. 13 August. <http://www.usatoday.com/news/nation/2003-08-13-insidemissile-usat_x.htm>

BBC Monitoring International Reports. 2003. 'Israeli Airline Installs Anti-Missile System on Some Planes.' Israeli TV Channel 1, Jerusalem. 1900 GMT, 27 October

BBC World Edition. 2003. 'Russian Press Hails Missile Sting.' 14 August. <http://news.bbc.co.uk/2/hi/europe/3151195.stm>

Bellaby, Mara. 2003. 'Twelve ex-Soviet Republics agree to increase controls on sale of anti-aircraft missiles.' *Associated Press*. 18 September.

Blackman, Major R. R. 1985. *Ground Air Defense in the Marine Air-Ground Task Force*. Quantico: Marine Corps Command and Staff College. <http://www.globalsecurity.org/military/library/report/1985/BRR.htm>

Bolkcom, Christopher, Bartholomew Elias, and Andrew Feickert. 2003. *Homeland Security: Protecting Airliners from Terrorist Missiles*. Washington, DC: Congressional Research Service. Library of Congress.

Bonner, Raymond. 2003. 'Saddam's Stingers Unaccounted For: Hundreds Missing, Posing Airport Risk.': *International Herald Tribune* (New York). 8 October.

Boucher, Richard. 2000. 'Member states of Wassenaar Arrangement Adopt Controls on Circulation of Man-Portable Anti-Aircraft Missiles.' Press release. US Department of State. 5 December.

Brooke, Micool. 'South-East Asian Targets for Russian Igla and Kilo.' *Asia Pacific Defence Reporter* (Canberra). June–July, p. 34.

Burns, Jimmy and Mark Turner. 2002. 'Allies Buy Back Missiles in Afghanistan.' *Financial Times*. 2–8 April, p. 4.

Byman, Daniel and Roger Cliff. 1999. *China's Arms Sales: Motivations and Implications. Appendix: An Overview of China's Arms Sales*. Washington, DC: RAND.

Charbonneau, Louis. 2003. Arms states vow to stop terrorists getting weapons. *Reuters Foundation Newsdesk*. 12 December. <http://www.alertnet.org/thenews/newsdesk/L12522770.htm>

CNN. 1999. 'Cold War Postscript: Legacy of Afghanistan Haunts Both Cold War Superpowers.' 7 March. <http://www.clw.org/atop/media/cnn030799.html>

Creedy, Steve. 2003. 'New Attacks on Planes "Inevitable".' *Australian* (Sydney). 4 September.

Daly, John. 2003. 'The Threat of Surface-to-Air Missiles.' Washington, DC: United Press International. 28 November.
<http://washingtontimes.com/upi-breaking/20031128-040741-3314r.htm>

Dror, Marom. 2003. 'Elta Anti-missile System Chosen to Protect Passenger Aircraft.' *Globes [online]*. 4 September.
<http://www.globes.co.il/DocsEn/did=720992.htm>

Eagle Picher. 2003. *Thermal Batteries*.
<http://www.epcorp.com/NR/rdonlyres/FEB03316-8021-4DBD-AB3F1E9E3E7D193C/0/ThermalAboutUs.pdf>

FAS (Federation of American Scientists). 2004. *MANPADS Proliferation*. Issue Brief 1. Washington, DC: FAS. January.
<http://www.fas.org/asmp/campaigns/MANPADS/MANPADS.html>

Fiorino, Frances. 2003. 'ICAO Lobbies for Manpads Control.' *Aviation Week and Space Technology*. Vol. 159, No. 12. 22 September, p. 15.

Forecast International. 2003a. 'Analysis 2: The Market for Surface-to-Air Missiles through 2012.' *Missiles Forecast*. Newtown: Forecast International/DMS. June.

—. 2003b. 'Surface to Air Missiles.' *Missiles Forecast*. Newtown: Forecast International/DMS. April.

Foss, Christopher. 2001. 'Close Support.' *Jane's Defence Weekly*. Coulsdon: Jane's Information Group. 3 October.

—. 2003. 'South Africa Orders Starstreak Missile.' *Jane's Defence Weekly*. Coulsdon: Jane's Information Group. 2 July.

G8. 2003. 'Enhance Transport Security and Control of Man-Portable Air Defence Systems—MANPADS—A G8 Action Plan.' *Summit Documents*, Article 1.6. Evian: Sommet d'Evian. <http://www.g8.fr/>

Gall, Carlotta. 2003. 'U.S. Troops in Afghanistan Kill 4 Taliban Suspects Near Border.' *New York Times*. 11 June, p. A5.

Gander, Terry. 2003. *Portable Launchers*. Background Paper. Geneva: Small Arms Survey.

Gething, Michael. 1998. 'Asian Aerospace: 23rd Mistral and first export ASRAAM.' *Jane's Missiles and Rockets*. Coulsdon: Jane's Information Group. 1 March. p. 14.

Goodenough, Patrick. 2003. 'Australia Mulls Terrorist Missile Threat to Airlines.' Cybercast News Service. 5 September.

Hordern, Nick. 2003. 'On a Wing and a Flare.' *Australian Financial Review* (Sydney). 13 September, p. 31.

Hunter, Thomas. 2001. 'The Proliferation of MANPADS.' *Jane's Intelligence Review*, Vol. 13, No. 9. 1 September.

IISS (International Institute for Strategic Studies). 2003. *The Military Balance 2003/2004*. Oxford: IISS.

Interfax. 2003. 'Ukraine Ready to Discuss Russia's Proposals on Tightening MANPAD sales.' 29 July.

Jane's Defence Weekly. 2002. 'In Brief: Lithuania buys Stingers.' Coulsdon: Jane's Information Group. 20 November.

Karniol, Robert. 1999. 'Anti-aircraft Boost for Tamil Tiger Rebels.' *Jane's Defence Weekly*. Coulsdon: Jane's Information Group. 7 April.

Kirby, Steve. 2003. 'Airport in Striking Distance: Baghdad facility scene of hit on DHL freighter.' *Washington Times*. 28 November, p. 17.

Kuhn, David. 2003. 'Mombasa Attack Highlights Increasing MANPADS Threat.' *Jane's Intelligence Review*, Vol. 15, No. 2. 1 February.

Kuperman, Alan. 1999. 'The Stinger Missile and U.S. Intervention in Afghanistan.' *Political Science Quarterly*, Vol. 114, No. 2, pp. 219–63.

—. 2001. 'Will Missiles Return to Sting?'. *USA Today*. 14 November, p. 17A.

Lapan, David. 2002. 'Pentagon Spokesman. Speaking on 6 August.' Cited in Paul Caffera, *The Air Industry's Worst Nightmare*. New York: Salon.com. 22 November. <http://www.salon.com/news/feature/2002/11/22/missiles/index_np.html>

Laurenzo, Ron. 2003. 'BAe Proposes System to Protect Airliners.' *Defense Week*, Vol. 24, No. 49. 15 December.

Lyall, Kimina. 2003. 'Thai Police Confess they Can't Find SAM Missiles'. *Australian* (Sydney). 2 October.

Lumpe, Lora. 1994. 'Preliminary Policy Option for Monitoring/Restricting Exports of Light Arms.' Paper prepared for UNIDIR meeting on Small Arms and Internal Conflict, 7–8 November. <http://www.fas.org/asmp/campaigns/smallarms/options.html>

Lumpkin, John. 2001. 'Stinger Missiles Said Unlikely to Threaten U.S. Troops in Afghanistan.' New York: Associated Press. 24 September.

Malaysia. 2002. *Report to the UN Register of Conventional Arms*. Kuala Lumpur: Government of Malaysia. 6 May.

Molecular Expressions. 2003. 'Thermal Batteries.'. National High Magnetic Field Laboratory (NHMFL), Tallahassee: Florida State University.
<http://micro.magnet.fsu.edu/electromag/electricity/batteries/thermal.html>

Moscow Times. 2003. 'Strelas Stolen.' Translation in Associated Press. 16 July.

Myers. Steven. 2002. 'Russia Says Missile Downed Copter, but Faults its Military.' *New York Times*. 31 August, p. A3.

NASA. 2003. 'Accident Mitigation and Fuel Tank Inerting.' Presentation for the International Aircraft Systems Fire Protection Working Group Workshop. Atlantic City, NJ, 5–6 November. <http://www.fire.tc.faa.gov/ppt/systems/McKnight-NASAworkupdate.ppt>

National Defense. 2003. 'Man-Portable Missiles Imperil Both Military, Civilian Aircraft.' Arlington, VA. August, p. 28.

NISAT (Norwegian Initiative on Small Arms Transfers). 1999. *Stinger Missile System*. Oslo: NISAT.
<http://www.nisat.org/weapons%20pages%20linked/US/stinger_missile_system.htm>

O'Halloran, James and Christopher Foss. 2002. *Jane's Land-based Air Defence*. Coulsdon: Jane's Information Group.

OSCE (Organization for Security and Co-operation in Europe). 2003. 'OSCE Security Conference Considers Fresh Options.' Vienna: OSCE News. 26 June. <http://www.osce.org/news/show_news.php?id=3382>

Pyadushkin, Maxim. 2003. *SALW Production in Russia*. Background paper. Geneva: Small Arms Survey.

Qantas. 2003. Fact File: Qantas at a Glance. ACN 009 661 901. Queensland: Qantas Airways Ltd. October.
<http://www.qantas.com.au/infodetail/about/FactFiles.pdf>

Redstone Arsenal. 2003. *Stinger/Avenger*. Redstone, AL: US Army Materiel Command.
<http://www.redstone.army.mil/history/systems/STINGER.html>

Richardson, Doug. 2002. 'Igla-S Can Engage Cruise Missiles and UAVs.' *Jane's Missiles and Rockets*. Coulsdon: Jane's Information Group. 1 June.
—. 2003. 'China Unveils Apache Killer.' *Jane's Missiles and Rockets*. Coulsdon: Jane's Information Group. 1 August.
Russia Reform Monitor. 2002. 'Chechens in Russia Face Backlash; Death Toll Mounts in War Against Corruption.' No. 981. Washington, DC: American Foreign Policy Council. 1 November. <http://www.afpc.org/rrm/rrm981.htm>
Saleem, Farrukh. 2001. 'Where are the Missing Stinger Missiles?' *Friday Times* (Lahore). 17–23 August.
Schrader, Esther and Alissa Rubin. 2003. 'Portable Missiles MAY Rise as a Threat.' *Los Angeles Times*. 4 November, p. 1.
Shaffer, Marvin B. 1993. 'Concerns about Terrorists with Man portable SAMs.' Rand Corporation Reports. Santa Monica, CA: RAND. October, p. 3.
Silverstein, Ken and Judy Pasternak. 2003. 'A Market in Missiles for Terror.' *Los Angeles Times*. 6 March.
SIPRI (Stockholm International Peace Research Institute). 2002. 'Transfers and Licensed Production of Major Conventional Weapons: Exports to Pakistan, Sorted by Supplier. Deals with Deliveries or Orders Made 1993–2002.' <http://projects.sipri.se/armstrade/PAK_MPTS_93-02.pdf>
—. 2003. *SIPRI Yearbook 2003: Armaments, Disarmament and International Security. Appendix 13C: Register of the Transfers and Licensed Production of Major Conventional Weapons, 2002*. Oxford: Oxford University Press.
Small Arms Survey. 2003. *Small Arms Survey 2003: Development Denied*. Oxford: Oxford University Press.
Time Magazine. 2003. 'How Secure Are the Skies?' New York. 25 August.
UN Comtrade. 2003. 'Data Availability: Reporters by Years.' New York: United Nations Statistics Division. <http://unstats.un.org/unsd/comtrade/mr/daReportersResults.aspx?bw=A>
United Nations. 2003a. *Resolution adopted by the General Assembly. Transparency in Armaments*. A/RES/58/54 of 8 December.
—. 2003b. *Continuing Operation of the United Nations Register of Conventional Arms and its Further Development*. A/58/274 of 13 August.
—. 2003c. *Report of the Panel of Experts on Somalia Pursuant to Security Council Resolution 1474 (2003)*. S/2003/1035 of 4 November.
USA Today. 2003. 'Threat Is "No Longer Theoretical": Portable Missiles are Easy to Hide, Easy to Use.' 13 August, p. 3.
US (United States). Department of the Army. 1984. 'Stinger Team Operations.' *Field Manual No. 44-18-1*. Washington, DC: US Department of the Army. 31 December. <http://www.globalsecurity.org/military/library/policy/army/fm/44-18-1/toc.htm>
—. 2000. 'Air Defense Artillery Reference Handbook.' *Field Manual No. 3-01.11 (FM 44-1-2)*. Washington, DC: US Department of the Army. 31 October. <http://www.army.mil/usapa/doctrine/DR_pubs/dr_a/pdf/fm3_01x11.pdf>
US. WRA (Office of Weapons Removal and Abatement). 2003. <http://www.state.gov/t/pm/wra/>
U.S. Newswire. 2003. 'Shoulder-Launched Surface-to-Air Missiles a Threat to Commercial Aviation, Says Coalition of Airline Pilots Associations.' Washington, DC: USNewswire.com. 13 August.
Wall, Robert and David Hughes. 2003. 'Missile Quandary.' *Aviation Week and Space Technology*, Vol. 159, No. 22. 1 December, p. 46.
Wassenaar. 2003. 'Elements for Export Controls of Man-Portable Air Defence Systems (MANPADS).' Agreed at the WA Plenary. Vienna: The Wassenaar Arrangement on Export Controls for Conventional Arms and Dual-Use Goods and Technologies. 11–12 December.
Waterman, Shaun. 2004. '3 Firms Tapped for Anti-Missile Project.' Washington, DC: United Press International. 1 January. <http://www.upi.com/view.cfm?StoryID=20040106-064321-5282r>
White House. 2003. 'Aviation Security Fact Sheet.' Washington, DC: Office of the Press Secretary, White House. 2 June.
Withington, Thomas. 2003. 'Terrorism: Stung by Stingers.' *Bulletin of the Atomic Scientists*. Vol. 59, No. 3. May/June, pp. 16–17. <http://www.thebulletin.org/issues/2003/mj03/mj03withington.html>
Wright, Robin and John Broder. 1993. 'Fearing Attacks, U.S. Acts to Rebuy Afghan Missiles.' *International Herald Tribune* (New York). 25 June, p. 5.
Wurst, Jim. 2003. 'U.N. Committee Approves Expansion of Arms Register.' New York: UN Wire. <http://www.unwire.org/UNWire/20031029/449_9888.asp>
Yousaf, Mohammad and Mark Adkin. 2001. *Afghanistan the Bear Trap: The Defeat of a Superpower*. Havertown, PA: Casemate.
Zaloga, Steven. 1989. *Soviet Air Defence Missiles*. Coulsdon: Jane's Information Group.
Zeller, Tom. 2003. 'Shoulder-Fired: Cheap and Lethal, It Fits in a Golf Bag.' *New York Times*. 26 October.

ACKNOWLEDGEMENTS

Other contributors
Philip Alpers, Peter Batchelor, Aaron Karp, Anna Khakee, Keith Krause, Emile LeBrun, Maxim Pyadushkin, and Siemon Wezeman.

Inspectors conduct UN-mandated searches for contraband in containers in February 2003.
(© AP/Leila Gorchev, Pool)

Back to the Sources:
INTERNATIONAL SMALL ARMS TRANSFERS

4

INTRODUCTION

In late 2003, human rights organizations brought a case against the British government's arms sales (including small arms sales) to Indonesia. They argued that these exports violated the UK export criteria, as there was a 'patent' risk that the weapons would be used for internal repression (Norton-Taylor and Agionby, 2003). This incident illustrates that much controversy still surrounds the issue of arms sales to countries where serious human rights violations take place, something that this chapter also shows.

Previous editions of the *Small Arms Survey* tried to identify main exporters and importers of small arms,[1] to examine the level of transparency in the small arms trade,[2] and to explore the links between legal and illicit arms transfers. This chapter continues to follow developments in the small arms and light weapons trade and state transparency. However, it does so in a slightly different way than in previous years. For the first time, it contains extensive listings of both main importers and exporters, with their most important trading partners and principal categories of weapons traded. The section on main exporters also systematically compares data from different sources (customs data and national reports on exports of military goods). The comparison shows that we are still far from a clear and coherent picture of the authorized trade in small arms. This is an important reason for introducing a second novelty: the **Small Arms Trade Transparency Barometer.** The barometer assesses the transparency of the main exporting states on a 20-point scale. It will be a recurrent feature of the *Small Arms Survey*. In subsequent editions, it should thus be possible to assess to what extent individual states are becoming more or less transparent over time, and hence whether we are moving towards a clearer picture of the authorized trade. As noted in previous editions of the *Small Arms Survey*, a good understanding of the legal (or authorized) trade is crucial for understanding the illicit market.

It is with a view to better comprehend the authorized trade that the chapter also sets out to examine the relationship between production and trade for the first time. The goal is to assess to what extent the small arms industry is dependent on trade for survival. Future editions of the *Survey* will deal with the other main source of small arms transfers, namely pre-existing state stockpiles.[3]

Lastly, in line with the theme of the 2004 edition of the *Small Arms Survey*, the chapter also examines the links between human rights violations and small arms transfers. Here, the goal is to detail small arms transfers to states where serious violations of human rights take place. In fact, there are surprisingly many such transfers.

The chapter seeks to answer the following questions:

- What are the recent trends in the authorized international small arms trade?
- Who are the leading international exporters and importers of small arms?
- How transparent is the authorized trade in SALW?
- How export-dependent are small arms producers?
- What are the links between the small arms trade and human rights violations?

SMALL ARMS SURVEY 2004

A number of issues pertaining to transfers will remain unexplored. Some of these are discussed elsewhere in this volume, such as questions related to the illicit trade in small arms (BROKERING), and the trade in MANPADS (MANPADS). The main findings of the chapter include the following:

- The largest small arms exporters by value, according to the latest available data as well as estimates, are the US, Italy, Belgium, Germany, Russia, Brazil, and China.
- The largest known small arms importers by value are the US, Saudi Arabia, Cyprus, Japan, South Korea, Germany, and Canada.
- According to the Small Arms Trade Transparency Barometer, the most transparent states *among the larger exporters of small arms and light weapons* are the United States, Germany, and France. However, even they are not fully transparent.
- Despite the Economic Community of West African States, (ECOWAS) moratorium on small arms, states in the region import significant amounts of firearms from Western and other sources.
- Small arms manufacturers of large producer countries, such as Brazil, Germany, and (to a lesser extent) Russia, are dependent on exports for their survival. US manufacturers, in contrast, produce mainly for domestic consumption.
- European exporters of civilian small arms are heavily dependent on the US market.
- The ability of states classed as having serious human rights problems to import arms is quite uneven. At one extreme, Russia—although involved in a war marred by human rights violations in Chechnya—has unlimited access to small arms of all types and from almost all states; at the other, no transfer of small arms was recorded to Iraq while it was embargoed under Saddam Hussein.

THE AUTHORIZED GLOBAL SMALL ARMS TRADE: ANNUAL UPDATE

This section provides an update and new information on the authorized global small arms trade. It focuses on the largest exporters and importers globally, their trading partners, and main products traded. It includes information on parts, whenever available, as well as on small arms ammunition, but does not cover grenades and mines. Moreover, it should be noted that, given gaps in the current data on light weapons ammunition, trade in ammunition is almost certainly underestimated (see Box 4.1 for details of an effort to circumvent this problem). The same is true of the trade in military small arms and light weapons, due to limited transparency on the part of many states.

The largest exporters of small arms by value in 2001 were the United States, Italy, Belgium, Germany, Russia, Brazil, and China.

The value of exports of small arms for 2001 documented in international customs data is approximately USD 2.4 billion.[4] This is slightly more than for 2000, when documented exports amounted to USD 2.1 billion (Small Arms Survey, 2003, p. 97), at least partly because, in a departure from previous practice, small arms parts are included in the calculations. There are therefore no reasons to modify the estimated total value of the authorized trade in small arms, namely USD 4 billion a year. The largest exporters by value in 2001 were the United States, Italy, Belgium, Germany, Russia, Brazil, and China. The largest importers in 2001 were the United States, Saudi Arabia, Cyprus, Japan, South Korea, Germany, and Canada.

As always, the data presented in tabular form in this section should be interpreted with caution. Information (customs data and national export reports) is available from the most transparent states; the exports and imports of less

Small arms exports

Of several sources of information on small arms exports, the two most important are national reports on exports of military goods and international customs data (as reported to UN Comtrade).[5] Here, we have attempted to systematically compare data from these two sources; where available, both sets are presented in Table 4.1. The comparison reveals that international customs data and export reports usually diverge significantly. Some of the possible reasons for this have been detailed in the 'remarks' column of Table 4.1. The most important reasons are: unequal reporting (a state might publish a rather detailed export report, but not report all its customs statistics internationally); different definitions of small arms and light weapons in the two sources; and the fact that some transfers do not go through customs (direct state-to-state transfers) and hence appear only in national export reports. Other possible reasons are that transfers to peacekeeping operations abroad sometimes go through customs but would not appear in export reports, and customs data at times includes guns returned to producers for repairs and refitting or servicing. The comparison suggests an urgent need for international standardization of national export reports. It is paradoxical that national export reports, which are published mainly for reasons of transparency, are at times less transparent on the small arms trade than international customs data, which were not designed as an arms trade transparency device.

The comparison also shows that, unless all states report their authorized imports and exports through customs and publish export reports, only a partial understanding of the trade can be obtained. Romania illustrates this point. Romania published a first export report in 2002 (see Box 4.3 and Table 4.5), in which it lists its main trading partners for arms generally: US, Israel, India, Pakistan, and Turkey. Small arms (including small arms ammunition) form a large part of total Romanian arms exports (about 63 per cent of the total or USD 15.4 million in 2001). As Romania has not provided its customs data for 2001 to international customs databases, we rely on importers' customs reports on their small arms trade with Romania (a total of USD 4.2 million only). While the US still is the largest customer, Switzerland comes second, followed by Senegal, Italy, and the Czech Republic. It is quite possible that an accurate list would include Israel, India, Pakistan, or Turkey, but among these countries only Turkey provides detailed import data to international customs databases. Hence, if we have to rely on importers' reports of their small arms trade with Romania, we are left with only a partial understanding of Romanian trade, in which the role of transparent states, such as Switzerland, Senegal, Italy, and the Czech Republic, probably is overstated.

To begin circumventing problems such as these, our data on exports, for the first time, makes use of estimates for China, a major producer of small arms (PRODUCERS), which provides very limited information on its exports.[6] The estimation technique is simple, and is based on other states' ratios of small arms exports to total arms exports. Details on the estimation technique are given in Annex 4.I, available on the Small Arms Survey Web site.[7]

To make full use of international customs data, we have used both exporters' reports on their exports, and so-called mirror data, i.e. importer's declarations on the same transactions (the two should in principle be identical). As is evident in Table 4.1, mirror data is particularly important for determining exports of non-reporting countries.

Our analysis shows that, globally, the US, Italy, Belgium, Germany, Russia, Brazil, and China were the top exporters of small arms and light weapons in terms of value in 2001. Other important exporters were Austria, Canada, the Czech Republic, Japan (non-military small arms only), and Spain. Countries that are known to be medium producers of small

It is paradoxical that national export reports, which are published for reasons of transparency, are less transparent than international customs data, which were not designed as an arms trade transparency device.

arms (Small Arms Survey 2003, Table 3.1), but about whose exports very little is known, include Iran, Pakistan, and Singapore. Some countries, such as Pakistan, are making strong efforts to increase their arms exports, including of small arms, although it is unclear whether they have been successful to date (Siddiqa-Agha, 2002).

Countries that are known to be medium producers of small arms, but about whose exports very little is known, include Iran, Pakistan, and Singapore.

A Canadian crew in Pakistan loads a consignment of machine guns, mortars, and rocket-propelled grenades with ammunition into a plane destined for Afghanistan in February 2003.

Some points emerging from the table are worthy of particular mention. Saudi Arabia is a very large recipient of small arms from countries such as Belgium, Brazil, Bulgaria, France, Spain, the UK, and the US. In 2003, there were news reports of leakages of small arms from Saudi stocks to terrorist organizations, in particular al Qaeda (STOCKPILES). Given the closed nature of the Saudi regime, it is possible to assume that such reports might constitute only the tip of an iceberg.

Exports from the Czech Republic to Yemen have been substantial for several years, and have been criticized for almost as long. Yemen is a particularly sensitive destination given its role as a regional hub in small arms trafficking. In a recent UN Security Council report on violations of the arms embargo against Somalia (a country experiencing a protracted civil war), Yemen is labelled 'Somalia's arms supermarket' (UNSC, 2003b, p. 19). Yemen is also allegedly a source of weapons for terrorists operating in Saudi Arabia. According to Saudi authorities, the weapons and explosives used in the 12 May 2003 bombings of housing compounds in Riyadh, which killed 35 people, were smuggled in from Yemen (*Al Jazeerah*, 2003). Since then, border control between the two countries has been substantially reinforced.

Another point worthy of mention is Brazilian and Russian exports of small arms to Algeria (see Table 4.13 for further exports, including by other countries, to Algeria over the past years), whose human rights situation is one of the worst in the world, and where both government-controlled and Islamist forces are accused of grave violations. Moreover, small arms are often directly involved in these human rights violations (Amnesty International, 2003b).

TRANSFERS

As noted above regarding medium producers such as Iran, Pakistan, and Singapore, some countries are noteworthy for the lack of information on exports. Examples of less important producers include Serbia and Montenegro and Moldova/Transdniestria. Serbia is home to the well-known Zastava Arms Company. Even considering that the industry is in crisis, Serbian officially declared exports are conspicuously small. At the same time, reports of Serbian firearms ending up in war zones have started to emerge: a Belgrade arms broker recently diverted Serbian-made assault rifles (manufactured in 2001 and 2002) to Liberia. The Serbian authorities withdrew the broker's licence when confronted with the evidence gathered by UN experts investigating violations of the arms embargo against Liberia (UNSC, 2003a; Vines, 2003). Moldova, in particular the breakaway Transdniestria area, is a 'black hole', with large known arsenals and very little transparency. In a recent report, Associated Press claimed to have obtained a copy of a confidential 1998 agreement, in which 'Russia and Trans-Dniester would share profits from the sale of 40,000 tons of "unnecessary" arms and ammunition stored in an arms depot in the breakaway region'. Until December 2003, the depot also contained hundreds of portable surface-to-air missiles, which Russia now claims have been withdrawn because of concerns that they could end up in terrorists' hands (Jahn, 2004; for similar stories relating to both surplus stocks of arms and production, see BBC Worldwide Monitoring, 2003). The same could in principle be true for other smaller producers with few known exports, even though fewer reports exist on dubious weapons exports from these countries.

Table 4.1 Annual authorized small arms exports of the most important known exporters, 2001 (most recent complete yearly data available)

Country	USD value customs data (Comtrade)*/ Export report[x] (2001 if not otherwise stated)	Main known recipients (listed in order of importance)	Main known types of SALW exported	Remarks
Australia	11.3m*	UK, US, Japan, New Zealand, Thailand*	Ammunition, pistols/ revolvers, shotguns, sporting/hunting rifles*	Publishes an export report, but does not detail the SALW share of arms exports.
Austria	At least 77.7m*	US, Germany, Sweden, Venezuela, Canada*	Pistols/revolvers, ammunition, parts pistols/revolvers, sporting/hunting rifles, parts sporting/hunting weapons*	Reports its trade neither in military weapons nor in pistols and revolvers to Comtrade. Hence the value for these categories (based on importers' reports) is likely to be underestimated.
Belgium	234.0m* EUR 82.0m (USD 73.5m)[x]	Saudi Arabia, US, France, Portugal, UK*	Military weapons, shotguns, parts sporting/hunting weapons, ammunition, sporting/ hunting rifles*	The discrepancy between customs and export report data is difficult to explain. It could be partly because the customs data includes repairs and refurbishing. Export report does not detail recipients of small arms.
Brazil	At least 99.1m*	US, Germany, Saudi Arabia, Colombia, Algeria*	Sporting/hunting rifles, pistols/revolvers, ammunition, shotguns*	Does not report trade in military weapons, pistols, parts of revolvers and pistols, parts of military weapons, or small arms ammunition to Comtrade. Hence the value is likely to be underestimated.[8]
Bulgaria	At least 17.1m*	Saudi Arabia, Macedonia, US, Austria, Italy*	Ammunition, parts sporting/hunting weapons, military weapons, shotguns*	Does not report on its SALW trade at all to Comtrade. Figures are based on importers' reports. Hence the value is likely to be underestimated.

103

SMALL ARMS SURVEY 2004

Table 4.1 (cont.)   Annual authorized small arms exports of the most important known exporters, 2001 (most recent complete yearly data available)

Country	USD value customs data (Comtrade)*/ Export report (2001 if not otherwise stated)	Main known recipients (listed in order of importance)	Main known types of SALW exported	Remarks
Canada	53.6m* CAD 25.8m (USD 16.7m)ˣ	US, Denmark, Netherlands, UK, France* Denmark, UK, Netherlands, Germany, Thailandˣ	Military weapons, ammunition, sporting/hunting rifles, pistols/revolvers*	International customs data and the national report diverge largely because the latter does not take into account exports to the US, which according to the export report are 'estimated to account for over half of Canada's exports of military goods' (Canada, 2002, p.8).
China	9.0m* SAS estimate: USD 100m	US, Bangladesh, Iran, Germany, Canada*	Sporting/hunting rifles, shotguns, pistols/revolvers, parts sporting/hunting weapons, ammunition*	International customs data probably underestimate actual exports, as China does not report on many of its exports, and hence figures are based on importers' reporting.
Czech Republic	52.3m*	US, Germany, Yemen, France, Slovakia*	Ammunition, pistols/revolvers, sporting/hunting rifles, parts pistols/revolvers*	
Finland	30.7m* EUR 2.9m (USD 2.6m)ˣ	US, Sweden, Germany, UK, Italy* Sweden, Italy, Germany, US, New Zealandˣ	Ammunition, sporting/hunting rifles, shotguns, parts sporting/hunting weapons, military weapons*	Customs and export report data diverge probably largely because civilian weapons are excluded from the export report.
France	At least 33.7m* EUR 18.5m (USD 16.6m)ˣ	Saudi Arabia, US, Norway, Portugal, Russia* Romania, Belgium, Saudi Arabia, Germany, Malaysia, USˣ	Military weapons, ammunition, parts sporting/hunting weapons, sporting/hunting rifles*	The discrepancy between customs and export report data is difficult to explain. Does not report trade in military weapons, pistols, parts of revolvers and pistols to Comtrade. Hence the value is likely to be underestimated. The export report data excludes ammunition and parts, but includes some non-SALW because certain categories do not contain purely SALW.
Germany	At least 156.7m*	US, Switzerland, France, Spain, Austria*	Pistols/revolvers, ammunition, sporting/hunting rifles, parts sporting/hunting weapons, parts pistols/revolvers*	Does not report trade in military weapons to Comtrade. Hence, the value is likely to be underestimated. Publishes an export report, but it includes information on granted export licences, not actual deliveries of SALW.
Iran	Medium producer, but little is known about its exports			
Israel	At least 23.2m*	US, Botswana, Brazil, Guatemala, Germany*	Pistols/revolvers, ammunition, military weapons, parts pistols/revolvers, parts sporting/hunting weapons*	International customs data probably underestimates actual exports, as Israel does not report most of its exports, and hence figures are based on importers' reports.
Italy	At least 298.7m*	US, Belgium, France, Germany, UK*	Shotguns, ammunition, pistols/revolvers, parts sporting/hunting weapons*	Does not report trade in military weapons to Comtrade. Hence, the value is likely to be underestimated. Publishes an export report, but it includes information on licences, not deliveries of SALW.

Table 4.1 (cont.) Annual authorized small arms exports of the most important known exporters, 2001 (most recent complete yearly data available)

Country	USD value customs data (Comtrade)*/ Export report (2001 if not otherwise stated)	Main known recipients (listed in order of importance)	Main known types of SALW exported	Remarks
Japan	70.3m*	US, Belgium, France, Germany, Canada*	Sporting/hunting rifles, parts sporting/hunting weapons, shotguns, shotgun barrels, ammunition*	Produces only non-military firearms.
Mexico	At least 14.2m*	US, Venezuela, Argentina, Paraguay, France*	Parts sporting/hunting weapons, shotgun barrels, ammunition, shotguns*	Does not report trade in military weapons, pistols, and some parts to Comtrade. Hence the value is likely to be underestimated.
Norway	13.7m* NOK 0.5m (USD 60,000)[x]	Switzerland, US, Italy, Sweden, Finland*	Ammunition, military weapons, shotguns, pistols/revolvers*	Customs and export report data diverge probably largely because it is difficult to fully distinguish SALW from non-SALW (especially ammunition) in the export report.
Pakistan	Medium producer, but little is known about its exports			
Portugal	At least 44.8m*	US, Belgium, Spain, Italy Greece*	Sporting/hunting rifles, parts sporting/hunting weapons, shotguns, shotgun barrels, ammunition*	Does not report trade in military weapons to Comtrade. Hence, the value is likely to be underestimated. Publishes an export report, but it does not detail the SALW share of arms exports.
Romania	At least 4.2m* 15.4 m[x]	US, Switzerland, Senegal, Italy, Czech Republic*	Sporting/hunting rifles, military weapons, ammunition, parts sporting/hunting weapons, pistols/revolvers*	The export report figure and the Comtrade figure diverge because Romania does not report its customs data to Comtrade, and hence figures are based on importers' reporting.
Russia	At least 42.2m* Estimate based on official information: no more than 130m (Pyadushkin, 2003, p. 24).	US, Cyprus, Algeria, Germany, Lebanon* Vietnam, Malaysia, Bhutan, Indonesia, Afghanistan (Northern Alliance), Ethiopia (Pyadushkin, 2003, p.24)	Shotguns, ammunition, sporting/hunting rifles, pistols/revolvers*	International customs data probably underestimate actual exports, as Russia does not report its exports, and hence figures are based on importers' reporting. This explains the large discrepancy between the customs data figure and the figure obtained through exporting companies.
Saudi Arabia	13.2m*	Germany, France, US, United Arab Emirates, Kuwait*	Parts sporting/hunting weapons, shotguns, ammunition, military weapons, shotgun barrels*	Does not produce large quantities of weapons. Much of the apparent exports are probably transfers due to servicing and repairs. Some might also be re-export or transit.
Singapore	Medium producer, but little is known about its exports			
South Africa	At least 12.5m* ZAR 81m (USD 9.5m)[x]	US, Colombia, Germany, India, Mexico*	Ammunition, military weapons, pistols/revolvers, sporting/hunting rifles*	The discrepancy between customs and export report data is difficult to explain. Does not report customs data to Comtrade. Hence, the value is likely to be underestimated.

SMALL ARMS SURVEY 2004

Table 4.1 (cont.) Annual authorized small arms exports of the most important known exporters, 2001 (most recent complete yearly data available)

Country	USD value customs data (Comtrade)*/ Export report (2001 if not otherwise stated)	Main known recipients (listed in order of importance)	Main known types of SALW exported	Remarks
South Korea	29.7m*	Venezuela, US, Ethiopia, Australia, Turkey*	Ammunition, military weapons, parts pistols/revolvers, parts sporting/hunting weapons, pistols/revolvers*	
Spain	At least 65.3m* EUR 42.9m (USD 38.5m)[x]	Saudi Arabia, US, Portugal, UK, France*	Ammunition, shotguns, parts pistols/revolvers, pistols/revolvers*	Does not report trade in military weapons to Comtrade. Hence, the value is likely to be underestimated. The discrepancy between the export report figure and the Comtrade figure is most likely due to differing definitions of SALW.
Sweden	At least 24.1 m* SEK 5m (USD 0.5m)[x]	US, Norway, Austria, Denmark, Finland*	Ammunition, military weapons, parts sporting/hunting weapons, sporting/hunting rifles*	Does not report trade in military weapons to Comtrade. Hence, the value is likely to be underestimated. Discrepancies probably arise because Sweden uses a restrictive definition of SALW in its export report (excluding light weapons), and does not separate small arms ammunition from other types of ammunition.
Switzerland	48.1m* CHF 11.7m (USD 6.9m)[x]	Germany, Singapore, Romania, US, Canada* Germany, US, Malaysia, Italy, France[x]	Ammunition, parts sporting/hunting weapons, pistols/revolvers, military weapons, sporting/hunting rifles*	Discrepancies in total amounts of SALW exports and main destinations may arise because SALW ammunition cannot be distinguished from other types of ammunition in the export report, and is therefore not included in the export report numbers.
Turkey	21.4m*	US, Italy, Germany, Lebanon, France*	Shotguns, parts sporting/hunting weapons, ammunition, sporting/hunting rifles, military weapons*	
UK	44.8m*	US, Saudi Arabia, Australia, Denmark, Belgium*	Military weapons, ammunition, shotguns, sporting/hunting rifles*	Publishes an export report, but does not detail the value of SALW exports. Instead it provides numbers of certain types of SALW exported.
US	741.4m*	Japan, South Korea, Saudi Arabia, Canada, Italy*	Military weapons, ammunition, pistols/revolvers, sporting/hunting rifles*	Publishes an export report, but it includes information on granted export licences, not actual deliveries of SALW.

Notes: Only countries with known or estimated yearly sales of more than USD 10 million have been included in the listing.

* UN Comtrade, 2001 figures (the latest available), customs codes 930100 (military weapons), 930200 (revolvers and pistols), 930320 (shotguns), 930330 (sporting and hunting rifles), 930510 (parts and accessories of revolvers and pistols), 930521 (shotgun barrels), 930529 (parts and accessories of shotguns or rifles), 930590 (parts and accessories of military weapons), 930621 (shotgun cartridges), 930630 (small arms ammunition).

[x] Export report

Source: NISAT (2003)

Box 4.1 Defining and counting SALW: A proposal for a new approach

Cased, palletized, or containerized, SALW are routinely forwarded by commercial carriers, along with (and sometimes inside) cargoes of other more innocent goods coming either from the more than 90 countries where their main manufacturers are located (PRODUCERS) or from second-hand markets. In previous research on the logistics of arms transfers and the transport companies servicing the arms trade,[9] we attempted to evaluate the market size of SALW transport and developed a database on SALW flows and trade lanes for 1994-2001. We based the flow-charts on the records in UN Comtrade, according to a methodology based on the cross-analysis of importer and exporter declarations.[10]

In this box we present some of our findings and, in particular, data on trends and flows of (a) goods under those customs categories that mostly include SALW and related ammunition (here referred to as the A9 Group[11]); (b) goods under those customs categories that include SALW among other items (B2 Group[12]); and (c) goods under those customs categories for which we believe there is a SALW association even though they are not usually considered as such (C2[13]).

The overall size of SALW trade obviously depends on how they are defined but, given the total value of A9 and C2 Groups and part of B2's, its value could be said to range, in annual average, between USD 5 billion and 7 billion, similar to the trade, for example, in sports footwear (USD 5 billion-6 billion) or frozen fish (USD 7 billion-8 billion).

Our findings show that, in 1994-2001 and in constant 2001 terms,[14] transfers of SALW of the A9 Group totalled USD 24.9 billion, with an annual average of USD 3.1 billion. In the same period, transfers of weapons of the B2 Group reached USD 37.4 billion, at an annual average of USD 4.7 billion. Transfers of C2 Group totalled USD 3.1 billion, at an annual average of USD 385 million. The A9 Group is most similar to the definition of SALW used elsewhere in this chapter. The difference in value (2.4 billion versus 2.8 billion) is mainly due to the fact that the two include slightly different categories of SALW.

Table 4.2 A9/B2/C2 Groups: value of transfers 1994-2001, in constant 2001 USD millions

Group	1994	1995	1996	1997	1998	1999	2000	2001	Total	Average
A9	3,477	3,515	3,409	2,344	3,097	2,857	2,827	2,839	**24,365**	3,046
B2	4,787	4,207	4,516	5,175	5,532	4,749	4,935	3,482	**37,383**	4,673
C2	599	566	804	178	253	209	227	248	**3,084**	386
Total	8,863	8,288	8,729	7,697	8,882	7,815	7,989	6,569	**64,832**	8,104

Source: Authors' database; see fn. 10

Within the A9 Group, transfers of parts and accessories account for nearly 27 per cent of the total; non-military firearms for 21 per cent; cartridges and parts thereof for nearly 20 per cent; and military revolvers and pistols account for an additional 12 per cent. The United States, Italy, and Germany ranked in the first positions as exporters, with USD 6.7 billion, 3 billion, and 2 billion, respectively, in sales during 1994-2001. In the first ten positions ranked also the United Kingdom, Belgium–Luxembourg (reporting jointly), Brazil, France, Austria, Switzerland, and Japan, together accounting for more than 70 per cent of the trade.

The B2 Group is composed of military weapons and munitions, which include SALW items such as machine guns, military rifles, rocket and grenade launchers, mines, mortars, and man-portable guided missiles[15] and their ammunition. It also includes howitzers, aircraft bombs, anti-tank air-to-air missiles, anti-submarine torpedoes, parts, and munitions, which obviously cannot be considered SALW. It is not possible to know the SALW proportion in the B2 Group for the relevant years, but in the only separate account that exists, for 2002,[16] out of an overall total of USD 525.6 million, transfers of self- and non-self-propelled artillery were worth USD 175.7 millions; transfers of rocket and grenade launchers, torpedo tubes, and similar items reached USD 159.6 million; and items such as military rifles, shotguns, and machine guns totalled USD 190.3 million. Failing to consider at least part of B2 Group transfers as SALW trade leads to a severe underestimation of the value of SALW and renders items included in the UN definition of SALW unaccounted for. The United States (USD 17 billion) and United Kingdom (USD 5.2 billion) ranked in the first two positions, accounting for nearly 60 per cent of the trade.

The C2 Group combines swords, bayonets, and so forth, with air guns, rifles, pistols, and truncheons. The former are considered 'arms of war', the latter non-military arms. Neither comes under the UN definition.[17] Nevertheless, knives and bayonets are standard complements of many assault rifles and are widely used by special forces and insurgents,[18] while machetes have found tragic use in civil wars in countries such as Algeria, Angola, Liberia, Sierra Leone, and Uganda, to name just a few. Airguns, rifles, and pistols not only could be as lethal as firearms over a certain energy level,[19] but are regularly used for military and law-enforcement training[20] in addition to being a fast-growing 'introductory' market for prominent SALW manufacturers.[21]

> **Box 4.1 (cont.)** **Defining and counting SALW—a proposal for a new approach**
>
> It seems unlikely that, between 1994 and 2001, countries such as Algeria, Angola, Indonesia, and Sri Lanka, all involved in bloody civil wars, bought millions of dollars of cutlasses and bayonets for peaceful purposes, and air guns and pistols for the enjoyment of their youth. Imports of swords and bayonets reached USD 1.6 million in Algeria (1.2 million from China in 1998) and USD 14.2 million in Sri Lanka (13.7 million from Iran in 2000), while imports of airguns totalled USD 2.3 million in Algeria (1.8 million from Belarus in 1998), USD 4.5 million in Angola (3.9 million from Belarus in 1998), USD 9.3 million in Indonesia (mostly from the Republic of Korea), USD 5.3 million in Sri Lanka (3.8 million from Czech Republic between 1997 and 1998). Finally, a testimony of the worrisome side of C2 Group trade is that in 1994-2001 the Netherlands, Germany, and the United Kingdom, among others, classified hundreds of millions of dollars of imports and exports of these items. Between 1994 and 1998, in particular, the Netherlands kept the origin of USD 633 million of imports and the destinations of USD 732 million of exports classified.
>
> Written by Sergio Finardi and Carlo Tombola

Small arms imports

The largest importers by value in 2001 were the United States, Saudi Arabia, Cyprus, Japan, South Korea, Germany, and Canada.

It is even more difficult to give a complete picture of imports than of exports, for several reasons. First, estimates such as that made for China above cannot easily be made for imports, as demand is harder to model than supply. Modelling demand would require thorough knowledge of the procurement levels of civilians, armed forces, and law enforcement agencies worldwide. Second, although arms export reports are becoming increasingly common, they only very rarely detail arms imports (although this may be about to change).[22] Reliable sources are hence fewer. In Table 4.3, therefore, we rely on international customs data only. Such data do not record all state-to-state transfers since these do not always pass through customs. Similarly to the export data presented above, the picture of imports is incomplete also because some states do not report imports at all, and some under-report them (that is, report only on certain categories of small arms). Again, we have relied on mirror data to complement deficient import reports.

Table 4.3 shows that the largest importer of small arms by value in 2001 was, perhaps unsurprisingly, the US. It was followed by Saudi Arabia, Cyprus, Japan, South Korea, Germany, and Canada. The structure of imports for these countries varied substantially: while in Saudi Arabia, Cyprus, Japan, and South Korea military weapons were the most important import category, US imports were topped by shotguns, and Germany and Canada imported mostly small arms ammunition.

Of these importers, Cyprus is perhaps the most astonishing, given the small size of the island. The value of the guns is simply too large to be explained by local demand or international peacekeeping operations—1,248 men in 2003 (IISS, 2003)—but probably reflects an important, though opaque, transit trade. As noted in Small Arms Survey (2003, p. 105), Cyprus is a problematic destination for small arms transfers, not only because of the unsettled status of the island, but also as it is very unclear what happens to the large quantities of weapons that enter it every year. Russia, Italy, and Spain are important exporters to this country. As noted in the previous section, Saudi Arabia is a prominent importer, even though some of the small arms imports recorded in the customs data might have gone to US troops stationed in the country until recently.

Among medium-sized importers, Colombia, Israel, Lebanon, and Venezuela are problematic because of their internal situations. In a press release from August 2003, the Latin American organization Desarme (2003) strongly criticized European exports to Venezuela under the title 'European Firearms in Venezuela: No Code, No Conduct'. The organization claims that exports from EU countries such as Austria and Belgium violate the EU Code of Conduct (EU, 1998), given that firearms owned by state structures often end up in the hands of the pro-President Hugo Chávez Círculos Bolivarianos, the recently created Frente Bolivariano de Liberación, and the Colombian guerrilla group Fuerzas Armadas Revolucionarias de Colombia (FARC). The widespread civilian unrest in the country should also lead to restraint in small arms exports, Desarme argues.

Other possibly large importers on which little data is available, and whose imports are likely illicit rather than authorized (and which do not figure in Table 4.3) are those states involved in (internal or international) conflict, such as Liberia, Ivory Coast, Russia (Chechnya), Democratic Republic of Congo, Nepal, Burundi, Algeria, Sierra Leone, Somalia, Uganda, Sudan, and Sri Lanka. Details of exports to some of these countries and insurgent groups are found in the section on small arms transfers and human rights below.

Table 4.3   Annual authorized small arms imports, by country with most recent yearly data available (2001)

Country	USD value	Main known suppliers (top five)	Main known types of SALW imported	Remarks
Argentina	13.8m	US, Brazil, Italy, Switzerland, Spain	Ammunition, pistols/revolvers, hunting/sporting rifles, shotguns	
Australia	62.8m	US, Belgium, Italy, UK, Germany	Ammunition, military weapons, shotguns, pistols/revolvers, hunting/sporting rifles	
Austria	22.9m	Germany, Sweden, Belgium, Italy, Switzerland	Ammunition, shotguns, hunting/sporting rifles, parts of hunting/sporting rifles, military weapons	Does not report on its imports of military weapons and pistols/revolvers through international customs data. Hence the value is possibly underestimated.
Belgium	64.3m	Italy, Portugal, US, Japan, Germany	Shotguns, ammunition, hunting/sporting rifles, pistols/revolvers	Does not report on its imports of military weapons and pistols/revolvers through international customs data. Hence the value is possibly underestimated. Parts of imports might actually be returns for repairs.
Brazil	11.3m	US, Israel, Chile, Italy, France	Military weapons, ammunition, shotguns, hunting/sporting rifles, parts pistols/revolvers	Does not report on its imports of military weapons through international customs data (reliance on mirror data). Hence the value is possibly underestimated.
Canada	99.9m	US, Switzerland, Austria, Italy, Germany	Ammunition, parts sporting/hunting weapons, hunting/sporting rifles, pistols/revolvers	
Colombia	21.6m	US, Brazil, Italy, South Africa, Czech Republic	Military weapons, ammunition, pistols/revolvers, shotguns	Does not report on its imports of shotguns through international customs data (reliance on mirror data). Hence the value is possibly underestimated.
Cyprus	159.8m	Unspecified country, Russia, Italy, Spain, Japan	Military weapons, shotguns, ammunition, hunting/sporting rifles	'Unspecified country' means that the exporter is kept classified.
Denmark	20.5m	Germany, Canada, UK, Sweden, Italy	Ammunition, parts sporting/hunting weapons, shotguns, hunting/sporting rifles	
Finland	14.0m	Italy, Germany, Sweden, US, Norway	Ammunition, shotguns, parts of sporting/hunting weapons, hunting/sporting rifles	

Table 4.3 (cont.) Annual authorized small arms imports, by country with most recent yearly data available (2001)

Country	USD value	Main known suppliers (top five)	Main known types of SALW imported	Remarks
France	72.5m	Italy, Belgium, Germany, US, Saudi Arabia	Shotguns, hunting/sporting rifles, ammunition, parts sporting/hunting weapons	Does not report on its imports of military weapons and pistols/revolvers through international customs data. Hence the value is possibly underestimated. Saudi Arabia probably appears as supplier because of repairs/refitting.
Germany	104.2m	US, Italy, Switzerland, Saudi Arabia, Belgium	Ammunition, parts sporting/hunting weapons, shotguns, pistols/revolvers, hunting/sporting rifles	Does not report on its imports of military weapons and shotguns through international customs data. Hence the value is possibly underestimated. Saudi Arabia probably appears as supplier because of repairs/refitting.
Greece	48.2m	US, Italy, Germany, Portugal, Spain	Military weapons, shotguns, ammunition, pistols/revolvers	Does not report on its imports of military weapons and pistols/revolvers through international customs data. Hence the value is possibly underestimated.
Honduras	10.8m	Italy, US, Uruguay, Israel, Argentina	Military weapons, pistols/revolvers, ammunition, hunting/sporting rifles	
Israel	18.7m	US, Italy, South Korea, Czech Republic, Spain	Military weapons, parts of sporting/hunting weapons, ammunition, parts pistols/revolvers, pistols/revolvers	Does not report any imports through international customs data (reliance on mirror data). Hence the value is probably underestimated.
Italy	74.3m	US, Germany, Belgium, Turkey, Switzerland	Military weapons, ammunition, hunting/sporting rifles, parts hunting/sporting weapons, pistols/revolvers	Does not report on its imports of military weapons through international customs data (reliance on mirror data). Hence the value is possibly underestimated.
Japan	151.0m	US, Germany, Italy, Spain, Australia	Military weapons, ammunition, shotguns, pistols/revolvers	
Kuwait	11.8 m	US, Spain, Italy, Cyprus, Australia	Military weapons, ammunition, parts pistols/revolvers shotguns	Does not report any imports through international customs data (reliance on mirror data). Hence the value is probably underestimated.
Lebanon	12.3m	Italy, Cyprus, Russia, Turkey, France	Shotguns, hunting/sporting rifles, ammunition, parts sporting/hunting weapons	Does not report on its imports of military weapons through international customs data (reliance on mirror data). Hence the value is possibly underestimated.
Mexico	20.0m	US, Greece, Italy, Spain, Belgium	Ammunition, pistol/revolvers, military weapons, shotguns	
Netherlands	12.1m	US, Canada, Switzerland, Germany, Belgium	Ammunition, parts sporting/hunting weapons, military weapons, shotguns	Does not report on its imports of military weapons and pistols/revolvers through international customs data. Hence the value is possibly underestimated.
Norway	23.3m	Sweden, US, Germany, Italy, France	Ammunition, hunting/sporting rifles, shotguns, parts sporting/hunting weapons	
Portugal	33.6m	Belgium, Spain, Italy, US, Germany	Parts sporting/hunting weapons, shotguns, shotgun barrels, ammunition, hunting/sporting rifles	

Table 4.3 (cont.) Annual authorized small arms imports, by country with most recent yearly data available (2001)

Country	USD value	Main known suppliers (top five)	Main known types of SALW imported	Remarks
Saudi Arabia	261.3m	Belgium, US, Spain, Bulgaria, France	Military weapons, ammunition, parts pistols/revolvers, shotguns	
South Korea	105.7m	US, Italy, Germany, Russia, Spain	Military weapons, ammunition, pistols/revolvers, shotguns	
Spain	36.7m	Italy, US, Germany, Belgium, Portugal	Shotguns, hunting/sporting rifles, pistols/revolvers, ammunition	Does not report on its imports of military weapons through international customs data. Hence the value is possibly underestimated.
Sweden	22.2m	Finland, US, Germany, Austria, Italy	Ammunition, shotguns, hunting/sporting rifles, parts of sporting/hunting weapons, military weapons	Does not report on its imports of military weapons through international customs data (reliance on mirror data). Hence the value is possibly underestimated.
Switzerland	36.0m	Germany, Norway, US, Italy, Austria	Ammunition, pistols/revolvers, parts sporting/hunting weapons, military weapons, shotguns	
Taiwan	19.7m	US, South Korea, Italy, Spain, Germany	Military weapons, ammunition, shotguns, pistols/revolvers, parts pistols/revolvers	
Thailand	18.7m	US, Czech Republic, Germany, Singapore, Greece	Pistols/revolvers, ammunition, military weapons, shotguns	Does not report on its imports of military weapons through international customs data (reliance on mirror data). Hence the value is possibly underestimated.
Turkey	20.1m	Italy, Singapore, Poland, Slovakia, Spain	Military weapons, ammunition, pistols/revolvers, parts sporting/hunting weapons	
United Arab Emirates	32.4m	US, Switzerland, Germany, Brazil, Czech Republic	Military weapons, ammunition, pistols/revolvers hunting/sporting rifles	Does not report any imports through international customs data (reliance on mirror data). Hence the value is probably underestimated.
United Kingdom	78.3m	US, Italy, Belgium, Spain, Germany	Shotguns, military weapons, ammunition, hunting/sporting rifles	
US	602.5m	Italy, Brazil, Japan, Austria, Germany	Shotguns, pistols/revolvers, hunting/sporting rifles, ammunition, parts sporting/hunting weapons	
Venezuela	31.0m	South Korea, US, Austria, Italy, Spain	Ammunition, pistols/revolvers, shotguns, hunting/sporting rifles	

Source: NISAT (2003)

Box 4.2 Business as usual? The ECOWAS moratorium and authorized transfers

On 31 October 1998, the heads of state of ECOWAS proclaimed a moratorium on the import, export, and production of all small arms and light weapons within the region.[23] The moratorium, which originally ran for three years, was renewed for another three years in 2001, and it will be up for renewal yet again in the autumn of 2004. The ban is far-reaching: not only private companies but also ECOWAS governments that want to import small arms need an exemption in order to do so. The UN Programme for Coordination and Assistance for Security and Development (PCASED) is supposed to support the implementation of the moratorium. International support for the measure has been widespread, particularly at the outset. A number of EU governments (including France and the UK) as well as Canada have been among the financial supporters of the moratorium (Ogunbanwo, 2002). Support has also come from the UN and its various specialized agencies (UNSC, 2000b, p. 31).

West African leaders stand as the ECOWAS anthem is played at a meeting in Ghana in September 2002.

The moratorium notwithstanding, officials in the region 'acknowledge the existence of a large, and largely uncontrolled informal weapons trade and outright illicit trafficking' going 'far beyond normal levels of informal trade' (quoted in UNSC, 2000b, p. 31). This illicit trade is probably best documented in a series of UN Security Council reports on embargo violations in Liberia, Sierra Leone, and Angola (UNSC 2000a, 2000b, 2001, 2002) as well as in reports by Global Witness (2001, 2003) and Human Rights Watch (2001a, 2003). These reports show that there are well-organized networks trading simultaneously in arms, diamonds, timber, and other commodities, and making use of the lax regulations in particular in transport systems surveillance. In March 2003, the UN Security Council expressed 'its profound concern at the impact of the proliferation of small arms and light weapons, as well as mercenary activities, on peace and security in West Africa' (UNSC, 2003c).

However, there is also an ongoing authorized trade between the countries under the ECOWAS moratorium and the outside world, which has not been mentioned in assessments of the moratorium such as by Ebo and Mazal (2003) and Ogunbanwo (2002). For a transfer to the region to be in agreement with the moratorium, the importer has to request an exemption from the moratorium from other ECOWAS governments before importing small arms. Some exporting countries have adopted a policy of seeking assurances that exemptions have been granted before authorizing exports to ECOWAS countries. Table 4.4 lists transfers to the ECOWAS region, reported in international customs data, which shows a rather substantial authorized trade in small arms and ammunition with ECOWAS states. The data on transfers does not square with publicly available information on exemptions granted (Ebo with Mazal, 2003, p. 20; Ogunbanwo 2002, p. 14).

Table 4.4 is not meant to be exhaustive. The true extent of the authorized trade is in all likelihood greater, given that many ECOWAS states do not report their customs data internationally. Other sources, such as British and other export reports as well as, for example, Berman (2003), report on additional authorized transfers. It is therefore unclear what, if any, effects the moratorium has had on authorized transfers in the region.

> It is unclear whether the moratorium has had any effects on authorized transfers in the ECOWAS region.

Box 4.2 (cont.)   Business as usual? The ECOWAS moratorium and authorized transfers

Table 4.4   Authorized imports of SALW to ECOWAS countries, 1999–2002

Importing ECOWAS country	Main exporting countries, value in USD, years	Comments (types of SALW traded, quantities/values)
Benin	Burkina Faso: 21,840 in 1999–2001 France: 10,900 in 1999–2001	Reported imports of mostly revolvers and pistols from Burkina Faso Revolvers and pistols, sporting rifles, and shotguns from France.
Burkina Faso	Italy: 856,315 for 1999–2002 Czech Republic: 155,384 for 1999–2001 France: 75,982 in 1999–2002 Spain: 66,645 in 1999–2001 Senegal: 55,394 in 2002	Italy reported exports of mainly cartridges, but also revolvers and pistols and sporting rifles.
Cap Verde	Czech Republic: 27,595 in 2001 Portugal: 13,101 in 1999–2001	Reported imports of revolvers and pistols.
Côte d'Ivoire	South Africa: 1,225,081 in 1999 Spain: 76,391 in 2001 Italy: 60,550 in 1999–2001 US: 48,889 in 1999–2001 Czech Republic: 38,051 in 2001–02 France: 27,886 in 1999–2001 Switzerland: 12,104 in 1999–2001	South Africa reported exports of mostly cartridges but also military weapons, revolvers/pistols, and shotguns. Spain and the Czech Republic reported exports of only cartridges. Revolvers/pistols and shotguns reported from Italy. Military weapons and cartridges reported from the US. France reported exports of mainly shotguns and Switzerland revolvers/pistols.
The Gambia	United Kingdom: 449,145 in 1999 Czech Republic: 120,961 in 1999–2002 Russia: 31,134 in 1999 Poland: 28,107 in 2000 Lebanon: 10,760 in 2001	UK reported exports of parts and accessories of military weapons, cartridges. Reported imports of cartridges from the Czech Republic, Russia, and Poland. Lebanon reported exports of sporting rifles.
Ghana	Spain: 7,249,315 for 1999–2001 US: 2,823,245 in 1999–2002 UK: 2,156,203 in 1999–2001 Cyprus: 2,093,385 in 1999–2001 South Africa: 1,473,985 in 1999 Germany: 131,099 in 1999–2000 France: 52,909 in 1999	Spain's and France's reported exports consist of cartridges, and the UK's of mainly cartridges. US reported exports mainly of shotguns, cartridges, and military weapons. Cyprus and Germany report exporting mainly shotguns. South Africa reports exports of cartridges, military weapons, and shotguns.
Guinea	France: 3,342,698 in 1999–2001 Spain: 1,563,183 in 1999–2001 United Kingdom: 325,601 in 1999 Croatia: 258,949 in 2000 Portugal: 231,845 in 1999–2001 Germany: 83,358 in 1999–2000 Brazil: 42,731 in 1999 Senegal: 20,580 in 2000 Czech Republic: 15,391 in 1999 Georgia: 12,000 in 2000	France exported cartridges, sporting rifles, military weapons, shotguns, and parts and accessories from France. Only cartridges from Spain and the UK. Croatia reported exporting military weapons. Portugal reported exporting cartridges and shotguns. Only shotguns from Germany. Only cartridges from Brazil and Senegal. Czech Republic reported exporting cartridges. Georgia reported exporting parts and accessories.
Guinea-Bissau	Portugal: 332,054 in 1999–2001 Spain: 168,912 in 2000–1 France: 104,620 in 1999–2002	Portugal reported exports of cartridges, shotguns, revolvers/pistols, and sporting rifles. Spain and France reported exports of cartridges.
Liberia	*Under UN embargo, no imports therefore authorized*	
Mali	France: 72,327 in 1999–2002	France reported exports of mainly parts and accessories.
Niger	South Korea: 492,500 in 1999 France: 92,134 in 1999–2002 Italy: 60,643 in 1999–2001	South Korea reported exports of military weapons. Reported imports of revolvers, shotguns, parts and accessories, and cartridges from France; France reported exporting sporting rifles, cartridges, and shotguns. Reported imports of shotguns from Italy; Italy reported exporting revolvers.

SMALL ARMS SURVEY 2004

Table 4.4 (cont.)	Authorized imports of SALW to ECOWAS countries, 1999-2002	
Importing ECOWAS country	Main exporting countries, value in USD, years	Comments (types of SALW traded, quantities/values)
Nigeria	India: 2,799,653 in 2001 Israel: 2,385,595 in 1999 South Korea: 1,056,356 in 1999-2001 Indonesia: 597,500 in 1999 US: 246,007 in 1999-2002 Brazil: 126,793 in 2000-01 UK: 90,953 in 1999-2002 Italy: 49,074 in 2001 Australia: 20,243 in 2001 Germany: 13,062 in 1999	India reported exporting cartridges. Reports imports of shotguns from Israel. Reports imports of military weapons and revolvers from South Korea; South Korea reports exports of military weapons. US reported exporting mainly cartridges. Germany and Indonesia reported exporting revolvers/pistols. Brazil reported exporting sporting rifles and cartridges. UK reported exporting shotguns, cartridges, and parts. Italy reported exporting revolvers and shotguns. Australia reported exporting only revolvers.
Senegal	France: 2,246,810 in 1999-2002 US: 959,420 for 1999-2002 Spain: 426,508 for 2000-2002 Italy: 232,992 for 1999-2002 Brazil: 203,754 for 1999-2002 Germany: 116,770 for 1999-2002 Czech Republic: 81,996 in 2001-02	Only cartridges from Spain. Mainly revolvers and cartridges from Germany. Diversified imports from France, US, Italy, and Brazil. Cartridges, revolvers/pistols and shotguns from the Czech Republic.
Sierra Leone (only rebels are under UN embargo)	Lebanon: 196,949 in 2001 US: 29,542 in 2001 Spain: 13,398 in 2001 UK: 10,139 in 2000	Lebanon reported exports of military weapons. The US reported exports of parts and accessories. Spain and the UK reported exports of cartridges.
Togo	Spain: 41,212 in 2000	Spain reported exporting cartridges.

Note: The figures are likely underestimates of the total trade, as some important exporters and some of the ECOWAS states do not report on their trade, and we have thus had to rely on mirror data. Cut-off point for inclusion in table: USD 10,000 over four-year period covered.

Source: UN Comtrade, download date: July-August 2003

DEVELOPMENTS IN TRANSPARENCY: ANNUAL UPDATE

Transparency in the arms trade has three dimensions: intergovernmental transparency, parliamentary transparency, and public transparency (Bauer, 2003). Intergovernmental transparency consists of exchanges of information between governments, such as the information exchange on small arms and light weapons imports and exports among participating states of the Organization for Security and Cooperation in Europe (OSCE), or the exchange of information on various types of armaments within the Wassenaar Arrangement. Neither of these organizations makes public the information exchanged, even if individual states can choose to make their contributions to the exchange public (and have done so). Parliamentary transparency means that the government shares information on its export and import decisions with national parliamentarians. Both these forms of transparency can be combined with public transparency, meaning that information about arms transfers is released to the general public.

Transparency in the trade in small arms can constitute an important early-warning and confidence-building device, in particular in contexts where few major weapons are available (for example, in some parts of Africa and in many internal conflicts). It is important in enabling the general public to effectively monitor whether states follow international agreements and guidelines as well as their own laws and regulations on small arms exports and imports. Without transparency, citizens, parliamentarians, NGOs, and other governments cannot verify whether international commitments

TRANSFERS

are being met (Bauer, 2002), nor can they check whether arms transactions are free from corruption (Courtney, 2002).[24] More generally, without transparency, it is impossible to obtain an accurate picture of the small arms trade.[25]

The importance of transparency in the small arms and light weapons trade is increasingly acknowledged in multilateral forums. In December 2003, the Wassenaar Arrangement participating states added small arms and light weapons, including MANPADS, to the list of strategic goods on which they exchange information (Wassenaar Arrangement, 2003).

There have also long been calls to include small arms into the UN Register of Conventional Arms, especially from the African continent, where these types of weapons are crucial tools of war. In summer 2003, a group of governmental experts from more than 20 countries charged with the periodic review of the functioning of the Register proposed that the large-calibre artillery category be expanded to include smaller artillery pieces equal to or above 75mm (such as the very common 81mm and 82mm mortars). The expert group also proposed that the missile/launcher category should encompass MANPADS. The proposal won the UN General Assembly's approval in December 2003 (UNGA, 2003a). This means that some light weapons are now included in the information exchange, while all small arms (as per the UN definition) remain outside its scope. However, the group of experts recommended a voluntary sharing of information through the UN on transfers of all small arms and light weapons 'made or modified to military specification and intended for military use' (UNGA, 2003b, para. 113(e)). The main argument underlying such efforts is that it is important to push transparency levels in the SALW trade to the same level as trade in major conventional weapon systems. This is already the case in some regional forums. As already noted, since 2002 the OSCE participating states have exchanged information yearly on a number of small arms issues, notably transfers.[26]

Here, key information on levels of transparency of the larger small arms exporters (hence not all states) has been assembled in a Small Arms Trade Transparency Barometer (Table 4.5). A discussion on transparency on the small arms issue generally is found elsewhere in this volume (MEASURES).

> Both the Wassenaar Arrangement and the UN Register of Conventional Arms introduced some type of information exchange on light weapons in 2003.

The Small Arms Trade Transparency Barometer

Assessing and comparing countries' export reports is complicated, as their formats differ widely: from a few pages of statistics to several hundred pages of text and tables. The basic question around which the Small Arms Trade Transparency Barometer is constructed is: how useful is the export report for understanding a country's small arms exports? The barometer is divided into two main categories: *(a)* access, clarity, and comprehensiveness; and *(b)* information on granted and refused licences and on deliveries. The first category assesses how easy it is to obtain and understand the data provided by a state, and how comprehensive it is in general terms. The underlying assumption is that data which is difficult to access (because it is not available in any major language, not found on the Internet, and/or is not free of charge), difficult to decipher (because there is no methodology, no information on end-users, and it is impossible to distinguish small arms and small arms ammunition from other types of weapons and ammunition), or incomplete (because it does not cover all types of transactions, or all kinds of small arms and parts) is of limited use in understanding a country's small arms trade.

The second cluster of criteria relates to the detail of the data provided in a report on granted licences, denied licences, and actual deliveries. The analysis of granted and denied licences and deliveries is subdivided in the same way: values and volumes disaggregated by weapon type and by both country and weapon type. The data is disaggregated by weapon type if the share of arms exports of different categories of weapons is detailed (in the Romanian export report, for example, the breakdown of arms exports is shown: 15 per cent aircraft and related equipment, 13 per cent bombs, rockets, and

115

missiles, and so forth). The data is disaggregated both by country and by weapon if it is possible to read out the quantity/value of weapons of each category transferred to individual recipients (for example the Swiss report shows it exported CHF 880,000 (USD 570,000) of *small arms* to Egypt in 2002).[27] As a rule, one point is given to an export report for each criterion fulfilled.[28] A criterion that is only partly fulfilled is given half a point. For example, under the Wassenaar Arrangement's classification system, the first category of weapons consists purely of small arms, while the second category contains both small arms and light weapons and larger weapons systems. Hence, it is only partially possible to distinguish small arms and light weapons from other types of weapons, and only half a point is attributed on that particular criterion.

It is important to stress that the barometer evaluates the reporting, and cannot independently verify the veracity of the information given. In other words, the barometer assesses the quantity, precision, and usefulness of the data made public, but not its truthfulness.

The number of countries releasing some form of public data on their arms exports continues to increase. Countries that produce arms export reports generally provide the most comprehensive information, but some countries that do not (yet) publish such reports provide valuable information on small arms transactions through the international release of customs data. Although international customs data is not necessarily thought of as a transparency device, it provides important insights into trade, and is therefore included in the analysis on transparency in this section.

Customs data fills some of the gaps in many export reports, such as very general statistics that make no mention of small arms and that are not standardized. It has shortcomings of its own.[29] First, customs codes were obviously not designed with a definition of small arms and light weapons in mind, and some codes include both small and other (larger) arms (for example, the code 9301 includes both military small arms and items such as torpedo tubes and large mortars). Other small arms and light weapons, such as MANPADS, are not included in any category. However, most categories of firearms and ammunition are comparatively well covered by the customs codes (Marsh, 2003). Second, not all state-to-state transfers go through customs, which of course affects total numbers. Third, exporters and customs officials do not always interpret customs codes in the same way. For example, for the customs code 'pistols and revolvers', Brazil consistently reports 'nil', although import data from other countries suggests that it exports large quantities. The handguns must therefore be (mis-)classified under some other heading (Lessing, 2003). Notwithstanding such problems, customs data is probably the most important tool for arriving at a general picture of the small arms trade. This is why, in a departure from previous Small Arms Survey practice, this form of transparency, and not only export reports, is included in the Small Arms Trade Transparency Barometer.

The barometer is thus based on *(a)* export reports and *(b)* international customs data. The full, disaggregated table is found in Annex 4.4, available on the Small Arms Survey web site. It is important to note that, because of its focus on small arms exports, the barometer cannot be used as a general measure of arms export transparency. It includes only those countries that are significant exporters of small arms and light weapons (see Table 4.1), and so excludes some rather transparent countries, such as, for example, Denmark and the Netherlands. This also necessarily means that the focus is mainly (although not only) on Western and Eastern European as well as North American states, given that it is mostly among their ranks that significant exporters are found. As is shown in the barometer, the most transparent among the main exporting countries are those states that both publish export reports and report their customs data internationally. Top of the list are the United States, Germany, and France. The average score (out of 20) is 8.5. This rather low average means that states generally, and even those countries ranking at the top of the barometer, still have some way to go before their reporting is fully transparent.[30]

Table 4.5 Small Arms Trade Transparency Barometer, covering known or estimated top exporters, based on the latest export report made publicly available and on 2001 international customs data (UN Comtrade)[31]

Country and source(s) available (E = export report, C = customs data)		Total points (20 points max)	Access (2 points max)	Clarity (4 points max)	Compre-hensiveness (4 points max)	Information on deliveries (disaggregated by weapons type, and by country and weapons type) Value of deliveries (V) Quantity of weapons (Q) (4 points max)	Information on licences granted (disaggregated by weapons type and by country and weapons type) Value of licences (V) Quantity of weapons (Q) (4 points max)	Information on licences refused (disaggregated by weapons type and by country and weapons type) Value of weapons (Q) (2 points max)
United States	E C	15	2	3	4	2	4	0
Germany	E C	14.5	2	3	4	2	3	0.5
France	E C	13	2	3.5	3.5	4	0	0
Italy	E C	12	2	3	3	2	2	0
Czech Rep.	EC	11.5	2	2.5	4	3	0	0
Sweden	E C	11	2	2	3	2	2	0
UK	E C	11	2	3	4	2	0	0
Canada	E C	10.5	2	3	3.5	2	0	0
Spain	E C	10.5	2	3	3.5	2	0	0
Finland	E C	10	2	3	3	2	0	0
Belgium	E C	9.5	2	2.5	3	2	0	0
Australia	E C	9	2	2	3	2	0	0
Norway	E C	9	2	2.5	2.5	2	0	0
Switzerland	E C	8.5	2	2	2.5	2	0	0
Portugal	E C	7.5	2	2	1.5	2	0	0
Turkey	C	7.5	1.5	2	2	2	0	0
Austria	C	7	1.5	2	1.5	2	0	0
Brazil	C	7	1.5	2	1.5	2	0	0
Romania	E	7	2	1.5	2.5	1	0	0
Japan	C	6.5	1.5	2	1	2	0	0
Russian Federation	C	6.5	1.5	2	1	2	0	0
South Korea	C	6.5	1.5	2	2	1	0	0
Mexico	C	6	1.5	2	0.5	2	0	0
China	C	5.5	1.5	2	0	2	0	0
Israel	C	5.5	1.5	2	0	2	0	0
South Africa	E	4	2	1	1	0	0	0
Bulgaria		0	0	0	0	0	0	0

Information as of December 2003.
Please check
www.smallarmssurvey.org/barometer
for regularly updated and revised information.

Sources: UN Comtrade, download date 31 Oct 2003, Australia (2003), Belgium (2003), Canada (2002), Finland (2002), France (2003), Germany (2002), Italy (2003), Norway (2003), Portugal (2002), Romania (2002), South Africa (2002), Spain (2003), Sweden (2003), Switzerland (2003), UK (2003), United States Department of State (2003)

Notes: Includes the following parameters:
(a) **Access:** Information is: available on Internet (half point); available in a UN language (1 point); free of charge (half point);
(b) **Clarity:** The reporting includes methodology (1 point); small arms and light weapons distinguishable from other types of weapons (1 point); SALW ammunition distinguishable from other types of ammunition (1 point); reporting includes information on end-user categories (military; police; other security forces; civilians directly; civilian retailers) (1 point).
(c) **Comprehensiveness:** The reporting covers: government as well as industry-negotiated transactions (1 point); civilian as well as military SALW (1 point); information on SALW parts (1 point); summaries of export laws and regulations as well as international commitments (1 point).

SMALL ARMS SURVEY 2004

> **Box 4.3 Transparency developing in leaps: Romanian arms export reporting**
>
> For the countries that entered the European Union on 1 May 2004,[32] export reports are few and far between, although some are quite generous in sharing their customs data.
>
> In fact, to date, one of the most ambitious countries in this respect seems to be Romania, which is not scheduled to become a member of the Union until 2007 at the earliest. The Romanian export report was published for the first time in mid-2002 and is available in English online (Romania, 2002). Challenges facing the author are very frankly noted in the foreword to the report. In particular, there was a 'genuine "confrontation" between the necessity of transparency and the conservative approach of some senior Romanian experts' (Romania, 2002, p. iv).
>
> The report covers both private and public sector exports. It lists the numbers of companies authorized to trade in various categories of weapons. The information provided on export licences is rather sparse. While total numbers of licence applications, denials, and approvals are noted and—unlike in most other export reports—values for all three categories are given, they are broken down only by region, not by country or weapon type. The part on licensing also quantifies permits issued for non-commercial operations. ML1, ML2, and ML3 are said to be among the main categories of these operations.
>
> In fact, the report uses the weapons categories of the Wassenaar Arrangement. There, the first category, ML1, covers 'arms and automatic weapons with a calibre of 12.7 mm or less and accessories… and specially designed components therefore'; and the second, ML2, 'armament or weapons with a calibre greater than 12.7 mm, projectors and accessories… and specially designed components therefore'. ML3 encompasses 'ammunition and specially designed components therefore, for the weapons controlled by ML1, ML2, or ML12'. In principle, ML1 is the only pure SALW category, with ML2 and ML3 containing important elements of non-SALW. However, the report states that 'in the structure of Romanian arms exports, the small calibre arms (ML1) represent the most important segment, [together with] light weapons (ML2) and the related munitions (ML3)' (Romania, 2002, p.35). This seems to indicate that, in the Romanian case, ML1, ML2, and ML3 contain only, or primarily, SALW.
>
> The report notes that in 2000 ML1 and ML2 (presented together) accounted for 34 per cent of actual exports, whereas ML3 covered 36 per cent. Based on total arms exports (USD 37.8 million according to the report), ML1 and ML2 accounted for USD 12.85 million, and ML3 USD 13.61 million. Totals for 2001 were: ML1 and ML2 55 per cent, and ML3 only 8 per cent, which gives values of USD 13.48 million and USD 1.96 million (total exports were USD 24.5 million). The report does not detail shipments by country.
>
> Although far from perfectly transparent, the report provides more SALW-relevant information than, say, the Australian or the Portuguese reports (Romania obtains a lower ranking on the Small Arms Trade Transparency Barometer than these two countries because it does not report customs data internationally).
>
> Overall, the report is a positive example of an emerging export transparency measure, and significant efforts have been devoted to its preparation. It remains to be seen, however, to what extent the practice is sustained over time. The Czech Republic published a special report on small arms exports in 2001, in time for the UN Small Arms Conference (see Small Arms Survey, 2002, p. 118), and has continued reporting since. Without sufficient political will, the same might not be true for Romania.
>
> Source: Kytömäki (2003)

Romania's first report on arms exports.

© Romanian National Agency for the Control of Strategic Exports and of Prohibition of Chemical Weapons/image: Nicolae Grigorescu

EXPORTING SMALL ARMS: A QUESTION OF SURVIVAL FOR PRODUCERS?

As many analysts have noted, arms production has been transformed in recent decades. It is no longer an industry catering largely to internal needs and exporting selectively (based on political considerations), but a for-profit, export-oriented industry like many others (Naylor, 1998). More wide-ranging exports are thought essential to maintaining a technological edge and economic viability. To what extent is this true for military (as well as non-military) small arms and light weapons production? Does the fact that the US is the top exporter (see previous section) mean that its small arms industry is dependent on exports for its long-term viability? To answer questions such as these, exporting has to be seen in the context of production.

The top small arms producing countries have been listed in previous editions of the *Small Arms Survey*. Focusing on two of the three major producers (Russia and the US) as well as a few medium producers (Germany and Brazil), this section shows that the degree of export dependency varies among producing countries and firms.

US: limited dependence, but for military weapons [33]

In general, US small arms manufacturers are not very dependent on exports for their revenue—manufacturers export on average only about 5–6 per cent of total small arms production, according to the US Bureau of Alcohol, Tobacco, Firearms and Explosives (ATF) data (see Table 4.6).[34] Using customs data slightly increases this share, to 9.7 per cent of all small arms produced in 2001. However, there are problems with using data from two different sources, as methodologies differ. Whatever the sources used, the export dependency of the US small arms industry is less than 10 per cent.

Table 4.6   Total quantity of firearms produced and exported by US manufacturers, 1998–2001

Year	Quantity produced	Quantity exported	% exported
1998	3,724,546	215,873	5.8
1999	4,070,237	242,573	6.0
2000	3,840,941	184,346	4.8
2001	2,989,022	182,632	6.1
Total 1998-2001	14,624,746	825,424	Average: 5.6

Source: US, ATF (1998, 1999, 2000, 2001)

However, when one looks at specific years, companies, or types of weapons, the picture seems slightly different. In fact, there are significant variations in export dependency among companies. In 2001, the latest year for which data is available, pistol producer Davis Industries exported 100 per cent of its production, while a large producer of pistols such as Bryco Arms did not export any arms. Among the most important producers, Smith and Wesson was by far the most export dependent in 2001, exporting 15.5 per cent of pistols and 28.6 per cent of revolvers produced. Its competitor Sturm Ruger & Co, in contrast, exported between 1.5 per cent (pistols) and 3.8 per cent (rifles) of its total production in 2001 (for more details, see Annex 4.2 available on the Small Arms Survey Web site).

In addition, certain types of small arms are exported to a larger extent than others. This is outlined in Figure 4.1 below. Machine guns, short-barreled rifles and shotguns, and 'miscellaneous firearms' (generally muzzle loading) are exported to a much higher degree than other types of small arms (pistols, revolvers, rifles, and shotguns), although data varies from year to year (exact percentages are presented in Annex 4.3 available on the Small Arms Survey Web site).

A close look at the data in Table 4.6 above reveals that US production and export levels have gone very largely hand in hand. Hence, in 1998, when 3.7 million weapons were produced, 0.22 million (5.8 per cent) were exported. Three years later, in 2001, production had decreased substantially, to 3.0 million weapons. Export numbers followed suit, to 0.18 million. The percentage share has remained more or less constant, at 6.1 per cent SALW exported in 2001

There are significant variations in export dependency among US companies.

(the average for 1998–2001 is 5.6). Declines in recent years in US exports of both military and civilian small arms should therefore be interpreted in the context of declining total domestic production: declining exports in absolute numbers do not necessarily signify that the US is becoming less dependent on export markets.

Figure 4.1   Export dependence of US small arms manufacturers, by type of weapon, 1998–2001

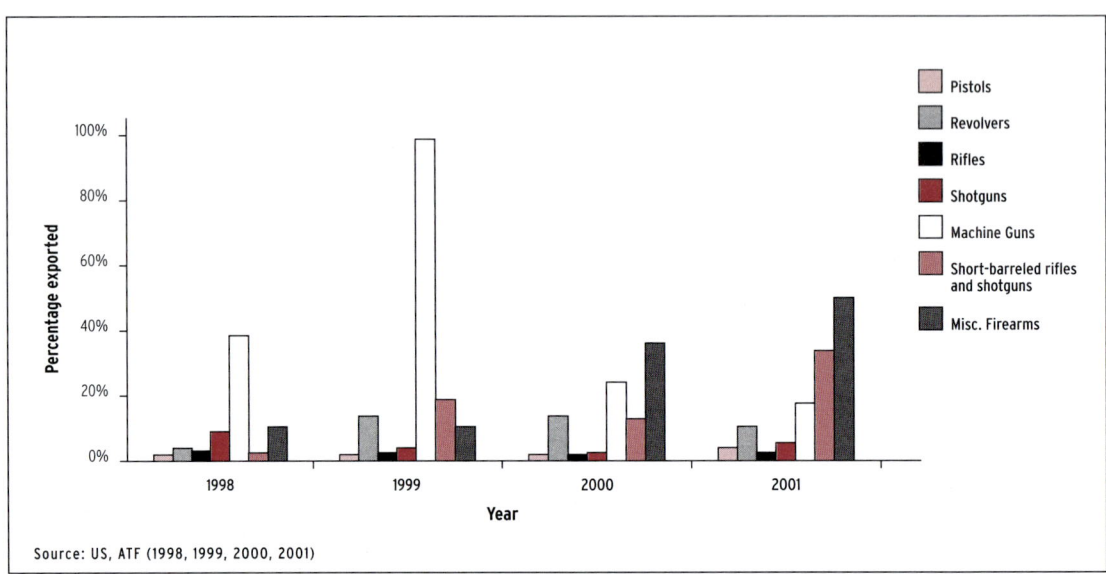

Source: US, ATF (1998, 1999, 2000, 2001)

Although not particularly dependent on exports generally, US exporters tend to rely on a few markets only: of the 115,950 sporting shotguns and combination shotgun-rifles exported in 2002, 32 per cent were imported by the United Kingdom, 15 per cent by Spain, and 9 per cent by Canada; these top three importers thus accounted for 56 per cent of the US exports of these weapons (US, Department of Commerce, 2003). The United Kingdom was also the top importer of military shotguns, with 36 per cent of the market, followed by New Zealand with 23 per cent. As for military rifles, the US exported 73 per cent of these to Middle Eastern countries in 2002. Kuwait was the major destination with 35 per cent, followed by Israel with 21 per cent. Another significant importer was Nepal (10 per cent). The top destination of US machine guns was South Korea, which imported 48 per cent of the 21,465 total machine guns that were exported by the US in 2002. After South Korea come Colombia (23 per cent) and Malaysia (18 per cent) (US, Department of Commerce, 2003). US exports of pistols and revolvers (73,262 weapons exported in 2002) are less concentrated; however, the top five importers account for 50 per cent of the US export market. Belgium is at the top with 19 per cent, followed by Japan (12 per cent), Germany (8 per cent), Thailand (6 per cent), and Venezuela (5 per cent). As for hunting and sporting rifles of a value less than USD 50 each, the United Kingdom is the largest importer, importing 63 per cent of the 17,721 such weapons exported by the US in 2002. For hunting and sporting rifles valued at over USD 50, Canada is the top importer with 34 per cent of the 72,025 rifles exported globally (US, Department of Commerce, 2003).

As mentioned elsewhere in this chapter, there are caveats to this data. It is not always clear when arms pass through customs whether they have actually arrived at their final destination. In some cases, weapons are sent back to the manufacturer for repair or refurbishing, and returned once the repairs are completed. This may explain why

Belgium has a high rate of imports, as it is a major exporter of handguns to the US. Also, sometimes weapons passing through customs may be used by military troops deployed abroad. It is possible that some of the weapons being sent to the Middle East are assigned to the US troops presently stationed there. Finally, the US and Canada jointly manufacture some types of small arms, and some of the US–Canada trade that appears in customs data could consist of weapons that are crossing the border to be finished in Canada.

Although US exports depend on single destinations, top customers seem to change over time. Table 4.7 shows sharp declines in exports of pistols and revolvers to Thailand and the Philippines since 1995. Similarly, the two countries made large purchases of military rifles in the late 1990s and, since then, imports have decreased dramatically. While Israel had seen a steady decline in imports of military rifles from the US over the past few years, 2002 goes against this trend.

Table 4.7 Emerging and declining customers for US exports (quantity of weapons exported), 1995–2003

Year	Thailand (pistols and revolvers)	Thailand (military rifles)	Philippines (pistols and revolvers)	Philippines (military rifles)	Israel (military rifles)	Nepal (military rifles)
1995	43,595	0	17,407	0	740	0
1996	20,362	510	18,860	0	62,277	0
1997	7,066	685	9,640	6,054	32,625	4,000
1998	7,962	10,100	2,817	20,256	40,350	0
1999	7,330	19,428	5,410	924	10,055	0
2000	6,003	16,645	50	0	2,843	0
2001	6,553	1	1,046	328	3,442	0
2002	4,230	0	1,883	76	6,375	3,000
2003*	1,437	102	788	184	40	3,400

* January–July

Source: US ATF, various years

Russia: important export share[35]

Since the early 1990s, Russian small arms manufacturers have substantially restructured their production (PRODUCERS). From the late 1980s and up until the last couple of years, the Russian armed forces basically did not acquire any new arms, and government orders for ammunition plummeted (Pyadushkin, 2003). At the same time, current Russian legal regulations make legal, large-scale sales of small arms to ordinary Russians impossible (Pyadushkin, 2003). Hence today most Russian small arms producing companies are not operating at their full capacity, and the serial production of military small arms has virtually stopped (Pyadushkin, 2003, p. 3). Moreover, companies have increasingly turned to production of cars, machine tools, instruments, and other purely civilian products.

All these problems with the internal market notwithstanding, Russia remains a top producer of small arms and light weapons, thanks in no small part to a successful turn to exporting them. Current knowledge about the Russian small arms industry suggests that approximately half of production is exported (Table 4.8; the main recipients are listed in Table 4.1). However, information is scarce about the two state-owned companies, KBP and Kolomna MBDB.

SMALL ARMS SURVEY 2004

Table 4.8 Exports of civilian and combat SALW from Russia in 2002, by manufacturer

Company (products)	SALW sales/production volume, USD m	Export volume, USD m	Exports as % of total sales/production
Izhevsk Arms Factory (Izhmash) (automatic sniper rifles, hunting and sporting shotguns and rifles)	13.1	3.2	24
IMZ (hunting and sporting shotguns)	52	15.7	30.2
TOZ (handguns, automatic and sniper rifles, anti-tank guided missiles, hunting and sporting shotguns and rifles)	29.2*	1.2**	4 (most likely an underestimate)
Kovrov Mechanical Plant (machine guns, grenade launchers, ATGMs)	2.5	No data available	
V.A. Degtyaryov Plant (MANPADS, machine guns)	108.5	86.8***	80
Molot (ATGM, hunting weapons)	16.4	1.2	7.3
Total	221.7	108.1	

Note: As more detailed information is currently unavailable, export volumes may include other products besides SALW.
* Total sales, including combat and civilian SALW as well as civilian goods.
** Only civilian firearms.
*** Calculated on the basis of the correlation between different types of production in 2001. Military production: 50% of total, 80% of military production is exported. See Interfax (2003).

Source: CAST (2003)

Interestingly, Russian small arms producers are less export-dependent than was previously thought.

Interestingly, Russian small arms producers are less export-dependent than previously thought (Pyadushkin, 2003). Hunting and sporting rifles are finding domestic customers. For example, according to the (imperfect) figures currently available, 70 per cent of IMZ's civilian weapons are sold to Russian amateur hunters, most probably in the larger cities. The Izhevsk Arms Factory exported 24 per cent of its production of civilian firearms in 2002; the rest were sold domestically. The largest foreign customer was the US, which received about 23 per cent of the exports. Combat small arms also seem to have found domestic customers recently (in the form of the Russian Ministry of Defence). While Izhevsk Arms Factory exported 71.3 per cent of its production of combat small arms in 2000, and 88.3 per cent in 2001, the figure had fallen to 26.5 per cent in 2002. However, it is probably too early to speak of a trend towards production for domestic army consumption.

Table 4.9 Combat small arms export by Izhevsk Arms Factory, 2000–02

Year	2000	2001	2002
Value of exports (in USD millions)	3.4	1.7	0.85
% of total combat small arms production	71.3	88.3	26.5

Note: Calculated on the basis of the correlation between different types of production in 2001. Military production: 50 per cent of total, 80 per cent of military production is exported. See Interfax (2003).

Source: CAST (2003)

Some other large producers: the importance of being an exporter

As discussed in further detail elsewhere in this volume (PRODUCERS), *Brazil*[36] is the largest producer of small arms and light weapons (including ammunition) in Latin America, and its output is the most diversified in the entire hemisphere after the US. It is heavily dependent on exports. According to Brazilian government statistics for 2001, the total sales of nationally produced non-military firearms (including ammunition and parts) amounted to approximately USD 100.3 million (IBGE, 2002).[37] Total exports for the same year were USD 62.5 million, or 62.3 per cent of total sales.[38] The actual export share may be even higher, given that the publicly available trade statistics do not include state-to-state transfers. Not all Brazilian companies are equally dependent on exports. For example, while for Companhia Brasileira de Cartuchos (CBC, producing ammunition, shotguns, and rifles) exports amounted to approximately 34 per cent of total sales in 2002, Taurus, Brazil's largest exporter of guns and a major supplier of handguns to the United States, reported exports of USD 38.1 million in 2002, totalling 74 per cent of its sales. For Amadeo Rossi, a small producer (of shotguns and rifles), the share was 77 per cent.[39]

Brazil is heavily dependent on exports to one market: the US. In 2000 and 2001, exports to the US accounted for 54 per cent (USD 37.6 million) and 59 per cent (USD 37 million) of total small arms exports, respectively.[40] In 2002, exports to the US increased to USD 55.7 million. Presumably, this is not because the US was more important for Brazilian exporters but because of an overall increase in exports as a consequence of the devaluation of the Brazilian currency, the *real*. Other significant recipients of Brazilian weapons in the last years have been Algeria, Colombia, and Germany (see Table 4.10).

By comparison, Argentina, the only other Latin American producer and exporter of any significance (close to USD 6 million in exports in 2001 and 7 million in 2002), is equally dependent on exports to the United States for its survival. The two main privately owned small arms producing companies, Bersa S.A. and Lasserre S.A. (also known as Rexio), are highly dependent on exports of their products (mainly pistols). Bersa, for example, exported 70 per cent of its production in 2002, and the United States overshadows all other recipients by far.[41]

> In 2000 and 2001, Brazilian exports to the United States accounted for about 55–60 per cent of its total small arms exports.

Table 4.10 Brazilian SALW-related commercial exports, top ten recipients, 1998–2002, in USD

1998		1999		2000		2001		2002	
US	27,621,389	US	36,258,797	US	37,645,729	US	36,959,632	US[42]	55,687,807
Belgium	3,380,755	Germany	2,677,782	United Arab Emirates	7,245,303	Colombia	3,858,170	Colombia	5,911,905
Argentina	3,128,677	Argentina	2,622,543	Argentina	2,662,638	Algeria	2,781,100	Germany	2,489,520
Peru	2,816,820	Peru	1,773,674	Venezuela	2,165,468	Germany	2,312,778	Algeria	2,486,360
Venezuela	2,611,164	Chile	1,397,566	Germany	2,077,718	Argentina	2,123,972	Singapore	2,107,306
Saudi Arabia	2,153,441	Angola	1,321,800	Angola	2,001,841	Belgium	1,864,062	Belgium	1,889,635
Germany	2,147,762	Philippines	977,809	Peru	1,919,267	United Arab Emirates	1,341,302	Pakistan	1,873,940
Colombia	2,128,483	Norway	889,069	Colombia	1,493,883	Yemen	1,096,240	Botswana	1,832,855
Paraguay	2,085,896	Paraguay	857,460	Chile	1,116,986	Angola	887,000	UK	1,758,934
South Africa	1,651,543	South Africa	704,627	New Zealand	1,010,384	Malaysia	816,312	Argentina	1,067,541

Source: SECEX (Secretaria de Comércio Exterior) database

Germany is one of the biggest European producers of small arms, and also one of the largest exporters. Its export share is even more impressive than that of Brazil: 92 per cent of all pistols and revolvers produced were exported in 2001; in 2002, 86 per cent of weapons in this category were sold abroad (see Table 4.12). For hunting and sporting rifles, export appear to be equally important for the industry.

German *imports* of pistols and revolvers are rather limited. In 2001, a little more than 35,000 pistols and revolvers were imported into Germany; in 2002, the figure was approximately 37,000. This means that, even if Germany put restrictions on imports, German companies could not continue producing at current levels. In contrast, import and export of hunting and sporting weapons reach similar levels. For hunting and sporting rifles, the import figures were a little more than 68,000 in 2001 and over 60,000 in 2002.

SMALL ARMS SURVEY 2004

Box 4.4 European export dependency on US civilian markets

The American market for firearms is the largest in the world, and has been growing in recent years, from 754,102 firearms (handguns, rifles, and shotguns) in fiscal year 1980 and 843,809 in 1990, to 1,096,782 in 2000 and 1,957,563 in 2002. All categories of firearms imports have grown, most spectacularly imports of handguns (*International Firearms Trade*, 2003, pp. 2, 10).

An important share of these imports comes from the member states of the European Union (see also Table 4.3 above). For example, out of the roughly 950,000 handguns imported in 2002, some 470,000—or 50 per cent—came from the EU (US, Department of Commerce, 2003). Ironically, given a tendency of Europeans to disapprove of the permissive US gun policies and gun culture,[43] many European companies would in all likelihood have some difficulty surviving without the US civilian market. Table 4.11 shows that around half of all EU exports of handguns, rifles, and shotguns are destined for the US. While some of these—handguns in particular—undoubtedly go to US law enforcement agencies and armed forces, many probably go to the US civilian market. Of the top five EU exporters of firearms (Austria, Belgium, Germany, Italy, and Spain), Austria is the most dependent on US markets (72 per cent of Austrian handguns, rifles, and shotguns go to the US). Italy comes second, with just over half of its total exports of these three categories of weapons going to the US. Belgium is least dependent on US markets, with only 19 per cent of weapons in the three categories exported to the US.

What is missing from this picture is, of course, total production (rather than exports) of handguns, rifles, and shotguns within the EU countries. Such figures would make it possible to determine the overall dependence of producers on exports to the US. Information on Germany presented above suggests that dependency on exports is high, but similar data is not readily available for other European countries. Also missing is the overseas production of European firms such as Heckler & Koch, and Beretta.

Table 4.11 Percentage of EU exports of non-military small arms (by value) destined for the US, 2001, ranked by total share of exports (three categories) going to the US

EU country	Pistols	Shotguns	Hunting rifles	All three weapons categories
Austria	78	21	6	72
United Kingdom	2*	71	63	65
Italy	40	60	35	56
Sweden	65*	29*	32*	41
Spain	68	34	44	41
Finland	4*	0*	43	40
Greece	0*	44*	0*	38*
Germany	44	25	16	34
Portugal	53	2	43	30
Netherlands	0*	90*	24*	26*
Belgium	59	4	34	19
Denmark	90*	0*	1*	14
France	12*	2	4	4
Ireland	0*	0*	0*	0*
Luxemburg	0*	No exports in this category	0*	0*
Total	**58**	**48**	**31**	**48**

Note: * Total sales in this category amount to less than USD 1 million.

Source: NISAT 2003

Table 4.12 German production and exports of selected civilian weapons, 2001-02 (numbers of weapons)

	2001			2002		
	Production	Export	% exported	Production	Export	% exported
Pistols and revolvers	159,571	147,379	92	197,688	169,029	86
Hunting and sporting rifles	48,400*	43,751	90	52,300*	50,264	96

* Production volumes of one category of hunting and sporting weapons (out of four), 'other hunting and sporting guns', has been estimated from production values.

Source: Production figures from Statistisches Bundesamt (2003), trade figures from Verband der Hersteller von Jagd-, Sportwaffen und Munition, private communication (compiled from Statistisches Bundesamt).

SMALL ARMS TRANSFERS AND HUMAN RIGHTS: MAKING THE CONNECTION

A number of regional and multilateral agreements explicitly cite human rights[44] as a criterion when deciding whether to authorize arms exports. Although most of these, including the European Union *Code of Conduct on Arms Exports* (EU, 1998), the OSCE *Principles Governing Conventional Arms Transfers* (OSCE 1993), the OSCE *Document on Small Arms and Light Weapons* (OSCE, 2000), and the Wassenaar Arrangement's *Best Practice Guidelines for Exports of Small Arms and Light Weapons (SALW)* (2002) are not legally binding, they are starting to generate legally binding commitments. For example, the rules included in the EU Code of Conduct have been integrated into Belgian law, so as to render it compulsory in Belgium (Belgium, 2003, p. 2).[45]

Some national legislation and regulations contain human rights criteria, such as for example the 'Leahy Law' in the United States and the Swedish guidelines for arms exports. Far from all do, however. Moreover, states interpret human rights criteria differently. A now almost classic example is the Belgian decision in 2002 to grant a licence for exports to Nepal, which had earlier been denied by Germany. The Belgian foreign minister found the sale 'eminently ethical' as it would help a weakened democracy fight terrorism (BICC, 2003, Box U.18).

International lawyers and activists argue that states are bound by existing international human rights law when deciding upon a transfer. A transferring state incurs derivative responsibility for violations of international law committed by the recipient, given that the transferring state is aware of the situation in the recipient state (see Gillard, 2000, and Small Arms Survey, 2003, pp. 224–5 for further details).

More specifically, there are at least two ways in which the human rights criterion can be interpreted with respect to transfers, which is illustrated in several of the above-mentioned documents. For example, the second criterion of the EU Code of Conduct states in its first paragraph that EU states will 'not issue an export licence if there is a clear risk that the proposed export might be used for internal repression'.[46] In the second paragraph, it is established that EU member states will 'exercise special caution and vigilance in issuing licences, on a case-by-case basis and taking account of the nature of the equipment, to countries where serious violations of human rights have been established by the competent bodies of the UN, the Council of Europe, or by the EU' (EU, 1998). The main principle is thus *not to deliver materiel which forseeably could be used in human rights violations.* However, the language also points to a second principle governing exports to human rights abusers, namely, that *all weapons exports to perpetrators of grave*

SMALL ARMS SURVEY 2004

violations of human rights are to be conducted with a high degree of caution. These two criteria implicitly or explicitly underlie much of the general debate on weapons transfers and human rights violations.

In what follows, examples will be given of exports of small arms to those countries in which some of the world's most serious human rights violations have occurred; it will also examine the use of specific imported firearms in human rights violations.

Tracing weapons from provider to perpetrator: good progress

A number of attempts to trace the use of specific imported small arms in human rights abuses have been made. Recently, Jürgen Grässlin (2003) has traced in detail the role of German Heckler & Koch G-3 guns in the individual destinies of a woman in Somaliland and a Kurdish man in Turkey, destinies marked by human rights violations.

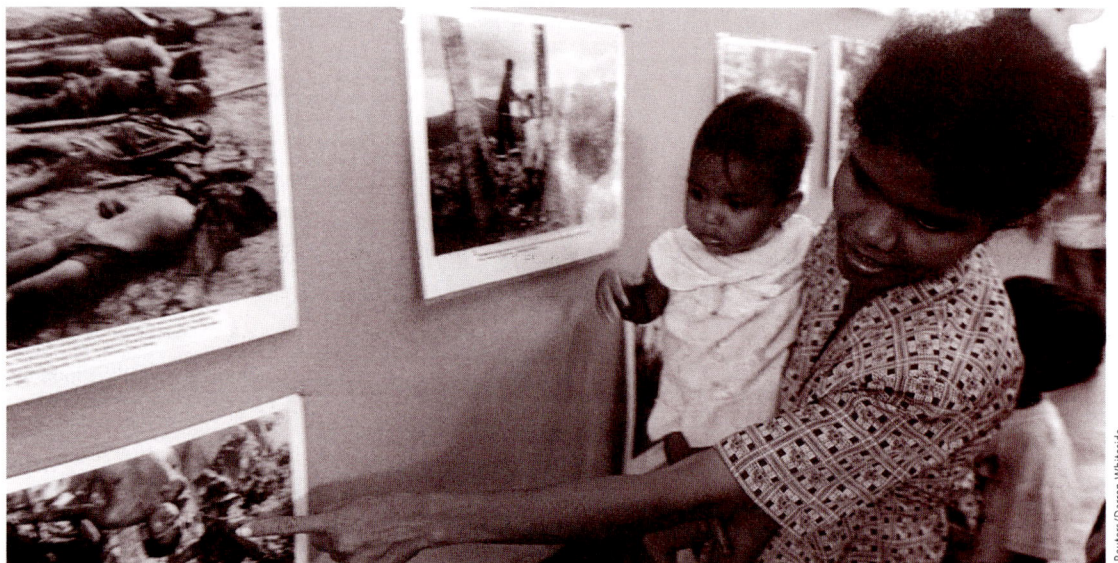

Carrying her baby, an East Timorese woman points to exhibition photos of human rights violations committed by Indonesian forces in East Timor.

Amnesty International has highlighted a range of cases in which human rights have been violated with imported arms. One of the first cases reported concerned Finnish bullets used in East Timor. Following an attack by a paramilitary militia in the capital of East Timor, Dili, on 17 April 1999, Amnesty researchers collected the casings of bullets reportedly fired by the militia at the scene. Amnesty later found that the casings had been manufactured in Finland by Patria Lapua Oy. The story created a considerable stir in Finland (Amnesty International, 1999). Amnesty has since continued its work with tracing weapons used in human rights violations. It traced munitions used in the fighting between Ugandan and Rwandese forces over Kisangani in north-eastern Democratic Republic of Congo in 2000, in which many civilians died. Amnesty researchers collected, amongst other things, North Korean and Russian 14.5mm cartridges (for heavy machine guns), Chinese 12.7mm cartridges (also for heavy machine guns), Russian cartridges for Nagant revolvers, South African (Armscor) 7.62mm ammunition (possible date 1981), and a Chinese (Norinco) cartridge from 37mm ammunition for type 55 anti-aircraft weapon (Amnesty International, 2002; Amnesty International and Oxfam, 2003, p. 10). Similar cases have involved Austrian Glock pistols in East Timor and 9mm Browning handguns in Jamaica (Amnesty International, 2003c, 2003d).

TRANSFERS

Human Rights Watch has also documented the origin of weapons used in human rights violations in both conflict and non-conflict situations. In an incident of excessive use of police force in Zambia in 1997, the organization traced the bullet used to seriously injure opposition leader Rodger Chongwe back to the manufacturing country, the former Yugoslavia. The bullet had reportedly been fired without prior warning and as the opposition leader was leaving a peaceful rally that the police had disrupted (HRW, 1998a, pp. 12–13). In a more recent case, the organization traced the origin of remnants of mortar rounds found in Monrovia, Liberia, after the indiscriminate killing of civilians by rebels during the 2003 fighting. It found that the mortar rounds (81mm and 60mm, produced in 2001 and 2002) had been purchased by Guinea (which at the time had a seat on the UN Security Council) from Iran earlier the same year and transferred to Liberia, which was under a UN embargo (HRW, 2003). Other cases have involved, for example, detailing the arms inventories of Sudanese government forces (in its 1998 report, Human Rights Watch found that the small arms came from a large number of states, including China, France, Hungary, Iran, Israel, Russia, South Africa, Sweden, United Kingdom, and the former Yugoslavia) (HRW, 1998b), and the ammunition used in extrajudicial executions in Kosovo in 1998.

Similarly, in an investigative newspaper report, Paul Salopek of the *Chicago Tribune* first described the harsh living conditions of a Romanian employee of a Kalashnikov factory. He then went on to outline the activities of Grace Ikombi, a Congolese rebel who is responsible for human rights violations and owns one of the Romanian guns, an AKM-47, serial number DA0889 1995 (Salopek, 2001, p. 1).

To date, such efforts,[47] however revealing, have involved varying investigative techniques and standards of evidence. They have not yet led to a systematic understanding of which weapons (from which countries and companies) are used in human rights violations worldwide, although progress has clearly been made. The United Nations Special Rapporteur on small arms and human rights, Barbara Frey, has called upon investigators of human rights abuse to identify the tools by which such abuses are committed (Frey, 2002, para. 31–4). The human rights community seems to be heeding this call: more and more reports of the kind described above have appeared in the last years.

Small arms transfers to states where gross violations of human rights occur

Amnesty International, Human Rights Watch, the International Peace Information Service, NISAT, and the various UN expert panel investigations on violations of UN arms embargoes have for some years published detailed information on arms transfers to states where gross human rights violations occur. This also follows the logic of some exporters, which, as noted above, vow to restrict exports to countries with poor human rights records.

Table 4.14 focuses on the most serious cases of human rights violations only, as measured on the Political Terror Scale (that is, those in which murders, disappearances, and torture are frequent). There are several rankings of human rights abuses, all of which are controversial, in part because ranking human suffering in this way is a debatable enterprise, and some rankings are perceived to be politically biased. The Political Terror Scale, updated yearly by an American scholar, uses Amnesty International reports and US State Department Country Reports on Human Rights Practices as the basis for the ranking. Both sources are widely used in the human rights community. The rankings take into account the human rights situation in the country generally, not only abuses committed by governments.

Table 4.14 lists known exports to states (and non-state actors active in those states) where serious human rights violations are systematic. It shows that, while some of these states were fairly isolated and received weapons from a few states only, others seem able to import small arms, ammunition, and parts fairly easily from a wide variety of

While isolated countries tend to import small arms from a limited number of states, others seem to import easily from a wide variety of sources.

sources. Iraq under Saddam Hussein, Myanmar, and North Korea are good examples of the former, and Algeria, China, Colombia, Indonesia, and Russia are examples of the latter.

Only some of these states were actually under a mandatory UN embargo during the period covered (1998–2002, that is, the most recent five-year period for which data is available), namely, Afghanistan (the Taliban) from 1999, Angola (UNITA) 1993–2002, Ethiopia 2000–01, Iraq from 1990, Liberia from 1992, Rwanda (non-state armed groups) from 1994, Sierra Leone (non-state armed groups) from 1997, Somalia from 1992, and the former Yugoslavia 1998–2001. Others have been under EU embargo. China, for instance, has been under EU embargo since the suppression of the pro-democracy movement at Tiananmen Square in 1989. It might therefore seem surprising that Austria, Finland, Germany, Italy, Spain, and the UK have all exported small arms to China. The reason for this apparent contradiction is that the EU did not originally define what would count as 'arms' under the embargo (SIPRI, no date). In December 1995, a common interpretation was issued which restricted the embargo to 'lethal weapons' (France, Ministère de la Défense, 2003, p. 72). Hence, the British explained their exports by stressing that 'the ammunition listed is in fact sporting gun ammunition (not covered by the UK's interpretation of the EU Arms Embargo) and the parts and accessories of military weapons refer to military firing sets for use in Explosive Ordnance Disposal work' (personal communication, 12 February 2004). Similar reasoning could lie behind the exports from Austria, Finland, Germany, Italy, and Spain.

It should be noted that the discussion here is rather restrictive in its scope—only the countries with extremely serious human rights problems have been included. A country such as Saudi Arabia, for instance, is not covered although its record on human rights is rather bleak and it has an increasingly ambiguous image when it comes to combating international terrorism. Saudi Arabia is the single largest customer of major EU exporters such as Belgium, France, and Spain and on the top five recipients list of many other important producers-exporters, including the US. In fact, Saudi Arabia is one of the top five known importers of small arms worldwide.

As always, the data should be interpreted with caution. Customs data, which is used in Table 4.14, does not tell us the reason for export. German exports to DRC are quite likely to have been destined for the UN mission established after the peace accord in 2001. However, all recorded customs figures have been included in the table. It is also important to note that the table does not aim to be exhaustive. Instead, it should serve to illustrate that small arms exports—both authorized and illicit—to states where gross human rights violations take place are still common.

Table 4.13   Known exports of small arms (in USD) to states where gross violations of human rights occur, 1998-2002[48]

Country	Exporters, years, and USD values
Afghanistan (Taliban government)	**Pakistan**,[49] **Saudi Arabia** provided funds for weapons purchases (public funds: after US protests, private funds only).[50]
Afghanistan (Northern Alliance)	**India**,[51] **Iran**,[52] **Russia**,[53] **US**,[54] non-state supplies from **Tajikistan**[55]
Algeria	**1998: China** (3.0m mainly hunting rifles), **France** (14,000 mainly shotguns), **Italy** (0.5m mainly handguns), **Russia** (3.5m shotguns), **UK** (0.2m ammunition) **1999: France** (18,000 mainly shotguns), **Italy** (0.5m mainly handguns), **Russia** (6.4m mainly shotguns and parts and accessories), **South Africa** 11.1m military weapons, **Switzerland** (28,000 handguns and parts and accessories) **2000: France** (29,000 mainly shotguns), **Russia** (0.6m mainly ammunition), **UK** (24,000 ammunition) **2001: Brazil** (2.8m ammunition), **France** (0.1m mainly shotguns), **Italy** (0.3m mainly handguns and shotguns), **Russia** (3.5m mainly shotguns) **2002: Brazil** (2.5m ammunition), **France** (0.9m mainly shotguns), **Italy** (USD 1.5m mainly handguns)

TRANSFERS

Table 4.13 (cont.)   Known exports of small arms (in USD) to states where gross violations of human rights occur, 1998–2002

Country	Exporters, years, and USD values
Angola	**1998: Portugal** (71,000 mainly shotguns) **1999: Brazil** (1.3m mainly shotgun cartridges), **Portugal** (16,000 mainly shotguns), **Slovakia** (0.5m mainly military weapons), **South Africa** (11,000 mainly military weapons) **2000: Brazil** (2m mainly shotgun cartridges), **Portugal** (50,000 mainly shotguns), **Russia** (2.4m ammunition), **Slovakia** (29,000 pistols and revolvers) **2001: Brazil** (0.9m shotgun cartridges), **Namibia** (16,000 mainly ammunition and hunting rifles), **Poland** (0.6m military weapons), **Portugal** (42,000 mainly pistols and revolvers) **2002: Portugal** (74,000 mainly shotgun cartridges, pistols and revolvers, and shotguns), **Spain** (49,000 ammunition), **France**,[56] **Russia**[57]
Angola (UNITA)	In the late 1990s, illicit supplies originating in **Bulgaria, Romania,** and **Ukraine** were supplied to UNITA. Chinese and Russian weapons have also been found in UNITA stockpiles.[58]
Burundi	**2000: Poland** (1.0m ammunition)
China	**1998: Austria** (26,000 mainly hunting rifles), **Belarus** (0.2m parts and accessories of military weapons), **Canada** (0.1m ammunition), **Germany** (0.2m mainly hunting rifles and ammunition), **Hong Kong** (11,000 pistols and revolvers), **Italy** (99,000 mainly shotguns), **Mexico** (64,000 ammunition), **Spain** (56,000 shotguns), **Switzerland** (61,000 mainly ammunition and shotguns), **US** (60,000 mainly shotgun cartridges) **1999: Canada** (0.1m ammunition), **Finland** (17,000 ammunition), **Germany** (0.3m mainly hunting rifles and ammunition), **Hong Kong** (28,000 mainly military weapons), **Italy** (71,500 mainly shotgun cartridges), **Mexico** (11,000 parts and accessories of military weapons), **Russia** (8.0m ammunition and parts and accessories for military weapons), **South Africa** (10,000 ammunition), **Switzerland** (0.2m parts and accessories of military weapons), **UK** (0.2m ammunition), **US** (0.1m mainly shotgun cartridges) **2000: Canada** (52,000 ammunition), **Finland** (0.1m ammunition), **Germany** (0.2m mainly hunting rifles), **Hong Kong** (26,500 mainly shotguns), **Italy** (0.1m mainly pistols and revolvers, and shotgun cartridges), **Russia** (9.0m mainly ammunition), **Switzerland** (1.8m mainly parts and accessories for military weapons), **UK** (0.45m ammunition), **US** (23,000 ammunition) **2001: Australia** (11,000 pistols and revolvers), **Canada** (94,000 ammunition), **Finland** (76,000 ammunition), **Germany** (0.3m mainly ammunition and rifles), **Italy** (57,000 mainly shotgun cartridges), **Serbia and Montenegro** (0.6m parts and accessories of military weapons), **Singapore** (0.6m parts and accessories of military weapons), **Switzerland** (4.0m mainly pistols and revolvers), **UK** (0.4m ammunition), **US** (0.2m mainly ammunition) **2002: Australia** (0.1m mainly shotguns), **Austria** (24,000 mainly parts and accessories for military weapons), **Canada** (57,000 mainly parts and accessories for military weapons), **Germany** (0.5m mainly sporting and hunting rifles), **Hong Kong** (58,000 mainly pistols and revolvers), **Italy** (0.35m mainly shotguns), **Russia** (44,000 parts and accessories of military weapons), **South Korea** (29,000 parts and accessories for military weapons), **Spain** (18,000 ammunition), **Switzerland** (0.9m mainly parts and accessories for military weapons), **UK** (1.0m parts and accessories of military weapons, and ammunition), **US** (0.2m mainly parts and accessories for military weapons)
Colombia	**1998: Austria** (0.3m pistols and revolvers), **Belgium-Luxembourg** (0.2m mainly parts and accessories for shotguns and rifles), **Brazil** (3.0m mainly shotgun cartridges), **Bulgaria** (1.9m military weapons), **Croatia** (1.2m military weapons), **Czech Republic** (0.5m mainly pistols and revolvers), **France** (78,000 mainly parts and accessories of military weapons), **Germany** (14,000 mainly ammunition and shotguns), **Israel** (6,3m mainly parts and accessories for military weapons), **Italy** (1,2m mainly pistols and revolvers), **Portugal** (0.1m parts and accessories for military weapons), **South Africa** (3,3m mainly military weapons), **Spain** (75,000 mainly parts and accessories for military weapons), **UK** (0.2m mainly parts and accessories for military weapons), **US** (24.0m mainly military weapons), **1999: Austria** (0.4m mainly pistols and revolvers), **Brazil** (1.0m mainly shogun cartridges and ammunition), **Croatia** (1.0m military weapons), **Czech Republic** (0.4m mainly pistols and revolvers), **Germany** (0.1m mainly pistols and revolvers), **Israel** (3.6m mainly parts and accessories for military weapons), **Italy** (3.8m mainly parts and accessories for military weapons), **Singapore** (12,000 military weapons), **South Africa** (1.0m mainly military weapons), **Spain** (0.3m mainly parts and accessories for military weapons), **UK** (0.1m mainly parts and accessories for military weapons), **US** (9.0m mainly military weapons and ammunition). **2000: Belgium** (1.5m military weapons), **Brazil** (1.9m mainly shotgun cartridges), **Bulgaria** (75,000 parts and accessories for military weapons), **Czech Republic** (0.9m mainly pistols and revolvers), **Germany** (0.2m mainly pistols and revolvers), **Israel** (2.8m mainly parts and accessories for military weapons), **Italy** (0.9m mainly pistols and revolvers), **Portugal** (31,000 ammunition), **South Africa** (0.6m mainly military weapons), **Spain** (38,000 mainly sporting and hunting rifles), **UK** (27,000 mainly ammunition), **US** (8.5m mainly ammunition and military weapons)

129

SMALL ARMS SURVEY 2004

Table 4.13 (cont.) Known exports of small arms (in USD) to states where gross violations of human rights occur, 1998-2002

Country	Exporters, years, and USD values
	2001: Belgium (23,000 mainly parts and accessories for military weapons), **Brazil** (4.4m mainly shotgun cartridges), **Czech Republic** (0.9m mainly pistols and revolvers), **Germany** (0.2m pistols and revolvers), **Israel** (3.3m mainly parts and accessories for military weapons), **Italy** (1.3m mainly pistols and revolvers), **Portugal** (49,000 ammunition), **South Africa** (1.3m mainly military weapons), **Spain** (0.2m mainly shotguns), **UK** (0.1m mainly ammunition), **US** (16.0m mainly military weapons). **2002: Argentina** (40,000 pistols and revolvers), **Brazil** (6.4m mainly shotgun cartridges), **Czech Republic** (1.3m mainly pistols and revolvers), **Germany** (0.4m pistols and revolvers), **Israel** (5.9m mainly military weapons and parts and accessories for military weapons), **Italy** (0.4m mainly sporting and hunting rifles, and shotgun cartridges), **Pakistan** (13,000 military weapons), **Portugal** (26,000 ammunition), **Russia** (37,500 sporting and hunting rifles), **South Africa** (2.7m mainly military weapons), **Spain** (60,500 military weapons), **UK** (0.2m mainly parts and accessories for military weapons), **US** (12.1m mainly military weapons and parts and accessories for military weapons)
Colombia (AUC, ELN, FARC)	**AUC:** Illicit supplies originating in **Nicaragua,**[59] **Panama**[60] **FARC, ELN:** Illicit supplies originating in **Brazil, Costa Rica, Ecuador, El Salvador, Honduras, Nicaragua, Panama, Paraguay, Peru, Suriname, Venezuela.**[61] IRA was allegedly supplying weapons to FARC in the 1990s and quite possibly beyond.[62]
Congo (RoC)	**1999: Italy** (83,000 pistols and revolvers), **Poland** (1.0m ammunition), **South Africa** (15,000 rifles) **2000: Austria** (20,500 rifles), **France** (0.1m mainly shotgun cartridges and shotguns), **Georgia** (0.6m ammunition) **2001: France** (0.1m shotguns), **Italy** (0.2m ammunition) **2002: Italy** (0.4m ammunition)
Congo DRC	**1998: China** (19.0m mainly military weapons and ammunition) **2000: Czech Rep.** (0.15m ammunition) **2001: Germany** (30,000 pistols and revolvers) **China,**[63] **Italy,**[64] **Libya,**[65] **Namibia,**[66] **Zimbabwe**[67]
Congo DRC (insurgents)	**Rwanda,**[68] **Uganda**[69]
Ethiopia	**1998: China** (0.9m ammunition) **1999: Russia** (6.5m mainly ammunition) **2000: Russia** (83,000 parts and accessories for military weapons) **2001: South Korea** (3.7m military weapons) **2002: China** (0.3m mainly military weapons and parts and accessories for military weapons), **Russia** (5.15m parts and accessories for military weapons), **Denmark** (0.2m parts and accessories for military weapons), **Netherlands** (12,500 parts and accessories for military weapons), **South Korea** (0.1m mainly hunting rifles)
Indonesia	**1998: Brazil** (0.1m mainly parts and accessories for revolvers and pistols), **China** (12,000 military weapons and parts and accessories for shotguns or rifles), **Czech Republic** (16,000 mainly pistols and revolvers), **France** (55,000 ammunition), **Germany** (0.7m mainly parts and accessories for military weapons), **India** (43,000 mainly shotgun cartridges), **Italy** (29,000 mainly pistols and revolvers), **Netherlands** (0.3m parts and accessories for revolvers and pistols, and parts and accessories for shotguns or hunting rifles), **Singapore** (15,000 mainly parts and accessories for shotguns or hunting rifles), **South Korea** (1.7m mainly parts and accessories for military weapons), **Spain** (14,000 pistols and revolvers), **Sweden** (0.2m mainly shotgun cartridges), **Thailand** (71,000 parts and accessories for revolvers or pistols), **Turkey** (0.4m mainly military weapons), **UK** (0.5m mainly parts and accessories for military weapons), **US** (70,000 mainly ammunition) **1999: Belgium** (13,000 parts and accessories for military weapons), **Brazil** (0.2m mainly hunting rifles), **China** (0.2m mainly parts and accessories for revolvers or pistols), **Czech Republic** (0.1m parts and accessories for military weapons), **France** (11,000 parts and accessories for military weapons), **Germany** (0.2m mainly parts and accessories for military weapons), **India** (35,000 parts and accessories for military weapons, and ammunition), **Italy** (37,000 mainly pistols and revolvers), **Japan** (12,000 mainly military weapons), **Malaysia** (0.1m parts and accessories for revolvers or pistols), **Netherlands** (19,000 parts and accessories for revolvers or pistols), **Singapore** (76,000 mainly shotgun barrels), **South Korea** (4.4m mainly parts and accessories for military weapons), **Spain** (91,000 mainly pistols and revolvers), **Sweden** (55,000 mainly parts and accessories for military weapons), **UK** (1.35m mainly parts and accessories for shotguns or hunting rifles), **US** (0.1m mainly ammunition) **2000: Austria** (35,000 mainly hunting rifles), **Brazil** (79,000 mainly hunting rifles), **China** (0.5m mainly military weapons and shotgun barrels), **Germany** (80,000 mainly pistols and revolvers), **Italy** (38,000 mainly military

TRANSFERS

Table 4.13 (cont.) Known exports of small arms (in USD) to states where gross violations of human rights occur, 1998–2002

Country	Exporters, years, and USD values
	weapons), **Japan** (0.1m pistols and revolvers), **Pakistan** (0.1m parts and accessories for revolvers or pistols), **Singapore** (0.2m mainly parts and accessories for military weapons), **Slovakia** (9.0m mainly ammunition), **South Korea** (0.1m mainly shotgun cartridges), **Sweden** (93,000 mainly parts and accessories for military weapons), **Turkey** (75,000 mainly parts and accessories for military weapons), **UK** (0.3m mainly parts and accessories for military weapons), **US** (49,000 mainly shotguns), **2001: Austria** (30,000 hunting rifles and parts and accessories for revolvers or pistols), **Brazil** (0.2m mainly hunting rifles), **Hong Kong** (14,000 ammunition), **Czech Republic** (0.1m mainly ammunition), **France** (21,000 parts and accessories for military weapons), **Germany** (0.1m mainly ammunition), **Italy** (15,000 mainly shotguns), **Japan** (30,000 pistols and revolvers), **Malaysia** (13,000 military weapons), **Singapore** (0.3m mainly military weapons), **Spain** (50,000 mainly pistols and revolvers), **Sweden** (0.2m parts and accessories for military weapons), **Turkey** (98,000 mainly parts and accessories for military weapons), **UK** (57,000 ammunition), **US** (29,000 mainly parts and accessories for shotguns or hunting rifles) **2002: Austria** (0.2m mainly military weapons), **Brazil** (0.6m mainly rifles), **China** (0.2m mainly parts and accessories for military weapons), **Czech Republic** (34,000 mainly pistols and revolvers), **Hungary** (11,000 pistols and revolvers), **Italy** (45,000 mainly shotguns), **Philippines** (0.4m parts and accessories for military weapons), **Russia** (17,000 military weapons), **Singapore** (4.4m mainly military weapons), **South Africa** (85,000 military weapons), **South Korea** (0.3m mainly ammunition), **Sri Lanka** (13,000 pistols and revolvers), **Sweden** (87,000 parts and accessories for military weapons), **Switzerland** (14,000 mainly pistols and revolvers, and parts and accessories for pistols or revolvers), **Turkey** (66,000 mainly parts and accessories for shotguns or rifles)
Indonesia (insurgents)	Ethnic Achenese living in **Malaysia**,[70] illicit supplies originating in **Thailand**[71]
Iraq	No information available on SALW transfers
Liberia	Illicit supplies originating in **Serbia**[72]
Liberia, (LURD)	Illicit supplies originating in **Guinea, Ivory Coast**[73]
Myanmar	**1998: China** (3.4m military weapons) **1999: China** (0.1m parts and accessories) **2001: China** (0.1m parts and accessories) **China**,[74] **Israel**,[75] **Pakistan**,[76] **Russia**,[77] **Vietnam**[78]
Myanmar (insurgents)	Allegations of illicit supplies originating in **Thailand, Laos, Cambodia,** and **China.**[79]
North Korea	**1998: China** (0.7m mainly ammunition and military weapons) **1999: China** (1.9m mainly hunting rifles) **2000: China** (81,000 mainly parts and accessories for military weapons) **2002: UK** (13,000 hunting rifles)
Pakistan	**1998: China** (3.5m mainly ammunition), **Czech Republic** (64,000 mainly pistols and revolvers), **Germany** (51,000 mainly pistols and revolvers, and shotguns), **Italy** (0.1m mainly shotguns), **Turkey** (0.4m ammunition), **UK** (18,000 mainly ammunition), **US** (0.1m mainly parts and accessories for shotguns or hunting rifles), **1999: China** (0.2m mainly parts and accessories for military weapons), **France** (34,000 parts and accessories for military weapons), **Germany** (16,000 mainly shotgun cartridges), **Italy** (92,000 mainly shotguns), **South Africa** (0.9m mainly ammunition), **Switzerland** (0.1m parts and accessories for military weapons), **UK** (0.1m mainly parts and accessories for military weapons), **US** (60,000 mainly military weapons) **2000: Brazil** (12,000 hunting rifles), **China** (0.5m mainly parts and accessories for military weapons), **Czech Republic** (40,000 mainly ammunition), **Germany** (84,000 mainly ammunition), **Italy** (22,000 mainly shotguns), **South Korea** (5.4m ammunition), **Switzerland** (70,000 mainly parts and accessories for military weapons), **UK** (57,000 mainly parts and accessories for military weapons and ammunition) **2001: China** (0.3m mainly shotguns), **Czech Republic** (0.1m mainly ammunition), **France** (22,000 parts and accessories for shotguns or hunting rifles), **Germany** (29,000 mainly ammunition), **Italy** (54,000 mainly shotguns), **Switzerland** (57,000 parts and accessories for military weapons) **2002: Brazil** (1.9m shotgun cartridges), **China** (0.1m mainly parts and accessories for shotguns or hunting rifles), **France** (74,000 parts and accessories for military weapons), **Italy** (27,000 mainly shotguns), **UK** (17,000 mainly ammunition), **US** (12,000 ammunition)

Table 4.13 (cont.) Known exports of small arms (in USD) to states where gross violations of human rights occur, 1998–2002

Country	Exporters, years, and USD values
Russia	**1998: Austria** (0.7m mainly sporting and hunting rifles), **Belarus** (12,500 mainly shotgun cartridges), **Belgium-Luxembourg** (0.5m mainly shotguns), **Cyprus** (0.3m mainly shotguns), **Czech Republic** (40,000 mainly sporting and hunting rifles), **Finland** (0.1m mainly shotguns), **France** (2.4m mainly shotguns), **Germany** (1.0m mainly shotguns, sporting and hunting rifles, and ammunition), **Italy** (1.1m mainly shotguns), **Kazakhstan** (0.9m mainly parts and accessories for military weapons), **Latvia** (11,000 mainly parts and accessories for military weapons), **Portugal** (13,000 shotguns), **South Korea** (11,500 sporting and hunting rifles), **Spain** (0.9m mainly ammunition), **Turkey** (29,000 mainly parts and accessories for military weapons), **UK** (0.3m mainly shotgun cartridges), **Ukraine** (0.1m mainly shotgun cartridges), **US** (1.0m mainly sporting and hunting rifles) **1999: Austria** (0.5m mainly sporting and hunting rifles), **Belgium** (0.2m mainly shotguns), **Cyprus** (15,500 mainly shotguns), **Czech Republic** (85,000 mainly sporting and hunting rifles), **Finland** (0.3m mainly shotguns), **France** (0.7m mainly sporting and hunting rifles), **Georgia** (16,000 mainly ammunition and military weapons), **Germany** (0.5m mainly shotguns and sporting and hunting rifles), **Italy** (0.9m mainly shotguns), **Nicaragua** (0.1m shotgun cartridges), **Switzerland** (76,000 mainly sporting and hunting rifles), **Turkey** (0.2m parts and accessories for shotguns or rifles), **Ukraine** (18,000 mainly parts and accessories for military weapons), **United Arab Emirates** (11,000 ammunition), **US** (57,000 mainly shotguns and parts and accessories for military weapons) **2000: Australia** (11,000 ammunition), **Austria** (0.7m mainly sporting and hunting rifles), **Belgium** (0.3m mainly shotguns), **Bulgaria** (88,000 ammunition), **Cyprus** (11,000 mainly shotguns), **Czech Republic** (0.2m mainly sporting and hunting rifles), **Finland** (0.1m mainly shotguns), **France** (1.2m mainly sporting and hunting rifles, and shotguns), **Georgia** (1.4m mainly military weapons), **Germany** (1.5m mainly shotguns), **Italy** (1.2m mainly shotguns), **Kazakhstan** (65,000 military weapons and parts and accessories for military weapons), **Spain** (46,000 mainly ammunition), **Turkey** (0.15m parts and accessories of shotguns or rifles), **UK** (0.1m mainly shotguns), **Ukraine** (0.1m mainly parts and accessories for military weapons), **US** (57,000 mainly sporting and hunting rifles, and ammunition) **2001: Austria** (1.5m mainly sporting and hunting rifles), **Belgium** (0.5m mainly shotguns), **Czech Republic** (0.3m mainly sporting and hunting rifles), **Finland** (0.3m mainly sporting and hunting rifles, and shotguns), **France** (1.2m mainly sporting and hunting rifles), **Germany** (2.8m mainly shotguns and sporting and hunting rifles), **Italy** (1.8m mainly shotguns), **Japan** (15,000 mainly shotguns), **Portugal** (64,000 shotguns), **Spain** (0.5m mainly parts and accessories for military weapons), **Sweden** (36,000 ammunition), **Switzerland** (51,000 mainly sporting and hunting rifles), **Turkey** (50,000 mainly parts and accessories for shotguns or rifles), **UK** (0.2m mainly shotguns), **Ukraine** (40,000 parts and accessories for shotguns or rifles), **US** (0.7m mainly ammunition) **2002: Austria** (1.7m mainly sporting and hunting rifles), **Belgium** (0.7m mainly shotguns), **Cyprus** (11,000 shotgun cartridges), **Czech Republic** (0.4m mainly hunting and sporting rifles), **Finland** (0.3m mainly hunting and sporting rifles), **France** (1.1m mainly hunting and sporting rifles, and shotguns), **Germany** (0.4m mainly sporting and hunting rifles), **Italy** (2.9m mainly shotguns), **Japan** (85,000 shotguns), **Portugal** (0.1m mainly shotguns), **South Korea** (0.1m ammunition), **Spain** (0.3m mainly shotgun cartridges), **Sweden** (39,000 mainly ammunition), **Switzerland** (69,000 sporting and hunting rifles), **UK** (45,000 mainly shotguns), **Ukraine** (0.7m parts and accessories for military weapons), **US** (82,000 mainly sporting and hunting rifles)
Russia (Chechen insurgents)	Illicit supplies originating with **Russian** military officials,[80] **Georgia**,[81] the **Taliban**,[82] various militant Islamic non-state actors,[82] **Turkey**[84]
Rwanda	**1998: China** (13,000 mainly shotguns) **2000: Russia** (0.8m parts and accessories for military weapons) **2002: Turkey** (37,500 ammunition), **Saudi Arabia** (11,000 military weapons) **US**,[85] although unclear whether US military aid includes SALW.
Sierra Leone	**2000: UK** (10,000 ammunition) **2001: Lebanon** (0.2m military weapons), **US** (29,500 parts and accessories), **Spain** (13,000 ammunition)
Sierra Leone (RUF)	**Liberia**,[86] **Burkina Faso**,[87] **Niger**,[88] **Ukraine**[89]
Sudan	**1998: China** (40,000 rifles) **1999: Cyprus** (22,000 mainly shotgun cartridges), **Iran** (0.8m ammunition) **2000: Cyprus** (17,000 mainly shotgun cartridges), **Iran** (2.5m parts and accessories for shotguns and hunting rifles, and ammunition) **2001: Austria** (26,000 mainly shotguns), **Cyprus** (11,000 mainly shotgun cartridges), **UK** (10,000 pistols and revolvers), **Ecuador** (10,500 parts and accessories for revolvers and pistols)

Table 4.13 (cont.) Known exports of small arms (in USD) to states where gross violations of human rights occur, 1998-2002

Country	Exporters, years, and USD values
	2002: China (1.0m mainly parts and accessories for shotguns or hunting rifles), **Egypt** (14,000 mainly pistols and revolvers), **Iran** (5.4m mainly ammunition, military weapons, and shotgun cartridges), **Saudi Arabia** (65,000 mainly military weapons), **Switzerland** (4.3m military weapons), **UK** (0.2m parts and accessories for revolvers and pistols), **Russia**,[90] although unclear whether Russian weapons include SALW. A Human Rights Watch report (1998b) shows that supplies in the earlier part of the 1990s were extremely varied.
Sudan (insurgents)	There is a significant amount of illicit trafficking in SALW between **Uganda**, **Sudan**, and **Kenya**.[91]
Yugoslavia	Allegations for 1998-2002 period do not include small arms.
Yugoslavia (KLA)	Illicit supplies originating in **Albania**, **Croatia**, **Germany**, **Iran**, **Switzerland**,[92] **Bosnia and Herzegovina**,[93] **Montenegro**[94]

Note: Cut-off point for inclusion in table: USD 10,000 per annum.

Source: Whenever not otherwise stated, UN Comtrade. Download date: 23 January 2004

Box 4.5 Using international law to curb arms transfers to human rights abusers?

In the autumn of 2003, a coalition of NGOs (Amnesty International, International Action Network on Small Arms (IANSA), and Oxfam) launched a campaign to control the international trade in arms, and in particular the small arms trade, and called for the adoption of the so-called Arms Trade Treaty (or the 'Framework Convention on International Arms Transfers').

The draft Arms Trade Treaty was first developed in 2000-01. It was a collaborative effort involving a number of international NGOs, the Commission of Nobel Peace Prize Laureates, and international lawyers. The treaty is informally supported by a number of states, and as of early December 2003 seven states had expressly pledged their support for a treaty of this kind: Brazil, Cambodia, Costa Rica, Finland, Macedonia, Mali, and the Netherlands (Control Arms, 2003).

As currently envisaged, it covers all arms transfers, not only small arms. It is a short text (comprising ten articles all in all), stipulating (a) that contracting states should not license exports of arms which would violate their express obligations under international law (such as UN Security Council decisions, international treaties, and customary law); (b) that contracting states should not license arms exports when the state 'has knowledge or ought reasonably to have knowledge' that transfers of arms of the kind under consideration are 'likely' to be used in violation of the prohibitions on the threat or use of force, or to commit serious violations of human rights or international humanitarian law; (c) that that there should be a 'presumption against authorization' when the arms to be exported are likely to be used in committing violent crimes or would undermine political stability, regional security, or economic development; and (d) that the states adhering to the Treaty should establish an international registry of international arms transfers to monitor compliance.[95]

In essence, the drafters and proponents of the Arms Trade Treaty have claimed that it assembles and consolidates into one single document those limitations on states' freedom to transfer weapons that can be derived from existing legally binding international agreements and norms on human rights, international humanitarian law, and peace and security. Some critics of the Arms Trade Treaty argue that, in fact, some of the provisions of the draft treaty go beyond current binding international law. Others, in contrast, argue that it is 'unambitious'. The many promoters of the project have argued that the Treaty and its format is a good way forward as it would be legally binding (rather than a political document such as the UN *Programme of Action*), valid internationally (hence preventing the case in which an irresponsible sale rejected by one state is accepted by another), and flexible (it is conceived as a framework convention, to which more specific legal provisions, such as on brokering or transport agents, can be added).

> As of December 2003, Brazil, Cambodia, Costa Rica, Finland, Macedonia, Mali, and the Netherlands had pledged their support for a treaty to control the arms trade.

CONCLUSION

This chapter introduces a couple of novelties in examining the authorized global small arms trade. For the first time, it gives information not only on the main exporting and importing countries but also on their most important trading partners and principal categories of weapons traded. Thus, some problematic cases which have not yet attracted much attention were revealed: known medium-sized producers without recorded authorized exports (Iran, Pakistan, and Singapore) and whose export activities thus remain 'black holes'; Czech exports of small arms to Yemen; Brazilian and Russian exports to Algeria; massive imports by Cyprus and Saudi Arabia (not least from Western states); and significant imports by Colombia, Israel, Lebanon, Venezuela, and others. Subsequent editions of the *Small Arms Survey* will try to map illicit transfers in a similar way.

The analysis of main exporters and importers is based on international customs data and export reports. The comparison of the two sources shows that we are still far from a clear and coherent picture of the authorized global trade in small arms. This is an important reason for introducing a second novelty: the **Small Arms Trade Transparency Barometer,** which assesses state export transparency on a 20-point scale. The barometer is based on the information made available by the main exporting states (that is, export reports and international customs data). The barometer will be a recurrent feature of the *Small Arms Survey*. In subsequent editions, it will thus be possible to assess whether individual states, as well as the international community as a whole, are becoming more or less transparent over time. This chapter has shown that, with an average of 8.5 out of 20, such developments would be more than welcome. Another issue that will have to be dealt with is the transparency of importing states.

It is with a view to better understanding the authorized trade that this chapter also sets out to examine the relationship between production and trade for the first time. We have shown that, for some of the world's largest producers of small arms, export is key to survival. Until recently, virtually all of Russia's military small arms production depended on international orders. Its civilian production is less export-dependent, although a considerable share is sold abroad. The same is true for Brazil, more than 60 per cent of whose production is exported. Germany, one of Europe's largest producers, follows the same pattern. The exception to what seems, albeit at a first glace, to be a uniformly export-dependent industry is the US, less than 10 per cent of whose production (but a higher share of military weapons) is exported. Future editions of the *Survey* will deal with the other main source of small arms transfers, namely pre-existing state stockpiles.

Lastly, in line with the theme of the 2004 edition of the *Small Arms Survey,* the chapter examines the links between human rights violations and small arms transfers. When examining transfers to countries with serious human rights problems, it becomes clear that many governments still have some way to go to achieve full consistency between their various foreign policy objectives: a relatively large number of states where human rights violations are widespread have no shortage of suppliers.

4. LIST OF APPENDICES

Appendices 4.1–4.4 are available on the Small Arms Survey Web site at www.smallarmssurvey.org/publications/yb_2004.htm.

4. LIST OF ABBREVIATIONS

ATF	US Bureau of Alcohol, Tobacco, Firearms and Explosives
BRL	Brazilian real
CAD	Canadian dollar
CHF	Swiss franc
DRC	Democratic Republic of Congo
ECOWAS	Economic Community of West African States
EU	European Union
EUR	Euro
FARC	Fuerzas Armadas Revolucionarias de Colombia
HRW	Human Rights Watch
HS	Harmonized system
IANSA	International Action Network on Small Arms
LURD	Liberians United for Reconciliation and Democracy
MANPADS	Man-portable air defence system
NOK	Norwegian kroner
OSCE	Organization for Security and Co-operation in Europe
PCASED	Programme for Coordination and Assistance for Security and Development
RoC	Republic of Congo
SALW	Small arms and light weapons
SEK	Swedish krona
SITC	Standard International Trade Classification
UNSC	United Nations Security Council
USD	United States dollar
WMEAT	World Military Expenditures and Arms Transfers
ZAR	South African rand

4. ENDNOTES

[1] In this chapter, 'small arms', 'guns', 'firearms', and 'small arms and light weapons' are used interchangeably unless explicitly stated otherwise.

[2] In this chapter, 'trade' and 'transfers' are used interchangeably, unless otherwise stated.

[3] More technically, production and pre-existing stockpiles of small arms are called primary and secondary levels of supply. There is also a tertiary level of supply, which indicates arms supplies from groups within the wider population (insurgents, ex-combatants, criminals, and so on) (Naylor, 1998, p. 232).

[4] In Box 4.1, Sergio Finardi and Carlo Tombola come to a slightly larger figure, USD 2.8 billion, also based on customs data, because they include slightly different categories in their definition of small arms.

[5] The international customs database employed here is UN Comtrade. For a more detailed discussion of this source, see Small Arms Survey (2001, ch. 4; 2003, Box 3.1).

[6] A major problem with estimating exports is that they fluctuate from year to year. For smaller exporters in particular, exports are dependent sometimes on a single transaction, and can hence go up or down several hundred per cent from one year to the next. Estimates are therefore restricted to major producers only, for whom such fluctuations should be relatively smaller.

[7] <www.smallarmssurvey.org/publications/yb_2004.htm>

[8] Brazil may also record its firearm exports in a somewhat unorthodox way, filing its pistols and revolvers exports under the customs category 'other sporting, hunting or target shooting rifles'. If this is correct, as some preliminary research by Dreyfus and Lessing (2003) seems to suggest, the above figures overestimate the actual trade.

[9] The research projects (Adriane's Thread: The Transport Networks of Arms Trade; and The Matchmakers: How Legal and Illegal Business Meet at Ports and Airports) were funded by the Program of Global Security and Sustainability of the John D. and Catherine T. MacArthur Foundation in 1999 and 2001.

[10] We reviewed all SALW-related 51,358 exporter and 56,442 importer declarations included in SITC Rev. 3 code 891 (SITC [Standard International Trade Classification] is a different coding system from the HS codes used elsewhere in this chapter). The cross-analysis of exporter and importer declarations was necessary for (a) amending gaps and inconsistencies in reporting and (b) trying to amend inconsistencies in coding, because 'the rules for the same products can be applied differently between countries... the registrations of imports and exports are done independently... and the commodity classification systems are likely to be different' (Ronald Jansen, Chief of the UN Statistics Division's Commodity Trade Statistics Section, personal communication, 9 October 2003). At the end

of this process, the database included about 82,545 entries relevant to SALW trade, selected according to the following criteria: *(a)* if available, matching exporter and importer declarations were compared and the higher value was chosen; *(b)* exporter's declarations were supplemented by the importer's when the former did not declare exports that were recorded by the latter. In theory, at world level, imports and exports should be of identical value, net of f.o.b. (free on board, excluding insurance and freight) and c.i.f. (cost including insurance and freight).

[11] SITC codes 891.14 (Revolvers and pistols); 891.22 (Cartridges for shotguns); 891.23 (Air gun pellets and parts of cartridges for shotguns); 891.24 (Cartridges and parts thereof, n.e.s.); 891.31 (Non-military firearms); 891.91 (Parts and accessories of revolvers or pistols); 891.93 (Sports shotgun barrels.); 891.95 (Parts of sports shotguns and rifles); 891.99 (Parts and accessories of military weapons other than revolvers and pistols, and nonmilitary arms other than firearms and side arms).

[12] SITC 891.12 (Military weapons, other than revolvers and pistols); 891.29 (Munitions of war and parts thereof, n.e.s.).

[13] SITC 891.39 (Non military arms other than firearms such as air guns, rifles and pistols, and truncheons); 891.13 (Swords, cutlasses, bayonets, lances and parts thereof).

[14] According to factors provided by the US Department of Defense.

[15] For example, the M-47 (Dragon), the 9K115 Metis (AT-7 Saxhorn), or the surface-to-air FIM-92 Stinger.

[16] Harmonized System 2002 (HS2002), codes 930111 and 930119; 930120; and 930190.

[17] For the UN definition, see PRODUCERS.

[18] Kalashnikov's AK-47s, AKM, AKS-74 are all outfitted with detachable bayonet-knives, as are Heckler-Koch's HK G36s and many other assault rifles. Widely traded bayonets and knives are, for example, Smith & Wesson SWAT, US combat M3 to M10, Beretta Model 92 knife, and Spanish FR7 bayonet, as well as the famous Gurkha Kukris and machetes, standard weapons for the Royal Gurkha Rifles.

[19] An energy in excess of 6ft/lbs for pistols and 12ft/lbs for rifles at the muzzle is considered very dangerous and, for example, the popular Webley & Scott Patriot and the Beeman Crow Magnum rifles produce 26–30ft/lbs at the muzzle, not to mention that some air weapons may be easily converted to use conventional ammunition.

[20] See, for example, the Prowler XS-B3, by China Xifeng, official training rifle for Chinese military youth.

[21] Such as Webley & Scott, Beretta, Walther, Smith & Wesson, and Colt. A list is available at <http://www.pyramydair.com>

[22] Exceptions include Belgium and Italy.

[23] For background information on the process, see Lodgaard and Rønnfeldt (1998).

[24] According to Courtney (2002, p. 8), '[d]espite accounting for less than 1% of total world trade... and less than 10% of the five most corruptible trades, sources from the US Department of Commerce indicate that [the overall arms trade] accounts for around 50% of all corrupt transactions'. The arms trade generally is the second most corruptible trade, after public works/construction, in terms of both frequency and value of bribes paid (Transparency International, 2002).

[25] It is important to note that transparency is only a first step to accountability. In future editions of the *Small Arms Survey*, accountability in the SALW trade will be addressed further. For more detailed arguments in favour of transparency, see Haug *et al.* (2002).

[26] The first information exchange in 2001 did not include transfers.

[27] This is the case when a country identifies both the recipient country and the type(s) of weapons exported to that particular country. This is different from reporting separately on trading partners and types of weapons exported. A country can report on both, but they do not necessarily have to be linked, in the sense that it is possible to tell which types of weapons are exported to which countries. Not included here are total numbers of deliveries and licences granted and denied, which refer to the global number for all arms exports (that is, including SALW as well as larger weapons and weapon systems, and summing up deliveries to all foreign countries). Also not included are deliveries disaggregated by country (that is, a list of figures for all arms transactions with one particular recipient state; for example, Sweden reports that its arms exports (all categories of arms) to Singapore in 2002 totalled SEK 419.8 million (USD 43.4 million) (Sweden 2003)). Neither tells us anything about small arms exports.

[28] The only exceptions are availability *(a)* on Internet *(b)* free of charge (worth half a point each) and information on licence denials, which has been weighted as being less important than information on licences granted and actual deliveries.

[29] For a thorough discussion on which the following is based, see Marsh (2003) and Lessing (2003).

[30] For a critique of the UK export report, see Saferworld (2003). A similar critique of the German report is published yearly by the Gemeinsame Konferenz Kirche und Entwicklung (GKKE).

[31] This table is based on the analysis made in Kytömäki and Firchow (2004). Its format is adapted from Haug *et al.* (2002, pp. 30–1).

[32] These are: the Czech Republic, Cyprus, Estonia, Hungary, Latvia, Lithuania, Malta, Poland, Slovakia, and Slovenia.

[33] This subsection is based on Haug (2003).

[34] All data in this paragraph is based on ATF reports, as they are the only source of data to list both production and exports of small arms.

[35] This subsection is based on CAST (2003) unless otherwise stated.

[36] The information on Brazil is based on Dreyfus and Lessing (2003).

[37] The actual amount listed is BRL 233,264,096, and includes pistols, revolvers, shotguns, carbines, and all other non-military firearms; ammunition and cartridges for such weapons; and parts, accessories, and services related to these items. In addition, the survey lists USD 38.5 million (BRL 89,624,377) under another heading, 'heavy military equipment', which includes military arms *(armas de guerra)*, bombs, grenades, and other projectiles; armoured combat vehicles; and parts, accessories, and services related to these items. Some of these items, particularly assault rifles, grenades, and mortar ammunition, may be small arms.

[38] SECEX database (Brazilian Ministry of Development, Industry, and Foreign Trade; Secretariat for Foreign Trade). This figure includes all customs subheadings of Chapter 93 except for those under the headings 9301 (military arms), 9303.90 (starting pistols, flare guns, and captive-bolt guns), 9304 (compressed air and spring-powered guns), 9305.91 (parts and accessories of military arms), 9306.90 (guided missiles, bombs, grenades, and munitions of war) and 9307 (swords, cutlasses, bayonets, etc.).

[39] Company information filed with the Securities and Exchange Commission of Brazil (Comissão de Valores Mobiliários, CVM). All information is taken from Annual Reports (Informações Anuais, IAN) and Standard Financial Reports (Demonstrações Financeiras Padronizadas, DFP). See <http://www.cvm.gov.br/ingl/indexing.asp>

[40] Data from SECEX database.

[41] For more details on Argentina and other Latin American countries, see Dreyfus and Lessing (forthcoming).

[42] In 2002, Brazil reported USD 117.6 million in arms exports to Malaysia, of which USD 67.5 million fell into non-military export headings. However, the anomalous size of these totals, along with corroborating press reports of a sale of an advanced missile system to the Malaysian government, suggest that most of these exports were not SALW. Consequently, we have not included them here.

[43] For an allusion to this European view of the US as 'a society plagued by guns and violence', see Blinken (2001).

[44] This section covers mainly human rights, rather than international humanitarian law.

[45] Belgium did so in the aftermath to the 'Arms to Nepal' row, over which a government minister resigned in August 2002 (BICC, 2003, Box U.18).

[46] Here, internal repression is taken to include, *inter alia*, 'torture and other cruel, inhuman and degrading treatment or punishment, summary or arbitrary executions, disappearances, arbitrary detentions and other major violations of human rights and fundamental freedoms as set out in relevant international human rights instruments, including the Universal Declaration on Human Rights and the International Covenant on Civil and Political Rights' (EU Code of Conduct, criterion two).

[47] The Latin American NGO Viva Rio has been doing the same kind of research, but is most well known for tracing guns used in crime.

[48] Four or more on average for 1998–2002 on the Political Terror Scale. This scale is based on two annual series of country reports: Amnesty International reports and the US State Department reports. Each report is classified on a 1–5 scale, on which grade 1 implies secure rule of law and no problem of political murders, torture, or imprisonment because of political opinion or beliefs. Grade 4 means that 'murders, disappearances, and torture are a common part of life. In spite of its generality, on this level terror affects those who interest themselves in politics or ideas'. For grade 5 'the terrors of level 4 have been expanded to the whole population. The leaders of these societies place no limits on the means or thoroughness with which they pursue personal or ideological goals'. <http://www.unca.edu/politicalscience/faculty-staff/gibney.html>
[49] Kanzhetaev (2001), HRW (2001b).
[50] HRW (2001b, p. 4).
[51] Davis (2001a).
[52] Davis (2001a), HRW (2001b).
[53] HRW (2001b).
[54] Fitchett (2001).
[55] HRW (2001b).
[56] Global Witness (2002).
[57] Amnesty International (2003a).
[58] UNSC (2000c).
[59] OAS 2003.
[60] Cragin and Hoffman. (2003).
[61] Cragin and Hoffman. (2003).
[62] McDermott and Harnden (2001); Akbar (2002).
[63] GRIP (2002, p. 2).
[64] Amnesty International and Oxfam (2003).
[65] GRIP (2002).
[66] GRIP (2002).
[67] GRIP (2002).
[68] GRIP (2002).
[69] GRIP (2002).
[70] Jane's Terrorism and Security Monitor (2000); Jakarta Post (2002).
[71] Davis (2001b); Jakarta Post (2002).
[72] UNSC (2003a).
[73] UNSC (2003a, p.14); HRW (2003, p. 15 ff.).
[74] Jane's Intelligence Digest (2001).
[75] Ashton (2000a).
[76] Jane's Intelligence Digest (2001); Ashton (2000b).
[77] Asia-Pacific Defense Reporter (2000, p. 34).
[78] Jane's Defense Weekly (2001).
[79] Thaitawat and Charoenpo (2000); Far Eastern Economic Review (2000, p. 10).
[80] Small Arms Survey (2002, p.137).
[81] Demetriou (2002, p.36).
[82] Small Arms Survey (2001).
[83] Small Arms Survey (2001).
[84] Small Arms Survey (2001).
[85] GRIP (2002, p. 15).
[86] UNSC (2000b).
[87] UNSC (2000b).
[88] UNSC (2000b).
[89] UNSC (2000b).
[90] Pronina (2002).
[91] Majtenyi (2001).
[92] Ripley (2000).
[93] UNSC (1999).
[94] Smith and Sagramoso (1999).
[95] The full text of the convention can be found at <http://www.arias.or.cr/fundarias/cpr/armslaw/fccomment.html> and also at <www.armslaw.org>

4. BIBLIOGRAPHY

Akbar, Arifa. 2002. 'IRA Arms Did Go to Columbia, Says Rebel.' *Independent* (London). 29 January.
Al Jazeerah. 2003. 'Yemenis Crack Down on Border Arms Trade.' 21 October. <http://www.aljazeerah.info/News%20archives/2003%21/10/2003>
Amnesty International. 1999. 'From Indonesia: East Timor Rapid Response Update 10: MSP Action, July 1999.' 21/121/1999 (internal AI document).
—. 2002. 'Britons Involved in Africa Gun-Running.' *Terror Trade Times*. No. 3. June.
—. 2003a. *A Catalogue of Failures: G8 Arms Exports and Human Rights Violations*. London: Amnesty International. 19 May.
—. 2003b. *Small Arms and Light Weapons and Human Rights Abuse: An Analysis of Amnesty International Documentation on 10 Countries from 1991–2002*. Background paper. Geneva: Small Arms Survey.
—. 2003c. 'UN Fails Timor-Leste Police in Firearms Training.' *Terror Trade Times*. No. 4. June.
—. 2003d. 'Jamaica: The Killing of the Braeton Seven—A Justice System on Trial.' AMR 38/005/2003. March.
—. and Oxfam. 2003. *Shattered Lives: The Case for Tough International Arms Control*. Eynsham: Information Press.
Arms Control Today. 2003. 'Russia Tops in Quantity of Arms Shipped in 2002.' Washington, DC: Arms Control Association. November. <http://www.armscontrol.org/act/2003_11/UNregister.asp?print>
Ashton, William. 2000a. 'Myanmar and Israel Develop Military Pact.' *Jane's Intelligence Review*. 1 March.
—. 2000b. 'Myanmar's Military Links with Pakistan.' *Jane's Intelligence Review*. 1 June.
Asia-Pacific Defense Reporter. 2000. 'South-East Asian Targets for Russia's Igla and Kilo.' June/July.
Australia. 2003. *Annual Report: Exports of Defence and Strategic Goods from Australia, 2001/2002*. Canberra: Defence Trade Control and Compliance Industry Division, Department of Defence. February.
Bauer, Sibylle. 2002. 'Transparency and Accountability of Arms Transfers—Implications of Europeanisation.' In Peter Brune and Lennart Molin, eds. *Arms Trade: Final Report from an Ecumenical Conference*. No.3. Sundbyberg: Sveriges Kristna Råds skriftserie.
—. 2003. 'Developing Transparency and Information Exchange as Essential Tools for Developing Collaborative Actions.' Presentation at EU–Belarus Cooperation meeting to increase security in a wider EU. Warsaw, 24–25 November.
BBC Worldwide Monitoring. 2003. 'Ministry Brings Case against Carrier for Alleged Arms Smuggling.' Kiev Unit. 11 April.
Belgium. 2003. *Rapport du Gouvernement au Parlement sur l'application de la loi du 5 août 1991 relative à l'importation, à l'exportation et au transit d'armes, de munitions et de matériel devant servir spécialement à un usage militaire, et de la technologie y afférente. Du 1er janvier au 31 décembre 2002*. July.
Berman, Eric G. 2003. 'The Provision of Lethal Military Equipment: French, UK, and US Peacekeeping Policies towards Africa.' *Security Dialogue*, Vol. 34, No. 2, pp. 195–210.
BICC (Bonn International Center for Conversion). 2003. *Conversion Survey 2003*. Baden-Baden: Nomos Verlagsgesellschaft.
Blinken, Anthony J. 2001. 'The False Crisis over the Atlantic.' *Foreign Affairs*, Vol. 80, No.3. May/June.
Canada. 2002. *Export of Military Goods from Canada Annual Report 2001*. Ottawa: Department of Foreign Affairs and International Trade.
CAST (Center for Analysis of Strategies and Technologies). 2003. *Russia's Exports of SALW*. Background paper. Geneva: Small Arms Survey.
Control Arms. 2003. 'The International Human Rights Day Sees World Support Build for International Arms Trade Treaty.' 10 December. <http://www.controlarms.org/latest_news/ihrd_pr2003.htm>
Courtney, Catherine. 2002. *Corruption in the Official Arms Trade*. Policy Research Paper 001. Transparency International UK. Sutton: Transparency International. April.

Cragin, Kim and Bruce Hoffman. 2003. *Arms Trafficking and Colombia*. Santa Monica, California: RAND.
Davis, Anthony. 2001a. 'Pakistan in Quandary over New Sanctions against the Taliban.' *Jane's Intelligence Review*. 1 February.
—. 2001b. 'Thailand Cracks Down on Arms for Aceh.' *Jane's Intelligence Review*. 1 June.
Demetriou, Spyros. 2002. *Politics from the Barrel of a Gun: Small Arms Proliferation and Conflict in the Republic of Georgia (1989–2001)*. Occasional Paper No.6. Geneva: Small Arms Survey.
Desarme. 2003. 'European Firearms in Venezuela: No Code, No Conduct.' 6 August. Carlanco/Caracas. <http://www.desarme.org/publique/cgi/cgilua.exe/sys/start.htm?infoid=1906&sid=8>
Dreyfus, Pablo and Benjamin Lessing. 2003. *Production and Exports of Small Arms and Light Weapons and Ammunition in South America and Mexico*. Background paper. Geneva: Small Arms Survey.
—. Forthcoming. *SALW Production and Exports in South America and Mexico*. Occasional Paper. Geneva: Small Arms Survey.
Ebo, Adedeji with Laura Mazal. 2003. *Small Arms Control in West Africa*. London: International Alert Security and Peacebuilding Programme, West Africa Series No.1. <http://www.international-alert.org/pdf/pubsec/MISAC_west_africa.pdf>
EU (European Union). 1998. *European Union Code of Conduct on Arms Exports*. 5 June. 8675/2/98 DG E – PESC 4. <http://ue.eu.int/pesc/ExportCTRL/en/8675_2_98_en.pdf>
Far Eastern Economic Review. 2000. 'Burma's Wa Run Guns.' 10 August, p. 10.
Finland. 2002. *Annual Report According to the EU Code of Conduct on Arms Exports: National Report of Finland for 2002*. Helsinki: Ministry of Defence.
Fitchett, Joseph. 2001. 'Success Paves Way for More Gains on Ground.' *International Herald Tribune*. 12 November.
France. Ministère de la Défense. 2002. *Rapport au Parlement sur les exportations d'armement de la France en 2000*. February.
—. 2003. *Rapport au Parlement sur les exportations d'armement de la France en 2001*. June.
Frey, Barbara. 2002. *The Question of the Trade, Carrying and Use of Small Arms and Light Weapons in the Context of Human Rights and Humanitarian Norms*. Working paper. Geneva: Sub-Commission on the Promotion and Protection of Human Rights, E/CN.4/Sub.2/2002/39.
Germany. Bundesregierung. 2002. *Bericht der Bundesregierung über ihre Exportpolitik für konventionelle Rüstungsgüter im Jahre 2002 (Rüstungsexportbericht)*. Berlin.
—. Statistisches Bundesamt. 2003. *Produzierendes Gewerbe. Reihe 3.1 Produktion im Produzierenden Gewerbe*. Wiesbaden: Statistisches Bundesamt.
Gillard, Emanuela-Chiara. 2000. 'What's Legal? What's Illegal?' In Lora Lumpe, ed. *Running Guns: The Global Black Market in Small Arms*. London: Zed Books, pp. 27–52.
Global Witness. 2001. *Taylor-made: The Pivotal Role of Liberia's Forests and Flag of Convenience in Regional Conflict*. London: Global Witness.
—. 2002. *All the Presidents' Men: The Devastating Story of Oil and Banking in Angola's Privatised War*. London: Global Witness. March.
—. 2003. *The Usual Suspects: Liberia's Weapons and Mercenaries in Côte d'Ivoire and Sierra Leone*. London: Global Witness. March.
Grässlin, Jürgen. *Versteck dich, wenn sie schiessen*. Munich: Droemer.
Grimmett, Richard F. 2002. *Conventional Arms Transfers to Developing Nations 1994–2001*. Washington, DC: Congressional Research Service, Library of Congress. August.
GRIP (Groupe de recherches sur la paix et la sécurité). 2002. *Transferts d'armes vers les acteurs impliqués dans le conflit en RDC*. Brussels: GRIP.
Haug, Maria. 2003. 'US Small Arms Exports in 2002.' Background paper. Geneva: Small Arms Survey.
—. and Martin Langvandslien, Lora Lumpe, and Nicolas Marsh. 2002. *Shining a Light on Small Arms Exports: The Record of State Transparency*. Geneva: Small Arms Survey/NISAT. January.
HRW (Human Rights Watch). 1998a. *Zambia: No Model for Democracy*. New York: HRW. May. <http://www.hrw.org/reports98/zambia/>
—. 1998b. *Sudan: Global Trade, Local Impact*. New York: HRW. August. <http://hrw.org/reports98/sudan/>
—. 2001a. *No Questions Asked: The Eastern Europe Arms Pipeline to Liberia*. Briefing paper. New York: HRW. 15 November.
—. 2001b. *Afghanistan: Crisis of Impunity*. New York: HRW.
—. 2003. *Weapons Sanctions, Military Supplies, and Human Suffering: Illegal Arms Flows to Liberia and the June–July 2003 Shelling of Monrovia*. Briefing paper. New York: HRW. 3 November.
International Firearms Trade. 2003. 'ATF/F.A.I.R. Trade Import Seminar a Huge Success: Heavily-attended Second Annual Import Regulation Conference Unveiled Wealth of Regulatory Data.' Vol. 2, No. 8. 1 August 2003.
IBGE (Brazilian Institute of National Statistics and Geography). 2002. *Pesquisa Industrial 2001*. Rio de Janeiro: IBGE.
IISS (International Institute for Strategic Studies). 2003. *The 2003 Chart of Armed Conflict*. London: IISS.
Interfax. 2003. 'V blizhaishiye tri goda obyom proizvodstva zavoda im. Degtyaryova uvelichitsya do 10–11 mlrd. Rub.' 20 February 2003.
Italy. Camera dei Deputati. 2003. *Relazione sulle operazioni autorizzate e svolte per il controllo dell'esportazione, importazione e transito dei materiali di armamento nonché dell'esportazione e del transito dei prodotti ad alta tecnologia (Anno 2002)*. March.
Jahn, George. 2004. 'AP Investigation: Soviet Weapons Cache, Arms Dealing and Dirty Bomb Cause Concern in Moldova's Separatist Enclave.' Associated Press. 9 January.
Jakarta Post. 2002. 'Illegal Guns Enter Indonesia through Four Countries.' 10 July.
Jane's Defense Weekly. 2001. 'More Bombs from Vietnam for Myanmar.' 25 July.
Jane's Intelligence Digest. 2001. 'Burma: A Special Report.' 2 March.
Jane's Terrorism and Security Monitor. 2002. 'Aceh: Indonesia's Continuing Headache.' 1 December.
Kanzhetaev, Marat. 2001. 'Arms Deliveries to Afghanistan in the 1990s.' *Vooruzsheni Export*. November–December.
Kytömäki, Elli. 2003. *Romanian Export Report 2001*. Background paper. Geneva: Small Arms Survey.
—. and Pamina Firchow. 2004. *Transparency in Arms Trade*. Background paper. Geneva: Small Arms Survey.
Lessing, Benjamin. 2003. 'Counting Guns. Customs Codes.' Mimeo. Small Arms Control Project, Viva Rio. Rio de Janeiro: Viva Rio.
Lodgaard, Sverre and Carsten F. Rønnfeldt. 1998. *A Moratorium on Light Weapons in West Africa*. Oslo: NISAT.
Majtenyi, Cathy. 2001. 'Government Officials Involved in Small Arms Flows.' *Africa News* (Nairobi). November.
Marsh, Nicholas. 2003. *Counting Guns: The Methodology of Aggregating Small Arms Customs Data*. Background paper. Geneva: Small Arms Survey.
McDermott, Jeremy and Toby Harnden. 2001. 'The IRA and the Columbian Connection.' *Daily Telegraph* (London). 15 August.
Naylor, R.T. 1998. 'The Rise of the Modern Arms Black Market and the Fall of Supply-Side Control.' *Transnational Organized Crime*, 4:3/4, pp. 209–36.
NISAT (Norwegian Initiative on Small Arms Transfers). 2003. *Various Calculations from the NISAT Database on Authorised Arms Transfers*. Background paper. Geneva: Small Arms Survey.
Norton-Taylor, Richard and John Aglionby. 2003. 'FO Faces Court over Arms to Indonesia.' *Guardian* (London). 10 December.
Norway. 2003. *Eksporten av forsvarsmateriell I 2002*. Oslo: Ministry of Foreign Affairs.
Ogunbanwo, Sola. 2002. 'Evaluation Study on the ECOWAS Moratorium on Importation, Exportation, and Manufacture of Small Arms in West Africa.' Submitted to ECOWAS on 21 October.
OAS (Organization of American States). 2003. *Report of the General Secretariat of the Organization of American States on the Diversion of Nicaraguan Arms to the United Defense Forces of Colombia*. OEA/Ser.G CP/doc.3687/03 of 6 June.
OSCE (Organization for Security and Co-operation in Europe). 1993. *Principles Governing Conventional Arms Transfers*. 25 November.
—. 2000. Forum for Security Co-operation. *OSCE Document on Small Arms and Light Weapons*. 24 November.

Portugal. 2002. *Anuário Estadístico da Defesa nacional 2001*. Lisbon: Ministry of Defence.
Pronina, Lyuba. 2002. 'Sudanese Shopping for Arms.' *Moscow Times*. 23 April.
Pyadushkin, Maxim, with Maria Haug and Anna Matveeva. 2003. *Beyond the Kalashnikov: Small Arms Production, Exports, and Stockpiles in the Russian Federation*. Occasional Paper 10. Geneva: Small Arms Survey.
Ripley, Tim. 2000. 'The UCK's Arsenal.' *Jane's Intelligence Review*. 1 November, pp. 22–23.
Romania. 2002. *Report on Arms Export Control 2000–2001*. Bucharest: National Agency for the Control of Strategic Exports and of Prohibition of Chemical Weapons. <http://www.ancesiac.ro/raport_arme/arms_rep.pdf>
Saferworld. 2003. *An Independent Audit of the 2001 UK Government Annual Report on Strategic Export Controls*. London: Saferworld.
Salopek, Paul. 2001. 'The Guns of Africa.' *Chicago Tribune*. 23 December.
Siddiqa-Agha, Ayesha. 2002. 'Pakistan's Export Plans Face Major Hurdles.' *Jane's Defence Weekly*, Vol. 37, No. 13. 27 March.
SIPRI (Stockholm International Peace Research Institute). 'European Union Arms Embargo on China.' <http://projects.sipri.se/expcon/euframe/euchiemb.htm>
Small Arms Survey. 2001. *Small Arms Survey 2001: Profiling the Problem*. Geneva: Small Arms Survey.
—. 2002. *Small Arms Survey 2002: Counting the Human Cost*. Oxford: Oxford University Press.
—. 2003. *Small Arms Survey 2003: Development Denied*. Oxford: Oxford University Press.
Smith, Chris and Domitilla Sagramoso. 1999. 'Small Arms Trafficking May Export Albania's Anarchy.' *Jane's Intelligence Review*. 1 January.
South Africa. 2002. *Annual Summary of Exports Statistics 2000/2001*. Pretoria: Directorate Conventional Arms Control.
Spain. 2003. *Informe sobre las estadísticas españolas de exportación de material de defensa y de doble uso*. Madrid: Subdirección General de Comercio Exterior de Material de Defensa y de Doble Uso.
Sweden. 2003. *Report on Sweden's Export Control Policy and Exports of Military Equipment in 2002*. Stockholm: Ministry of Foreign Affairs. March.
Switzerland. 2003. *Ausfuhr von Kriegsmaterial im Jahr 2002*. Berne: Staatssekretariat für Wirtschaft (SECO).
Thaitawat, Nusara and Anucha Charoenpo (2000). 'Ethnic Rebels Launch Arms Spree.' *Bangkok Post*. 1 July.
Transparency International. 2002. *Transparency International Bribe Payers Index 2002*. <http://www.transparency.org/cpi/2002/bpi2002.en.html>
UK (United Kingdom). 2003. *Strategic Export Controls Annual Report 2002*. London: Foreign and Commonwealth Office.
UN (United Nations). Comtrade (UN Commodity Trade Statistics Database). 2003. Geneva: Statistics Division. <http://unstats.un.org/unsd/comtrade/>
UNGA (United Nations General Assembly). 2003a. *Transparency in Armaments*. Resolution 58/54. Adopted 8 December. Reproduced in UN document A/RES/58/54 of 10 December.
—. 2003b. *Continuing Operation of the United Nations Register of Conventional Arms and its Further Development*. Note by the Secretary-General. A/58/274. 13 August.
UNSC (United Nations Security Council). 1999. *Report of the Security Council Committee Established Pursuant to Resolution 1160 (1998)*. S/1999/216. 4 March.
—. 2000a. *Report of the Panel of Experts on Violations of Security Council Sanctions Against UNITA*. S/2000/203 of 10 March.
—. 2000b. *Report of the Panel of Experts Appointed Pursuant to Security Council Resolution 1306 (2000), paragraph 19, in Relation to Sierra Leone*. S/2000/1195 of 20 December
—. 2000c. *Final Report of the Monitoring Mechanism on Angola Sanctions* S/2000/1225. 21 December.
—. 2001. *Report of the Panel of Experts pursuant to Security Council Resolution 1343 (2001), paragraph 19, concerning Liberia*. S/2001/1015 of 26 October.
—. 2002. *Report of the Panel of Experts Appointed Pursuant to Security Council Resolution 1395 (2002), paragraph 4, in Relation to Liberia*. S/2002/470 of 19 April.
—. 2003a. *Report of the Panel of Experts Appointed Pursuant to Paragraph 25 of Security Council Resolution 1478 (2003) concerning Liberia*. S/2003/937 of 28 October.
—. 2003b. *Report of the Panel of Experts on Somalia Pursuant to Security Council Resolution 1425 (2002)*. S/2003/223 of 25 March.
—. 2003c. *Proliferation of Small Arms and Light Weapons and Mercenary Activities: Threat to Peace and Security in West Africa*. S/RES/1467(2003) of 18 March.
US (United States). 2003. *FY 2002 Security Assistance Information for the Report on Military Assistance, Military Exports, and Military Imports*. Defense Security Cooperation Agency. 17 March.
—. ATF (Bureau of Alcohol, Tobacco, Firearms and Explosives). Various years. *Annual Firearms Manufacturing and Export Report*. Washington, DC: Department of the Treasury.
—. Department of Commerce. 2003. *US Imports History*. Historical Summary 1998–2002. Washington, DC: Foreign Trade Division, US Census Bureau. June.
—. Department of State, 2003. *Report by the Department of State pursuant to Sec. 655 of the Foreign Assistance Act: Direct Commercial Sales Authorizations for Fiscal Year 2002*. Washington, DC: United States Department of State.
Vines, Alex (2003). 'Hunting the Illegal Arms Traffickers.' *Gun Traffic*. BBC2. 7 December.
Wassenaar Arrangement. 2002. *Best Practice Guidelines for Exports of Small Arms and Light Weapons (SALW)* adopted on 11–12 December. <http://www.wassenaar.org/docs/best_practice_salw.htm>
—. 2003. *Public Statement: 2003. Plenary Meeting of the Wassenaar Arrangement on Export Controls for Conventional Arms and Dual-Use Goods and Technologies*. 12 December.
Wezeman, Pieter D. 2003. *Conflicts and Transfers of Small Arms*. Mimeo. Stockholm: SIPRI. March.

ACKNOWLEDGEMENTS

Other contributors
Sibylle Bauer, Center for Analysis of Strategies and Technologies (CAST), Pablo Dreyfus, Sergio Finardi, Pamina Firchow, Maria Haug, Elli Kytömäki, Benjamin Lessing, Nicholas Marsh, Sarah Meek, Lisa Misol, David Mutimer, Norwegian Initiative on Small Arms Transfers (NISAT), Stéphanie Pézard, Ruxandra Stoicescu, Carlo Tombola, and Brian Wood.

Many paramilitary fighters in Colombia's mountains have received weapons through complex deals arranged by specialized arms brokers.
(© Reuters/Albeiro Lopera)

Targeting the Middlemen:
CONTROLLING BROKERING ACTIVITIES

INTRODUCTION

On 5 November 2001, a Panama-registered ship, the *Otterloo*, offloaded 14 containers with 3,117 AK-47s and 5 million rounds of ammunition in the port of Turbo in Colombia. The weapons, which were previously owned by the Nicaraguan armed forces, reached the armed group Autodefensas Unidas de Colombia (AUC), for which they were intended (OAS, 2003b). The complex deal at the origins of this weapon transfer had been organized by an Israeli broker, Shimon Yelinek, and his associate, Marco Shrem, who both declared themselves brokers for the Panamanian National Police (PNP). Yelinek had bought the weapons under a false purchase order from the PNP; he then had been instrumental in arranging their transportation to the AUC. Yelinek called off a second order when word leaked out of a joint investigation by Panama, Colombia, and Nicaragua into the weapon purchase. He was arrested in Panama in November 2002 (OAS, 2003b). In August 2003, a Panamanian first-instance criminal court dismissed the charges against Yelinek on grounds of lack of jurisdiction, given that the weapons had been loaded in Nicaragua and delivered in Colombia. The court's decision was appealed by the Panama Fiscalia de Drogas, which took over the investigation (*El Panamá América*, 2003).[1]

As shown by this example, brokers and their activities are central in the illicit small arms trade, even if their role and functions, while new neither to the international sphere nor to the arms business, have remained relatively unnoticed for decades. This has changed in recent years, during which policy agendas and research conducted by various governmental and non-governmental institutions have increasingly focused on the issue of illicit brokering activities.

This research has developed in parallel with, and sometimes as a consequence of, increased concern expressed in international, regional, and national forums about the role of brokers in illicit transfers of small arms and light weapons. During the 2001 *United Nations Conference on the Illicit Trade of Small Arms and Light Weapons in All Its Aspects* (2001 UN Small Arms Conference), for example, 79 states mentioned the issue of illicit brokering in their opening statements.[2] These countries stressed that efforts to tackle the illicit small arms trade could not neglect the role played by brokers, and called for some form of regulation in this area. Some countries spoke of 'standards', while others advocated 'strict regulation' and, in a few cases, 'legally binding instruments' (Small Arms Survey, 2003, p. 231).

Existing research has highlighted how the ways in which brokers typically carry out illicit deals are grounded in a series of regulatory gaps that are present at both national and international levels. This chapter complements this research by analysing the attempts by individual states and regional and international organizations to prevent illicit arms brokering. It particularly focuses on countries that have established national regulations on brokering, and compares these regulations to identify differences and potential loopholes. Finally, the chapter assesses whether such national regulations are effective in controlling illicit arms brokering.

The main findings of this chapter are as follows:

- Brokers acting illicitly play a key role in diverting weapons to illicit destinations.
- Controls on legal and illicit brokering are closely linked: unless states regulate the former, they will be unable to prevent the latter.
- Activities on the issue of small arms brokering, promoted by states at both national and international levels, rely primarily on national capacities for adopting and implementing brokering controls.
- At the national level, only 25 states have explicit regulations on brokering. These differ widely, creating potential loopholes and the possibility of circumvention.
- Even in countries that have enacted relevant legislation, effective implementation of brokering controls presents a number of challenges.
- International cooperation is critical in preventing illicit brokering activities.

The first section of the chapter briefly describes brokers' activities and their modus operandi, thus identifying the regulatory gaps that allow illicit brokering to take place almost undisturbed; the second analyses the initiatives to control brokering that have been developed at the international, regional, and national levels; finally, the third section assesses the effectiveness of existing national controls on brokers. While the focus of this chapter is on brokering of small arms transfers, it should be noted that brokering is rarely restricted to small arms and light weapons, and often involves other arms technologies, including major weapon systems.

MAKING ILLICIT BROKERING POSSIBLE

In order to grasp the full significance of the role of brokers in arms transfers, a broad definition of the term is necessary (see Box 5.1). The *Small Arms Survey 2001* identified seven main services offered by brokers (Small Arms Survey, 2001, p. 100). These can be broadly divided into 'core' services—mediation in negotiations of weapon deals—and 'associated' brokering activities—transportation, financing, insurance, and technical assistance services. Brokers may facilitate one or more aspects of a weapon deal, from the identification of the weapons' sources to their delivery to the final recipient. Thanks to their expertise and contacts, especially in an increasingly large and complex global economic system, brokers have become an important resource for states and private companies involved in legal weapon transfers. In this sense, brokering cannot be considered an illicit activity *per se*. However, prominent cases revealed in recent years clearly point to brokers as key actors in carrying out illicit arms deals.

Brokers are key actors in illicit small arms deals.

A number of UN Panels found that brokers were instrumental in the diversion of weapons to embargoed countries such as Angola, Liberia, Sierra Leone, Somalia, and Rwanda. Other research has also stressed the role of brokers in transferring weapons to zones of conflict, such as Sri Lanka and the Democratic Republic of Congo (DRC). While arguably not in violation of international law when an arms embargo has not been imposed, arms transfers to zones of conflict violate many national regulations on arms exports, and may contradict states' obligations under international human rights and humanitarian law.

> **Box 5.1 Defining brokering activities**
>
> As an activity that is essentially intangible as well as encompassing diverse types of operations, brokering is hard to define in detail. Wood and Peleman (2000, p. 129) define brokers as 'middlemen who organize arms transfers between two or more parties. Essentially, they bring together buyers, sellers, transporters, financiers and insurers to make a deal'. While describing brokers' activities in a comprehensive and exhaustive way, such a definition would not serve the purpose of regulatory instruments, which aim to identify what clearly falls within their scope of control. This tension between the need for comprehensiveness and for precision is reflected at the international level where, even if some proposals have been made, no definition of 'brokering activities' has yet been agreed.
>
> A study conducted by the UN Group of Governmental Experts on the 'feasibility of restricting the manufacture and trade of small arms to the manufacturers and dealers authorized by States' (UN, 2001), which was presented during the 2001 UN Small Arms Conference, proposed distinctions between dealers, agents, brokers, and transportation agents in an attempt to capture the various types of brokering activities. While straightforward in theory, such distinctions prove difficult to frame in practice, since the boundaries between the four categories are often blurred. At the opposite extreme, the Model Regulations of the Organization of American States (OAS) define a large spectrum of activities as brokering, which range from manufacture to delivery of arms, and include 'exporting, importing, financing, mediating, purchasing, selling, transferring, transporting, freight-forwarding' (OAS, 2003a, art. 1). Broad definitions are also contained in the *EU Common Position on the Control of Arms Brokering* (EU, 2003) and in the *Protocol on the Control of Firearms, Ammunition and Other Related Materials in the Southern African Development Community (SADC) Region* (SADC, 2001).
>
> At the national level, a few countries provide an explicit definition of brokering activities. This is the case, among others, with Belgium, France, Slovakia, South Africa, Switzerland, Ukraine, and the United States.[3] Among these, the definition established in the South African legislation is both comprehensive and specific, and might offer a good legal basis for the scope of brokering controls. In the National Conventional Arms Control Act, brokering services are defined as:
>
> (a) acting as an agent in negotiating or arranging a contract, purchase, sale or transfer of conventional arms for a commission, advantage or cause, whether financially or otherwise;
> (b) acting as an agent in negotiating or arranging a contract for the provision of services for a commission, advantage or cause, whether financially or otherwise;
> (c) facilitating the transfer of documentation, payment, transportation or freight forwarding, or any combination of the aforementioned, in respect of any transaction relating to buying, selling or transfer of conventional arms; and
> (d) acting as intermediary between any manufacturer or supplier of conventional arms, or provider of services, and any buyer or recipient thereof (South Africa, 2002, Preamble, 1.i).
>
> The South African definition is broad enough to include the core activity of mediation and the arrangement of associated activities like transportation and financing. It does not limit the scope of controlled activities to those that facilitate transfers only between third countries. It recognizes that non-financial forms of payment can be made in exchange for brokering services. Finally, it is generic enough to include both those cases in which brokers directly possess the weapons they sell and those (the majority) in which they do not.

Illicit brokering presents a number of common features that highlight loopholes—regulatory gaps or inadequacies of existing controls—that make it possible.

Unregulated activities. In many cases, brokers do not acquire ownership of the weapons they sell. An important consequence of this is that brokers' activities, which are more intangible than those of importers and exporters, are rarely defined as a specific category under national arms export laws. They are, therefore, typically unregulated (Wood and Peleman, 2000, p. 129).

Lax control on weapon stocks. Various cases show that existing surplus or second-hand weapon stocks are valuable sources of supply for brokers acting illicitly. This is possible because the life cycle of small arms is notoriously long, and weapons that are considered old or unserviceable in some countries can nevertheless serve the purposes

Regulatory gaps and inadequate control mechanisms make illicit brokering possible.

of other countries engaged in conflict. As pointed out by a number of UN Panels' reports, weapons originating from existing government stocks, mainly but not exclusively from Eastern European countries, have found their way to African countries under embargo (UNSC, 2000a, para. 41; 2000b, paras 35–6). Lax controls on weapon stockpiles and government surplus weapons are then a primary loophole that brokers acting illicitly exploit.

Third-party brokering. In many instances so-called third party brokering takes place: deals are arranged without the weapons entering the territory in which the intermediary activity occurs. Often, in fact, brokers do not reside in the weapons' country of origin, nor do they live in the countries that the weapons pass through or ultimately arrive in (Clegg and Crowley, n.d., p. 5). This creates various monitoring and enforcement difficulties; many countries have problems enforcing their regulations outside their territories. More importantly, even some countries that have brokering regulations cannot apply them if the weapons traded do not cross the national territory.

Offshore financing. Brokers frequently establish their illicit activities in tax havens and countries with lax export or transit controls. From the point of view of financing illicit arms deals, the need to conceal payment trails and to launder money puts a premium on tax havens, offshore banks, and countries with strong bank secrecy systems. Financial tax havens are favourite choices of brokers acting illegally because of their strong confidentiality practices with money transactions, lax regulation, and lack of income tax, among other reasons (Small Arms Survey, 2001, p. 104). Offshore banks are attractive because they are exempt from the host country's rules relating to interest rates, capital adequacy, and liquidity. Offshore banks are often used to split the main transaction into a set of multiple payments between banks with lax controls or protected by secrecy, usually in the name of shell companies (Naylor, 2000, pp. 166–7).

Easily circumvented documentation requirements. Successful brokers have great expertise in obtaining the necessary official documentation, whether through forgery or by exploiting the negligence or active complicity of state officials. This is true particularly of end-user certificates (EUCs) without which, in principle, states would not authorize an arms export. For example, the Panel of Experts appointed by the UN Security Council (UNSC) to conduct a follow-up assessment on Liberia's compliance with the arms embargo of 2001[4] documented weapons sales to the country on the basis of a false Nigerian EUC (UNSC, 2003a, para. 69). The weapons, which included automatic rifles, automatic pistols, missile launchers, machine guns, pistols, and various types of ammunition, were delivered from Belgrade in six shipments from June to August 2002. These shipments were brokered by a Belgrade-based company, Temex, and the weapons were delivered by a Moldovan company, Aerocom, and by the Belgian affiliate of Ducor World Airlines (UNSC, 2003a, para. 70). During the investigation, Serbian authorities confirmed that all the weapons had been manufactured by a Serbian company, Zastava, between 2001 and 2002, and that the serial numbers found by the Panel corresponded with those of the weapons that Temex declared were destined for the Nigerian Ministry of Defence (para. 72). The Nigerian Ministry of Foreign Affairs, in an official letter transmitted to the Government of Serbia and Montenegro through its embassy in Lagos, stressed that the EUCs used for this deal were false documents (para. 72).

Ease of transport. Transportation is also a key aspect of brokering activities, and one that easily exploits difficulties of enforcement and monitoring. While the choice among transportation modes—by land, sea, or air (see Box 5.2)—depends on a number of factors, including the size of the weapons transferred and the geography of destinations, a number of tactics are commonly used by transport agents.

Box 5.2 Transporting weapons by air

Air freight is a popular mode of transport for illicit weapon deliveries, particularly small arms and light weapons. It is fast, and speed in delivery and turn-around may reduce the chances of detection (UNSC, 2003a, para. 104). Arms brokers looking to move their cargo by air often turn to *ad hoc* charter airlines, companies that will let their planes, or the cargo space on them, to the highest bidders. Much of the air charter industry consists of small companies that operate only one or a handful of aircraft that are usually old. It is most often the smaller cargo companies that operate to and in countries with weak law enforcement capacities, especially if these countries are politically unstable.

With an increasing number of older aircraft like the DC-8 and Boeing 707 coming onto the market, cargo planes have become relatively inexpensive, which in part explains the explosion in the number of small private companies willing to fly just about anything to just about anywhere. As a result of fierce competition, profits on regular flights tend to be marginal, and many of the smaller charter companies are struggling financially. Some are therefore hard-put to resist lucrative contracts, like those involving weapons and ammunition. According to industry sources, few charter companies have not been engaged, at one time or another, in arms shipments. However, some companies appear more willing than others to ship weapons to governments or non-state actors involved in armed conflict even if this violates an arms embargo.[5]

Because transporting arms can be very profitable, companies that do fly weapons are able to substantially underbid other companies for contracts carrying regular commercial cargo on the return flight. This means that airlines that refuse to fly weapons lose valuable general freight business. This then creates a vicious circle that drives some airlines that previously refused to ferry weapons to reconsider their opposition to the arms trade, as a way to keep their airlines in business. A UN Panel of Experts recognized this situation, stating: 'Operators can find themselves in a position where taking certain risks could well be one of only a few options available in order to stay afloat economically' (UNSC, 2000c, para. 116).

Source: Hogendoorn and Misol (2003)

Illicit arms deliveries to the final recipients are commonly broken into numerous shorter trips that involve many sub-contractors and different companies. Such complexity is designed to make it very hard to trace the exact route, and therefore the origin, of the weapons, or to identify the individuals or companies originally responsible for the shipment (Hogendoorn and Misol, 2003; Wood and Peleman, 2000).

Also, transport agents typically disguise the content of the goods they deliver. Arms have been described as a host of other innocuous goods, such as food, clothing, agricultural equipment, tents (Wood and Peleman, 2000, p. 140), technical equipment, or metalwork. In August 2003, for example, the UN Panel of Experts investigating the embargo violations in Liberia reported the offloading of cargo from a 'suspected arms flight' from Iran to Guinea. The cargo contained green boxes with green ropes that soldiers loaded onto military trucks. The cargo manifest indicated that 'detergent' material was contained in the boxes. The Panel's suspicions were confirmed by an oral testimony, according to which ammunition was in the cargo, which was forwarded to Liberia (UNSC, 2003b, para. 4; HRW, 2003).

Cover blown: Italian customs police find weapons in a truck whose manifest said it contained humanitarian aid for Kosovo refugees in April 1999.

SMALL ARMS SURVEY 2004

Other tactics used by transport agents include diversion from authorized routes, with 'emergency stops' that are used to load cargo different from that declared in the accompanying documentation or to offload concealed weapons to other means of transportation; the filing of false flight plans (Small Arms Survey, 2001, p. 113; Wood and Peleman, 2000, p. 141); and the establishment of companies in countries with lax regulations, as is the case with the so-called 'flags of convenience' (FOCs) (see Box 5.3).

Box 5.3   Flags of convenience

A major tactic used by brokers to transport weapons illicitly is through the establishment of business companies in countries that provide 'flags of convenience' (FOCs). Companies that own aircraft and ships are required to register these vessels with the relevant authorities of a national government, this giving each vessel the nationality of its country of registration and placing it under the legal jurisdiction of that country. Some countries serve as FOCs, offering easy registration, even to companies that have no ownership or operational link to the flag country. FOCs are popular because they are cheaper, impose fewer taxes, and offer maximum discretion and lack of transparency with minimal regulatory interference (ITF, 2003).[6] Many FOCs have shown themselves to be unable or unwilling to monitor and enforce companies' compliance with international rules and standards, and so attract arms traffickers seeking to register their transport companies with them (Vines, 2002). When arms-related scandals force one registry to clean up or close, as has happened with Liberia's civil aviation registry[7] and the maritime registry of Tonga,[8] another FOC stands ready to lend its flag. As noted by UN investigators, it takes 'only a matter of hours' for a company to register in another country (UNSC, 2000c, para. 144).[9]

Source: Hogendoorn and Misol (2003)

Transport agents exploit the difficulties in enforcing customs controls, particularly in countries with long borders and limited resources.

When delivering illicit cargo, transport agents exploit the difficulties in enforcing customs controls, particularly in countries with long borders and few resources. They also exploit the favourable situation created by the increasing scale of transnational commercial activities that, coupled with the lack of cooperation between customs authorities, makes systematic checks of cargoes very difficult. However, the transportation of weapons remains the most 'visible' part of an illicit arms deal and, therefore, one with great potential for monitoring. As pointed out by the UN Panel of Experts investigating violations of the embargo on UNITA, the transportation of goods creates a real 'paper trail', a long list of documents (for loading and offloading cargo, registering aircraft and ships, crossing borders, and obtaining landing permits) that, if adequately controlled, could help reconstruct and punish illicit arms transactions (UNSC, 2000a, para. 167).

Israeli Defence Force labels identify assault rifles, ammunition clips, and mortar equipment on the deck of the Karine-A, seized in the Red Sea in January 2002 with 50 tonnes of mainly Iranian-supplied weapons and explosives for the Palestinian Authority.

The preceding description of illicit brokering activities points to a number of implications for their control:

- It is clear that controlling the activity of arms brokers is not a matter just of the existence of regulations but also of their implementation and enforcement. In this respect, and given the inherently transnational nature of illicit brokering, international cooperation is critical.
- Controls on brokers cannot be divorced from the control of weapons generally. In this sense, controls on existing stockpiles, which serve as the main source of illicitly brokered deals, acquire great importance.

- Given that diversion from legal transfers is a common practice among brokers, brokering controls should be complementary to, not a substitute for, systems of regulation governing the export, import, and transit of weapons (Mason, 2003).

GLOBAL AND REGIONAL INITIATIVES FOR THE CONTROL OF BROKERING ACTIVITIES

As knowledge about the role and characteristics of illicit brokering activities has grown, international momentum has built around initiatives to control these. A great number of international and regional processes have been initiated, all of which are still under way, aimed at preventing illicit arms brokering. At the very least, these initiatives have aimed to bring states together to discuss the nature of the issue and possible solutions. In a few instances, these processes have led to the adoption of documents setting out the measures that states should adopt to counter illicit brokering. While these processes vary greatly in scope and strength, they all rely on national controls as the primary means of regulating arms brokering activities. International momentum on the issue is undoubtedly strong.

International momentum on the issue of illicit brokering is growing.

This could be considered surprising, given that, during the 2001 UN Small Arms Conference, while some states spoke of necessary common 'standards', 'strict regulation', and, in a few cases, 'legally binding instruments' for the control of illicit brokering activities (Small Arms Survey, 2003, p. 231), the issue of brokering was dealt with in relatively diluted terms in the UN *Programme of Action* (UNGA, 2001). At the national level, states were encouraged 'to develop adequate national legislation or administrative procedures regulating the activities of those who engage in small arms and light weapons brokering'. Measures such as 'registration of brokers, licensing or authorization of brokering transactions as well as the appropriate penalties for all illicit brokering activities' were listed as suitable (UNGA, 2001, II.14). At the global level, states agreed to 'develop common understandings of the basic issues and the scope of the problems related to illicit brokering in small arms and light weapons with a view to preventing, combating and eradicating the activities of those engaged in such brokering' (UNGA, 2001, II.39).

Far from dropping off the agenda, brokering was taken up again, at the global level, during the First Biennial Meeting of States (BMS) to consider the implementation of the UN *Programme of Action*, held in New York on 7–11 July 2003. Brokering was listed as a stand-alone issue on the informal agenda for the thematic discussion circulated by the chair of the meeting. This was an important development, since it created an opportunity for targeted discussions on the problem.[10] The Chairperson's Summary, which was annexed to the BMS final report, also stated that 'it is widely accepted that progress in addressing the question of illicit brokering depends largely on the level of international cooperation, particularly in information sharing, compliance, and law enforcement' (UNGA, 2003, Annex, para. 35).

An important indication of states' priority concerns around small arms was contained in the statements that countries gave, either on their own behalf or on behalf of regional groups, during the BMS. The issue of brokering was mentioned in 19 statements,[11] representing a total of 40 countries. Some of the national statements—Colombia, Germany, Sweden, and Italy for the European Union (EU)—contained an explicit call for the adoption of a legally binding international instrument on the subject.

Almost all the states that mentioned brokering in their national statements were members either of the EU and associated countries or of the Organization of American States (OAS). This is not surprising, as it is in these two regions that measures to control the illicit brokering of small arms are the most advanced. Statements by regional

147

groups during the BMS confirmed that it is primarily in the EU and the OAS that control of brokering activities is regarded as necessary, as no other region has given any priority to the issue at this stage.[12]

Outside the EU and the OAS, at least for the time being, developments have been absent or much slower because it is believed that illicit brokering is not a significant factor in the illicit spread of small arms. This is at odds with the findings of recent research, which have shown that brokers acting illegally have been crucial to the diversion of weapons to illicit destinations (such as embargoed countries), particularly in Africa. However, this situation might change, given that in some regions in Africa, attention is being focused on the problem of illicit brokering (see Box 5.4).

Positive influence, in this sense, might also be exerted by the latest UN General Assembly resolution on the illicit trade in small arms and light weapons, approved during the 58th session of the Assembly. In paragraph 11 of the resolution, the General Assembly requested the Secretary-General to hold broad-based consultations with all member states and interested regional and subregional organizations 'on further steps to enhance international cooperation in preventing, combating and eradicating illicit brokering in small arms and light weapons'. The Secretary-General is also requested to report to the next session of the Assembly on the results of these consultations (UNGA, 2004, para. 11).

Regional initiatives

As the issue of illicit brokering has attracted more attention within the UN Conference process, a number of other initiatives have been undertaken in some regions. Developments in the EU and the OAS have been particularly significant.

The European Union. In the EU, a *Common Position on the Control of Brokering Activities* was passed in June 2003 by the EU Council (EU, 2003). The Position, which is legally binding, established that EU Member States would enact or improve, as appropriate, national legislation to control brokering activities, and laid out the provisions that national regulations should contain, relating to, among other things, licensing, record-keeping, international exchange of information, and criminal sanctions. Some provisions, related to extraterritorial jurisdiction and registration, were indicated as optional.

Two elements of the Common Position are worth noting. First, brokering activities are defined as those of persons and entities 'negotiating or arranging transactions that may involve the transfer of items on the EU Common List of military equipment from a third country to any other third country'. The Position leaves it optional for states to include among the controlled brokering activities those that relate to weapons originating from their own territory (art. 2.3). Second, while making control of activities that occur within one state's territory a key provision, the Position 'encourages' Member States to 'consider controlling brokering activities outside of their territory carried out by brokers of their nationality resident or established in their territory' (art. 2.1).

As a result of the Common Position, EU states that do not yet have brokering controls (Denmark, Greece, Ireland, Italy,[13] Luxemburg, Portugal, Spain, and the UK) are in the process of discussing or adopting them (Anders, 2003).

The Organization of American States. Within the OAS, *Model Regulations for the Control of Brokers of Firearms, their Parts and Components and Ammunition* were approved during the Inter-American Drug Abuse Commission (CICAD) meeting in November 2003 in Montreal (OAS, 2003a). The regulations consist of nine articles, and two annexes that are intended as guidelines for the framing of national legislation. The articles cover definitions, competent national authorities, registration, licensing, prohibitions, offences, liability of legal entities, scope of controls, and reports and inspections. The annexes reproduce models of registration and licensing application forms, thus listing the information that national authorities should obtain from interested agents in considering their request to engage in brokering activities.

These regulations define brokering activities in very broad terms, covering, among other things, financing and transporting of weapons (art. 1). Licensing systems are viewed as the minimum requirement for effective control, with registration as an option. However, it is suggested that a *de facto* register of brokers be constructed with the information collected for licence applications (art. 3). Importantly, the regulations make people convicted of related serious crimes ineligible for registration and licensing, and require national authorities to exchange information on ineligibility, debarments, and denied applicants (arts. 3.1, 3.12, 4.5). The regulations spell out a number of criteria for assessing licence applications. These include the risk that the transferred weapons could result in genocide, crimes against humanity, or human rights violations; in the violation of UN Security Council arms embargoes or other sanctions imposed by international organizations; or in diversion for illicit activities (art. 5). Finally, the regulations require that violations of the arms brokering provisions be made offences under national legislation with appropriate criminal penalties (art. 6).

The OAS Model Regulations are specifically designed to control brokering of small arms and light weapons, not of weapon systems in general. The effectiveness of this instrument, therefore, and the risk of significant legal loopholes being created, will strongly depend on how small arms are defined. Moreover, the regulations are not legally binding; it will then be up to governments to choose to incorporate them into national laws making them binding. However, the Model Regulations represent an important step in the attempt to harmonize national approaches to the control of brokers and their activities.

Promising developments have also occurred within the framework of the Wassenaar Arrangement (WA) and of the Organization for Security and Co-operation in Europe (OSCE) even if, so far, they have produced political rather than legally binding documents.

The Wassenaar Arrangement. In a document adopted during the Plenary Meeting of 12 December 2003 in Vienna, states participating in the WA agreed to 'strictly control the activities of those who engage in the brokering of conventional arms by introducing and implementing adequate laws and regulations' (WA, 2003). The document was adopted following a series of WA initiatives on export (including brokering) controls, particularly the *Statement of Understanding on Arms Brokerage* of December 2002 (WA, 2002). It lists the measures that national regulations should include 'in order to ensure a common WA policy on arms brokering', as follows:

- mandatory licensing of arms-brokering activities to be carried out in the state where these take place, if the weapons are transferred from a third country to another third country;
- record-keeping of legal and natural entities that have obtained a brokering licence;
- prescribing adequate penalties, including administrative measures, for the punishment of illicit brokering activities;
- international exchange of relevant information; and
- assistance to other member states for the establishment of effective national controls on brokering activities.

The WA document also suggests optional measures, such as the regulation of brokers even when weapons originate from the state's territory (in addition to controls on the exporter), the establishment of national registers of brokers, and the extraterritorial application of brokering controls (WA, 2003).

The Organization for Security and Co-operation in Europe. Within the OSCE, and following the Forum for Security Cooperation (FSC) Decision No 11/02 (10 July 2002), a set of eight Best Practice Guides (BPG) were approved to help states identify regulatory options for the prevention of illicit small arms transfers. The BPG on brokering identified a set of measures—some essential, some optional—that states should adopt to exercise effective control over

> Promising developments for the control of illicit brokering have taken place within the Wassenaar Arrangement and the OSCE frameworks.

brokering activities, of which the most important was licensing systems. In particular, the BPG suggested that, to be effective, licensing systems should cover all 'core brokering activities' conducted on a state's territory, whether by nationals or by foreigners. 'Core activities' included:

- acquisition of small arms located in one third country for the purpose of transfer to another third country;
- mediation between sellers and buyers of small arms to facilitate their transfer from one third country to another third country; and
- the indication of an opportunity for such a transaction to the seller or buyer (in particular, the introduction of a seller or buyer in return for a fee or other consideration) (OSCE, 2003, p. 4).

The BPG treated the control of associated activities as optional. These included the arrangement of transportation, freight forwarding, and charter services; technical services; financial services; and insurance services (OSCE, 2003, p. 5). It also listed measures relating to the registration of brokers, criteria for assessing licence applications, mechanisms for enforcement, penalties for violations, and international cooperation.

These regional initiatives vary considerably in rigour. In particular, only the EU Common Position is legally binding. The degree to which the others influence national policies will therefore depend both on the follow-up to these processes within the same organizations and, to a great extent, on national decisions. However, these regional instruments, even where non-binding, are important for a number of reasons.

For a start, they reveal the salience that the issue of controlling brokering activities has gained on the international agenda. At the same time, they build on such salience and are an important means of furthering it. Second, these processes bring together diverse countries, some of which are vitally important for the control of the small arms trade. Third, they represent important steps in the harmonization of policies towards brokering issues, a necessary

---

Box 5.4   The Dutch–Norwegian Initiative on further steps to enhance international cooperation in preventing, combating, and eradicating illicit brokering in small arms and light weapons

Since April 2003, the Dutch and Norwegian governments have sponsored a series of international discussions on the problem of illicit small arms brokering, aimed at framing internationally agreed measures that states would adopt, at the national level, for its prevention. The first result of the Dutch–Norwegian Initiative (DNI) was an international conference held in Oslo on 22–24 April 2003, which brought together 71 experts, representing 28 states, in addition to international organizations, research institutes, and NGOs from around the world.

During the conference, key issues relating to the control of brokering activities were discussed. The report from the conference identified a number of measures that states should adopt within their jurisdictions to control brokering activities. These included systems of licensing and registration, penalty regimes, and mechanisms for international cooperation. The conference was important since it brought together governments from very different regions, and helped build on harmonized approaches to the prevention of illicit brokering.

As a follow-up to the DNI, the Dutch and Norwegian governments invited the main regional organizations to initiate discussions on arms brokering. Positive informal responses were received from many regional organisations.

Formal initiatives have been launched in cooperation with the Economic Community of West African States (ECOWAS) secretariat. ECOWAS hosted a regional conference to discuss small arms problems in the region with a particular emphasis on brokering. Conference participants tried to identify possible solutions as a basis for a regional plan of action. The initiative in ECOWAS was also supported by the UK government.

In the OSCE, the governments of the Netherlands and Norway have launched an initiative to formulate a common position for OSCE member states with respect to the adoption and implementation of legislation on brokering small arms. The government of Germany has joined this initiative.

step for effective control. Indeed, it has been pointed out that inconsistencies and strong differences among national regulatory systems are damaging to the effective prevention of illicit brokering activities as they undercut the value of national regulations. Brokers moving business from countries with strong regulations to countries with weaker ones provide compelling evidence of this.

A common feature of these regional instruments is their reliance on state regulations as the primary means for the control of brokering activities. While emphasizing the importance of international cooperation, they primarily underline the need for individual states to adopt, or improve, controls on brokers and their activities. The instruments also share a common focus on regulations and legislative frameworks as the primary means of controlling brokers. As well, some specific measures are consistently cited as the building blocks of national regulations on brokering, notably licensing systems. These are important developments, since they get to the heart of the issue of brokering controls, in two respects. First, the general regulatory void in which brokers operate is problematic and is a striking missing link in the chain of controls on the small arms trade. Second, controls on licit and illicit brokering are closely linked: unless states regulate the former, they will be unable to prevent the latter.

NATIONAL REGULATIONS ON BROKERING ACTIVITIES

Currently, only 25 countries have regulations governing the brokering of arms deals.

Some of these regulations are very recent, and their adoption has been spurred by recent debates over the central role of arms brokers in illicit arms transfers. This section gives an overview of existing national regulations on arms brokering. It will not treat each national system in detail but will rather compare national provisions in the following key issue areas:

Brokers make their deals behind the scenes. Only 25 countries have regulations that could curb such illicit transactions.

- licensing systems;
- extraterritorial jurisdiction;
- registration requirements;
- reporting obligations on the part of brokers; and
- penalties.

The purpose of this comparison is to highlight how different national approaches might affect actual control over brokering activities. Most of the analysis is of the relevant national legal texts (laws and regulations); it has also examined the reports on the implementation of the UN *Programme of Action* submitted for the BMS, with clarifications directly from national officials. It is important to stress that only those regulations that clearly define the activity of brokering as subject

SMALL ARMS SURVEY 2004

to national controls have been taken into account. That is, the analysis excludes the majority of national regulations, in which brokering activity is not explicitly defined but could be covered by existing export and import controls, because the use of export controls to regulate brokering activities, where the latter are not clearly defined, is not straightforward, but would depend on an extensive interpretation of the law. There is in fact a great difference between a national system that could be used to control brokers and one that considers brokering conducted without state authorization as illegal.

In total, 25 countries have brokering regulations in place: Austria, Belgium, Bulgaria, the Czech Republic, Estonia, Finland, France, Germany, Hungary, Israel, Italy, Japan, Latvia, Lithuania, the Netherlands, Norway, Poland, Romania, Slovakia, Slovenia, South Africa, Sweden, Switzerland, Ukraine, and the United States. Of these, 23 will be analysed in the next section.[14]

The geographical distribution of these countries is striking: 21 are in the European region, and one each from the Middle East, Africa, Asia, and North America (see Map 5.1).

> Of the 25 countries with brokering regulations, 21 are in the European region.

Also, although some additional countries have announced they are in the process of adopting or considering such regulations, the total number remains very low.[15] This, for the moment, seems unlikely to change, given that the establishment of brokering controls does not appear as a priority for the majority of states. As mentioned, government statements during the BMS indicated that the firmest support for such controls come from the OAS and EU regions. This was confirmed by the statements given during the Security Council debate on small arms, held in New York on 19 January 2004. During the debate, 16 statements, representing in total 47 states, mentioned the issue of illicit brokering.[16] Eight of these (including Ireland on behalf of the EU and associated countries) belong to the EU or OAS region. The remaining eight are unevenly distributed among the Arab League (Algeria and Egypt), ECOWAS (Benin and Sierra Leone), SADC (Angola and South Africa), plus Armenia and India. Among these eight states, there were vague references to the problem of illicit brokering or unscrupulous brokers (Egypt and India), the general call for controls in this area (Angola), and the stress on national registers and/or international cooperation as a means of preventing illicit brokering activities (Algeria, Benin, and Armenia).

Map 5.1   Countries with brokering controls

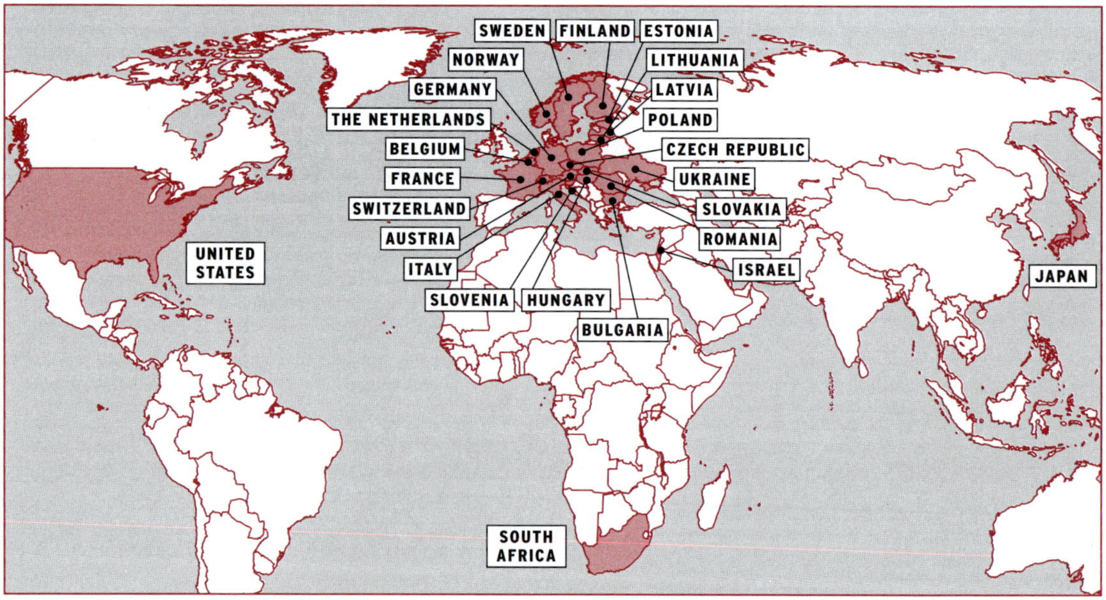

While, for the most part, the issue of brokering controls is simply ignored (for example, in the Association of South-East Asian Nations (ASEAN), as well as in some of the Arab League members' statements), in some instances it is explicitly mentioned as one that 'does not pose any problem', and therefore that does not need to be addressed with specific measures. In this group of states, particularly relevant is the attitude of big small arms producers, notably China and Russia.

Licensing of brokering activities

Licensing systems have been identified by the *UN Feasibility Study* as the principal means, along with registration and disclosure requirements, by which states can exercise effective control on brokering activities (UN, 2001, para. 64).

Arms broker licensing is in place when individual and/or commercial entities cannot legally engage in intermediary activities unless they have received explicit consent by the relevant national authorities. Without this consent, the relevant activity is automatically illicit and therefore liable to legal prosecution.

Given the opportunities they offer for state monitoring, it is not surprising that all of the 23 surveyed countries have brokering licensing systems. In three of these countries, Hungary, Italy, and the Netherlands, the licensing is not sanctioned by law but operates in practice (Hungary, 2003; Italy, 2003, p. 4; Netherlands, 1997, art. 9.1; 2003b, p. 6).[17] These licensing systems, however, vary greatly along five main dimensions: types of licensed activities, scope of brokering controls, types of goods for whose transfer brokering must be licensed, types of brokering licences (individual/open), and criteria for the assessment of licence applications.

> Licensing systems have been identified as the key means to control brokering activities.

Types of activities subject to licensing

While an internationally agreed definition of brokering activities has not yet emerged, the distinction between core and associated activities has become commonplace. Thus, the majority of the analysed national systems distinguish between licensing solely the activity of mediation and/or the related activities such as transportation and financing. While 22 countries require that the core intermediary activity be licensed, only 11 establish such a requirement also for associated activities (see Table 5.1).[18] In addition, in Latvia, only the associated activity of transportation must be licensed: Latvian companies wishing to transport strategic goods in transit outside Latvian territory must possess a licence (Latvia, 1997, art. 14).

Some countries—Bulgaria, the Czech Republic, Hungary, Romania, Slovenia, and Switzerland—have a system of what we might call 'double-licensing': brokers have to possess both an initial, general authorization (permit) and a specific licence (for each deal) to carry out the intermediary activity (Bulgaria, 1995, art. 5; Czech Republic, 1994, art. 6, 14; Hungary, 2003; Romania, 1999, arts. 10–11; Slovenia, 2003a, arts. 1, 14; Switzerland, 1996, arts. 9, 12, 15). In Switzerland, the Federal Law on War Material clearly states that any person who does not possess arms production facilities in the country and who wishes to broker the transfer of war materials to entities abroad needs an initial authorization and a specific licence for each individual deal (Switzerland, 1996, art. 15). The specification of production premises is important, since manufacturers in Switzerland need no specific authorization for brokering war material if they hold an initial permit for the brokering of war material similar to that produced in their own premises (Switzerland, 1998, art. 6.1). This provision covers situations in which a customer's order exceeds the current production capabilities of a Swiss manufacturer. In such cases, Article 6 of the War Material Ordinance allows those manufacturers with production branches abroad to supply the requested goods directly from their foreign branches to their customer, without having to apply for an individual brokering licence.[19]

In two other countries, Slovakia and France, brokers have to apply only for a general authorization or permit (France, 1992, art. 3; Slovakia, 1998, art. 5, 6). In France, this requirement applies to those operations (including the submission and acceptance of offers and the negotiation of contracts entailing the transfer or delivery of war materials abroad) in which the brokered weapons are exported from France.

As for associated activities, Italy and the Netherlands require any agent involved in the financing of arms deals to act under licence. While in Italy this requirement applies to any financial transaction related to the import into, export from, and transit through Italy of military material, and thus does not cover transfers between third countries (Italy, 1990, art. 27.1–2; 2003, p. 8), in the Netherlands the requirement applies to all financial transactions related to transfers of strategic goods—including military-style small arms—taking place outside the EU, carried out by Dutch nationals and residents (the Netherlands, 1996, art. 1; 2003a, p.13).

Bulgaria, Lithuania, Poland, and Slovenia require transportation of military material to be licensed, provided that they cross national territory (Bulgaria, 1995, art. 13a; Poland, 2000, art. 3.8.a; Slovenia, 2003a, art. 14.3).[20] In Germany, persons or entities wishing to transport war weapons that are loaded and unloaded outside German territory, and that do not transit German territory, on ships sailing under the German flag or in aircraft registered in Germany must obtain a licence to do so (1961a, art. 4.1). Estonia, South Africa, and the United States have particularly broad definitions of the associated activities that are subject to licence. In Estonia, for example, all brokering related to 'buying, selling, promoting, advertising, marketing, transporting, handling, developing, producing, testing, maintaining or other services related to WMD [weapons of mass destruction] or conventional arms and their parts' (including small arms) are subject to licence (Estonia, MFA, 2002). In the United States, it includes 'financing, transportation, freight forwarding, or taking of any other action that facilitates the manufacture, export, or import of a defense article or defense service, irrespective of its origin' (2003, sec. 129.2). (For the South African definition of brokering, which includes facilitation of various operations related to arms transfers, see Box 5.1.)

> Exemptions to licensing requirements for brokering activities are common.

It is important to note that exemptions to licensing requirements are common. In general, these are provided for transfers carried out by government agencies, including the armed forces. In two cases, however, the exemption is broader, since it refers to brokering of arms deals directed towards a specified list of countries. In the US, the *International Traffic in Arms Regulations* (2003, sec. 129.6) provide that '[b]rokering activities that are arranged wholly within and destined exclusively for the North Atlantic Treaty Organization, any member country of that Organization, Japan, Australia, or New Zealand' do not require a licence, although with some exceptions, mostly covering WMD and fully automatic firearms and their parts (sec. 127.a.1). In Switzerland the exemption refers only to specific authorizations (the general permit must therefore still be granted) and currently relates to a list of 25 countries (Switzerland, 1998, Annex 2).[21] Clearly, such exemptions are aimed at facilitating commercial transfers with friendly countries. However, as the degree of screening is reduced in these cases, the risk of diversion from the licit to the illicit market is correspondingly higher. This seems all the more important given that cases have occurred of illicit weapon diversions from legal transfers originally intended for friendly or allied countries.

In the case of Lithuania, the licensing exemption covers an entire class of goods. For a start, Lithuanian brokers are not allowed to possess the weapons they assist in selling. Weapons in the Lithuanian system fall under four categories: category A comprises military-style weapons, and categories B, C, and D civilian weapons. While brokers can facilitate deals involving all categories of weapons, they have to possess a licence only for civilian weapons. Only the government can buy or sell military-style weapons in Lithuania, subject to a licence from the Ministry of Economy. The government is considering extending the licensing requirement for brokering activities to the brokering of category A weapons.[22]

Types of goods subject to brokering licences

On the types of goods covered by brokering regulations, EU countries are largely similar, all referring to the Common List of Military Equipment covered by the EU code of conduct on arms exports (EU, 1998). This common list, as well as most national lists on controlled goods, include arms and automatic weapons with a calibre of 12.7 mm or less such as rifles, carbines, revolvers, pistols, machine pistols, and machine guns (sec. 1.1), as well as armaments and weapons with a greater calibre, including guns, howitzers, mortars, anti-tank weapons, projectile launchers, and recoilless rifles (sec. 2.1). Related ammunition is also included (sec. 3). As existing arms brokering legislation is usually integrated into export controls on military weapons, controls extend to the brokering of military small arms and light weapons. Civilian firearms such as hunting and sport shooting rifles are normally excluded from military export controls, and consequently the brokering of such civilian firearms is generally unregulated or subject to other controls (as already mentioned, Lithuania is an important exception in this respect). Also, the system in the Netherlands varies according to the type of brokered weapons. The brokering of transfers of automatic firearms, which are covered by the Arms and Ammunition Act, requires a licence; as for military small arms covered by the Decree on Exports of Strategic Goods, which are the same as those in the Wassenaar Arrangement Munitions List, only *financial transactions* for transfers outside the EU need a licence. Among non-EU countries, four—Bulgaria, Estonia, Norway, and Romania—refer to the Wassenaar Arrangement Munitions List and/or the EU Common List of Military Equipment. The remainder all apply nationally defined lists of armaments that generally cover military-style small arms and light weapons.

Types of brokering licences

Licences granted for brokering activities can be individual or open. Under an individual licence, national authorization is required for each arms transaction, and licences are assessed on a case-by-case basis. Under an open licence, a single authorization covers more than one transfer, usually for a class of goods and/or a set of specified destinations.

Fifteen of the surveyed countries, for instance Italy and South Africa, provide only for individual licences to be granted, and five, for example Germany and Ukraine, provide for both open and individual ones. In Slovakia, only open (general) licences are granted (see Table 5.1). Open licences are usually designed to facilitate certain arms transactions and to reduce the administrative burdens on agents. Their potential for screening, however, might be much less than for licences that are assessed and granted for each transaction. Consequently, the risk of arms diversion to the illicit market is greater with open licences.

> Open licences carry a greater risk of illicit arms diversion.

Scope of brokering controls

National licensing systems differ most in the scope of their application (or extent of their jurisdiction). Part of this issue is whether controls apply extraterritorially, and will be treated in detail below. In this subsection we analyse the types of transfers that require a brokering licence if the intermediary activity is carried out within the territory of the controlling state.

In general terms we can distinguish three basic models of the scope of brokering controls. Under the model with the narrowest jurisdiction, brokering activities must be licensed if they relate to *transfers from, into, or through the controlling state*. This system is found in Italy, Lithuania, and Poland. Thus, if a broker conducts the intermediary activity from the territory of the controlling state, but the weapons do not cross its territory, no licence is necessary. This system clearly creates a serious legal loophole, especially as so-called third-party brokering is a common aspect of illicit weapon transfers. In France, only brokering related to arms exports requires a licence for specific transactions (France, 1992, art. 3). However, brokers must possess an initial authorization to be able to operate, in the form of registration with relevant authorities (France,

1939, art. 2.1; 1995, art. 6). Following the adoption of the EU Common Position (EU, 2003), both France and Italy have started to revise their brokering controls, which will in the future be extended to arms transfers between third countries.

Under the second model, which allows for a greater degree of screening, brokering conducted on the territory of the controlling state and relating to the transfer of military equipment from *one third country to another third country* must be licensed. This model is found in the Czech Republic, Finland, Germany, the Netherlands,[23] Norway, Romania, and Slovakia. Under this system, brokering activities connected with the export from, and import into, the controlling state do not require state authorization. The logic of this model is that, when goods originate in the controlling state's jurisdiction, or are destined for it, it is sufficient to control the exporters and importers to ensure that the weapon transfer is licit. It also appears to be grounded in the intention to avoid administrative burdens linked to a double licensing system for each individual transaction. If import and export controls are efficiently applied, the system does not seem to pose any risks. In the Austrian case, however, the system is applied in a way that creates a potentially serious legal loophole. Under Austrian legislation, brokering activities must be licensed when they involve the transfer of goods *from one country outside the EU to another country outside the EU* (Austria, 1977, art. 1.4). In this sense, Austrian entities brokering weapon deals between EU countries enjoy great—perhaps too great—freedom of action.

Among the surveyed countries, Hungary, Slovenia, and Sweden impose controls whose scope combines versions of the first and second models described here. In Sweden, Swedish authorities and companies, and persons resident or permanently domiciled in the country, require licences to supply military equipment to a person or entity located abroad (Sweden, 1992, sec. 4). 'Supply' of military equipment includes its sale, transfer, offer for sale, loan, gift, or intermediary activity (sec. 2). This licensing requirement also exists for the supply of military equipment located abroad (sec. 5). Similar provisions exist in Hungary, where both the intermediation for weapon transfers between third countries and that for exports from Hungary must be licensed (Hungary, 2003). In Slovenia, brokering requires both a general permit and a specific licence for deals related to export from, import into, and transit through the country. Slovenian agents brokering a transaction between third countries do not need a specific licence. However, they do need a general permit for trading in military arms and equipment.[24] A system such as that of Hungary, Slovenia and Sweden allows, at least in principle and to different degrees, for the full control of brokering activities occurring on the national territory, whether or not the weapons originate there.

The third model has an even broader scope, and it is used in Belgium, Switzerland, Ukraine, and the United States. In these cases the law explicitly states that all brokering activity conducted on the national territory is subject to licensing, *irrespective of the origins of the weapons.* Swiss regulations have a particularly broad application, covering brokering conducted on their territory by any agent (Switzerland, 1996, art. 15). Foreign agents are also covered by Belgian and US legislation: for the first, all Belgian and foreign residents in Belgium need a brokering licence (Belgium, 2003, art. 10); for the second, licences are necessary for all US citizens and all foreign agents subject to the US jurisdiction (US, 2003, sec. 129.2.b). Similarly, in South Africa brokering subject to licensing includes mediation between any manufacturer or supplier of conventional arms, or provider of services, and any buyer or recipient of the same (2002, art. 1.i).

The cases of Bulgaria and Estonia lie outside these three main models. In Bulgaria, what is relevant is not the location of the brokered weapons but the nationality of the contractors. Under Bulgarian law licences are required for both Bulgarian and foreign brokers when the importer or the exporter is a Bulgarian company or citizen.[25] In Estonia, what counts is the link with the country, whether through citizenship or the location of the contractors. Services connected with the development, production, use, or maintenance of military equipment must be licensed, among other things, if they are supplied from or into Estonia and to a foreign recipient in Estonia or to an Estonian recipient abroad (1999, art. 2).

Criteria for assessing licences applications

As with controls on arms exports, those on brokering activities usually establish a number of criteria that national agencies must adopt in deciding on licence applications. In the surveyed systems, such criteria are always spelled out, either in the framework laws or in their implementing regulations. Criteria for licensing can also be established through government decisions or policy guidelines, or can derive from one state's membership in regional or international organizations. In many instances the relevant laws state only a general principle, whose interpretation may vary over time. For example, the majority of countries studied refer to obligations derived from international agreements, which might change over time and alter the corresponding specific criteria. In view of this, as well as the limited sources used, the criteria listed here should not be considered exhaustive. Despite these limitations, a number of general conclusions can be drawn.

In broad terms, criteria for the licensing of brokering closely follow those established by export controls and are indeed usually considered as belonging to broader export controls. Furthermore, states commonly make the national interest a criterion for licensing, and refuse licences for brokering transfers that might endanger national economic, foreign policy, or security interests. All EU countries have agreed on a minimum standard for evaluating licences, contained in eight criteria in the politically binding EU Code of Conduct (EU, 1998). At least in the EU region—and among EU associated countries and others that have joined the Code—a certain potential for uniformity is present.[26] Apart from these common features, national criteria for licensing differ widely.

In a few of the countries surveyed—Belgium, Bulgaria, the Czech Republic, France, Slovakia, and Slovenia—licences are not granted to agents who do not fulfil specified conditions of reliability and/or economic stability.[27] Importantly, in the Czech Republic past violations of trade regulations must be considered. Licences are refused if 'in carrying out foreign trade, or in connection with this trade, the applicant violated domestic or foreign legislation relating to this sphere' (1994, art. 18.b). Three countries—Lithuania, Poland, and the United States—establish lists of recipients for which brokering activities are prohibited or restricted. Usually these lists are established through government decision, and are subject to periodic revision (Poland, 2000, art. 6.3; US, 2003, sec. 129.5.a).[28]

For 12 countries—Austria, Belgium, Bulgaria, Estonia, Germany, Hungary, Italy, Lithuania, Norway, South Africa, Switzerland, and the United States—some criteria for licensing depend on the situation of the recipient of the arms. In particular, brokering licences are refused for transfers to countries under UN Security Council or other international embargo, countries in potential or actual conflict, or countries where weapons might contribute to the violation of human rights (see Table 5.1).

> In 12 countries, some licensing criteria depend on the situation of the arms recipient.

Finally, a few countries—Poland, Slovakia, and Ukraine—impose an obligation on brokers to refrain from facilitating trade in certain situations. In this sense, brokers are considered responsible for the application of the listed criteria, which include:

- the risk that the transferred weapons will be used in human rights violations, will threaten stability, or contribute to terrorist acts (Poland, 2000, art. 10.1);
- national—foreign policy, economic, and trade—interests and obligations rising from international agreements (Slovakia, 1998, art. 10.3); and
- the risk that the transferred weapons will be used for purposes, or by end-users, different from those stated in the contract (Ukraine, 2003, art. 17).

Extraterritorial jurisdiction

Extraterritorial jurisdiction on brokering normally refers to the application of the law to one state's nationals when they operate from abroad. Given the inherently transnational nature of brokering activities, extraterritoriality is a critical issue and one that might be problematic, as it pits one state's sovereignty against that of other states unless inter-state agreements set out principles or procedures under which foreign authorities can enforce controls on one another's territory. The rationale of extraterritorial provisions in brokering regulations is to prevent brokers from evading them merely by crossing the border.

> Extraterritorial jurisdiction helps prevent brokers from evading controls by moving across the border.

A common objection to extraterritorial jurisdiction is that it would not be needed if every state implemented export controls effectively. That is to say, the necessary screening of arms transfers should be carried out by those states from whose territory the weapons originate. While this argument is logical, it remains at odds with the reality that in many countries arms exports are poorly regulated and/or the regulations are poorly enforced, allowing brokers to send weapons to illicit end-users with the minimum of obstacles. Extraterritorial jurisdiction also poses important problems of practical implementation; even if states have the legal framework establishing extraterritorial provisions, how can they enforce them, for example regarding evidence gathering, overseas investigations, and seizing of suspects?

The United States presents the broadest application of extraterritorial provisions concerning brokering activities. The US Arms Export Control Act, as amended in 1996, applies to all US nationals operating in the United States or abroad. It also applies to all foreigners living in or operating from the United States, as well as foreigners who live abroad but *broker US-made weapons or work with US nationals* (Bondi and Keppler, 2001).

Zimbabwean policemen inspect weapons seized in March 1999 from three US citizens who allegedly worked as arms dealers in Congo, Tanzania, and Zimbabwe.

Among the countries surveyed, including the United States, 14 have extraterritorial provisions for the control of brokering activities (see Table 5.1). While the *principle* of extraterritorial controls is common to all these systems, the *degree* to which it is applied varies considerably. Short of the broad interpretation characteristic of the US system, there are in fact many ways in which extraterritoriality can be established.

In seven countries—the Czech Republic,[29] Finland, the Netherlands, Norway, Romania, Sweden, and Ukraine—brokers subject to national jurisdiction must possess a licence even when they conduct operations from abroad, and the weapons they deal with neither enter nor transit national territory. In these countries, arms brokering requires explicit authorization even when the only link between the transaction and the controlling state is the nationality or permanent residence of the broker (Finland, 1990, sec. 2a.2; the Netherlands, 2003b, p. 6; Norway, 2003; Sweden, 1992, sec. 4; Ukraine, 2003, art. 1).[30] In Estonia, reference is made only to the location of the broker's operations, and not to the location of the transferred weapons. Brokering activities subject to licensing include, among others, those by Estonian service suppliers, both legal and natural persons, respectively through the economic activities of or in the territory of a foreign state.[31] Arguably, this provision covers the brokering of weapon transfers between third countries that is conducted abroad by Estonian nationals.

In Poland, brokers operating abroad must possess a licence for operations relating to the transfer from (export), into (import), or in transit through Poland. In this case, therefore, Polish individuals and companies that act as brokers abroad must possess a state authorization, as long as the weapons they help to transfer touch Polish territory (Poland, 2000, art. 1.a-b).

In the remaining four cases, extraterritoriality is established through national judicial competence rather than through an explicit licensing requirement. In Belgium and South Africa, judicial authorities are competent for any violation of the arms brokering regulations, even if such violation occurs outside the national territory (Belgium, 1991, art. 13; South Africa, 2002, art. 26).[32] In both Bulgaria and Germany, the judiciary's competence is restricted to specific cases. A Bulgarian agent who operates outside Bulgaria and brokers a weapon transfer that does not cross Bulgarian territory does not need a licence. However, if such a broker conducts the transfer in breach of a UNSC or EU established embargo, he or she is liable under the Bulgarian Penal Code.[33] In Germany, finally, violations of the provisions on arms brokering in the War Weapons Control Act fall under the competence of German courts if at least one part of the brokering operation took place on German territory (Anders, 2003, p. 8).[34]

Registration of brokers

Registration is one important means by which states can maintain supervision over, and gather information about, companies and individuals engaged in the brokering of arms. The *UN Feasibility Study* identified it as one of the three main regulatory options—together with licensing systems and disclosure requirements—that would allow states to exercise more effective control over brokering activities (UN, 2001, para 64). Beyond the 23 surveyed countries, very few states have registration requirements for brokers. As a consequence, few states have records of the numbers of individuals and companies that are allowed to trade in military and security equipment. While estimates put this number in the order of thousands, the exact figure is not known. This lack of 'institutional memory' has a number of consequences, at both the national and international levels: at the national level because the lack of records makes it impossible for states to prevent individuals and/or companies that have violated national provisions on the trade in military equipment from continuing their activities; at the international level because states cannot exchange information on brokers involved in illicit deals (Small Arms Survey, 2001, p. 126). This means that brokers convicted in one state, or suspected of illicit arms activity, can simply move to another country to continue their activities.

The lack of brokers' registration has important negative consequences at the national and international levels.

Of the 23 surveyed countries, 21 have registration systems. In most of these, brokers must register before they can legally engage in brokering activities, and broker registration works both as an initial authorization and as a form of record-keeping by the state (see Table 5.1).[35] In Germany and the Netherlands the registration requirement is applied to selected cases. In Germany, prior registration is necessary for those seeking a general licence for the transport abroad of war weapons on ships or aircraft registered in Germany (Anders, 2003, p. 14). In the Netherlands, registration is necessary for those wishing to engage in the trade of controlled goods under the 1997 Arms and Ammunition Act, including the transfer of firearms between third countries, but no such requirement applies to the brokering of weapons covered by the 1963 Decree on Exports of Strategic Goods (Anders, 2003, p. 14). In Finland, Norway, Poland, and Sweden, registration of brokers is *de facto*: it does not work as an initial authorization, but simply as a form of data collection on granted licences.[36]

Reporting obligations

To facilitate continued monitoring by state authorities on brokering activities, some of the 23 surveyed countries ask brokers to keep transaction records to report periodically to the relevant institutions, or both. Eleven countries require individuals and companies engaging in brokering activities to keep records of their transactions. In addition, 12 require brokers to submit periodic reports on such transactions (see Table 5.1). Usually, brokers' records must contain information on the parties of the transactions and the weapons brokered, and must be available for inspection by relevant authorities. Where specified, the time period of such records varies from a minimum of three years (Lithuania) to five years (Slovakia), ten (Bulgaria and Switzerland), 15 (Romania), with a maximum of 20 years (Slovenia). As for mandatory reporting to national authorities, time intervals vary from a minimum of one month (Hungary), to three months (Sweden), to four months (the Czech Republic, Norway, and Slovakia), to six months (France and Poland), to a maximum of one year (Bulgaria and the United States). In South Africa, reporting is not automatic but can be requested by national authorities (South Africa, 2002, art. 22.1).

Both records and periodic reports can be a source of important information and can greatly assist effective state monitoring, depending on the type of information that brokers are required to keep and/or provide. For example, Bulgaria asks brokers to keep all transaction and transportation documents in addition to information on the execution of deals (Bulgaria, 1995, art. 14.1–3); France requires that records be updated constantly during the execution of the deal, and that they disclose the names of the parties involved, the contents of the operations, and their status (France, 1995, art. 16); in Germany, persons manufacturing, transporting (including through a third party), or trading weapons have to maintain an arms register indicating their whereabouts (1961a, art. 12.2). The registers must also provide information on people who transport and acquire exported weapons and the date of export (1961b, art. 9);[37] Slovenia generally requires documentation on the export of military weapons and equipment, including on the type, number, and identification code of the military weapons or equipment traded (Slovenia, 2003a, art. 19.1–2).[38]

Penalties: Administrative and criminal

The explicit definition of offences and the provision of corresponding penalties are important, since no action can be legally punished unless it has been defined as an offence. Of the 23 surveyed countries, all but one provide for legal penalties in relation to brokering controls.[39] The one exception is Slovenia, which has indicated that national provisions of the Penal Code will be revised to include crimes related to illicit brokering (Slovenia, 2003b).

Penalties for illicit brokering usually include both fines and imprisonment.

As a general rule, all countries make a distinction between minor and major offences, the first usually involving negligence. Countries usually also provide for both monetary penalties and imprisonment, according to the type of violation. Exceptions include Germany, Hungary, Lithuania, and Slovakia. In Germany, brokering an arms deal involving weapons located abroad, as well as the conclusion of such a contract without the required license, entails punishment by imprisonment of up to five years, and up to ten years in cases of serious violations (1961a, art. 22a.1.7, 22a.2). In Hungary, violations of brokering controls are classified in the Penal Code (arts. 261/A, 263, 263/A, 263/B, 264/C, and 287) and are punishable in the aggregate with up to 15 years of prison terms (Hungary, 2003). Neither Lithuania not Slovakia provides for imprisonment. In nine cases, penalties other than fines and imprisonment are established for some offences. These can include property seizure (Bulgaria, Estonia, and Switzerland), deregistration or debarment (the Czech Republic, Italy, Lithuania, Norway, Ukraine, and the United States), or the dissolution of the commercial activity (Estonia).

The Czech and Ukrainian systems contain the important offence of the granting of fraudulent documents by government officials. In the Czech Republic, '[a] person who has violated or failed to perform an important duty in his employment, profession, position or function thereby causing the illegitimate issue of a permit to trading in military material with a foreign country or a licence for a specific deal involving military material ... shall be punished by a prison term of from six months to three years' (Czech Republic, 1994, art. 124e). Similarly, Ukrainian law establishes

Table 5.1 Elements of national legislation on brokering activities

Country	Licensing requirement (core brokering activities)	Licensing requirement (related brokering activities)	Extraterritorial jurisdiction	Criteria for licensing: human rights	Criteria for licensing: embargoes	Criteria for licensing: conflict areas	Types of licences	Registration	Requirement to keep records (for the broker)	Obligation to report to national authorities	Penalties
1. Austria	Yes			Yes	Yes	Yes	I				F, P
2. Belgium	Yes		Yes	Yes		Yes	I and O	Yes			F, P
3. Bulgaria	Yes	Yes	Yes		Yes	Yes	I	Yes	Yes	Yes	F, P, Ot
4. Czech Rep.	Yes		Yes				I	Yes		Yes	F, P, Ot
5. Estonia	Yes	Yes	Yes	Yes	Yes	Yes	I				F, P, Ot
6. Finland	Yes		Yes				I	De facto	Yes[i]		F, P
7. France	Yes[ii]						I and O	Yes	Yes	Yes	F, P
8. Germany	Yes	Yes	Yes		Yes		I and O	Yes[iii]	Yes		P
9. Hungary*	Yes				Yes	Yes	I	Yes		Yes	P
10. Israel*											
11. Italy	Yes[iv]	Yes		Yes	Yes	Yes	I	Yes			F, P, Ot
12. Japan*											
13. Latvia		Yes						Yes			F, P
14. Lithuania	Yes	Yes		Yes	Yes		I	Yes	Yes		F, Ot
15. Netherlands	Yes[v]	Yes[vi]	Yes				I and O	Yes[vii]			F, P
16. Norway	Yes		Yes		Yes	Yes	I	De facto		Yes	F, P, Ot
17. Poland	Yes	Yes	Yes				I[viii]	De facto	Yes	Yes	F, P
18. Romania	Yes		Yes				I	Yes	Yes	Yes	F, P
19. Slovakia	Yes						O	Yes	Yes	Yes	F
20. Slovenia	Yes	Yes						Yes	Yes		
21. South Africa	Yes	Yes	Yes	Yes	Yes	Yes	I	Yes		Upon request	F, P
22. Sweden	Yes		Yes				I	De facto		Yes	F, P
23. Switzerland	Yes			Yes	Yes	Yes	I	Yes	Yes		F, P, Ot
24. Ukraine	Yes	Yes	Yes				I and O	Yes	Yes	Yes	F, P, Ot
25. United States	Yes	Yes	Yes		Yes	Yes		Yes		Yes	F, P, Ot

Notes: I = Individual licences   O = Open licences   F = Fines   P = Imprisonment   Ot = Other (e.g. confiscation, debarment)
* Details on legislation not available.
i The obligation to keep registers pertains only to civilian firearms.
ii Licensing is mandatory only for the brokering of weapons that originate in France.
iii Only for those seeking a general licence for the transport abroad of war weapons on German ships or aircraft.
iv In Italy, core brokering activities are subject to licensing by way of practice; this requirement so far applies to weapons transferred from, into, or through Italy.
v Only for weapons covered by the 1997 Arms and Ammunition Act, which include automatic firearms and related ammunition.
vi Only for weapons covered by the 1963 Decree on the Export of Strategic Goods and transferred outside the EU.
vii Needed for those trading in the controlled goods under the 1997 Arms and Ammunition Act.
viii Licences for dual-use goods can be both individual and open (general or global). Licences for trade in munitions can only be individual.

the disciplinary, administrative, criminal, as well as civil and legal responsibility of 'officials from duly authorized executive state export control body and other executive structures involved in decision making in the sphere of state export control, if [they] violate legislation in this sphere' (Ukraine, 2003, art. 28).

What this review of national legislations shows is that even if brokering controls are in place, sometimes their design is such that important loopholes remain. For a start, the regulations examined here usually cover military-style small arms, while civilian firearms are either covered by other instruments or remain unregulated.

Governments' screening of brokering activities is also sensibly reduced when exemptions to the licensing requirement for transfers with specific countries as well as open brokering licences are possible. In both cases the risks of arms diversion to the illicit market are greatly increased.

SMALL ARMS SURVEY 2004

Given the common practice of brokers to arrange deals for which weapons do not cross the territory of the state from where they operate, states where brokering licences are necessary only for deals related to weapons that are imported into, exported from, or transited through their territory can exert a lesser control than states for which brokering must be licensed irrespective of the origin of the weapons. While more difficult to enforce, these provisions diminish the ease with which brokers faced with constraints in one country can move their activities across the border.

ARE NATIONAL REGULATIONS EFFECTIVE?

This section deals with the effectiveness of national brokering regulations as measured by the extent and manner of the punishment of illicit activities. However, it cannot be considered exhaustive, for a number of reasons. Information about criminal prosecutions is rarely made public unless the case has been completely closed with a conviction or an acquittal. Information made available through media releases is seldom complete and often relies on unproven allegations. On the other hand, most media attention is skewed towards high-profile scandals, usually big-name brokers who have escaped justice in one way or another. These sources, therefore, rarely tell us whether 'minor' brokers manage to escape justice as easily as 'major' ones, or whether administrative sanctions (such as the revoking of brokering licences) are applied. Furthermore, investigations into illicit arms brokering are usually highly complex because, for example, they are conducted in numerous countries at the same time and involve other offences as well (individuals suspected of illicit arms trafficking are often alleged to have committed other, related crimes, such as money laundering, forgery, or smuggling of precious goods). In this sense, it is hard to keep track of the numerous and overlapping proceedings on individual cases. A full assessment of the effectiveness of national regulations in controlling brokering activities would therefore require direct contact with the national judicial authorities of those states in which brokering controls are in place, and future research in this issue would be a most welcome development. However, the few cases treated in this section will help us to reach some preliminary conclusions.

Convictions for violations of brokering regulations are rare.

It is striking that convictions for violations of brokering regulations are hard to obtain. In the United States, for example, where such regulations are among the most comprehensive, administrative sanctions have been used to 'debar' companies and individuals by revoking their licences and publicizing their names for violating arms trading regulations;[40] yet only one prosecution for the specific crime of violation of the brokering regulations is known to have occurred so far. This concerns the case of Hemant Lakhani, a British citizen who was arrested in August 2003 for allegedly selling an Igla-S man-portable surface-to-air missile system for import into the United States. According to the criminal complaint filed for the case, Lakhani was accused of attempting to 'engage in the business of brokering activities with respect to the import and transfer of a foreign defense article ... which was a non-United States defense article of a nature described on the United States Munitions

A US court indicted alleged arms dealer Hemant Lakhani (foreground) on new allegations in January 2004, less than half a year after he was arrested on charges relating to the attempted sale of a shoulder-launched missile to the FBI.

List, without having first registered with and obtained from the Department of State's Directorate of Defense Trade Controls a licence for such brokering or written authorization for such brokering' (US District Court, 2003). On 10 January 2004, the competent District Court in Newark scheduled pre-trial oral arguments for Lakhani for 26 April 2004 (*Reuters*, 2004).

US prosecutors, for example, have attributed the rare use of the national brokering statute to ignorance of the law among law enforcement officials and lack of coordination among government agencies. Lack of time and resources, coupled with meagre legal experience in the application of the law, work against the use of judicial proceedings to enforce brokering regulations.[41] On the other hand, plea bargains may lead to brokering charges being replaced by different charges. In such cases, the offences would still have occurred but would not appear in the convictions.[42]

In general, the apparent absence of convictions for brokering offences may be explained by the fact that broker-specific laws exist in only a few countries and in most of those, they have only recently come into force. However, other explanations may also play a role.

The complex schemes of illicit brokering pose serious difficulties for prosecution, of which a central one is time. It takes a lot of time to gather sufficient evidence, and national laws often do not foresee that it can take years for an illicit arms deal to be exposed and a trial initiated (Hogendoorn and Misol, 2003, p. 33). For example, after a long delay, in 1997 Latvian authorities initiated criminal proceedings against Janis Dibrants and his associates.[43] Five years earlier, in 1992, Dibrants, who at the time was Chief of Procurement for the Latvian Armed Forces, allegedly provided the official cover for a shipment of weapons to Somalia, in violation of a UN arms embargo. Dibrants agreed to sign a contract with Jerzy Dembrowski, then First Director of Cenrex, a Polish majority-government-owned arms trading company, that would allow the export of the cargo—40 TT pistols, 301 AK-47 rifles, 30 RP sub-machine guns, 160 RPG-2, 100 hand grenades, 3,450,000 rounds of 7.62mm ammo (for AK-74s), and 10,000 mortar bombs—to Somalia. In return for his cooperation, Dibrants claimed he had demanded that a share of the arms be provided free of charge to the Latvian armed forces, an allegation that the Latvian Minister of Defence (MOD) has since denied. On 10 June 1992, Polish customs authorities cleared the departure of the MS Nadia (a Honduran-flagged freighter) with documentation indicating that the entire shipment was intended for the Latvian MOD. However, there were two sets of forms, one for shipment to the MOD of Latvia, the other for onward shipment. The second set declared the arms cargo to be bound for Yemen. This documentation was with a Cenrex employee who presented it to Dibrants upon arrival in Latvia. On 14 June 1992, the MS Nadia docked in Liepāja, Latvia, and offloaded 300 AK-74 assault rifles and 250,000 rounds of 7.62mm ammunition. In Latvia, Dibrants signed a receipt for the entire cargo, but in fact the captain departed with most of the cargo still on board for a rendezvous off the coast of Somalia. There the cargo was transferred to a new vessel, apparently a fishing vessel owned by Shifco, a Somali company, and delivered to the embargoed warring factions in Somalia.[44] In May 2000 a criminal case was brought against Dibrants and his associates in Latvia, but the charges were ultimately dropped because of time limitations—too many years had elapsed since the alleged crimes had been committed (*Neatkariga Rita Avize*, 2002).

In most countries it is not illegal under domestic laws to broker otherwise illegal deals if the weapons do not pass through the territory of the state of which the broker is a national or an established resident. For instance, lack of jurisdiction allowed Leonid Minin, an Israeli citizen, to avoid conviction in Italy for illicit arms trafficking. Minin was first arrested in August 2000 and imprisoned for possession of drugs. While serving the sentence, Italian prosecutors turned their attention to the documents that had been found in Minin's possession at the time of his arrest. The documents—1,500 pages which included fake EUCs, copies of money transfers, faxed messages, and correspondence—

SMALL ARMS SURVEY 2004

all pointed to Minin's heavy involvement in illegal arms trafficking to Africa, specifically in arming the Revolutionary United Front (RUF) in Sierra Leone through Liberia and Liberia itself, in both cases in violation of UN arms embargoes (*RFE/RL Crime, Corruption and Terrorism Watch,* 2001; Warner, 2002). In November 2002 the Italian Supreme Court determined that Italy did not have jurisdiction to try Minin, for two reasons. First, the weapons transferred with Minin's connivance had not crossed Italian territory. Second, to be punished for an offence should be defined as such also in the state where the violation occurred (Tortorella, 2003; Tosi, 2003). Pending a final hearing, Minin was released in December 2002 (Tortorella, 2003). In January 2004, the Italian Supreme Court confirmed its previous sentence that Minin could not be tried in Italy (*Corriere della Sera,* 2004).

> Accused illicit brokers have been able to evade arrest by crossing the border into another jurisdiction.

Accused illicit brokers are also able to evade arrest by crossing a border into another jurisdiction. While they still may face conviction *in absentia* in some cases, illicit brokers can continue their activities by moving their operations to countries where they are protected from extradition. This strategy worked for a time for Geza Mezosy, a Belgian national of Hungarian origin. Belgian authorities first accused Mezosy in the 1990s of involvement in a number of arms smuggling operations from Central and Eastern Europe, and he lost his Belgian arms dealing licence in 1993 (Wood and Peleman, 1999, pp. 49–54). In 1996 a Belgian court sentenced him *in absentia* to a three-year prison term for smuggling operations that involved fraud and gun-running to and from Croatia and Bosnia (*Le Soir,* 2001a; Wood and Peleman, 1999, pp. 50–4). Belgium also issued an international warrant for his arrest (Wood and Peleman, 1999, p. 53).

By that time Mezosy had moved to South Africa, where he continued his arms brokering activities until South African police arrested him in 1998 on an international arrest warrant but also on suspicion of new illicit arms trafficking activities. Their investigation showed that Mezosy's import-export company obtained weapons, including thousands of handguns, in Central and Eastern Europe which it then supplied to various war-torn countries in Africa, including the Central African Republic, DRC, Ethiopia, Sudan, and Uganda (Wood and Peleman, 1999, p. 53). Mezosy was extradited in 1998 to Belgium, where he was imprisoned on the 1996 charges and served two years in jail (*Le Soir,* 2001a). Following his release Mezosy remained under investigation and was later charged, again in Belgium, with forgery and arms trafficking but remained free pending trial (*Le Soir,* 2001b).[45] Mezosy reportedly is also the subject of new legal proceedings in Belgium, opened in 2002 on the basis of suspicions he had supplied weapons to the Armed Islamic Group (GIA) in Algeria (*Le Soir,* 2002).

Poor international cooperation also adds to impunity. Investigators and prosecutors complain that responses to requests can take years, if they come at all. This is especially troublesome in cases involving countries in Africa and the former Soviet Union (Hogendoorn and Misol, 2003, p. 33). The same problem of scant international cooperation was stressed in connection with the investigations over Yelinek and the other Israeli citizens involved in the illicit diversion of Nicaraguan weapons to the AUC in Colombia.

It is also striking that, even when convicted, individuals accused of violations of arms brokering regulations often receive lenient punishment. This has led some analysts to suggest that political will is a critical element in the effective implementation of brokering regulations (Bondi and Keppler, 2001). This factor has been stressed particularly in connection with recent scandals involving brokers with alleged high-level contacts. Lenient sanctions, in these cases, would reflect a lack of will on the part of relevant governments to seriously punish individuals who enjoy close ties with them and who have sensitive information that could compromise their current or former government sponsors (Hogendoorn and Misol, 2003, p. 22ff.) (see Box 5.5).

Box 5.5 Impunity for brokers: Sarkis Soghanalian and Pierre Joseph Falcone

The press has recently given extensive coverage to a number of cases of brokers who, despite acting illegally, received lenient sanctions. Among these are the cases of Sarkis Soghanalian and Pierre Joseph Falcone, who both claim that their actions were not just known about but also supported by national governments.

Sarkis Soghanalian

Sarkis Soghanalian, a long-time arms dealer, asserts that he has always worked with US government approval, including when he illegally supplied arms to Saddam Hussein's Iraq in 1983, a crime for which he was convicted in the United States in 1991 (PBS Frontline/World, 2001). He has noted that ties to the US government have mostly kept him out of jail: 'I was convicted for six and a half years [for the Iraq arms sales, for which the prosecutor had sought a much higher sentence of 24 years]. But I did not serve six and a half years. When they needed me, the U.S. government that is, they immediately came and got me out' (PBS Frontline/World, 2001). His sentence was reduced to two years. Later, he was arrested in the United States and charged in connection with an alleged USD 3 million fraud involving stolen cashier's checks. He faced a sentence of five years, but in 2001 was sentenced to time served (ten months). The US attorney's office recommended he be released in exchange for his 'substantial assistance to law enforcement' related to an unspecified investigation (PBS Frontline/World, 2001). On Soghanalian's account: '[T]he $3 million charge was dropped. Why was it dropped? Because I was helping the secret service ... I'm chasing people doing wrong on behalf of the US government. And chasing them around and with the knowledge of the US government' (PBS Frontline/World, 2001). Soghanalian left the US for Jordan, where he remained in 2003 (Silverstein and Pasternak, 2003).

The 61-year-old international arms dealer Sarkis Soghanalian leaves federal court in Florida in October 1991, convicted of conspiracy to violate US laws by arming Iraq with military helicopters.

Pierre Joseph Falcone

Pierre Joseph Falcone, a broker of Algerian-French origin was taken into custody on the night of 2 December 2000, on the order of a French special prosecutor.[46] He was initially charged with brokered sales of weapons of Russian origin worth more than USD 1 billion to Angola in 1993 and 1994 without authorization from the French government agency that reviews weapon exports.[47] The first deal was worth approximately USD 47 million and took place on 7 November 1993, while a second deal, worth some USD 563 million, took place in 1994 (cited in Brunais, 2001).[48] In both cases, the weapon purchases were reportedly paid for with Angolan proceeds from oil sales—with Sonangol,[49] Angola's state oil company, for example, paying some of the money for the 1994 transaction to French bank accounts controlled by a Czech firm, ZTS Osos, that provided some of the weapons (HRW, 2001).[50] By late 1994, according to *Le Monde*, Falcone had been involved in the selling of weapons to Angola worth some USD 633 million (cited in Global Witness, 2002, p. 12).[51]

Falcone was let out of prison after serving one year—from 1 December 2000 to 1 December 2001. His release was contingent on posting a bail of FRF 105 million (USD 14,351,000, more than ten times France's previous highest bail demand) and on a number of conditions that prevented him from leaving Paris, from meeting with other people under investigation for his alleged crimes and a number of witnesses, and which obliged him to present himself periodically to the local judicial authorities (*Le Monde*, 2001b). A subsequent decision by the French Court of Appeal reduced the bail to about USD 6 million and allowed Falcone to move within French territory (Routier, 2002).

The discovery of new documents led to a second investigation on Falcone, beginning in late March 2002. The documents pointed to illicit weapon transfers to Angola post-1994 and at least until 2000, this time through another company, Vast Impex, which replaced ZTS-Osos (*Le Monde*, 2002).

In June 2003, Falcone was appointed Ambassador Plenipotentiary for Angola in UNESCO (*Le Monde*, 2003b). Only three days after receiving an Angolan passport and diplomatic status, he left France for Angola, purportedly with the intention of respecting the conditions of his bail agreement (*Le Monde*, 2003c).[52] However, he did not respect two convocation orders by the French investigator; this entailed the issuing of an international arrest warrant against him, which was declared on 14 January 2004 (*Le Monde*, 2004).

> Why countries have not used existing brokering-specific provisions more often remains a mystery.

It remains to be seen whether political considerations are relevant beyond those cases of brokers with high-level contacts. Yet one key question, which for the moment remains unanswered, concerns how much significance 'big brokers' such as Soghanalian and Falcone have in the overall illicit weapons trade, specifically of small arms.

While not an exhaustive account of criminal investigations and prosecutions around the world, this section could identify a number of obstacles and difficulties that hamper the effectiveness of national brokering regulations. Future research on proceedings that are still under way would be a welcome development. It is, however, worth noting that in some instances brokers acting illegally have been convicted, but for other offences, such as money laundering, forgery of documents, or violation of generic export controls (Hogendoorn and Misol, 2003). The puzzle, at this point, is why brokering-specific provisions have not been used more often in countries that have had them in place for several years.

CONCLUSION

Illicit arms brokering is by definition a clandestine activity. As such, information on it is usually scarce, incomplete, and anecdotal. However, research conducted in recent years by both governmental and non-governmental organizations has revealed that brokers often play a critical role in illicit arms transfers. While each brokering deal displays specific features, illicit brokering tends to follow a range of patterns, a typical modus operandi whose success strongly depends on regulatory gaps. While the most obvious of these is the paucity of countries that explicitly regulate brokering, more specific gaps range from lax controls on governmental weapon stockpiles to lack of controls of transport and financing agents to inadequate border and customs controls.

At the national level, only 25 countries have specific brokering regulations. Provisions in these countries vary considerably, particularly concerning their scope of application—both within and outside the national territory of controlling states—the definition of the activities subject to licensing and the criteria for assessing brokering licence applications. In some cases, national regulations create important loopholes, notably when they establish exemptions to the licensing requirements, or the possibility of granting open brokering licences.

The analysis of the use of national brokering regulations in the context of criminal proceedings begs the question of how effective such regulations are. Convictions for brokering-specific offences are rare; however, some brokers have been convicted for other violations, typically relating to money laundering, forgery, and arms exports or imports. While this might be largely because in some of the countries brokering regulations have come into force only very recently, other factors can be highlighted. Poor knowledge of the relevant laws and meagre legal practice in their application; lack of international cooperation; difficulties in conducting investigations; and sometimes legal loopholes all help explain the small number of brokering-specific convictions.

Arms brokering remains a largely unregulated activity. However, international attention on this issue is growing and a number of important initiatives, started at both the international and regional level, might have significant potential for affecting national policies on brokering controls. In this respect, the EU Common Position and the OAS Model Regulations, the first of which is legally binding, show great potential. At a minimum, increased international discussions on illicit brokering might bring forth harmonized understandings of the issue and of the possible means of dealing with it. More importantly, they might spur the adoption of brokering regulations by a larger number of states, thus closing the biggest gap that allows illicit brokering to take place.

8. LIST OF ABBREVIATIONS

ASEAN	Association of South-East Asian Nations
AUC	Autodefensas Unidas de Colombia
BMS	Biennial Meeting of States
BPG	Best Practice Guide
CICAD	Inter-American Drug Abuse Commission
DNI	Dutch–Norwegian Initiative
DRC	Democratic Republic of Congo
ECOWAS	Economic Community of West African States
EU	European Union
EUC	End-user certificate
FOCs	Flags of convenience
FSC	Forum for Security Cooperation
GIA	Armed Islamic Group
MFA	Ministry of Foreign Affairs
MOD	Ministry of Defence
OAS	Organization of American States
OSCE	Organization for Security and Co-operation in Europe
PNP	Panamanian National Police
RUF	Revolutionary United Front (Sierra Leone)
SADC	South African Development Community
UNESCO	United Nations Educational, Scientific and Cultural Organization
WA	Wassenaar Arrangement
WMD	Weapons of mass destruction

5. ENDNOTES

[1] For a full account of this weapons deal, see OAS (2003b).

[2] During the Conference, 134 opening statements were made, representing a total of 171 countries.

[3] See Belgium (1991, art. 10); France (1995, art. 1); Slovakia (1998, art. 3); Switzerland (1996, art. 6); Ukraine (2003, art. 1); US (2003, art. Sec. 129.2).

[4] The UN Security Council placed an arms embargo on Liberia in 1992 (UN S/RES/788 (1992)), which was tightened in 2001, with SC Resolution 1343(2001), because of the Liberian government's support of the Revolutionary United Front (RUF) in Sierra Leone. Beginning in 2001, reports of the UN Panel of Experts investigating the contravention of the embargo on Liberia documented, in detail, the role of air cargo companies in the embargo-breaching transfer of arms into Liberia (UNSC, 2001). The Panel's first case studies demonstrated the ease with which Liberia was able to procure quantities of weapons and arrange for their delivery by air.

[5] Information in this paragraph provided by Ernst Jan Hogendoorn based on interviews with air cargo personnel under the auspices of HRW.

[6] As of June 2003, the International Transport Workers' Federation considered 28 countries to be FOCs: Antigua and Barbuda, Bahamas, Barbados, Belize, Bermuda, Bolivia, Burma/Myanmar, Cambodia, Cayman Islands, Comoros, Cyprus, Equatorial Guinea, German International Ship Register, Gibraltar, Honduras, Jamaica, Lebanon, Liberia, Malta, Marshall Islands, Mauritius, the Netherlands Antilles, Panama, São Tomé and Príncipe, St Vincent and the Grenadines, Sri Lanka, Tonga, and Vanuatu (ITF, 2003, p. 12).

[7] Liberian-registered aircraft have been used to ferry arms in violation of UN arms embargoes. The systematic misuse of this registry, including by the air cargo network of known arms trafficker Victor Bout, led the UN Security Council to adopt an unprecedented resolution grounding all Liberian-registered aircraft until the problem could be addressed. Also in pursuance of the Security Council resolution, the Liberian Aircraft Registry underwent a UN and International Civil Aviation Organization overhaul between late 2001 and early 2002 (UNSC, 2001, paras. 4–5). At the time of writing, Liberia had opened a new registry for civil aircraft registration that was not yet in use (UNSC, 2002, para. 109).

[8] On 3 January 2002, the Israeli Navy seized control over Tonga-flagged ship *Karine A*, which was sailing in international waters towards the Suez Canal. Aboard the ship were found 50 tonnes of weapons, which the Israeli government believes were destined for the Palestinian Naval Police (Israel, MFA, 2002). The cargo included rocket launchers, mortars, bombs, sniper rifles, machine guns, AK-47 assault rifles, and small arms ammunition, among others (Israel, IDF, 2002). This seizure, coupled with some other incidents involving

9. Tonga-flagged ships, prompted the Tongan authorities to decide to close down its ship registry, which had been opened in 2000 and was headquartered in the Athens port of Piraeus (Frontline World, 2004; *Sydney Morning Herald*, 2003). According to one source, the Tongan registry had more than 180 ships signed up on it before it closed down. Its 'success' was said to depend on the very low level of control exercised over ships registered with Tonga (Frontline World, 2004).

9. The ease with which vessel registration controls can be evaded in some countries with low enforcement capacity has been exploited in the most ingenious ways. For example, aircraft have been reported to change their registration literally overnight, as soon as links with illicit activities have started to surface; another company used the logo and colours of a licensed firm to fly non-licensed planes; yet another operator used an old licence, cancelled by aviation authorities, to fly its planes to illicit destinations in Africa (Wood and Peleman, 2000, p. 141). Names and logos of shipping companies have also been changed in cases of transportation by sea. In 1993, for example, an international arrest warrant was issued for a ship registered in Greece under the name *Maria*, allegedly transporting a cargo of illicit arms. En route, however, the ship's name had been illegally changed to *Malo* (Wood and Peleman, 2000, p. 141).

10. During the thematic discussions, the following countries spoke on brokering: Belgium, Brazil, Finland, Germany, Italy (for the EU), Mali, and the Netherlands. Italy gave an overview of the *EU Common Position on the Control of Arms Brokering*, which will be described in detail below. Finland and Germany stressed two important points, namely, that the absence of controls is 'clearly a potential loophole' and that brokers may play a role in the diversion of weapons from licit to illicit markets. Importantly, Mali called for international assistance to deal with the issue of arms brokering.

11. Argentina, Armenia, Austria, Italy (on behalf of the EU), Brazil, China, Colombia, Cuba, Germany, Guatemala, the Holy See, Hungary, the Netherlands, Nicaragua, Niger, Norway, Rwanda, Sweden, and the United Kingdom. During the BMS, 102 countries gave general statements (two of them, Lithuania and Luxemburg, did not take the floor, but circulated written statements), representing in total 144 states.

12. During the BMS the following regional organizations made statements: OSCE, African Union, Pacific Islands Forum Group, the Nairobi Secretariat on Small Arms and Light Weapons in the Great Lakes Region and the Horn of Africa, SADC, ASEAN, and the League of Arab States.

13. In Italy explicit controls, in the form of a licensing requirement, currently exist only on financial activities related to arms deals. Other controls, notably on the core activity of mediation, are exercised by practice as they are not formally established in the law. Furthermore, they apply only to weapons originating in Italian territory. The Italian government has established an inter-agency group, chaired by the Ministry of Justice, to extend controls to brokering activities between third countries, thus bringing Italian legislation in line with the EU Common Position (Anders, 2003, p. 24).

14. Israel and Japan are not included in this comparative analysis since details of their relevant regulations were not available.

15. As well as the EU countries listed above, Botswana, Serbia, and Thailand have declared to be in the process of consideration or adoption of brokering regulations.

16. All the statements can be found in the UN Small Arms Conference 'Government Documents and Statements' Database, <http://129.194.160.20:8080/examples/servlet/FMProXMLSearch>

17. In Hungary, revisions to the export control system, with inclusion of explicit brokering controls, will enter into force during 2004 (Hungary, 2003).

18. See Austria (1977, art. 1.4); Bulgaria (1995, art. 5.2); Norway (1987, para. 1; 1989, sec. 1.i), and Finland (1990, sec. 2; presentation of 2003, p. 2). For the provisions relating to licensing of core brokering activities in other countries see: Czech Republic (1994, 6.1, 14.1); Estonia (MFA, 2002), France (1939, art. 2.1; 1995, art. 6), Germany (1961a, art. 4a.1), Hungary (2003), Lithuania (2002, art. 7.1), Netherlands (1997, art. 9.1), Poland (2000, art. 6.1), Slovakia (1998, arts. 5-6), Slovenia (2003a, art. 1.1-3), South Africa (2002, art. 13), Sweden (1992, sec. 4), Switzerland (1996, arts. 2, 9, 12, 15; 1998, 6), Ukraine (2003), US (1976, (b)(A)(ii); 2003, sec. 129.6, 129.7.a.1).

19. E-mail communication with the Swiss State Secretariat for Economic Affairs, January 2004.

20. Concerning Lithuania, this information was provided by the Lithuanian MFA, Security Policy Department, e-mail communication of January 2004.

21. These countries are all the EU members, plus Argentina, Australia, Canada, the Czech Republic, Hungary, Japan, New Zealand, Norway, Poland, and the United States.

22. Information provided by the Lithuanian MFA, December 2003.

23. In the Netherlands, brokering must be licensed for transfers of weapons covered by the Arms and Ammunition Act from one country outside Benelux to another outside Benelux (Anders, 2003).

24. Information provided by the Slovenian MFA, e-mail communication, February 2004.

25. E-mail communication with the Bulgarian MFA, January 2004.

26. Lithuania also provides that the EU Code of Conduct will be followed in decisions to grant or refuse brokering licences (2002, art. 8.1).

27. See Belgium (1991, art. 10); Bulgaria (1995, art. 6.2); Czech Republic (1994, arts. 7–8); France (1995, art. 9.II.b.) ; Slovakia (1998, art. 6); Slovenia (2003a, art. 4).

28. For Lithuania, this information was provided by the Lithuanian MFA, e-mail communication, January 2004.

29. E-mail communication with the Czech Ministry of Industry and Trade, January 2004.

30. In Sweden, this requirement does not cover overseas activities of Swedish nationals who are established residents abroad (Anders, 2003, p. 8).

31. E-mail communication with the Estonian MFA, December 2003.

32. In Belgium, this competence by the judiciary can be exercised if the accused is found on Belgian territory, even if the Belgian authorities have not received a complaint or official notification by the authorities in the country in which the alleged violation took place, and even if the activity is not punishable in the country where it was carried out (Belgium, 1991, art. 13). In South Africa, any national court may also try a foreign citizen for similar violations committed within the country (South Africa, 2002, art. 26).

33. E-mail communication with the Bulgarian MFA, January 2004.

34. Such a link to German territory exists if, for example, a meeting for negotiations takes place in Germany, or if phone calls, letters, or faxes related to the weapons transfer in question originate or are received in German territory (Anders, 2003, p. 8).

35. See Belgium (2003, art. 1.1); Bulgaria (1995, art. 5.1); Czech Republic (1994, art. 12); France (1995, art. 6.3); Hungary (2003); Italy (1990, art. 3.1-2); Latvia (MFA, 2002); Lithuania (2002, art. 25; 2003); Romania (1999, art. 10); Slovakia (1998, art. 10.6–7); Slovenia (2003a, art. 1.7); South Africa (2002, art. 13); Switzerland (1996, art. 9); Ukraine (2003, art. 12); and US (2003, sec. 129.3).

36. See Finland (2003); Norway (2003); Poland (2000, art. 21); Sweden (Anders, 2003, p. 14).

37. However, there is no requirement to provide information on weapons that are bought, sold, or mediated abroad (Anders, 2003, p. 15).

38. This information on the weapons must be kept permanently.

39. In Italy and the Netherlands, penalties are the same as those applied in the case of violations of general arms exports regulations. See Italy (1990, art. 25.2; 2003) and the Netherlands (2003b, p. 5).

40. US Department of State, 'Defense Trade Controls—List of Debarred Parties, July 1988–March 2002,' available at <http://www.pmdtc.org/debar059.htm>. For example, in September 2003, the US government announced sanctions against a Russian company for transferring arms to Iran, which it considers to be a 'sponsor of terrorism'. Under the sanctions, the US government blocked the company for a period of one year from receiving any US aid, importing or exporting weapons or defence services from the United States, or taking part in any US procurement (*Reuters*, 2003). Numerous people have been prosecuted in the United States for attempted and actual illegal arms deals, often in connection with sting operations, but prosecutors have not relied on the brokering law in such cases (*Agence Presse*, 2003). Instead, they have often charged

41 Interview and e-mail communications with a US Department of Justice official, November 2003.
42 Interview and e-mail communications with a US Department of Justice official, November 2003.
43 Interview by E. J. Hogendooorn with prosecutor Mariussz Marciniak, Gdansk, Poland, 18 November 2002.
44 Interview by E. J. Hogendooorn with prosecutor Mariussz Marciniak, Gdansk, Poland, 18 November 2002, and interview with Somali involved in the transaction, Somalia, February 2002.
45 Mezosy reportedly confessed to the charges.
46 Letter from Pierre Joseph Falcone, Prison Register Number: 298073 T D-5, Fleury-Merogis Prison to Special Prosecutor Courroye, Special Prosecutor Prevost-Desprez, Tribunal de grande instance de Paris, Financial Division, 5/7 rue des Italiens, 75009 Paris, 7 May 2001.
47 At that time the agency that approved French weapons sales to other countries was SOFREMI (French Company for Export of Materiel, Systems, and Services Under Ministry of Interior). Falcone served as a consultant to SOFREMI (Silverstein, 2001). As of February 2001, SOFREMI ceased to exist and was replaced by a new structure within the Interior Ministry called Civipol, which will no longer be involved in the sale of arms (*Le Monde*, 2001a).
48 One news report states that there was actually just one sale, which was amended 20 April 1994 to raise it to a total value of USD 463 million (*Le Figaro*, 2002).

brokers with violations of other provisions of US arms export law (Hogendoorn and Misol, 2003, p. 30).

49 For details on Sonangol see its Web site <http://www.sonangol.com/Home.jsp>.
50 According to a journalist at CTK Publications, the Slovak state registry of companies records a name change from 'ZTS-Osos Martin' to 'Osos Vrutky' in December 1994 (Global Witness, 2002, p. 17).
51 Illicit arms trafficking is only one of the charges that Falcone has to face. Investigations into arms sales to Angola uncovered a complex business network which involved, among other things, crimes of corruption and fiscal fraud (*Le Monde*, 2003a). Furthermore, Falcone's illicit activities involved prominent politicians (Angolan and French, among others), some of whom are subject of current investigations. For a full account of 'Angolagate' and the related scandals, see Global Witness (2002).
52 Falcone's appointment to UNESCO spurred a debate over the nature and extent of the diplomatic immunity he was entitled to and on the effects this would have on the investigation that was being conducted against him. Falcone's lawyers argued that as the immunity would be total, Falcone could not be subject to any judicial order. The investigating judge, to the contrary, maintained that such immunity would be limited, and hence would cover only acts that Falcone would carry out in his official capacity as a UNESCO ambassador (*Le Monde*, 2004). The French MFA seconded the latter interpretation (*Le Monde*, 2003d).

5. BIBLIOGRAPHY

Agence Presse. 2003. 'Two indicted on arms sting deal'. 20 March.
Anders, Holger. 2003. *Controls on Arms Brokering in the EU Member States: A Comparative Overview of Existing and Planned Legislation*. Background paper. Geneva: Small Arms Survey.
Austria. 1977. *Bundesgesetz vom 18. Oktober 1977 über die Ein-, Aus- und Durchfuhr von Kriegsmaterial (Kriegsmaterialgesetz—KMG: War Material Act) BGBl. Nr. 540/1977 idF BGBl. I Nr. 125/2001*.
Belgium. 1991. *Loi du 5 août 1991 relative à l'importation, à l'exportation et au transit et à la lutte contre le trafic d'armes, de munitions et de matériel devant servir spécialement à un usage militaire et de la technologie y afférente (Loi du 5 août 1991) modifié par la Loi du 26 mars 2003 et la Loi du 25 mars 2003*.
——. 2003. *Arrêté royal du 16 mai 2003 relatif à la licence visée à l'article 10 de la loi du 5 août 1991 relative à l'importation, à l'exportation, au transit et à la lutte contre le trafic d'armes, de munitions et de matériel devant servir spécialement à un usage militaire ou de maintien de l'ordre et de la technologie y afférente*.
Bondi, Loretta and Elise Keppler. 2001. *Casting the Net? The Implications of the U.S. Law on Arms Brokering*. Washington, DC: Fund for Peace report. January.
Brunais, Alexandra. 2001. 'Mitterrand's Son Posts Bail in Arms Case: Inquiry Sullies Fame Of French Ex-Leader.' *Washington Post*. 13 January, p. A16.
Bulgaria. 1995. *Law on the Control of Foreign Trade Activity in Arms and in Dual-Use Goods and Technologies adopted in 1995, in force from 1996; amended and complemented on 19 July 2002, in force from 3 September 2002*.
Clegg, Elizabeth and Michael Crowley. n.d. *Controlling Arms Brokering and Transport Agents: Time for International Action*. Briefing Paper No. 8, Biting the Bullet.
Corriere della Sera (Milano). 2004. 'Il trafficante d'armi ucraino non puo' essere processato in Italia.' 10 January.
Czech Republic. 1994. *Act No 38/1994 of 15 February 1994 to regulate trade in military material with foreign countries and to supplement Act No. 455/1991, on Small Businesses (Small Business Act), amended by later legislation, and Act No. 140/1961, Penal Code, amended by later legislation*.
El Panamá América. 2003. 'Declaran nulas las pesquisas sobre armas'. 6 August.
Estonia. 1999. *Strategic Goods Import, Export and Transit Act*. 16 June.
——. MFA (Ministry of Foreign Affairs). 2002. 'Export Controls in Estonia.' 15 February. <http://www.vm.ee/eng/kat_153/893.html>
EU (European Union). 1998. *European Union Code of Conduct on Arms Exports*. 8 June. Reproduced in UN Document A/CONF.192/PC/3 of 13 March 2000. < http://www.smallarmssurvey.org/resources/reg_docs.htm#europe>
——. 2003. *Council Common Position 2003/468/CFSP of 23 June 2003 on the control of arms brokering*. Official Journal L 156. 25 June.
Finland. 1990. *Act on the Export and Transit of Defence Materiel 242/1990*; amendments up to 900/2002 included.
——. 2003. 'Licensing of Other Types of Goods or Transfers Than Standard Exports of Standard Military List Goods—Finnish Experiences.' Presentation by the Finnish MFA during the Conference Arms Export Controls in an Enlarged European Union. Dublin, 12 December.
France. 1939. *Décret du 18 avril 1939 fixant le régime des matériels de guerre, armes et munitions, modifié par Loi 2001-1062 du 15 novembre 2001, Loi 92-1336 du 16 décembre 1992, Loi 77-7 du 3 janvier 1977, Ordonnance 58-917 du 7 octobre 1958 et Décret 48-1986 du 9 décembre 1948*.
——. 1992. *Arrêté du 2 octobre 1992 relatif à la procédure d'importation et d'exportation des matériels de guerre, armes et munitions et des matériels assimilés, modifié par Arrêté 2002-03-28, Arrêté 2000-08-25 et Arrêté 1999-12-20*.
——. 1995. *Décret n° 95-589 du 6 mai 1995 relatif à l'application du décret du 18 avril 1939 fixant le régime des matériels de guerre, armes et munitions, modifié par Décret 2002-933 du 13 juin 2002, Décret 2002-23 du 3 janvier 2002, Décret 2000-376 du 28 avril 2000, Décret 98-1148 du 16 décembre 1998 et Décret 96-831 du 20 septembre 1996*.

Frontline World. 2004. *Hiding behind the Flag: Tonga*. January. <http://www.pbs.org/frontlineworld/stories/spain/tonga.html>
Germany. 1961a. *War Weapons Control Act BGBl I 1961, 444, last amended by §3 Gesetz vom 11.10.2002, I 3970*.
—. 1961b. *Order on General Licenses under War Weapons Control Act, Nr. 150 of 8.8.1961, last amended by Verordnung vom 8. Januar 1998, BGBl. I S.59*.
Global Witness. 2002. *All the President's Men: The Devastating Story of Oil and Banking in Angola's Privatised War*. March. <http://www.globalwitness.org/reports/show.php/en.00002.html>
Hogendoorn, Ernst Jan and Lisa Misol. 2003. *The Role of Transport Agents in Illicit Arms Brokering and Prosecutions of Illicit Arms Brokers*. Background paper. Geneva: Small Arms Survey.
Hungary. 2003. E-mail communication with Hungarian government. December.
HRW (Human Rights Watch) 2003. *Weapons Sanctions, Military Supplies, and Human Suffering: Illegal Arms Flows to Liberia and the June-July 2003 Shelling of Monrovia*. Briefing paper. New York: HRW. November 3.
Israel. IDF (Israel Defence Forces). 2002. *The Weapons Seized on the Karine A Ship*. <http://www.idf.il/english/news/karinea.stm>
Israel. MFA (Ministry of Foreign Affairs). 2002. 'Seizing of the Palestinian weapons ship Karine A.' Communiqué by the IDF. 4 January. <http://www.mfa.gov.il/mfa/go.asp?MFAH0l0k0>
Italy. 1990. *Legge 09/07/1990 n° 185 Nuove norme sul controllo dell'esportazione, importazione e transito dei materiali di armamento (Legge 185/90)*. Gazzetta Ufficiale, n. 163. 14 July.
—. 2003. *Information provided by Italy on the implementation of the UN 2001 Programme of Action to Prevent, Combat and Eradicate the Illicit Trade in Small Arms and Light Weapons in All Its Aspects*.
ITF (International Transport Workers' Federation). 2003. *Steering the Right Course: Towards an Era of responsible flag States and Effective International Governance of Oceans And Seas*. June. <http://www.itf.org.uk/publications/pdfs/steeringrightcourse.pdf>
Latvia. 1997. *Regulations on the control of goods of a strategic nature*. No. 421, adopted 16 December.
—. MFA (Ministry of Foreign Affairs). 2002. *Export, Import and Transit Control of Strategic Goods in the Republic of Latvia*. Information paper published by the Latvian MFA. 25 November. <http://www.am.gov.lv/en/index.html?id=58>
Le Figaro (Paris). 2002. 'Paris Daily Cites Confidential Police Report on Dealings of Angolagate Figures.' 20 August.
Le Monde (Paris). 2001a. 'Status of French Ties with Angola Analyzed.' 17 March, pp. 1, 20.
—. 2001b. 'Pierre-Joseph Falcone a été remis en liberté après un an de détention.' 4 December.
—. 2002. 'Le traffic d'armes vers l'Angola s'est poursuivi jusqu'à l'été 2000.' 3 April.
—. 2003a. 'L'hommes d'affaires Pierre Falcone a été mis en examen dans l'enquête sur la Sofremi ; Il avait été un apporteur d'affaires pour la société.' 7 January.
—. 2003b. 'Nommé ministre de l'Angola à l'Unesco, Pierre Falcone obtient une immunité qui lui permet de quitter la France.' 20 September.
—. 2003c. 'Pierre Falcone a quitté la France grace à son passeport diplomatique angolais.' 22 September.
—. 2003d. 'Justice : l'immunité dont jouit Pierre Falcone concerne les seuls actes accomplis dans le cadre de sa mission au sein de la délégation angolaise à l'UNESCO.' 24 September.
—. 2004. 'Un mandat d'arrêt international a été livré contre Pierre Falcone.' 16 January.
Le Soir (Brussels). 2001a. 'Belgian Arms Trafficker Violated UN Croatia Embargo.' 20 April, FBIS translation.
—. 2001b. 'Press Profiles "Key" Belgian Arms Trafficker Mezosy.' 20 April, FBIS translation.
—. 2002. 'Arms Trafficking: Brussels Initiates Proceedings Against Hungarian.' 9 March.
Lithuania. 2002. *Law on Amending the Law on the Control of Import, Transit and Export of Strategic Goods and Technologies*. No. IX-1051, 5 July.
—. 2003. *Government decision of 27 May 2003 on arms brokers registration regulations*.
Mason, Peggy. 2003. 'Brokering Controls: Building on the Work of the UN Group of Governmental Experts.' Paper presented during the Lancaster House Conference on Strengthening Export Controls. London. 14–15 January.
Naylor, R.T. 2000. 'Gunsmoke and Mirrors: Financing the Illegal Trade.' In Lora Lumpe, ed. *Running Guns: The Global Black Market in Small Arms*. London: Zed Books.
Neatkariga Rita Avize (Riga). 2002. 'Latvian firm did not break arms embargo on Somalia as UN claims.' 19 July.
The Netherlands. 1996. *Financial Transactions of Strategic Goods Order*. 24 October.
—. 1997. *Arms and Ammunition Act*. 5 July.
—. 2003a. *Handboek strategische goederen*. Groningen: Centrale Dienst voor In- en Uitvoer. February.
—. 2003b. 'Implementation and Support for the UN Programme of Action an SALW in The Netherlands.' <http://disarmament2.un.org/cab/salw-nationalreports.html>
Norway. 1987. *Act of 18 December 1987 nr. 93 on Control of Export of Strategic Goods, Services and Technology*.
—. 1989. *Ministry for Foreign Affairs Ordnance of 10 January 1989 to implement export regulations for strategic goods, services and technology*.
—. 2003. *National report on the implementation of The United Nations Programme of Action to Prevent, Combat and Eradicate the Illicit Trade in Small Arms and Light Weapons in All Its Aspects*. 30 April.
OAS (Organization of American States). 2003a. *Amendments to the Model Regulation for the Control of the International movement of Firearms, their Parts and Components and Ammunition, proposed by the Group of Experts—Broker Regulations*. OEA/Ser.L/XIV.2.34, CICAD/doc1271/03. 13 November. Approved during the CICAD 34th regular session, Montreal, Canada, 17–20 November.
—. 2003b. *Report of the General Secretariat of the Organization of American States on the diversion of Nicaraguan arms to the United Defense Forces of Colombia*. OEA/Ser.G, CP/doc. 3687/03. 29 January.
OSCE (Organization for Security and Co-operation in Europe). 2003. *Handbook of Best Practices on Small Arms and Light Weapons*. Vienna: OSCE. Ch. IV.
PBS Frontline/World. 2001. 'Sarkis Soghanalian: The Cold War's Largest Arms Merchant.' Interview by William Kistner. March. <http://www.pbs.org/frontlineworld/stories/sierraleone/soghanalian.html>
Poland. 2000. *Law of 29 November 2000 concerning international trade in goods, technologies and services of strategic significance for state security and maintenance of international peace and security, and amending selected laws*.
Reuters. 2004. 'Lakhani pleads not guilty to U.S. terrorism charges.' 10 January.
RFE/RL Crime, Corruption, and Terrorism Watch. 2001. 'Breaking the embargo: Arms sales to Liberia-Part 2.' Vol. 1, No. 4. 22 November. <http://www.rferl.org/reports/corruptionwatch/2001/11/4-221101.asp>
Romania. 1999. *Emergency Government Ordinance no. 158/1999 on the strategic goods export and import regime, that repeals the Government Ordinance no. 31/1994, approved by the Law no. 93/1994*. 19 October.

Routier, Airy. 2002. 'Le juge Courroye déjugé?' *Le Nouvel Observateur,* Magazine No. 1942. 24 January.
SADC (Southern African Development Community). 2001. *Protocol on the Control of Firearms, Ammunition and Other Related Materials in the Southern African Development Community (SADC) Region ('SADC Firearms Protocol').* Blantyre, Malawi. 14 August.
Silverstein, Ken. 2001. 'The Arms Dealer Next Door: International billionaire, French prisoner, Angolan weapons broker, Arizona Republican. Who is Pierre Falcone?' *In These Times.* Chicago. 22 December. <http://inthesetimes.com/issue/26/04/feature4.shtml.>
—. and Judy Pasternak. 2003. 'A Market in Missiles for Terror: Portable surface-to-air weapons—SAMs—can be had by buyers legal and illegal. They already have been used to attack commercial flights.' *Los Angeles Times.* 6 March.
Slovakia. 1998. Act No 179/1998 Coll. *(on trading in military material and on amendment to Act No 455/1991 Coll. On trade business (Trade Act), as altered and amended), as last amended by Act No 26/2002 Coll. and 496/2002 Coll. On trading in military material.*
Slovenia. 2003a. *Government Decree on permits and consents for the trade in and production of military weapons and equipment.* 6 February.
—. 2003b. *Report of the Republic of Slovenia on Implementation of the United Nations Programme of Action to Prevent, Combat and Eradicate the Illicit Trade in Small Arms and Light Weapons in All Its Aspects.* Ljubljana. May.
Small Arms Survey. 2001. *Small Arms Survey 2001: Profiling the Problem.* Oxford: Oxford University Press.
—. 2003. *Small Arms Survey 2003: Development Denied.* Oxford: Oxford University Press.
South Africa. 2002. *National Conventional Arms Control Act.* No. 41 of 2002.
Sweden. 1992. *Military Equipment Act (1992:1300),* last amended by Law 2000:1248.
Switzerland. 1996. *Federal Law on War Material.* 13 December.
—. 1998. *War Material Ordinance.* 25 February.
Sydney Morning Herald. 2003. 'The ships that died of shame'. 14 January. <http://www.smh.com.au/articles/2003/01/13/1041990234408.html>
Tortorella, Maurizio. 2003. 'Tutti lo inseguono, noi lo liberiamo.' *Panorama* (Milan). 23 January <http://www.panorama.it/italia/politica/articolo/ix1-A020001017223>
Tosi, Giorgio. 2003. 'Il diritto e il suo rovescio: due sentenze'. *QuestoTrentino* (Trento). 22 March. <http://www.questotrentino.it/2003/06/sentenze.htm>
Ukraine. 2003. *Law of Ukraine 'On State Control of international Transfers of Goods Designated for Military Purposes and Dual-Use Goods.'*
UN (United Nations). 2001. *Report of the Group of Governmental Experts established pursuant to General Assembly resolution 54/54 V of 15 December 1999, entitled 'Small arm' ('UN Feasibility Study').* Reproduced in UN Document A/CONF.192/2, 11 May.
UNGA (United Nations General Assembly). 2001. *Programme of Action to Prevent, Combat and Eradicate the Illicit Trade in Small Arms and Light Weapons in All Its Aspects ('Programme Of Action').* 20 July. Reproduced in UN Document A/CONF.192/15, Annex.
—. 2003. *Report of the United Nations First Biennial Meeting of States to Consider the Implementation of the Programme of Action to Prevent, Combat and Eradicate the Illicit Trade in Small Arms and Light Weapons in All Its Aspects.* Reproduced in UN Document A/CONF.192/BMS/2003/1.
—. 2004. *The Illicit Trade in Small Arms and Light Weapons in All its Aspects.* Resolution 58/241. Adopted 23 December 2003. Reproduced in UN document A/RES/58/241 of 9 January 2004.
UNSC (United Nations Security Council). 2000a. *Report of the Panel of Experts on Violations of Security Council sanctions against UNITA.* S/2000/203 of 10 March.
—. 2000b. *Report of the Panel of Experts Appointed Pursuant to Security Council Resolution 1306 (2000), paragraph 19, in relation to Sierra Leone.* S/2000/1195 of 20 December.
—. 2000c. *Final Report of the Monitoring Mechanism on Angola Sanctions.* S/2000/1225 of 21 December.
—. 2001. *Report of the Panel of Experts pursuant to Security Council Resolution 1343 (2001), paragraph 19, concerning Liberia.* S/2001/1015 of 26 October.
—. 2002. *Report of the Panel of Experts appointed pursuant to Security Council resolution 1408 (2002), paragraph 16, concerning Liberia.* S/2002/1115 of 25 October.
—. 2003a. *Report of the Panel of Experts appointed pursuant to paragraph 4 of Security Council resolution 1458 (2003), concerning Liberia.* S/2003/498 of 24 April.
—. 2003b. *Report of the Panel of Experts appointed pursuant to paragraph 25 of Security Council resolution 1478 (2003) concerning Liberia.* S/2003/937 of 28 October.
US (United States). 1976. *Arms Export Control Act.* Sec. 38, as Amended. Title 22, United States Code, Section 2778. Washington, D.C.
—. 2003. *International Traffic in Arms Regulations (ITAR).*
—. District Court. 2003. District of New Jersey. *Criminal Complaint v. Hemant Lakhani.* 11 August.
Vines, Alex. 2002. 'Flags of Convenience and the Illicit Arms Trade.' Statement before the US House of Representatives Armed Services Committee Special Oversight Panel session on 'The Merchant Marine Vessel Operations under "Flags of Convenience" and National Security Implications.' 13 June.
WA (Wassenaar Arrangement). 2002. *Statement of Understanding on Arms Brokerage.* Adopted during the 11–12 December Plenary Meeting, Vienna.
—. 2003. *Elements for Effective Legislation on Arms Brokering.* Adopted during the 12 December Plenary Meeting, Vienna.
Warner, Tom. 2002. 'The African connection—missiles to Liberia.' *Financial Times.* 21 October, p. 27.
Wood, Brian and Johan Peleman. 1999. *The Arms Fixers: Controlling the Brokers and Shipping Agents.* PRIO Report No. 3/99. Oslo.
—. 2000. 'Making the Deal and Moving the Goods: The Role of Brokers and Shippers.' In Lora Lumpe, ed. *Running Guns: The Global Black Market in Small Arms.* London: Zed Books.

ACKNOWLEDGEMENTS

Other contributors
Holger Anders, Ernst Jan Hogendoorn, Aaron Karp, Anna Khakee, Glenn McDonald, Lisa Misol, Ruxandra Stoicescu, and Herbert Wulf.

A woman holds up the photo of her son, who fell victim to gun violence in 1993, during a news conference in Los Angeles in May 1999. (© AP/Nick Ut).

A Common Tool:
FIREARMS, VIOLENCE, AND CRIME

6

INTRODUCTION

Highly publicized mass shootings such as the 1999 Columbine High School massacre or the 2002 Washington, DC, sniper attacks tend to generate a skewed picture of firearm-related violence, focusing on extreme personalities in unusual contexts. Yet small arms are misused on a daily basis in many communities around the world, making gun violence too banal and too frequent for the international media to cover it all. To those involved, the effects of everyday gun violence are no less dramatic than they would be in a mass shooting. Innocent people are killed and injured, while fear and perceptions of insecurity often spread through society as a whole.

State agents have used small arms to violate, directly and indirectly, the entire spectrum of human rights, including rights to life, liberty, and security of person (UNECOSOC, 2002). Moreover, a growing human security movement aims to hold states accountable for controlling high levels of armed violence, particularly in the absence of basic measures to promote the safety and security of citizens.[1] Others see armed violence as justification for an individual's right to self-defence, a concept frequently used to legitimize private gun ownership.[2] These diverse interpretations highlight the need for a deeper understanding of the complex relationship between small arms and societal violence, defined here as the use of firearms in crime, suicide, and unintentional shootings.

This chapter considers the following questions:
- How prevalent is non-conflict-related gun violence, globally and regionally?
- Does the accessibility of firearms affect overall levels of violence?
- How do communities experience and react to gun violence?

The debate over the relationship between firearms and violence has, for the most part, remained a North American academic and public policy issue. Most of the relevant data, research methodologies, and findings have emerged from that region, with its distinct cultural and socio-economic characteristics. While acknowledging the valuable insights included in such literature, this chapter brings a global perspective to the debate, drawing both on existing international evidence[3] and new field research.[4]

The first section draws on criminal justice and public health datasets to measure the extent of gun violence at the global and regional levels, relying primarily on rates of firearm use in homicide and suicide. It also establishes gender and age profiles of the victims of gun violence. The second section reviews recent developments in the academic and public policy debate with respect to the use of small arms in violence. It offers an overview of recent studies assessing the impact of gun availability on violence and crime levels, and discusses the economic costs incurred by gun misuse. The main findings of field research conducted in African communities and other local contexts are presented in the third section. Common patterns discussed include the recycling of military weapons in criminal activity, as well as the emergence of various private responses to cope with high levels of gun violence. The following are among the most important findings:

- At least 200,000 non-conflict-related firearm deaths occur each year, worldwide. These include firearm homicide, firearm suicide, and unintentional shooting deaths.
- Globally, firearms are used in six per cent of suicides and in almost 40 per cent of homicides.
- Firearm homicides are most common in Latin America and the Caribbean, with a rate five times higher than the world average.
- Almost half the world's firearm suicides occur in North America and Western Europe.
- The relationship between firearm accessibility and overall levels of violence is not clear-cut. Guns facilitate violent outcomes but can also deter crime in some contexts.
- Communities confronted with gun violence in Africa and elsewhere often adopt a variety of responses to gain a greater sense of security. These include reliance on formal and informal private security providers, as well as personal (often illegal) gun ownership.

MAPPING THE PROBLEM: GLOBAL AND REGIONAL PATTERNS OF SMALL ARMS USE IN VIOLENCE AND CRIME

It is generally believed that on average half a million people are killed each year with small arms. Among these, 300,000 people are said to die in armed conflicts, and 200,000 in events not attributed to conflict situations (Small Arms Survey, 2001, 2002, 2003). Because they are routinely cited, these estimates need to be regularly re-evaluated.

This section revisits the figure of 200,000 annual, non-conflict-related firearm deaths. These include fatalities recorded as firearm homicides, firearm suicides, unintentional firearm deaths, and firearm deaths of undetermined intent. Deaths that occur in conflict situations will be considered in subsequent editions of the *Small Arms Survey* (see Box 6.1). This section also identifies regional patterns of firearm use in violence and crime, and establishes the gender and age profile of victims.

Reassessing the estimate of 200,000 annual non-conflict-related firearm deaths

There is an ongoing debate as to whether 200,000 deaths actually result from firearm-related violence and crime each year.[5] A considerable limitation of this estimate is its reliance on firearm mortality rates for less than 40 countries,[6] which account for only one-sixth of the world's population, and are extrapolated globally (Cukier, 1998; Krause, 1999). Critics argue that the data used in these estimates essentially covers developed countries where firearm availability is arguably the highest. As a result, extrapolating these rates to countries with lower levels of gun ownership is likely to produce an overestimate (Kopel, Gallant, and Eisen, 2003). Here, we present the findings of an estimate that extrapolates on a regional basis (see Appendices 6.1 and 6.2), drawing on data available for 110 countries that account for more than half the world's population (see Appendix 6.3).

Available data confirm that at least 200,000 non-conflict-related firearm deaths occur every year globally.

The 200,000 estimate, however unsatisfactory the methodology on which it was originally based, appears to mirror figures obtained by the regional approach presented here. Moreover, 200,000 is likely to be a conservative estimate;

as reported in Appendix 6.1, the available data suggest a minimum of 180,000 annual deaths from firearm homicides and suicides, and an upper threshold of 250,000 deaths if under-reporting and under-recording are taken into account. If we add to these estimates the 18,000 documented unintentional firearm deaths and firearm deaths of undetermined intent (see Table 6.5 in Appendix 6.3), the range increases to 200,000–270,000 annual non-conflict-related firearm deaths. Consequently, it appears that 200,000 represents a conservative estimate of the number of non-conflict-related firearm deaths occurring annually.

> **Box 6.1 How many die in armed conflict?**
>
> In 2001, the *Small Arms Survey* cited the established estimate of 300,000 small arms-related deaths in armed conflict each year. In contrast to the number of non-conflict-related firearm deaths, which our assessment has shown to be reasonable, conflict deaths now show evidence of a decline.
>
> There seems little doubt that the global estimate will be revised downward. A number of studies and databases have already reported recent reductions in armed conflicts around the world (Marshall, 2003; IISS, 2004). Indeed, the *Small Arms Survey 2003* noted a decline in armed conflicts in sub-Saharan Africa, a region that contributed a disproportionate number of armed conflict deaths in the 1990s, the years that formed the basis of the original global estimate. There is also a trend towards more thorough counting and better sourcing, which is likely to further refine the overall figure.
>
> This reduction is undoubtedly good news, and cause for hope. However, it should be reiterated that conflict-related deaths are only the tip of the iceberg of the human cost linked to the proliferation and misuse of small arms. As the Survey has documented in recent years, the range of attributable effects is much wider than deaths from fighting. There are also the indirect deaths and injuries resulting from increased insecurity during and after armed conflict, elevated disease morbidity, reduced access to health services, and malnutrition, many of which are not included in conflict death tolls. The effects of a reduction in small arms conflict deaths on these wider impacts will be challenging, but important, to determine.

Global and regional patterns of firearm use in homicide and suicide

Globally, suicides outnumber homicides by a ratio of 3 to 2 (WHO, 2002).[7] But the ratio is radically different when considering homicides and suicides committed with firearms. At the global level, there are four times as many firearm homicides as firearm suicides (see Appendix 6.1). Firearms are used in approximately six per cent of suicides worldwide and in almost 40 per cent of homicides (see Figure 6.1). At the global level, firearms seem to be primarily a tool for committing homicide rather than suicide.

Non-conflict-related firearm deaths vary tremendously from region to region.[8] There appears to be a global annual rate of 2.8 to 4 non-conflict-related firearm deaths per 100,000; firearm deaths (homicide and suicide combined) seem most common in Latin America and the Caribbean. In fact, this region carries 36 per cent of the global burden at an estimated rate of between 13.6 to 16.6 firearm deaths per 100,000. Given the relatively modest number of weapons in circulation in the region (STOCKPILES), this finding contradicts assumptions that extrapolation from 'well-armed' developed countries would lead to an overestimation of the numbers. Second comes Africa, carrying 18 per cent of the global burden with an estimated rate of 4.2 to 6.5 firearm deaths per 100,000. On the lower end, the Middle East, Western Europe, South-East Asia, and the Asia Pacific region all experience firearm mortality rates below 2 per 100,000.

At the global level, there are four times as many firearm homicides as firearm suicides.

SMALL ARMS SURVEY 2004

Figure 6.1: Putting numbers in perspective: Firearms vs. other means of committing homicide and suicide worldwide (number of deaths)

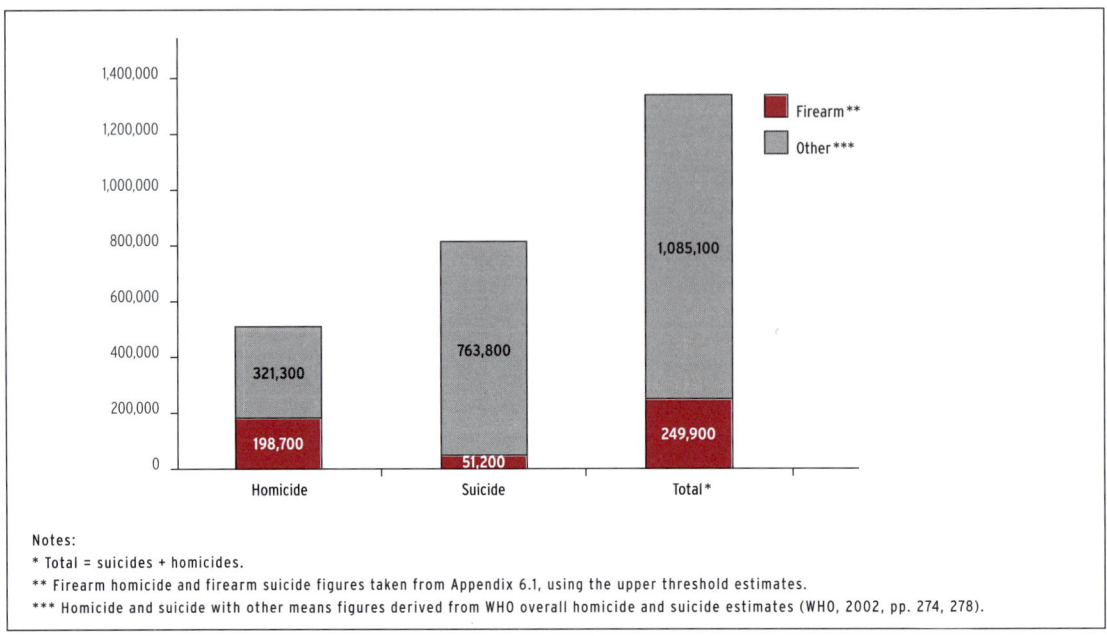

Notes:
* Total = suicides + homicides.
** Firearm homicide and firearm suicide figures taken from Appendix 6.1, using the upper threshold estimates.
*** Homicide and suicide with other means figures derived from WHO overall homicide and suicide estimates (WHO, 2002, pp. 274, 278).

Figure 6.2: Regional distribution of global firearm homicides and suicides (in % of global firearm deaths)*

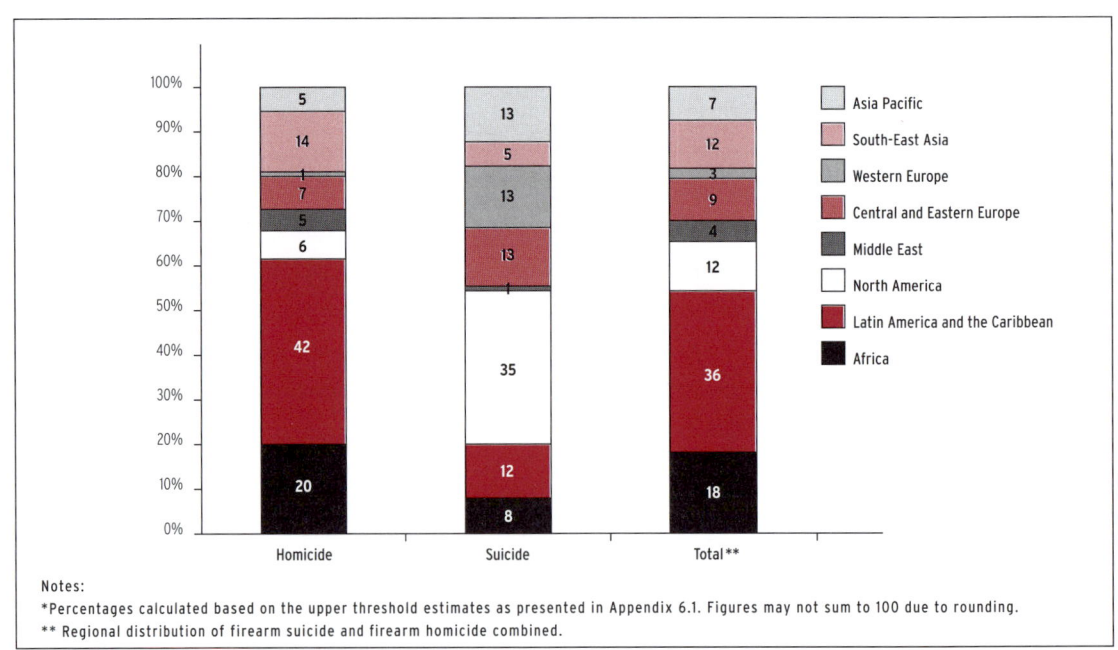

Notes:
*Percentages calculated based on the upper threshold estimates as presented in Appendix 6.1. Figures may not sum to 100 due to rounding.
** Regional distribution of firearm suicide and firearm homicide combined.

The majority of firearm suicides affect industrialized and developed countries. Indeed, almost half the world's firearm suicides occur in North America and Western Europe (Figure 6.2). Western Europe and North America also stand out as the only two regions where firearm suicides are more prevalent than firearm homicides (Figure 6.3). North America, however, experiences the highest regional firearm suicide rate (more than five per 100,000). At the low end, firearm suicide seems to be a comparatively minor problem in South-East Asia, the Middle East, and the Asia-Pacific regions, all of which have estimated rates below 1 per 100,000. It is important to note that the potential distortion of reported suicide data in different religious contexts is highlighted repeatedly in the public health literature (Connolly, 1997; Sayil, 1991). For example, in Muslim and Catholic communities, where people fear that family honour, a religious burial, and even a place in heaven could be denied as a result of suicide, sympathetic officials regularly subsume such deaths among other categories, or simply fail to record them. The suicide estimates presented here should therefore be treated with caution.

Firearm suicide levels are the highest in North America and Western Europe.

A 13-year-old gang member who has killed five people exhales smoke in Medellin, Colombia, a city known as the most dangerous place in the Western hemisphere.

Firearm homicides appear to be most highly concentrated in Latin America and the Caribbean (40 per cent of estimated global cases) and in Africa (20 per cent). Latin America and the Caribbean also register the highest firearm homicide rate, ranging between 12.8 and 15.5 per 100,000. This largely reflects the high overall homicide rates in the region and the fact that firearms are used in 60 per cent of estimated cases. It is also consistent with findings presented in Table 6.1, which suggest that Latin American urban areas experience the highest rates of assaults, threats, robberies, and sexual offences committed with firearms. Western Europe is last, with only one per cent of estimated global firearm homicides, and the lowest rate per 100,000 (0.3 to 0.4).

Latin America and the Caribbean make up the region most affected by firearm homicide.

Firearms appear to be more commonly used in homicide than in suicide both globally and across all regions (see Appendix 6.1). In North America and Latin America and the Caribbean, as many as 60 per cent of all homicides are committed with a firearm. At the lower end, it appears that firearms are used in 16 and 20 percent of homicides in the Asia Pacific and Central and Eastern Europe regions, respectively. Firearms are also widely used in North American suicides (50 per cent of all cases). In the Middle East, South-East Asia, and the Asia-Pacific region, less than two per cent of all suicides appear to be committed with firearms.

Figure 6.3: Levels of firearm mortality across regions (per 100,000)*

Note: *Per 100,000 rates reflect the upper threshold estimates as presented in Appendix 6.1.

Figure 6.4: Homicide and suicide victims by gender (% of total cases)

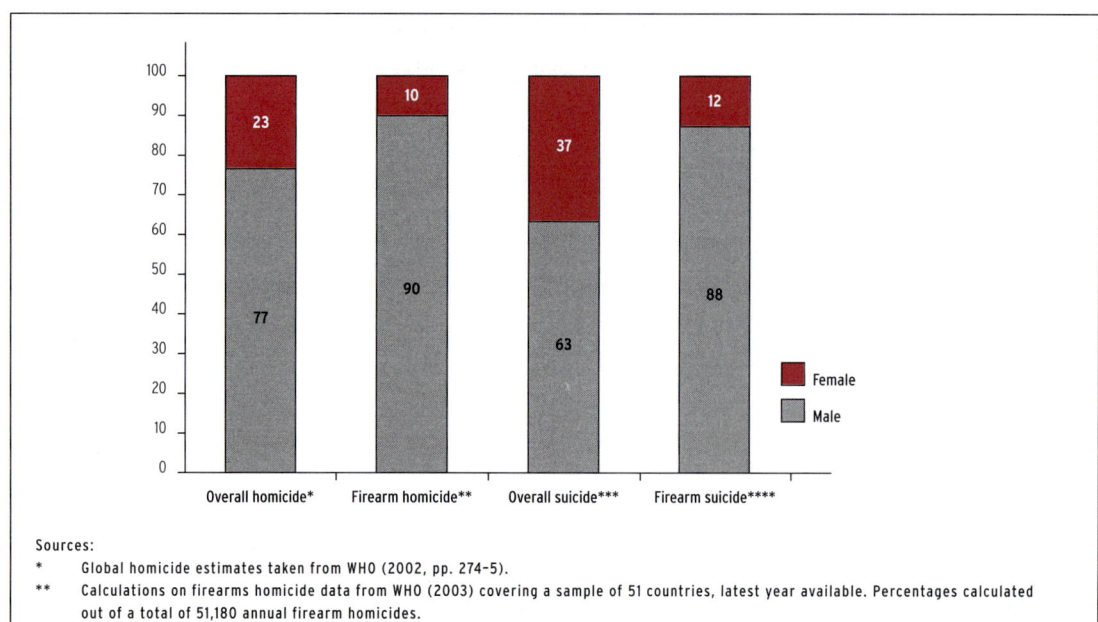

Sources:
* Global homicide estimates taken from WHO (2002, pp. 274-5).
** Calculations on firearms homicide data from WHO (2003) covering a sample of 51 countries, latest year available. Percentages calculated out of a total of 51,180 annual firearm homicides.
*** Global suicide estimates taken from WHO (2002, pp. 278-9).
**** Calculations on firearms suicide data from WHO (2003) covering a sample of 51 countries, latest year available. Percentages calculated out of a total of 22,778 annual firearm suicides.

Demographic profile of victims

Non-conflict-related firearm deaths are an overwhelmingly male phenomenon. The gendered direct effects of firearms have long been studied and trends appear to be consistent across time and space (Small Arms Survey, 2001, p. 213). What is more striking, however, is that the gender imbalance of victims is more marked for firearm deaths than for overall violent deaths. As shown in Figure 6.4, men account for fewer than 80 per cent of overall homicide victims but for more than 90 per cent of firearm homicide victims. Also noteworthy is the fact that men account for fewer than 65 per cent of overall suicide victims but close to 90 per cent of firearm suicide victims. These contrasts suggest that, whereas small arms are a preferred tool for committing violent acts against men, violence against women might involve a wider array of tools and means.

> Young men are the primary victims of firearm homicide.

Box 6.2 The use of firearms in non-fatal violent crimes: Preliminary findings from the International Crime Victim Surveys

The United Nations Interregional Crime and Justice Institute (UNICRI) has carried out the *International Crime Victim Surveys* (ICVS) in 75 countries since 1989. ICVS respondents are randomly selected and asked whether they have been victims of 11 types of non-fatal crime in the previous five years. When respondents answer in the affirmative, they are asked more specific questions. For violent crimes (robberies, assaults and threats, and sexual offences), respondents are asked whether the perpetrator used a firearm.[9]

The ICVS allows for international comparisons due to its standardized methodology.[10] As a result of logistical and resource constraints, the surveys are administered nationally in developed countries (n=2,000) and in capital cities among developing countries (n=1,000-1,500). In order to ensure comparability, the victimization rates presented here are for urban areas only.

Table 6.1 illustrates how firearms, at the regional level, appear to be more commonly used in robberies and assaults than in sexual offences. When compared with Appendix 6.1, these findings also show that firearms are a much more common tool for committing homicide than the non-fatal violent crimes discussed here. There are two possible explanations for this finding: First, criminals may prefer using firearms for committing crimes that pose great risks to their personal safety. Second, the use of firearms in violent crime may increase the risk of a fatal outcome; robberies and assaults that turn into a homicide would be recorded as homicide and cannot be reported in victim surveys.

The regional patterns of firearm homicide identified in this chapter also apply to the other types of violent crime discussed here. As with firearm homicides, Latin America and Africa experience the highest rates of firearm robberies and assaults. The lowest victimization rates are experienced in Western Europe and Asia. Latin America and Africa also experience the highest levels of gun use in both robberies (25 and 13 per cent of all cases, respectively) and assaults and threats (nine per cent for both regions). In the 'New World' region, comprised of the United States, Canada, Australia, and New Zealand, seven per cent of robberies and four per cent of assaults are committed with a firearm. At the lower end, small arms appear to be a relatively unpopular tool for committing non-fatal violent crimes in Asia.

Table 6.1 Regional victimization rates (urban areas only)*

Regions**	Robbery			Assaults and threats			Sexual offences***		
	Overall	Firearm	%	Overall	Firearm	%	Overall	Firearm	%
Western Europe	1.45	0.08	5.52	4.02	0.05	1.24	3.10	0.03	0.97
'New World'****	1.24	0.09	7.26	5.84	0.23	3.94	2.50	0.00	0.00
CE Europe	1.81	0.09	4.97	3.20	0.20	6.25	2.02	0.02	0.99
Asia	1.32	0.02	1.52	2.04	0.04	1.96	2.70	0.00	0.00
Africa	4.18	0.54	12.92	5.42	0.48	8.86	5.19	0.11	2.12
Latin America	7.89	1.96	24.84	5.13	0.44	8.58	5.35	0.03	0.56

* Figures represent the percentage of respondents who experienced the stated crime in the five years prior to the surveys (which were conducted between the early 1990s and 2001). Figures in the % columns represent the percentage of crimes committed with a firearm.
** Regions are defined slightly different from in the rest of the chapter.[11]
*** Only female respondents were asked about sexual offence victimization.
**** The 'New World' is comprised of Australia, Canada, New Zealand, and the United States.

Source: van Kesteren (2003)

Figure 6.5: Homicide and suicide victims by age group (% of total cases)

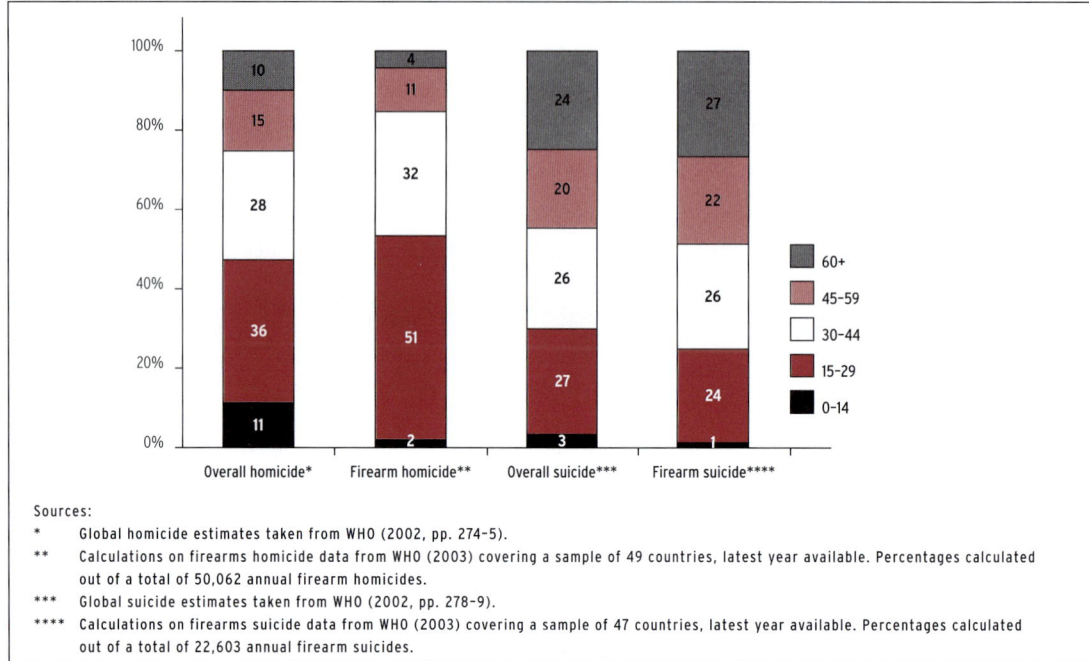

Sources:
* Global homicide estimates taken from WHO (2002, pp. 274-5).
** Calculations on firearms homicide data from WHO (2003) covering a sample of 49 countries, latest year available. Percentages calculated out of a total of 50,062 annual firearm homicides.
*** Global suicide estimates taken from WHO (2002, pp. 278-9).
**** Calculations on firearms suicide data from WHO (2003) covering a sample of 47 countries, latest year available. Percentages calculated out of a total of 22,603 annual firearm suicides.

There are striking differences with respect to the age of homicide and suicide victims. Figure 6.5 shows that 85 per cent of firearm homicide victims are under the age of 44. In contrast, half of those committing suicide with a firearm appear to be aged 45 or more. As with gender, these patterns are more pronounced for victims of firearm deaths than for victims of overall homicide and suicide. This clearly shows that firearm homicides are concentrated primarily among relatively young, physically strong, and potentially productive individuals. With more than one-quarter of firearm suicide victims aged 60 or more, small arms appear to be a common weapon for committing suicide among the elderly.

BEYOND NUMBERS: THE ROLE OF SMALL ARMS IN VIOLENCE AND CRIME

The debate over gun violence has been most lively in North American academic and public policy circles.

The first section of this chapter established that small arms are a common tool for committing homicide and suicide, although to varying degrees across regions and demographic groups. The fact that small arms are used in violence, however, does not necessarily mean that they cause it or make it worse. This section reviews the existing literature on the implications of the accessibility and misuse of small arms.

A considerable proportion of the research undertaken on the empirical relationships between small arms availability and crime and violence has been produced by North American academics and public policy specialists. Their interest in the issue should come as no surprise, as the region is greatly affected by firearm violence: North America registers the third-highest rate of firearm homicides (3.5 per 100,000) and the highest rate of firearm suicides in the world (5.5 per 100,000).

Box 6.3: Self-defence under international law: Two perspectives.

The right to self-defence is often cited in the US context as a justification for private gun ownership and defensive gun use. This box presents two different, though not necessarily competing, perspectives on the right to self-defence under international law.

The Various Aspects of Self-Defence Under International Law, by Antonio Cassese

The right of self-defence under international law governs relations between states as opposed to groups and individuals. Pursuant to Article 51 of the *Charter of the United Nations and Statute of the International Court of Justice* (UN, 1945) and corresponding customary international law, states have a right to defend themselves against an 'armed attack' if the UN Security Council fails to take effective action to stop it.

Rebels, insurgents, and other organized armed groups do not have a right to use force against governmental authorities, except in three cases. Liberation movements can use force in order to resist the forcible denial of self-determination by (1) a colonial state, (2) an occupying power, or (3) a state refusing a racial group equal access to government. These situations, however, are not considered ones of 'self-defence' under international law.

Individuals who are not organized in groups have even less scope for the use of force under international law. Individuals have no legal right to use force to repel armed violence by oppressive states. This includes governments that commit acts of genocide or other serious human rights violations. Nor does international law grant individuals a right to defend themselves against other individuals. This right is provided for by states in their national legal systems as each state determines the conditions under which individuals can use force for these purposes.

It is not surprising that states have refused to legitimize the resort to armed violence by individuals given the threat this would pose to their own authority. International law is made by states and tends to reflect their interests and concerns. The *Universal Declaration of Human Rights* nevertheless provides a moral endorsement of the violent reaction of individuals to political oppression or other forcible denial of fundamental human rights: 'it is essential, if man is not to be compelled to have recourse, as a last resort, to rebellion against tyranny and oppression, that human rights should be protected by the rule of law' (UNGA, 1948, third pream. para., emphasis added).

Individuals' Right to Self-Defence Under International Law, by Don Kates

The right of individuals to defend themselves has been and remains fundamental to international law. In the first instance, this is a matter of simple logic. Nation states are the embodiment of the people living within them. Their right of self-defence, expressed in Article 51 of the UN Charter, can only derive from the right of self-defence held by their people.

This right of individual self-defence was, in fact, a key starting point for international law. Many of the first international law treatises included long discussions of individual self-protection. The right of individual self-defence is also implicit in current international instruments. The right to life, enunciated in the *Universal Declaration of Human Rights* (UNGA, 1948, art. 3), has no substance unless it includes the right to preserve life.

The right to individual self-defence is also accepted by modern philosophers, many of whom also argue that this right entitles individuals to own guns, the only effective means of defence. While pacifist philosophers hold that individuals cannot use force in any circumstances, they also deny this right to nation states. Throughout history, however, the world's major religions—including Christianity, Judaism, and Islam—have equally recognized a right (even a duty) to kill in self-defence.

A universal right of self-defence for individuals has strong practical justification. Police have no legal duty to protect endangered individuals. They deter crime by patrolling and by apprehending perpetrators after crime occurs. The law does not require police to help specific individuals under attack or under a general threat of death. This principle has been upheld by US courts, for example in the case of *Warren v District of Columbia* (US, District of Columbia Court of Appeals, 1981). This, in fact, reflects police resource limitations that apply not only in the United States but also in other industrialized countries with significant levels of violent crime, including Australia, Canada, and England.

Sources: Cassese (2003); Kates (2003)

This section highlights three dimensions of the gun-control debate. The most controversial has to do with the so-called 'accessibility' question: does the availability of firearms increase overall levels of violence and/or does it enhance security through deterrence and defensive gun use? A second theme relates to the 'instrumentality' versus the 'substitution' of firearms. In other words, given their lethality and other attributes, do firearms actually facilitate and create more opportunities for violent outcomes? If small arms were no longer available, would criminals 'substitute' them with other types of weapons? A third perspective has emerged from the fields of economics and criminology, and attempts to measure the net costs imposed on societies affected by high rates of firearm violence.

More guns, more or less violence? The 'accessibility thesis' debate

Proponents of the accessibility thesis argue that when there is ready access to a firearm (handgun, rifle, or shotgun), a violent outcome is more likely.[12] Opponents of this position argue that the availability of firearms deters and therefore reduces violent outcomes. Citizens fearful of violent crime will acquire guns for self-defence (see Box 6.3) and, as a result, gain a greater sense of security. Resolving the accessibility debate requires an understanding of whether increased arms availability increases violence and/or personal security.

Methodological challenges

A number of methodological challenges have prevented the research community from providing clear answers to the accessibility question. One of the key obstacles has been the definition of 'accessibility' itself. Studies have typically advanced three indicators to measure whether weapons are accessible: the percentage of households possessing firearms; the extent to which firearms are regulated; and the number of firearms in civilian hands (Kates and Polsby, 2000).

Each of these measures has limitations. For example, the number of households with a gun does not necessarily reflect people's ability to access firearms they do not own. Furthermore, this type of data is usually collected through voluntary surveys, which are likely to underestimate prevalence given the sensitive nature of the question. Using firearm regulations as indicators of availability is equally problematic: strict firearm laws are often passed as a result of gun availability and violence. Areas with tougher gun legislation may therefore actually have more guns than areas with more flexible laws but lower levels of violence. As for the total number of firearms in civilian hands, it too is controversial as the indicator does not adequately reflect the overall distribution of weapons within a given society (i.e. the number of weapons per gun owner).

> One major challenge to resolving the accessibility thesis debate lies in demonstrating a causal link between gun accessibility and violence.

Demonstrating a causal link between gun accessibility and violence is not methodologically straightforward. Where increased firearm availability is accompanied by higher rates of violent death, how can one determine which came first? It is possible in such situations that civilians arm themselves as a response to increasing crime rates. When studies are conducted over a period of time, it is also extremely difficult to determine whether the variations in overall levels of violence are the consequence of reduced arms availability or of developments affecting other plausible factors of violence.[13]

Another major obstacle to resolving the accessibility issue has to do with the availability and reliability of statistical data. As shown in Appendix 6.3, basic aggregate data such as national annual firearm homicide rates are not available for many countries. Even in countries with comparatively sophisticated data collection systems such as the United States, researchers there argue that even more comprehensive data is needed to adequately tackle the issue (Dahl, 2003). This was made clear with the release of findings from the Task Force on Community Preventive Services, which found 'insufficient evidence' to determine the effectiveness of eight different types of firearms legislation (CDC, 2003a).

State of the debate

Notwithstanding these limitations, the literature has produced a number of 'qualified' findings since the issue was last examined in the 2001 *Small Arms Survey*. These fall into three main categories: studies showing that firearm availability among specific population segments increases the likelihood of a violent outcome, research emphasizing the number of crimes that are deterred by responsible gun ownership, and studies seeking to measure the effectiveness of gun control legislation.

The most pertinent studies seeking to establish a relationship between small arms availability and a higher incidence of violence focus on specific age groups (primarily youth and the elderly) and on the gender dimensions of violence (with gun availability posing an increased risk of violence against women). With respect to age groups, Miller *et al.* (2002, p. 273) find that, where there are more guns, children aged 5–14 are much more likely to become victims of lethal violence than to be protected from it. Using the Life Experiences Survey, Slovak (2002) finds that increasing access to guns coupled with lack of parental monitoring heightens the risk of exposure to gun violence. There is also growing evidence that the availability of firearms at home increases the risk of impulsive suicide among youth, especially when combined with other risk factors such as alcohol and drug abuse.[14] In this regard, Kellerman *et al.* (1992) showed that youth under 24 with a firearm in the home are 10.4 times more likely to commit suicide than youth from the same age group whose household does not possess a firearm. In the United States, the elderly, and in particular white men, are also at a higher risk of suicide when they have access to handguns (Conwell *et al.*, 2002). Wiebe (2003a, 2003b) finds that younger and older people, men and women, whites and non-whites are all at an increased risk of violent death if guns are kept at home.

> A number of studies suggest that access to guns increases the likelihood that women, youth, and the elderly become victims of violence.

This police photo shows a gunman robbing Barclays Bank in north London in February 2002.

Gender-focused research has also generated revealing findings. A study that compares 25 high-income countries has found that female homicide victimization rates are significantly associated with firearms availability (Hemenway *et al.*, 2002). This correlation is strengthened by the United States, where firearms are used in 59 per cent of all intimate partner homicides of women (US Bureau of Justice Statistics, 2002). Kellermann and Heron (1999), in an examination of firearms and family violence, have shown that women are much more likely to be murdered by a firearm than to be protected by one. This confirms the results of a study by Bailey *et al.* (1997), which shows that women in homes with one or more guns are 7.2 times more likely to be the victims of homicide. The use of firearms in intimate partner violence is becoming an increasingly well-documented issue. Wintemute *et al.* (2003) find that handgun purchase among women in

California is associated with a 50 per cent increase in homicide risk compared with all adult women in California. This increased risk is of intimate partner homicide, not of homicide involving other assailants.

College students practice at the Smith and Wesson shooting range in Massachusetts in May 2002.

However, there appears to be little relationship between gun prevalence and general crime, because most crimes do not involve guns (see Box 6.2). For example, it is still unclear whether gun availability increases or prevents burglary and robbery. Gun advocates believe that criminals are deterred by gun ownership in private houses (Kopel, 2001), while others believe that it may increase burglaries because guns are considered valuable loot (Duggan, 2001; Ludwig and Cook, 2003). A number of studies, however, have shown that higher levels of gun ownership appear to be associated with higher rates of robbery with guns, but not of overall robbery (Cook, 1979, 1987; Kleck, 1997).

In the last decade, considerable research has focused on the frequency of legitimate gun use in the United States. Surveys have generated estimates of the annual number of such defensive uses ranging from 64,000 (McDowall and Wiersema, 1994; Cook and Ludwig, 1997) to 2.5 million (Kleck and Gertz, 1995). The true figure of defensive gun use is likely to lie somewhere in between; some have suggested a figure of between 200,000 to 500,000 instances annually (Wintemute *et al.*, 1999, quoting T. Smith, 1997).[15] Supporters of defensive gun use have pointed out that defensive gun use saves lives: guns used against criminals may not necessarily kill the criminal. Even when a criminal is killed, this might have saved more lives if the criminal intended to kill more than one person (Kleck, 1997). Sceptics of defensive gun use contend that victims are seldom able to deploy a gun against intruders even when they have one available (Cook and Ludwig, 2000). They believe that guns are not widely used for defensive purposes in moments when they are needed and that self-reported defensive gun use includes instances of perceived rather than real threat.

Box 6.4: The impact of gun control measures in Australia

Despite reports of a crime wave in Australia following recent restrictions on the private ownership of firearms, evidence actually shows sweeping reductions in gun-related death, injury, and crime.

On 10 May 1996, 12 days after 35 people were shot dead by a single gunman at Port Arthur, Tasmania, Australia's state and federal governments agreed to enact wide-ranging gun control measures. Between June 1996 and August 1998, new restrictions were progressively brought into force. These included the 1996-97 Australian Firearms Buyback, in which 643,726 newly prohibited semi-automatic and pump-action rifles and shotguns were purchased at market value for destruction by the government. Thousands of gun owners also volunteered additional, non-prohibited firearms for free, and more than 700,000 guns were destroyed (Australia, CAGD, 2002; Giles, 2002[16]).

Following the gun buy-back, the number of firearm-related homicides (see Figure 6.6) fell sharply between 1996 and 1999 (Reuter and Mouzos, 2002). By 2001, Australia's rate of 0.25 gun-related homicides per 100,000 population was at its lowest since 1950, having fallen to one-sixteenth that of the United States (ABS, 2001; Arias *et al.*, 2003). Although by 2002 overall homicides (by any method) had risen once again almost to pre-buyback levels, the use of guns in homicide had fallen to its lowest proportion since 1915 (Mouzos, 2003). This suggests a substitution effect to weapons of lower lethality.

In the seven years from 1996 to 2002, total firearm-related deaths from all causes in Australia (homicide, suicide, unintentional shootings, and justifiable homicide) fell from 521 to 299–a reduction of 43 per cent since the new gun laws were introduced and well under half the annual gun death toll that prevailed two decades earlier. As a result, in 2001 the country's overall rate of gun death reached a new low of 1.75 per 100,000 population, or one-sixth that of the United States. In 2002, the Australian rate dropped once more, to 1.5 per 100,000 (Bell, 2003; ABS, 1998-2003; Research Centre for Injury Studies, 2000; Arias *et al.*, 2003). Similar reductions were reported in non-fatal firearm-related injury (Mouzos, 2001a).

Those who claim that Australia suffered a 'crime wave' following restrictions on private gun ownership often cite as evidence unrelated figures for common assault, sexual assault, or robbery (no weapon), armed robbery (any weapon), unrepresentative regional figures, and short-term spikes. In reality, Australia's robbery victimization rate in 2002 (106 per 100,000 population) was the lowest since 1995 (ABS, 2003b).

In recent years, 94 per cent of robberies in Australia did not involve firearms. When a robber did use a weapon, it was less and less likely to be a gun. In 2002, a ten-year low was reached when only 5.6 per cent of robberies involved a firearm (ABS, 2001, 2003a). By comparison, 41 per cent of robberies in the United States in 2000 involved a gun, usually a handgun (Australian Institute of Criminology, 2002).

Handguns account for half the firearms used to commit homicide in Australia. Between 10 per cent and 27 per cent of the perpetrators of homicide were licensed gun owners (Mouzos, 2001b, 2002a, 2003b). In July 2003, Australian states and territories launched a new initiative to remove potential crime guns from private ownership. The National Handgun Buyback targets readily concealable pistols and revolvers, offering market prices during an amnesty period, followed by prohibition of several hundred models of handgun based on calibre, barrel length, and magazine/shot capacity (Council of Australian Governments, 2003).

The debate over the predominant source of Australian crime guns involves much heat but little evidence. While some claim that firearms used by criminals must be smuggled into Australia (O'Malley, 2003), others cite Customs and Police testimony that crime guns are most often obtained from licensed Australian gun owners (Toohey, 2002; O'Malley, 2003; Australian Customs Service, 2003). An average of 4,200 firearms are reported stolen each year in Australia, with an unknown number unreported. More than 3,500 easily concealed handguns were reported stolen from licensed gun dealers, police stations, security firms, shooting clubs, and private premises in the years 1994-2000 alone (Mouzos, 2002b).

Figure 6.6: 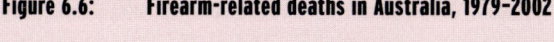 Firearm-related deaths in Australia, 1979-2002

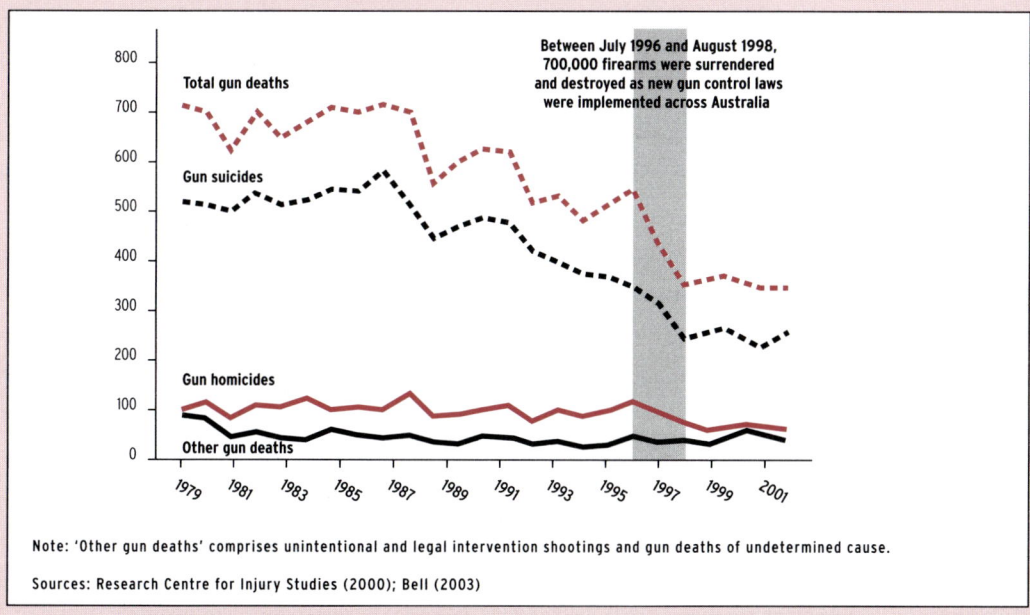

Note: 'Other gun deaths' comprises unintentional and legal intervention shootings and gun deaths of undetermined cause.

Sources: Research Centre for Injury Studies (2000); Bell (2003)

In a trend that preceded the Australian Firearms Buyback but seems to have been greatly accelerated by it, private gun ownership fell by 45 per cent between 1989 and 2000, leaving an Australian household three times less likely to own a firearm than a US household (Australian Institute of Criminology, 2002). By destroying one-fifth of their country's estimated stock of firearms—an equivalent figure in the United States would be 40 million (Reuter and Mouzos, 2002)—Australians have chosen to significantly shrink their private arsenal. All remaining guns must now be individually registered to their licensed owners, private firearm

> sales are no longer permitted, and each gun purchase through a licensed arms dealer is scrutinized by the police to establish a 'genuine reason' for ownership. Possession of firearms for self-defence is specifically prohibited, and very few civilians are permitted to own handguns. Australia's state governments, police forces, and police unions all support the tightened gun laws, while opinion polls show strong voter approval.
>
> In the ten years to 1996, culminating in the massacre at Port Arthur, Australia saw 11 mass shootings in each of which five or more victims died. In these events alone, 100 people were shot dead and another 52 wounded (Alpers, 1996). In the eight years since Port Arthur and the new gun laws, no mass shootings have occurred. Even among gun homicides, these events are rare, and causality cannot be claimed from such a small sample. Yet Australians have reason to be encouraged by the results of recent measures to curb the proliferation of small arms.
>
> Source: Alpers (2004)

There is a persistent belief in some quarters that the open possession of firearms by civilians can decrease the likelihood of crime occurring. For example, Lott and Mustard (1997) and Lott (1998) contend that permissive laws allowing civilians to carry firearms outside their home (Right-to-Carry or RTC laws) have led to a substantial reduction in violent crime. In their view, if potential victims arm themselves, they are not only better equipped to defend themselves but the deterrent effect is greater as criminals will think twice before attacking a victim who might be carrying a firearm. Duggan (2001) and Kovandzic and Marvell (2003), however, find that there is no credible evidence, statistical or otherwise, that allowing citizens to carry concealed handguns produces greater deterrent effects.[17] Nevertheless, the findings of Lott and Mustard have proven enormously influential: lawmakers in a number of US states have recently passed a series of RTC laws (Donohue, 2003).[18]

Gun control has registered some notable successes in reducing the proportion of crimes committed with firearms.

The effectiveness and efficiency of firearm legislation in reducing overall crime and violence is also still very much an open debate. For example, a recent CDC report presented the findings of the evaluation of eight types of gun-control laws, including: bans on specific firearms or ammunition; restrictions on firearms acquisition; firearm registration and licensing of firearm owners; concealed weapon-carry laws; child-access prevention laws; zero tolerance laws for firearms in schools; and combinations of firearms-regulation legislation. The evaluation found 'insufficient evidence to determine the effectiveness of any of the firearms laws or combinations of laws reviewed on violent outcomes' (CDC, 2003a, pp. 1–2). Even though the report also contains a disclaimer specifying that 'insufficient evidence to determine effectiveness should not be interpreted as evidence of ineffectiveness', this report has been seized upon by anti-gun control advocates who seek to highlight not only the ineffectiveness but also the perceived harmful impacts of gun laws (Wheeler, 2003). There is, however, a growing body of evidence indicating that gun control measures contribute to reducing levels of firearm violence without necessarily affecting overall violence (see Boxes 6.4 and 6.5).

A tool among others? Guns, their instrumentality, and the substitution effect

A debate closely related to the accessibility thesis concerns the instrumentality of firearms versus their substitution effect.[19]

Adherents of the instrumentality theory argue that firearms, because of their specific attributes (e.g. simplicity and lethality), increase the likelihood of serious injury or death. In their view, the availability of guns might increase overall homicide and suicide rates irrespective of the aggressor's motivation. By way of contrast, proponents of the substitution effect argue that if a person intends to kill, the method is irrelevant: if they did not have access to firearms, criminals and those aiming to commit suicide will merely substitute another weapon or means to carry out the act. The overall level of violence would, therefore, remain unaffected by the availability of guns.

Do any attributes of firearms make them different from other means of committing violent acts? It is regularly pointed out that virtually no physical competence is required to deliver violence with a gun. Moreover, a criminal act committed with a gun poses virtually no risk to the perpetrator and can kill at a distance thereby endangering 'all in the vicinity' (Cook and Ludwig, 2000, p. 35). The greater lethality of guns compared with other weapons is comparatively obvious with respect to violent crime (Rennison, 2002). Gun robberies are three times more likely to result in death than robberies committed with knives, and ten times more fatal than robberies in which other weapons are used (Cook, 1987, quoted in Cook and Ludwig, 2000, p. 35). It has also been argued that suicide attempts by gunshots are more likely to be effective than suicide attempts by other means (Zimring, 1991). Studies conducted in the United States and Canada show that suicides committed with firearms have the highest likelihood of a lethal outcome; 90 per cent of suicide attempts with a gun are fatal, compared with around 20 per cent with drug overdoses (see Table 6.2). A more recent study shows even higher firearm lethality and reduced poisoning lethality: 96.5 per cent and 6.5 per cent, respectively (Shenassa, Catlin, and Buka, 2003).

Table 6.2 Lethality of suicide attempts by means

	US* (%)	Canada** (%)
Firearm	90	92
Hanging	80	78
Carbon Monoxide	77	78
Drowning	77	67
Drug overdoses / poisoning	23	23

Sources:
* Kleck (1991), quoted in Mouzos (1999)
** Chapdelaine, Samson, and Kimberly (1991), quoted in Miller and Hemenway (1999)

Supporters of the 'substitution effect' interpretation contend that the method is of little significance compared to the intent: the perpetrator will persevere until he or she achieves his or her goal. Though firearms at home appear to increase the risk of suicide among certain age groups, the case for substitution seems to be compelling with respect to suicides. In his exhaustive survey of the literature on the relationship between firearms and suicide, Kleck (1997) finds that, of 13 studies, nine found the aforementioned significant correlation between levels of gun availability and rates of gun suicide, but only one study claimed to find a significant association between the level of gun ownership and the rate of total suicide. This seems further illustrated by the case of Japan, which has an extremely small total stockpile of firearms but a suicide rate similar to that of the United States; in Japan, suicides are almost always accomplished with means other than guns (see Kopel, 1992). A recent study by Killias, van Kesteren, and Rindlisbacher (2001) also shows that, at the cross-national level, gun ownership is associated with the proportion of suicides committed with a firearm; but gun ownership is not found to be correlated with overall suicide rates. In other words, where firearms are available, they are the preferred tool for committing suicide, but do not appear to increase overall rates of suicide within a whole country.

Box 6.5   A handgun ban in the United Kingdom

The 1997 ban on civilian handgun possession in the United Kingdom is a case study in preventing gun violence that is being closely watched by policy-makers and advocates in other countries. But while the law appears to have reduced the number of banned weapons in circulation, its overall effect on gun crime is unclear.

Prior to the ban, England and Wales (grouped together by the Home Office for statistical purposes) already had some of the lowest rates of firearm mortality among the high- and upper-middle income nations of the world, and the lowest of 21 surveyed European countries (Krug, Powell, and Dahlberg, 1998). Since the police began publishing figures for gun homicides in 1977, fewer than 100 fatal shootings have been recorded each year, and the rate has not exceeded 0.18 per 100,000 people (see Figure 6.7).

Figure 6.7:   Homicide and firearm homicide in England and Wales

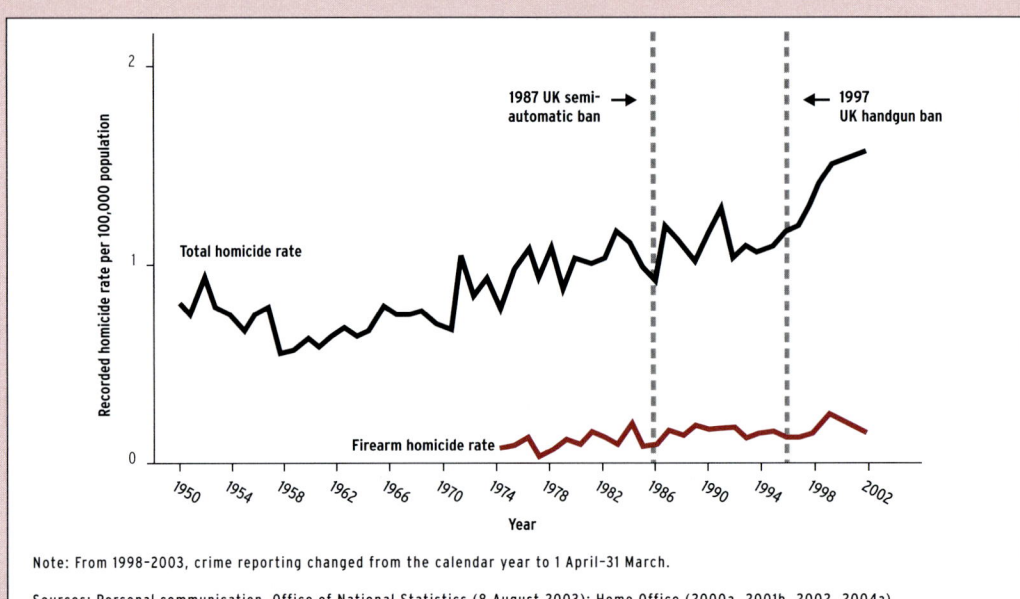

Note: From 1998–2003, crime reporting changed from the calendar year to 1 April–31 March.

Sources: Personal communication, Office of National Statistics (8 August 2003); Home Office (2000a, 2001b, 2002, 2004a)

But in a culture unaccustomed to widespread gun violence, sporadic mass shootings have proven deeply disturbing to the public. Two massacres in particular—the 1987 assault weapon and handgun attack that left 18 people dead in Hungerford, England, and the 1996 handgun killing of 16 schoolchildren and their teacher in Dunblane, Scotland—generated a public outcry and calls for gun control policies that led to revisions to the 1968 Firearms Act governing civilian firearm ownership. Since both of these shootings were committed by licensed gun owners with legally acquired weapons, the amendments sought to further limit the kinds of weapons that could be acquired and the people who could own them.

Legislative changes in response to these shootings built on the 1968 Firearm Act's ban on automatic weapons and licensing and 'good reason' requirements for long guns (rifles and shotguns). After the Hungerford incident, all semi-automatic firearms were prohibited, except for .22 calibre semi-automatic long guns. Then, in response to the Dunblane shooting, Parliament in 1997 banned all handguns except for very limited purposes (for example, to slaughter animals or to start races, but not for self-protection). The ban, effective 1 March 1998, did not extend to all hand-held weapons, however. In particular, deactivated handguns, hand-held airguns, and replica weapons were exempted. Amnesty programmes were instituted to remove existing, now illegal handguns from general circulation. The government paid market prices for handguns, accessories, and ammunition. At least 159,701 now illegal handguns have been surrendered in this way since 1998; however, an estimated 250,000 deactivated firearms that can readily be reactivated remain widely available (UK, NCIS, 2003; Muir and Carter, 2003).

As of 2000, the legal handgun ownership rate is 0.02 per 100 persons (UK, Home Office, 2004b). Despite this low level of ownership, Home Office statistics report an increase in the gun homicide rate from 0.09 per 100,000 in 1998 to 0.15 per 100,000 in 2002, while the use of guns in all violent crime increased from 12.8 to 23.3 per 100,000 (UK, Home Office, 2004a).

What kinds of firearms are being used to commit this post-ban violence? Airguns that have not been banned appear to predominate in gun crime, accounting for at least 40 per cent of all gun assaults, and they are over three times more likely than genuine handguns to be used in causing or threatening injury (see Figure 6.8). In 2002, airguns were responsible for 30 per cent of non-fatal serious gun injuries (UK, Home Office, 2004a).

Figure 6.8: Recorded use of guns to injure and threaten in England and Wales, by weapon type

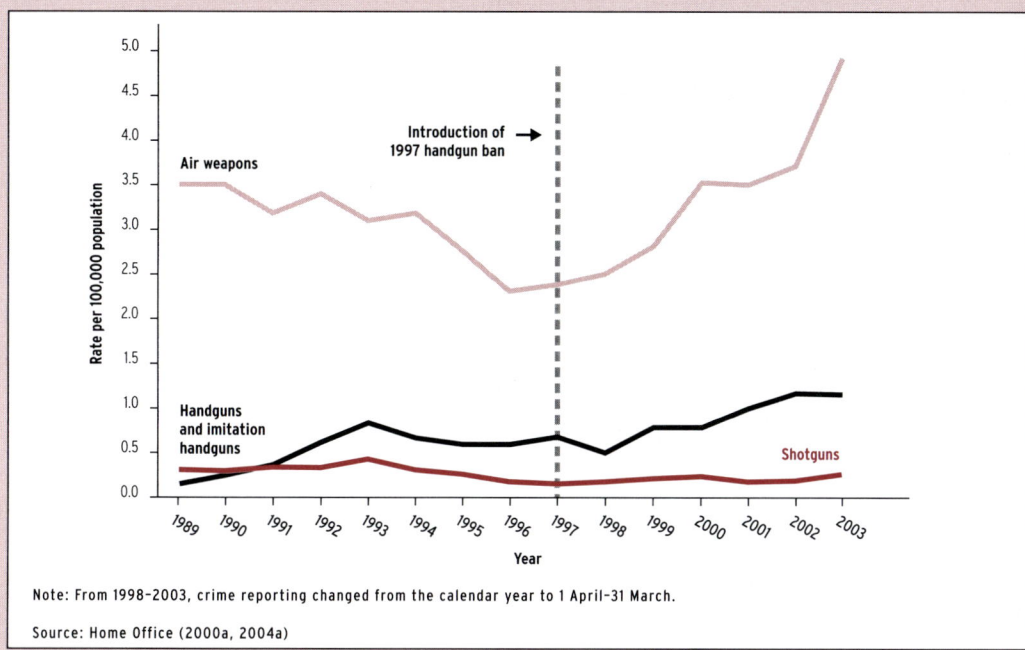

Note: From 1998–2003, crime reporting changed from the calendar year to 1 April–31 March.

Source: Home Office (2000a, 2004a)

The picture is less clear with respect to gun homicides, the majority of which were committed with handguns (49 per cent), then shotguns (17 per cent), rifles (6 per cent), airguns (1 per cent), and unidentified firearms (26 per cent) in 2002 (UK, Home Office, 2004a). The 'handgun' and 'unidentified' categories are likely to contain some, and possibly many, formerly deactivated or replica guns, as there has been a 50 per cent increase in seizures of converted replicas in the wake of the ban (UK, NCIS, 2003). Since the gun homicide data do not shed light on whether guns were once deactivated or replicas, however, it is difficult to assess the full impact of the ban. Given the low number of gun homicides and the modest fluctuations since the ban, it does not appear to have been statistically significant.

What became increasingly clear to police and government officials in the wake of the ban was that lawful airguns, replicas, and deactivated firearms were still a significant crime problem. This realization led to the inclusion of provisions in the Anti-Social Behaviour Act of 2003 (effective 20 January 2004) that prohibit certain types of convertible airguns commonly used in crime and raise the minimum age for purchase of any airgun from 14 to 17, which is also the minimum age for firearms. These restrictions, if aggressively enforced, will complement the handgun ban by addressing weapons that are far more common in UK crime than genuine firearms.

Source: Howard and LeBrun (2004)

With respect to weapon substitution in violent crime, it is interesting to note how different types of firearms may or may not influence overall levels of violence. In the United States at least, handguns (pistols and revolvers) are the type of firearm most commonly used by criminals (US, Department of the Treasury, 2002, p. 10). Anderson and Kates (2003)

A burglar holds a gun to his head, threatening to commit suicide unless the police provide an escape vehicle in Buenos Aires in June 2003.

argue that, should handguns become unavailable to criminals, the homicide rate would remain steady at least and might even increase, as some professional criminals would switch to knives (roughly equivalent in lethality to small-calibre handguns) or other methods, while others would switch to rifles and shotguns (of greater lethality than handguns). The experience of the United Kingdom, however, shows that one of the outcomes of the 1997 handgun ban has been the increased reliance on airguns, handgun imitations, and replicas (as opposed to shotguns) in violent acts (see Box 6.5).

A conciliatory approach? The economic costs of gun violence

The relationship between small arms availability and overall violence is not a simple one. On the one hand, it is important to acknowledge the valuable and policy-relevant contributions made by the accessibility debate: firearm availability does pose a risk to specific demographic groups such as women, male youth, and the elderly in specific contexts. On the other hand, one cannot ignore the deterrent effects of small arms on crime when they are in the hands of law-abiding citizens. The injection of more resources into research and data collection would undoubtedly generate more focused and policy-relevant findings—especially the identification of population groups most at risk.

These qualified findings must not overshadow the fact that violence is a complex phenomenon that cannot be reduced by focusing on guns alone. A review of the crime prevention literature demonstrates that violence reduction is contingent upon a range of factors, with guns representing only part of the puzzle (Waller, 2003). Blumstein and Wallman (2000), for instance, emphasize that much of the growth in violent crime in the United States from 1970 to 1980 and then the decline to 1985 was due to the 'movement of the baby-boom generation into and then out of the high crime prone age groups' of 15–25. They warn that demographic trends could lead to an increase in crime rates in the next decade.

Crime prevention and reduction programmes that 'work' do not necessarily target guns exclusively. A recent evaluation of such interventions found only one 'promising' gun-focused programme. This programme involved proactive arrests of individuals carrying concealed weapons in Kansas City's gun-crime hot spots. The evaluation found that gun buy-backs were ineffective and not a single gun-related programme was listed among those that actually successfully reduced crime according to rigorous scientific standards (Sherman *et al.*, 1998, quoted in Waller, 2003).

Whether such programmes work or not, a growing literature indicates that the use of guns in violence is especially problematic because of their disproportionately high social costs in comparison with other types of weapons. As has been reported in previous editions of the *Small Arms Survey* (2001; 2002; 2003), firearm injuries are more costly to public health systems than those occasioned by other types of weapons. In the United States, for instance, it was estimated that the medical treatment for a gunshot injury is on average 12 times more costly than treating cuts or stab wounds (Miller and Cohen, 1996). Other quantifiable costs incurred by gun violence include lost productivity due to premature death or disability arising as a result of firearm injuries. These tangible or 'victimization' costs can be given a monetary value using the 'cost of illness' approach, an accounting framework that adds up the medical costs of treating injuries and lost earnings from injury or death (Small Arms Survey, 2003; Cook and Ludwig, 2000).

Box 6.6   Non-measurable? The intangible impacts of gun violence

Fatal and non-fatal injuries are the most frequently cited evidence of armed violence. But other costs are hidden, difficult to quantify, and thus often go unrecorded. In order to begin understanding these intangible impacts, the Small Arms Survey supported a participatory research project in 12 countries from 2001-04. Participatory Rural Appraisal (PRA) focuses on the 'subjective' consequences of armed violence by those most affected, and on their own understandings of how to improve their personal safety and well-being (Banerjee and Muggah, 2002).

As is well documented, small arms are used in a wide range of crimes, such as rape, robbery, or kidnapping. The mere display of a weapon often suffices to give its bearer the power to intimidate and coerce. PRA studies conducted in various settings provide valuable insights into the effects of armed violence based on gender and age. For example, research carried out with internally displaced persons in Aceh, Indonesia, shows that while women are primarily worried about risks of rape and sexual harassment, men voiced concern about abduction at gun-point and forced disappearance (Muggah and Moser-Puangsuwan, 2003). In Kosovo, men highlighted 'political uncertainty' as the main factor contributing to their personal insecurity, while women indicated a greater concern about poor infrastructure and the risks of crime and violence (Khakee and Florquin, 2003).

Participatory research suggests that women are often the direct victims of violence; in crime-ridden areas of Jamaica, for instance, their main fears are being tagged as informers by gangs (amounting to a death sentence in some cases), being raped, and being robbed (Moser and Holland, 1997). Youth is another category at risk. Participatory studies have shown how growing up surrounded by armed violence can lead to a 'culture of violence', in which notions of status and identity are linked to the possession of a gun. This tendency is aggravated by the lack of alternatives: 'area stigma' lowers the chances of finding a job, and community associations such as clubs and sports facilities often cease to function.[20]

Depending on the culture in which it is manifested, armed violence can also have more hidden but equally devastating effects: Bangladeshi women who are raped or kidnapped for prostitution can never come back to their community, since they would be rejected and their family would lose face (Banerjee and Muggah, 2002). Fear of retaliation by gangs is the reason most rapes go unreported in some urban areas of Jamaica (Moser and Holland, 1997). Disappearances in Aceh provoke all the more anxiety as it is believed the dead have to be buried quickly for their spirits to avoid suffering (Muggah and Moser-Puangsuwan, 2003).

Source: Pézard (2003)

Often underestimated, however, are the intangible costs of gun violence, including declines in physical and mental health amongst victims and witnesses of gun violence (Greenspan and Kellermann, 2002; Brent *et al.*, 1993a). Although challenging to quantify (see Box 6.6), these costs must be taken into account to reveal the true extent of the impacts inflicted by armed violence on societies. A promising attempt was made in the United States with the 'willingness to pay' approach, which relies on contingent-valuation survey methods: respondents are asked how much they would be willing to pay in additional taxes for a programme resulting in a 30 per cent reduction in gun injuries. It was ultimately estimated that the total cost of gun violence amounted to USD 80 billion annually, which represents a USD 50 billion increase over estimates that only take quantifiable impacts into account (Cook and Ludwig, 2000). While this method has the potential to produce revealing international comparisons, it remains to be tested in other contexts.

Comparable research on the relative costs of gun violence and overall violence is urgently needed to advance the debate. If firearm violence imposes greater costs than other types of violence, then reducing the proportion of total violence committed with small arms would trigger net benefits. Regardless of overall levels of crime and violence, reducing the percentage of violent acts committed with firearms would diminish the burden of violence by removing the additional intangibles or side effects incurred by gun violence. As a result, policies and interventions that succeed in reducing this ratio can be seen as especially effective and worthwhile even though overall violence levels, which appear to be contingent upon a range of risk factors, may remain steady or even increase. One consequence is that gun control laws seem much more effective in reducing levels of gun violence than overall levels of violence. In Canada, the ratio of crimes committed with firearms has gone down steadily since the introduction in 1977 of a firearm certificate programme (Waller, 2003, citing Canadian Centre for Justice Statistics, 2003a, 2003b). By 2002, the proportion of homicides committed with guns had dropped to 26 per cent, and stabbing became the most prevalent means of committing homicide, representing 31 per cent of recorded cases (Hung, 2003). Similar patterns can be observed following the introduction of gun control legislation in Australia (see Box 6.4) and the United Kingdom (see Box 6.5).

EXPERIENCES AND RESPONSES TO SMALL ARMS-RELATED CRIME IN AFRICAN COMMUNITIES AND OTHER LOCAL SETTINGS

Homicide and suicide rates are useful indicators for assessing the use of small arms in violence and crime, but it is important to recognize that they reflect only a fraction of what occurs at the local level. Various connections emerge between small arms and crime in selected urban and rural communities in six African countries under review: Cameroon, Ghana, Kenya, Nigeria, Senegal, and Zambia.[21] Findings from studies undertaken in Peshawar and Kosovo are also presented to illustrate the global nature of some of the trends identified in Africa.

Regional overview: Small arms and crime in the sub-Saharan continent

According to available data, Africa appears to be significantly affected by firearm violence, carrying approximately 18 per cent of the global burden of firearm homicides and suicides (see Figure 6.2). This is also reflected in the relatively high level of use of firearms in violent crime, with small arms used in 35 per cent of homicides (Figure 6.4), 13 per cent of robberies, 5 per cent of assaults and threats, and 2 per cent of sexual offences (Table 6.1). Within the region, South Africa seems to be the country most affected by gun violence, with an annual rate of 30 firearm homicides per 100,000, placing it second in the world only to Colombia (Small Arms Survey, 2004). South Africa also seems to lead the region in the proportion of violent crimes committed with firearms (Table 6.3), although this data is only available for a limited number of countries.

These regional statistics, however limited, confirm that firearm use in violent crime is an important issue on the continent. With an estimated 30 million small arms (a mere 5 per cent of the global stockpile), about 80 per cent of which are in civilian hands (Small Arms Survey, 2003, pp. 80–1), however, Africa is not as awash with small arms as commonly believed. On the other hand, Table 6.3 suggests that some subregions, countries, and communities are clearly more affected than others.

Table 6.3 Percentage of violent crimes committed with firearms in selected African countries

Country*	Homicides (%)	Robberies (%)	Assaults and threats (%)	Sexual offences (%)
Botswana	N/A	7.3	0	0.8
Guinea	8.0	N/A	N/A	N/A
Burkina Faso	9.5	N/A	N/A	N/A
Lesotho	55.7	4.8	12.4	3.2
Mozambique	N/A	4.4	7.31	4.6
Namibia	N/A	7.3	5.1	2.5
Nigeria	N/A	27.3	9.4	N/A
South Africa	48.0	58.5	28.3	14
Swaziland	N/A	7.2	6.9	2.2
Tanzania	7.5	N/A	N/A	N/A
Uganda	N/A	9.9	5.9	3.0
Zambia	50.0	5.9	2.5	0
Zimbabwe	65.5	6.1	2.0	2.3

Note: * Use of firearms in homicide figures is at the national level and calculated from Small Arms Survey (2004). Use of firearms in other types of violent crime is drawn from 1,000–1,500-respondent ICVS surveys administered in the capital cities of the respective countries (van Kesteren, 2003).

The vast bulk of the academic literature on crime in Africa tends to focus on the role of the state (Mthembu-Salter, 2003). A pioneer in this field is the French author Jean-François Bayart, who wrote the seminal *The State in Africa: The Politics of the Belly*, in 1993. A later text co-written by Bayart, *The Criminalisation of the State in Africa* (1999), is also an important reference, as is Patrick Chabal's book, *Africa Works: Disorder as Political Instrument* (1999). The literature available on the role of small arms in crime in Africa is limited to a number of countries, such as South Africa, Tanzania, and Kenya (Chetty, 2000; Jefferson and Urquhart, 2002; Muchai and Jefferson, 2002). One emerging research theme in the region has been the phenomenon of the illicit production of small arms (Small Arms Survey, 2003, pp. 29–31; Aning, 2003b).

This section of the chapter represents a modest attempt to improve our understanding of the role of small arms in crime in a region with limited data collection systems. In order to address issues of lack of availability and poor reliability of official statistics in the region, the Small Arms Survey uses a similar methodological framework in all six case-study countries, drawing on a combination of qualitative and quantitative data collection approaches.[22]

Local experiences of armed criminality in selected African urban and rural contexts

The types of crime involving small arms are numerous and vary between urban and rural areas. In urban contexts, small arms tend to be used primarily in violent crimes (homicides, armed robberies, assaults). Small arms are also used in politically motivated killings in Douala (Atanga, 2003) and Nairobi (Sabala and Mkutu, 2003), as well as in ethnic and religious clashes in Nigeria.[23] In Dakar, most recorded cases involve the illicit possession or use of firearms.[24] In rural areas, small arms-related crime appears to be more varied and linked to the local context. In the Northern Region of Cameroon, small arms are typically used in highway banditry (Atanga, 2003). Gun crime in Kitale is usually linked to land disputes and livestock rustling (Sabala and Mkutu, 2003), while armed poachers threaten wildlife in Zambia's Kafue National Park (Mthembu-Salter, 2003).

Given the variety of crimes concerned, criminals are found to use a number of different weapons. While in other contexts, such as in the United States, crime weapons are primarily handguns, military assault rifles are often found in the hands of African criminals. Poachers in Zambia's Kafue National Park, for instance, use AK-47 assault rifles allegedly brought into the country by Angolan refugees (Mthembu-Salter, 2003). In Cameroon's Northern Region, more than half the highway bandits are former combatants primarily from the Central African Republic, Chad, and Nigeria. Based on the weapons seized by the police, these bandits use assault rifles allegedly smuggled in from the above-mentioned neighbouring countries (Atanga, 2003). Illicitly manufactured firearms are also being used for criminal purposes. This situation is pronounced in Ghana, where about 30 per cent of firearm-related crimes are perpetrated with home-made weapons (Aning, 2003a). This proportion was even higher in Dakar, where more than half the crime guns seized by the police were identified as craft small arms. It must be noted, however, that firearms were secondary as weapons of crime in Dakar, far behind bladed weapons (Agboton-Johnson, 2003).

> African criminals rely on a wide variety of weapons, including military assault rifles and illicitly manufactured guns.

The demographic profiles established in all case studies usually confirm the common belief that the primary offenders are young males. In Ghana, however, it was noted that women often play a supportive role in criminal activity, helping with the general planning of operations, spying or approaching particular targets, caring for sick or wounded accomplices, or acting as intermediaries between wanted criminals and traditional healers (Aning, 2003a).[25] Another gendered finding was that close to 80 per cent of the gun criminals surveyed in Kitale, Kenya, were married.[26] In most cases, perpetrators tended to be nationals of the countries studied. In Cameroon's Northern Region and in Kaolack, Senegal, however, former combatants from troubled neighbouring countries were also involved (Agboton-Johnson, 2003; Atanga, 2003). As will be discussed further, law-enforcement officials and even politicians are also involved in various aspects of armed crime.

Contributing factors to armed crime? Conflict weapons and lack of governance

Proximity to zones of armed conflict as well as issues of governance and institutional capacity seem to affect the prevalence of armed crime.[27]

Proximity to unstable areas appears to facilitate armed crime, as weapons that were originally used in conflict (hereafter 'conflict weapons') are often found in the hands of criminals. A revealing case is that of Senegal. In the capital city Dakar, only about 4.5 per cent of weapon injuries treated in the emergency room at Le Dantec hospital were caused by firearms. In the Kaolack suburban area, however, 20 per cent of the injuries caused by a weapon were inflicted by firearms.[28] Kaolack's proximity to zones of armed conflict such as Casamance and Guinea Bissau might help explain these higher rates of firearm injuries. The situation is similar in the Northern Region of Cameroon, which borders

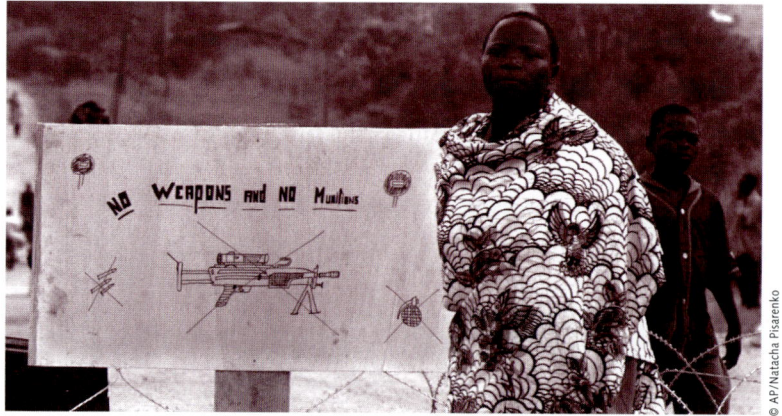

A Congolese woman walks past a 'no weapons' sign at the edge of the north-eastern town of Bunia in June 2003. Enforced by international troops, the gun ban is to help curb crime involving weapons formerly used in conflict.

VIOLENCE AND CRIME

troubled states such as Chad and the Central African Republic. Highway banditry in the region is often perpetrated by former combatants from neighbouring countries, most often involving the use of military assault rifles such as AK-47s and FN FALs (Atanga, 2003).

Box 6.8 Small arms and crime in Peshawar District, Pakistan

The number of criminal cases increased by 23 per cent from 1998 to 2001 in Pakistan's North-West Frontier Province (NWFP), home to some 15 million people and located on the border with Afghanistan (Aziz Khan, 2003). Statistics obtained from the Police Department of Peshawar suggest that the Peshawar District, one of the NWFP's 22 districts, experiences high levels of violent crime: homicide rates range from 8 per 100,000 in urban areas to 12 per 100,000 in rural areas.[29] The police believe that around 90 per cent of these homicides are committed with small arms. Small arms are also used in robberies, sectarian violence, terrorist acts, and other personal and tribal disputes.

An arms dealer demonstrates a handgun in a gun shop in Darra Adam Khel, Pakistan.

Illicitly manufactured small arms are cheap and widely available in the district, with an estimated 200 illicit workshops and 1,900 illegal arms shops located in the Bara, Darra Adam Khel, and Jamrud black markets.[30] Between USD 10 and USD 70 can buy anything from revolvers to shotguns, USD 6 is enough for a grenade or a landmine, while rocket launchers and heavy machine guns cost, respectively, USD 500 and USD 1,000. AK-47s are also easily accessible and are reportedly smuggled in from Afghanistan or manufactured locally in Darra Adam Khel. The types of weapons seized by the police confirm the availability of all these types of weapons (see Figure 6.9).

Figure 6.9: Small arms seized by the Peshawar District Police, by category

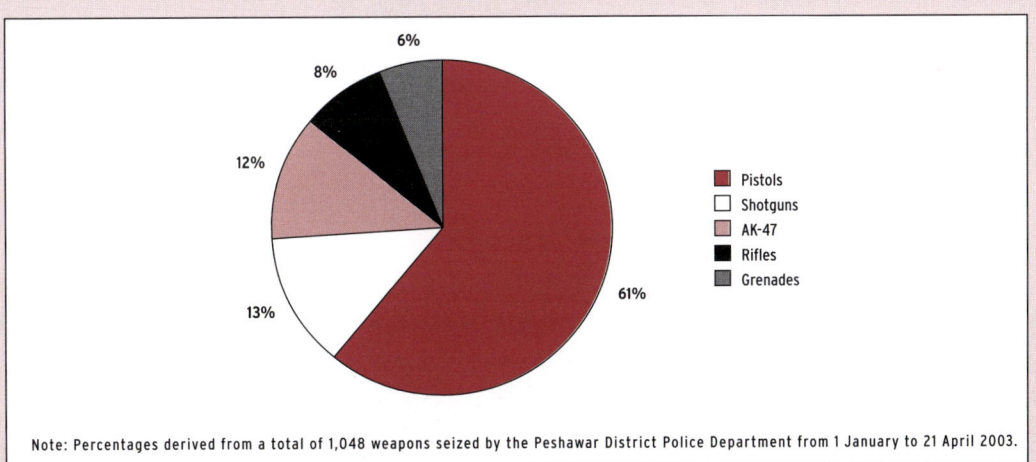

- Pistols: 61%
- Shotguns: 13%
- AK-47: 12%
- Rifles: 8%
- Grenades: 6%

Note: Percentages derived from a total of 1,048 weapons seized by the Peshawar District Police Department from 1 January to 21 April 2003.

Rising crime rates and small arms availability are overwhelming the police force, which can only count on one police officer per 28,000 people. Residents and businesses in Peshawar are responding by relying increasingly on private security means: out of the 35 private security companies registered with the local government, 28 were created between 1997 and 2002, in the heat of the crime wave. This privatization is partly formal, with banks and upper-class residents resorting to the services of private security guards armed with pistols or shotguns. On the other hand, residents with more limited means appear to turn to gun ownership for protection.

Source: SPADO (2003)

The use of conflict weapons in criminal activities highlights the importance of effective disarmament, demobilization and reintegration of ex-combatants.

Conflict weapons tend to be used as criminal implements, particularly where there is no adequate disarmament, demobilization, and reintegration (DDR) programme at the end of the conflict. In Borno state, north-east Nigeria, both the weapons and the criminals often come from across the border in Chad, an arena of internecine conflict. Chadian fighters come across the border to sell their weapons when they need money for food and other essentials (Ebo, 2003). This same practice is common in the Mano river states of Liberia, Sierra Leone, and Guinea (Obasi, 2002). The problems caused by conflict weapons, both in post-conflict settings and in neighbouring countries and areas, highlight the importance of undertaking effective DDR programmes. The use of conflict weapons in crime, however, appears to be a global phenomenon (see Boxes 6.7 and 6.8) and should not be interpreted as being limited to Africa.

The second factor is related to the issue of governance, which is characterized by the lack of capacity and, in several instances, the lack of accountability of the police forces.[31] These shortcomings can be measured through impunity or conviction rates. In Senegal, 40 per cent and 38 per cent of criminal cases are not prosecuted in Kaolack and Dakar.[32] In 2002 in the Southern Province of Zambia, a comparison of police and court statistics shows that only 25 per cent of recorded murders were actually prosecuted by the High Court (Mthembu-Salter, 2003). In Kaduna, Nigeria, the proportion of firearm-related cases that were ultimately prosecuted for the period 1997–2001 was even lower, at a mere 18 per cent.[33]

These limitations of the public security sector often result in inadequate police services, but also in the lack of professionalism on the part of public security agents, sometimes reflected by their personal involvement in crime. In Douala, Cameroon, a security report issued in 2000 listed 84 members of the police, gendarmerie, and army involved in cases of armed banditry that were subsequently prosecuted (Atanga, 2003). Some policemen in Ghana collaborate with robbers by lending them their weapons and clothing, enabling what are often referred to as 'pobbers' (police-robbers) (Aning, 2003a). Several Nigerian army soldiers and police officers have been sentenced to death for armed robbery (Ebo, 2003), but more shocking is the role of politicians in arms proliferation and armed crime. In Nigeria's Cross River state, of the 54 illegal guns seized by the police in the first half of 2002, 16 were recovered from politicians, and another 8 from politically motivated murders (Chigbo, 2002).

Armed criminality and the privatization of security

Given the above-mentioned shortcomings of the public security sector, the fact that security is being privatized comes as no surprise in areas where armed criminality is prevalent. As the services of private security guards are relatively expensive and therefore used mainly by businesses and wealthy social classes, the low-income classes have turned to so-called vigilante groups[34] or informal community-based organizations providing security services.

The increasing role of private security companies (PSCs) was noted in all urban areas studied. In Zambia, for instance, it was estimated that the criminal justice system's budget (including the police, the judiciary, prisons, and so forth) was roughly equivalent to 1 per cent of the GDP, which represents only half of what is spent annually for the services of private security guards (Mthembu-Salter, 2003). The private security sector appears to be booming in areas where small arms crime is more prevalent. In Kaduna city, Nigeria, the number of clients of a sample of five PSCs[35] tripled from 1997 to 2001, while the number of guards hired has multiplied by five (Ebo, 2003). Ghana has also experienced a boom in the sector, with more than 110 such companies now in operation in the country (Aning, 2003a). While no such firms existed in Cameroon in 1980, more than 180 could be counted in 2002, employing about 15,000 staff (Atanga, 2003).

VIOLENCE AND CRIME

Box 6.8 Conflict weapons and crime in Kosovo

Between 330,000 and 460,000 of the guns left over by several years of armed conflict in Kosovo are estimated to have found their way into civilian hands. Many arms are kept by civilians for self-defence, while others are being used for criminal purposes. With a murder rate of 4.45 per 100,000 for 2001, however, violent crime is not more prevalent in Kosovo than in other Central and Eastern European countries. Reported crime levels even seem to be decreasing in the aftermath of the conflict, although this could be due in large part to the presence of international police and to a tendency to under-report criminal offences.

More worrying, however, is the extent to which firearms are used. Almost three out of four murders and close to a third of robberies are committed with a small arm. When compared to Estonia and Hungary's much lower ratios (13 and 15 per cent in Estonia, 11 and 8 per cent in Hungary), this suggests that remaining conflict weapons in Kosovo created more opportunities for the use of guns in crime than in contexts where the transition from communism occurred in a more peaceful manner (Khakee and Florquin, 2003, pp. 36-7).

Figure 6.10   Small arms and light weapons seized by the Kosovo Police Service, 2000-02

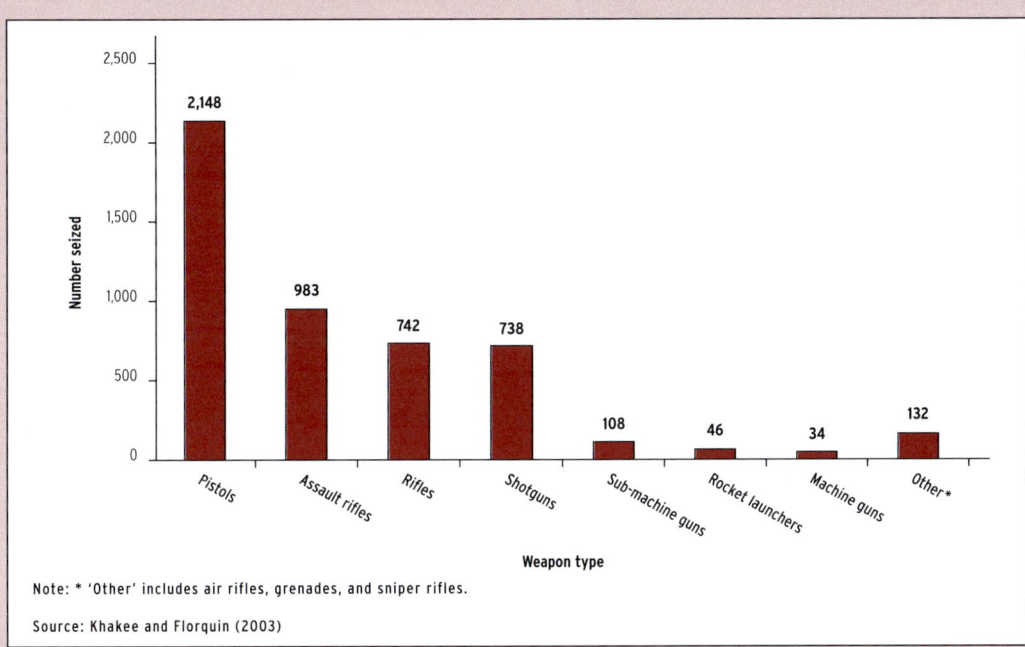

Note: * 'Other' includes air rifles, grenades, and sniper rifles.

Source: Khakee and Florquin (2003)

Many of the small arms found in the hands of criminals are military weapons. Pistols and AK-47 assault rifles are the most commonly used small arms in homicides and robberies. Pistols and automatic weapons were also cited during participatory focus group discussions among the three most dangerous weapons (together with knives), and are also the weapon types most commonly seized by the police (see Figure 6.10). The assault rifles that are confiscated are primarily AK-47 Kalashnikovs, with a few Zastavas. The use of combat assault rifles in crime indicates clearly that many of the weapons that were once used in conflict (the Kosovo Liberation Army's AK-47s, and the Yugoslav Zastavas) have now become prominent tools in criminal activity.

Source: Khakee and Florquin (2003)

SMALL ARMS SURVEY 2004

Private security takes on a ghastly dimension: Residents of a working-class suburb of Lagos, Nigeria, look on as the body of an alleged armed robber burns in the street in May 1999. By catching and killing alleged criminals themselves, vigilante groups such as this one are taking law and order into their own hands.

Another manifestation of the privatization of security in Africa as a response to armed criminality has been the emergence of informal vigilante groups in low-income and rural areas. This phenomenon reflects the inability of state agents to cope with armed criminality, but it is also due to the fact that formal PSCs are too costly for the average citizen. Vigilante groups consist of volunteers organized at the community level to patrol communities. They are usually paid small monthly fees by each household. In Kaduna city, Nigeria, for instance, vigilante services cost about USD 4 per month per household. Residents of rural Zonkwa have to pay less than USD 0.15 a month, although wealthier community members and local authorities also contribute larger sums (Ebo, 2003).

The last aspect of the privatization of security concerns the increasing reliance on small arms ownership for self-defence. In Nigeria, for instance, when asked about their perception of the private ownership of guns in small-scale (n=100) community surveys, most respondents saw it as 'good' both in urban Kaduna (62 per cent vs. 38 per cent 'bad') and in rural Zonkwa (45 per cent vs. 32 per cent who answered 'bad' and 21 per cent who said they did not know) (Ebo, 2003). Private guns can be legal but also illicit given the booming illicit manufacturing sector, a phenomenon that appeared in all case studies. Home-made pistols and rifles cost USD 60 and USD 80, respectively in Kaduna in 2001, although prices have been continually climbing, reflecting an increase in demand (Ebo, 2003). Illicit guns can also be smuggled in from neighbouring countries. In Senegal, a handgun costs only around USD 40 along the border with Gambia, but up to USD 100 by the time it is smuggled into urban black markets (Agboton-Johnson, 2003).

CONCLUSION

Used in almost 40 percent of all homicides, but also in assaults, threats, robberies, sexual offences, and suicides, firearms are clearly a common tool for perpetrating societal violence. Whether gun accessibility affects overall levels of violence is, however, more difficult to assess. The lethality of guns increases the risk of injury and death and raises perceptions of threat, but firearm ownership by law-abiding citizens can also contribute to deterring crime. The balance between these two effects is the subject of ongoing debate.

The impacts of gun violence, however, are not limited to fatal and non-fatal firearm injuries. A wide variety of small arm-related crimes—committed either by individuals or by the state—can threaten a community's physical, economic, social, political, and cultural security. While quantifying these impacts can be challenging, recent research suggests that the societal costs of gun violence are substantially higher than those associated with other means. Further work in this area is critical, as it provides a rationale for reducing violence committed with small arms, a goal that gun control measures seem able to achieve.

Gun violence can challenge a state's monopoly on the maintenance of law and order. Particularly in contexts where the state appears unable to provide an effective response to armed violence, the privatization of security is emerging as a common response to firearm-related crime. While big businesses and the wealthy can afford the services of registered companies and guards, many others must rely on informal vigilante groups or on private gun ownership to gain a greater sense of security. Unless effective responses to gun violence are put in place, the range of actors taking arms for self-defence can only increase.

APPENDIX 6.1: ESTIMATED ANNUAL FIREARM HOMICIDE AND SUICIDE BY REGION*

Region	Number		Per 100,000		% firearm use in violent act
	Lower threshold	Upper threshold	Lower threshold	Upper threshold	
Africa firearm homicide	26,385	40,600	3.83	5.90	35
Africa firearm suicide	2,227	4,050	0.33	0.59	15
Africa Total	**28,612**	**44,650**	**4.16**	**6.49**	**31**
LA and Caribbean firearm homicide	69,460	84,000	12.80	15.47	60
LA and Caribbean firearm suicide	4,270	6,090	0.79	1.12	21
Latin America and Caribbean total	**73,700**	**90,090**	**13.59**	**16.59**	**53**
North America firearm homicide	10,300	11,400	3.17	3.50	60
North America firearm suicide	17,400	18,000	5.34	5.52	50
North America total	**27,700**	**29,400**	**8.51**	**9.02**	**53**

SMALL ARMS SURVEY 2004

Region	Number		Per 100,000		% firearm use in violent act
	Lower threshold	Upper threshold	Lower threshold	Upper threshold	
Middle East firearm homicide	2,690	9,300	0.52	1.8	30
Middle East firearm suicide	120	300	0.02	0.06	1
Middle East total	**2,800**	**9,600**	**0.54**	**1.26**	**17**
CE Europe firearm homicide	7,800	14,800	1.63	3.09	20
CE Europe firearm suicide	3,370	6,750	0.70	1.41	5
CE Europe total	**11,170**	**21,550**	**2.33**	**4.50**	**10**
Western Europe firearm homicide	1,280	1,390	0.32	0.35	32
Western Europe firearm suicide	6,080	6,630	1.52	1.66	13
Western Europe total	**7,360**	**8,020**	**1.84**	**2.01**	**15**
South-East Asia firearm homicide	16,778	27,300	1.04	1.45	30
South-East Asia firearm suicide	964	2,520	0.06	0.10	1
South-East Asia total	**17,742**	**29,820**	**1.1**	**1.55**	**12**
Asia Pacific firearm homicide	8,930	9,940	0.51	0.54	16
Asia Pacific firearm suicide	2,310	6,880	0.13	0.39	2
Asia Pacific total	**11,240**	**16,820**	**0.64**	**0.93**	**4**
World firearm homicide	143,623	198,730	2.27	3.14	38
World firearm suicide	36,741	51,220	0.58	0.81	6
World total	**180,364**	**249,950**	**2.85**	**3.96**	**19**

*Note: Regions are based on the regional divisions used in WHO (2002, pp. 262–9). Following are the lists of countries included in each region:

Africa (includes countries categorized by the WHO as 'African region'): Algeria, Angola, Benin, Botswana, Burkina Faso, Burundi, Cameroon, Cape Verde, Central African Republic, Chad, Comoros, Côte d'Ivoire, Democratic Republic of Congo, Equatorial Guinea, Eritrea, Ethiopia, Gabon, Gambia, Ghana, Guinea, Guinea-Bissau, Kenya, Lesotho, Liberia, Madagascar, Malawi, Mali, Mauritania, Mauritius, Mozambique, Namibia, Niger, Nigeria, Republic of Congo, Reunion, Rwanda, São Tomé and Principe, Senegal, Seychelles, Sierra Leone, South Africa, St. Helena, Swaziland, Tanzania, Togo, Uganda, Zambia, Zimbabwe.

Latin America and the Caribbean (includes countries categorized by the WHO as 'region of the Americas, low and middle income'): Anguilla, Antigua and Barbuda, Argentina, Aruba, Barbados, Belize, Bermuda, Bolivia, Brazil, Cayman Islands, Chile, Colombia, Costa Rica, Cuba, Dominica, Dominican Republic, Ecuador, El Salvador, French Guiana, Grenada, Guadeloupe, Guatemala, Guyana, Haiti, Honduras, Jamaica, Martinique, Mexico, Montserrat, Netherlands Antilles, Nicaragua, Panama, Paraguay, Peru, Puerto Rico, St. Kitts and Nevis, St. Lucia, St. Vincent and the Grenadines, Suriname, Trinidad and Tobago, Turks and Caicos Islands, Uruguay, Venezuela.

North America (includes countries categorized by the WHO as 'region of the Americas, high income'): Bahamas, Canada, St. Pierre and Miquelon, United States, Virgin Islands.

Middle East (includes countries categorized by the WHO as 'Eastern Mediterranean region'): Afghanistan, Bahrain, Cyprus, Djibouti, Egypt, Iran, Iraq, Jordan, Kuwait, Lebanon, Libya, Morocco, Oman, Pakistan, Qatar, Saudi Arabia, Somalia, Sudan, Syria, Tunisia, United Arab Emirates, Yemen.

Central and Eastern Europe (includes countries categorized by the WHO as 'European region, low and middle income'): Albania, Armenia, Azerbaijan, Belarus, Bosnia and Herzegovina, Bulgaria, Croatia, Czech Republic, Estonia, Former Yugoslav Republic of Macedonia, Georgia, Hungary, Kazakhstan, Kyrgyzstan, Latvia, Lithuania, Malta, Moldova, Poland, Romania, Russian Federation, Serbia and Montenegro, Slovakia, Slovenia, Tajikistan, Turkey, Turkmenistan, Ukraine, Uzbekistan.

Western Europe (includes countries categorized by the WHO as 'European region, high income'): Andorra, Austria, Belgium, Channel Islands, Denmark, England and Wales, Faeroe Islands, Finland, France, Germany, Gibraltar, Greece, Greenland, Holy See, Iceland, Ireland, Isle of Man, Israel, Italy, Liechtenstein, Luxemburg, Monaco, the Netherlands, Northern Ireland, Norway, Portugal, San Marino, Scotland, Spain, Sweden, Switzerland.

South-East Asia (includes countries categorized by the WHO as 'South East Asia region'): Bangladesh, Bhutan, Democratic People's Republic of Korea, India, Indonesia, Maldives, Myanmar, Nepal, Sri Lanka, Thailand.

Asia Pacific (includes countries categorized by the WHO as 'Western Pacific region'): Australia, Brunei Darussalam, Hong Kong, Japan, New Zealand, Republic of Korea, Singapore, Taiwan, Cambodia, China, Cook Islands, Federated States of Micronesia, Fiji, French Polynesia, Guam, Kiribati, Lao PDR, Macao, Malaysia, Marshall Islands, Mongolia, Nauru, New Caledonia, Niue, Northern Mariana Islands, Palau, Papua New Guinea, Philippines, Samoa, Solomon Islands, Tokelau Island, Tonga, Tuvalu, Vanuatu, Vietnam.

APPENDIX 6.2: METHODOLOGY FOR ESTIMATING GLOBAL FIREARM SUICIDES AND HOMICIDES

The estimate of firearm homicide and suicide presented in this chapter (see Appendix 6.1) is based on several existing data sets that have been combined on a regional basis (see Appendix 6.1 for a description of the regional divisions used). Official statistics on firearm suicides and homicides were used to establish a lower threshold of regional firearm homicides and suicides. Adjusted data that takes into account epidemiological surveys and cause of death statistical models combined with official statistics provided the basis for upper thresholds. Estimates were calculated separately for each region using a regional firearm suicide and homicide rate.

The estimate presented in this chapter relies on the regional division adopted by the World Health Organization (WHO, 2002) to estimate global homicides and suicides. A regional approach is an improvement over previous estimates based on a global approach. Moreover, WHO (2002) estimates of overall violent deaths provide a useful comparative basis for estimating firearm mortality. As explained below, the WHO estimates are central in generating the upper-threshold firearm death estimate, which makes a similar regional approach necessary.

Establishing lower thresholds

Data sets on international public health and criminal justice that monitor firearm mortality include the WHO (2002, 2003), the UN (1998, 1999), the UNODC (2003), SAFER-NET and HELP Network (2001), and a number of government and research reports (see Appendix 6.3). Rates of firearm suicide and homicide per 100,000 were compared and the most recent figure was entered into a database. In cases where considerable discrepancies between public health and criminal justice data were found, further sources, when available, were sought to help make a judgement. Based on the countries for which firearm mortality data was available, regional firearm homicide and suicide rates per 100,000 were calculated from UN Population Division (2002). This rate was then applied to the population of those countries for which no documented firearm data existed and is quoted as the lower threshold. Countries experiencing firearm mortality rates significantly higher (or lower) than the regional average were discarded as outliers so that they would not influence regional rates.

Adjusting for under-reporting and under-recording to establish the upper threshold

The official statistics used to establish the lower threshold are very likely to produce an underestimate due to under-reporting by the population and under-recording by authorities in official statistics (Fajnzylber, Lederman, and Loayza 2000; MacDonald, 2002). Individual and socio-economic factors comprising age, gender, ethnicity, community victimization rates, perceptions of the police, and employment status (MacDonald, 2000) influence under-reporting. Under-recording is often a factor of development levels and institutional capacity (Fajnzylber, Lederman, and Loayza 2000).

The estimate presented here used available public health and criminal justice data on both overall and firearm homicides and suicides to establish regional patterns of firearm use in violent deaths (computed as the percentage of homicides and suicides committed with firearms). These ratios were then applied to WHO regional estimates for overall homicide and suicide to establish the upper threshold. The WHO estimates were used as they adjust homicide and suicide rates for under-reporting and under-recording by taking into account epidemiological surveys and cause of death statistical models (WHO, 2002, p. 258).

SMALL ARMS SURVEY 2004

Unintentional firearm deaths and firearm deaths of undetermined intent

Global unintentional firearm deaths and firearm deaths of undetermined intent were not estimated as the data is too limited and inconsistent from year to year. The 18,000 such deaths documented annually are, however, added to the final global estimate, which implies that global annual non-conflict-related firearm deaths may even be higher than the 200,000–270,000 range suggested in this chapter.

APPENDIX 6.3: SOURCES AND AVAILABILITY OF FIREARM MORTALITY DATA

Data sources

The national firearm mortality data used for estimating non-conflict-related firearm mortality in this chapter are posted on the Small Arms Survey Web site (see Small Arms Survey, 2004). Table 6.4 shows the main data sources. The large majority of statistics were taken from WHO/public health data sets (WHO, 2002, 2003), although these were cross-checked for reliability with criminal justice sources when available. Criminal justice data—that is, data recorded by the police—was drawn from the UN (1998, 1999), UNODC (2003), SAFER-NET and HELP NETWORK (2001); a number of reports from research institutes citing recent national statistics were also used.

Table 6.4   Data sources

Data source	Homicide	Suicide	Unintentional	Undetermined
WHO (2002, 2003)	47	61	64	63
UN (1998, 1999)	10	10	13	1
UNODC (2003)	26	N/A	N/A	N/A
SAFER-NET and HELP NETWORK (2001)	3	2	3	1
Other	19	3	2	1

Note: Figures represent the number of countries for which data from the indicated source was used.

Most of the data used in this estimate, therefore, originates from WHO statistics, which provide the most reliable measure of committed homicides. In effect, subtractions and triangulation are required with criminal justice sources (UN, 1999; UNODC, 2003) as attempted homicides are sometimes, but not systematically, included. While there are some limitations when comparing WHO and UN sources at the national level, research has shown that UN and WHO homicide rates are significantly correlated when data is aggregated to produce global estimates (UNODCCP, 1999, Box 0.7, p. 12). In other words, mortality statistics are suitable for making global and regional comparisons, but must be treated with caution in cross-national analyses as they emanate from different sources and years.

Data availability by manner of death

Drawing from the main international public health and criminal justice data sets and a series of national reports and sources, the Small Arms Survey is able to document 160,000 annual firearm deaths in some 110 countries. Table 6.5 shows the extent of available data for the main four categories of non-conflict-related firearm deaths.

Table 6.5 Availability of firearm death statistics by manner of death

Manner of firearm death	Homicide	Suicide	Unintentional	Undetermined	All manners*
Number of documented annual deaths	110,370	31,065	6,903	11,308	159,646
Documented annual deaths per 100,000	3.32	1.01	0.22	0.65	4.66
Number of countries documented	105	76	82	66	110
Population covered	3,320,957,782	3,071,805,782	3,155,425,782	1,727,061,782	3,430,697,782

Note: *A few countries have data only for total firearm deaths, which explains why the 'all manners' number is slightly larger than the sum of 'homicide,' 'suicide,' 'unintentional', and 'undetermined' figures.

Data availability by region

While the temptation is great to apply the documented ratio of 4.66 per 100,000 firearm deaths to the global population of 6.3 billion people (which would give a rate of some 295,000 firearm deaths annually), this would seriously overlook important disparities between countries. For example, only four countries (Brazil, Colombia, South Africa, and the United States) carry more than 60 per cent of the (documented) burden with approximately 98,000 annual firearm deaths and a combined rate of 17.5 firearm deaths per 100,000.

Moreover, the availability of data differs greatly by region: while data is available for the majority of the large North American and Western European countries (see Small Arms Survey, 2004), the available data covers only 18 per cent and 19 per cent of the populations of the Middle East and Africa, respectively. These regional differences in data availability (and reliability) are reflected in the variation between the upper threshold and lower threshold at the regional level as presented in Appendix 6.1: the relative difference[36] between the lower and upper thresholds is much higher in Central and Eastern Europe (93 per cent) and the Middle East (133 per cent) than for North America (6 per cent) and Western Europe (9 per cent). This is because, in regions where little data was available, more arbitrary judgements were made to establish regional rates and ratios, thereby increasing the error margin.

Data availability by year

The national firearm mortality statistics used in the estimate reflect the most recent available year. Due to data scarcity, the available data was drawn from a wide range of years (1994–2002). However, and as shown by Table 6.6, more than 86 per cent of the annual statistics used to produce the estimate related to years between 1997 and 2001. The estimate presented in this chapter can therefore be said to reflect the situation in the late 1990s.

Table 6.6 Firearms mortality data by year

Year	Homicide	Suicide	Unintentional	Undetermined	Total
2002	2	0	0	0	2
2001	7	4	4	4	19
2000	36	23	25	23	107
1999	18	22	19	17	76
1998	8	9	10	9	36
1997-2001*	11	0	0	0	11
1997	12	7	8	7	34
1996	3	1	5	1	10
1995	7	8	8	3	26
1994-96**	0	0	1	1	2
1994	1	2	2	1	6

Notes: Figures represent the number of countries for which data from the indicated year was used. For example, the estimate used firearm homicide data for the year 2000 in 36 countries.
*Data taken from Alpers and Twyford (2003) on a number of Pacific Island countries. Average annual rates were computed based on five-year figures.
**Annual average taken from WHO (2002).

6. LIST OF ABBREVIATIONS

CDC	Centers for Disease Control
DDR	Disarmament, demobilization, and reintegration
GDP	Gross Domestic Product
ICVS	International Crime Victim Surveys
NWFP	North-West Frontier Province (Pakistan)
PRA	Participatory Rural Appraisal
PSC	Private security company
RTC laws	Right-to-carry laws
UNICRI	United Nations Interregional Crime and Justice Institute
WHO	World Health Organization

6. ENDNOTES

1. See UNECOSOC (2003, Para. 30, 36-39), International Council on Human Rights Policy (2003), and Centre for Humanitarian Dialogue (2003).
2. See Kates' perspective in Box 6.3.
3. These include the *United Nations International Study on Firearms Regulation* (UN, 1999), the *United Nations Surveys on Crime Trends and the Operations of Criminal Justice Systems* (UNODC, 2003), and the World Health Organization mortality database (WHO, 2002, 2003).
4. Includes field research undertaken by the Small Arms Survey in six African countries (Ghana, Zambia, Nigeria, Senegal, Kenya, and Cameroon), the Peshawar District of Pakistan, and Kosovo.
5. See, for example, Kopel, Gallant, and Eisen (2003).
6. This data was usually drawn from UN (1998) and Krug *et al.* (1998). A more recent WHO (2001) study on 52 high- and middle-income countries concluded that more than 115,000 people died in these countries annually from firearm homicide, suicide, or accident.

7   Violent deaths in this chapter refer to deaths from homicide and suicide, following the approach used in WHO (2002). Violent deaths from conflict are not considered in this chapter but will be in future editions of the *Small Arms Survey* (see Box 6.1).
8   See appendix 6.1 for details about the regional approach used.
9   The full questionnaire can be found at <http://www.unicri.it/icvs/data/questionnaires/Face_to_Face_2000.pdf >
10 Its standardized methodology deals with the main limitations of official crime statistics, such as differences in the definition of crimes between countries, differences in official recording procedures, and the population's willingness to report crimes to authorities.
11 Selected urban areas and/or capital cities of the following countries were used to establish the regional estimates presented in this box: *Western Europe:* Austria, Belgium, Denmark, England and Wales, Finland, France, Italy, Malta, the Netherlands, Portugal, Scotland, Spain, Sweden, Switzerland; *'New world':* Australia, Canada, New Zealand, United States; *Africa:* Botswana, Egypt, Lesotho, Mozambique, Namibia, Nigeria, South Africa, Swaziland, Tanzania, Tunisia, Uganda, Zambia, Zimbabwe; *Asia:* Azerbaijan, China, India, Indonesia, Japan, Mongolia, Philippines; *Latin America:* Argentina, Bolivia, Brazil, Colombia, Costa Rica, Panama, Paraguay; *Central and Eastern Europe:* Albania, Belarus, Bulgaria, Croatia, Czech Republic, Georgia, Hungary, Kyrgyzstan, Latvia, Lithuania, Macedonia, Poland, Romania, Russia, Serbia and Montenegro, Slovakia, Slovenia, Ukraine.
12 Sub-section adapted from Mihorean (2003); Wille (2003).
13 See WHO (2002, pp. 12–13) for a description of the various categories of factors affecting levels of violence.
14 See Brent *et al.* (1988, 1991, 1993a, 1993b, 1994, 2001, 2003) and Buckstein *et al.* (1993).
15 A number of reviews, however, note that certain data limitations make it impossible to determine a plausible precise figure of the number of defensive gun uses (Hemenway, 1997). The analysis of self-protective gun use data, for example, has shown that the majority of reported self-defence gun uses are the consequence of escalating arguments and would be interpreted under the law as illegal, even though the gun users thought they were acting in self-defence (McDowall, Loftin, and Presser, 2000; Hemenway and Azrael, 2000).
16 Note that this report from Victoria is typical. Across all jurisdictions, thousands of non-prohibited firearms were surrendered in addition to those covered by the Australian Firearms Buyback.
17 See, for example, Ludwig (1998), Black and Nagin (1998), Duwe, Kovandzic, and Moody (2002), and Maltz and Targonski (2002). Kovandzic and Marvell (2003), Duggan (2001), and other recent work has demonstrated that RTC laws do not reduce crime. Manning (2003), as cited in Donohue (2003), suggests that correcting Lott and Mustard's (1997) results for autocorrelation would render all of their results statistically insignificant.
18 The Lott hypothesis has become influential not only in the United States but also at the international level. A study by Wesson (2000) sought to apply the Lott model in the South African context, and suggests that the increase in the number of licensed weapons for the years 1994–99 contributed to a reduction in violent crime and a move towards non-confrontational crimes for personal gain.
19 Subsection adapted from Wille (2003) and Anderson and Kates (2003).
20 See Muggah and Moser-Puangsuwan (2003), Banerjee and Muggah (2002), Moser and Holland (1997).
21 This section of the chapter is based on field research conducted for the Small Arms Survey by Atanga (2003), Aning (2003a), Sabala and Mkutu (2003), Ebo (2003), Agboton-Johnson (2003), and Mthembu-Salter (2003).
22 Researchers were asked to investigate two sites in each country, preferably one urban and one rural area, and to focus on three broad themes: the nature and prevalence of small arms use in crime, the impacts of small arms crime in these communities, and public and private responses to armed criminality. The methods used ranged from desk research, collection of official statistics, key informant interviews, focus groups, and small-scale community and/or purposive surveys. This combination of quantitative and qualitative methods was deemed necessary given the well-recognized limitations affecting official statistics in the region. The sites surveyed are *Cameroon:* Douala and the Northern Region; *Ghana:* Accra and Madina; *Ethiopia:* Nairobi and Kitale; *Nigeria:* Kaduna and Zonkwa; *Senegal:* Dakar and Kaolack; *Zambia:* Livingstone and Kafue National Park.
23 100,000 persons are believed to have been killed in Nigeria in more than 50 ethnic and religious crises since May 1999, with small arms being used frequently in such clashes (CLEEN/OMCT, 2002).
24 Dakar Police data quoted in Agboton-Johnson (2003).
25 Traditional healers are believed to have powers to provide protection against, among other things, bullets and police arrest. They are also perceived by many as being able to treat bullet injuries.
26 Data based on a survey (Sabala and Mkutu, 2003) of the law court files of 77 perpetrators of armed crime in Kitale (30) and Nairobi (47).
27 This finding, however, can not be generalized to the entire continent. South Africa is the best counter-example, suffering the highest armed crime rates despite relatively lower levels of corruption and stable neighbours.
28 Data obtained from Kaolack and Dakar (A. le Dantec) hospitals and quoted in Agboton-Johnson (2003).
29 Annual per 100,000 rates were calculated by multiplying by three the number of homicides recorded by the police from January to April 2003. As a result, these rates may not reflect any seasonal crime trends.
30 Other estimates suggest as many as 3,000 'father and son' operations selling, trading, and manufacturing small arms in Darra Adam Khel (Small Arms Survey, 2003, p. 32).
31 The lack of capacity of the public security sector was noted in Ghana, with the police service falling 10,000 officers short of the recommended figure of 25,000 (Tong, 2003). In Zambia, it was estimated that the criminal justice system's budget (including the police, the judiciary, prisons, and so forth) was roughly equivalent to 1 per cent of GDP, which represents only half of what is spent annually for the services of private security guards (Mthembu-Salter, 2003).
32 Dakar and Kaolack criminal justice data quoted in Agboton-Johnson (2003).
33 Kaduna State Ministry of Justice data quoted in Ebo (2003).
34 The term 'vigilante groups' in this chapter does not refer to organized groups of citizens who punish criminals after the fact, as in the United States. In the African context, they are considered as informal private security patrols organized at the community level to prevent and sometimes react to crime.
35 The five companies are Nigerguards Limited, Blackstar Security Company Limited, Profile Security Services, HNB Security and Protective Company Limited, and Havard Security Services Limited.
36 Computed as (upper threshold – lower threshold) / lower threshold x 100.

6. BIBLIOGRAPHY

ABS (Australian Bureau of Statistics). 1998–2003 (six volumes). *Causes of Death, Australia 1997–2002*. Canberra: ABS.

—. 2001. *Recorded Crime, Australia 2000*. Canberra: ABS.

—. 2003a. *Recorded Crime, Australia 2002*. Canberra: ABS.

—. 2003b. *Recorded Crime, Australia 2002—Main Findings*. Canberra: ABS.

Agboton-Johnson, Christiane. 2003. *Armes et criminalité: Le cas du Sénégal*. Background paper. Geneva: Small Arms Survey.

Alpers, Philip. 1996. 'Mass Gun Killers: Ten-Year Survey Challenges Myths.' *Mental Health Quarterly. New Zealand Mental Health Foundation*. Winter, June, pp. 22–3.

—. 2004. *Gun Crime and Injury Drop in Australia. Trend Coincides with Recent Gun Control Measures*. Background paper. Geneva: Small Arms Survey.

—. and Conor Twyford. 2003. *Small Arms in the Pacific*. Occasional Paper 8. Geneva: Small Arms Survey.

Anderson, Gary and Don Kates Jr. 2003. *Guns and the Substitution Effect: An Overview*. Background paper. Geneva: Small Arms Survey.

Anderson, Jack. 1996. *Inside the NRA. Armed and Dangerous: An Expose*. Beverly Hills, California: Penguin USA.

Aning, Kwesi. 2003a. *Small Arms and Crime in Africa: The Ghana Case*. Background paper. Geneva: Small Arms Survey.

—. 2003b. 'Local Craft Production and Legislation on Small Arms in Ghana.' *West Africa*. 7–13 July, pp. 17–18.

Arias, Elizabeth *et al.* 2003. *Deaths: Final Data for 2001*. National Vital Statistics Reports 52/3. Atlanta: Centers for Disease Control & Prevention.

Atanga, Mufor. 2003. *Small arms and Criminality in Cameroon*. Background paper. Geneva: Small Arms Survey.

Australia. CAGD (Commonwealth Attorney-General's Department). 2002. *The Australian Firearms Buyback: Tally for Number of Firearms Collected and Compensation Paid*. Canberra: CAGD.

Australian Customs Service. 2003. *Customs and Handguns—Frequently Asked Questions*. <http://www.customs.gov.au> (accessed 11 January).

Australian Institute of Criminology. 2002. *Australian Crime: Facts and Figures 2001*. Canberra: Australian Institute of Criminology.

Aziz Khan, Javed. 2003. 'Crime rate in NWFP on the rise.' *The News International* (Karachi). 19 April.

Bailey, J., A. Kellermann, G. Somes, J. Banton, F. Rivara, and N. Rushforth. 1997. 'Risk Factors for Violent Death of Women in the Home.' *Archives of Internal Medicine*. Vol. 157, No. 7. 14 April, pp. 777–82.

Banerjee, Dipankar and Robert Muggah (eds.). 2002. *Small Arms and Human Insecurity*. Colombo, Sri Lanka: Regional Centre for Security Studies. <http://www.smallarmssurvey.org/copublications/PRAinSouthAsia.pdf>

Bayart, J.-F. 1993. *The State in Africa: The Politics of the Belly*. English translation. London: Longman.

—. S. Ellis, and B. Hibou. 1999. *The Criminalisation of the State in Africa*. Oxford: James Currey.

Bell, Geoff. 2003. 'Underlying Causes of Death (ICD10): Firearm Related Deaths, 1999–2002.' Unpublished dataset. Canberra: ABS.

Black, D. and D. Nagin. 1998. 'Do Right-to-Carry Laws Deter Violent Crime?' *Journal of Legal Studies*, Vol. 27, pp. 209–19.

Blumstein, A. and J. Wallman. 2000. *The Crime Drop in America*. Cambridge: Cambridge University Press.

Brent, David *et al.* 1988. 'Risk Factors for Adolescent Suicide: A Comparison of Adolescent Suicide Victims with Suicidal Inpatients.' *Archives of General Psychiatry*, Vol. 45, pp. 581–8.

—. 1991. 'The Presence and Accessibility of Firearms in the Homes of Adolescent Suicides: A Case Control Study.' *Journal of American Medical Association*, Vol. 266, pp. 2989–95.

—. 1993a. 'Firearms and Adolescent Suicide: A Community Case-Control Study.' *American Journal of Disease of Children*, Vol. 147, pp. 1066–71.

—. 1993b. 'Suicides in Adolescents with No Apparent Psychopathology.' *Journal of the American Academy of Child and Adolescent Psychiatry*, Vol. 32, pp. 494–500.

—. 1994. 'Suicide in Affectively Ill Adolescents. A Case Control Study.' *Journal of Affective Disorders*, Vol. 31, pp. 193–202.

—. 2001. 'Firearms and Suicide.' *Annals of the New York Academy of Sciences*, Vol. 932, pp. 225–40.

—. 2003. 'Firearms and Suicide.' <http://www.angelfire.com/ga4/suicideawareness/16.html> (accessed July).

Buckstein, O. *et al.* 1993. 'Risk Factors for Completed Suicide Among Adolescents with a Lifetime History of Substance Abuse: A Case-Control Study.' *Acta Psychiatrica Scandinavia*, Vol. 88, pp. 403–8.

Campbell, J. *et al.* 2003. 'Risk Factors for Femicide in Abusive Relationships: Results from a Multisite Case Control Study.' *American Journal of Public Health*, Vol. 93, pp. 1089–97.

Canadian Centre for Justice Statistics. 2003a. 'Crime Statistics in Canada, 2002.' *Juristat 23*, No. 5. Ottawa: Statistics Canada.

—. 2003b. 'Homicide in Canada, 2002'. *Juristat 23*, No. 8. Ottawa: Statistics Canada.

Cassese, Antonio. 2003. *The Various Aspects of Self-Defence*. Background paper. Geneva: Small Arms Survey.

CDC (Centers for Disease Control). 1997. 'Rates of Homicide, Suicide and Firearm-Related Death Among Children--26 Industrialized Countries.' *Morbidity and Mortality Weekly Report*, Vol. 46. 7 February, pp. 101–5.

—. 2003a. 'First Reports Evaluating the Effectiveness of Strategies for Preventing Violence: Firearms Laws.' *Morbidity and Mortality Weekly Report*, Vol. 52, 3 October, pp. 11–20. <http://www.cdc.gov/mmwr/preview/mmwrhtml/rr5214a2.htm>

—. 2003b. *Letter to Grantees: Restriction of Funding*. <http://www.cdc.gov/ncipc/res-opps/restrictions.htm> (accessed 15 January).

Centre for Humanitarian Dialogue. 2003. *Putting People First: Human Security Perspectives on Small Arms Availability and Misuse*. Geneva: Centre for Humanitarian Dialogue. <http://www.hdcentre.org/Programmes/smallarms/publications.htm>

Chabal, P. and J.-P. Daloz. 1999. *Africa Works: Disorder as Political Instrument*. Oxford: James Currey.

Chapdelaine, Antoine, E. Samson, and M. Kimberly. 1991. 'Firearm Related Injuries in Canada: Issues for Prevention.' *Canadian Medical Association Journal*, Vol. 145, pp. 1217–23.

Chetty, Robert, ed. 2000. *Firearm Use and Distribution in South Africa*. Pretoria: The National Crime Prevention Centre Firearm Programme.

Chigbo, Maureen. 2002. 'Danger: Politicians Stockpile Arms to Fight Their Ways Into Political Offices in 2003'. *Newswatch* (Lagos). 12 August, pp. 20-27.

CLEEN/OMCT (Centre for Law Enforcement Education/World Organization Against Torture). 2002. *Hope Betrayed? A Report On Impunity and State-Sponsored Violence In Nigeria*. Lagos: CLEEN/OMCT.

Conetta, Carl. 2003. *The Wages of War: Iraqi Combatant and Noncombatant Fatalities in the 2003 Conflict*. Research monograph No. 8. Washington, DC: Project on Defense Alternatives. 20 October.

Connolly, J. 1997. 'Suicide and the Irish problem: Comments on Under-reporting.' *Archives of Suicidal Research*, Vol. 3, No.1, pp. 25–9.

Conwell, Y. *et al.* 2002. 'Access to Firearm and Risk for Suicide in Middle-Aged and Older Adults.' *American Journal of Geriatric Psychiatry*, Vol. 10, pp. 407–16.

Cook, Philip. 1979. 'The Effect of Gun Availability on Robbery and Robbery Murder.' In R. Haveman and B. Zellner, *Policy Studies Review Annual*. Beverly Hills, California: Sage, pp. 743–81.

—. 1987. 'Robbery Violence'. *Journal of Criminal Law and Criminology*, Vol. 70, No. 2, pp. 357–76.

—. and Jens Ludwig. 1997. *Guns in America: National Survey on Private Ownership and Use of Firearms*. Research in Brief. Washington, DC: National Institute of Justice. May.

—. 2000. *Gun violence. The Real Costs*. Oxford: Oxford University Press.

—. 2001. 'The Costs and Benefits of Reducing Gun Violence.' *Harvard Health Policy Review*, Vol. 2, No.2, pp. 23–8. <http://hcs.harvard.edu/~epihc/currentissue/Fall2001/cook.htm>

Council of Australian Governments. 2003. *National Handgun Buyback*. <http://www.handgunbuyback.gov.au> (accessed 25 October).

Cukier, Wendy. 1998. *International Fire/Small Arms Control: Finding the Common Ground*. Discussion Paper. Toronto, Montreal, and Ottawa: Coalition for Gun Control and Canadian Center for Foreign Policy Development.

Dahl, Dick. 2003. 'CDC Report Highlights Need for Better Research.' Join Together Online. <http://www.jointogether.org/gv/news/features/reader/0,2061,567328,00.html>

Donohue, John. 2003. 'The Final Bullet in the Body of the More Guns, Less Crime Hypothesis.' *Criminology and Public Policy*, Vol. 2, No.3. July, pp. 397–410.

Dowdney, Luke. 2003. *Children of the Drug Trade: A Case Study of Children in Organised Armed Violence in Rio de Janeiro*. Rio de Janeiro: 7 Letras.

Duggan, M. 2001. 'More Guns, More Crime.' *Journal of Political Economy*, Vol. 109, No. 5. October, pp. 1086–14.

Duwe, G., T. Kovandzic, and C. Moody. 2002. 'The Impact of Right-to-Carry Concealed Firearm Laws on Mass Public Shootings.' *Homicide Studies*, Vol. 6, pp. 271–96.

Ebo, Adedeji. 2003. *Small Arms and Criminality in Nigeria: Focus on Kaduna State*. Background paper. Geneva: Small Arms Survey.

Fajnzylber, Pablo, Daniel Lederman, and Norman Loayza. 2000. 'Crime and Victimization: An Economic Perspective.' Paper presented at the first meeting of the Latin America Economic Policy Review, New York, 12–13 May.

Giles, Tanya. 2002. 'Amnesty Tally 40,000 Guns.' *Herald-Sun (*Melbourne), 22 April.

Greenspan, A and A. Kellermann. 2002. 'Physical and Psychological Outcomes After Serious Gunshot Injury.' *Journal of Trauma*, Vol. 53, pp. 709–16.

Hemenway, David. 1997. 'The Myth of Millions of Self-Defense Gun Use: An Explanation of Extreme Overestimates.' *Chance*, Vol. 10, pp. 6–10.

—. and D. R. Azrael. 2000. 'The Relative Frequency of Offensive and Defensive Gun Use: Results from a National Survey.' *Violence and Victims,* Vol. 15, pp. 257–72.

—. Tomoko Shinoda-Tagawa, and Matthew Miller. 2002. 'Firearm Availability and Female Homicide Victimization Rates among 25 Populous High-Income Countries.' *Journal of the American Medical Women's Association,* Vol. 57, Issue 2. Spring, pp. 100–4.

Howard, Alun and Emile LeBrun. 2004. *A Handgun Ban in the United Kingdom*. Background paper. Geneva: Small Arms Survey.

Hung, Kwing. 2003. *Firearm Statistics (Supplementary Tables)*. Ottawa: Research and Statistics Division, Department of Justice Canada.

IISS (International Institute for Strategic Studies). 2004. *The armed conflict database*. <http://www.iiss.org/databases.php> (accessed January)

International Council on Human Rights Policy. 2003. *Crime, Public Order and Human Rights*. Versoix: International Council on Human Rights Policy.

Interpol. 2003. International Crime Statistics. <http://www.interpol.int/Public/Statistics/ICS/downloadList.asp>

Jefferson, Clare and Angus Urquhart. 2002. *The Impact of Small Arms in Tanzania*. Pretoria: Institute for Security Studies.

Join Together Online. 1999. www.jointogether.com (accessed 15 November).

Kates, Don, Jr. 2003. *Genocide, Murder and the Right to Defend One's Life*. Background paper. Geneva: Small Arms Survey.

—. and Daniel D. Polsby. 2000. 'Long-term Nonrelationship of Widespread and Increasing Firearm Availability to Homicide in the United States.' *Homicide Studies,* Vol. 4, Issue 2. May, pp. 185–201.

Kellermann, A. and S. Heron. 1999. 'Firearms and Family Violence.' *Emergency Medicine Clinics of North America*, Vol. 17, pp. 699–717.

—. et al. 1992. 'Suicide in the Home in Relation to Gun Ownership.' *The New England Journal of Medicine*, Vol. 327, pp. 467–72.

van Kesteren, John. 2003. *Firearms Ownership and Crime Data from the International Crime Victim Surveys*. Background paper. Geneva: Small Arms Survey.

Khakee, Anna and Nicolas Florquin. 2003. *Kosovo and the Gun: A Baseline Assessment of Small Arms and Light Weapons in Kosovo*. Special Report. Geneva: Small Arms Survey.

Killias, Martin, John van Kesteren, and Zorrin Rindlisbacher. 2001. 'Guns, Violent Crime, and Suicide in 21 Countries.' *Canadian Journal of Criminology,* Vol. 43, pp. 429–48.

Kleck, Gary. 1991. *Point Blank: Guns and Violence in America*. New York: Aldine De Gruyter.

—. 1997. *Targeting Guns: Firearms and their control*. New York: Aldine de Gruyter.

—. and Marc Gertz. 1995. 'Armed Resistance to Crime: the Prevalence and Nature of Self-Defense with a Gun.' *Journal of Criminal Law and Criminology,* Vol. 86, pp. 150–85.

Kopel, David. 1992. *The Samurai, the Mountie, and the Cowboy: Should America Adopt the Gun Control of Other Democracies?* Buffalo, New York: Prometheus Books.

—. 2001. 'Lawyers, Guns, and Burglars,' 43 *Arizona Law Review* 345 (2001). <http://www.davekopel.com/2A/LawRev/LawyersGunsBurglars.htm>

—. and Paul Blackman. 2000. 'Firearms Tracing Data from the Bureau of Alcohol, Tobacco and Firearms: An Occasionally Useful Law Enforcement Tool, but a Poor Research Tool.' 11 *Criminal Justice Policy Review* 44. March.

—. Paul Gallant, and Joanne D. Eisen. 2003. 'Global Deaths from Firearms: Searching for Plausible Estimates.' *Texas Review of Law and Politics*. Vol.8, No.1, Fall, pp. 114-140. <https://webspace.utexas.edu/starrbd/articles/Kopel.pdf>

Kovandzic, Tomislav V. and Thomas B. Marvell. 2003. 'Right-to-Carry Concealed Handguns and Violent Crime: Crime Control Through Gun Decontrol?' *Criminology and Public Policy,* Vol.2, No.3. July, pp. 363–96.

Krause, Keith. 1999. 'Human Dimension of the Issue of Small Arms and Light Weapons.' In Swiss Federal Department of Foreign Affairs. *Report of Workshop on Small Arms*. Geneva, 18–20 February.

Krug, E., K. Powell, and L. Dahlberg. 1998. 'Firearm-Related Deaths in the United States and 35 Other High- and Upper-Middle-Income Countries'. *International Journal of Epidemiology*, Vol. 27, pp. 214–21. <http://ije.oupjournals.org/cgi/reprint/27/2/214.pdf>

Lott, John R., Jr. 1998. *More Guns, Less Crime*. Chicago: University of Chicago Press.

—. and David Mustard. 1997. 'Crime, Deterrence, and Right-to-Carry Concealed Handguns.' *Journal of Legal Studies,* Vol. 26, pp. 1–68.

Ludwig, J. 1998. 'Concealed-gun-carrying Laws and Violent Crime: Evidence from State Panel Data.' *International Review of Law and Economics,* Vol. 18, pp. 239–54.

—. and Philip Cook, eds. 2003. *Evaluating Gun Policy: Effects on Crime and Violence*. Washington, DC: Brookings Institution..

MacDonald, Ziggy. 2002. 'Official Crime Statistics: Their Use and Interpretation.' *The Economic Journal,* Vol. 112. February, F85–106.

Maltz, M. and J. Targonski. 2002. 'A Note on the Use of County-Level UCR Data.' *Journal of Quantitative Criminology,* Vol. 18, pp. 297–318.

Manning, Willard. 2003. 'Comment to John J. Donohue.' In Ludwig and Cook, 2003, pp. 331–41.

Marshall, Monty G. and Ted Robert Gurr. 2003. *Peace and Conflict 2003: A Global Survey of Armed Conflicts, Self-Determination Movements, and Democracy*. College Park, Maryland: Center for International Development and Conflict Management.

McDowall D. and B. Wiersema. 1994. 'Incidence of Defensive Firearms Use by US Crime Victims, 1987–1990.' *American Journal of Public Health,* Vol. 84, No. 12, pp. 1982–4.

—. C. Loftin, and S. Presser. 2000. 'Measuring civilian defensive firearm use: A methodological experiment.' *Journal of Quantitative Criminology,* Vol. 16, pp. 1–19.

Mihorean, Stephen. 2003. *The Accessibility Thesis Debate*. Background paper. Geneva: Small Arms Survey.

Miller, Mathew and David Hemenway. 1999. 'Relationship between Firearms and Suicide: A Review of the Literature.' *Aggression and Violent Behavior,* Vol. 4, No. 1, pp. 59–75.

—. et al. 2002. 'Firearm Availability and Unintentional Firearm Deaths, Suicide, and Homicide among 5–14 Year Olds.' *Journal of TRAUMA Injury, Infection, and Critical Care,* Vol. 52, No. 2. February, pp. 267–75.

Miller, Ted and Mark Cohen. 1996. 'Costs of Gunshot Injury and Cut/Stab Wounds in the United States, with Some Canadian Comparisons.' *Accident Analysis and Prevention,* Vol. 29, pp. 329–41.

Moser, Caroline and Jeremy Holland. 1997. *Urban Poverty and Violence in Jamaica*. Washington, DC: The World Bank.

Mouzos, Jenny. 1999. *Firearm-related Violence: The Impact of the Nationwide Agreement on Firearms*. Canberra: Australian Institute of Criminology

—. 2001a. *Firearm-related Morbidity in Australia, 1994–95 to 1998–99*. Canberra: Australian Institute of Criminology, March

—. 2001b. 'Homicide in Australia 1999–2000.' *Trends and Issues in Crime Control and Criminal Justice,* No.187. Australian Institute of Criminology. Canberra, February.

—. 2002a. *Homicide in Australia 2000–2001: National Homicide Monitoring (NHMP) Annual Report*. Research & Public Policy Series No.40. Canberra: Australian Institute of Criminology, March.

—. 2002b. *Firearms Theft in Australia*. Trends & Issues in Crime & Criminal Justice No 230. Canberra: Australian Institute of Criminology, June.

—. 2003. *Homicide in Australia 2001–2002: National Homicide Monitoring (NHMP) Annual Report*. Research & Public Policy Series No.46. Canberra: Australian Institute of Criminology, April.

Mthembu-Salter, Gregory. 2003. *Small Arms and Crime in Zambia: Focus on Livingstone, Namwala and the Kafue National Park*. Background paper. Geneva: Small Arms Survey

Muchai, Augusta and Clare Jefferson. 2002. *Kenya Crime Survey 2002*. Nairobi: Security Research and Information Centre (SRIC).

Muggah, Robert and Eric Berman. 2001. *Humanitarianism Under Threat. The Humanitarian Impacts Of Small Arms And Light Weapons*. Special Report. Geneva: Small Arms Survey

Muggah, Robert and Yeshua Moser-Puangsuwan, eds. 2003. *Whose Security Counts? Participatory Research on Armed Violence and Human Insecurity in Southeast Asia*. Geneva: Small Arms Survey, Nonviolence International.

Muir, Hugh and Helen Carter. 2003. 'Lethal Replicas Fuel Gun Crime Fears'. *Guardian* (London). 11 October.

NRA (National Rifle Association). 1999. <http://www.nra.org> (accessed 12 June).

Obasi, Nnamdi K. 2002. *Small arms proliferation and disarmament in West Africa: Progress and prospects of the ECOWAS Moratorium*. Abuja, Nigeria: Apophyl Productions.

O'Malley, Nick. 2003. 'Security Industry Targeted by Carr'. *Sydney Morning Herald*. 22 October.

Peters, Rebecca. 2002. 'A Plague of Small Arms'. *International Herald Tribune*. 28 October. <http://www.iht.com/articles/75028.html>

Pézard, Stéphanie. 2003. *The Intangible Costs of Small Arms*. Background paper. Geneva: Small Arms Survey.

Rennison, C. 2002. *Criminal Victimization 2001. Changes 2000–2001 with trends 1993–2001* NCJ No 194610. Washington, DC: Bureau of Justice Statistics, US Department of Justice.

Research Centre for Injury Studies. 2000. *Numbers of Firearm-related Deaths, Australia, 1979–1999 by Intent*. Adelaide: Australian Institute of Health and Welfare/NISU.

Reuter, Peter and Jenny Mouzos. 2002. 'Australia: A Massive Buyback of Low-Risk Guns.' In Ludwig and Cook, pp. 121–41.

Sabala, Kizito and Kennedy Mkutu. 2003. *The Impact of Armed Criminality in Rural and Urban Kenya: Case Studies of Nairobi and Kitale Municipality*. Background paper. Geneva: Small Arms Survey.

SAFER-NET and HELP NETWORK. 2001. *Nation Status Report on Violence and Small Arms*. Chicago and Ontario: SAFER-NET and HELP NETWORK.

Sayil, I. 1991. 'Turkey.' *IASP Newsletter*, Vol. 2, No 3, pp. 3–4.

Shenassa, E., S. Catlin, and S. Buka. 2003. 'Lethality of firearms relative to other suicide methods: A population based study.' *Journal of Epidemiology and Community Health*, Vol. 57, pp. 120–4.

Sherman, Lawrence *et al.* 1998. *Preventing Crime: What Works, What Doesn't, What's Promising*. Research in Brief. Washington, DC: National Institute of Justice. July.

Slovak, Karen. 2002. 'Gun Violence and Children: Factors Related to Exposure and Trauma.' *Health and Social Work*, Vol. 27, No. 2. May, pp. 104–12.

Small Arms Survey. 2001. *Small Arms Survey 2001: Profiling the Problem*. Oxford: Oxford University Press.

—. 2002. *Small Arms Survey 2002: Counting the Human Cost*. Oxford: Oxford University Press.

—. 2003. *Small Arms Survey 2003: Development Denied*. Oxford: Oxford University Press.

—. 2004. *Firearms mortality database*. <http://www.smallarmssurvey.org>

Smith, T. 1997. 'A Call for a Truce in the DGU War.' *Journal of Criminal Law and Criminology*, Vol. 87, pp. 1462–9.

SPADO (Sustainable Peace and Development Organization). 2003. *Crimes Related to Small Arms: A Case Study of Peshawar*. Background paper. Geneva: Small Arms Survey

Toohey, Paul. 2002. 'States Won't Pay Gun Buyback Bill'. *Australian* (Sydney). 6 November.

Tong, Castro Zangina. 2003. 'Cops paid fake cash as bribe'. *Ghanaian Times* (Accra). 28 August

UK (United Kingdom). Home Office. 2000. *Criminal Statistics, England and Wales 1999*. London: Office for National Statistics.

—. 2001. *Firearm Certificates England and Wales, 1999 and 2000*. London: Office for National Statistics.

—. 2002. *Crime in England and Wales 2001/2002*. London: Office for National Statistics.

—. 2003. *Recorded Crime Statistics 1898—2001/2002*. <http://www.homeoffice.gov.uk/rds/pdfs/100years.xls>

—. 2004a. *Crime in England and Wales 2002/2003: Supplementary Volume 1*. London: Office of National Statistics.

—. 2004b. *Firearm Certificates England and Wales, 2002/2003*. London: Office for National Statistics.

—. NCIS (National Criminal Intelligence Service). 2003. *Threat Assessment of Serious and Organised Crime 2003*. London: NCIS.

UN (United Nations). 1945. *Charter of the United Nations and Statute of the International Court of Justice*. Adopted in San Francisco, 26 June. Entered into force on 24 October. <http://www.un.org/aboutun/index.html>

—. 1998. *International Study on Firearm Regulation*. New York: UN.

—. 1999. 'International Study on Firearm Regulation database, 1999 updated data.' <http://www.uncjin.org/Statistics/firearms/>.

UNECOSOC (United Nations Economic and Social Council). 2002. *The question of the trade, carrying and use of small arms and light weapons in the context of human rights and humanitarian norms: Working paper submitted by Ms. Barbara Frey in accordance with Sub-Commission decision 2001/120*. UN document no. E/CN.4/Sub.2/2002/39 of 30 May.

—. 2003. *Prevention of human rights violations committed with small arms and light weapons: Preliminary report submitted by Barbara Frey, Special Rapporteur, in accordance with Sub-Commission resolution 2002/25*. UN document no. E/CN.4/Sub.2/2003/29 of 25 June.

UNGA (United Nations General Assembly). 1948. *Universal Declaration of Human Rights*. Adopted and proclaimed by UNGA Resolution 217A (III) of 10 December. <http://www.unhchr.ch/udhr/>

UNODC (United Nations Office on Drugs and Crime). 2003. 'Surveys on Crime Trends and the Operations of Criminal Justice Systems.' <http://www.unodc.org/unodc/crime_cicp_surveys.html>

UNODCCP (United Nations Office for Drug Control and Crime Prevention) 1999. *Global Report on Crime and Justice*. New York and Oxford: Oxford University Press.

UN. Population Division. 2002. *World Population Prospects: The 2002 Revision.*
    <http://www.un.org/esa/population/publications/wpp2002/wpp2002annextables.PDF>

US (United States). Bureau of Justice Statistics. 2002. *Homicide Trends in the US. Intimate Homicide and Homicides by Relationship and Weapon Type.* Washington, DC: Department of Justice.

—. Department of the Treasury. 2002. *Gun Crime Trace Reports.* Youth Crime Gun Interdiction Initiative. Washington, DC: Bureau of Alcohol, Tobacco and Firearms.

—. District of Columbia Court of Appeals. 1981. *Warren v. District of Columbia. Atlantic Reporter.* 2nd Series, Vol. 444. p. 1.

Waller, Irvin. 2003. *Main Lessons from Evaluations of North American Crime Prevention and Gun Violence Reduction.* Background paper. Geneva: Small Arms Survey.

Wesson, Richard. 2000. 'Does the Lott Model Apply to South Africa?' October.
    <http://www.crimefree.org.za/Role-players/Criminologist/R-Wesson/SAMURDER.htm>

Wheeler, Timothy. 2003. 'A Light Goes On at the CDC; No Escaping Gun-Control Reality.' *National Review.* 23 October.

WHO (World Health Organization). 2001. *Small Arms and Global Health.* Geneva: WHO.

—. 2002. *World Report on Violence and Health.* Geneva: WHO.

—. 2003. *Mortality Database.* <http://www3.who.int/whosis/mort/text/download.cfm?path=whosis,whsa,mort_download&language=english> (accessed 10 June)

Wiebe, Douglas. 2003a. 'Homicide and Suicide Risks Associated with Firearms in the Home: A National Case-Control Study.' *Annals of Emergency Medicine,* Vol. 41, Issue 6. June, pp. 771–82.

—. 2003b. 'Guns in the Home: Risky Business.' *Leonard Davis Institute of Health Economics (LDI) Issue Brief,* Vol. 8, No. 8. May.

Wille, Christina. 2003. *Firearms Use in Homicides and Suicides.* Background paper. Geneva: Small Arms Survey.

Wintemute, Garen *et al.* 1999. 'Mortality among Recent Purchasers of Handguns.' *New England Journal of Medicine,* Vol. 341. 18 November, pp. 1583–9.

—. 2003. 'Increased Risk of Intimate Partner Homicide Among California Women who Purchased Handguns.' *Annals of Emergency Medicine,* Vol. 41. February, p. 2.

Wright, James and Peter Rossi. 1986. *Armed and Dangerous: A Survey of Felons and their Firearms.* New York: Aldine de Gruyter.

Zimring, Franklin. 1991. 'Firearms, Violence and Public Policy.' *Scientific American,* Vol. 265, No. 5. November, pp. 48–54.

ACKNOWLEDGEMENTS

Other contributors
Christiane Agboton-Johnson, Philip Alpers, Gary Anderson, Kwesi Aning, Mufor Atanga, Antonio Cassese, Adedeji Ebo, Alun Howard, Don Kates, John van Kesteren, Emile LeBrun, Glenn McDonald, Stephen Mihorean, Kennedy Mkutu, Robert Muggah, Gregory Mthembu-Salter, Stéphanie Pézard, Kizito Sabala, the sustainable Peace and Development Organization (SPADO), and Irvin Waller.

A police officer draws his gun during clashes between police and demonstrators in Gothenburg, Sweden, in June 2001.
(© AP/Tor Wenstroem/Lehtikuva)

Critical Triggers:
IMPLEMENTING INTERNATIONAL STANDARDS FOR POLICE FIREARM USE

INTRODUCTION

Pull the trigger or not? Police decisions to use force have broad repercussions for the societies they are meant to protect.

The first casualty of police firearm misuse is the bond between citizen and state. Under international law, the state is sworn to respect the human rights of its citizens. National policing is a key testing ground of that commitment—and of the state's commitment to the rule of law generally. Policing, good or bad, also influences individual decisions about security: to trust in the state or rely on private security providers.

Against the backdrop of relevant international standards, this chapter examines the issues associated with police use of force and firearms. Among its major conclusions are the following:

- Police use of force and firearms is a core human rights issue.
- The twin principles of necessity and proportionality underpin the legitimate use of force by law enforcement officials under international and national law.
- A broad range of factors, such as equipment and training, condition police use of force and firearms.
- Although there is some good news, policing in many countries appears to fall well short of international standards.
- While resources are important for good policing, political commitment is the key.

This chapter aims to highlight critical issues relating to the implementation of international standards for police use of force and firearms. It does not attempt to assess state implementation in a systematic way, yet its sample of high, middle, and low-income countries from all parts of the world illustrates the many challenges and problems arising in this area.

The next two sections examine the normative framework that governs the use of force and firearms by law enforcement officers at both the international and national levels. The chapter points out that police firearm misuse involves a violation of such fundamental human rights as the right to life and the right not to be tortured or subjected to cruel, inhuman, or degrading treatment or punishment. The chapter then moves to specifics—comparing state practice with relevant norms in a wide range of areas that shape the legitimate and illegitimate use of force by police.[1]

INTERNATIONAL STANDARDS

National policing practices must fulfil international human rights obligations. The 1948 *Universal Declaration of Human Rights* (UNGA, 1948) contains a number of provisions that are directly relevant to the use of firearms in law enforcement work, in particular Article 3, which reads: 'Everyone has the right to life, liberty and security of person.'

Other provisions of the *Universal Declaration,* such as the ban on torture along with 'cruel, inhuman or degrading treatment or punishment' (art. 5), are also relevant to the use and misuse of firearms by state agents.

While the *Universal Declaration* is not a legally binding instrument, provisions such as those cited above are commonly held to form part of customary international law, which is legally binding. Many of the *Universal Declaration's* provisions have also been incorporated, in legally binding form, in human rights treaties, most notably the *International Covenant on Civil and Political Rights* (ICCPR) (UNGA, 1966). Article 6 of the ICCPR, enunciating 'the inherent right to life', is one of a limited number of provisions from which no derogation is permitted, even '[i]n time of public emergency which threatens the life of the nation' (art. 4). Other treaties, such as the 1984 *Convention against Torture and Other Cruel, Inhuman or Degrading Treatment or Punishment* (UNGA, 1984), have since reinforced the normative framework sketched out in the *Universal Declaration.*

International efforts to create a code of practice for police that is consistent with international human rights obligations can be traced back to 1957, when the International Federation of Senior Police Officers adopted a code of ethics (Heijder, 1984). Two decades later, in June 1975, a seminar organized by Amnesty International (AI) at the Hague resulted in a set of proposals for an international code of conduct on policing (the 'Declaration of The Hague').

Shortly afterwards, a process was launched under UN auspices for the development of a non-binding *UN Code of Conduct for Law Enforcement Officials* (UNGA, 1979b). The 1979 UN Code comprises a Commentary intended to guide interpretation of its eight articles.

Article 1 defines the Code's scope of application, specifying that the term 'law enforcement officials' embraces 'all officers of the law, whether appointed or elected, who exercise police powers, especially the powers of arrest and detention.' This definition explicitly encompasses 'military authorities' and 'State security forces' that exercise such powers.

Article 3 of the UN Code presents the fundamental principles that, as discussed below, underlie more specific rules governing the use of force and firearms by police, namely necessity and proportionality: 'Law enforcement officials may use force only when strictly necessary and to the extent required for the performance of their duty.' The Commentary to the article specifies that such force 'should be exceptional' and '[i]n no case ... disproportionate to the legitimate objective to be achieved' (paras a–b). The Commentary adds, in paragraph (c):

> The use of firearms is considered an extreme measure. Every effort should be made to exclude the use of firearms, especially against children. In general, firearms should not be used except when a suspected offender offers armed resistance or otherwise jeopardizes the lives of others and less extreme measures are not sufficient to restrain or apprehend the suspected offender. In every instance in which a firearm is discharged, a report should be made promptly to the competent authorities.

While this chapter reviews a wide range of standards governing the use of force and firearms by state agents exercising a policing function,[2] it will focus mainly on the most specific formulation of norms in this area, the *Basic Principles on the Use of Force and Firearms by Law Enforcement Officials,* adopted in September 1990 (UN, 1990). Although this instrument is not legally binding, many of the Basic Principles reflect states' existing obligations under international human rights law in the law enforcement context.

Basic Principles 4 and 5 articulate the fundamental considerations that apply to the use of force and firearms by police. Basic Principle 4 specifies that any such use must be a last resort. Police 'may use force and firearms only if other means remain ineffective or without any promise of achieving the intended result.' Basic Principle 5 stipulates that any use of force or firearms must be restrained and proportionate to the seriousness of the offence and the objective being pursued by the police officer (para. a). Law enforcement officials must minimize any harm arising from their use of force or firearms (para. b). They also have a duty of care to any injured or affected persons, extending necessary medical assistance (para. c) and notifying close friends and relatives (para. d).

Basic Principle 9 builds on the principles of necessity and proportionality articulated in Basic Principles 4 and 5 (and in the 1979 *UN Code of Conduct*), specifying that law enforcement officials 'shall not use firearms against persons' except in the following circumstances, and then 'only when less extreme means are insufficient to achieve these objectives':

- in self-defence or defence of others against the imminent threat of death or serious injury;
- to prevent the perpetration of a particularly serious crime involving a grave threat to life;
- to arrest a person presenting such a danger and resisting the police officer's authority, or to prevent his or her escape.

Basic Principle 9 also stipulates that, '[i]n any event, intentional *lethal* use of firearms may only be made when strictly unavoidable in order to protect life' (emphasis added).

According to Basic Principle 10, 'law enforcement officials shall identify themselves as such and give a clear warning of their intent to use firearms, with sufficient time for the warning to be observed,' unless the particular circumstances dictate otherwise.

Guidelines listed in Basic Principle 11 are intended to underpin national rules and regulations governing the use of firearms by law enforcement officials.

In order to meet these standards, Basic Principle 19 states that '[t]hose law enforcement officials who are required to carry firearms should be authorized to do so only upon completion of special training in their use.' Standards for such training are set out in Basic Principle 20.

Basic Principle 2 also calls upon governments and law enforcement agencies to 'develop a range of means as broad as possible ... that would allow for a differentiated use of force and firearms'. Basic Principles 13 and 14 set strict limits to the use of force and firearms by police in dispersing unlawful assemblies, even when these are violent. Many of these specific issues are discussed below.

> The *UN Basic Principles* articulate key standards governing the use of force and firearms by police.

NATIONAL REGULATION

Police have the difficult task of preventing, combating, and investigating crime, maintaining public order, and protecting the population within their jurisdiction. These men and women have a direct interest in clear rules for the use of force—particularly lethal force—when apprehending violent suspects or otherwise protecting the public.

States, in other words, need to set out the basis of legitimate force in national legislation and more specific operational guidance for police. Basic Principle 11 indicates that such rules should:

(a) Specify the circumstances under which law enforcement officials are authorized to carry firearms and prescribe the types of firearms and ammunition permitted;

(b) Ensure that firearms are used only in appropriate circumstances and in a manner likely to decrease the risk of unnecessary harm;

(c) Prohibit the use of those firearms and ammunition that cause unwarranted injury or present an unwarranted risk;

(d) Regulate the control, storage, and issuing of firearms, including procedures for ensuring that law enforcement officials are accountable for the firearms and ammunition issued to them;

(e) Provide for warnings to be given, if appropriate, when firearms are to be discharged;

(f) Provide for a system of reporting whenever law enforcement officials use firearms in the performance of their duty. (UN, 1990)

Legal frameworks

The levels of force that police can use in the performance of their duties are generally defined both administratively and by statute. National courts also play an important role in interpreting, and in some cases establishing, these rules. These may (or may not) reflect relevant international norms, such as those found in the *UN Code of Conduct,* the *UN Basic Principles,* and the ICCPR.

A Manila police officer disperses two opposing political factions in the Philippines in May 1998.

Although most countries have ratified the ICCPR, about one-quarter have not.³ Moreover, the laws and regulations of states that have ratified the treaty do not always mirror its provisions. The *UN Code of Conduct* and *UN Basic Principles* are also imperfectly and partially reflected in national legislation around the world.

National rules do not always reflect international human rights norms.

For example, in July 2003, the UN Human Rights Committee, which monitors state compliance with the ICCPR, noted with concern that Portuguese regulations on the use of firearms by police were not compatible with the *UN Basic Principles*. This discrepancy was reported to have been a factor in a series of lethal shooting incidents involving the Portuguese police. The Committee asked the government to ensure that Basic Principles 9, 14, and 16 were 'fully integrated into Portuguese law and implemented in practice, and that adequate training [was] effectively conducted' (UN, Human Rights Committee, 2003).

The UN reported in 1998 that written standards for training and the use of force were generally high among police departments in the United States. These appeared to reflect relevant international standards, including the *UN Code of Conduct* and *UN Basic Principles*, 'despite the fact that there [was] little, if any, awareness of the existence of these international standards' (UN, Commission on Human Rights, 1998, para. 130).

Many developing countries inherited their policing structures from the colonial era. Laws and practices on the use of force by police in many African, Asian, and Caribbean countries derive from quasi-militaristic approaches to policing developed by the British in Ireland and subsequently Northern Ireland. French, Portuguese, and Spanish traditions of gendarme policing were similarly imposed on former colonies.

For example, the traditions of 19th-century British-run constabulary policing in Ireland were exported to South Africa after the Anglo-Boer War, so shaping the militaristic South African Police Service for most of the 20th century (Brogden, 1985). Similarly repressive models of colonial internal security influenced professional policing in El Salvador, Guatemala, and Haiti (Neild, 1995; 2001).

Some regional agreements on police use of force and firearms are still drafted in a way that permits national laws and practices to fall below international standards. For example, in July 2001 the Southern African Regional Police Chiefs Co-operation Organisation (SARPCCO) adopted a *Code of Conduct for Police Officials* as a 'minimum standard for police forces/services in the region' (SARPCCO, 2001). While the Code contains many essential policing standards in line with UN human rights instruments, it does not specifically refer to the use of firearms or the *UN Basic Principles*. Article 3 regarding the 'Use of Force' is formulated in broad terms, leaving the development of specific guidelines to national authorities.[4] These may or may not be consistent with international standards.

Several of the national police agencies covered by this Code, such as those in Zimbabwe and Swaziland, have reportedly used firearms to commit human rights violations, while at least three governments in southern Africa retain laws that allow impunity for such violations.[5] Other countries, such as Malawi, have yet to upgrade colonial-era policing legislation to incorporate the *UN Basic Principles* and other international standards concerning police use of firearms.

Self-defence

Several fundamental principles underpin and inform almost all national legislation governing the use of force and firearms by law enforcement officials. These are also reflected in the international instruments and standards described in the preceding section. The first of these principles is self-defence. UN Basic Principle 9 restricts the police use of firearms to situations that include 'self-defence or defence of others against the imminent threat of death or serious injury' (UN, 1990). This concept is very similar to that of 'risk of serious physical harm or loss of life', codified in US law after the US Supreme Court, in a 1985 ruling, set narrow limits to the use of deadly force by police.[6] For example, current rules in Cincinnati, Ohio, stipulate:

> Respect for human life requires that police officers exhaust all other reasonable means before resorting to the use of firearms and then only when an officer reasonably believes that such use of firearms is necessary to protect the officer or another from the risk of serious physical harm or loss of life. (Cincinnati Police Department, 2003)

Other US police departments have similar rules.[7] In fact, the principle of self-defence is universally established, as noted by South Africa's Constitutional Court:

> Self-defence is recognised by all legal systems. Where a choice has to be made between the lives of two or more people, the life of the innocent is given preference over the life of the aggressor ... To deny the innocent person the right to act in self-defence would deny to that individual his or her right to life.[8]

Although the approach to self-defence varies between countries, there appears to be near universal agreement that a police officer has a legal right to use lethal force to stop an aggressor who poses a direct and immediate threat to the life of the officer or another person, if necessary under the circumstances.

Courts in Canada, Germany, and the UK have reached conclusions that are very similar to those of the US Supreme Court. In each country, the degree of force police can use in making an arrest is determined not only by the seriousness of the offence, but also by the threat or danger posed by the suspect to the police or to others in society.[9]

Necessity and proportionality

Necessity and proportionality underpin national rules for the use of force and firearms by police.

Two further principles underpin national rules for the use of force and firearms by police: necessity and proportionality. French law requires that any use of force be proportionate to the severity of the threat or attack. Pursuant to Article 9 of the *Code of Professional Ethics of the French National Police*, '[w]hen lawfully authorized to use force and, in particular, to use weapons, the police officer must only do so when strictly necessary and in proportion to the objective to be achieved.'[10] The rules governing the use of weapons by police derive from Article 122-5 of the French penal code concerning the broader right of self-defence.[11]

All States Parties to the European Convention on Human Rights (Council of Europe, 1950), including France, Germany, and the UK, are bound by the Convention's Article 2, which articulates many of the principles already discussed, in particular necessity:

> Deprivation of life shall not be regarded as inflicted in contravention of this article when it results from the use of force which is no more than absolutely necessary:
> a. in defence of any person from unlawful violence;
> b. in order to effect a lawful arrest or to prevent the escape of a person lawfully detained;
> c. in action lawfully taken for the purpose of quelling a riot or insurrection.

The Article 2 requirement of 'absolute necessity' involves a stricter application of the proportionality principle than one finds in other parts of the Convention. The relevant use of force must not be merely 'reasonable', it must be 'absolutely necessary'.

Pursuant to South Australia's *Police Issue 3375*, resort to the use of a firearm must only occur when the police officer 'believes on reasonable grounds such use is necessary to protect life or prevent serious injury and only then when satisfied no other means are available' (Sarre, 1993).

Notions of what is 'necessary' and 'proportional' in this regard have evolved over time. Under old British common law, a 'fleeing felon' could be killed, but this approach dates back to the period, centuries ago, when almost all felonies were punishable by death. Prior to the 1985 US Supreme Court decision described above, most of the 50 US states had laws approving the so-called 'any-felony' policy, allowing police to use firearms, or other means of deadly force, to arrest persons suspected of committing any felony. Some states allowed police officers to shoot fleeing persons, including those suspected of such property offences as cheque forgery and auto theft. Other states had somewhat more restrictive rules, limiting the use of deadly force to persons suspected of having committed 'forcible' felonies, such as a robbery. About 12 states had no statute at all on the use of deadly force by police.[12]

Common law states have now distanced themselves from the old 'fleeing felon' rule. The relevant felony must be punishable by life imprisonment and police must have no other means of apprehending a suspect before they can use force or firearms.[13]

> **Box 7.1 Replacing apartheid-era legislation in South Africa**
>
> Under apartheid-era legislation, police in South Africa were allowed to shoot suspected thieves, drug dealers, and other offenders posing no direct threat to the life of the officer or the public (Hartley, 2002).[14] The central provision at issue was Section 49 of the Criminal Procedure Act of 1977.
>
> In November 1998, the South African Parliament adopted a revised draft Section 49 to bring the rules governing the use of force by police into line with South Africa's new Constitution and international human rights law (South Africa, Parliament, 1998). With backing from the Minister of Safety and Security and the Vice President, however, the South African Police Service (SAPS) won a delay in the implementation of the new law in order to allow police to be retrained in its requirements. In 1997 and 2002, the SAPS issued interim orders that significantly tightened the rules governing officers' use of firearms. The SAPS claimed, in early 2004, that its firearms training had largely been brought into compliance with the standards contained in the 1998 amendment,[15] although this assertion was questioned by a leading expert.[16]
>
> The South African government finally put the 1998 legal amendment into effect in July 2003. The new law allows police to use lethal force where there are reasonable grounds to believe that a person presents a danger of 'future death or grievous bodily harm'. While this is a considerable improvement on the apartheid-era legislation, the new law's use of the term 'future' is at odds with the requirement of an '*imminent* threat of death or serious injury' contained in the *UN Basic Principles* (UN, 1990, Basic Principle 9, emphasis added).

A critical issue for the regulation of police firearm use—but which the *UN Basic Principles* do not address—is whether police officers should be allowed or encouraged to fire warning shots. In South Africa, under the post-apartheid Constitution, the government issued a directive requiring that police officers only use potentially deadly force after 'a warning and/or a warning shot'. Police in countries such as the UK, and some states and counties in the United States, no longer use warning shots because of the danger they may pose to innocent bystanders.

For instance, police in Houston are told, 'Never fire warning shots.' Rule 8 of the Police Firearms Policy prohibits Houston police officers from 'drawing or otherwise displaying their firearms without probable cause to believe there is a threat to the officers' life or safety.' The reason for this is that 'drawing or displaying a firearm can limit officers' alternatives in controlling situations, as well as create unnecessary anxiety on the part of citizens and result in unwarranted or accidental discharges' (Houston Police Department, 1984, 'Use of Firearms', Rule 8).

While the Cincinnati Police Rules and Regulations do not prohibit warning shots, they stipulate: 'Officers should only use warning shots if convinced a warning shot will possibly save a life or alleviate the need of taking a life. As with any shot an officer fires, the officer must know it will not endanger innocent bystanders' (Cincinnati Police Department, 2003).

> A critical issue for the regulation of police firearm use is whether police officers should be allowed or encouraged to fire warning shots.

STATES OF EMERGENCY

Human rights are often compromised during states of emergency.

UN Basic Principle 8 stipulates that '[e]xceptional circumstances such as internal political instability or any other public emergency may not be invoked to justify any departure from these basic principles' (UN, 1990). There are strict limits to the kinds of restrictions that may be imposed in a state of emergency. Some rights are so fundamental they may never be suspended, even during a state of emergency. These include the right to life, the right not to be tortured or subjected to cruel, inhuman, or degrading treatment or punishment, and the right to freedom of thought, conscience, and religion.[17]

In practice, however, human rights are often compromised during states of emergency. Violations of the rights to life and freedom from torture frequently occur when police and other security forces are authorized to maintain public order in the absence of safeguards designed to uphold these rights.

The People's Republic of China has adopted martial and anti-terrorism laws that give wide powers to the security forces and enable the excessive use of force by armed police (see Box 7.2).

Box 7.2   China's martial and anti-terrorism laws

A new *Martial Law of the People's Republic of China*, promulgated on 1 March 1996 by the Standing Committee of the National People's Congress, reportedly allows martial law enforcement personnel to use 'guns and other weapons ... if police instruments prove to be of no avail' in various situations where violence occurs or there is a threat of violence. These rules apply, for example, if a person who is detained or transported under escort commits a physical assault or 'attempts to get away'. Significantly, the law sets no limit on the amount of force to be used in such situations (AI, 1997). The *Martial Law* has been applied in the Tibet Autonomous Region, the Inner Mongolia Autonomous Region, and the Xinjiang Uighur Autonomous Region (XUAR).

At the end of December 2001, China amended the provisions of its criminal law for the stated purpose of making more explicit certain existing punishments for 'terrorist' crimes. It appears that the new law nevertheless creates considerable uncertainty about what conduct is prohibited and how it will be punished. Several of its articles are vaguely worded, the terms 'terrorism', 'terrorist organization', and 'terrorist crime' are not defined despite being used in several places, and no maximum punishment is specified for some offences (HRW, 2003b).

This law has since been applied in the context of the Chinese government's current campaign against 'separatist, terrorist and religious extremist forces' in XUAR, with hundreds of armed police units mobilized for this purpose (AI, 2002d).

Policing practices also appear to have fallen short of international standards in Israel, where a state of emergency has been in force since 1948. Numerous human rights groups have reported that in policing the demonstrations of September–October 2000, in Israel proper and the Occupied Territories, Israeli security forces tended to use military methods rather than more appropriate policing methods. Although Palestinian demonstrators, many of whom were younger than 18 years old, threw stones, and occasionally petrol bombs, at Israeli security forces, these posed little or no threat to the Israelis who occupied secure positions and were well-protected. Nevertheless, Israeli security forces frequently responded with lethal weaponry, including rubber or plastic-coated metal bullets and live ammunition.[18]

DIFFERENTIATED USE OF FORCE

The *UN Basic Principles* stress the need for police to be given the means to perform their various law enforcement functions without having to resort to the use of potentially lethal force.

> Governments and law enforcement agencies should develop a range of means as broad as possible and equip law enforcement officials with various types of weapons and ammunition that would allow for a differentiated use of force and firearms. These should include the development of non-lethal incapacitating weapons for use in appropriate situations, with a view to increasingly restraining the application of means capable of causing death or injury to persons. For the same purpose, it should also be possible for law enforcement officials to be equipped with self-defensive equipment such as shields, helmets, bullet-proof vests and bullet-proof means of transportation, in order to decrease the need to use weapons of any kind. (UN, 1990, Basic Principle 2)

In the same spirit, Basic Principle 3 stipulates:

> The development and deployment of non-lethal incapacitating weapons should be carefully evaluated in order to minimize the risk of endangering uninvolved persons, and the use of such weapons should be carefully controlled.

Basic Principle 11 requires governments to '[p]rohibit the use of those firearms and ammunition that cause unwarranted injury or present an unwarranted risk'. This prohibition, applicable in peacetime, is distinct from the similar wartime prohibition, under international humanitarian law, of the use of military weapons that are inherently indiscriminate in nature or cause unnecessary suffering.

Regardless of whether they include equipment allowing for the non-lethal use of coercion, police holdings of small arms vary enormously between countries with similar characteristics, and sometimes within the same country. Depending on their roles, different units or forces may possess very different types of equipment. Security forces in many developing countries, especially those affected by civil war, often use powerful assault rifles for policing in non-conflict situations, posing an increased risk of excessive force.

A threshold question is whether police are issued firearms as regular equipment. Norway and the UK are two of the few countries around the world with a largely unarmed police force. Firearms and other powerful weapons are stored at police armouries or in patrol cars and may be used in self-defence or in case of need with the permission of a police commissioner. The tendency, however, is to rely on the rapid deployment of specialist firearms officers. In contrast, Swedish police officers carry handguns whenever they are in uniform.

In order to determine whether this difference in police access to guns affects the number of shootings, a recent study compared data from Norway and Sweden from 1985 to 1999. The study examined all reported incidents of firearms use by on-duty police officers. While about 450 shooting incidents occurred in Sweden, with 15 people killed by police officer's fire, in Norway there were only around 50 such incidents and 4 persons killed. Given that Sweden has about twice Norway's population, and that the two countries share many social characteristics, the study suggests that police shootings and killings increase where police have regular access to firearms (Knutsson and Strype, 2000). More research is needed, however, before any firm conclusions can be reached on this question.

Since rubber bullets were first used against crowds in 1970 by UK forces in Northern Ireland, security forces around the world have used them as a form of riot control considered 'less lethal' than regular firearm munitions.

> **Box 7.3   UK police weapons**[19]
>
> UK police forces hold 9mm pistols (Browning and SIG Sauer), revolvers (Smith & Wesson), and 9mm semi-automatic carbines ('short rifles', including the Heckler & Koch MP5), as well as a few 'specialist munitions' such as high-velocity sniper rifles, shotguns, and 'less lethal' weapons such as baton guns. The 9mm pistols and revolvers are usually accurate over a range of 50m, although the rounds can cause serious injury at distances up to 500m, while the MP5s can be accurate over 200m. Sniper rifles are normally used over a 200m to 500m range, though some models are accurate and lethal at distances up to 1km. Fully automatic rifles are not issued to UK police as they pose an unwarranted risk to the public. A burst of fire from these weapons—containing multiple rounds and travelling 2 to 3km—can be especially dangerous in densely populated areas.
>
> The type of weapon to be used in a specific operation is determined by taking a series of factors into consideration:
>
> - the type of situation or threat
> - the level of force needed to meet the threat
> - the likely distance between the police officers and the source of the threat (affecting the time police have to react to a developing threat)
> - the weapon(s) used by the source of the threat
> - the operational environment (e.g. extent of cover, room for manoeuvre)
> - the training and experience of the armed firearms officers involved.
>
> At shorter ranges, revolvers, self-loading pistols, and carbines firing handgun ammunition may be appropriate. At greater distances, rifles and carbines using rifle ammunition may be more suitable.
>
> Armed officers also have a range of munitions that can be used when carrying out specific tasks. 'Specialist munitions' include shotgun CS gas (tear gas) rounds, baton rounds, exploding distraction devices, and shotgun breaching rounds. Specialist munitions have the potential to cause injury, including fatal injury, even when used correctly, with secondary fragments posing a particular danger. Police officers handling or using such munitions are therefore given special training in their characteristics and proper use.
>
> UK police use the term 'less lethal options' to refer to weapons, devices, and tactics that are intended to induce compliance by a subject without posing a substantial risk of serious or permanent injury or death to that person. The aim, in other words, is to control and then neutralize a threat without resorting to lethal force (though the actual outcome may, on occasion, be lethal). These 'less lethal options' are also designed to minimize the risk of unwarranted injury and any treatment that could be considered torture or cruel, inhuman, or degrading treatment or punishment.[20] The development of 'less lethal options' requires ongoing research. In the UK, this work is being conducted by the Police Scientific Development Branch.

Both, the Israeli police and the Israeli Defence Forces, which exercise a policing function in the Occupied Territories, use rubber bullets. These can be lethal if used at short range and cause great trauma if fired at the head, for example. In May 2002, a group of doctors based in hospitals in Israel published the results of a study examining injuries from rubber bullets sustained by 152 Arab citizens of Israel during riots in early October 2000, at the start of the second Palestinian intifada (Mahajna *et al.*, 2002). The authors examined 201 injuries, and identified the effects of two types of rubber bullet fired by Israeli police, both manufactured by TAAS (Israel Military Industries):

Rubber bullets and plastic baton rounds are controversial 'less lethal' munitions.

- RCC-95, a 'blunt cylindrical missile composed of three metal cores that are coated by a hard rubber shell 0.2cm thick with a diameter of 1.8cm. The bullet is mounted in a special canister that fits on the muzzle of a US-manufactured M-16 assault rifle ... The missile dissociates into its three components after shooting'.
- MA/RA 88, composed of '15 rubber balls with a metal core, each weighing 17g ... When fired, the bullets form a circle with a diameter of 7m at a range of 50m'.

Three of the people in the doctors' study died: two from injuries sustained when rubber bullets entered their brains through an eye; one from post-operative complications. The doctors categorized 71 of the 201 injuries as 'moderately severe' and 38 as 'severe'. They recovered RCC-95 bullets from all of the severe injuries and most of the moderately severe.

This type of inaccurate ammunition—one missile that breaks into three components immediately after firing—and the resulting ricochets evidently make it difficult or impossible to avoid severe injuries to vulnerable body regions such as the head, neck and upper torso, leading to substantial mortality, morbidity, and disability. (Mahajna *et al.*, 2002)

Plastic baton rounds (PBRs) are another controversial 'less lethal option'. Their use by British police in Northern Ireland has resulted in several deaths and injuries, prompting calls for their withdrawal. PBRs are held by a number of police departments worldwide. The Patten Commission on policing reform in Northern Ireland recommended that '[t]heir use should be confined to the smallest necessary number of specially trained officers, who should be trained to think of the weapon in the same way as they would think of a firearm, that is as a weapon which is potentially lethal' (Patten Commission, 1999, para. 9.17).

A British police officer demonstrates a baton gun in August 2002 in Essex, England.

Many alternatives to firearms were considered to be inappropriate by the UK Home Office, but even products approved for police use have attracted criticism. For example, a 1999 report by the UK Police Complaints Authority indicated that, in contravention of relevant guidelines, CS (tear) gas had not been used in self-defence in 40 per cent of the 135 cases it had reviewed (AI, 2001c).

While the use of 'less lethal' weapons by police is intended to reduce police use of firearms, it is unclear whether this is the result. The US-based International Association of Chiefs of Police (IACP) has established a National Police Use of Force Database in an attempt to record the most common types of force used by US police. In 1999–2000, the IACP reported that physical force was the most common type of force used by US police officers, followed by the use of chemical sprays, kinetic impact force (batons), and firearms. During the same period, US police use of chemical force—primarily products using Oleoresin Capsicum (OC), the principal ingredient of pepper spray—exceeded the combined total for electronic (stun guns, taser guns), impact, and firearm force. The IACP argues that as US police have increased their use of chemical force, they have decreased their use of firearms, but this finding is based on reporting from a relatively small number of (mostly municipal) police forces nationwide (IACP, 2001, pp. ii, 9–10).[21]

Although US-produced OC spray has been promoted as a safer, more effective alternative to other chemical agents, there is some concern about its health risks. Since the early 1990s, more than 100 people are reported to have died in custody in the United States after being exposed to OC spray. While other causes, such as drug intoxication or positional asphyxia, have been blamed for most of these deaths, OC spray appears to have contributed to some of them (AI, 2003h, p. 65).

A differentiated range of police equipment with which to apply appropriate minimal force in varying circumstances, as required by the *UN Basic Principles,* is chronically lacking in most developing countries. Police in developing countries

SMALL ARMS SURVEY 2004

usually have to choose between using, or threatening to use, their own bodily strength, handcuffs, a baton or stick, tear gas canisters, or a firearm. This may seem sufficient, but use of force experts argue that police officers need a suitable, non-lethal instrument 'that provides sufficient stand off so that they can outrange a rock thrown by a strong teenager' (Alexander, 2002, p 17).

In Malawi, for example, district police stations, in 2001, still had little elementary equipment, such as adequate protective clothing or means of force other than hands and guns. This problem was compounded by an absence of vehicles, radios, telephones, stationery, and other means needed to organize and record police responses (Wood, 2001).

Clearly, the ability of police forces to meet international standards, such as those spelled out in the *UN Basic Principles*, depends in large measure on the availability of financial and other resources. Equipping police officers with a range of appropriate 'less-than-lethal' means of coercion and rigorously training them in the use of these instruments can be costly. Yet even less developed societies with minimal resources can develop effective policing practices consistent with international standards, given committed police leadership and reasonably good governance and accountability. For example, certain community-based policing initiatives in Botswana, Malawi, and South Africa have seen local communities and police successfully cooperate in the development and implementation of crime reduction plans (AI, 2002f).

SELECTION AND TRAINING

The careful selection and rigorous training of police officers is essential in limiting police misuse of firearms. UN Basic Principle 18 requires governments and law enforcement agencies to:

> ensure that all law enforcement officials are selected by proper screening procedures, have appropriate moral, psychological and physical qualities for the effective exercise of their functions and receive continuous and thorough professional training. Their continued fitness to perform these functions should be subject to periodic review. (UN, 1990)

Pursuant to Basic Principle 19:

> Governments and law enforcement agencies shall ensure that all law enforcement officials are provided with training and are tested in accordance with appropriate proficiency standards in the use of force. Those law enforcement officials who are required to carry firearms should be authorized to do so only upon completion of special training in their use.

Basic Principle 20 stipulates that such training should emphasize 'issues of police ethics and human rights, especially in the investigative process' and 'alternatives to the use of force and firearms, including the peaceful settlements of conflicts, the understanding of crowd behaviour, and ... methods of persuasion, negotiation and mediation'. Basic Principle 20 also calls on law enforcement agencies to 'review their training programmes and operational procedures in the light of particular incidents.'

Other human rights instruments also underline the importance of police training. For example, the third UN *Principle on the Effective Prevention and Investigation of Extra-Legal, Arbitrary and Summary Executions* states:

> Governments shall prohibit orders from superior officers or public authorities authorizing or inciting other persons to carry out ... extralegal, arbitrary or summary executions. All persons shall have the right and the duty to defy such orders. Training of law enforcement officials shall emphasize the above provisions. (UNECOSOC, 1989)

Training is essential in limiting police misuse of firearms.

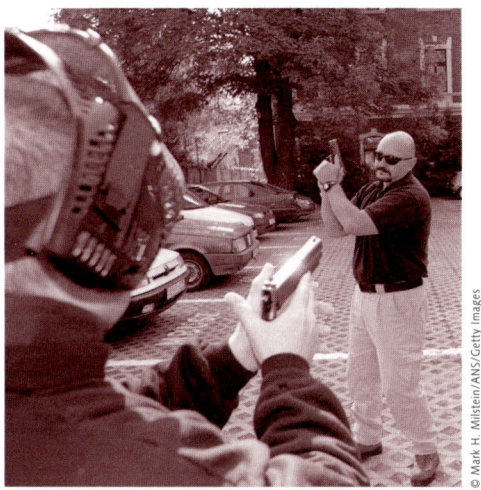

An FBI agent instructs a police officer on appropriate firearm use in threatening situations at an international academy in Hungary.

In many countries, however, relatively little attention is given to the development of police training courses. The translation of international standards into practical instruction is often neglected in favour of technical competence. As a result, while police officers become adept at operating and cleaning their weapons and hitting targets, they are unable to properly assess threat levels and the correct level of force needed in actual incidents. Nor are they taught how to carry out an armed operation with minimum risk.

In the Philippine city of Cebu, 194 of 300 policemen who took a firearms proficiency test reportedly failed (Taghoy, 2003). These officers were required to undergo retraining, and even threatened with dismissal if they did not improve their performance. This training, however, was based solely on shooting accuracy.

In contrast, an effort has been made to provide practical guidance to French police concerning when to use firearms. The principle of proportionality between the means of defence and the seriousness of the threat is explained in the French police training manual:

> If there is the slightest possibility of the police officer avoiding, without serious consequences for himself or others ... an unjustified attack ... he must opt for that solution rather than use his weapon. For example, if a vehicle is driven intentionally at the officer and he has the time and is physically able to move aside ... he should do so rather than use his weapon. Once the vehicle has passed, the criteria for self-defence no longer existing, the use of the weapon by the officer is forbidden.[22]

Many police institutions with colonial roots continue to emphasize more militaristic modes of police training, such as drill and armaments training. Policing institutions in these countries also tend to stress hierarchy and military-type discipline, as opposed to the high level of discretion associated with modern, professional policing. In Indonesia, efforts are now underway to wean the national police force off Suharto-era militarism (see Box 7.4).

> **Box 7.4   Police training in Indonesia**
>
> Following the end of General Suharto's regime in 1998 and the independence of East Timor in 1999, Indonesia's political leaders moved to create a national police force that would take over responsibility for regular law enforcement from the army. During 1999–2001, the national police corps was separated from the Indonesian armed forces and placed under civilian authority.
>
> Training facilities for the new Indonesian National Police were, however, apparently very modest, consisting largely of benches with blackboards and chalk. Training materials and practices at the country's main police college were strongly militaristic in tone, reinforcing 'a trigger-happy approach to the use of force'. New police recruits were given target practice, but no operational training reflecting the requirements of the *UN Basic Principles*.[23]
>
> International observers reported that the whole notion of training in the Indonesian police was poorly regarded. New recruits to the police had often failed to get into the military, which was seen as a more prestigious profession. Consequently, they paid to enter police college, paid for exam papers, and then for postings and promotions. Trainers did not appear to make much money.[24]
>
> In recent years, international donors have directed their attention to the Indonesian police. Assistance programmes with a training component have been conducted by the Australian, Japanese, UK, and US governments, as well as the UN High Commissioner for Human Rights.[25]

Resources for police training are often limited, especially in developing countries. For example, in Zamboanga City, in the Philippines, private gun club members rather than professional firearms officers were allowed to train police because of a lack of public funds. The programme focused on proficiency in hitting targets, as well as firearms handling and safety (*Minda News*, 2003).

Countries with adequate resources do not necessarily have better police training, yet many of the better programmes are in fact found in the developed world. Some police organizations in the North instruct officers in tactics that are useful in averting violence where confrontation is necessary. Several police departments in the United States have developed 'officer survival', 'hostage negotiation', conflict resolution, and verbal skills courses. These have been credited with preventing physical conflict and saving the lives of officers and suspects alike (United States, Department of Justice, 2002).

> **Box 7.5   Firearms training for UK police**[26]
>
> In most UK county police forces, roughly five per cent of trained police are 'authorised firearms officers'. These officers are increasingly trained in a sophisticated range of methods that are broadly compatible with the *UN Basic Principles*.
>
> New firearms officer recruits are selected annually for initial training from a pool of officers who have already completed their two-year probationary period and, in addition, pass certain IQ, health, fitness, and psychological tests. The initial firearms training is very intensive. It takes place over a period of around two weeks, with recruits required to pass a number of additional proficiency tests relating to all aspects of the use of standard issue firearms. The essential elements of the training involve:
>
> ▶ *Technical and mechanical proficiency*, e.g. cleaning and maintaining guns so as to avoid misfires; the safe handling of weapons and ammunition;
> ▶ *Practical and tactical efficiency*, e.g. accurate multi-positional shooting; police firearms tactics;
> ▶ *Applied decision-making*, i.e. meeting the requirements of law, including human rights law, applicable in the UK (e.g. under what conditions can the weapon be aimed and the trigger pulled? How can effective warnings be given before shooting?)
>
> Those who qualify as 'authorised firearms officers' are assigned to the crew of an 'armed response vehicle' where they are mentored and subjected to regular refresher training courses, varying in duration from one day to one week. Experienced firearms officers may graduate, via further higher-level training, to using specialist weapons, or eventually become firearms instructors and commanders of armed-response operations.

POLICING

As civil society organizations become more involved in educating the public about policing and in monitoring certain police actions from a human rights or human security perspective, the need to familiarize civil society representatives in the basic concepts and provisions of the *UN Basic Principles* has become evident. With this goal in mind, NGOs and the Malawi Police Service jointly organized local workshops in 2000–02 to introduce civilian members of the country's many 'Community Policing Forums' to basic policing issues. In an effort to create mutual understanding and respect, the subjects taught included basic standards for the use of force by police and the need for communities to report suspected illegal firearms possession or use.[27]

COMMUNITY LINKS

A positive, helpful, and dynamic relationship between the police and surrounding community greatly diminishes the prospect of the police using excessive force. In its resolution adopting the *UN Code of Conduct*, the UN General Assembly emphasized that law enforcement agencies 'should be representative of and responsive and accountable to the community as a whole' (UNGA, 1979a, para. a). Police selection, recruitment, and career structures often fall short of this standard, however, particularly with regard to women and ethnic minorities.

The UN *Declaration on the Elimination of Violence against Women* requests all states to '[t]ake measures to ensure that law enforcement officers and public officials responsible for implementing policies to prevent, investigate and punish violence against women receive training to sensitize them to the needs of women' (UNGA, 1993). UN standards that promote non-discrimination and protection from sexual harassment require police services to:

- ensure that female officers are able to submit complaints and recommendations on gender-related issues of concern to them;
- discourage gender-insensitive conversations and jokes; and
- review recruitment, hiring, training, and promotion policies to remove any gender bias. (UN, OHCHR, 2002b)

Institutional practice along such lines cannot be effectively organized without recruiting and training women police officers at all levels of command. Rather than mainstreaming female officers into all parts of the police service, however, some countries tend to deploy them to 'vulnerable persons units' or 'victim support units', which specialize in domestic violence and child abuse. Such assignments do not take their skills or suitability for such work into consideration.

An armed Pakistani policewoman guards the venue of a forthcoming summit in Islamabad in January 2004.

The extent to which ethnic minorities are represented in police forces is another key determinant of the police–community relationship. A 1998 report by the UN Special Rapporteur on Extrajudicial, Summary or Arbitrary Executions states that:

> Many [US] police departments are trying to have a more balanced ethnic representation among their personnel in an effort to make them more representative of the local population. The Special Rapporteur was informed that in Miami, 50 per cent of the police officers are Hispanic, 25 per cent are African American and 25 per cent white. ... Balancing the composition of police departments according to the ethnic distribution of the local population may also have a positive impact in reducing allegations of racial bias. (UN, Commission on Human Rights, 1998)

'Community-based policing', involving the cultivation of decentralized, co-operative, and consultative ties between police forces and the communities they serve, gradually emerged in the UK and United States in the 1970s and 1980s.[28] A 1999 report indicated that 75 per cent of police chiefs in a large, representative sample of US departments said they were relatively far along in implementing this 'new paradigm' (Parks et al., 1999).

For example, beginning in the mid-1990s, the Boston Police Department launched a strategic planning process involving community stakeholders. Both supporters and critics of the department were asked to identify problems in their neighbourhoods and contribute to the development of crime-fighting strategies. City-wide surveys were conducted to assess levels of fear and gather recommendations for improved policing. In an effort to improve diversity, almost 300 new officers were added to the ranks of the force in 1994–99. Training for new recruits and serving officers emphasized the importance of respect and civility in police interactions with the public. The Boston police claim a decline in complaints of nearly 50 per cent against officers during this time.[29]

Police in Maryland similarly contend that an emphasis on police courtesy in dealings with citizens improved public attitudes towards the force. This approach did not preclude 'aggressive enforcement', so long as the latter was backed up by intensive officer training.[30] Nevertheless, as discussed below, such changes occurred against a backdrop of federal government scrutiny.

The use of force and firearms can be reduced where the police pursue policies and practices that have the consent of the public—especially the poor, who are the most vulnerable, and often the most alienated from the police. Where partnerships with the public are developed in undemocratic or factional ways, however, poor and vulnerable groups may be excluded. Some partnership institutions have consequently fallen under the sway of powerful local groups and political associations which seek to influence these institutions (and ultimately the police) for their own ends. Preventing the exclusion or domination of particular groups or interests requires careful stakeholder analysis and the prudent development of partnership relationships.[31]

Where police forces have persistently used excessive or inappropriate force, especially with firearms, they have been slow to adopt community-based policing strategies. Senior police management and politicians have been afraid that such policing, while useful in terms of enhancing the public image of police forces, could undermine their effectiveness in combating crime. Despite some success in integrating community-based policing into training programmes, many forces have failed to understand that such an approach requires a radical change in police–public relationships. Frequently, the police have preferred to set the terms for public involvement, as opposed to negotiating these; and many projects have not secured the participation of all stakeholders.[32]

POLICING

Many police forces have been slow to fully integrate community-based policing into their policies and practices. Projects aimed at lessening dependence on force and firearms have failed to consider the needs and interests of those most vulnerable to crime and to develop full partnerships with these groups. Some new projects in South Africa show that, with relatively strong government, police, and public commitment, it is possible to build effective police–public partnership institutions and to begin to develop a different approach to policing. Yet, where vulnerable groups (the poor, ethnic groups, women) have been marginalized or excluded, such efforts have had minimal impact on crime rates or police dependence on firearms.

Two different cases, both in urban South Africa, illustrate this point.[33] Kwamashu township and surrounding area in Durban, with roughly one million residents, has been plagued by unemployment and high levels of violence for many years. Criminal gangs armed with firearms have become entrenched in this area. In the late 1990s, there were relatively few local police, and their equipment and training was quite poor. In 1999, the South African government began 'Operation Ventilation'. This involved house-to-house sweeps by heavily armed police in armoured vehicles, from outside the township, but low levels of cooperation with existing local police. The result was that, by February 2000, very few firearms had been recovered, gang violence was just as pervasive, and police morale was very low.

In contrast, the Police Task Team sent in to Edendale township, in Pietermaritzburg, adopted a community-based policing strategy with an intelligence-led anti-firearms programme. Edendale, another large, low-income township, faced high levels of armed violence of a political nature during the late apartheid and immediate post-apartheid period, and now confronts increasing violence perpetrated by organized criminal gangs. The Police Task Team, formed in early 2000, was made up of highly trained officers from other parts of South Africa, as well as a significant number of local police officers trusted by the community. Consequently, the Task Team obtained extremely valuable information on the activities and whereabouts of the armed gangs, resulting in a high number of arrests.

As the leader of the Edendale Police Task Team recounted in 2002:

> Apartheid policing broke down community trust of the state. Under the new democratic government, crime escalated—we saw running gun battles between gangs—until community-based policing took root. After four years, we have solved over 500 murder cases, recovered stolen vehicles and confiscated illegal weapons—AK-47s, handguns, shotguns, rifles and home-made pipe-guns. Police officers are responding rapidly to community reports, trying to avoid the use of firearms.[34]

Another South African scheme points to the success of community-based approaches. Police and community leaders in Cator Manor, a former squatter camp in Durban, adopted a strategy very similar to that used in Edendale. This resulted in a significant reduction in armed and other violence by both community residents and police.[35]

FIREARM STORAGE

UN Basic Principle 11(d) requires governments to develop guidelines that '[r]egulate the control, storage and issuing of firearms, including procedures for ensuring that law enforcement officials are accountable for the firearms and ammunition issued to them' (UN, 1990). This provision is routinely ignored in many countries. For example, firearms and ammunition may be issued to police officers without adequate recording of gun and ammunition markings, or there may be no

International standards regarding the storage and record-keeping of police firearms are routinely ignored in many countries.

comprehensive system for reviewing the security and effectiveness of equipment, or any means of safely storing and guarding it. In 2003, an audit of firearms control laws in 12 of the countries belonging to the Southern African Development Community (SADC)[36] found that only Mauritius and South Africa had legislation providing for the control and management of state firearm stockpiles, notwithstanding widespread concern over leakages of state holdings (Cross, *et al.*, 2003).

> **Box 7.6   Failure to safeguard police weapons in the Solomon Islands**
>
> Armed conflict broke out in the Solomon Islands at the end of 1998, with native Guadalcanal men attacking a second group, originally from the island of Malaita, on the main island of Guadalcanal. Malaitans formed their own militia, the Malaita Eagle Force (MEF), and in January and June 2000 staged separate raids on police armouries on both Malaita and Guadalcanal islands, gaining possession of high-powered assault rifles.
>
> The seizure of weapons from the armouries was principally the result of complicity between many members of the paramilitary police force and the MEF, but police advisers who subsequently visited the storage facilities indicated that their rudimentary nature had greatly facilitated the thefts. The Police Act contained no clear rules on the storage of weapons or indeed professional standards for the conduct of police. By mid-2000, the police service was effectively no longer functioning on the islands of Guadalcanal and Malaita, as MEF members had deprived it of almost all weapons, most vehicles, and equipment.
>
> Not surprisingly, law and order had broken down, leaving the population vulnerable to the excesses of paramilitary groups and criminal opportunists. The Townsville Peace Agreement (TPA), signed in October 2000, established an International Peace Monitoring Team and local Peace Monitoring Council, and provided for the disarmament of combatants. The TPA brought about a cessation of overt violence, but serious law and order problems, including human rights violations, persisted. In mid-2003, an international peacekeeping force led by Australia was assisting with the implementation of the TPA.

PERSONS IN CUSTODY OR DETENTION

Rules for the use of force and firearms by law enforcement officials also apply after arrests have been made and convictions secured. UN Basic Principle 15 states that:

> Law enforcement officials, in their relations with persons in custody or detention, shall not use force, except when strictly necessary for the maintenance of security and order within the institution, or when personal safety is threatened. (UN, 1990)

UN Basic Principle 16 specifies that these officials shall not use firearms against detainees 'except in self-defence or in the defence of others against the immediate threat of death or serious injury', or when strictly necessary to prevent the escape of a person in custody or detention who presents a grave threat to life.

The *Principles on the Effective Prevention and Investigation of Extra-legal, Arbitrary and Summary Executions* are also relevant:

> In order to prevent extra-legal, arbitrary and summary executions, Governments shall ensure strict control, including a clear chain of command over all officials responsible for apprehension, arrest, detention, custody and imprisonment, as well as those officials authorized by law to use force and firearms (UNECOSOC, 1989, Principle 2).

Extrajudicial execution remains a problem in many parts of the world.

Extrajudicial execution remains a problem in many parts of the world. Mozambique is a case in point. In late 2001 and early 2002, there were allegations that police officers were removing detainees from their place of custody and extrajudicially executing them. Three detainees were reportedly shot by police in December 2001 (AI, 2002c).

In order to ensure that weapons do not fall into the hands of prisoners, current thinking argues against the carrying of firearms by staff, including police, in prisons. Officials who need to be armed should be well trained and have a clear understanding of the circumstances in which they may use their firearms (Coyle, 2002, p. 28). This approach is reflected in Rule 54(3) of the UN *Standard Minimum Rules for the Treatment of Prisoners,* which states:

> Except in special circumstances, staff performing duties which bring them into direct contact with prisoners should not be armed. Furthermore, staff should in no circumstances be provided with arms unless they have been trained in their use. (UNECOSOC, 1955)

This rule is even more stringent when applied to juvenile prisoners and detainees—i.e., those less than 18 years old. According to the *UN Rules for the Protection of Juveniles Deprived of their Liberty,* 'The carrying and use of weapons by personnel should be prohibited in any facility where juveniles are detained' (UNGA, 1990, rule 65).

Police shoot at inmates during a raid at a prison in Guatemala in April 2003. One guard and three inmates were killed in the clash.

UK prison regulations are consistent with the *UN Basic Principles* in that they allow the lethal use of firearms only where there is an immediate and clearly perceived threat to human life. Thus, in the UK, an officer cannot use a firearm simply because a prisoner is escaping (Coyle, 2002, p. 28). The standards of many countries fall well short of the requirements found in the *UN Basic Principles*. A particular problem is the present lack of international standards governing the use of firearms during inmate insurrections. Such situations, involving a risk of serious harm to police, wardens, and other persons, also pose a threat of firearms misuse by security personnel. The *UN Basic Principles* relating to firearm use and policing of unlawful assemblies can, however, be applied in such situations to reduce the risk of abuses.

> **Box 7.7 Killings of prisoners in Brazil**
>
> In September 2002, Brazil's Carandiru prison complex was closed. The prison achieved widespread notoriety in October 1992, when members of the São Paulo military police killed 111 inmates following a riot at the prison.
>
> Similar violence was averted in February 2001, when human rights observers and Brazilian politicians helped negotiate an end to a prisoner rebellion at 29 detention centres throughout São Paulo state. While 16 inmates died during the revolt, these deaths were mostly the result of prisoner-on-prisoner violence (AI, 2001b, 2002a, 2003a).
>
> In early 2004, the UN Special Rapporteur on Extrajudicial, Summary or Arbitrary Executions pointed to an apparent decline in deaths in custody in São Paulo and Rio de Janeiro state prisons in recent years, but she also noted that judicial or other enquiries into such deaths were, in general, 'superficially carried out' (UN, Commission on Human Rights, 2004).

POLITICAL MANIPULATION

State repression of fundamental political and civil rights usually involves the threat—though not necessarily the use—of deliberate and arbitrary force that contravenes the spirit of the *UN Code of Conduct* and the letter of such instruments as the *UN Basic Principles* and the *Principles on the Effective Prevention and Investigation of Extra-Legal, Arbitrary and Summary Executions*.

The political manipulation of police or other public security forces will often involve the use of force and firearms for the express purpose of suppressing political opposition. For example, the Government of Zimbabwe has reportedly used youth militia, sometimes armed, to attack and even kill actual or perceived opposition supporters. These militia have seized control of some rural areas, denying access to the political opposition, especially during elections (AI, 2002e).[37] Under Zimbabwe's Public Order and Security Act, police have also been granted the power to restrict the movement of anyone above the age of 16 if they are unable to produce their identity documents. Police can easily misuse this provision to intimidate and discourage people from attending political gatherings and rallies (AI, 2003d).

In some countries, the use of excessive force by armed police at the behest of political authorities may be primarily intended as a public demonstration of unrestrained state power. Police can also be used to uphold the rule of authoritarian regimes (rather than the rule of law) under the guise of 'fighting violent crime'. Militaristic policing methods involving flagrant violations of international standards may, in fact, have political aims, though they are presented as a response to citizens' concerns over violence and crime. Moreover, the boundaries between politics and crime

> **Box 7.8 Crackdown on drug dealers in Thailand**
>
> On 28 January 2003, the Prime Minister of Thailand, Thaksin Shinawatra, announced the government was launching a three-month 'war on drugs'. Yet this campaign was soon criticized as 'a de facto shoot-to-kill policy of anyone believed to be involved in the drugs trade' (AI, 2003b). By 24 April, more than 2,270 alleged drug criminals had reportedly been killed since the start of the crackdown on 1 February. According to Thai police sources, 51 of these had been killed by police in self-defence, with the rest dying in battles among dealers. More than 50,000 suspected drug traffickers had been arrested (Adams, 2003).
>
> International observers, including Amnesty International, the Asian Legal Resource Centre, and Human Rights Watch (HRW), rejected government claims that drug dealers were killing each other. They attributed the high number of casualties to a combination of financial incentives and government pressure on police to 'produce results'(AI, 2003b). In their view, disregard for the lives of alleged drug traffickers had also been fostered by incendiary remarks made by high-ranking government officials, including the Prime Minister. Subsequent investigation of the shooting incidents was widely perceived as inadequate, with active obstruction by the authorities reported in certain cases (Adams, 2003; AI, 2003g; Asian Legal Resource Centre, 2003).

may be deliberately blurred. One study of crime in transitional societies noted: 'Generally, ... police in authoritarian regimes made an effort to control some aspects of criminal behaviour, although in most cases there was an overlap between what constituted a crime and what was the stuff of politics' (Shaw, 2002, p. 27).

CORRUPTION AND CRIMINALITY

Police corruption and criminality can have a major impact on the control and use of firearms. Article 7 of the *UN Code of Conduct* requires law enforcement officials to 'rigorously oppose and combat' corruption, while paragraph (a) of the Commentary to this Article calls for the full enforcement of the law regarding any official who commits an act of corruption (UNGA, 1979b). UN Basic Principle 1 requires governments to 'keep the ethical issues associated with the use of force and firearms constantly under review' (UN, 1990). This is not mere rhetoric. The rule of law, which rests on impartial and accountable policing, can be fatally undermined where police institutions are riddled with corruption.[38]

> Corruption among low-ranking police officers can undermine efforts to control access to and use of firearms.

Corruption among low-ranking police officers can sometimes directly undermine efforts to control access to and use of firearms. For example, in northern Kenya, an inadequate state presence has led to the arming of local pastoral communities through the 'home guard' system or as Kenya Police Reservists (KPR). In some districts, the 'home guards' or KPR act on behalf of powerful individuals. The KPR often become alternative sources of small arms supply, compounding the problem of insecurity. In recent years, some of the KPR have themselves become involved in banditry and arms trafficking at the local level (HRW, 2002; Khadiagala, 2003).

Arguably, where police officers are deeply involved in organized crime, they will be more inclined to resort to the use of lethal force to protect their interests. This appears to be the case in Indonesia, where an international environmental group has implicated both police and military in illegal logging activities (EIA and Telapak, 2003). Armed police have allegedly tortured and arbitrarily arrested individuals they accuse of carrying out attacks on logging companies. In 2001, 27 people arrested during such operations claimed they were tortured; they were given jail terms after unfair trials. As of the end of 2002, no investigation had been carried out into their allegations (AI, 2003a).

Death squads with links to police reportedly operate in several parts of Brazil. In many cases, these groups are involved in organized criminal activity, including drug trafficking and extortion. In the coastal state of Espírito Santo, for example, death squads are said to have penetrated all branches of the state government. While several investigations have been carried out on these groups over the past decade, their impact has been limited to date. In March 2003, a judge who was presiding over several cases against members of one squad was murdered. He had received repeated threats against his life (UN, Commision on Human Rights, 2004, paras 42–7).

CROWD CONTROL

Demonstrations, especially violent ones, pose a formidable challenge to police forces around the world. On the one hand, police are asked to confront specific threats to life, limb, and property; on the other hand, they must limit their use of force and firearms to what is strictly necessary and proportional in the circumstances.

A lesson in crowd control: Czech police officers in riot gear train in August 2000.

UN Basic Principle 13 requires law enforcement officials who are dispersing unlawful, but non-violent, assemblies to avoid the use of force. If force needs to be used, for example, to secure the safety of others, they are to use the minimum amount of force necessary (UN, 1990). According to Basic Principle 14, '[i]n the dispersal of violent assemblies, law enforcement officials may use firearms only when less dangerous means are not practicable and only to the minimum extent necessary.' Basic Principle 14 specifies that any use of firearms in these circumstances is governed by the general principles examined earlier. Police officers can therefore use firearms to defend themselves, demonstrators, or members of the public 'against the imminent threat of death or serious injury' (Basic Principle 9). But they cannot use firearms for the sole purpose of dispersing an unlawful assembly, even where violent (Basic Principle 14).

This rule can be difficult to apply in extreme circumstances, where the actions of a group of individuals may, as a group, pose an imminent threat to life, but police cannot distinguish between those who pose the threat and those who do not. A few examples serve to show the range of contexts in which police have resorted to firearms to control (sometimes violent) crowds and the varying responses by governments to these events.

Police in Mauritius were accused of using excessive force in response to demonstrations that followed the death in custody of a well-known singer in February 1999. Three people were shot dead, at least one by the police, with many others injured. The resulting government inquiry criticized police handling of the protests (AI, 2002f).

Box 7.9 Crowd control in Belize

The Belize government and police have conducted several investigations of disputed police shootings in recent years, including in situations involving crowd control. In November 2002, for example, the Solicitor General reviewed a case of alleged excessive use of force by police during a demonstration by civilians from the Cayo District of Belize. On 24 April 2002, 200–250 demonstrators, including schoolchildren in uniform, assembled to protest against fare increases imposed by bus operators.[39] The demonstration was authorized, but apparently took place after the agreed time. A section of the crowd demanded that police allow them to march to one of the bus companies, but the police refused, citing the stoning of the company's premises on 19 April. The refusal prompted some 100 demonstrators to throw stones, bottles, and sticks at the police, inflicting minor injuries on 29 police officers. According to the police version of events, officers then fired warning shots into the air. Nevertheless, a 15-year-old student was reportedly shot in the chest, and another in the leg. In addition, three other demonstrators were severely beaten. Police or friends took the injured to nearby hospitals, and some civilians were arrested and charged. As of mid-2003, this incident was still being reviewed by the Solicitor General.[40]

A highly controversial aspect of public order policing in Northern Ireland has been the use of plastic baton rounds in place of regular ammunition. PBRs were introduced into the UK police service in the 1970s, replacing rubber bullets. The Patten Report (1999) indicated that a total of 41,657 PBRs had been discharged by police and 14,572 by the UK army in Northern Ireland since 1981. Eleven deaths and 615 injuries were attributed to PBRs during this period, with the last death occurring in 1989 (Patten Commission, 1999, p. 54).

PBRs are also held by police services in mainland Britain, as well as Canada and the United States. Rather than being employed in public order policing, however, they are used against individuals posing a threat of death or serious injury to police or others—as in many hostage-taking incidents. Their utilization against rioters in Northern Ireland can be explained by the rioters' use of petrol bombs, blast bombs, and firearms against police. Crowd control methods requiring close proximity between police and rioters, such as baton charges or the use of mounted police, are ineffective in such situations (Patten Commission, 1999, p. 54). Northern Ireland police have emphasized that PBRs are only employed against 'individuals behaving in a way that brings risk to life', not for crowd control in a broader sense.[41]

The use of CS (tear) gas canisters has also proven controversial in Northern Ireland. As noted by the Patten Commission, they are relatively indiscriminate in their effects. While useful in dispersing crowds, they may also affect innocent bystanders and people in their homes. They cannot be used against particular individuals posing a specific threat to public order and safety (Patten Commission, 1999, p. 54).

> **Box 7.10   Attempted reform of crowd control in Indonesia**
>
> During 2000, an expatriate training adviser introduced modern policing techniques for crowd control to the Indonesian police. In line with the requirements of the *UN Basic Principles,* the role of firearms was minimized. Instead of placing armed police officers at the front of a police line—which increases the chances of police shooting unruly, but unarmed, demonstrators—police with assault rifles were placed at the rear, behind another line of police in protective clothing carrying shields and batons. At the very front, lightly clothed police without guns talked and engaged with the crowd. These methods were credited with the absence of deaths or serious injuries in demonstrations outside the Indonesian Parliament in August 2001.[42]
>
> Nevertheless, there are reports of police later dealing brutally with other protesters. On 19 August 2002, two trade unionists were apparently shot and seriously injured by police in Bandung, the capital of West Java, during large peaceful demonstrations against two proposed labour laws (HRW, 2003a).

VULNERABLE PERSONS

International human rights standards have increasingly addressed the specific needs of especially vulnerable groups of people, such as women, children, and minorities. These standards have implications for conduct by police and other state actors.[43]

Under the terms of the UN *Declaration on the Elimination of Violence against Women,* 'States should pursue by all appropriate means and without delay a policy of eliminating violence against women', whether physical, sexual, or psychological in nature, and whether occurring in public or private life (UNGA, 1993, arts 1, 4). In particular, states are to:

> Take measures to ensure that law enforcement officers and public officials responsible for implementing policies to prevent, investigate and punish violence against women receive training to sensitize them to the needs of women. (art. 4(i))

Nonetheless, Human Rights Watch has reported that violence against women, often facilitated and perpetrated by police, was a prominent aspect of the sectarian violence that swept through the Indian state of Gujarat in February–March 2002 (HRW, 2003c, pp. 27–30).

The *UN Code of Conduct for Law Enforcement Officials* acknowledges the need to protect children[44] from the excessive use of force by police: 'The use of firearms is considered an extreme measure. Every effort should be made to exclude the use of firearms, especially against children' (UNGA, 1979b, art. 3, commentary c). This provision is reflected in police regulations at the national level. For example, Cincinnati police rules stipulate: 'A police officer will not discharge a firearm at a person known to be or suspected of being a juvenile (person less than 18 years of age)' except in self-defence, meaning the defence of the police officer or others from a threat of 'death or serious physical harm' (Cincinnati Police Department, 2003).

Nevertheless, there have been persistent reports of police shootings of children in certain countries—for example, Honduras. The UN Special Rapporteur on Extrajudicial, Summary or Arbitrary Executions travelled to the country in August 2001 to investigate allegations of extrajudicial executions of a large number of children from 1998–2000. She concluded that it was 'abundantly clear that children have been killed in Honduras by members of the security forces. In most of the cases the child was unarmed and did not provoke the police to use force, let alone lethal force.' These killings, she added, were fostered by a climate of 'institutionalized impunity' that rendered investigations, trials, and convictions in these cases exceptional (UN, Commission on Human Rights, 2002, para. 73).

> Police mistreatment of ethnic minorities is a recurring problem in many countries.

Police mistreatment of ethnic minorities is a recurring problem in many countries. In Greece, allegations of human rights violations committed by police officers from the mid-1990s to mid-2002 included eight cases of fatal shootings. Persons with vulnerable social identities made up most of the victims: three Roma, two ethnic Albanians, a 17-year-old Serbian high school student, a Pontic Greek, and a member of the majority Greek population. Human rights groups reported that no police officers were convicted of torture or ill-treatment between 1996 and 2000. Judicial bodies handed down decisions in five cases of fatal police shootings from January 2000 to June 2002. In two of these cases, no indictments were brought against the officers concerned. While the other three cases produced convictions for manslaughter, two of the accompanying prison sentences were suspended, while the third (four-and-a-half years) was subsequently appealed. As of the end of June 2002, no indictments had been issued in connection with a series of border incidents cited by these organizations (AI and IHF, 2002).

The UN has begun to promote Guidelines for Command and Supervisory Officials in police training. These emphasize, among other things, the responsibility of police commanders and supervisors to 'issue clear orders on the special vulnerability and protective needs of refugees and non-nationals' and to 'develop cooperative schemes with community representatives to combat racist and xenophobic violence and intimidation' (UN, OHCHR, 2002b, p. 167).

Human rights groups have documented the police harassment and abuse of sexual minorities (homosexuals, bisexuals, or transgendered persons) in, for example, Egypt and southern Africa. Firearms are often used as instruments of intimidation or coercion in these cases (HRW, 2004; HRW and IGLHRC, 2003). Moreover, it appears that some law enforcement officials have failed to protect sexual minorities in their custody from violence. They have also failed to provide needed assistance to victims or witnesses of hate crimes against sexual minorities. In some instances, police have further mistreated those who have reported such violence to the authorities (AI, 2001d; HRW, 2001b).

Police are frequently called to scenes involving mentally disabled people; however, police rules and practices regarding the use of force and firearms do not usually reflect their particular circumstances. On 20 September 2000, two police officers shot to death a 28-year-old mentally disabled man of Vietnamese origin in a wooded area near the town of Ulm, Germany. The man was a long-term resident of a home for the mentally disabled and had been reported missing earlier in the afternoon. The two officers reportedly shot at the man 21 times, hitting him eight times. It appears they used little or no restraint in using their firearms against a suspect who had not fired upon them. The 'gun' he was carrying was, in fact, a toy (AI, 2001a).

Once a suspect has been shot and the threat they posed ended, they become a vulnerable person to whom police owe a duty of care. Basic Principle 5(c) stipulates that '[l]aw enforcement officials shall … [e]nsure that assistance and medical aid are rendered to any injured or affected persons at the earliest possible moment' (UN, 1990).

If basic first aid is not provided, minor gunshot wounds may become fatal injuries. In East Timor, for instance, recruits to the new (post-independence) police force received no training in treating gun-shot wound trauma, nor were they equipped with battle dressings, despite being armed and frequently posted to locations where there was little or no possibility of trauma assistance.[45]

OVERSIGHT SYSTEMS

Systems designed to oversee the use of force and firearms by police officers and hold the latter accountable for improper or illegal conduct are essential in curbing abuses and upholding the rule of law generally.

The *UN Basic Principles* stress the need for prompt reporting of incidents involving the use of force or firearms. Basic Principle 6 requires police officers promptly to inform their superiors of any injury or death caused by their use of force and firearms (UN, 1990). Basic Principle 11(f), more broadly, requires governments to '[p]rovide for a system of reporting whenever law enforcement officials use firearms in the performance of their duty.'

Prompt reporting is only one step in the overall process. In many cases, an internal investigation is required. External review of police actions—by other branches of the government, including the judiciary—is also an essential element of the broader system. Basic Principle 22 requires governments and law enforcement agencies to establish effective reporting and review procedures for all incidents in which injury or death is caused by the use of force and firearms by police, or where the latter use firearms in the performance of their duty. Government and police authorities must also 'ensure that an effective review process is available and that independent administrative or prosecutorial authorities are in a position to exercise jurisdiction in appropriate circumstances.'

Basic Principle 23 specifies that persons affected by the police use of force and firearms or their legal representatives 'shall have access to an independent process, including a judicial process.'

Accountability of superior officers is essential to preventing the misuse of firearms by subordinates. Basic Principle 24 states:

> Governments and law enforcement agencies shall ensure that superior officers are held responsible if they know, or should have known, that law enforcement officials under their command are resorting, or have resorted, to the unlawful use of force and firearms, and they did not take all measures in their power to prevent, suppress or report such use.[46]

This principle does not absolve individual police officers of responsibility for the unlawful use of force and firearms. Basic Principle 26 stipulates that '[o]bedience to superior orders shall be no defence' to such conduct. Basic Principle 25 specifies that governments and law enforcement agencies shall not punish police officers who refuse to carry out an order to use force or firearms that is in conflict with UN policing standards, or who report such use by other officers.

The *UN Basic Principles* stress the need for prompt reporting of incidents involving the use of force or firearms.

SMALL ARMS SURVEY 2004

> **Box 7.11   Unlawful police shootings in Jamaica**
>
> Since at least 1983, Jamaica has seen an exceptionally high rate of police killings. In 2003, Jamaican police took the lives of 114 people, yet trials of officers accused of unlawful killings are exceedingly rare. Police describe most fatal shootings as the result of exchanges of gunfire that were initiated by armed civilians. It is true that Jamaica has a high level of crime and police officers face armed criminals daily, often leaving them no alternative but the use of lethal force to protect their own lives and those of the public. There were 1,045 murders in Jamaica during 2002. Sixteen of the dead were officers of the Jamaica Constabulary Force. Others were seriously injured. At least 112 police officers were killed between 1991 and 2001 (AI, 2001d, 2004).
>
> Nonetheless, human rights groups have documented many incidents that point to indiscriminate fire by the Jamaican police (HRW, 2001c). Such abuses are apparently a particular feature of 'emergency' anti-crime operations, which have involved the use of paramilitary-style tactics since 1999. Per capita rates of police killings indicate that Jamaican police kill at a rate almost five times that of their counterparts in South Africa, a country also suffering from high levels of violent crime (AI, 2001d).
>
> The 'Braeton Seven' incident has contributed, more than any other case, to publicizing the problem of Jamaican police killings. On 14 March 2001, armed police officers from the Crime Management Unit (CMU) approached a house in Braeton to arrest one of its occupants. A short time later, seven boys and young men aged between 15 and 20 (the 'Braeton Seven') were shot dead. The police subsequently claimed they came under heavy fire from within the house. Yet neighbours said they heard the boys pleading for their lives before being shot one at a time (AI, 2003c).
>
> In April–June 2003, following an intense campaign by human rights groups, as well as diplomatic interventions from several governments, the Jamaican government committed itself to a series of measures designed to prevent and punish unlawful police killings. These included:
>
> - improving autopsies on civilians killed by police;
> - reducing the backlog in Coroner's Court inquiries into police killings;
> - explicitly and publicly stating that unlawful killings by police officers will not be tolerated;
> - publicly requesting the Director of Public Prosecutions to decide whether to prosecute members of the CMU involved in the 'Braeton Seven' shootings;
> - seeking and receiving expert assistance from the Canadian, UK, and US governments in investigating the killing of four persons in Crawle by CMU officers on 7 May 2003; and
> - disbanding the CMU (AI, 2003e).

While most states around the world have established systems to oversee and review the use of force and firearms by police, there are considerable variations worldwide, especially with respect to actual practice. The robustness and independence of investigations, and the transparency with which they are conducted, differ considerably. Independent judicial review is often lacking. Even if low-ranking officers are punished for firearm misuse, their superiors may escape justice.

The excessive use of force by police, including unjustified shootings, has been a problem in many parts of the United States (HRW, 1998). In 1994, the US Congress authorized the Justice Department to conduct investigations into city police departments alleged to have committed systematic civil rights violations. Where investigators decide that changes are needed to police practices, the Justice Department can either negotiate an agreement with the city for the implementation of necessary reforms or file a lawsuit to force changes. As of September 2002, the Justice Department had agreements or consent decrees for eight cities.

Agreements were reached in 2002 with Cincinnati, Ohio, and Buffalo, New York. The Cincinnati investigation followed protests and rioting that were sparked by the shooting of an unarmed African-American man, Timothy Thomas, in April 2001. The Cincinnati agreement required the police department to institute improvements in a wide range of areas, including complaint procedures, training, use-of-force policies, and supervision. The agreement with the Buffalo Police Department focused on the force's improper use of pepper spray, complaint procedures, use-of-force reporting procedures, and training (IHF, 2003).

Box 7.12   Investigative procedures in the UK

Recent police reforms in the UK[47] have included changes designed to improve accountability. For example, the ACPO firearms guidance manual has been published (UK, ACPO, 2001) with only a few tactical sections removed from public view. UK citizens are now able to ascertain their rights and responsibilities, along with those of the UK police, with respect to the use of force and firearms.

Under procedures in force in 2003, any use of force by police that results in the death of a person will usually culminate in a formal Public Inquest by a public coroner. The purpose of the Coroner's Court is to establish the cause of death and not apportion blame or determine guilt.

In addition to the civil remedies they may have in the UK court system, victims can make complaints against individual officers through the UK Police Service's complaints procedure (UK, ACPO, 2001, ch. 6). Investigations of complaints are usually conducted by the police agency directly concerned. Depending on the situation, however, another UK police force, usually from another county, may carry out the investigation in order to enhance its independence.

Any instance during which UK police officers discharge a firearm while on duty is usually voluntarily referred to the Police Complaints Authority under Section 71 of the Police Act 1996. If death or serious injury results, this referral is mandatory. The Authority approves the appointment of an Investigating Officer (nominated by the relevant Chief Officer) and oversees the investigation.

These investigations tend to be wide-ranging, examining not only the specific circumstances of the firearms injury or death, but also the circumstances leading to the shooting and other surrounding factors. Among the issues that may need to be investigated are:

1. **Intelligence:** What intelligence or evidence was available before the operation and who was in possession of it? What decisions were taken as a result and why? What steps were taken to verify the information?
2. **Briefing:** Was available information accurately relayed at the briefing, or subsequently as events unfolded?
3. **Authorization:** Who granted the authority for the issue of firearms? Who authorized the operation (if different)?
4. **Threat/risk assessment:** What assessments were carried out? What conclusions were reached?
5. **Armed Response Vehicles (ARVs):** What use was made of ARVs? What were their terms of reference in the relevant police force?
6. **Firearms Teams:** What use was made of Firearms Teams? What were their terms of reference in the relevant police force?
7. **Specialist munitions:** Were any used—shotgun or tear gas rounds, distraction devices, shotgun breaching rounds—and what internal Force instructions exist for their use?
8. **Command structure:** Who occupied which positions within the structure?
9. **Strategy:** What was the strategic intention of the 'Gold Commander' (the most senior officer in charge of strategy, policy, and tactics)?
10. **Tactical parameters:** Were any set by the 'Gold Commander'? What were they?
11. **Tactical plan:** What tactical options did the 'Silver Commander' (the officer in charge of policy and tactics) consider? What was the reasoning behind the decisions that were taken?
12. **Negotiator:** Was one used? What was his or her input?
13. **Tactical advisor:** Was one used? What was his or her input?
14. **Rendezvous points:** Where were they?
15. **Communications:** What arrangements were made?
16. **Records:** Is there any video footage/photographs of the incident?
17. **Medical:** What were the paramedic/ambulance/first aid training arrangements? How was the police duty of care to the injured person met?
18. **Scene management:** What steps were taken to preserve public safety?
19. **Tours of duty:** What were their lengths?
20. **Firearms training:** Were police officers authorized to use the particular weapon(s) they were carrying or fired? What records relating to firearms training are available?
21. **Fitness:** Are records of health/eyesight/fitness tests available? (UK, ACPO, 2001)

Although the Police Complaints Authority monitors these investigative procedures and distributes leaflets telling citizens how to file a complaint, the system has been criticized for a lack of independence. For example, in a May 2001 case concerning alleged violations of the right to life by UK security forces in Northern Ireland, the European Court of Human Rights found that investigating police officers were not sufficiently independent of the accused officers whose conduct they were examining (European Court of Human Rights, 2001).

The costs of establishing and maintaining effective investigative and judicial review bodies are significant. Governments of developed countries can devote greater resources to the development and operation of such systems, yet these do not always function well. In 1999, for instance, Amnesty International concluded that courts in France 'feel uneasy about convicting police officers for crimes of violence or excessive force to anything but nominal sentences' (AI, 1999). While it is more difficult for less-developed countries to find the necessary funds, they sometimes prioritize the effective oversight of policing. Even more important than the question of resources is a government's commitment to international human rights norms.

> A government's commitment to international human rights is essential to the establishment of effective oversight systems.

The Constitution of Mauritius, for instance, contains human rights guarantees that prohibit arbitrary arrest and detention, along with torture and inhuman treatment. In 1999, the police established a Complaints Investigation Bureau, which investigates allegations of abuses by police officers. A National Human Rights Commission, set up in 2001, oversees these investigations. At least 13 deaths in police custody occurring between January 1996 and April 2002, some the result of police shootings, have been or are the subject of judicial inquiries (AI, 2002 f).

POST-CONFLICT REFORM

Police reform in the aftermath of conflict has a mixed history. Reform efforts conducted since the end of the Cold War, though useful in many respects, have often failed to yield lasting change consistent with international policing standards. Two of the largest UN-supervised transitions, conducted in Namibia in 1989–90 and Mozambique in 1993–94, included limited police reforms; nevertheless, post-transition reviews of police practice in these countries found that police still tended to use excessive force (AI, 2002 f).[48] Likewise, in El Salvador, national laws and training programmes for police were not fully reformed following the 1992 peace accord. Despite some UN assistance with these reforms, it appears they produced little change in Salvadoran police tactics, which still emphasized enforcement (O'Rawe and Moore, 1997, pp. 105–6, 265–6).

A recognition that UN civilian police trainers needed to be better prepared for this work led the UN Department of Peacekeeping Operations (DPKO) and the United Nations Centre for International Crime Prevention to develop standardized training materials in 1995–96 (Broer and Emery, 1998). In recent years, human rights training programmes for both military and police personnel regularly feature in UN-led post-conflict rehabilitation efforts. Key players in these efforts have included DPKO, the Office of the High Commissioner for Human Rights (OHCHR), and the UN High Commissioner for Refugees. Target countries (and peace operations) have included: Bosnia and Herzegovina, Croatia, East Timor, and Mozambique (UN, OHCHR, 2002a).

OHCHR has also worked with the Palestinian National Authority (PNA) to improve police adherence to international standards governing the use of force and firearms in the Palestinian territories (UN, OHCHR, 2002a). Since 1996, the PNA has been criticized for allowing a broad array of armed officials to commit serious human rights abuses, including extrajudicial executions and torture.[49] During 2001, OHCHR supported the development of guidelines on arrest, detention, and the use of force and firearms for the Palestinian police. These were adopted by the PNA Higher Security Council in 2002. OHCHR has also drafted a human rights curriculum for use in training courses aimed at members of the Palestinian security forces (UN, OHCHR, 2002a).

In October 1999, a UN transitional administration was created to assist East Timor in its transition to independence after decades of Indonesian rule. A key objective was the rapid establishment of a professional police force.[50] Recent killings of civilians by East Timorese police have, however, highlighted the limitations of the UN-supervised training programme. In the most widely-publicized event, police shot two people dead and injured several others during disturbances in the capital, Dili, in December 2002 (AI, 2003f, pp. 1–2, 9–12). More generally, complaints of assaults and excessive use of force by Timorese police were on the rise in 2003.

Though highly motivated, nearly 90 per cent of recruits to the East Timor Police Service have had no prior policing experience. Police officers in the new force were issued pepper spray, batons, and Austrian Glock pistols. The UN-supervised training in the handling of firearms, notably the Glock pistols, did not review in any serious way the circumstances in which police should use their weapons. New recruits were simply sent out onto the streets after receiving target practice.[51]

Box 7.13 Reform in the Balkans

A recent study conducted for the Small Arms Survey (Grillot, 2004) has reviewed ongoing police reforms in five Balkan countries (Albania, Bosnia and Herzegovina, Croatia, Macedonia, and Serbia and Montenegro) and one territory (Kosovo).[52] Police reform has been a particular focus of efforts to rebuild the Balkans after a decade of civil war and political instability. Law enforcement officials played an important role in perpetrating and perpetuating violence and repression before, during, and even after this decade of crisis, leading, in many cases, to a complete breakdown of the police–community relationship.

Reforms in the Balkans have been directed at many of the elements of good practice previously highlighted in this chapter, including, in addition to the controlled use of force and firearms: police force representation, depoliticization, demilitarization, and accountability. In pursuing these goals, governments in the subregion, in cooperation with a wide range of international and local actors, have undertaken a series of overlapping initiatives. The training of new recruits and retraining of serving officers have been central to these efforts. Training materials typically cover such issues as human rights and professional ethics. In some cases, they have specifically incorporated the *UN Basic Principles*. Other initiatives designed to improve policing in the Balkans include police restructuring, new laws and regulations, and surveys of public perceptions.

In some cases (Bosnia, Kosovo), international actors have had a relatively free hand in designing and implementing these programmes. In most countries, however, national governments have retained direct control over this work, with international and local actors playing more of a facilitating role.

It is presently unclear how successful these efforts are in bringing Balkan policing into line with international standards. Government officials and many of their international partners are upbeat, claiming that these standards are having an impact on policing practice. In particular, these officials assert that police relations with the public are now vastly better than they were even a few years ago.

The available evidence indicates, at a minimum, that more and more police in the subregion are being trained to respect human rights and exercise caution in their use of force and firearms. Yet, it appears that not all Balkan countries have taken up police reforms wholeheartedly. Some of the international officials involved in reform have expressed concern, even scepticism, about the lasting impact of this work. There is a fear that old, bad practices will reassert themselves in some countries once the international community directs its attention elsewhere. Moreover, there is a question as to how far existing practices have been altered. For example, Western police officers working alongside Kosovo police have indicated that new human rights training has not conquered a culture of law enforcement that emphasizes the use of force.

It is unclear whether such problems are isolated or indicative of broader trends. For the moment, the evidence suggests that the Balkans, collectively, has some way to go before its policing truly meets international standards. Yet at least the subregion now seems to be moving in the right direction.

Source: Grillot (2004)

CONCLUSION

Modern, professional policing is a complex task. This chapter focuses on a specific, yet crucial aspect of this task, namely the use—and misuse—of force and firearms by law enforcement officials. This subject lies at the heart of several key governance and security concerns.

In the first instance, police use of force and firearms is a core human rights issue. Gun misuse by police and other state agents involves a violation of such fundamental human rights as the right to life and the right not to be tortured or subjected to cruel, inhuman, or degrading treatment or punishment.

The use of firearms by police also features prominently in the governance debate. While policing is just one component of public security—along with judicial and penal systems—it is arguably the state's most visible expression of commitment (or lack of commitment) to the rule of law.

The use or misuse of firearms by police is equally a factor in small arms proliferation. When civilians do not trust the state to provide security, they often fall back on local structures—and on themselves—to fill the gap. The most immediate consequences are a rise in individual gun ownership and the risk of spiralling levels of armed violence. If the public has little or no confidence in state security forces, measures to control small arms and remove surpluses from society are unlikely to succeed.

As awareness of the importance of public perceptions has spread, modern policing has begun to emphasize the need for police officers to develop and sustain the trust of the communities in which they work. Such an approach contrasts with the more militaristic policing traditions still prevalent in many parts of the world, especially in post-colonial societies, which frequently concentrate on the protection of the state and ruling elites, rather than that of citizens. As the chapter indicates, strong links between the police and the community are crucial to promoting good policing practices, minimizing the recourse to firearms, and enhancing human security.

Though by no means perfect,[53] the normative framework governing the use of force and firearms by law enforcement officers is increasingly well-developed at both the international and national levels.

At the international level, several instruments now specifically govern the use of force and firearms by police, above all the *UN Basic Principles*. A number of other human rights norms are also relevant. These rules apply both to societies at peace and to those that have declared states of emergency.

Although national rules vary considerably in their formulation, it appears that certain critical principles are ever more widely shared. In general, states are accepting that any use of force by police must be limited to what is necessary under the circumstances and proportional to the objective at hand. In almost all states that have signed up to international civil and political rights standards, these principles (necessity and proportionality) restrict any form of firearm use by police to situations involving self-defence or defence of members of the public against a direct threat to life or limb.

As the chapter describes, specific rules govern the use of firearms against persons in custody or detention, vulnerable persons, and crowds. Standards and practices relating to the selection and training of police officers, their links to the community, equipment, and weapons storage are all essential to preventing recourse to excessive or inappropriate force. Other measures subsequently intervene to punish violations by public security forces, deter further abuses, and generally uphold the rule of law. Especially important in this regard are systems that oversee police conduct and ensure that officers are held accountable for excessive force or firearm misuse.

The chapter also examines instances where security and policing systems break down as a result of political manipulation or institutionalized corruption and criminality. Yet policing institutions—even when devastated by civil war—can be rebuilt. The final section of the chapter illustrates some of the difficulties of reforming police structures and practices in post-conflict societies.

The chapter's selection of national practice from various regions of the world, though useful in illustrating the challenges and problems arising in specific areas, does not allow us to map implementation with precision. The chapter's many examples nonetheless demonstrate that a large number of states around the world are not adhering to these standards.

POLICING

Policing that is consistent with the requirements of the *UN Basic Principles* requires significant resources—not least for training, equipment, and the establishment and operation of oversight mechanisms. A number of developing countries, however, are succeeding in their efforts to comply with such standards, with or without international assistance. Resources are clearly important for good policing, but ultimately it is political commitment that determines whether it is firmly rooted in respect for human rights.

7. LIST OF ABBREVIATIONS

ACPO	Association of Chief Police Officers
AI	Amnesty International
ARV	Armed Response Vehicle
CMU	Crime Management Unit (Jamaica)
DPKO	Department of Peacekeeping Operations (United Nations)
HRW	Human Rights Watch
IACP	International Association of Chiefs of Police
ICCPR	International Covenant on Civil and Political Rights
ICITAP	International Criminal Investigative Training Assistance Program (United States)
KPR	Kenya Police Reservists
MEF	Malaita Eagle Force
OC	Oleoresin Capsicum
OHCHR	Office of the High Commissioner for Human Rights
PBR	Plastic baton round
PNA	Palestinian National Authority
SADC	Southern African Development Community
SAPS	South African Police Service
SARPCCO	Southern African Regional Police Chiefs Co-operation Organisation
TPA	Townsville Peace Agreement (Solomon Islands)
XUAR	Xinjiang Uighur Autonomous Region (People's Republic of China)

7. ENDNOTES

[1] For further background, see: AI, IANSA, and Oxfam International (2004); Crawshaw, Devlin, and Williamson (1998); de Rover (1998); Crawshaw (1994).

[2] These standards include: *Principles on the Effective Prevention and Investigation of Extra-Legal, Arbitrary and Summary Executions; Declaration on the Protection of All Persons from Enforced Disappearance; Standard Minimum Rules for the Treatment of Prisoners; United Nations Rules for the Protection of Juveniles Deprived of Their Liberty; Declaration on the Elimination of Violence against Women;* and *Declaration of Basic Principles of Justice for Victims of Crime and Abuse of Power.* References and full text are available at <http://www.unhchr.ch/html/intlinst.htm>

[3] As of 2 November 2003, 43 states had not ratified the ICCPR, although some of these had signed: Andorra (signed), Antigua and Barbuda, Bahamas, Bahrain, Bhutan, Brunei Darussalam, China (signed), Comoros, Cook Islands, Cuba, Fiji, Guinea-Bissau (signed), Holy See, Indonesia, Kazakhstan, Kiribati, Laos (signed), Liberia (signed), Malaysia, Maldives, Marshall Islands, Mauritania, Micronesia, Myanmar (Burma), Nauru (signed), Niue, Oman, Pakistan, Palau, Papua New Guinea, Qatar, Saint Kitts and Nevis, Saint Lucia, Samoa, Sao Tome and Principe (signed), Saudi Arabia, Singapore, Solomon Islands, Swaziland, Tonga, Tuvalu, United Arab Emirates, and Vanuatu. Source: OHCHR (www.unhchr.ch).

[4] 'Police officials may only use force when strictly necessary and to the extent required for the performance of their duties adhering to national legislation and practices.' SARPCCO (2001, art. 3).

[5] For a comprehensive look at this issue, see AI (2002f).

[6] 'Where the suspect poses no immediate threat to the officer and no threat to others, the harm resulting from failing to apprehend him does not justify the use of deadly force to do so ... Where the officer has probable cause to believe that the suspect poses a threat of serious physical harm, either to the officer or to others, it is not constitutionally unreasonable to prevent escape by using deadly force. Thus, if the suspect threatens the officer with a weapon or there is probable cause to believe that he has committed a crime involving the infliction or threatened infliction of serious physical harm, deadly force may be used if necessary to prevent escape, and if, where feasible, some warning has been given.' United States, Supreme Court (1985).

7. See, for example, Houston Police Department (1984).
8. From Judge Chaskalson's leading judgement in the South African death penalty case *State v. Makwanyane and Mchunu*. South Africa, Constitutional Court (1995).
9. A review of jurisprudence and legislation in these countries was carried out by the South African government in 1996 and analysed by Judge Olivier in the case of *Govender v. Minister of Safety and Security*. South Africa, Supreme Court of Appeal (2001).
10. Author's translation of the French original: 'Lorsqu'il est autorisé par la loi à utiliser la force et, en particulier, à se servir de ses armes, le fonctionnaire de police ne peut en faire qu'un usage strictement nécessaire et proportionné au but à atteindre.' France (1986, art. 9).
11. See France (2004, art. 122-5).
12. The city of Seattle claims to have been the first major US city to legislate the use of deadly force by police officers. A May 1978 ordinance overturned state law dating from the 19th century, which allowed police to use deadly force to arrest persons suspected of committing any felony. See Wilma (2000).
13. See Sarre (1993).
14. Interview with Capt. Bongani Mbhele, Head of Human Rights Unit, Division of Policing Standards, South African Police Service, 13 December 2002.
15. Interview with Assistant Commissioner, South African Police Service, Pretoria, 15 January 2004.
16. Interview with Professor Anthony Minnaar, Institute for Human Rights and Criminal Justice Studies, Pretoria, 19 March 2004.
17. See UNGA (1966, article 4(2)).
18. See for example: AI (2000); HRW (2001a); Physicians for Human Rights (2000).
19. Information in this section is derived from interviews conducted by author Brian Wood with UK police experts during 2002–03 and from UK, ACPO (2001, especially chs. 3, 5).
20. For examples of so-called non-lethal or 'legitimate' policing equipment whose use has contributed to unwarranted injury, torture, or serious ill-treatment, see AI (2001c).
21. Note that while the IACP argues that data collected for 2000 (the most recent year covered in the report) is representative of the United States as a whole, this is probably not true for previous years (1991–99). See pp. ix, 2–3.
22. *Gestes et techniques professionnels d'intervention: Direction du personnel et de la formation de la police*. Translation from the French original, quoted in AI (1998).
23. Information from police advisers provided to author Brian Wood, in 2000–01.
24. Ibid.
25. The US programme, run by the US government's International Criminal Investigative Training Assistance Program (ICITAP), is summarized in Newsweek (2002). For a critique of US foreign police training, see AI (2002b).
26. Information in this section is derived from discussions with UK police officers during 2002–03, and from the Association of Chief Police Officers (2001).
27. Sources: author Brian Wood's notes and unpublished reports on regional training workshops by the Malawi Centre for Human Rights and Rehabilitation, the Public Affairs Committee, and the Malawi Police Service, 2000–2002.
28. For more information, see Neild (1998).
29. Paul Evans, Commissioner of Police, Boston, Massachusetts, 9 April 1999. Quoted in US, Dept of Justice (2002, sec. III).
30. John Farrell, Chief of Police, Prince George's County, Maryland, February 1999. Quoted in US, Dept of Justice (2002, sec. IV).
31. See Neild (1998) for examples in Baltimore, Boston, Denver, Detroit, and Los Angeles in the United States, as well as Australia and the Netherlands.
32. Many pilot schemes for community policing in post-apartheid South Africa, for instance, failed because the (as yet unreformed) police sought to dominate and control these structures, while community groups tried to use them for their own ends. See Shaw (2002, pp. 41–47).
33. Sources: interviews and documents obtained in KwaZulu-Natal, South Africa, February 2000 and April 2002.
34. Captain Pillay, Police Special Investigations Task Team, addressing 30 AI and local NGO representatives, Edendale, South Africa, 29 April 2002.
35. Cator Manor Project reports and local interviews conducted by author Brian Wood in February 2000 and April 2002.
36. The 12 SADC countries surveyed were Botswana, Lesotho, Malawi, Mauritius, Mozambique, Namibia, Seychelles, South Africa, Swaziland, Tanzania, Zambia, and Zimbabwe.
37. In 2002, election observer teams noted that threats and intimidation were used to prevent independent investigators from entering these areas. AI (2002e)
38. See Crawshaw (1994, chs. 1, 9).
39. Letter from the Solicitor General of Belize to AI, 11 November 2002 (confidential).
40. Ibid. See also AI (2003a).
41. Royal Ulster Constabulary Chief Constable Sir Ronnie Flanagan. Quoted in BBC (2001).
42. Interview with AI researcher, August 2001.
43. See the police training manual produced by the Office of the High Commissioner for Human Rights for chapters on juveniles, women, and refugees: UN, OHCHR (2002b).
44. Defined in the *UN Convention on the Rights of the Child* as anyone under 18 years of age. UNGA (1989, art. 1).
45. Information from a policing consultant after a mission to East Timor in late 2002.
46. See also UN (1990, Basic Principle 26, last sentence).
47. These were set in motion by the Sheehy Report and the White Paper on police reform, both published in 1993: Sheehy et al. (1993); UK, Home Office (1993).
48. See also Woods (1998).
49. For detailed criticism of the Palestinian police in the initial, post-Oslo period, see AI (1996).
50. The following account of police reforms in East Timor is largely based on AI (2003f).
51. Information from a policing consultant after a mission to East Timor in late 2002.
52. Research, both in-country and desk-based, was conducted during 2003. For more information on policing reforms in the six Balkan countries/territory covered in this box, see Grillot (2004).
53. See UN, Commission on Human Rights (2003, para. 28).

7. BIBLIOGRAPHY

Adams, Brad. 2003. 'Thailand's Crackdown: Drug "War" Kills Democracy, Too.' *International Herald Tribune*. 24 April.

AI (Amnesty International). 1996. *Palestinian Authority: Prolonged Political Detention, Torture and Unfair Trials*. AI Index: MDE 15/68/96. December.

—. 1997. *People's Republic of China: Law Reform and Human Rights*. AI Index: ASA 17/14/97. 1 March.

—. 1998. *France: Fatal Shooting of Abdelkader Bouziane and Alleged Ill-Treatment of Djamel Bouchareb by Law Enforcement Officers*. AI Index: EUR 21/007/1998. 11 September.

—. 1999. *Concerns in Europe, January–June 1999*. AI Index: EUR 01/002/1999. 1 August.

—. 2000. *Israel and the Occupied Territories: Excessive Use of Lethal Force.* AI Index: MDE 15/41/00. 19 October.
—. 2001a. *Report 2001.* AI Index: POL 10/001/2001
—. 2001b. *Reforming São Paulo's Prison System: Tackle the Cause Not the Symptom.* AI Index: AMR 19/008/2001. 20 February.
—. 2001c. *Stopping the Torture Trade.* AI Index: ACT 40/002/2001. 26 February.
—. 2001d. *Jamaica: Killings and Violence by Police: How Many More Victims?* AI Index: AMR 38/003/2001. 10 April.
—. 2002a. *Report 2002.* AI Index: POL 10/001/2002.
—. 2002b. *Unmatched Power, Unmet Principles: the Human Rights Dimensions of US Training of Foreign Military and Police Forces.* Washington, DC: Amnesty International USA.
—. 2002c. *Mozambique: Amir Ali Mahomed (m), 25 Years Old.* Urgent Action. AI Index: AFR 41/001/2002. 13 February.
—. 2002d. *People's Republic of China: Anti-terrorist Legislation and Repression in the Xinjiang Uighur Automomous Region.* AI Index: ASA 17/010/2002. 22 March.
—. 2002e. *Zimbabwe: The Toll of Impunity.* AI Index: AFR 46/034/2002. 25 June.
—. 2002f. *Policing to Protect Human Rights: A Survey of Police Practice in Countries of the Southern African Development Community, 1997-2002.* AI Index: AFR 03/004/2002. 9 July.
—. 2003a. *Report 2003.* AI Index: POL 10/003/2003.
—. 2003b. *Thailand: Extrajudicial Killing Is Not the Way to Suppress Drug Trafficking.* Press Release. AI Index: ASA 39/001/2003. 20 February.
—. 2003c. *Jamaica: The Killing of the Braeton Seven: A Justice System on Trial.* AI Index: AMR 38/005/2003. 13 March.
—. 2003d. *Zimbabwe: Rights under Siege.* AI Index: AFR 46/012/2003. 2 May.
—. 2003e. *Jamaica: Welcome Developments: Is an End to Police Impunity in Sight?* AI Index: AMR 38/015/2003. 25 June.
—. 2003f. *The Democratic Republic of Timor-Leste: A New Police Service, A New Beginning.* AI Index: ASA 57/002/2003. 1 July.
—. 2003g. *Thailand: Grave Developments: Killings and Other Abuses.* AI Index: ASA 39/008/2003. 5 November.
—. 2003h. *The Pain Merchants: Security Equipment and Its Use in Torture and Other Ill-Treatment.* AI Index: ACT 40/008/2003. 2 December.
—. 2004. *Jamaica: Janice Allen Case Demonstrates Lack of Political Will to End Police Killings.* AI Index: AMR 38/005/2004. 16 March.
—. and IANSA (International Action Network on Small Arms) and Oxfam International. 2004. *Guns and Policing: Standards to Prevent Misuse.* February. <http://www.controlarms.org>
—. and IHF (International Helsinki Federation for Human Rights). 2002. *Greece: In the Shadow of Impunity: Ill-treatment and the Misuse of Firearms.* AI Index: EUR 25/022/2002. 24 September.
Alexander, John. 2002. 'An Overview of the Future of Non-Lethal Weapons.' In Lewer, ed.
Asian Legal Resource Centre. 2003. *Special Report: Extrajudicial Killings of Alleged Drug Dealers in Thailand.* Article 2, Vol. 2, No. 3. June.
Association of Chief Police Officers. 2001. *Manual of Guidance on Police Use of Firearms.* United Kingdom: Association of Chief Police Officers. January.
BBC (British Broadcasting Corporation). 2001. *BBC News.* 'The Trouble with Plastic Bullets.' 2 August. <http://news.bbc.co.uk/1/hi/northern_ireland/1460116.stm>
Bennett, Tom, *et al.*, eds. 1985. *Acta Juridica.* Cape Town: Juta & Company Limited.
Broer, Harry and Michael Emery. 1998. 'Civilian Police in UN Peacekeeping Operations.' In Oakley, Dziedzic, and Goldberg.
Brogden, Michael. 1985. 'The Origins of the South African Police: Institutional Versus Structural Approaches.' In Bennett *et al.*
Butterfield, Fox. 1999. 'Citizens as Allies: Rethinking the Strong Arm of the Law.' *New York Times.* 4 April.
Cincinnati Police Department. 2003. 'Discharging of Firearms by Police Personnel.' *Procedure Manual.* Section 12.550. 23 September.
Council of Europe. 1950. *Convention for the Protection of Human Rights and Fundamental Freedoms, as amended by Protocol No. 11.* Adopted in Rome on 4 November. Entered into force on 3 September 1953. *European Treaty Series*, No. 5. <http://conventions.coe.int/Treaty/EN/CadreListeTraites.htm>
Coyle, Andrew. 2002. *A Human Rights Approach to Prison Management.* London: International Centre for Prison Studies.
Crawshaw, Ralph. 1994. *Human Rights and the Theory and Practice of Policing.* Colchester: University of Essex Human Rights Centre.
—. Barry Devlin, and Tom Williamson. 1998. *Human Rights and Policing: Standards for Good Behaviour and a Strategy for Change.* The Hague: Kluwer Law International.
Cross, Peter, *et al.* 2003. *Law of the Gun: An Audit of Firearms Control Legislation in the SADC Region.* Pretoria and London: SaferAfrica and Saferworld. June.
de Rover, Cess. 1998. *To Protect and To Serve.* Geneva: International Committee of the Red Cross.
EIA (Environmental Investigation Agency) and Telapak. 2003. *Above the Law: Corruption, Collusion, Nepotism and the Fate of Indonesia's Forests.* January.
European Court of Human Rights. 2001. *Kelly and Others v. The United Kingdom.* Application No. 30054/96. <http://hudoc.echr.coe.int/>
France. 1986. *Code de déontologie de la Police nationale.* Décret no. 86-592 du 18 mars 1986 portant code de déontologie de la police nationale. <http://www.legifrance.gouv.fr/WAspad/UnCode?code=CDPOLIC0.rcv>
—. 2004. *Code pénal.* 101e édition. Paris: Dalloz. <http://www.legifrance.gouv.fr/WAspad/UnCode?code=CPENALLL.rcv>
Grillot, Suzette. 2004. *The Police and Their Guns in the Balkans: Implementing the 1990 UN Basic Principles on the Use of Force and Firearms.* Background paper. Geneva: Small Arms Survey. January.
Hartley, Wyndham. 2002. 'New Non-lethal Force Law Still Not Implemented.' *Business Day.* 25 November.
Heijder, Alfred. 1984. 'Codes of Professional Ethics Against Torture.' In AI, *Codes of Professional Ethics.* New York: Amnesty International USA.
Houston Police Department. 1984. *Firearms Rules and Regulations.* Training Bulletin. 3 May.

HRW (Human Rights Watch). 1998. *Shielded from Justice: Police Brutality and Accountability in the United States.* July.
—. 2001a. *Center of the Storm: A Case Study of Human Rights Abuses in Hebron District.* April.
—. 2001b. *No Escape: Male Rape in U.S. Prisons.* April.
—. 2001c. *Jamaica: Investigate Police and Military Killings.* 12 July.
—. 2002. *Playing With Fire: Weapons Proliferation, Political Violence and Human Rights in Kenya.* 31 May.
—. 2003a. *World Report 2003.*
—. 2003b. *In the Name of Counter-Terrorism: Human Rights Abuses Worldwide.* Briefing Paper for the 59th Session of the United Nations Commission on Human Rights. 25 March.
—. 2003c. *Compounding Injustice: The Government's Failure to Redress Massacres in Gujarat.* Vol. 15, No. 3 (C). July.
—. 2004. *In a Time of Torture: The Assault on Justice in Egypt's Crackdown on Homosexual Conduct.* March.
—. and IGLHRC (International Gay and Lesbian Human Rights Commission). 2003. *More than a Name: State-Sponsored Homophobia and Its Consequences in Southern Africa.* New York: Human Rights Watch.
IACP (International Association of Chiefs of Police). 2001. *Police Use of Force in America.* <http://www.theiacp.org/documents/pdfs/Publications/2001useofforce.pdf>
IHF (International Helsinki Federation for Human Rights). 2003. *Human Rights in the OSCE Region: Europe, Central Asia and North America: Report 2003.* 24 June. Report on the United States. <http://www.ihf-hr.org/documents/index.php>
Khadiagala, Gilbert. 2003. *Protection and Poverty: The Experiences of Community Weapons Collection Initiatives in Northern Kenya.* Nairobi: Oxfam GB.
Knutsson, Johannes and Jon Strype. 2000. 'Police Use of Guns in Norway and Sweden.' Paper presented to the American Society of Criminology Conference.
Lewer, Nick, ed. 2002. *The Future of Non-Lethal Weapons: Technologies, Operations, Ethics and Law.* London: Frank Cass.
Mahajna, Ahmad, *et al.* 2002. 'Blunt and Penetrating Injuries Caused by Rubber Bullets During the Israeli-Arab Conflict in October 2000: A Retrospective Study.' *The Lancet.* Vol. 359, No. 9320: 1795–1800. 25 May.
Minda News. 2003. 'Gun Club to Train Zambo Police on Marksmanship.' 16 March.
Neild, Rachel. 1995. *Demilitarizing Public Order: The International Community, Police Reform and Human Rights in Central America and Haiti.* Washington, DC: Washington Office on Latin America.
—. 1998. *Community Policing: Themes and Debates in Public Security Reform: A Manual for Civil Society.* Washington, DC: Washington Office on Latin America.
—. 2001. 'Democratic Police Reforms in War-Torn Societies.' *Journal of Conflict, Security and Development,* Vol. 1, No. 1. <http://csdg.kcl.ac.uk/Publications/html/journal.htm>
Newsweek. 2002. 'Asian War Games.' 29 April.
O'Rawe, Mary and Linda Moore. 1997. *Human Rights on Duty: Principles for Better Policing: International Lessons for Northern Ireland.* Belfast: Committee for the Administration of Justice. Publication No. 37. December.
Oakley, Robert, Michael Dziedzic, and Eliot Goldberg, eds. 1998. *Policing the New World Disorder: Peace Operations and Public Security.* Washington, DC: National Defense University Press. <http://www.ndu.edu/inss/books/Book_authors.htm>
Parks, Roger, *et al.* 1999. 'How Officers Spend Their Time with the Community.' *Justice Quarterly.* 16 September.
Patten Commission (Independent Commission on Policing for Northern Ireland). 1999. *A New Beginning: Policing in Northern Ireland,* September.
Physicians for Human Rights. 2000. *Medical Group Examines Use of Force in Israel, Gaza and West Bank; Issues Conclusions on Death of 'Issam Judeh.* 3 November.
SARPCCO (Southern African Regional Police Chiefs Co-operation Organisation). 2001. *Harare Resolution on the SARPCCO Code of Conduct for Police Officials.* Adopted at the Sixth Annual General Meeting. Mauritius, 27–31 August. <http://www.apt.ch/africa/Sarpcco.pdf>
Sarre, Rick. 1993. 'Police Use of Firearms: Issues in Safety.' Paper presented at the Second National Conference on Violence. Canberra: Australian Institute of Criminology. 15-18 June. <http://www.aic.gov.au/conferences/ncv2/sarre.pdf>
Shaw, Mark. 2002. *Democracy's Disorder? Crime, Police and Citizen Responses in Transitional Societies.* Johannesburg: South African Institute of International Affairs. September.
Sheehy, Patrick, *et al.* 1993. *Inquiry into Police Responsibilities and Rewards.* London: HMSO.
South Africa. Constitutional Court. 1995. *State v. Makwanyane and Mchunu.* Case No. CCT/3/94. 1995 (3) SA 391 (CC); 1995 (6) BCLR 665 (CC).
—. Parliament. 1998. *Judicial Matters Second Amendment Act.* Section 7.
—. Supreme Court of Appeal. 2001. *Govender v. Minister of Safety and Security.* Case No. 342/99. 2001 (4) SA 273 (SCA).
Taghoy, Jovy. 2003. '12 PNP Officials Fail Gun Proficiency Test.' *Cebu Daily News.* 15 April. <http://www.inq7.net/globalnation/sec_cdn/2003/apr/new/apr15_02.htm>
United Kingdom. ACPO (Association of Chief Police Officers). 2001. *Manual of Guidance on Police Use of Firearms.* January.
—. Home Office. 1993 *Police Reform: A Police Service for the Twenty-first Century.* London: HMSO.
United Nations. 1990. *Basic Principles on the Use of Force and Firearms by Law Enforcement Officials ('UN Basic Principles').* Adopted by the Eighth United Nations Congress on the Prevention of Crime and the Treatment of Offenders, Havana, Cuba, 27 August–7 September. <http://www.unhchr.ch/html/menu3/b/h_comp43.htm>

—. Commission on Human Rights. 1998. *Report of the Special Rapporteur on Extrajudicial, Summary or Arbitrary Executions, Mr Bacre Waly Ndiaye, Submitted Pursuant to Commission Resolution 1997/61*. Addendum: Mission to the United States of America. UN document E/CN.4/1998/68/Add.3 of 22 January.

—. Commission on Human Rights. 2002. *Report of the Special Rapporteur on Extrajudicial, Summary or Arbitrary Executions, Ms. Asma Jahangir*. Addendum: Mission to Honduras. UN document E/CN.4/2003/3/Add.2 of 14 June.

—. Commission on Human Rights. 2003. *Report of the Special Rapporteur on Prevention of Human Rights Violations Committed with Small Arms and Light Weapons, Barbara Frey*. Preliminary Report. UN document E/CN.4/Sub.2/2003/29 of 25 June.

—. Commission on Human Rights. 2004. *Report of the Special Rapporteur on Extrajudicial, Summary or Arbitrary Executions, Asma Jahangir*. Addendum: Mission to Brazil. UN document E/CN.4/2004/7/Add.3 of 28 January. <http://www.unhchr.ch/pdf/chr60/7add3AV.pdf>

—. Human Rights Committee. 2003. *Concluding Observations of the Human Rights Committee: Portugal*. CCPR/CO/78/PRT. 5 July.

—. OHCHR (Office of the High Commissioner for Human Rights). 2002a. *Annual Report 2002: Implementation of Activities and Use of Funds*. Geneva: OHCHR.

—. OHCHR (Office of the High Commissioner for Human Rights). 2002b. *Human Rights and Law Enforcement: A Trainer's Guide On Human Rights for the Police*. Professional Training Series No.5/Add.2. New York and Geneva: United Nations. <http://www.unhchr.ch/html/menu6/2/train5add2.pdf>

UNECOSOC (United Nations Economic and Social Council). 1955. *Standard Minimum Rules for the Treatment of Prisoners*. Adopted by the First United Nations Congress on the Prevention of Crime and the Treatment of Offenders, held in Geneva in 1955. Approved by ECOSOC in its Resolutions 663 C (XXIV) of 31 July 1957 and 2076 (LXII) of 13 May 1977. <http://www.unhchr.ch/html/menu3/b/h_comp34.htm>

—. 1989. *Principles on the Effective Prevention and Investigation of Extra-legal, Arbitrary and Summary Executions*. Recommended by ECOSOC in its Resolution 1989/65 of 24 May. <http://www.unhchr.ch/html/menu3/b/54.htm>

UNGA (United Nations General Assembly). 1948. *Universal Declaration of Human Rights*. Adopted and proclaimed by Resolution 217A (III) of 10 December. <http://www.unhchr.ch/udhr/>

—. 1966. *International Covenant on Civil and Political Rights*. Adopted by Resolution 2200A (XXI) of 16 December. Entered into force on 23 March 1976. Reproduced in General Assembly Official Records, Twenty-first Session, Supplement No. 16 (A/6316). <http://www.unhchr.ch/html/menu3/b/a_ccpr.htm>

—. 1979a. Resolution 34/169 of 17 December.

—. 1979b. *Code of Conduct for Law Enforcement Officials*. Adopted by UNGA Resolution 34/169 of 17 December. <http://www.unhchr.ch/html/menu3/b/h_comp42.htm>

—. 1984. *Convention against Torture and Other Cruel, Inhuman or Degrading Treatment or Punishment*. Adopted by Resolution 39/46 of 10 December. Entered into force on 26 June 1987. <http://www.unhchr.ch/html/menu3/b/h_cat39.htm>

—. 1989. *Convention on the Rights of the Child*. Adopted by Resolution 44/25 of 20 November. Entered into force on 2 September 1990. <http://www.unhchr.ch/html/menu2/6/crc/treaties/crc.htm>

—. 1990. *United Nations Rules for the Protection of Juveniles Deprived of their Liberty*. Adopted by UNGA Resolution 45/113 of 14 December.

—. 1993. *Declaration on the Elimination of Violence against Women*. Resolution 48/104 of 20 December. Reproduced in UN document A/RES/48/104 of 23 February 1994.

United States. Department of Justice. Community Relations Service. 2002. *Police Use of Excessive Force: A Conciliation Handbook for the Police and the Community*. June. <http://www.usdoj.gov/crs/pubs/pdexcess.pdf>

—. Supreme Court. 1985. *Tennessee v. Garner*. 471 US 1 (1985).

Wilma, David. 2000. 'Seattle is First Major City to Legislate a Police Shooting Policy on May 1, 1978: Seattle/King County.' *HistoryLink.org*. 19 May. <http://www.historylink.org/output.cfm?file_id=2433>

Wood, Brian, with Undule Mwakasungura and Robert Phiri. 2001. *Report of the Malawi Community Safety and Firearms Control Project*. Lilongwe, Malawi. August.

Woods, James. 1998. 'Mozambique: the CIVPOL Operation.' In Oakley, Dziedzic, and Goldberg.

ACKNOWLEDGEMENTS

Other contributors
James Bevan, Pamina Firchow, Suzette Grillot, Lisa Misol, Stéphanie Pézard, and Ruxandra Stoicescu.

A steam roller crushes rifles and machine guns in front of Belgrade's City Hall in May 2002.
(© Reuters/Ivan Milutinovic)

Under the Spotlight:
MONITORING IMPLEMENTATION OF SMALL ARMS MEASURES

INTRODUCTION

The First Biennial Meeting of States (BMS),[1] held in New York on 7–11 July 2003, marked a key second step in the UN Small Arms Conference process, following the adoption of the *UN Programme of Action* two years earlier (UNGA, 2001b). Largely judged a success, or relative success, by independent observers, the BMS saw a large number of states, as well as international organizations, report on their implementation of the nascent, but far from stillborn, *Programme of Action*.

Reporting, monitoring, and verification will almost certainly be essential to the success of ongoing efforts to tackle the small arms problem—as they have been in other areas.[2] The effective implementation of small arms measures, including the *Programme of Action* and arms embargoes, will depend on the sharing of information and independent scrutiny that are inherent in these processes. Reporting, monitoring, and verification appear especially important at the global level, where some governments may feel less inclined to meet the expectations of fellow states in relation to small arms.

The chapter's major conclusions include the following:

- The July 2003 Biennial Meeting was largely successful in generating significant information and analysis on the implementation of the *UN Programme of Action*.
- However, existing efforts do not provide a complete picture of *Programme* implementation, nor of implementation challenges and solutions.
- Verification of compliance with UN arms embargoes has become more resolute in recent years, but this improvement remains vulnerable to weakening political will.
- Governments, international organizations, and civil society, working both independently and in partnership, have key roles to play in ensuring that small arms measures are effectively implemented.
- Reporting, monitoring, and verification will be essential to these efforts.

The chapter makes frequent use of the terms 'reporting', 'monitoring', and 'verification'. Although their exact meaning may vary according to the particular context, the basic concepts are fairly straightforward. When 'reporting', states and other actors give an account of action they have taken to implement particular agreements. 'Monitoring' involves the independent observation and evaluation of implementation efforts, while 'verification' usually refers to a process of information gathering and analysis to establish whether specific commitments, especially legal ones, have been complied with.[3]

The chapter is divided into two main parts. The first part looks at the UN Conference process, highlighting key developments from the BMS and other small arms processes, including regional ones. It examines the roles of reporting and monitoring in the UN Conference process, and reviews a few important initiatives in this area. The second part of the chapter reviews efforts to verify compliance with mandatory UN Security Council arms embargoes. It looks at the institutions and mechanisms that underpin verification efforts, considers the question of their effectiveness, and briefly describes some of the key proposals for improving these systems.

The effective implementation of Security Council arms embargoes is critical to achieving the goals of the *UN Programme of Action*—and not only because the issue is mentioned in the *Programme* itself. While UN arms embargoes typically cover a broad range of weapons, including weapons of mass destruction and major conventional systems, many of the arms that wreak havoc in embargoed zones are, in fact, small arms and light weapons.

Although UN member states are legally bound to implement mandatory Security Council embargoes, we will see that verification systems have a crucial role to play in bolstering state compliance with these measures—just as reporting and monitoring appear essential to the effective implementation of the *UN Programme of Action*.

THE UN CONFERENCE PROCESS[4]

The small arms issue moved squarely onto the international agenda with the convening, on 9–20 July 2001, of the *United Nations Conference on the Illicit Trade in Small Arms and Light Weapons in All Its Aspects*. This Conference, and more specifically the *Programme of Action* which emerged from it (UNGA, 2001b), provide key reference points for activity around the world on small arms.[5] The next sections of the chapter briefly review some of this activity before examining, in greater depth, the issues of transparency, reporting, and monitoring.

The *Programme of Action* provides a key reference point for activity around the world on small arms.

The First Biennial Meeting of States

In the *UN Programme of Action,* states agreed to meet every two years 'to consider the national, regional and global implementation of the Programme of Action' (UNGA, 2001b, sec. IV, para. 1(b)). The first of these meetings was held in New York on 7–11 July 2003. The First BMS gave the international community, including governments, international organizations, and NGOs, an opportunity to exchange information, share experience, and assess what progress had been made in implementing the *Programme of Action* in its first two years. There was no mandate to negotiate new instruments or reopen issues on which no agreement could be reached in July 2001.[6]

The five-day Meeting consisted of ten plenary sessions. In the first five, devoted to national implementation, representatives of 102 governments,[7] speaking on behalf of 144 states, gave statements outlining the steps they had taken to counter the proliferation and misuse of small arms, specifically within the framework of the *Programme of Action*. During the BMS, 98 states also distributed national reports outlining their implementation of the *Programme*.[8] Most of the rest of the Meeting was taken up with statements from civil society and regional/international organizations, along with thematic discussions. During the tenth and final session, Meeting Chairperson, Ambassador Kuniko Inoguchi, presented government delegations with a revised version of her 'Chairperson's Summary'. However, the document failed to gain the support

Ambassador Kuniko Inoguchi chairs the First Biennial Meeting of States in July 2003.

of all states and does not form part of the Meeting Report proper (UNGA, 2003b, Annex). As a result, it will have little impact on the next phases of the UN Conference process (Batchelor, 2003).

NGOs, states, and international organizations, sometimes in partnership, also organized a series of side events in the margins of the BMS. These were designed to raise awareness around small arms issues and promote common understandings in a few key areas imperfectly addressed in the *Programme*, such as controls over small arms transfers and brokering.

The 2003 BMS has paved the way to the next stages of the UN Conference process, which include a second biennial meeting in 2005 and a review conference in 2006. Most significantly, the Meeting appears to have helped sustain the momentum generated around small arms in July 2001, keeping the issue firmly on the international agenda in the new, post-11 September era.[9]

The Broader Picture

The period following the 2001 UN Conference has seen considerable activity on the small arms issue. The following review, covering the period from July 2001 to the end of 2003, presents, very briefly and selectively, some of the key international and regional initiatives that have been undertaken since the Conference.

In the months following the 2001 Conference, consultations of mostly regional scope were held in such countries as Belgium, Chile, Costa Rica, and South Africa to review the outcome of the Conference and discuss how to implement the *Programme of Action*. A meeting held in Tokyo, Japan, in January 2002, brought together governments, international organizations, and civil society from around the world for this same purpose.[10] In advance of the July 2003 BMS, UN regional meetings were held in Asia-Pacific (Indonesia), south-eastern Europe (Slovenia), and central Africa (Republic of Congo) in order to look at *Programme* implementation in these regions and help participants prepare for the 2003 BMS. A fourth UN regional meeting on small arms, co-hosted by the League of Arab States, was held in Egypt in December 2003.

Since July 2001, the UN General Assembly has continued to shepherd the UN Conference process. In December 2003, pursuant to the recommendation of a Group of Governmental Experts,[11] the General Assembly decided to establish an 'open-ended working group' to negotiate an international tracing instrument (UNGA, 2003d, para. 8). The UN Security Council has also taken up the small arms issue, adopting resolutions on such topics as the protection of children affected by armed conflict, and small arms proliferation and mercenary activities in West Africa (UNSC, 2003a, 2003b). Statements made by the Council President have focused on responsibility in small arms transfers and the effective implementation of arms embargoes (UNSC, 2002d, 2004).

In the two years since the July 2001 Conference, the broader UN system has gone some ways towards integrating the letter and spirit of the *Programme of Action* into its work. The United Nations Development Programme (UNDP) has provided technical assistance and funding for weapons collection and destruction efforts in various parts of the world. The United Nations Children's Fund (UNICEF) and the World Health Organization (WHO) have piloted their own small arms initiatives. Much of this work involves action-oriented research. For example, the United Nations Institute for Disarmament Research (UNIDIR) is conducting an assessment of selected weapons collection programmes. Various UN agencies and departments are collaborating on many of these projects.[12]

Other international initiatives have contributed to the implementation of the *Programme of Action*, although they are not formally part of the UN Conference process. For example, the United Kingdom has led in-depth discussions on integrating small arms issues into development programmes (UK, DFID, 2003). In a similar vein, in 2003 a UN

Group of Governmental Experts began a review of the relationship between disarmament and development, including the UN's role in this area. The *UN Firearms Protocol,* an international treaty designed to combat the illicit firearms trade (UNGA, 2001a), continues to gather the ratifications it will need in order to enter into force.[13]

Since July 2001, the Wassenaar Arrangement has strengthened its controls over small arms transfers and moved to increase their transparency. Specific initiatives include the adoption, in December 2002, of guidelines for the export of small arms and, in December 2003, of measures aimed at tightening controls over the transfer of MANPADS (MANPADS), exchanging information on small arms transfers (TRANSFERS), and ensuring that arms brokering is effectively regulated (BROKERS).

While the *Programme of Action* provides an essential framework for international action on small arms, it is only a starting point. Several international initiatives have been launched in the period since the 2001 Conference in an effort to build upon the minimum standards articulated in the *Programme*. An important example in the area of brokering, led by the Dutch and Norwegian governments, is described in the chapter dealing with this theme (BROKERS). An initiative launched by the UK at a meeting at Lancaster House, London, in January 2003, seeks to build consensus among states on the strengthening of controls over small arms transfers (UK, DFID *et al.,* 2003). A Consultative Group Process, initiated by the Biting the Bullet project, also in 2003, brings together government and civil society experts for the purposes of developing shared understandings on guidelines for the authorization of small arms transfers and on transfers to non-state actors.

> While the *Programme of Action* provides an essential framework for international action on small arms, it is only a starting point.

As Brazil adopts sweeping gun control legislation, President Luis Inácio Lula da Silva joins relatives of gun victims in Brasilia in December 2003.

Activity at the regional level continues to make an essential contribution to overall efforts to tackle the small arms problem. Among the highlights since July 2001 are the following:[14]

- the adoption, by the Southern African Development Community (SADC), of a *Firearms Protocol* (SADC, 2001);
- the development of model legislation for weapons control by the Pacific Islands Forum;
- the establishment of the South Eastern Europe Clearinghouse for the Control of Small Arms and Light Weapons (SEESAC)[15];

- the development of a regional legal protocol on small arms control by the Eastern Africa Police Chiefs Cooperation Organisation (EAPCCO); and
- annual exchanges of small arms-related information among participating States of the Organization for Security and Co-operation in Europe (OSCE) and the development, by the OSCE, of a *Handbook of Best Practices* (OSCE, 2000, 2003).

Important initiatives on arms brokering, mounted by such regional organizations as the European Union (EU) and the Organization of American States (OAS), are covered elsewhere (BROKERS).

Transparency

The importance of transparency is increasingly recognized across a wide range of fields (Haug *et al.*, 2002, p. 5). Yet it remains somewhat controversial with respect to small arms, even though most observers ground this issue firmly in human—as opposed to national—security.

The arguments for transparency in the small arms trade are presented elsewhere in this edition of the *Survey* (TRANSFERS).[16] This section focuses on the importance of transparency for monitoring implementation of the *Programme of Action* and other small arms measures. In brief, transparency allows states to demonstrate that they are abiding by their commitments in the *Programme* and other instruments. It also allows third parties to assess such implementation independently. If specific successes, problems, and challenges are to be shared among all stakeholders in the UN Conference process, including other states, relevant and specific information on states' implementation of the *Programme* is essential.

There is no single transparency mechanism for small arms and light weapons. The issue receives some attention in the *UN Programme of Action* (UNGA, 2001b), notably in section II, para. 31, where states agree:

> To encourage regions to develop, where appropriate and on a voluntary basis, measures to enhance transparency with a view to combating the illicit trade in small arms and light weapons in all its aspects.[17]

In fact, transparency on small arms is much better in many regions than at the global level—though here, too, it has its limits. While regional organizations, such as the OSCE, the EU, and the OAS, have exchanged information on the implementation of their small arms measures, much of this data is restricted to states participating in these processes (Small Arms Survey, 2003, pp. 236–7).

Some recent developments herald further improvements in transparency for small arms. In December 2003, the UN General Assembly decided, for the first time, to expand the scope of the UN Register of Conventional Arms to include certain types of light weapons (TRANSFERS). Information in the UN Register is public. This is not, however, the case with the Wassenaar Arrangement, which, as mentioned earlier, also in December 2003, decided to expand its information exchange arrangements to include small arms transfers.

The UN Conference process has so far proven to be quite open. The provision the *Programme of Action* makes for 'voluntary' reporting appears to assume at least some degree of transparency as a result of its use of the word 'circulate':

SMALL ARMS SURVEY 2004

> [States] request the Secretary-General of the United Nations, within existing resources, through the Department for Disarmament Affairs, to collate and circulate data and information provided by States on a voluntary basis and including national reports, on implementation by those States of the Programme of Action. (UNGA, 2001b, sec. II, para. 33)[18]

In 2003, 103 states reported on their implementation of the *Programme of Action*.

So far, no restrictions have been placed on the information generated in the context of the UN Conference process. The reports that states have submitted on their implementation of the *Programme*, along with the statements they gave at the BMS, are posted on the UNDDA website.[19]

Reporting

Whereas, in 2002, only 16 states submitted reports to UNDDA on their implementation of the *Programme of Action*, 103 did so in 2003 (as of 31 December). This is slightly up from the figure of 98 reports submitted at the time of the July 2003 BMS. Each of the numbers from 2003 represents just over half of all 192 states worldwide.

Table 8.1   State reporting on implementation of the UN *Programme of Action* as at end 2003

Regions	Total states*	2002 Reports	2002 Regional percentage	2003 Reports	2003 Regional percentage
Africa	52	3	6	23	44
Americas	35	3	9	18	51
Asia	29	2	7	12	41
Europe	48	7	15	37	77
Middle East	14	0	0	10	71
Oceania	14	1	7	3	21
Totals	**192**	**16**	**8%**	**103**	**54%**

Notes: For the current list of reports, see <http://disarmament2.un.org/cab/salw-nationalreports.html>

*Comprising all 191 UN Member States, plus the Holy See (observer to the UN).

The BMS served to catalyse activity on small arms. In the months preceding the Meeting, there was a sudden flurry of conferences and workshops. UNDP and UNDDA also launched phase 1 of their reporting project, assisting 25 less-developed countries in the preparation of their national reports (Box 8.1). Many of the reports submitted by states at the BMS were specifically prepared for that meeting. To some extent, it appears this pressure also fed into actual implementation, with several national points of contact established in the run-up to the BMS. However, by the time of the BMS, two years after the adoption of the *Programme of Action*, it appeared that many countries had yet to establish a national point of contact, arguably the simplest of the *Programme's* requirements.[20]

The July 2003 BMS also spurred reporting by regional and international organizations on their implementation of the *Programme of Action*. The statements and reports of these bodies, including many UN departments and agencies, highlight initiatives taken or under way and, in some cases, point to challenges and lessons learned in addressing the small arms problem.[21]

MONITORING

National reporting in 2003

There were few constants in national reporting in 2003. Some reports were several dozen pages long, while others took the form of brief letters to the UN. Some countries followed the *Programme of Action* paragraph by paragraph. Others offered only the broadest overview of national implementation. Many reports included annexes with additional, detailed information. Two states produced 'nil reports', indicating they had nothing to report on their implementation of the *Programme*.

Comparison among states and the identification of gaps in implementation is made more difficult as a result of the different formats states used for reporting. No format was provided or formally approved by the UN. The US developed a matrix for reporting that matched government action on small arms, including the provision of assistance and other cooperation, to specific sections of the *Programme* (US, 2003). Several other states adopted this reporting framework in 2003. Other countries opted for a set of guidelines distributed by the Geneva Forum (see below). These also formed the basis of a more extensive set of guidelines used in the UNDP–UNDDA reporting assistance project (see Box 8.1). Many states followed no set format.

> There were few constants in national reporting in 2003.

As one would expect, some reports were far more informative than others. Many countries simply asserted, in general terms, that they were meeting their *Programme* commitments—reproducing relevant language from the *Programme of Action* without additional explanation or elaboration. In many cases, there appears to have been no genuine attempt to grapple with the small arms issue as it affected the particular country.[22] Whether national reports were detailed or superficial, states only rarely acknowledged and explained specific difficulties they had encountered in implementing the *Programme*, limiting the instructive potential of the reporting exercise.

The following discussion, organized by *Programme* issue area, gives some idea of the quantity and quality of information that was presented by states in 2003. It is based on an analysis of the 103 reports submitted by states in 2003 (Kytömäki, 2003).

National point of contact, national coordination agency. As noted above, as of July 2003, many countries had established a national point of contact to liaise with other governments on small arms issues, and this was indicated in most of the national reports. Many reports also referred to national coordination agencies, though most often to indicate that these were being established or were under consideration. Some countries also reported that, while they had not set up a dedicated coordination agency, different government departments were meeting and cooperating for this purpose.

> States rarely acknowledged and explained specific difficulties they encountered in implementing the *Programme*.

National laws, regulations, and administrative procedures. In general, states either provided fairly detailed information about their national laws and regulations or simply noted that they had 'taken the necessary measures' in accordance with the requirements of the *Programme*. Many states gave a detailed account of legislative changes under way or initiated following the adoption of the *Programme* in July 2001. Some reports were mostly devoted to the question of legislation.

Criminalization. States tended to neglect the issue of criminal offences and penalties in their reports. Many countries did not address the question at all, or instead indicated that there were penalties (without more detail) when discussing legislation. Several countries, however, provided considerable detail on relevant offences and corresponding penalties.

Stockpile management. Along with legislation (especially export controls), stockpile management and security was an area that states seemed comfortable in addressing in their reports. Yet, in this area as well, transparency varied considerably. Some states simply acknowledged the importance of the issue in general terms, while others described applicable security measures and procedures in detail.

255

SMALL ARMS SURVEY 2004

Older rebel fighters wrestle a gun from a younger peer over a disciplinary matter in the Liberian capital of Monrovia in August 2003.

Transfers. The subject of transfer controls was also widely covered in the national reports. Some countries dealt with the issue as part of their discussion of legislation, while others provided information on transfer practices in a separate section. The issues of end-use certification and delivery verification were mentioned less often, though some countries described the steps they took to ensure that small arms that were exported from the country reached intended recipients.

Brokering. Many states reported that, while they did not yet have legislation specifically addressing the problem of illicit brokering, they were taking steps to fill this gap.

Marking, record-keeping, and tracing. This topic also received widespread attention, though once again the depth of reporting varied considerably. Some states simply noted that all weapons manufactured within their jurisdiction were marked. Many others, however, gave detailed information on the content of marks and methods of marking. Many states also indicated that they supported the negotiation of an international instrument for tracing illicit small arms.

Collection and disposal. Many countries also discussed the collection and disposal of small arms (illicit or surplus) in their reports. Detailed information on numbers and types of weapons seized and/or destroyed during 2002 was provided in several cases, often in the form of annexes to the main report. Means of disposal of surplus stocks included destruction, transfer to other ministries within the government, and sale to friendly third countries. Some countries said they had no surplus to dispose of. Destruction methods varied widely and included smelting, melting, shredding, cutting, and severing. Several states noted that amnesty periods were in force in order to encourage the surrender of weapons.

DDR. While several countries—both donor and assisted states—discussed disarmament, demobilization, and reintegration (DDR) in their reports, in general, the reports do not give a full picture of all of the activity now under way in this area.

Public awareness and confidence-building programmes. Most states had little to say on this issue, though several developing countries noted the existence of radio and TV programmes designed to broaden public awareness.

Civil society. As one might expect, some countries mentioned NGOs and civil society in their reports, while others did not. Where states raised this issue, it was mostly in terms of projects and project funding. Donor governments noted the NGOs they were supporting, while developing countries referred to NGOs that were working in the country.

Implementation at the regional and global levels. Most states devoted relatively little space to regional and global action in their reports. Some countries addressed the issue in discussing national-level implementation. In general, states using the US matrix or the Geneva Forum reporting guidelines took greater account of international action than those using some other format. The most commonly cited international activities included adhesion to international instruments and participation in meetings and conferences. Many of the reports reflected the importance of terrorism in the post-11 September world. Transnational organized crime was another focus of attention, with several countries indicating they had signed and/or ratified the *UN Firearms Protocol* (UNGA, 2001a). Many countries noted that they complied with UN arms embargoes and exchanged information with Interpol. States mentioning cooperation at the regional level often cited information-sharing and similar projects as examples—specifically between customs and border officials of neighbouring countries.

Assistance. Many governments discussed assistance for small arms work in their reports, though donor countries tended to provide more detailed information on the projects they had funded or coordinated. While countries which had received assistance did not generally reveal much about ongoing projects or existing needs, there were some exceptions. In particular, some countries indicated quite clearly where they needed technical or financial assistance in implementing the *Programme of Action*.

> Many of the reports reflected the importance of terrorism in the post-September 11 world.

Reporting and implementation

Before examining various efforts to monitor implementation of the *Programme of Action*, it is worth considering the role played by national reporting in the UN Conference process, and in particular its relationship with *Programme* implementation.

While reporting is not implementation, they may be related in several ways. In the first instance, publicity surrounding reporting may raise awareness of the UN Conference process and the *Programme of Action* among government officials responsible for implementation. For example, at a wide range of events held in the run-up to the 2003 BMS, Chairperson Inoguchi repeatedly called upon states to prepare reports in time for the Meeting. The first phase of the UNDP reporting project also helped bring the UN Conference process to the attention of governments that were not aware of it, or at least were not focused on reporting and the BMS. The monitoring processes described in the next sections of the chapter have fulfilled the same function.

Related to this first catalyst for implementation is a second, no less important one. Specifically, the task of reporting, when taken seriously, can build capacity to implement across different government agencies. The *Programme of Action* covers a wide range of activity. Ministries such as foreign affairs, defence, the interior, and industry all need to be brought together to generate the information required for the report—just as they need to work together for the effective coordination, development, and implementation of national small arms policy. Enhancing the capacity of governments for inter-ministerial cooperation, including information sharing, was in fact one of the key outcomes of the UNDP reporting project, especially its field-assistance component.

Third, reporting can spur implementation for the simple reason that states want to have something to report on. This may have been less of a factor to date than it will be later on, as countries which have lagged behind in implementing the *Programme of Action* are prodded through positive example (the reporting of other states) and critical scrutiny (third-party monitoring) to take action to implement the *Programme* and report on these efforts.

> **Box 8.1 Capacity development for reporting**
>
> In April 2003, UNDP and UNDDA, in collaboration with UNIDIR, launched a project which aimed to build the capacity of states to report on their implementation of the *UN Programme of Action*. The first phase of the project was timed to coincide with the July 2003 BMS, offering support to selected countries as they prepared their inputs for this meeting. Phase II of the project began in September 2003 and is scheduled to continue until September 2006. This second phase aims to develop the long-term capacity of those countries most affected by the small arms problem, allowing them to participate in the UN Conference process through reporting, information sharing, and implementation of the *Programme*.
>
> During the first phase of the project, 25 states requested and received assistance. This included the provision of a Reporting Assistance Package (all 25 states), dedicated desk-bound assistance (five states), and field missions (two states). Twenty-three phase 1 participants responded by submitting a report to the 2003 BMS, making a national statement, and/or appointing a national point of contact. Twenty participating states submitted reports to the BMS, representing almost one-third of reports received from developing countries.
>
> Phase II of the project will retain its focus on reporting while stepping up efforts to promote implementation of the *Programme of Action* over the longer term. This work will include raising awareness of the *Programme*, involving new partners in the project, and integrating it into broader UNDP programmes and activities.
>
> Further information on the project, including the full text of the Assistance Package, can be obtained from <http://www.undp.org/bcpr/smallarms/PoA.htm>
>
> Source: Wille (2003)

Fourth, the reporting task affords governments an opportunity to review their implementation efforts, identifying gaps, as well as needs to be met in filling these gaps. This 'stock-taking exercise' can also extend, beyond the national level, to the regional and global ones, as states collectively identify gaps in implementation and resolve to address these (matching needs and assistance).

Finally, the exchange of information inherent in the reporting process can allow states, collectively, to learn from the experience of others in implementing the *Programme of Action*. Of course, if lessons are to be learned and shared, governments need to provide a complete and detailed account of the challenges and problems they have encountered in implementation, along with the measures (successful or not) they have taken to address these. As indicated in the preceding section, current reporting efforts fall short of what is needed in this regard.

Monitoring processes

Monitoring involves the independent observation and evaluation of efforts to implement particular commitments. National reporting feeds into this process. The information that states provide in their reports and statements mostly focuses on their own implementation of the *Programme of Action*. The bigger picture—implementation across the board—must be derived through a systematic review and analysis of all national reports. These need to be supplemented with other sources of information, as independent assessments of national implementation clearly cannot rely on national reporting alone.

The responsibilities of the UN under the *Programme of Action* with respect to monitoring are quite modest, namely 'to collate and circulate data and information provided by States ... on implementation by those States of the Programme of Action' (UNGA, 2001b, sec. II, para. 33). The task of analysing such information has been taken up by other actors, especially NGOs.

The role of civil society in monitoring the implementation of the *Programme of Action* is key. NGOs, in the first instance, can undertake the kind of systematic and intensive review of *Programme* implementation that no single state has an interest in providing. Clearly, NGOs are also better placed than states themselves to undertake impartial evaluations of state behaviour—though NGO independence is far from absolute. NGOs are important players in the UN

The role of civil society in monitoring the implementation of the Programme of Action *is key.*

Conference process, helping, for example, to set agendas and provide information (Small Arms Survey, 2002, pp. 242–3). They are also increasingly involved in implementation (BtB and IANSA, 2003). Yet they are not states, and it is states that have primary responsibility for implementing the *Programme*—and whose conduct requires monitoring.

Given their relative independence, NGOs are usually able to point to problems of implementation in a more direct and forthright way than states themselves or the organizations they are part of, including the UN—praising and shaming individual governments as they deem necessary. Nevertheless, the relationship between governments and civil society in particular countries can affect quite dramatically the capacity of NGOs to fulfil their informal monitoring function.

Monitoring is often *ad hoc*. For example, the Centre for Humanitarian Dialogue, in the first issue of its *Small Arms and Human Security Bulletin,* analysed the national reports submitted to the July 2003 BMS (Widmer and Buchanan, 2003). International Alert has examined control practices in selected regions as part of its project for Monitoring the Implementation of Small Arms Controls (MISAC).[23] The Small Arms Survey also reviews progress in the development and implementation of small arms measures at the national, regional, and global levels (BROKERS).

To launch the 'Swords into Ploughshares' exhibit in London in January 2002, a Mozambican artist 'plays' a saxophone sculpture made from an AK-47 assault rifle.

The next two subsections will look at two other mechanisms. The first, the report produced by the Biting the Bullet (BtB) project and the International Action Network on Small Arms (IANSA) involves something close to a classic NGO monitoring exercise, while the second, the so-called 'Geneva Process', brings states, international organizations, and NGOs together in an information-sharing arrangement which fulfills many, though not all, of the functions of a traditional monitoring mechanism.

The BtB–IANSA report[24]

The lack of formal monitoring provisions in the *Programme of Action* led the BtB project team (Bradford University, International Alert, and Saferworld) and IANSA to join forces to provide a civil society contribution to monitoring efforts. The resulting report (BtB and IANSA, 2003), launched at the 2003 BMS, draws together information on a large number of states, highlighting weaknesses and broad trends in *Programme* implementation.

Project aims

The BtB–IANSA project sought to assess progress by states and civil society in implementing the *Programme of Action*. Specific goals included:

- identifying measures taken around the world to meet *Programme* commitments and exposing emerging gaps;
- identifying and highlighting key lessons and good practices that could be learned to enhance future implementation;

- examining international cooperation and assistance related to the *Programme* in order to identify emerging successes and problems;
- improving understanding of the role played by partnerships between states, regional/international organizations, and civil society; and
- enhancing the capacity of civil society organizations throughout the world to undertake research and advocacy related to small arms and the *Programme of Action*.

Methods and activities

Due to funding constraints, the report was produced and published in only five months. Much of the information it contains was collected in-country, largely by civil society organizations. With the support of IANSA networks, more than 100 NGOs in all regions provided primary information and research support. In the first stage of the research, a questionnaire was distributed to NGOs in the IANSA network and to other experts from civil society, international organizations, and governments. Expert consultants were contracted to produce the regional and country case studies. Regional workshops were also held in Jordan, Malawi, Peru, and Sri Lanka for purposes of building the capacity of participants to contribute to the report and research and monitor implementation in their areas.

The BtB–IANSA team compiled and validated the information returned by civil society and expert partners, and augmented it with information drawn from a wide range of sources, including the Geneva Process (see next subsection). A draft report was reviewed by an expert advisory panel and selected consultants before being finalized and released to governments at a Geneva Forum meeting, in Geneva, in June 2003. The report was formally launched a month later, in New York, at the First BMS.

All measures that contributed to the implementation of the *Programme of Action*, whether or not directly inspired by the UN Conference process, were, in theory, of interest to the BtB–IANSA team. The project nevertheless focused

> *The BtB-IANSA project focused on a narrow range of Programme commitments that it considered essential first steps towards broader implementation.*

Box 8.2   Key findings of the BtB-IANSA report

The report (BtB and IANSA, 2003) focuses on identifying emerging strengths and weaknesses in the implementation of the *Programme of Action* at the national, regional, and international levels, including examples of good (and bad) practices. An important question is the extent to which there has been positive movement since 2001, and whether appropriate linkages and partnerships are developing between issues and actors. On the basis of these assessments, the report makes a number of conclusions and recommendations.

Overall, the report finds that a number of promising steps have been taken since July 2001 in many countries and most regions that contribute to *Programme* implementation and provide useful lessons or precedents for the future. These gains, however, remain modest. Much more needs to be done to address the various aspects of the small arms problem as reflected in the *Programme*. In particular:

▶ Implementation of the first steps in the process has been limited and mixed, with many national points of contact officially established (though often with limited capacity), but few reviews of laws and procedures or national action plans.
▶ There is considerable regional variation in the implementation of the *Programme of Action*, with greater—if limited—successes correlating with the presence of substantial regional agreements and cooperative relationships between governments and civil society.
▶ Donor responses to the *Programme* have been mixed, with increased assistance available, but concentrated in a few areas and often poorly coordinated.

Source: Bourne and Greene (2003)

on a narrower range of *Programme* commitments that it considered essential first steps towards broader implementation. These included:

- the creation of national points of contact and national coordination agencies;
- governmental reviews of national laws and procedures;
- the formulation of national action plans; and
- the development of strategic partnerships across government, and between civil society, government, and regional or international organizations.

Contributions to the UN Conference process

The BtB–IANSA report was welcomed by governments, international organizations, and NGOs as a valuable contribution to the 2003 BMS and the broader *Programme of Action* review process. It continues to serve as a resource for governments and civil society in their implementation and monitoring efforts.

The BtB–IANSA project makes several important contributions to the review and promotion of *Programme* implementation. In the first instance, the process of gathering information for the report helped increase awareness among governments of their responsibilities under the *Programme* and of the concerns and activities of local NGOs. The identification of measures—or lack of measures—by particular states in the final report also prompted officials from those countries to come forward with additional information on their initiatives and plans. Perhaps most significantly, the report's emphasis on good initiatives and practices will contribute to lessons learned processes.

The BtB–IANSA project equally underlines the role that civil society can play in monitoring implementation of the *Programme of Action*. The process of preparing the report was explicitly designed to develop IANSA and wider civil society networks and to build the capacity of NGOs in developing and transitional societies to engage with their governments on small arms issues and monitor their implementation of the *Programme*. The four regional training workshops were particularly important in this respect.

The time and resource constraints faced by the project were, however, a key limitation. These precluded the kind of detailed and comprehensive civil society monitoring that, for example, the Landmine Monitor has provided in relation to the *Mine Ban Convention* (Convention, 1997). As a result, although the BtB–IANSA report identifies whether national coordination mechanisms or relevant laws are in place, it does not systematically investigate their underlying substance and effectiveness. Moreover, while the report notes strengths, gaps, and weaknesses in national implementation of the *Programme*, it does not assess compliance by states with all of their commitments. While such an assessment may be premature at this early stage of the UN Conference process, it will require more far-reaching efforts if attempted later on.

Another drawback of the final report is its limited use of the 2003 national reports on *Programme* implementation. Those national reports that were available as the BtB–IANSA report was being finalized, in the spring of 2003, were taken into account. However, the majority of the 2003 reports were released shortly afterwards, during and around the time of the July BMS.

A lack of NGO capacity in much of the world was a further constraint on the BtB–IANSA reporting exercise. This is often more than a problem of resources. In certain parts of the world, governments remain reluctant to provide information on small arms. Their relationship with civil society is strained at best. NGOs in these countries and regions face huge obstacles in gathering information on *Programme* implementation.

The BtB–IANSA team plans further monitoring initiatives for the 2005 BMS and 2006 Review Conference. Although the details remain to be worked out, BtB and IANSA are convinced that it will be necessary to go beyond monitoring the initial steps in *Programme* implementation—the approach taken in 2003—to undertake a more critical and comprehensive assessment of performance in each of the *Programme's* key areas. This would, in particular, provide the basis for a review of the adequacy of existing *Programme* commitments and mechanisms. A key element of these new initiatives will be the further development of civil society's capacity to monitor and review implementation of the *Programme of Action* (Bourne and Greene, 2003).

The Geneva Process [25]

What has become known as the Geneva Process on small arms brings together governments, international organizations, and NGOs in regular informal consultations for purposes of promoting and monitoring implementation of the *Programme of Action*. An initiative of the Geneva Forum,[26] the Geneva Process was established in order to help maintain political momentum on the small arms issue between UN biennial meetings and, at the same time, draw on the resources present in this area in Geneva.

Between May 2002, when the mechanism was launched, and the July 2003 BMS, the Geneva Process met nine times. As of October 2003, 25 states, seven international organizations, and seven NGOs were participating. Governments, international organizations, and NGOs participate on an equal footing and share chairing and planning responsibilities.

> The Geneva Process was established to help maintain political momentum on the small arms issue between UN biennial meetings.

Monitoring Programme *implementation*

The Geneva Process has played an important role in encouraging and facilitating regular reporting on the implementation of the *Programme of Action* and in making this information publicly available. At each meeting, Geneva Process participants—governments, international organizations, and NGOs—report on implementation activities in which they are involved. A researcher also presents independently gathered data on *Programme* implementation. All of this information is fed into a public, searchable database which is continuously updated (see Box 8.3).

Box 8.3   The Geneva Process database

In cooperation with the Geneva Forum, the Small Arms Survey has established a database containing information on measures taken to implement the *UN Programme of Action* since its adoption in July 2001.

The database (*Implementation of the UN Programme of Action*) includes documents circulated as part of the Geneva Process, as well as statements and reports from regional and international meetings—including the national reports and statements submitted in connection with the 2003 BMS. Various press sources provide additional information on small arms-related action.

As of the end of November 2003, the database contained over 1,100 documents. It can be accessed at <http://www.smallarmssurvey.org/databases.htm>

The Geneva Process is not a fully-fledged monitoring instrument. As noted already, only a limited number of countries and organizations participate. Its independent data-gathering capacity is also modest. Nor has the Geneva Process sought to analyse or evaluate the information it has generated in any systematic way. While participants have reviewed progress made in implementing the *Programme of Action* in general terms, the monitoring role of the Geneva Process has mostly been limited to the gathering and dissemination of information. The information the Process provides has, however, fed into other monitoring initiatives, such as the BtB–IANSA project (see above).

MONITORING

Information-sharing and implementation

Much of the work of the Geneva Process has focused on promoting implementation of the *Programme of Action*. The sharing of information and experience from around the world has been central to this activity. At one session, officials from South Africa briefed Geneva Process participants on their country's experience in implementing small arms collection and destruction projects. In addition to highlighting the many 'hidden costs' associated with these programmes, this discussion also revealed that much practical small arms work can be carried out by developing countries without outside financial assistance.

The Geneva Process has also sought to promote *Programme* implementation by helping states prepare their national reports. For example, as a result of discussions initiated by the Geneva Process in June 2002, the Small Arms Survey developed a set of reporting guidelines, which the Geneva Forum then informally circulated to all UN member states. These subsequently formed the basis of the more detailed guidelines used in the UNDP–UNDDA reporting assistance project (see Box 8.1).

The Geneva Forum initially envisaged the Geneva Process as a temporary mechanism, which would serve, above all, to help participants prepare for the First BMS in July 2003. At their last meeting before the 2003 BMS, however, participants decided to continue the Geneva Process beyond the First BMS. Governmental participants, in particular, saw the Process as a means of keeping international attention focused on the small arms issue in the years between the 2003 and 2005 biennial meetings.

> The monitoring role of the Geneva Process has mostly been limited to the gathering and dissemination of information.

UN ARMS EMBARGOES[27]

Separate yet related to the UN Conference process discussed above is the topic of UN arms embargoes. This section first explores some of the links between the two processes, before reviewing, in some detail, the various ways that monitoring and verification bolster state compliance with arms embargoes.

Arms embargoes aim at halting the flow of weapons and the provision of training and related services to a 'target' government or faction. Part of the 'targeted' or 'smart' sanctions toolbox, they are often accompanied by transport-related sanctions, including aviation sanctions and naval blockades, designed to reduce the cross-border movement of weapons through inspections and, more generally, to deter embargo violations. While arms embargoes are sometimes stand-alone measures, they often form part of a broader sanctions regime comprising restrictions on trade (including trade in lucrative commodities, such as oil and diamonds), the movement of funds, travel, and/or diplomatic representation.

UN Secretary-General Kofi Annan addresses the UN Security Council, which voted to impose an arms embargo on armed groups in eastern Congo, on 28 July 2003.

Multilateral arms embargoes long predate international efforts to address the small arms problem, which began in earnest in the mid-1990s and reached a milestone with the adoption of the *UN Programme of Action* in July 2001. The two instruments, though separate, nevertheless complement and reinforce one another. The effective implementation of one furthers the aims of the other.

The *Programme* takes up the question of arms embargoes in several of its provisions. It comes up indirectly in section II of the *Programme*, which sets out a series of national-level commitments, including one relating to the licensing of small arms exports:

> [States agree] To assess applications for export authorizations according to strict national regulations and procedures that cover all small arms and light weapons and are consistent with the existing responsibilities of States under relevant international law, taking into account in particular the risk of diversion of these weapons into the illegal trade. (UNGA 2001b, sec. II, para. 11)

The term 'relevant international law' would encompass all arms embargo regimes, including any regional ones, that the state is legally bound to implement. Box 8.4 highlights three provisions of the *Programme of Action* which mention arms embargoes specifically. In each case, the reference is to arms embargoes adopted by the UN Security Council.

Box 8.4   The UN *Programme of Action* on arms embargoes

Preamble:
12. Recalling the obligations of States to fully comply with arms embargoes decided by the United Nations Security Council in accordance with the Charter of the United Nations,

Section II: [States undertake:]
At the national level
15. To take appropriate measures, including all legal or administrative means, against any activity that violates a United Nations Security Council arms embargo in accordance with the Charter of the United Nations.

At the global level
32. To cooperate with the United Nations system to ensure the effective implementation of arms embargoes decided by the United Nations Security Council in accordance with the Charter of the United Nations.

Security Council arms embargoes are not 'small-arms specific' in that they typically cover a wide range of weapons (and related materials and services), including, in addition to small arms and light weapons, major conventional systems and weapons of mass destruction (including precursor material). Yet the link between UN arms embargoes and the UN small arms process is strong, since small arms are very often the weapons of primary concern in embargoed zones. A good example is Somalia, under UN arms embargo since January 1992. Small arms and light weapons have driven the insecurity that has plagued the country since the overthrow of the Siad Barre regime in January 1991.[28] Nevertheless, it was only after the terrorist attacks of 11 September, 2001 that the Security Council made a serious effort to ensure the embargo was being respected—specifically through improved monitoring.[29]

The Somalia arms embargo was part of a flurry of Security Council activity that occurred in the years following the end of the Cold War. This activity involved much more than arms embargoes, but arms embargoes have been the Council's preferred sanctions measure throughout this period (see Box 8.5).

A crisis in UN sanctions policy in the mid-1990s gave way to an increased emphasis on 'targeted' or 'smart' sanctions, including arms embargoes. These developments are reviewed in the recent sanctions literature (Brzoska, 2003; Cortright and Lopez, 2002). This section focuses on one crucial component of this recent evolution in UN sanctions policy: monitoring and verification.

Small arms are very often the weapons of primary concern in embargoed zones.

Box 8.5 Security Council arms embargoes

UN Security Council arms embargoes that are mandatory, not mere recommendations,[30] legally bind all UN member states. In accordance with Article 25 of the UN Charter, all UN member states are obliged to abide by these embargoes (UN, 1945). This includes the adoption of necessary national implementing legislation.[31] The Security Council's 'law-making power' is a rarity in international law; states normally decide, on a case-by-case basis, whether or not to undertake particular legal obligations. In the case of the UN, it is the Security Council, with its restricted membership[32]—not the UN membership as a whole—that decides whether and when to impose a mandatory arms embargo upon a particular state or faction.

During the Cold War, the frequent clash of interests between the US and USSR meant that the Security Council only rarely imposed mandatory sanctions. Such sanctions, including arms embargoes, were applied in only two cases: Southern Rhodesia (now Zimbabwe)[33] and South Africa.[34] The Council has been far more active since the end of the Cold War. Since 1990, it has imposed mandatory arms embargoes against the states of Afghanistan,[35] Ethiopia and Eritrea,[36] Haiti,[37] Iraq,[38] Liberia,[39] Libya,[40] Rwanda,[41] Sierra Leone,[42] Somalia,[43] and Yugoslavia (former Yugoslavia[44] and Serbia and Montenegro[45]).

The Security Council has also imposed mandatory arms embargoes against non-governmental forces operating in Angola,[46] Democratic Republic of Congo,[47] Rwanda,[48] and Sierra Leone.[49] In addition, the Council has prohibited the supply of weapons to Osama bin Laden, members of al Qaeda, the Taliban, and their associates,[50] as well as 'terrorists' in general.[51] During the post-Cold War period, the Security Council has recommended arms embargoes in relation to conflicts in Afghanistan,[52] Armenia and Azerbaijan,[53] Ethiopia and Eritrea,[54] and Yemen.[55]

The report of the expert panel set up to investigate violations of sanctions against the Angolan rebel movement União Nacional Para a Independência Total de Angola (UNITA), released in March 2000 (UNSC, 2000a), was a watershed in UN sanctions verification. The report identified a specific country (Bulgaria) as the principal source of weapons to UNITA in contravention of the embargo. It named other governments, heads of state, and private actors it considered complicit in a broad range of sanctions violations, highlighting the role of brokers in this activity (BROKERS). The example of the Angola experts report has been followed by subsequent expert panels, as these have continued to provide detailed and specific information on sanctions violations.

In the next subsections of the chapter we inquire into where these recent efforts to improve the monitoring and verification of arms embargoes (and sanctions generally) have brought us. We first examine verification systems in general terms (including relevant institutions) before turning to the specific mechanisms that underpin them.

A UN report accused Presidents Blaise Compaoré of Burkina Faso (left) and Gnassingbé Eyadéma of Togo (right) of helping Angola's UNITA rebels to circumvent international sanctions.

Verification systems

Verification systems serve to determine whether states are abiding by particular commitments, such as the implementation of UN Security Council arms embargoes, which, though decided by the Security Council, must be implemented by UN member states. Where effective, these systems detect and deter non-compliance, facilitate parties' demonstration of compliance, and generally build confidence that the relevant commitment is being effectively implemented by all parties. Where the commitment amounts to a legal obligation and the organization's legal framework so provides, the body imposing the obligation may elect to take further action to ensure that compliance is achieved and transgressors punished. Whereas negotiated arms limitation agreements usually lay down procedures for dealing with confirmed cases of non-compliance,[56] this is at the discretion of the Security Council under its own sanctions regimes.

Using its UN Charter powers, the Security Council has established a range of *ad hoc* institutions to verify compliance with mandatory sanctions, either at the time the sanctions are adopted or some months—or even years—afterwards. These bodies may oversee sanctions implementation, collect and assess compliance reports from UN member states, and/or make recommendations for improving the effectiveness of sanctions regimes. In several instances, the Council has used monitoring mechanisms to gather and generate information on implementation. Regional organizations monitoring conflicts in their region, including the flow of weapons, have often contributed to these processes.

> The Security Council has established a range of *ad hoc* institutions to verify compliance with mandatory sanctions.

The Sanctions Committees are among the most important of these institutions. Made up of states represented on the Security Council, these bodies oversee the implementation of UN sanctions regimes. Among other tasks, they compile and analyse compliance information received from UN member states (in the form of national reports) and other sources. The UN Secretariat assists them in their work. The Council has created Sanctions Committees for most of the mandatory arms embargoes it has adopted since 1990 (though not always promptly). Sanctions Committees have varied considerably in their effectiveness over the years, often as a function of the Committee chair and the number of staff the Committee has at its disposal.

The Sanctions Committees' limitations were especially evident in the case of Rwanda. That Sanctions Committee's failure to gain the cooperation of Rwanda's neighbours in investigating sustained and widespread violations of the sanctions regime led the Security Council to establish an Independent Commission of Inquiry (INCOI) (UNSC, 1995c) with substantially more intrusive investigative powers. Since 1999, the Council has made increasing use of sanctions monitoring bodies of this kind, establishing independent Panels of Experts for sanctions in Angola,[57] Liberia,[58] Sierra Leone,[59] and Somalia.[60] The Security Council has also set up a Monitoring Group[61] and Counter-Terrorism Committee[62] to monitor implementation of measures, including arms embargoes, against international terrorism.

> Sanctions Committees have varied considerably in their effectiveness.

The Security Council deployed its most far-reaching verification body in Iraq following the 1990–91 Gulf War. The United Nations Special Commission (UNSCOM)[63] conducted on-site weapons verification and destruction from June 1991 to December 1999. Its successor, the United Nations Monitoring, Verification and Inspection Commission (UNMOVIC),[64] operated from November 2002 to March 2003. Although small arms were covered under the broad arms embargo imposed on Iraq in August 1990 (UNSC, 1990), both UNSCOM and UNMOVIC focused on Iraq's weapons of mass destruction and long-range missile systems. The invasive on-site inspection powers granted UNSCOM and UNMOVIC have no parallel in UN sanctions history and are unlikely to feature in other UN monitoring efforts any time soon.

Verification mechanisms

The Security Council has employed a range of mechanisms, in varying combinations, to assess implementation of its mandatory arms embargoes. These include the following:[65]

- national reporting;
- compilation and analysis of information;
- remote or on-site monitoring; and
- clarification.

MONITORING

In the final stage of the verification process, the Security Council decides whether a particular state is in breach of its obligation to uphold the embargo. Non-implementation, as determined through the mechanisms outlined above, may be attributed to private traffickers operating beyond governmental control. Or the Council may decide that the government is itself involved in embargo-busting and take corrective action.

Verification systems for arms embargoes are often part of broader sanctions regimes. In many of the cases reviewed below, the text will therefore refer to 'sanctions' rather than 'embargoes'.

National reporting

National reporting is a common feature of embargo verification systems. The Security Council requests or requires UN member states to provide the UN Secretary-General or relevant Sanctions Committee with an initial report (or 'declaration') on measures taken to implement the embargo, and to submit additional reports on further action. The Security Council usually also asks states to forward any information they may possess on suspected sanctions violations.

The amount of information countries are expected to provide in their reports differs across the various sanctions regimes. In the context of sanctions imposed on rebel groups in Sierra Leone, UN member states were to notify the Sierra Leone Sanctions Committee of all arms they exported to the country, while the Sierra Leone government was to inform the Committee of any arms it imported. The latter were to be marked and registered in order to facilitate compliance monitoring (UNSC, 1998b, para. 4). However, the standard reporting requirement is simply to: 'seek from all States information regarding the action taken by them concerning the effective implementation of the general and complete embargo on all deliveries of weapons and military equipment to' the embargoed destination or actors (UNSC, 1992d, para. 11(a)).

In principle, by enabling states to demonstrate their compliance with an arms embargo, these reports can reduce doubts or suspicions about implementation, encourage other states to report, and help build confidence in the embargo (UNIDIR and VERTIC, 2003, pp. 3–4). However, as many Sanctions Committees have discovered,[66] states often fail to fulfill their reporting obligations.[67] Nor can the reports that states do submit necessarily be taken at face value. The Sanctions Committee for the Ethiopia and Eritrea sanctions, for example, indicated its work had been 'constrained' by the lack of a mechanism to verify reported data (UNSC, 2001b, para. 8).

> **National reporting is a common feature of embargo verification systems.**

Compilation and analysis of information

At this stage of the verification process, the monitoring body (usually the Sanctions Committee) collects and analyses available information in order to detect any inconsistencies or ambiguities. Successive reports from the same state are checked against each other and against those submitted by other states. In practice, Sanctions Committees receive much of their information from sources other than the national reports. Other material fed into the verification system includes reports of any monitoring mechanisms that are part of the sanctions regime, information from the media and NGOs, and intelligence collected and forwarded by states.

> **States often fail to fulfil their reporting obligations.**

Monitoring

Monitoring serves to verify and supplement information received from national reports and other sources on arms embargo implementation. It may be *ad hoc* or continuous, and conducted remotely or on-site. Specific monitoring activities that have been authorized by the Security Council include: the establishment of expert panels to investigate sanctions violations; border monitoring of the movement of goods into a target state (including naval and air blockades); and on-site sanctions coordinators.

The specific form that monitoring takes varies widely among sanctions regimes. In many cases, the Sanctions Committee, alone, has had responsibility for monitoring. However, many Sanctions Committees have interpreted their mandates restrictively, effectively precluding an active monitoring role. A good example is the Libya Sanctions Committee. While it had a standard mandate to examine state reports on sanctions implementation and receive and consider reports on violations, it did not seek out the reports of states which failed to submit them and largely left investigation of alleged violations to UN member states (Cortright and Lopez, 2000, p. 117). This can be contrasted with the approach of the Sierra Leone Sanctions Committee, which actively sought the compliance and cooperation of governments and organizations in the subregion (Cortright and Lopez, 2000, p. 174).

Monitoring has been most extensive when conducted as part of comprehensive sanctions regimes. The monitoring of such sanctions depends for its effectiveness on the cooperation of states neighbouring the target and, as always, the provision of adequate resources. The comprehensive sanctions against the former Yugoslavia in the early 1990s were backed by an array of mechanisms designed to assess, enforce, and improve implementation. These included a naval blockade, sanctions assistance missions (SAMs), a Sanctions Assistance Missions Communications Center (SAMCOMM), and a Sanctions Coordinator. The EU, NATO, the OSCE, and the WEU conducted these operations in partnership with the UN. Extensive monitoring was also a feature of the comprehensive sanctions imposed on Iraq in 1990–91. Yet, monitoring of this scale has been, and is likely to remain, exceptional—particularly with the Security Council now shying away from the comprehensive sanctions it imposed, almost reflexively, in the early 1990s.[68]

Since the late 1990s, the Security Council has taken something of a middle road between bare-bones monitoring (Sanctions Committees) and the sophisticated efforts that it mounted for some of the comprehensive sanctions regimes. Beginning with the UNITA sanctions investigations, in 1999–2000, the Council has increasingly looked to expert panels to generate independent information on compliance with its sanctions regimes. These panels are typically mandated to investigate sanctions violations, and recommend measures to end specific breaches and improve implementation generally. Their reports have been made public, putting pressure on parties named as complicit in sanctions violations to mend their ways. At the same time, the independence of these panels from the Security Council allows Council members to distance themselves from panel findings and recommendations when seeking to resolve compliance problems through 'quiet diplomacy' (Cortright and Lopez, 2002, p. 206).[69]

Clarification

Any ambiguities or inconsistencies detected through the information collection, analysis, and verification processes must be resolved if the verification system and the sanctions regime in general are to retain their credibility. False evidence of non-compliance may be deliberately fed into the verification system for political reasons. This needs to be weeded out, while well-founded allegations of non-compliance should be confirmed and publicized so that further breaches of the embargoes regime can be deterred.

For these purposes, the sanctions oversight body (Sanctions Committee) may seek clarification from the state concerned or conduct additional verification activities, including fact-finding missions or on-site inspections. A key issue at this stage of the verification process is whether non-implementation, once confirmed, amounts to non-compliance. In other words, is there evidence that a particular government is complicit in sanctions-breaking detected from or across its territory?

Determining non-compliance

Once the overall assessment of implementation is complete, the Security Council must decide whether any instances of non-implementation detected through the processes outlined above amount to non-compliance. This determination may not be straightforward. Can and should a particular state be held accountable for the acts of individual traffickers who have evaded its control? Is government complicity or active involvement in such trade established?

Then President Charles Taylor of Liberia: The subject of 'secondary' UN sanctions.

Strictly speaking, verification stops at the Security Council's determination of non-compliance. Further action to punish transgressors and/or ensure that they comply with UN sanctions is a separate matter. While several expert panels have recommended that the Council impose sanctions on governments found to have been complicit in arms embargo violations,[70] as of the end of 2003 the Security Council had imposed such 'secondary sanctions' in only one case—against the Charles Taylor government in Liberia as a result of its violation of sanctions against Sierra Leone rebels (UNSC, 2001a).

Verification and compliance

States care about their reputations.[71] Evidence that a state is breaching a mandatory arms embargo can jeopardize its standing in the international community. While Bulgaria protested loudly when the Angola sanctions panel identified the country as the principal source of weapons to the UNITA rebel movement, it subsequently strengthened its controls over arms transfers. The naming of specific companies and individuals in expert panel reports has also directed international attention to their activities. Although this has not put an end to these operations,[72] it has at least made them more difficult.

The practice begun by the Angola sanctions panel of 'naming and shaming' governments and individuals involved in UN sanctions-breaking has been continued by subsequent panels. While this practice has met opposition in some quarters—particularly among developing countries, worried that it could be used to withhold development assistance—many observers consider it a key means of improving sanctions compliance (Cortright and Lopez, 2002, pp. 172, 205–7).

This new openness in UN sanctions monitoring can be expected to enhance the deterrent effect that verification normally brings. States and other actors not only run the risk that sanctions-busting will be detected, they can anticipate that such activity will be widely publicized. Perhaps most important, this allows interested NGOs to keep up the pressure on transgressors, pushing for a change of behaviour and/or punishment. Arguably, the prospect of being 'named and shamed' is of greater concern for most states than the threat of UN enforcement action. As noted above, the Security Council has so far been reluctant to take enforcement action in response to confirmed instances of sanctions-breaking, though the precedent that exists, with respect to Liberia, is recent.

Of course, no verification or enforcement system, no matter how effective, can ensure perfect compliance with UN sanctions. States may decide to breach an arms embargo for a variety of reasons. The violating state may have some special affinity with the target, such as ethnic or religious ties. States neighbouring the target may decide that overriding national security, economic, or other interests dictate a breach of the sanctions regime—for example, arming factions under embargo

> Evidence that a state is breaching a mandatory arms embargo can jeopardize its standing in the international community.

for purposes of wielding influence or protecting national territory. Factors leading to inadvertent sanctions breaking include unclear Security Council resolutions and a lack of capacity, including legislative capacity, in the implementing state.[73]

Improving verification

In his *Supplement to An Agenda for Peace* (UN, 1995), former UN Secretary-General Boutros Boutros-Ghali called for enhanced monitoring and implementation of sanctions at a time when many UN sanctions regimes were quite ineffective. Since then, a series of studies have considered how to improve the design, implementation, and monitoring of sanctions regimes. These have direct or indirect application to arms embargoes, depending on the study. Several of these initiatives have been launched by governments, in collaboration with NGOs and scholars. They include:

- the *Interlaken process*, initiated by Switzerland, on targeted financial sanctions;[74]
- the *Bonn–Berlin process*, launched by Germany and coordinated by the Bonn International Center for Conversion (BICC), on the design and implementation of arms embargoes and travel- and aviation-related sanctions;[75] and
- the *Stockholm process*, initiated by Sweden, focusing on the implementation of targeted sanctions, with specific recommendations for arms embargoes.[76]

Expert panels have issued their own recommendations for improving UN sanctions. Most often, these focus on the sanctions the particular panel is dealing with;[77] yet some panels have suggested improvements to broader UN sanctions practice.[78] Civil society has also led several recent evaluations of arms embargo implementation. Among these are the BICC project 'Evaluating the effectiveness of arms embargoes',[79] the reports of sanctions experts David Cortright and George Lopez (Cortright and Lopez, 2000, 2002), and a briefing paper by the Biting the Bullet project (Kirkham and Flew, 2003).

> Experts panels have issed their own recommendations for improving UN sanctions.

Several key recommendations[80] emerge from these studies regarding the improvement of sanctions (and arms embargo) monitoring and verification. One of the most important is that Sanctions Committees and other oversight bodies can do little if they lack the authority to carry out their mandates, especially *vis-à-vis* concerned governments. Many of the studies similarly underline the crucial role played in sanctions monitoring by expert panels and independent commissions of inquiry, and the importance of giving these bodies the competence, authority, and capacity they need to carry out in-depth investigations of the highest standard. The studies also underline the importance of reviewing sanctions implementation throughout the life of the regime, and making any changes that may be needed.

Another issue raised in the sanctions evaluations—one which in fact lies at the heart of compliance—is the clarity, or lack of clarity, in the underlying terms of the sanctions. Language regarding weapons is not usually a source of confusion in the arms embargo resolutions. Rather, the Security Council may leave states in doubt as to their applicability to dual-use items and weapons-related services. Where interpretation is left to the discretion of individual states, there is a risk that a 'lowest common denominator approach' will prevail as states opt for the least onerous interpretation of their obligations.

A central theme throughout the sanctions literature is the need to ensure that sanctions oversight bodies have the resources they need to do their job. Many commentators, noting the limitations inherent in the present, *ad hoc* system of sanctions adoption and verification, advocate the establishment of standing bodies and information systems. Often mentioned in this context is the establishment of a UN Sanctions Coordinator and sanctions assistance missions, modelled on the initiatives conducted in the former Yugoslavia. Increasing the capacity of sanctions oversight mechanisms would, in particular, allow these bodies to systematically review national implementation measures, including national legislation and penalties.

Capacity is also a key determinant of sanctions implementation by *states*, especially those neighbouring the target. Lack of capacity of neighbouring countries to control land, sea, and air space has been a major problem in the implementation of UN sanctions. Yet only very exceptionally have UN verification bodies been mandated to provide technical or other assistance to states for sanctions implementation. Important precedents include the SAMs, deployed by the EU and OSCE in support of UN sanctions in the former Yugoslavia, and the Counter-Terrorism Committee, mandated to build capacity among UN member states for the implementation of Security Council Resolution 1373 (UNSC, 2001c).

Where national implementation lags, outside pressure can be useful. Many of the sanctions studies stress the important role civil society has to play in monitoring arms embargo implementation. Human Rights Watch and other NGOs have scrutinized state compliance with specific embargoes (Human Rights Watch, 2003). Civil society experts have also participated in UN verification efforts and in broader discussions of sanctions reform.

Capacity is a key determinant of sanctions implementation by states, especially those neighbouring the target.

CONCLUSION

The UN Conference process, though still in its early stages, is showing encouraging signs of life. A key indication of this is the development of arrangements and mechanisms for reporting and monitoring of *Programme of Action* implementation. The chapter highlighted important developments at the 2003 BMS in this regard—particularly with respect to national reporting—and examined a few significant reporting and monitoring initiatives mounted by civil society, international organizations, and governments. It stressed the crucial role civil society plays in evaluating *Programme* implementation.

The verification of UN member state compliance with mandatory Security Council arms embargoes, examined in the second part of the chapter, is a separate, though related, process. Here, too, the aim is to see whether states are adhering to their commitments, though in this case the underlying commitment is legally binding. UN member states are required, under the law of the UN Charter, to implement arms embargoes decided by the Security Council. As a result, the same states (Security Council members) that establish a sanctions regime also decide on the verification measures that will accompany it.

Where political interest in ensuring compliance with sanctions regimes is strong, associated verification systems can be quite far-reaching (for example, the sanctions in Iraq and the former Yugoslavia). Yet the problem with these systems is precisely that they tend to be weak where political will itself is weak (for example, the Somalia embargo in the pre-11 September period). Civil society monitoring does not share this limitation.

Of course, in practice, the dichotomy just outlined—civil society monitoring for the UN Conference process, state-driven verification for mandatory UN arms embargoes—breaks down, to some extent. As discussed in the chapter, state reporting of *Programme of Action* implementation is a key component of the broader monitoring task. Similarly, civil society is an important part of efforts to verify compliance with UN arms embargoes. Reports of embargo violations by NGOs play a crucial role in reinforcing verification (and compliance) across the board.

Thus, the chapter's first main conclusion is that governments, international organizations, and NGOs all have essential roles to play in ensuring that small arms measures are effectively implemented. In some contexts, for example the Geneva Process, states and civil society (together with international organizations) work towards this common end in relatively close partnership. In others, the relationship is more adversarial, as with independent NGO monitoring of state compliance with arms embargoes. Other situations, such as the BtB–IANSA monitoring project, fall somewhere in between.

Yet in all cases—and this is the chapter's second conclusion—reporting, monitoring, and verification are crucial components of these efforts. An arms embargo without a serious verification system is not a serious initiative. The absence of verification betrays states' lack of interest in abiding by their (legal) obligations. While there are some encouraging signs in the evolution of sanctions verification practice over the past decade or so, verification efforts, along with the sanctions regimes themselves, remain vulnerable to weakening political will. Civil society could potentially enhance its role in filling this gap, as and when it appears.

The UN Conference process also depends on national reporting and independent monitoring for its success. Judging from the large number of national statements and reports presented to the 2003 BMS—along with the monitoring efforts now emerging from civil society—the Conference process is in reasonable health. Yet we are still a long way from full implementation of the *Programme*, and the reduction in small arms proliferation and misuse that this can be expected, over the long term, to bring. Sustained reporting and monitoring of *Programme* implementation will be essential to the continuing viability of this process.

8. LIST OF ABBREVIATIONS

BICC	Bonn International Center for Conversion
BMS	United Nations First Biennial Meeting of States to Consider the Implementation of the Programme of Action to Prevent, Combat and Eradicate the Illicit Trade in Small Arms and Light Weapons in All Its Aspects
BtB	Biting the Bullet (joint project of Bradford University, International Alert, and Saferworld)
DDR	Disarmament, demobilization, and reintegration
DFID	Department for International Development (UK)
EAPCCO	Eastern Africa Police Chiefs Cooperation Organisation
ECOWAS	Economic Community of West African States
EU	European Union
IANSA	International Action Network on Small Arms
IGAD	Intergovernmental Authority on Development
MISAC	Monitoring the Implementation of Small Arms Controls (project of International Alert)
NATO	North Atlantic Treaty Organization
OAS	Organization of American States
OSCE	Organization for Security and Co-operation in Europe
SADC	Southern African Development Community
SAM	Sanctions Assistance Mission
SAMCOMM	Sanctions Assistance Missions Communications Center
UNDDA	United Nations Department for Disarmament Affairs
UNDP	United Nations Development Programme
UNICEF	United Nations Children's Fund
UNIDIR	United Nations Institute for Disarmament Research
UNITA	União Nacional Para a Independência Total de Angola
UNMOVIC	United Nations Monitoring, Verification and Inspection Commission
UNSCOM	United Nations Special Commission on Iraq
WEU	Western European Union
WHO	World Health Organization

8. ENDNOTES

[1] United Nations First Biennial Meeting of States to Consider the Implementation of the Programme of Action to Prevent, Combat and Eradicate the Illicit Trade in Small Arms and Light Weapons in All Its Aspects.

[2] With respect to international environmental commitments, see, for example, Victor, Raustiala, and Skolnikoff (1998, pp. 676–84).

[3] For more on these concepts, particularly 'verification', see UNIDIR and VERTIC (2003).

[4] This section draws on information and analysis in Stohl (2003).

[5] For a comprehensive review of the Conference and its outcomes, see Small Arms Survey (2002, ch. 5).

[6] These issues, which included the regulation of civilian possession of small arms and transfers to non-state actors, were nevertheless mentioned by several states, as well as NGOs. See: Widmer and Buchanan (2003, p. 3); Batchelor (2003).

[7] Lithuania and Luxembourg, counted here among the 102 states, did not take the floor, but circulated written statements at the Biennial

8 Meeting. For the text of the national statements, see the UNDDA website <http://disarmament2.un.org/cab/salw-2003/statements.html>
8 These were issued as conference room papers: A/CONF.192/BMS/2003/CRP.1 to 98. For the current list of reports, see <http://disarmament2.un.org/cab/salw-nationalreports.html>
9 For further analysis, see: Batchelor (2003); Griffiths-Fulton (2003); Widmer and Buchanan (2003).
10 For more on this first round of post-July 2001 meetings, see Laurance and Stohl (2002, pp. 9–10).
11 For the report of the Group, see UNGA (2003a).
12 For more information on the activities of UN agencies, see the UNDDA website <http://disarmament2.un.org/cab/salw-2003/statements-Organizations.html> <http://disarmament2.un.org/cab/salw-orgs.html>
13 For more on the *UN Firearms Protocol*, see Small Arms Survey (2002, pp. 237–41). As of 31 January 2004, 52 states had signed this instrument, while 12 had ratified or acceded to it. For the latest information, see <http://www.unodc.org/unodc/crime_cicp_signatures_firearms.html>
14 For more information on regional initiatives in 2002–03, see UNGA (2003c).
15 See <http://www.seesac.org/>
16 See also Haug *et al.* (2002).
17 See also: sec. II, paras. 23, 27; sec. III, paras. 11–12.
18 This request has been reaffirmed by the UN General Assembly, most recently in its Resolution 58/241 (UNGA, 2003d, para. 13).
19 See <http://disarmament2.un.org/cab/salw.html>. This site also contains information submitted by states on their national legislation and points of contact, plus information from international agencies and NGOs.
20 The BtB–IANSA report on *Programme* implementation was able to confirm the existence of national points of contact in 111 states. As of 23 July 2003, the DDA website listed points of contact for 112 states. BtB–IANSA researchers could confirm the establishment or designation of national coordination agencies in only 37 states. This compares with a total of 192 states in the world in 2003. See BtB and IANSA (2003, pp. 25–27, 172–74).
21 The statements and reports of regional and international organizations can be found on the UNDDA website: <http://disarmament2.un.org/cab/salw-2003/statements-Organizations.html> <http://disarmament2.un.org/cab/salw-orgs.html>
22 See Widmer and Buchanan (2003, pp. 2–3).
23 For project reports, see <http://www.international-alert.org/policy/misac.htm>
24 This subsection is based on Bourne and Greene (2003).
25 This subsection is based on Mc Carthy (2003).
26 The Geneva Forum is a joint undertaking of the Quaker United Nations Office, UNIDIR, and the Programme for Strategic and International Security Studies of the Graduate Institute of International Studies, all based in Geneva.
27 This section draws on information and analysis in Woodward (2003).
28 See, for example, UNSC (2003g, paras. 71–73).
29 The Security Council first established a Team of Experts, which laid the groundwork for a subsequent Panel of Experts and an initial report (UNSC, 2002b; 2002c; 2003d). The Panel of Experts was re-established in April 2003 and given a range of tasks aimed at improving implementation of the arms embargo, including investigating violations and assessing the capacity of states in the region for implementation (UNSC, 2003e). It reported in November 2003 (UNSC, 2003g).
30 The terms the Security Council uses in an arms embargo resolution indicate whether the measure is mandatory or not. If the embargo is mandatory, the Council will 'decide that states shall', or 'demand' or 'order' states to take particular action in the operative part of the resolution. Reference is also usually made, in the resolution's preamble, operative section, or both, to Chapter VII of the UN Charter, from which the Security Council derives its enforcement powers. Where, by contrast, the Council is only recommending an embargo, it will 'request', 'urge', or 'call upon' UN member states to take such action.
31 States must typically transform international obligations into domestic law in order for these to have effect at the national level. Some states have adopted laws which give the government the power to issue regulations giving effect to UN Security Council decisions. This aspect of the national-level implementation of arms embargoes, previously overlooked, is now receiving greater attention. See, for example, BtB and IANSA (2003, chs. 3.1.2 and 3.1.3).

32 The Security Council has 15 member states, including five permanent members (China, France, the Russian Federation, the UK, and the US).
33 UNSC (1966).
34 UNSC (1977).
35 UNSC (2000d). This applied to 'the territory of Afghanistan under Taliban control', as designated by the Committee established under UNSC (1999c).
36 UNSC (2000b).
37 UNSC (1993a).
38 UNSC (1990).
39 UNSC (1992e; 2001a).
40 UNSC (1992c).
41 UNSC (1994a).
42 UNSC (1997).
43 UNSC (1992b).
44 UNSC (1991b; 1992a).
45 UNSC (1998a).
46 UNSC (1993c).
47 UNSC (2003f).
48 Non-governmental forces were the sole target from 1995: UNSC (1995a; 1995b).
49 Non-governmental forces were the sole target from 1998: UNSC (1998b).
50 UNSC (2002a).
51 UNSC (2001c).
52 UNSC (1996).
53 UNSC (1993b).
54 UNSC (1999a).
55 UNSC (1994b).
56 Note, however, that when all other procedures are exhausted, the matter is often referred to the UN Security Council for further action. See, for example, the *Biological Weapons Convention* (Convention, 1972, Article VI).
57 UNSC (1999b, para. 6).
58 UNSC (2001a, para. 19).
59 UNSC (2000c, para. 19).
60 UNSC (2002c, para. 3; 2003e, para. 3).
61 UNSC (2002a; 2003a), concerning sanctions against Osama Bin Laden, members of al Qaeda, the Taliban, and their associates.
62 UNSC (2001c), concerning measures against international terrorism.
63 Established under UNSC (1991a).
64 Established under UNSC (1999d).
65 For more information on verification systems, technologies, and techniques, see UNIDIR and VERTIC (2003).
66 In relation to the Rwanda sanctions, see UNSC (2002e, para.7).
67 This is also true of verification systems for negotiated arms limitation agreements. Where no provision is made for overseeing implementation (through a standing verification agency or treaty secretariat) or for assisting states in implementation, the rate of reporting tends to be low. An exception is the *Mine Ban Convention* (Convention, 1997). Although it lacks a treaty secretariat, a high percentage of States Parties have submitted the transparency reports due under the Convention's Article 7. For more information, see <http://disarmament2.un.org/MineBan.nsf>
68 See Brzoska (2003).
69 For more on the expert panels, see: Brzoska (2003); Vines (2003).
70 See, for example, UNSC (2000a, para. 179).
71 See Small Arms Survey (2003, p. 220).
72 See Vines (2003, p. 260).
73 For more on the factors influencing compliance and non-compliance, see Woodward (2003).
74 The process consisted of two expert seminars: Interlaken I, 17–19 March 1998, and Interlaken II, 29–31 March 1999, both held in Interlaken, Switzerland. For final reports, see <http://www.smartsanctions.ch>
75 See Brzoska (2001).
76 See Wallensteen, Staibano, and Eriksson (2003).
77 See, for example, the report of the Somalia experts panel: UNSC (2003g, paras. 173–92).
78 See, for example, the report of the Angola/UNITA sanctions panel: UNSC (2000a).
79 For more information, see the BICC website <http://www.bicc.de/projects/project_files/616_armsemb.html>
80 These are reviewed in more detail in Woodward (2003).

8. BIBLIOGRAPHY

Batchelor, Peter. 2003. 'The First Biennial Meeting of States on Small Arms: Building Momentum for Global Action.' *Disarmament Diplomacy*. No. 72. August–September. <http://www.acronym.org.uk/dd/dd72/72op1.htm>

Bourne, Mike and Owen Greene. 2003. *The BtB–IANSA Report on Implementation of the Programme of Action*. Background paper. Geneva: Small Arms Survey.

Brzoska, Michael (ed.). 2001. *Design and Implementation of Arms Embargoes and Travel and Aviation Related Sanctions: Results of the 'Bonn-Berlin Process'*. Bonn: BICC, in cooperation with the German Foreign Office and the United Nations Secretariat. <http://www.bicc.de/events/unsanc/index.html>

—. 2003. 'From Dumb to Smart? Recent Reforms of UN Sanctions.' *Global Governance*, Vol. 9, No. 4. October–December, pp. 519–35.

BtB (Biting the Bullet Project) and IANSA (International Action Network on Small Arms). 2003. *Implementing the Programme of Action 2003: Action by States and Civil Society*. <http://www.iansa.org/documents/report>

Convention. 1972. *Convention on the Prohibition of the Development, Production and Stockpiling of Bacteriological (Biological) and Toxin Weapons and on Their Destruction*. Adopted in London, Moscow, and Washington on 10 April. Entered into force on 26 March 1975. <http://www.state.gov/t/ac/trt/4718.htm>

Convention. 1997. *Convention on the Prohibition of the Use, Stockpiling, Production and Transfer of Anti-personnel Mines and on Their Destruction*. Adopted in Oslo on 18 September. Entered into force on 1 March 1999. <http://www.icbl.org/treaty/text.php3>

Cortright, David and George Lopez, with Richard Conroy, Jaleh Dashti-Gibson, and Julia Wagler. 2000. *The Sanctions Decade: Assessing UN Strategies in the 1990s*. Boulder, Colorado: Lynne Rienner.

—. with Linda Gerber. 2002. *Sanctions and the Search for Security: Challenges to UN Action*. Boulder, Colorado: Lynne Rienner.

Griffiths-Fulton, Lynne. 2003. *Moving Things Forward? The UN Biennial Meeting of States on Small Arms and Light Weapons*. Project Ploughshares Report. <http://www.ploughshares.ca/CONTENT/CONTROL%20WEAPONS/BMS%20report.pdf>

Haug, Maria, Martin Langvandslien, Lora Lumpe, and Nicholas Marsh. 2002. *Shining a Light on Small Arms Exports: The Record of State Transparency*. Occasional Paper No. 4. Geneva: Small Arms Survey. January.

Human Rights Watch. 2003. *Weapons Sanctions, Military Supplies, and Human Suffering: Illegal Arms Flows to Liberia and the June–July 2003 Shelling of Monrovia*. Briefing paper. 3 November. <http://www.hrw.org/arms/index.php>

Kirkham, Elizabeth and Catherine Flew. 2003. *Strengthening Embargoes and Enhancing Human Security*. Biting the Bullet Project. Briefing No. 17. <http://www.international-alert.org/pdf/pubsec/BB_Briefing171.pdf>

Kytömäki, Elli. 2003. *Review and Analysis of National Reports Submitted to the First Biennial Meeting of States, New York, 7–11 July 2003*. Background paper. Geneva: Small Arms Survey.

Laurance, Ed and Rachel Stohl. 2002. *Making Global Public Policy: The Case of Small Arms and Light Weapons*. Occasional Paper No. 7. Geneva: Small Arms Survey. December.

Mc Carthy, Patrick. 2003. *The Geneva Process on Small Arms: Monitoring and Promoting Implementation of the UN Programme of Action*. Background paper. Geneva: Small Arms Survey.

OSCE (Organization for Security and Co-operation in Europe). Forum for Security Co-operation. 2000. *OSCE Document on Small Arms and Light Weapons*. 24 November. FSC.DOC/1/00. <http://www.osce.org/docs/english/fsc/2000/decisions/fscew231.htm>

—. 2003. *Handbook of Best Practices on Small Arms and Light Weapons*. <http://www.osce.org/events/mc/netherlands2003/handbook/salw_all.pdf>

SADC (Southern African Development Community). 2001. *Protocol on the Control of Firearms, Ammunition and Other Related Materials in the Southern African Development Community (SADC) Region*. Blantyre, Malawi. 14 August. <http://www.smallarmssurvey.org/resources/reg_docs.htm#africa>

Small Arms Survey. 2002. *Small Arms Survey 2002: Counting the Human Cost*. Oxford: Oxford University Press.

—. 2003. *Small Arms Survey 2003: Development Denied*. Oxford: Oxford University Press.

Stohl, Rachel. 2003. *The Biennial Meeting of States: An Assessment*. Background paper. Geneva: Small Arms Survey.

UK (United Kingdom). DFID (Department for International Development). 2003. *Tackling Poverty by Reducing Armed Violence*. Recommendations from a Wilton Park Workshop. 14–16 April.

—. DFID, FCO (Foreign and Commonwealth Office London), and MoD (Ministry of Defence). 2003. *Strengthening International Export Controls of Small Arms and Light Weapons: Implementing the UN Programme of Action*. Conference report. Lancaster House, London. 14–15 January.

UN (United Nations). 1945. *Charter of the United Nations and Statute of the International Court of Justice*. Adopted in San Francisco, 26 June. Entered into force on 24 October. <http://www.un.org/aboutun/index.html>

—. 1995. *Supplement to an Agenda for Peace: Position Paper of the Secretary-General on the Occasion of the Fiftieth Anniversary of the United Nations*. UN document A/50/60–S/1995/1 of 25 January.

UNGA (United Nations General Assembly). 2001a. *Protocol against the Illicit Manufacturing of and Trafficking in Firearms, Their Parts and Components and Ammunition, Supplementing the United Nations Convention against Transnational Organized Crime ('UN Firearms Protocol')*. Adopted 31 May. Reproduced in UN document A/RES/55/255 of 8 June.

—. 2001b. *Programme of Action to Prevent, Combat and Eradicate the Illicit Trade in Small Arms and Light Weapons in All Its Aspects ('UN Programme of Action')*. 20 July. Reproduced in UN document A/CONF.192/15.

—. 2003a. *Report of the Group of Governmental Experts Established Pursuant to General Assembly Resolution 56/24 V of 24 December 2001, Entitled 'The Illicit Trade in Small Arms and Light Weapons in All Its Aspects'*. Reproduced in UN document A/58/138 of 11 July.

—. 2003b. *Report of the United Nations First Biennial Meeting of States to Consider the Implementation of the Programme of Action to Prevent, Combat and Eradicate the Illicit Trade in Small Arms and Light Weapons in All Its Aspects*. A/CONF.192/BMS/2003/1 of 18 July.

—. 2003c. Report of the Secretary-General. A/58/207 of 1 August.

—. 2003d. *The Illicit Trade in Small Arms and Light Weapons in All Its Aspects*. Resolution 58/241. Adopted 23 December. Reproduced in UN document A/RES/58/241 of 9 January 2004.

UNIDIR (United Nations Institute for Disarmament Research) and VERTIC (Verification Research, Training and Information Centre). 2003. *Coming to Terms with Security: A Handbook on Verification and Compliance*. Geneva: UN. UNIDIR/2003/10.

UNSC (United Nations Security Council). 1966. Resolution 232, adopted 16 December.

—. 1977. Resolution 418, adopted 4 November.

—. 1990. Resolution 661, adopted 6 August.

—. 1991a. Resolution 687, adopted 3 April.
—. 1991b. Resolution 713, adopted 25 September.
—. 1992a. Resolution 727, adopted 8 January.
—. 1992b. Resolution 733, adopted 23 January.
—. 1992c. Resolution 748, adopted 31 March.
—. 1992d. Resolution 751, adopted 24 April.
—. 1992e. Resolution 788, adopted 19 November. S/RES/788 (1992).
—. 1993a. Resolution 841, adopted 16 June. S/RES/841 (1993).
—. 1993b. Resolution 853, adopted 29 July. S/RES/853 (1993).
—. 1993c. Resolution 864, adopted 15 September. S/RES/864 (1993).
—. 1994a. Resolution 918, adopted 17 May. S/RES/918 (1994).
—. 1994b. Resolution 924, adopted 1 June. S/RES/924 (1994).
—. 1995a. Resolution 997, adopted 9 June. S/RES/997 (1995).
—. 1995b. Resolution 1011, adopted 16 August. S/RES/1011 (1995).
—. 1995c. Resolution 1013, adopted 7 September. S/RES/1013 (1995).
—. 1996. Resolution 1076, adopted 22 October. S/RES/1076 (1996).
—. 1997. Resolution 1132, adopted 8 October. S/RES/1132 (1997).
—. 1998a. Resolution 1160, adopted 31 March. S/RES/1160 (1998).
—. 1998b. Resolution 1171, adopted 5 June. S/RES/1171 (1998).
—. 1999a. Resolution 1227, adopted 10 February. S/RES/1227 (1999).
—. 1999b. Resolution 1237, adopted 7 May. S/RES/1237 (1999).
—. 1999c. Resolution 1267, adopted 15 October. S/RES/1267 (1999).
—. 1999d. Resolution 1284, adopted 17 December. S/RES/1284 (1999).
—. 2000a. *Report of the Panel of Experts on Violations of Security Council Sanctions against UNITA*. S/2000/203 of 10 March.
—. 2000b. Resolution 1298, adopted 17 May. S/RES/1298 (2000).
—. 2000c. Resolution 1306, adopted 5 July. S/RES/1306 (2000).
—. 2000d. Resolution 1333, adopted 19 December. S/RES/1333 (2000).
—. 2000e. *Report of the Security Council Committee Established Pursuant to Resolution 918 (1994) Concerning Rwanda.* S/2000/1227 of 22 December.
—. 2001a. Resolution 1343, adopted 7 March. S/RES/1343 (2001).
—. 2001b. *Report of the Security Council Committee Established Pursuant to Resolution 1298 (2000) Concerning Eritrea and Ethiopia.* S/2001/503 of 18 May.
—. 2001c. Resolution 1373, adopted 28 September. S/RES/1373 (2001).
—. 2002a. Resolution 1390, adopted 16 January. S/RES/1390 (2002).
—. 2002b. Resolution 1407, adopted 3 May. S/RES/1407 (2002).
—. 2002c. Resolution 1425, adopted 22 July. S/RES/1425 (2002).
—. 2002d. *Statement by the President of the Security Council*. S/PRST/2002/30 of 31 October.
—. 2002e. *Report of the Security Council Committee Established Pursuant to Resolution 918 (1994) Concerning Rwanda.* S/2002/1406 of 24 December.
—. 2003a. Resolution 1455, adopted 17 January. S/RES/1455 (2003).
—. 2003b. Resolution 1460, adopted 30 January. S/RES/1460 (2003).
—. 2003c. Resolution 1467, adopted 18 March. S/RES/1467 (2003).
—. 2003d. *Report of the Panel of Experts on Somalia Pursuant to Security Council Resolution 1425 (2002)*. S/2003/223 of 25 March.
—. 2003e. Resolution 1474, adopted 8 April. S/RES/1474 (2003).
—. 2003f. Resolution 1493, adopted 28 July. S/RES/1493 (2003).
—. 2003g. *Report of the Panel of Experts on Somalia Pursuant to Security Council Resolution 1474 (2003)*. S/2003/1035 of 4 November.
—. 2004. *Statement by the President of the Security Council*. S/PRST/2004/1 of 19 January.
US (United States). Bureau of Political–Military Affairs. 2003. *United States Support for the United Nations Program of Action to Prevent, Combat and Eradicate the Illicit Trade in Small Arms and Light Weapons in All Its Aspects*. 24 July.
Victor, David, Kal Raustiala, and Eugene Skolnikoff (eds.). 1998. *The Implementation and Effectiveness of International Environmental Commitments: Theory and Practice*. Cambridge, Massachusetts: MIT Press.
Vines, Alex. 2003. 'Monitoring UN Sanctions in Africa: The Role of Panels of Experts'. In VERTIC (Verification Research, Training and Information Centre), *Verification Yearbook 2003*. London, pp. 247–61.
Wallensteen, Peter, Carina Staibano, and Mikael Eriksson (eds.). 2003. *Making Targeted Sanctions Effective: Guidelines for the Implementation of UN Policy Options*. Uppsala, Sweden: Uppsala University. <http://www.smartsanctions.se/Reports.htm>
Widmer, Mireille and Cate Buchanan. 2003. 'Moving from Words to Deeds: the UN Programme of Action on Small Arms.' *Small Arms and Human Security Bulletin*. No. 1. October; pp. 1–3.
Wille, Christina. 2003. *UNDP Capacity Project*. Background paper. Geneva: Small Arms Survey.
Woodward, Angela. 2003. *Verification of Mandatory Multilateral Arms Embargoes*. Background paper. Geneva: Small Arms Survey.

ACKNOWLEDGEMENTS

Other contributors
Mike Bourne, Owen Greene, Elli Kytömäki, Patrick Mc Carthy, Rachel Stohl, Christina Wille, Angela Woodward, and Valerie Yankey.

A former member of the Malaitan Eagle Force carries his gun after the group agreed to surrender their weapons in the Solomon Islands in August 2003. (© Reuters/Str DG/RCS)

Trouble in Paradise:
SMALL ARMS IN THE PACIFIC

INTRODUCTION

Recent events in the Pacific offer clear lessons, both in success and failure. Innovative links between disarmament and national aspirations for autonomy, clear-cut contrasts between weapon collection methods deployed in adjacent island communities, the 'good neighbour' traditions of the region, and relative transparency of information all combine to provide a small laboratory of ideas and examples.

Pacific nations are no strangers to small arms. During the Second World War, island states in the region were home to thousands of armed troops, and suffered many bloody conflicts. More recently, small arms have reappeared as vectors of human rights abuse, death, and injury in the Solomon Islands, Papua New Guinea, Fiji, and even Australia.

Unlike its neighbours in South-east and South Asia, the region is not afflicted with large-scale trafficking. Yet the Pacific experience demonstrates how deeply even a small number of small arms can damage small communities. Armed conflict and violent crime have had profound social and economic effects in the region, not least on the prospects of young Pacific Islanders.

The line between the legal and illegal small arms trade is as blurred in the Pacific region as it is anywhere. The great majority of firearms used in violence were legally imported, then diverted to crime from civilian, military, and police holdings.

Among the chapter's principal findings are the following:

- *Civilian gun ownership in the Pacific is higher than the global average.* There are some 3.1 million privately owned firearms, the great majority of which are in Australia (11 per 100 people) and New Zealand (22 per 100 people).
- *Security stockpiles in the Pacific are moderate.* Police and armed forces hold an estimated 226,046 firearms, or one-fourteenth the civilian stockpile.
- *At least 26 nations export small arms to the Pacific.* The US is the largest exporter and provides more than half of all known Pacific imports.
- *Gun smuggling is rare,* though Papua New Guinea remains a hot spot.
- *Gun laws are inconsistent and contain many loopholes.* Until firearm legislation in the Pacific is harmonized, the region remains vulnerable to gun-running.
- *Safe storage is a real concern.* Most firearms used in crime or conflict were obtained locally from lawful gun owners or leaked from state or police armouries.
- *Craft manufacture is common.* Crude home-made guns are locally manufactured in times of scarcity and conflict, but their relative importance is often overrated.
- *Weapon disposal efforts have had positive results.* In the recently conflict-torn Solomon Islands and Bougainville, disarmament is now firmly linked to progressive political change, social stability, and economic development.

> Most guns used in violence began as legal weapons owned by civilians, military, and police.

SMALL ARMS SURVEY 2004

In the Pacific, disarmament is firmly linked to social stability and development.

This chapter summarizes and updates *Small Arms in the Pacific* (Alpers and Twyford, 2003), a recent study of 20 nations[1] sprinkled across the largest stretch of water on the globe (see Map 9.1). A comprehensive examination of firearm ownership, legislation, and gun violence in the Pacific, this 14-month study assembled the insights and experience of more than 100 organizations and communities.

Map 9.1   Pacific Islands Forum countries

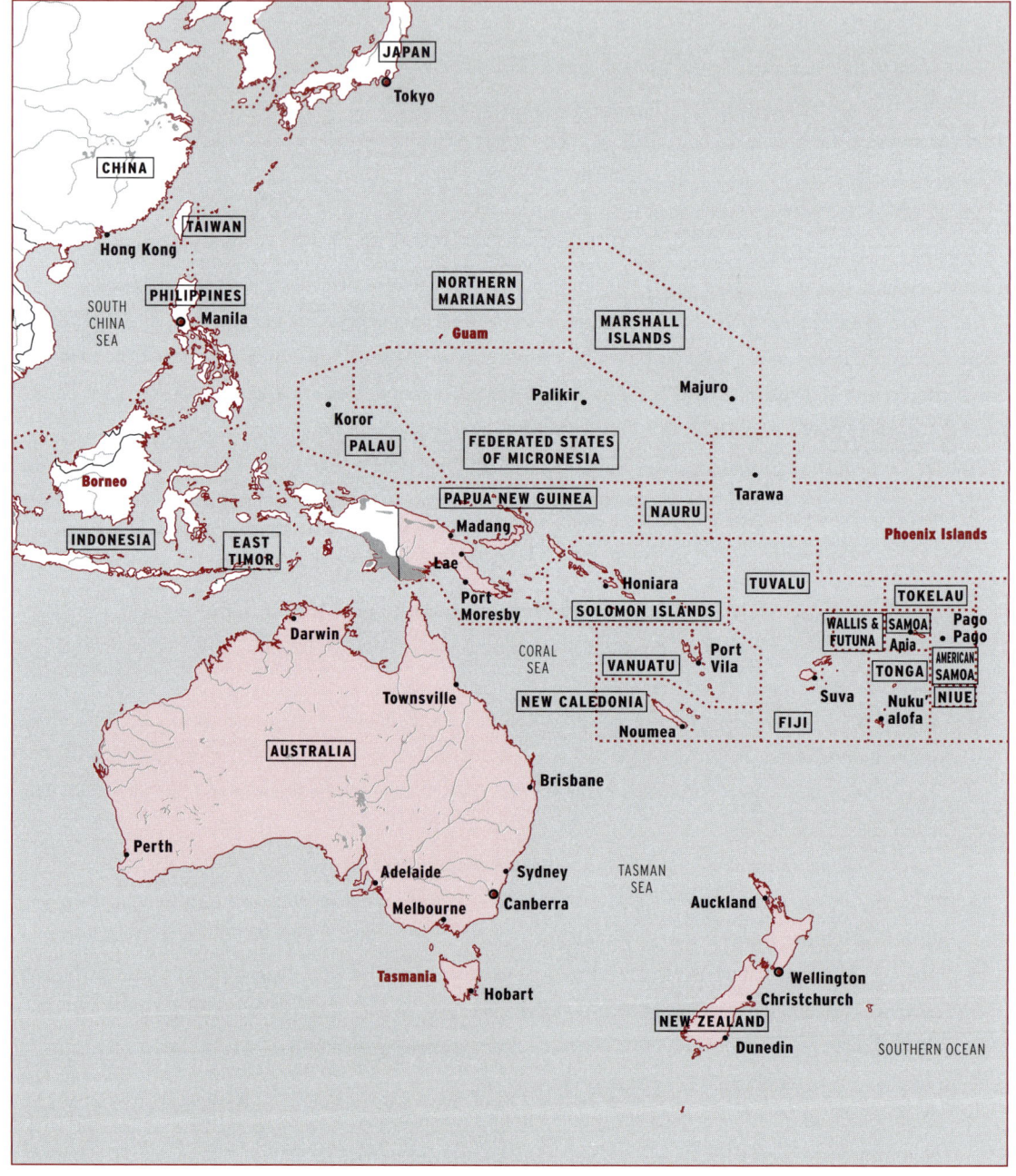

PACIFIC

The first section of this chapter considers the scale and volume of legal exports, imports, and known holdings among civilians and security forces. The second section turns to some of the vectors of the illegal trade, including smuggling, leakage from civilian and official stockpiles, and armed crime. The third section reveals the human costs associated with firearm availability and misuse in the Fiji Islands, the Solomon Islands, and Bougainville, an island province of Papua New Guinea. The fourth section relates recent experiences with weapon collection and destruction in Bougainville and the Solomon Islands, while the final section summarizes arms-related legislation in the Pacific.

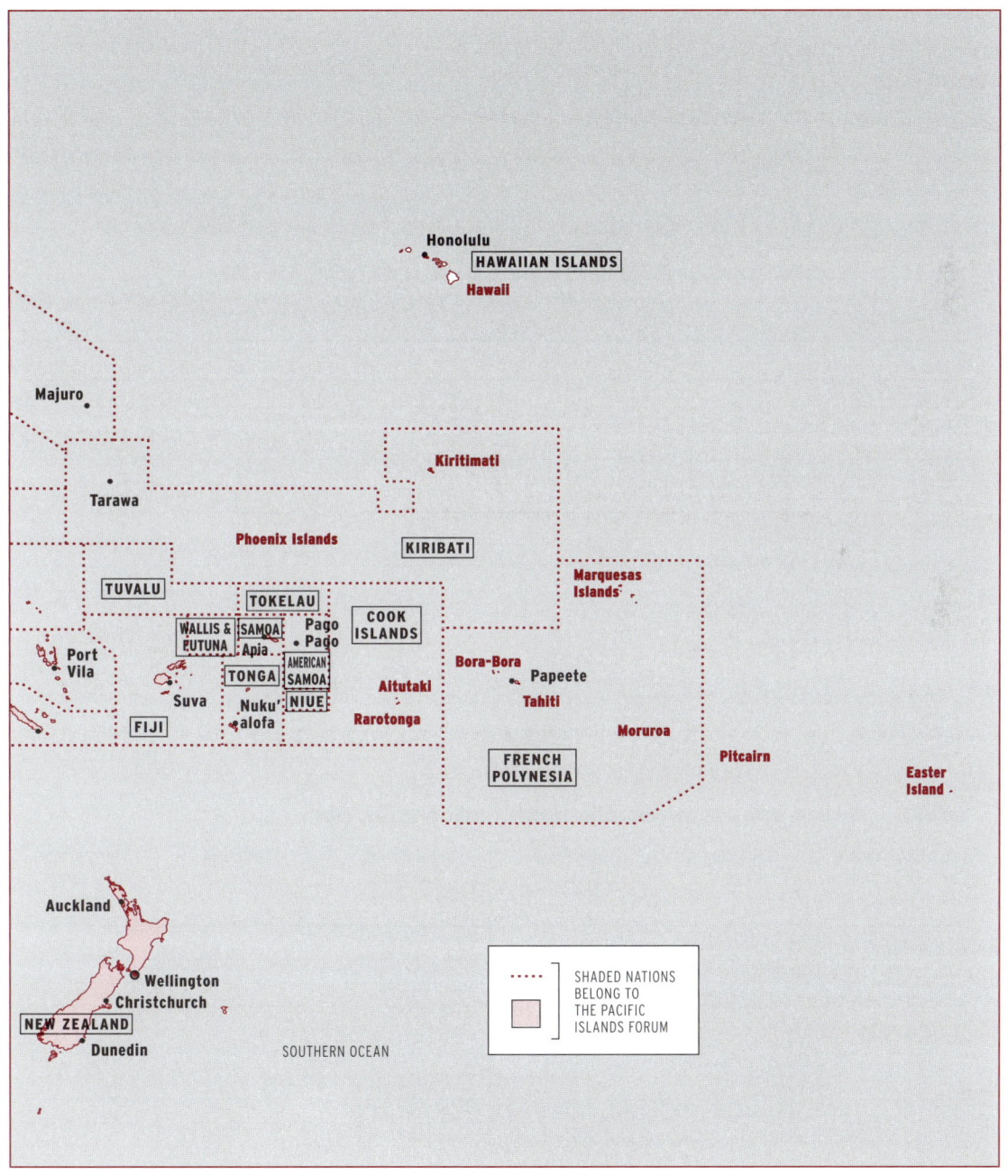

SMALL ARMS SURVEY 2004

LAWFUL GUN TRADE AND STOCKPILES IN THE PACIFIC

The legal trade in small arms in the southern Pacific region is surprisingly dynamic. Demand varies widely with population size, purchasing power, local firearm laws and their enforcement, the presence or absence of regular military forces or routinely armed police, and social attitudes to gun ownership and use. With the largest military and police forces, 3.1 million legal firearms between them, and the lion's share of annual arms imports into the region, Australia and New Zealand dwarf the rest of the Pacific in this respect.

Who buys?

Figures on commercial and military arms imports are rarely published, though some legal weapon transfers from the US are openly documented. Table 9.1 lists a range of Pacific countries for which US small arms and ammunition export licence approvals were granted between 1998 and 2000.[2] Note that export licences are often not fulfilled to the approved value, resulting in lower import figures declared in the receiving country (see Table 9.2).

Table 9.1   US small arms and ammunition export licence approvals to the Pacific, 1998-2000

Importing country	Licence value (nominal USD)
Australia	127,137,186
New Zealand	8,123,120
New Caledonia	804,898
Papua New Guinea	325,769
Solomon Islands	199,406
Tonga	34,514
Federated States of Micronesia	3,131
Nauru	2,514
Vanuatu	1,517
Total	136,632,055

Source: Federation of American Scientists (2002)

Limited commercial sales data from other exporting states and some information on government sales are also available, mainly from customs authorities (Marsh, 2003). Table 9.2 indicates the extensive network of suppliers of small arms and light weapons dealt with by Pacific states in 2000.

Table 9.2   Declared small arms and ammunition imports, Pacific countries, 2000[3]

Importing country (% of known imports into the region)	Exporting country	Small arms USD value	Ammunition USD value	Combined USD value	Country total USD known imports
Australia (76.8)	Austria	32,000	194,000	226,000	33,953,700
	Belgium	21,000	537,000	558,000	
	Bosnia & Herzegovina		814,000	814,000	
	Brazil	251,000	637,000	888,000	
	Canada	41,200	302,000	343,200	
	China	15,500		15,500	
	Cyprus		75,000	75,000	
	Czech Republic	472,000	69,000	541,000	
	Finland	289,000	69,000	358,000	

280

Table 9.2 (cont.)   Declared small arms and ammunition imports, Pacific countries, 2000[3]

Importing country (% of known imports into the region)	Exporting country	Small arms USD value	Ammunition USD value	Combined USD value	Country total USD known imports
	France		16,000	16,000	
	Germany	436,000	1,967,000	2,403,000	
	Italy	1,344,000	835,000	2,179,000	
	Japan	542,000		542,000	
	Korea, Republic of		1,134,000	1,134,000	
	Netherlands	39,000		39,000	
	Philippines	50,000	55,000	105,000	
	Portugal	78,000		78,000	
	Spain	165,000	544,000	709,000	
	Switzerland	36,000		36,000	
	UK	96,000	2,658,000	2,754,000	
	US	2,362,000	17,778,000	20,140,000	
New Zealand (17.87)	Australia	67,000	529,000	596,000	7,898,000
	Austria	16,000		16,000	
	Belgium	192,000		192,000	
	Bosnia & Herzegovina		300,000	300,000	
	Brazil	47,000	966,000	1,013,000	
	Canada		16,000	16,000	
	China	29,000		29,000	
	Czech Republic	30,000	11,000	41,000	
	Finland	153,000	149,000	302,000	
	France		1,487,000	1,487,000	
	Germany	91,000	30,000	121,000	
	Italy	180,000	200,000	380,000	
	Japan	206,000		206,000	
	Korea, Republic of		53,000	53,000	
	Philippines	15,000	33,000	48,000	
	Portugal	37,000		37,000	
	Mexico		15,000	15,000	
	Spain	35,000	176,000	211,000	
	Sweden	10,000		10,000	
	UK		884,000	884,000	
	US	907,000	1,034,000	1,941,000	
French Polynesia (2.89)	Unspecified	566,000	12,000	578,000	1,277,000
	France		681,000	681,000	
	New Zealand		18,000	18,000	
New Caledonia (1.7)	Australia		43,000	43,000	750,000
	China	21,000		21,000	
	Czech Republic	58,000		58,000	
	Finland	49,000		49,000	
	France	51,000	198,000	249,000	
	Germany	50,000		50,000	
	US	171,000	109,000	280,000	
Papua New Guinea (0.36)	Australia	19,000	101,000	120,000	160,000
	US	40,000		40,000	
Fiji (0.25)	Australia	110,000		110,000	110,000
Tonga (0.06)	Australia		11,000	11,000	28,000
	New Zealand		17,000	17,000	
Nauru (0.03)	Thailand	15,000		15,000	15,000
Samoa (0.03)	UK		13,000	13,000	13,000
Vanuatu (0.01)	Australia	2,368		2,368	2,368
TOTALS		**9,437,068**	**34,770,000**	**44,207,068**	**44,207,068**

Source: Marsh (2003)

Australia and New Zealand, the dominant economic powers in the region, are by far the largest importers of small arms and ammunition in the Pacific. Between 1998 and 2000 they accounted for virtually all (99 per cent) of imports into the region from the US and almost 95 per cent of recorded small arm and ammunition deliveries from any source (see Tables 9.1 and 9.2). Demand in these countries is fuelled by relative affluence, the region's largest military and police forces, agricultural pest control, and strong hunting and sport shooting traditions. Although permissive firearm legislation has until recently facilitated private gun ownership in Australia and New Zealand, Australian figures to June 2002 show a 66 per cent decrease in average annual firearm imports since gun laws were tightened in 1996–97 (ACS, 2003a).

Papua New Guinea maintains the next largest defence and police forces in the region, but lacks the resources to import proportionate quantities of small arms and ammunition. In 2000, the French territories of New Caledonia and French Polynesia imported 86 per cent of all known small arms and ammunition destined for countries in the Pacific other than Australia and New Zealand.

Who supplies?

Small arms and ammunition are supplied to the region from a global range of nations. In 2000, 26 countries are recorded as having delivered arms and ammunition worth over USD 44 million to the Pacific. Major suppliers other than the United States included Belgium, Finland, France, Germany, Italy, Spain, and the UK, reflecting closer political and economic ties to Europe than to Asia, as well as long-standing trade patterns and familiarity with European and US brands. Brazil and Australia were also in the top ten, while in the military sphere, Singapore, Israel, and South Korea are important suppliers to the defence forces in the Pacific.[4]

> At least 26 countries export arms and ammunition to the Pacific.

Surprisingly, some of the world's leading arms suppliers are only minor players in the Pacific. Of the Eastern European and Balkan arms-producing countries, only the Czech Republic and Bosnia and Herzegovina featured in reported exports, suggesting that their marketing reach does not extend far into the Pacific. Chinese small arms are far less common in the Pacific than in other regions, both in imports declared and in numbers of illegal weapons discovered.

Private gun ownership

Lawfully held civilian stockpiles of small arms in the Pacific include 3.1 million firearms, or ten privately held guns for every 100 people. This is more than 50 per cent higher than the global average (Alpers and Twyford, 2003, p. 12). In the Pacific, per capita rates of gun ownership vary considerably from country to country (see Figure 9.1).

> With one firearm for every ten people, the Pacific's rate of private gun ownership is 50 per cent higher than the global average.

A police officer stacks guns with crushed barrels on the last day of the Australian gun buy-back programme in September 1997. Australians surrendered more than 700,000 guns in the wake of the country's worst shooting massacre, which killed 35 people at Port Arthur in April 1996.

Figure 9.1   Rate of lawful civilian firearm ownership per 100 population in 20 Pacific nations

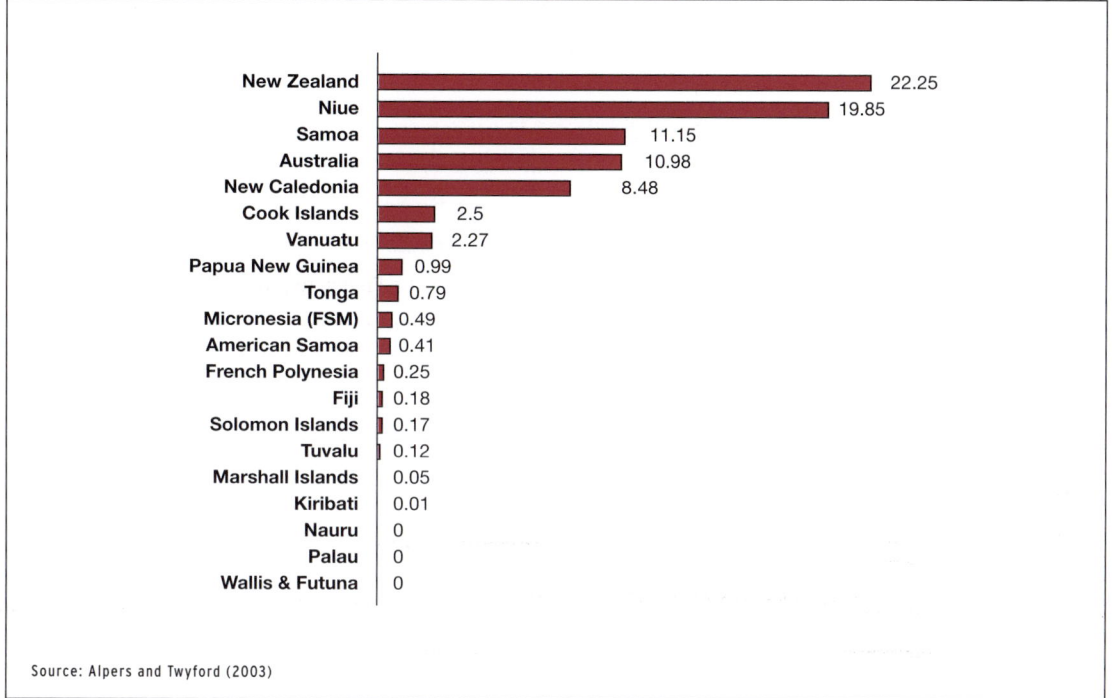

Source: Alpers and Twyford (2003)

Heavily armed Pacific people

The vast majority of firearms in the Pacific are owned by Australians and New Zealanders, who rank among the most heavily armed civilians in the industrialized world. With some 2.1 million registered firearms (Mouzos, 2002a, p. 5), Australia has eleven legal guns for every 100 head of population. New Zealand's ratio of 22 legal guns per 100 people is twice that of Australia. This is a conservative figure,[5] with NZ Police citing a higher estimate of one million guns in a population approaching four million (Green, 2002).

Per capita gun ownership in some of the smaller Pacific states is also surprisingly high. Almost one in five people in Niue, for instance, owns a registered firearm, while the rate of legal gun ownership in Samoa is slightly higher than in Australia. In Nauru and Palau, private guns are prohibited.

Firearm ownership estimates for all Pacific nations remain low in comparison with the US, where four per cent of the world population possesses 50 per cent of the planet's privately owned firearms, or 67 guns per 100 people (Alpers, 2002, p. 262; Alpers and Twyford, 2003, p. 11).

> Australians and New Zealanders rank among the most heavily armed civilians in the industrialized world.

State security force stockpiles

The combined military and law enforcement holdings of the southern Pacific are estimated to be 226,046 small arms, or seven per cent of the civilian stockpile (see Table 9.3). As military inventories are rarely published, this figure was derived using a multiplier technique developed by the Small Arms Survey (STOCKPILES).[6] These are conservative estimates, and much more can be done to refine the assumptions on which they are based.

SMALL ARMS SURVEY 2004

Table 9.3   State security forces in the Pacific, 2002

State-owned small arms in the Pacific are estimated at 226,046, or seven per cent of the civilian stockpile.

	Population	Sworn police officers	Police routinely armed?	Regular military
Australia	19,707,200	43,722	Yes	50,700
Papua New Guinea	5,028,000	5,311	Yes	4,400
New Zealand	3,820,749	7,038	No	8,695
Fiji	840,000	1,970	No	3,500
Solomon Islands	479,000	1,442	Yes	0
French Polynesia	241,000	220	Yes	530
New Caledonia	224,000	268	Yes	704
Vanuatu	207,000	319	No	256
Samoa	160,000	490	No	0
Federated States of Micronesia	124,000	500	Yes	0
Tonga	101,000	418	No	390
Kiribati	92,000	458	No	0
American Samoa	61,000	200	No	0
Marshall Islands	54,000	130	No	0
Cook Islands	20,000	100	No	0
Palau	20,000	75	Yes	0
Wallis and Futuna	14,700	20	Yes	46
Nauru	12,000	80	No	0
Tuvalu	10,000	72	No	0
Niue	2,000	16	No	0
Totals	**31,217,649**	**62,849**	**Yes 82%** **No 18%**	**69,221**

Source: Alpers & Twyford (2003)

Military inventories: In 2000, it is conservatively estimated that defence and paramilitary forces of the south-western Pacific supported 69,221 active personnel. Combining this figure with the standard small arms multiplier of 2.25 yields a conservative estimate of 155,747 military small arms in the Pacific. It is quite likely that total troop numbers have declined since then,[7] though it is also probable that total stocks have increased since ageing firearms tend to be retained rather than destroyed.

Routinely unarmed police protect more than 5 million citizens in 12 of 20 nations surveyed.

Police inventories: Not all Pacific police officers carry guns. As shown in Table 9.3, routinely unarmed police protect more than five million citizens in 12 of the 20 nations surveyed. Combining a standard small arms multiplier of 1.3 weapons for each of 51,558 routinely armed police officers[8] yields a figure of approximately 67,025 police firearms. Adding guns stored for officers who are routinely unarmed, as in New Zealand, increases the total to 70,299.

Table 9.4   Civilian, military, and police firearms in the Pacific, 2002

Firearms	Number held
Lawfully held civilian firearms	3,112,272
Military firearms	155,747
Police firearms	70,299
Total	**3,338,318**

THE ILLICIT TRADE: GUN SMUGGLING, LEAKAGE, AND CRIME

> Illicit trade in small arms is simply an extension of the legal trade. It's good trade gone bad.
> (Warren A. Paia, Secretary of Foreign Affairs, Solomon Islands.
> Pacific Islands Small Arms Seminar, Tokyo, January 2003)

Crime and conflict are, as elsewhere, the main drivers of demand for illegal small arms in the Pacific region. The key centres of gun trafficking for the purposes of armed crime are those with the largest populations—Australia and Papua New Guinea. Yet, when compared with the legal trade, illicit firearm imports into the Pacific appear to be minor.

The great majority of illicit, commercially manufactured small arms in the Pacific began as legal weapons in the hands of local civilians, military, and police. Firearms seized following crime and conflict, collected during gun amnesties, and turned up in routine policing are commonly sourced to licensed gun owners and dealers and to state-owned armouries. With the possible exception of Papua New Guinea, domestic leakage of legally held guns greatly exceeds the volume of firearms smuggled into the region.

Domestic leakage of legally held guns greatly exceeds the volume of firearms smuggled into the region.

Smuggled weapons

Conflicts in the region have generated organized gun-running in the past, such as a container of small arms intercepted on its way to Fiji in the late 1980s.[9] Less organized gun-running from South-east Asia and Australia to Papua New Guinea undoubtedly occurs and continues to cause alarm. Gun smuggling into Australia, New Zealand, and the smaller island states is invariably revealed to be small-scale, opportunistic, and relatively uncommon.

The Australian Institute of Criminology found that most firearms smuggled into Australia were imported as parts by mail from the United States (Mouzos, 1999, p. 4). In a country of 20 million, the Australian Customs Service intercepted a modest 204 handguns in fiscal year 2000–01, and later reported 'no significant evidence or intelligence to suggest that large numbers of handguns are being illegally imported into Australia' (ACS, 2003b). According to Australia's federal Justice and Customs Minister Chris Ellison, most firearms that fell into the wrong hands were stolen from licensed gun owners (Toohey, 2002).

Claims of systematic smuggling of illicit firearms into New Zealand surface from time to time but have not been substantiated. In an extensive judicial review of firearm regulation, Sir Thomas Thorp (1997, pp. 25–6) concluded that '[b]oth Customs and the Police believe that illegal [firearm] imports into New Zealand have at least until recently been at low volume, and that large-scale imports would have become apparent were they occurring'. In the past decade, New Zealand Police and Customs have discovered only a few dozen smuggled firearms, all one-off imports or in very small numbers, trafficked by opportunistic individuals.

Law-enforcement officers also speak of illicit handgun possession in the Samoan fishing fleet and illegal long guns in Nauru, Niue, and the Cook Islands. Again, evidence is scarce or non-existent.

Illegal trafficking in small arms is a pressing issue in Papua New Guinea. A number of smuggling routes appear to be active, sourcing firearms from South-east Asia and Australia. Illicitly produced firearms from the Philippines and military-issue weapons from Vietnam and other South-east Asian countries have been discovered in Papua New Guinea. Visiting forestry contractors are among those suspected of smuggling handguns.

Illegal trafficking in small arms is a pressing issue in Papua New Guinea.

SMALL ARMS SURVEY 2004

Hand in hand with a recognized trade in drugs, arms trafficking is also allegedly taking place along the rugged, rarely patrolled border between Papua New Guinea and the Indonesian province of Irian Jaya, or West Papua. It is nevertheless difficult to be sure in which direction the arms are flowing, as both countries claim to be the target of local gun-runners.[10]

The narrow, island-studded Torres Strait between Australia and Papua New Guinea is recognized as a favourite smuggling route for both commodities and people, and so is carefully monitored. Despite this attention, small arm seizures have been few in number and small in scale. In testimony to a parliamentary inquiry, Australian Federal Police described Torres Strait smuggling as 'ad hoc, opportunistic, unsophisticated, albeit effective' (Saunders, 2000).

It is rumoured that quantities of illegal firearms have been smuggled into the Pacific region from elsewhere, perhaps from China. While this remains unsupported by any evidence of smuggled guns, such guesswork continues to fuel a debate beyond resolution. Until adequate samples of crime guns have been traced back to their last lawful owners, whether domestic or foreign, evidence-based policy options are likely to remain elusive.

Leakage from civilian stocks

In Australia, 25,171 firearms were reported stolen in the six years to June 2000. Of these, 81 per cent were taken from private homes while an unknown number of additional thefts went unreported. One South Australian licensed gun dealer lost up to 600 handguns in a single robbery, and 'highly organized' raids on firearm dealers and private collectors in Victoria and New South Wales netted at least 500 more (Mouzos, 2002b; *The Advertiser,* 1999). Several licensed gun dealers have also been prosecuted for large-scale, organized firearm sales to criminals.

Theft of privately owned firearms is the most important source of illegal guns in Australia.

A Fijian soldier enforces martial law at a checkpoint just before curfew during the fourth week of the civilian coup in June 2000 in Suva.

In the second half of 2003, a spate of burglaries and armed robberies netted 60 handguns from licensed security guards in Sydney alone (Geohegan, 2003). Australia's federal Justice and Customs Minister declared the theft of privately owned firearms to be 'the major source of illegal guns in Australia' (ABC, 2003).

In New Zealand, a survey of prison inmates indicated that the bulk of firearms available on the black market had been stolen from legitimate owners (Newbold, 1999, p. 73, cited in Chatvick, 1999, p. 2). Another study found that 54 per cent of firearms reported stolen were rifles, 34 per cent shotguns, and five per cent handguns. Sixty per cent of these guns had been stolen from urban dwellings, while 52 per cent of incidents of gun theft involved firearms that had not been securely stored by their owners (Alpers and Walters, 1998).

An officer in charge of the New Zealand Police Firearms Licensing Task Force once wrote: 'I have no doubt that in the overwhelming majority of cases, those firearms [used in crime] came into this country lawfully, and their original New Zealand owners were the holders of firearms licences or permits.'[11]

In the island nations of the Pacific, figures on gun theft from private owners are rarely collected. It is known that, of the commercially manufactured firearms surrendered during the Solomon Islands and Bougainville disarmament campaigns, most had been diverted from a legitimate civilian or state purpose. Firearms used in peacetime for hunting, pest control, and policing had been pressed into service during conflict, then surrendered to authorities by former combatants.

Leakage from police and military holdings

> I'm the most powerful man in the country. I hold the key to the armoury.
> (A Pacific Island delegate, speaking at a small arms seminar in Tokyo.)[12]

In Fiji, the Solomon Islands, and Papua New Guinea, groups bent on rebellion, intimidation, and profit have treated state-owned armouries as gun supermarkets, helping themselves to weapons when needed. Stolen military small arms have fuelled a variety of police and defence force insurrections, made possible the overthrow of elected governments, and greatly increased the lethality of armed crime and tribal and ethnic conflict. Resource constraints, corruption, and ethnic loyalties limited the capacity of authorities to retrieve lost weapons, many of which quickly found their way into criminal hands. In recent years the most destructive firearms used in crime and conflict in Pacific island nations were provided by soldiers and police.

Fiji Islands: The May 2000 raid on parliament could hardly have been executed without assault rifles stolen from the Fiji Military Force armoury. The number of firearms used in Suva was small—only seven gunmen executed the coup, later providing arms to perhaps another 100 young rebels—yet this was sufficient to unseat a democratically elected government. Members of Fiji's Counter-Revolutionary Warfare Unit—ironically, a crack military team established in the wake of two earlier coups in 1987—were implicated in providing the guns.

Solomon Islands: In January and June 2000, Malaitan militants raided Royal Solomon Islands Police (RSIP) armouries at Auki and Honiara, the latter in collusion with the RSIP's own paramilitary force. More than 500 assault rifles and machine guns were taken, some of which were used to overthrow the elected government. Quickly diverted to criminals, the guns then enabled armed gangs to embark on a three-year spree of intimidation and violence. Hundreds of civilians were injured and killed, and thousands were driven from their homes.

The relative importance of home-made weapons in the Pacific is often overstated.

> Groups bent on rebellion, intimidation, and profit have treated state-owned armouries as gun supermarkets.

> **Box 9.1   Home-made firearms**
>
> Home-made firearms added significantly to the combatants' arsenal in both the Bougainville and the Solomon Islands conflicts, primarily as a substitute for unobtainable commercial firearms. In Bougainville, home-made weapons made up more than half of those surrendered to peace monitors in the first 11 months of disarmament (BPMG, 2002a). In the Solomon Islands, they made up 35 per cent of the weapons confiscated in the three years to January 2004 (Solomon Islands IPMT, 2001; RAMSI, 2004).
>
> In both conflicts, home-made weapons were produced in greater quantities by the side with proportionately less access to high-powered firearms. For example, in the Solomon Islands close relations with the police meant that the Malaita Eagle Force (MEF) sourced many of its firearms directly from the police armoury. By contrast, the Isatabu Freedom Movement (IFM), from an opposing ethnic group, had fewer claims on police support and so augmented its arsenal by producing home-made weapons.
>
> There remains a thriving market for home-made guns in Papua New Guinea, where police collections of confiscated weapons are littered with primitive, one-off, locally made firearms used in clan conflict and crime (Dorney, 2000). Yet the relative importance of home-made weapons in the Pacific has often been overstated. In reality, a length of water pipe firing mismatched and/or ancient ammunition can be as dangerous to the user as it is to the target, and craft manufacture is seen as a last resort.
>
> Single-shot, smoothbore pistols and long guns are the only home-made firearms discovered to date, and these cannot be compared in terms of range, accuracy, and firepower to mass-produced, repeating firearms with rifled barrels and matched ammunition. There is no evidence of local production of rifled barrels, nor of multi-shot firing mechanisms such as pump-action or lever-action, semi-automatic or automatic firearms in the south-western Pacific.
>
> Source: Alpers and Twyford (2003, pp. 25–6)

Papua New Guinea: In December 2000 almost 100 police firearms were reported missing, including assault rifles, semi-automatic pistols, and shotguns, along with thousands of rounds of ammunition. An audit the following year reported that as many as 600 firearms had disappeared from the police armoury. In March 2001 a quantity of military weapons and ammunition were taken from the Papua New Guinea Defence Force (PNGDF) headquarters, followed a year later by large-scale firearm thefts from Moem Barracks at Wewak. During nine years of armed conflict on the islands of Bougainville, PNGDF forces and police either supplied or lost many hundreds of small arms to combatants on both sides.

> **Box 9.2   World War II small arms**
>
> Firearms and ammunition salvaged from World War II stockpiles provided a small but significant proportion of firepower in the Bougainville and Solomon Islands conflicts. Both Japanese and Allied troops dumped thousands of tonnes of war materiel in the region, yet 60 years on, less than ten per cent of the firearms documented in recent years in Bougainville—many of them no longer capable of being fired—came from wartime stocks. In the Solomon Islands, the 'handful' of war relics handed in were all degraded and unusable (BPMG, 2002b). Although ex-combatants possibly retain some carefully preserved World War II small arms for future use, relics from the 1940s remain less desirable, and ammunition for them harder to obtain, than modern equivalents.

Most of the firearms used in the Fiji coup appear to have been returned. However, in Papua New Guinea and the Solomon Islands hundreds of former security force firearms remain in circulation, adding to the challenges of disarmament and fuelling fears of continued armed violence.

In recent years Australia and New Zealand have prioritized development assistance for armoury management in Pacific Island nations, providing training and funding to secure small arms held by military and police. Both nations see disarmament and weapon destruction programmes as essential prerequisites for peace, human security, and development.

Box 9.3 After the shooting stops: The recirculation of leftover weapons

Following conflict, former combatants commonly trade their weapons into black markets, which then transfer them to the next centre of demand. This has been most apparent among three of the region's closest island neighbours: the Solomon Islands, Bougainville, and mainland Papua New Guinea.

Community leaders in the Papua New Guinea islands of Bougainville report that, when transport links reopened following conflict, PNG mainlanders began travelling to Buka to purchase firearms. The going rate for a self-loading military rifle was as high as USD 250, and could make the trip worthwhile. Papua New Guinea police and customs occasionally check ships, but only in ports. Further down the main island of Bougainville, long-time residents working closely with ex-combatants report a 'steady stream' of weapons out of Buka, particularly since the beginning of the 2002 peace-building and election period. Prices allegedly ranged from USD 500 for an M-16 assault rifle to USD 2,500 for an M-60 machine gun.

Close cultural ties exist between the people of Bougainville and the western Solomon Islands, and no doubt there is some trafficking across the narrow border strait between them. In addition to known movements of armed criminals, caches of Bougainville Revolutionary Army weapons are still believed to exist in parts of Gizo and Western Province. Nevertheless, despite a few isolated incidents, there is little evidence to support claims of serious trafficking. Authorities in Honiara have not observed any 'new or unusual' influx of firearms to the Solomon Islands.

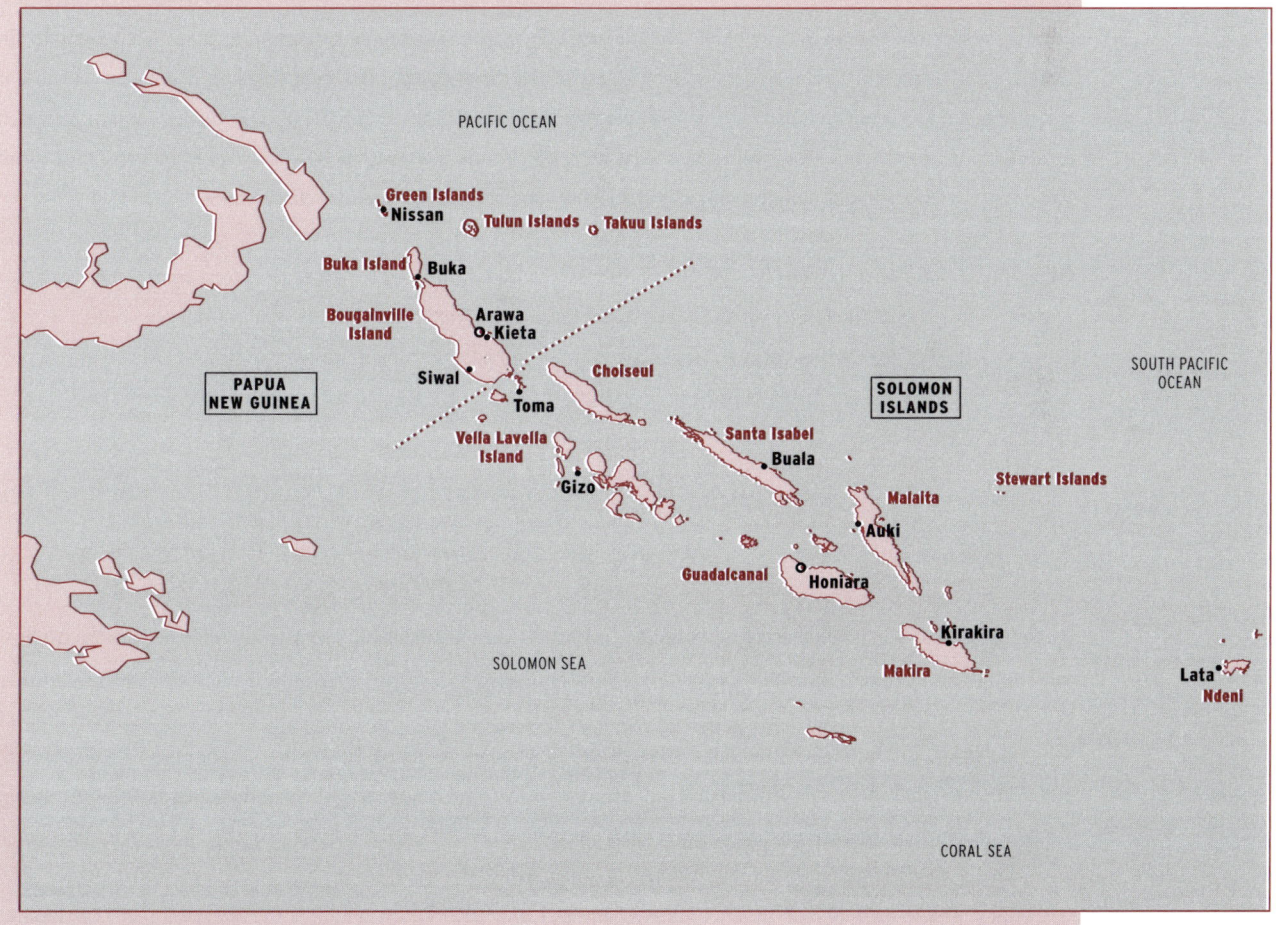

Source: Alpers and Twyford (2003, pp. 26–7)

> We were once able to draw tourists from across the globe, tourists who were in search of the perfect Pacific paradise—warm, friendly people, clear blue waters, white beaches, a wealth of custom and culture found nowhere else in the world. However, I fear that this image has been shattered by the recent crises in our region. We shouldn't be surprised if people view our region as one characterised by coups, militancy, instability and general lawlessness.
>
> (Sir Peter Kenilorea, Chairman, Peace Monitoring Council
> Honiara, Solomon Islands, 2001)

THE HUMAN COST OF FIREARM MISUSE IN THREE PACIFIC COMMUNITIES

In many of the smaller Pacific Island countries, development processes are fragile. States such as the Solomon Islands and Papua New Guinea, which rank alongside Cambodia and Zimbabwe as two of the 'least developed' countries in the world, lack the resources or capacity to deliver basic services such as health and education adequately to their citizens (UNDP, 2003). Where inequality, lack of economic opportunity, and long-standing disputes over land and resources lead to violence, the availability of firearms makes conflict more lethal, more protracted, and more difficult to resolve.[13] Clearly, small arms alone do not cause states to fail. Yet ready access to small arms can quickly bring weak states to the brink of collapse and spark humanitarian and developmental crises.

Fiji

> It's a sad situation—one our military was not trained for. To combat internally. But here we're seeing our own soldiers kill at random, indiscriminately… When we see the bullet marks, we cannot believe this is happening in our own country. It's something you expect to see in the Middle East or elsewhere, but never in our own country.
>
> (Major Howard Politini, spokesman, Fiji Military Forces, 2000)

The availability of firearms has made Pacific conflicts more lethal, more protracted, and more difficult to resolve.

In Fiji, longstanding social inequalities and ethnic tensions built a tinderbox, with the sudden availability of small arms providing the spark. The 1999 election of Mahendra Chaudry, the country's first Indo-Fijian prime minister, encountered bitter opposition from many in the indigenous Fijian establishment. Already unsettled by two coups in 1987 and the adoption of an explicitly multi-racial constitution in 1997, an increasingly radicalized opposition began to foment insurrection.

Following two violent protests against the newly established government, a small group of men armed themselves with Uzi and Galil assault weapons from state armouries. On 19 May 2000, led by local businessman George Speight, the gang stormed parliament buildings, where for 56 days they held hostage the Prime Minister and most of Fiji's elected government. Five people were killed.

Unprecedented rioting and looting broke out across Fiji, with 20 shops set alight in the capital, Suva, alone. Indo-Fijians were targeted in widespread mob violence, evictions, rape, and arson. Many hundreds fled their homes, farms, and businesses, some never to return. Tourist resorts, police stations, and a military base were taken over by nationalists, while power cuts and prolonged roadblocks added to the chaos. Then on 2 November the Counter-Revolutionary

Warfare Unit of the Fiji Military Force—many members of which had been involved in the coup—attempted to murder the military Chief of Staff. Eight soldiers were killed and scores more, including civilians, were hit by stray bullets.

The economic costs of armed violence in Fiji were severe. The vital tourism sector collapsed (see Box 9.4), albeit briefly, mass redundancies and shorter working hours followed across most other sectors, and unemployment doubled to 15 per cent. Even 18 months after the coup, the Fijian government estimated that at least 9,000 workers had been made redundant as a result of the crisis. In addition, by May 2002 more than 11,500 people had left Fiji since the coup (population 840,000). The great majority of those who left permanently were Fijians of Indian extraction (Gurdayal, 2002; *Port Vila Presse,* 2002).

George Speight stands beside weapons used during the 2-month coup he led in Suva, Fiji, in July 2000. The weapons were handed over to the Great Council of Chiefs later that day.

Fiji's economy contracted sharply following the crisis, with an overall decline in 2000 of between 2.8 and 4 per cent of GDP.[14] While the crisis remained unresolved, major donor countries such as Australia and New Zealand introduced a range of sanctions. Official aid was reduced by 30 per cent, and most humanitarian programmes were cut. At the request of Fijian trade unions, both Australian and New Zealand unions imposed temporary bans on the loading and unloading of cargo to and from Fiji, resulting in losses of approximately USD 57 million. The threat of further trade sanctions led to falling export demand, and export levels fell by more than 20 per cent in the three months following the coup. Health and education funding dried up, and schools were closed for months. In 2000, the overall costs of the armed coup were estimated at USD 300 million, or more than one-third of GDP (Alpers and Twyford, 2003, pp. 35–8). Despite a temporary decline in revenue after 11 September 2001, however, a recovering tourism sector and a modest growth in exports have been features of continued growth in the Fijian economy from 2000 to 2004 (ADB, 2003, p. 44).

> The economic costs of armed violence in Fiji were severe, collapsing the country's vital tourism sector.

> **Box 9.4 The effects of armed violence on Fiji's tourist industry**
>
> Tourism is Fiji's primary source of foreign currency. In 1999, the industry generated USD 250 million, or 30 per cent of GDP, directly and indirectly employing more than 45,000 people. That year, 410,000 tourists arrived in Fiji, an increase of ten per cent on the previous year.
>
> Following the May 2000 coup, massive decreases were recorded for visitors from all major markets. In the third quarter of 2000, tourist numbers dropped by 62 per cent to just 45,000, compared with 119,300 in the same quarter of 1999. Over 2,000 employees of the tourism and hospitality sector lost their jobs. Financial losses were estimated at USD 500,000 daily, or USD 46 million over the crisis period. Two years on, employment figures for the tourism accommodation industry were still 5.2 per cent lower than before the conflict. Nevertheless, by 2003 tourist arrival figures had reached 430,800—more than the 1999 figure—and were predicted to rise to 445,000 in 2004.
>
> Sources: Alpers and Twyford (2003, pp. 35-8); Fiji Government (2004)

The Solomon Islands

> ... the problem lies deep within our hearts. A relatively small number of men are establishing a new way of acting. The gun and what it stands for—intimidation and power—is creating a society where the culture of violence rules.
>
> (John Roughan, Solomon Islands NGO leader, 2001)

Four years of armed conflict and instability in the Solomon Islands brought into sharp focus the extent of underdevelopment, and quickly reversed a decade of social and economic gains. The outbreak of violence in 1998 was initiated by young men from the main island of Guadalcanal, who, frustrated with the failure of successive governments to address local problems, armed themselves with privately owned hunting rifles, home-made firearms, World War II relics, and ammunition. Their frustrations were focused on long-standing, smouldering disputes over the occupation of land in Guadalcanal by settlers from the island of Malaita, aggravated by one-off incidents of Malaitan violence against people from Guadalcanal.

Small groups of organized 'Gualese' began attacking Malaitan households in the capital, Honiara, and surrounding areas. By the end of 1998, a Gualese militant group with as many as 2,000 members had been formed, initially called the Guadalcanal Revolutionary Army but later renamed the Isatabu Freedom Movement (IFM). By mid-1999, at least 50 people had been killed by armed militants, and about 20,000 people, including 13,000 Malaitans, had fled Guadalcanal.

Malaitans reacted by forming the Malaita Eagle Force (MEF), which in January 2000 raided the police armoury at Auki, greatly augmenting its firepower with 34 military assault rifles and ammunition. By late 1999, open confrontations were occurring between the IFM and the MEF. At the request of the Solomon Islands government, the Commonwealth Secretariat deployed a contingent of police officers from Fiji and Vanuatu, but this failed, as did other attempts to facilitate a peace process.

On 5 June 2000 the MEF colluded with police to raid the Rove armoury in Honiara, stealing over 1,000 assault rifles and machine guns and forcing the resignation of the Prime Minister. In August 2000 the two factions agreed to a ceasefire, and in mid-October a peace agreement was signed in Townsville, Australia. The Townsville Peace Agreement established an International Peace Monitoring Team and a local Peace Monitoring Council, with provision for weapon surrender (see below).

Four years of armed conflict in the Solomon Islands reversed a decade of social and economic gains.

Armed violence continued, with an estimated 100 deaths in 2000 and 30 'post-conflict' firearm fatalities in the first half of 2003 alone (Muggah and Alpers, 2003). Many more are believed to have died due to limited access to basic health services. Police retreated or joined the rebels, villages were burnt, armed crime and rape became commonplace, and, in a nation of 480,000 people, 40,000–50,000 residents had been displaced from their homes. Of these, 23,000 were Malaitans fleeing Guadalcanal. Forced dislocation of families left enduring scars on the islands' traditional, village-based society. The number of single-headed households increased dramatically, and ruptured social structures heralded long-term disempowerment for youth. An estimated 100 child soldiers fought in the conflict, and many other children were forced to abandon their schooling.

Financial resources that would ordinarily have been devoted to development were spent instead on emergency relief. New Zealand ceased the vast majority of its development programmes, and over the next two years redirected 73 per cent of its USD 3.2 million aid budget to humanitarian assistance and conflict resolution. Australia redirected extra funds to the Solomons, increasing its assistance from an average of USD 8.6 million a year over the previous six years to more than USD 22 million a year in the three budget years following the coup. The European Union, however, suspended its USD 72 million 1998/99 development assistance funding to the Solomons for more than two years.

> The *Economist* headlined the Solomon Islands as 'The Pacific's First Failed State?'

Armed conflict and official mismanagement pushed the already fragile Solomon Islands economy into ruin. Most industries ceased operations, prompting a dramatic fall in export earnings and a sharp decline in GDP. At the end of 2001, gross external reserves were sufficient to cover only a month of imports, while external reserves continued to decline in 2002 at the rate of USD 10 million a week. On 15 February 2003, *The Economist* headlined the Solomon Islands as 'The Pacific's First Failed State?'

Bougainville

> Without warning one day [the BRA] came to my village firing shots indiscriminately. It was chaos and nightmare. Families were separated. The next day I gave birth prematurely with the assistance of a local doctor in an abandoned bank. A few minutes later on the same morning, another pregnant woman came in—she was not so fortunate. She died from loss of blood. Her baby survived. After her came another pregnant mother who needed to give birth by Caesarean method. Her stomach burst open—she died. Her baby survived. What could the doctor do without equipment and medicine? He was helpless. Ten days later our village was completely burnt and we had to run into the jungle to hide.
>
> (Helen Hakena, Bougainville peace activist, UN Small Arms Conference, New York, July 2001)

The nine-year crisis in Bougainville was the longest and most devastating conflict in the Pacific since the Second World War. The roots of the violence in this mountainous island province of Papua New Guinea extend back to the colonial era.[15] Tensions between the indigenous population and the Papua New Guinea government worsened as a result of Rio Tinto's development of the Panguna gold and copper mine on Bougainville Island. Between 1972 and 1989, production at the mine accounted for 40–50 per cent of Papua New Guinea's foreign exchange, with few visible benefits to local inhabitants. Growing inequalities, environmental damage, and disputes over compensation payments to traditional landowners sowed the seeds of the conflict that eventually erupted in the late 1980s.

In November 1988, mining operations were brought to a standstill after a coordinated attack by armed landowners. By June 1989 the conflict had escalated into a war between the Papua New Guinea Defence Force (PNGDF) and the newly formed Bougainville Revolutionary Army (BRA). Although the PNGDF was by far the better equipped of the two forces, the BRA, armed with World War II relics, home-made weapons, and stolen PNGDF firearms, forced a ceasefire in March 1990. For four years, Papua New Guinea imposed a total blockade of the island.

From 1992, the PNGDF began to recapture parts of the province. It was aided by the Bougainville Resistance Forces (BRF), local groups formed in reaction to the at times unrestrained violence of the BRA. Gradually a secessionist conflict evolved into a much more complex internal war. Most factions fought each other, and small arms-related human rights atrocities were committed by all sides.

> Small arms-related human rights atrocities were committed by all sides.

Several attempts had been made since 1990 to negotiate an end to the conflict, but none was successful. Ironically, a heavy-handed move by the Papua New Guinea government, in 1997, to hire British and South African mercenaries to crush the BRA and recapture the mine provided the catalyst for a peace process to begin. Amidst public outrage, the then Papua New Guinea Prime Minister was forced to resign, and the Sandline mercenaries never reached the shores of Bougainville. Military solutions had been effectively discredited.

With his pistol drawn, a major urges PNGDF troops not to join anti-government protests in March 1997. Disillusionment was at a high after the dismissal of an army commander who had demanded the resignation of the prime minister for hiring foreign mercenaries to quash a nine-year secessionist rebellion in Bougainville. © Reuters

In October 1997 a truce was negotiated at Burnham, New Zealand, followed by a ceasefire in 1998. Deployment of a New Zealand-led Truce Monitoring Group was followed by an Australian-led Peace Monitoring Group (PMG)[16] endorsed by the UN Security Council. The Bougainville Peace Agreement, finalized at Arawa in August 2001 between the Papua New Guinea Government, the BRA, and the BRF, included provisions for a transition to autonomy and a deferred referendum on independence, as well as a complex plan for weapon disposal (Regan, 2002). In March 2002 Papua New Guinea's parliament cleared the way for elections for an autonomous Bougainville. By late 2003 both the international Peace Monitoring Group and a smaller civilian group that replaced it had withdrawn from the province, and a new constitution and elections had been scheduled for 2004.

> In Bougainville, peace negotiations explicitly link weapon destruction to autonomy and an eventual referendum on independence from Papua New Guinea.

Throughout these negotiations, disarmament was a paramount concern, with explicit conditions linking the destruction of small arms to any eventual independence from Papua New Guinea (see next section).

The nine-year Bougainville conflict is commonly reported to have caused 12,000 to 15,000 deaths, though no clear methodology for this estimate has been advanced. Most observers agree that at least several thousand Bougainvillean civilians were killed, as well as several hundred PNGDF personnel, along with similar numbers from the two combatant groups, the BRA and the BRF.

The four-year blockade of Bougainville by the Papua New Guinea government led to the complete collapse of the health system and contributed significantly to the casualties of war. Malaria, whooping cough, and malnutrition spread unchecked, tuberculosis and leprosy made a comeback, and immunization, medicines, and health care were simply not available. In central and southern Bougainville, 100,000 people lived from 1992 to 1998 without access to a doctor.

Armed conflict forced thousands of civilians into the bush, where many hid for months, even years. Others were forced into 'care centres' run by the Papua New Guinea government. By mid-1995, some 64,000 displaced Bougainvilleans (population approximately 160,000) had taken refuge in 39 such centres. As many as 9,000 fled as refugees to the neighbouring Solomon Islands.

For many families in Bougainville, the war has not ended. One of the most common forms of human rights abuse was gender-based violence, and many cases of sexual violation and abuse are only now coming to light as women and children report events long suppressed by fear.

Prior to 1988, Bougainville had one of the highest rates of literacy in the Pacific. Armed conflict collapsed the best-achieving primary and secondary school system in Papua New Guinea, and 15,000–20,000 young people were denied the opportunity of learning. Recovery is slow, and young men in particular have difficulty resuming normal life, their memory of atrocities never far from the surface.

Funds allocated to the Bougainville peace process and associated weapon-disposal efforts represent an opportunity cost to donor partners, who might otherwise have spent them on ongoing development assistance. In 2001–02, New Zealand spent more than a fifth of its entire Bougainville assistance budget of USD 1.58 million on weapon disposal. During the five years following the start of formal peace talks in mid-1997, Australia spent at least USD 12.4 million, or more than 15 per cent of its entire Bougainville budget, on direct support to the peace process.

The widespread destruction of infrastructure, the collapse of the mining, copra, and cocoa industries, and years of lost education in Bougainville constitute a major, long-term economic setback to the province once known as the country's most productive. Bougainville's provincial government now lacks the financial and human capacity to

> Bougainvilleans see the destruction of small arms as essential to renewed development, good health, education, and prosperity.

Box 9.5 Gun violence and crime in Australia, New Zealand, and Papua New Guinea

Australia's gun death rate has declined considerably since the 1980s (see Box 6.5). Of the 299 firearm-related deaths recorded during 2002 in Australia, 217 (73 per cent) were suicides, 45 (15 per cent) were homicides, 31 (ten per cent) were unintentional, and six (two per cent) were law enforcement shootings (Bell, 2003). In the five years to June 2001, handgun homicide as a proportion of firearm homicide grew from 13 per cent to 50 per cent. Handgun violence has emerged as a serious problem in some suburbs of Sydney and Melbourne, and public concern at the level of illicit firearm trafficking in Australia—particularly the trade in handguns, which were used in 67 per cent of all armed robberies in 2001—has risen accordingly.

In 2000, **New Zealand** recorded 53 murders. Firearms were used in six of these, one of which involved a handgun. In the period 1988-98, there were 1,046 gun-related deaths, an average of 95 per year. Of these, 76 per cent were suicides, 13 per cent homicides, and seven per cent unintentional shootings. Violent robberies totalled 1,657 in 2000-1, of which 164 involved firearms. Both New Zealand's and Australia's per capita rates of firearm violence are moderate by world standards.

In **Papua New Guinea,** although figures are scarce and unreliable, firearm-related violence has by all accounts reached epidemic proportions. In the rural highlands, where guns are rapidly replacing traditional weapons, tribal fighting claims an average of 200 lives per year. A UN survey of three major towns, Port Moresby, Lae and Goroka, found rates of violent crime to be twice those of Johannesburg and Rio de Janeiro.

Source: Alpers and Twyford (2003, pp. 25–6)

undertake many of its core functions. Throughout all this, observers, donor agencies, governments, and many Bougainvilleans see disarmament and the destruction of small arms as essential and urgent prerequisites to renewed development, good health, education, and prosperity.

DISARMAMENT PACIFIC STYLE: EXPERIENCES IN BOUGAINVILLE AND THE SOLOMON ISLANDS

In Bougainville and the Solomon Islands, disarmament is seen as an essential pillar of durable stability. Without comprehensive disposal of small arms, challenges to law and order persist, and the threat of armed violence undermines any restoration of peace.

No two conflicts are alike, nor are they resolved in exactly the same way. In Bougainville, the war was long and its resolution involved a wide range of actors. A complex three-stage 'weapons disposal plan' is now intricately linked to aspirations for political autonomy and possible independence.

The Solomon Islands conflict was more acute, its outrages in the end more criminal than political, its gun-fuelled anarchy resolved only by the collapse of government and unprecedented outside intervention. Prior to this, peace processes focused almost exclusively on weapon disposal, arguably at the expense of broader conflict resolution, justice and law reform, corruption control, and a more integrated peace-building process.

This section considers the problems and challenges encountered in two very different disarmament processes. The people involved, however, remain culturally and ethnically north and south Solomon Islanders, their nation cut in half, annexed in 1899 by Germany, with the North Solomons (Bougainville) more recently declared a province of Papua New Guinea. Their contrasting experiences illustrate disarmament, Pacific style.

Bougainville: Getting the house in order

> After ten years of war, we have had these weapons too long . . . to achieve what we want, we have to lose our weapons. Tomorrow we will be free; the country will be free. The house will be in order.
>
> (Komoiki, Bougainville ex-combatant; UNDP, 2002)

Weapon disposal is now intricately linked to aspirations for political autonomy and independence.

In Bougainville, following the agreement of an agenda for successful peace negotiations in mid-1997, weapon disposal remained one of the more sensitive issues on the table. Due to mistrust between combatant factions and continuing fear of the PNGDF, disarmament was sidelined until January 2001, when factional leaders met the Papua New Guinea government to establish a set of principles for a referendum on Bougainville's political status. Now weapon disposal took centre stage, and in August 2001 the Bougainville Peace Agreement included provisions for a transition to autonomy and a deferred referendum on independence, both linked to a complex weapon disposal process (see Box 9.6). The three-stage disarmament plan was launched in December 2001, then gradually implemented across Bougainville.

In March 2002, the Papua New Guinea parliament unanimously passed a set of constitutional amendments to give effect to the Bougainville Peace Agreement. In the months preceding the vote, ex-combatants made remarkable progress on disarmament, mindful that support for the passage of legislation was contingent on visible progress being made on weapon disposal. Though progress was variable in both time and place, by late October 2002 1,639 firearms had been surrendered—304 'high-powered' firearms,[17] 284 sporting rifles, 892 home-made guns, and 159 Second World War relics.

> **Box 9.6   From weapon disposal to independence: The three-stage arms disposal plan**
>
> **Stage One:** Small arms are handed in to regional faction commanders for storage in portable containers. These are then publicly sealed by representatives of the UN Observer Mission on Bougainville (UNOMB).
>
> **Stage Two:** Senior commanders from each faction move the weapons to larger, secure containers in central locations. Following the passage of amendments to the Papua New Guinea Constitution, the arms are secured with two locks: one key held by the ex-combatant commander, the other held by UNOMB. This stage ends after constitutional amendments come into force, and UNOMB has verified that sufficient arms have been collected and safely secured. Only then can preparations for the first autonomous elections begin.
>
> **Stage Three:** Discussions on the final disposal of weapons are held within four-and-a-half months of autonomy legislation coming into effect. If no decision is made, the BRA, BRF, and Papua New Guinea government can decide whether or not sufficient weapons have been collected to allow elections to proceed. UNOMB may also be called upon to determine whether sufficient weapons have been collected for free and fair elections to take place, a decision which binds all parties. After this, a referendum on independence for Bougainville is to be held no fewer than ten, but no more than 15, years after the first autonomous elections.

The most positive development in the latter half of 2002 was the widespread shift of all ten Bougainville districts from Stage One to Stage Two containment. But there had also been a number of direct challenges to the weapon disposal initiative. These included the theft of hundreds of firearms from Stage Two containers, issues of amnesty and pardon for former combatants, political hesitation during the 2002 PNG national elections, crisis-related compensation payments, the non-participation of some factions, and the complications of individual versus group weapon ownership. At several stages of the bargaining process, threats were made against weapon containers.

Donors and civil society groups also had reservations. Ex-combatants and their groups had built up a formidable position within the process, sometimes impeding both disarmament and recovery. Large segments of the community were being excluded, most notably women. But the chief concern among donors related to their 'exit strategy'—or lack thereof. The peace process, some feared, had become so comfortable that there was little incentive to complete it.

By mid-2002, funding for weapon disposal had lost much of its impetus, and frustrations simmered over the way in which initial funds had been disbursed. Given the uncertainty surrounding political negotiations, donors became reluctant to contribute to Stage Two. Yet despite a number of setbacks, the momentum for weapon disposal remained.

Following the verification of Stage Two by the UN in August 2003, the constitutional amendments implementing the peace agreement became law in Papua New Guinea. By October of that year the total number of guns held in containers exceeded 1,900. In December 2003, the parties met to discuss Stage Three and agreed that the ultimate fate of the weapons would be destruction. By early 2004, nearly one-third of the collected firearms had been destroyed in the presence of UN observers. Bougainville was 'getting the house in order'.

The Solomon Islands: A society in armed collapse

> Many militants and villages were reluctant to hand over weapons for fear of being attacked when their defences were down. The other factor was sense of balance. Each side wanted to know what the other was handing back. If one side knew what the other had, and what was, or was not, handed over, then they could calculate the threat to their village or area.
>
> (RNZAF Flt.-Sgt. John Phillips, former IPMT armourer, June 2002)

After several failed attempts, peace—or at least an end to overt hostilities—finally came to the Solomon Islands with the signing of the Townsville Peace Agreement (TPA) in October 2000. The nine-part agreement covered a broad spectrum of issues,[18] including two provisions for amnesty. An initial *weapon amnesty* required all arms and ammunition used during the conflict to be handed over to the respective commanders within 30 days. In return, former militants and police would be granted immunity from prosecution with respect to the theft or illegal possession of firearms. In the event that the weapon amnesty was fully complied with, those concerned could then potentially be granted a *general amnesty* regarding unlawful acts committed in connection with the conflict.

To facilitate the peace and disarmament process, an International Peace Monitoring Team (IPMT)[19] was established, along with an indigenous Peace Monitoring Council (PMC). The IPMT was to assist with confidence-building, receive and monitor weapon surrenders, maintain an arms inventory, and monitor and report breaches of the TPA. The PMC provided local leadership, liaised closely with communities throughout Guadalcanal and Malaita, and ran a spirited media campaign to encourage militants to comply with the terms of the TPA.

As with the peace monitors in Bougainville, neither the IPMT nor the PMC had any enforcement authority, instead focusing on building community confidence to make arms secure. Relations with the influential Anglican Melanesian Brothers and Sisters were especially important when negotiating weapon surrenders with militants.

The early stages of the disarmament initiative were promising. By June 2001, some nine months after the signing of the TPA, over 1,000 firearms and 3,600 rounds of ammunition had been surrendered, including 141 military firearms, 62 commercially manufactured guns, and 831 home-made guns. As expected, most of the police-issue firearms came from the MEF, military firearms were returned from Malaita, and home-made guns were mainly handed in by Gualese ex-combatants. But by July 2001 there was concern about the declining number of guns surrendered. Authorities were aware that 500–600 high-powered police firearms remained in circulation, yet there was no sign of them.

A number of deterrents existed to the complete disarmament of ex-combatants. Persistent insecurity fuelled by armed crime, issues of compensation, the low morale of police forces, and uncertainty associated with the amnesty all acted as disincentives. Many ex-combatants, especially Gualese groups in Honiara and villagers in rural Malaita, feared retribution if they disarmed. As in Bougainville, a man's firearm could be his most potent, and perhaps only, source of social and economic power. As the Solomon Islands government sought to appease armed men with essentially corrupt 'disarmament allowances', expectations grew of continued financial incentives for those with access to guns.

Demoralization had also spread through the police force. Many senior officers refused to return their weapons or were pardoned under the provisions of the TPA, despite their role in human rights abuses. The recruitment by the Solomon Islands government of hundreds of former militants into the police as 'special constables' created a whole new raft of problems. Prior to the coup, only about 200 of these unarmed, village-based police had existed. By the second half of 2001, the number of untrained special constables, newly armed with police weapons and many with criminal records, had swollen to 2,000. The UN Development Programme (UNDP) and the Solomon Islands government began to reduce their numbers in 2002, but the special constables continued to generate disorder, on occasion using their guns to demand payment directly from the Treasury. A flawed attempt at demobilization and reintegration had backfired badly, leaving the police force in worse shape than ever.

Despite these challenges, in early 2002 community support for disarmament developed fresh momentum. Some 10,000 people participated in a 'Wokabaot for Pis' (Walkabout for Peace) organized by civil society groups in Honiara. Backed by a vigorous radio and media campaign, the Peace Monitoring Council and the Solomon Islands government launched a new effort to recover small arms, ammunition, explosives, and stolen property. More importantly, senior police officers were outspoken in their support for revitalizing the police force and the weapon surrender campaign. Two weeks after the expiry of the amnesty, 2,043 weapons were held in IPMT containers. In June 2002, the IPMT dumped hundreds of guns into the aptly named Iron Bottom Sound off the coast of Honiara under the watchful eye of Melanesian Brothers and to the cheers of Solomon Islanders.

In the event, piecemeal attempts at disarmament were overtaken by national collapse. On 18 July 2003, mired in an economic and social crisis—largely of its own making—which could no longer be ignored, the Solomon Islands parliament voted without dissent to request foreign intervention. One week later the Regional Assistance Mission to Solomon Islands (RAMSI) landed in Honiara with the first of 2,250 military, police, and civilian personnel from Australia, New Zealand, Fiji, Papua New Guinea, Tonga, Samoa, and other neighbouring nations. Their first order of business was to quarantine and destroy small arms.

> On occasion, police 'special constables' used their guns to demand payment directly from the Treasury in Solomon Islands.

An Australian soldier of the Regional Assistance Mission cuts up 12 guns handed in by rebels at Avu Avu, Solomon Islands, in August 2003.

In all the international debate and preparation surrounding the Pacific's first solicited invasion, nothing was accorded more urgency by governments, the intervention force, development agencies, and news media than the drive to collect and destroy firearms and ammunition. The proliferation and misuse of firearms had long been identified as the most immediate impediment to recovery in the Solomon Islands, and there was to be no dispute about disarmament.

Five days after its arrival, the multinational RAMSI force launched a national weapon amnesty, followed by determined enforcement of a ban on private guns. The most recent assessment of remaining small arms in the Solomon Islands had counted a high figure of 3,520 missing, illicit firearms (Muggah and Alpers, 2003). Five months later, in January 2004, the RAMSI weapon surrender campaign had collected 3,713 small arms, 386 of which had been stolen three years earlier from police armouries (RAMSI, 2004). This brought the total to 6,000 guns surrendered since November 2000. Destruction followed quickly, with no exceptions.

Although swift intervention, coupled with widespread community goodwill, had delivered a remarkable result, in early 2004 as many as 240 looted modern military assault rifles and machine guns were still missing in the Solomon Islands.

DOMESTIC AND REGIONAL ARMS CONTROL LEGISLATION

Comprehensive firearm legislation, though not sufficient in itself, forms the foundation of effective small arms control, both domestically and regionally. Stringent rules on firearm ownership and use, limits on access to ammunition, careful background checks of licence applicants, and regularly updated firearm registers are just some of the components of such legislation, underpinning national security and sustaining effective law enforcement.

Like most transnational crime, illicit small arms trafficking thrives on the ability to exploit differences between and inefficiencies in jurisdictions. Countries seeking to combat small arms proliferation thus need to focus not only on improving local and national laws but also on harmonizing key components of firearm laws across states. Uniform import–export laws and penalties for illegal trafficking are particularly important, as are common rules on marking, tracing, and record-keeping for arms and ammunition.

The many inconsistencies among small arms-related laws in the Pacific leave the region vulnerable to gun-running. Loopholes and permissive attitudes to small arms encourage illicit traffickers to mark countries as soft entry points, thus gaining access to whole regions. Wide variations in legislation have created holes in the Pacific's net for traffickers to exploit.

Domestic regulation of firearms

Six Pacific states have either banned the private ownership of firearms entirely or have suspended civilian firearm ownership for an indefinite period. Rules regarding civilian possession vary widely, from outright bans in Nauru, Palau, and the Marshall Islands to suspension of private gun ownership in the Solomon Islands and Fiji, a licensing moratorium in Papua New Guinea, multi-tiered registration systems in the French territories, and widespread licensed ownership in Australia and New Zealand.

Of the 20 nations surveyed,[20] 15 prohibit the private ownership of handguns (pistols and revolvers), while the remainder allow licensed handgun ownership only in exceptional cases. Semi-automatic weapons commonly attract tighter regulations, with many varieties banned altogether. Australia in particular has made sweeping recent efforts to reduce its civilian arsenal of semi-automatic long guns and short-barrelled handguns (see CRIME).

Fully automatic firearms (machine guns and sub-machine guns) are either prohibited in civilian possession or restricted to thousands of licensed gun collectors, as in Australia and New Zealand.

As the only two fully industrialized nations in the Pacific, with 75 per cent of the region's population between them, Australia and New Zealand enjoy greater capacity for legislative reform. Through their foreign policies, both countries also play a leading role in small arms policy development in the Pacific. Australia has led by example, comprehensively tightening its own gun laws since 1996. Although New Zealand encourages its island neighbours to curb the proliferation of small arms and supports their efforts to do so, the country's domestic gun laws remain, overall, the most permissive in the Pacific. With the region's highest per capita rate of firearm ownership, New Zealand is nevertheless the only Pacific nation to have abandoned registration of most firearms. In this regard, New Zealand stands almost alone with the US among the world's industrialized nations.

Although governments are committed at a regional level to addressing small arms issues in the Pacific by way of the *Nadi Framework* (see Box 9.7), there remain glaring inconsistencies in domestic firearm legislation. With few exceptions, such as Papua New Guinea and Vanuatu, smaller states have not significantly altered their firearm legislation since independence. Existing gun laws tend to reflect the legislative style and attitudes to firearm control of former colonial administrations—as they stood in Europe in the early 1900s (see Box 9.8).

Fifteen out of 20 Pacific nations prohibit the private ownership of handguns. Only two permit private firearms for self-defence.

Box 9.7 The Nadi Framework: A regional approach to arms control

Recognizing that domestic and regional controls are crucial to any international effort to curb the illicit trade in firearms, the 16 member states of the Pacific Islands Forum have worked since 1996 to develop a common regional approach to weapon control. In March 2000, this culminated in the *Nadi Framework* agreement (SPCPC and OCO, 2000), which seeks to encourage cross-border cooperation and harmonize legislation throughout the region.

The *Nadi Framework* is premised on two basic ideas: that the possession and use of firearms, ammunition, other related material, and prohibited weapons is a privilege that is conditional on the overriding need to ensure public safety, and that public safety will be enhanced by imposing harmonized controls on the importation, possession, and use of these commodities.

To achieve these objectives, the *Nadi Framework* and its draft legislation would require that individual applicants for a licence demonstrate 'genuine reason' for arms ownership. Stringent controls over the importation, possession, and use of weapons are also recommended. If uniformly adopted, these would significantly improve the firearm laws of many states, and provide a common regional deterrent to small arms traffickers. In August 2003, the *Nadi Framework*'s draft model legislation for the Pacific was unanimously accepted for consideration by all 16 member states of the Pacific Islands Forum.

Common themes in Pacific gun laws

Licensing of gun owners, as in most nations, is the primary public safety measure regulating firearms in the Pacific. The requirements for a licence to possess firearms vary according to the type of weapon concerned and any 'genuine reason' required for ownership. Gun safety training and safe storage requirements are components of several licensing regimes.

Most of the smaller Pacific Island nations tightly restrict firearm licences regardless of gun type or calibre, permitting only a narrow range of acceptable uses. In recognition of the subsistence lifestyles still practised by many Pacific citizens, genuine reasons for gun ownership often include hunting, farming, and pest control. Only Papua New Guinea and the French territories permit the possession of private firearms for self-defence.

> In New Zealand, police interview the spouse of each gun licence applicant.

Background checks on licence applicants vary widely, and are often not specified in law. Police attempt to discover previous violent, criminal, and mental histories where available, and character references are often required. In New Zealand, one referee must be the applicant's current or most recent spouse or partner.

Firearm registration is the second pillar of information-based policing, allowing law-enforcement authorities to track the flow of small arms within and between countries. Of the Pacific countries that permit civilian firearm ownership, Australia, Papua New Guinea, Fiji, the Cook Islands, the Federated States of Micronesia, Kiribati, Samoa, Tonga, Tuvalu, and Vanuatu all maintain comprehensive firearm registers under legislation. Firearm registers are also kept in Niue, American Samoa, and the Solomon Islands, even though there is no express legal requirement. In the French territories, gun dealers must transmit information on each firearm transfer to the police each month. New Zealand is the only Pacific nation without comprehensive firearm registration.

Access to ammunition is controlled in most Pacific jurisdictions, where gun owners can legally obtain and possess ammunition only for the specific type of firearm for which they are licensed. Only New Zealand, the Cook Islands, and the Australian state of Queensland have no such requirement. Most jurisdictions also place a legal ceiling on the amount of ammunition that may be purchased during the life of a firearms licence.

Marking and identification regimes also form a crucial element of effective small arms management, enabling accurate record-keeping, improving inventory security, and strengthening police capacity to track missing weapons. Though many states have provisions allowing (though not requiring) marking of individual firearms if no serial number exists, only the Federated States of Micronesia, American Samoa, the French territories, and the Solomon Islands legally require a serial number or identifying mark to be recorded.

Box 9.8 The origins of Pacific small arms legislation

Legislative arrangements in place at the time of independence or transition to self-governance have largely determined the complexion of existing firearm laws in most Pacific Island countries.

Former British protectorates such as Fiji, Kiribati, the Solomon Islands, and Tuvalu share almost identical small arms legislation, copied from the UK. Three countries with direct colonial links to New Zealand—the Cook Islands, Niue, and Samoa—exhibit a wide degree of variation in the wording, structure, and content of their gun laws, perhaps reflecting a looser style of colonial administration. Several former trust territories of the US—including the Federated States of Micronesia, the Republic of Palau, and the Republic of the Marshall Islands—possess virtually identical arms control legislation. American Samoa, still a US territory, appears to have developed its laws quite separately. All have chosen far more stringent controls than would be tolerated on the US mainland.

The French Pacific territories of New Caledonia, French Polynesia, and Wallis and Futuna have modified gun laws based on complex French legislation dating back to the Second World War.

Small arms legislation in the former British colonies of Australia and New Zealand was originally based on British law, but in both countries has evolved considerably over the last few decades. While one law covers all of New Zealand, there is no uniform national firearm legislation in Australia. Australian federal law controls imports, but each state and territory has separate legislation regarding civilian ownership and use of firearms. Most progressive reform in Australia has been initiated at the federal level, primarily by negotiating uniformity between states.

Papua New Guinea and Vanuatu have some of the most comprehensive small arms legislation in the Pacific. The former, which became independent from Australia in 1975, and the latter, which was jointly administered by the British and French until 1980, are almost alone among Pacific developing states in having extensively revised and adapted their legislation in recent years.

The tiny state of Nauru (population 12,000) has perhaps the most idiosyncratic small arms legislation in the Pacific. A former Australian-administered British protectorate, its Arms and Opium Prohibition Ordinance (1936-1967) bans 'natives and Chinamen' from possession of firearms, and clearly has not been updated since independence in 1968.

Manufacture and trade in arms are controlled, although with wide variations between countries. All non-commercial firearm transfers—private sales, exchanges, and even loans—are also generally legislated for in Pacific law. In Australia, civilian firearm transfers may be carried out only by licensed arms dealers or the police, in Vanuatu or Tuvalu there are no legal provisions for transfers, while New Zealand does not require any record-keeping for most gun transfers.

In many of the smaller states, controls on manufacturing are a formality to allow for the unlikely prospect of legal mass production of arms within their borders. Licensed manufacturing is permissible only in Australia, New Zealand, the Federated States of Micronesia, Samoa, and Vanuatu. Of these, only Australia has the capacity to manufacture small arms in any quantity (PRODUCERS).

Import and export controls are far from uniform across the Pacific, with Australia and New Zealand setting the standard for the most rigorous regimes. Most other Pacific states have only rudimentary import and export controls, and many do not stipulate any controls at all. Several have some restrictions on imports, but none on exports. This is one of the key areas where harmonization appears essential if a uniform regional deterrent to trafficking is to be established.

Penalty regimes provide a key legislative mechanism to deter small arms proliferation. Once again there is great inconsistency across the Pacific, with many penalties set too low to act as a serious deterrent.

Weapon collection and destruction can reduce the overall number of weapons in circulation, and are designed to improve the overall security of civilians. Many countries in the Pacific have legislation providing for compulsory weapon 'call-ins', with or without compensation. Fiji, Kiribati, the Solomon Islands, Tonga, Tuvalu, and Vanuatu all have provisions within their arms laws for the responsible minister to declare a prohibited area and to order the surrender of any or all arms and ammunition within its boundaries. In Palau and the Marshall Islands, compulsory surrender orders were enforced in 1982 and 1983.

Box 9.9   Gun amnesties: More style than substance?

Particularly in the wake of conflict, weapon amnesties and buy-backs are commonly promoted in an attempt to reduce the number of illegal small arms in circulation. In Fiji, the Solomon Islands, and Papua New Guinea, the results of amnesties have varied widely (see above).

In nations at peace, a growing body of evidence suggests that amnesties rarely succeed in removing targeted weapons from circulation (Plotkin, 1996; Sherman, 2001). Although widely favoured by policymakers as an instinctive and inexpensive option, firearm amnesties have been found to achieve better results in public relations and community building than in preventing future gun injury (Romero et al., 1998; Wintemute, 1999). Two leading US researchers have referred to gun amnesty and buy-back initiatives as 'a triumph of wishful thinking over all the available evidence', and 'the programme that is best-known to be ineffective' in reducing firearm violence (Dorning, 2000). Although authorities periodically promote gun amnesties, in reality unwanted firearms are accepted for disposal at any time, resulting in a year-round amnesty in most countries.

CONCLUSION

Most Pacific nations are at peace. Despite surprisingly high per capita civilian gun ownership in a handful of nations, rates of firearm-related violence in the region range from low to moderate.

Australia and New Zealand differ so markedly from their smaller island neighbours in wealth, stability, and per capita firearm ownership as to render many regional comparisons invalid. In weaker Pacific states, armed conflict has arisen where community control of small arms has been relinquished or usurped.

Though they feature only rarely in international headlines, several Pacific states are seen as potential tinderboxes for future armed conflict. Fiji, the Solomon Islands, and Papua New Guinea have all suffered recently from small arms-related violence, and firearm misuse has had profound direct and indirect consequences.

Neither the recent conflicts in the Pacific nor criminal activity have generated sufficient demand to prompt an influx of arms from countries outside the region, or even from Pacific neighbours. To date few combatant groups have had the money to procure a shipment of any size, while criminals seem satisfied with the rich and easy domestic supply of firearms available in larger Pacific states.

The ease with which firearms and ammunition leak from state armouries is a red flag for all states. Recent experience has shown that the injection of such weapons into fragile island communities can spark widespread, even regional, instability. It should be emphasized that existing domestic stockpiles, and not cross-border trafficking and smuggling, are the primary source of firearms misused in crime, conflict, and intentional and unintentional death and injury.

Although country-by-country legislative improvements may be on the horizon in the wake of the *Nadi Framework,* domestic and regional small arms-related legislation in the Pacific varies widely. The most comprehensive and up-to-date firearm legislation in the region is Australia's. By the standards of its 19 Pacific neighbours, New Zealand's domestic firearm laws are the most permissive, facilitating easy ownership and undocumented transfer of the region's largest unregistered stockpile of private guns. Despite these differences, the two nations experience similar rates of gun crime and injury.

Worryingly, most Pacific states lack basic firearm-related health and justice information. Accurate data are the lifeblood of informed policy-making and, without base-level knowledge of the impacts of firearm-related violence in affected communities, or the origins and trafficking routes of misused weapons, the small arms problem in the Pacific could become much worse before it improves. To avoid the sudden influxes of weapons common in less fortunate regions, donor partners in the Pacific have an important role to play in prevention.

Recent experiences with weapon disposal in Bougainville and the Solomon Islands have yielded positive results, and a number of lessons emerge. The early stages of the intervention yielded the best results, home-made or other less desirable weapons made up the majority of surrendered guns, the innovative linkage between weapon destruction and national aspirations for autonomy in Bougainville seem to have worked well, and the trust and involvement of community actors was essential in every case.

Grass-roots community involvement, in particular empowering partnerships between governments, donors, church, and women's groups, have been and remain the key to weapon collection, disposal, and peace in the Pacific.

9. LIST OF ABBREVIATIONS

BPMG	Bougainville Peace Monitoring Group
BRA	Bougainville Revolutionary Army
BRF	Bougainville Resistance Forces
FSM	Federated States of Micronesia (also 'Micronesia')
IFM	Isatabu Freedom Movement
IPMT	International Peace Monitoring Team
MEF	Malaita Eagle Force
PMC	Peace Monitoring Council
PMG	Peace Monitoring Group
PNG	Papua New Guinea
PNGDF	Papua New Guinea Defence Force
RAMSI	Regional Assistance Mission to Solomon Islands
RNZAF	Royal New Zealand Air Force
RPNGC	Royal Papua New Guinea Constabulary
RSIP	Royal Solomon Islands Police
TPA	Townsville Peace Agreement
UNDP	UN Development Programme
UNOMB	UN Observer Mission on Bougainville

9. ENDNOTES

[1] American Samoa, Australia,* Cook Islands,* Fiji,* French Polynesia, Kiribati,* Marshall Islands,* Federated States of Micronesia,* Nauru,* New Caledonia, New Zealand,* Niue,* Palau,* Papua New Guinea,* Samoa,* Solomon Islands,* Tonga,* Tuvalu,* Vanuatu,* and Wallis and Futuna. Note: an asterisk denotes each of the 16 member states of the Pacific Islands Forum.

[2] The US government produces a range of reports on military and commercial small arms transfers, including the Pentagon Defence and Security Assistance Agency's Foreign Military Sales (FMS) report, the State Department's Section 655 Report (which contains a country-by-country listing of the value of all direct commercial sales, DCS, approvals), FMS export approvals, excess defence article (EDA) agreements, and the Department of Treasury's Export Commodity Reports (Lumpe and Donarski, 1998).

[3] Although Table 9.2 includes Australian exports of 'Non-military Lethal Goods' declared in 2000 to Fiji (USD 110,000) and Vanuatu (USD 2,368), these figures lack transparency. The small arms and ammunition component of such transfers remains uncertain, but could be significant in the case of Fiji, where 100 per cent of that year's known arms trade was declared under this catch-all category. Due to uncertainty over their content, additional transfers of 'Non-military Lethal Goods' in 2000 from Australia to Papua New Guinea (USD 871,723), New Zealand (USD 358,000), and New Caledonia (USD 23,000) have not been included in Table 9.2.

[4] In a 2001 survey of Pacific state armouries, small arms analyst David Capie identified Singaporean Ultimax-100 light machine guns and SR-88s in Papua New Guinean armouries, and Uzis, MP5s, Galils, and K2s (a South Korean copy of the M-16) in Fiji (Capie, 2003).

[5] Alone among Pacific nations, New Zealand has ceased to register most firearms owned by licensed gun owners. For this reason, authorities can only estimate the number of lawfully held firearms.

[6] The STOCKPILES chapter adopts a multiplier of 2.25, which is based on the number of small arms known to be possessed by the Canadian armed forces. This methodology has important limitations. It is a conservative estimate, and ratios are subject to change. If personnel are retrenched, for example, the ratio can increase because there are more small arms per soldier.

[7] Trends in the Pacific are towards smaller military forces. Fiji's UN peacekeeping force has been downsized, and a Commonwealth review recommended that Papua New Guinea's armed forces be reduced by more than half.

[8] Survey data from around the world indicate that the ratio of firearms to sworn police is lower than military weapon-to-troop ratios. In Norway, the ratio is 1.2 guns per officer, while in Belgium and Sweden it is 1.3. This rises to 1.45 in the case of South Africa (Small Arms Survey, 2001, p. 71). The Pacific region multiplier is conservatively calculated at 1.3 firearms per officer.

[9] In May 1988, only months after two military coups in Fiji, customs officers in Sydney seized a 12-ton container of second-hand Czechoslovakian small arms labelled 'used machinery' en route to Fiji from North Yemen. In London, expatriate Fijian Indian Mohammed Raffia Khan was arrested in connection with the shipment and

served jail terms in Britain for other offences (Ross, 1993, p. 128). Although Fijian authorities claimed that another ten-ton shipment of primarily Soviet arms had arrived on the Suva wharves a month earlier, no evidence of this emerged. While a conclusive explanation was never provided, the weapons are widely suspected to have been connected with the organizers of the 1987 coup.

[10] The Papua New Guinea National Intelligence Organisation believes the West Papua border is PNG's main entry point for smuggled guns. There is also evidence of weapon trafficking from PNG to West Papua, to supply the local independence movement *Organisasi Papua Merdeka* (OPM).

[11] Personal correspondence with Inspector Phil Gubb, Coordinator, NZ Police Firearms Licensing Task Force, Wellington, 4 February 1994.

[12] Comment made at the Pacific Islands Countries Regional Seminar on the Illicit Trade in Small Arms and Light Weapons in All Its Aspects, held in Tokyo, 20–22 Jan. 2003. The delegate, who shall remain nameless, was reflecting on the responsibility he feels at holding the key to his nation's armoury.

[13] See, for example, Muggah and Brauer (2004).

[14] Nevertheless, GDP increased by an estimated 1.5 to 4 per cent in 2001, and 4.4 per cent in 2002. Consult ADB, 2002, p.43; ADB, 2003, p.44; WDI Online, 2004.

[15] In 1899, what is now the PNG province of Bougainville was arbitrarily annexed from the Solomon Islands by Germany. Bougainvilleans are culturally quite distinct from the people of Papua New Guinea, and are now separated by an international border from their kin in the Solomon Islands.

[16] The Bougainville PMG, 300-strong at its peak, was a neutral, unarmed organization of civilian commanders, negotiators, and monitors, supported by military personnel from Australia, New Zealand, Fiji, and Vanuatu.

[17] Although 'high-powered' is an official term routinely used to describe certain firearms in both the Solomon Islands and Bougainville, no standard definition exists. In Bougainville, peace monitors loosely defined these as factory-manufactured military-style weapons (M-16, AR-15, SLR, FAMAS, SIG, and so on). In the Solomon Islands, the IPMT defined a military weapon as 'any high-powered centre-fire semi-automatic, automatic, bolt action, magazine-fed shotgun, riot gun, or signal pistol issued to members of the Solomon Islands police'. In practice, 'high-powered' firearms were mass-manufactured military weapons of World War II or later design.

[18] Reconciliation, restructuring of the police force, rehabilitation of militants, compensation for loss and damages, increased autonomy for Malaita and Guadalcanal, and promises of infrastructure development in both provinces.

[19] Civilian-led and unarmed, the IPMT drew its 50 personnel from Australian and New Zealand police and defence forces, civilian government departments, and police forces in Tonga and Vanuatu.

[20] For a comprehensive list of domestic gun laws, comparisons between states, and an analysis of small arms-related legislation on export-import, marking and tracing, brokering, and other provisions in 20 Pacific nations, see Alpers and Twyford (2003).

9. BIBLIOGRAPHY

ABC (Australian Broadcasting Corporation). 2003. 'Minister Blames Theft for Gun Crime Rise.' ABC NewsOnLine. Canberra, 28 December. http://www.abc.net.au/news/newsitems/s1016961.htm

ACS (Australian Customs Service). 2003a. *Commercial Importation and Commercial/private Export of Firearms*. Canberra: ASC. <http://www.customs.gov.au/site/index.cfm?nav_id=670&area_id=5> (accessed 23 February).

—. 2003b. *Customs And Handguns—Frequently Asked Questions*. Canberra: ASC. <http://www.customs.gov.au> (accessed 11 January).

Advertiser (Adelaide). 1999. '350 Handguns Stolen from Army Store.' 29 July.

Alpers, Philip. 2002. 'Yes, Americans Are Often Shot—And So Are Many Others.' *Injury Prevention*, Vol. 8, No. 4, p. 262.

—. and Conor Twyford. 2003. *Small Arms in the Pacific*. Occasional Paper No. 8. Small Arms Survey. Geneva, March 2003. <http://www.smallarmssurvey.org/OPapers/OPaper8Pacifics.pdf>

—. and Reece Walters. 1998. 'Firearms Theft in New Zealand: Lessons for Crime and Injury Prevention.' *Australian and New Zealand Journal of Criminology*, Vol. 31, No. 1, pp. 85–95.

Asian Development Bank. 2002. 'Asian Development Outlook 2002: Trends, Analysis, Projections.' Manila: ADB.

Bell, Geoff. 2003. 'Underlying Causes of Death (ICD10): Firearm Related Deaths, 1999–2002.' Unpublished dataset. Canberra: Australian Bureau of Statistics, 10 December.

BPMG (Bougainville Peace Monitoring Group). 2002a. 'Bougainville Weapons Containment Update.' Unpublished document. 24 October.

—. 2002b. 'Bougainville Weapons Containment Update.' Unpublished document. 31 July.

Chatvick, Andre. 1999. *A Report on Firearm Registration Issues*. Wellington: Office of the Commissioner, New Zealand Police.

Dorney, Sean. 2000. *Papua New Guinea: People, Politics and History since 1975*, revised edn. Sydney: ABC Books.

Dorning, Mike. 2000. 'Gun Buybacks Fail to Cut Crime, Killings: Programs Attract Wrong Weapons, Study Says.' *Chicago Tribune*. 9 June.

Federation of American Scientists. 2002. *2002 Section 655 Report*. <http:///www.fas.org/asmp>

Fiji Government. 2004. News Brief. Suva. 17 February. <http://www.fiji.gov.fj/publish/page_1968.shtml>

Geohegan, Andrew. 2003. *The 7.30 Report*. ABC TV. Sydney, 23 December. <http://www.abc.net.au/7.30/content/2003/s1015505.htm>

Green, Inspector Joe. 2002. 'Kiwis Could Own Nearly One Million Firearms.' *The Dominion* (Wellington). 15 June.

Gurdayal, Mithleshni. 2002. '10,000 Migrate, Leave Fiji $1 Billion Poorer.' *Daily Post* (Suva). 21 January, p. 1.

Lumpe, Lora and Jeff Donarski. 1998. *The Arms Trade Revealed: A Guide for Investigators and Activists*. Washington, DC: Federation of American Scientists Fund.

Marsh, Nicholas. 2003. *Small Arms Database*. Oslo: Norwegian Initiative on Small Arms Transfers (NISAT) and the International Peace Research Institute. March.

Mouzos, Jenny. 1999. *International Traffic in Small Arms: An Australian Perspective*. Trends and Issues in Crime and Criminal Justice No. 104. Canberra: Australian Institute of Criminology.

—. 2002a. *Homicide in Australia: 2000–2001 National Homicide Monitoring Programme (NHMP) Annual Report*. Canberra: Australian Institute of Criminology.

—. 2002b. *Firearms Theft in Australia*. Trends and Issues in Crime and Criminal Justice No. 230. Canberra: Australian Institute of Criminology.

Muggah, Robert and Philip Alpers. 2003. *Reconsidering Small Arms in the Solomon Islands*. Small Arms Survey policy briefing. Honiara, 1 August.

Muggah, Robert and Jürgen Brauer. 2004. 'Diagnosing Demand: An Economic Framework.' Small Arms Survey background paper. Geneva.

Newbold, Greg. 1999. 'The Criminal Use of Firearms.' *Australian and New Zealand Journal of Criminology*, Vol. 32, No. 1, pp. 61–78.

Plotkin, Martha, ed. 1996. *Under Fire: Gun Buy-Backs, Exchanges and Amnesty Programs*. Washington, DC. Police Executive Research Forum.

Port Vila Presse. 2002. 'Loss of Skilled People Threatening Stability, Says Fiji Minister.' 4 May, p. 8.

RAMSI (Regional Assistance Mission to Solomon Islands). 2004. *Weapon Hand-in Cover Page*. Honiara, 11 January.

Regan, Anthony. 2002. 'The Bougainville Political Settlement and the Prospects for Sustainable Peace.' Draft paper for the *Pacific Economic Bulletin*. May.

Romero, Michael P., Garen J. Wintemute, and Jon S. Vernick. 1998. 'Characteristics of a Gun Exchange Program, and an Assessment of Potential Benefits.' *Injury Prevention*, No. 4, pp. 206–10.

Ross, Ken. 1993. *Regional Security in the South Pacific: The Quarter-century 1970–95*. Canberra: Strategic and Defence Studies Centre, Australian National University.

Saunders, Megan. 2000. 'PNG Smugglers Swap Drugs for Guns'. *Weekend Australian* (Sydney). 4 November, p. 10.

Sherman, Lawrence W. 2001. 'Reducing Gun Violence: What Works, What Doesn't, What's Promising.' *Criminal Justice*, No. 1. February, pp. 11–25.

Small Arms Survey. 2001. *Small Arms Survey 2001: Profiling the Problem*. Oxford: Oxford University Press.

Solomon Islands International Peace Monitoring Team (IPMT). 2001. 'Weapons Containment Data.' July.

SPCPC (South Pacific Chiefs of Police Conference) and OCO (Oceania Customs Organisation). 2000. *Towards a Common Approach to Weapons Control ('Nadi Framework')*. Nadi. 10 March.

Thorp, Sir Thomas. 1997. *Review of Firearms Control in New Zealand: Summary and Conclusions*. Wellington: Government Printer.

Toohey, Paul. 2002. 'States Won't Pay Gun Buyback Bill'. *Australian* (Sydney). 6 November.

UNDP (United Nations Development Programme). 2002. 'Weapons Disposal Advancing.' *Tok Save*. UNDP Bougainville Rehabilitation, Reconstruction and Development Project Newsletter. May.

—. 2003. *Human Development Report 2002*. New York and Oxford: Oxford University Press.

Wintemute, Garen J. 1999. 'The Future of Firearm Violence Prevention: Building on Success.' *Journal of the American Medical Association*, 282:5, p. 2. 4 August.

WDI Online. 2004. World Development Indicators. Fiji: GDP per capita growth (annual %). Washington: World Bank Group. <http://devdata.worldbank.org/dataonline/>

ACKNOWLEDGEMENTS

Other contributors
Rod Alley, James Bevan, David Capie, Aaron Karp, and Emile LeBrun.

Kyrgyz police officers drag away a demonstrator in Bishkek in November 2002. Police detained more than 100 protesters who demanded punishment of government officials responsible for the shooting deaths of five civilians in Aksy eight months earlier. (© Reuters/Valdimir Pirogov)

An Anomaly in Central Asia?
SMALL ARMS IN KYRGYZSTAN

10

INTRODUCTION

The southern regions of the former Soviet Union (the Caucasus and Central Asia) are widely viewed as forming an arc of instability fuelled by state weakness, economic decline, social fragmentation, civil conflicts, national and translational crime, and the spillover of conflicts from neighbouring regions. For all of these reasons, one would expect a high demand for and easy availability of small arms throughout the area.

A Small Arms Survey study carried out in mid-2003 (MacFarlane, Neil, and Torjesen, 2004), on which this chapter is based, indicates that the degree of small arms possession, use, and proliferation in Kyrgyzstan is less serious than appears to be the case in other Central Asian states. There is no firm evidence of a link between trafficking in small arms and that in drugs and people. Furthermore, small arms violence and casualty rates are limited. The study highlights the need to question regional generalizations and points to some factors that appear to prevent serious small arms proliferation. It suggests the following explanations for why small arms problems in Kyrgyzstan appear to be less serious than expected:

- The stockpile of arms in Kyrgyzstan at the time of independence was smaller than in neighbouring republics such as Tajikistan and Uzbekistan.
- The general level of security in the country has remained high. Individuals have had few incentives to arm themselves for their own protection.
- In the absence of civil war and collapse, the authorities have been able to maintain control of the arms issue more effectively than their counterparts in states such as Georgia or Tajikistan.
- Kyrgyzstan does not appear to have a particular cultural demand for arms. Nor is small arms possession in the country obviously linked to gender identities, unlike in some other parts of the former Soviet Union.
- There is no obvious reason to smuggle arms through Kyrgyzstan to nearby concentrations of demand. Russia has plentiful supplies of its own, as do Tajikistan and Afghanistan.

A TROUBLED STATE IN A VOLATILE REGION

Kyrgyzstan displays many signs of trouble. Its economy, although growing, is characterized by industrial stagnation, high unemployment, and very wide income differentials. Per capita income levels remain far below the levels that people were accustomed to in the Soviet era. There is widespread and considerable frustration and political disillusionment. The government lacks capacity and its democratic institutions and processes are weak. Ethnic minorities are underrepresented in government. The state is unaccountable to its citizens and shows signs of creeping authoritarianism. It appears to be incapable of consistently providing essential public services. For these reasons, the people of Kyrgyzstan increasingly view their government as illegitimate.

Kyrgyzstan is situated in a region where many countries have suffered significant political unrest and civil conflict. Tajikistan, in the south, experienced civil war from 1992 to 1997, and a number of Tajik regions remain outside government control even after the peace agreement of May 1997. Afghanistan, further to the south, suffered foreign invasion and civil war in the period from 1979 to 2001. It is widely believed that substantial numbers of arms remain beyond government control.

Radical Islamism has contributed to insecurity in Afghanistan, where the pre-2002 Taliban regime granted sanctuary to an array of terrorist and insurgent groups including not only al Qaeda but also Uighur separatist groups challenging Chinese rule in Xinjiang. The Islamic Movement of Uzbekistan (IMU), which had grown out of the Uzbek government's suppression of Islamic movements in the Ferghana Valley, tried to penetrate Uzbekistan via Tajikistan and southern Kyrgyzstan, mounting raids into the Batken District of the Ferghana Valley in 1999–2000 (see Box 10.5).[1]

> The general level of security in Kyrgyzstan has remained high. Individuals have had few incentives to arm themselves for their own protection.

Box 10.1 Methodology: Challenges and solutions

This study is based on a broad array of sources. These include a thorough desk review of primary and secondary sources (academic, governmental, and those of international organizations and NGOs) and a commissioned summary of reports on crime and criminality published in *Delo No*, the principal Kyrgyz newspaper. Official statistics on possession, use, and impact were complemented with a wide range of interviews in Bishkek and in southern Kyrgyzstan. Interview subjects included officials from the National Security Service and the ministries of Foreign Affairs, the Interior, and Defence, as well as a selection of medical personnel, journalists, academics, and civil society representatives. In addition, research staff interviewed a wide range of diplomatic personnel and representatives of international organizations and NGOs. The breadth of the interview sample was designed to provide an adequate basis for triangulation of interview results.

In order to discover public views about the small arms issue, the research team carried out a household survey in the south, where political tension and criminality have been relatively high. The 236 survey respondents were selected so as to reflect a balance between Kyrgyz and minority communities. To complement the survey, the researchers attended village meetings.

To gain a better understanding of regional dynamics of arms flows, as well as the link between these flows and trafficking in goods and people, research was also carried out in Kazakhstan and Tajikistan.

Challenges

The research project encountered a number of methodological problems related to official data. Kyrgyz authorities were reluctant to provide data. There is reason to question the capacity of official organs to generate complete data on various arms issues, such as the size of stockpiles or crime rates. During interviews there was evidence of motivated bias: government personnel in Kyrgyzstan had both an interest in projecting an image of stability, security, and effective control and in inflating the dimensions of exogenous threats to its security (for example, terrorism and narcotics trafficking) because external flows of assistance are influenced by outside perceptions of the dimensions of such problems. Opposition figures and the NGO community may have countervailing biases that inflate their estimates of the small arms problem. Household survey data suffered because people might have been reluctant to talk to strangers about gun possession and use. Respondents in Kyrgyzstan often inquired who was behind the survey and whether the information would be handed to government authorities.

Nevertheless, the variety of sources taken together should give a fairly reliable impression of the small arms issues in Kyrgyzstan today.

Kyrgyzstan lies along major routes for the trafficking of drugs and people. In 2000, Afghanistan produced 70 per cent of the world's supply of illicit opium. Between 1994 and 2001, the Central Asian share of seizures of heroin originating in Afghanistan grew from 0.1 per cent to 23.0 per cent (UNODC, 2003, p. 5; UNODCCP, 2002, p. 14).

These internal and external factors create conditions in which it is reasonable to expect that small arms constitute a significant problem for Kyrgyzstan. For example, Pirseyedi (2002: 85–6) argues that the combination of latent tension and conflict and the easy availability of small arms in the region could have explosive consequences.

The existence of a considerable infrastructure for illicit small arms trafficking in Central Asia suggests that a breakout of armed internal conflict in Uzbekistan, Kazakhstan, Turkmenistan, or Kyrgyzstan would lead to immediate and massive shipments of small arms to the conflict region. However, given the proportions the proliferation of small arms has already assumed within these countries, it can be argued that the easy availability of small arms itself may become the decisive factor transforming political disagreements into full-scale armed confrontations.

However, there is little evidence that the economic and political pressures facing Kyrgyzstan are producing major political instability within the country. This reflects not only the effectiveness of informal coping mechanisms in the economy but also the absence of any obvious political alternatives to the present government. The opposition remains weak and divided, and generates little enthusiasm among the population as a whole. Although much is made of the danger of Islamism in Central Asia, there is no substantial evidence that radical Islamist movements are taking hold within the Kyrgyz majority of the country.

The incidence of political violence is sporadic and low. During a period of unrest in the region of Aksy in 2002, the government was barely able to retain control over the situation (see Box 10.2).[2] In general, however, there is little evidence that economic deprivation and social and political frustration have produced increasing levels of crime.

> The people of Kyrgyzstan increasingly view their government as illegitimate.

This remote Kyrgyz checkpoint at Kyzyl-Art poses a feeble threat to traffickers who navigate the windy road into and out of neighbouring Tajikstan.

> Although much is made of the danger of Islamism in Central Asia, there is no substantial evidence that radical Islamist movements are taking hold within the Kyrgyz majority of the country.

SMALL ARMS SURVEY 2004

> **Box 10.2**   'For those who perished by the bullets of the authorities'[3]
>
> Kyrgyz police forces fired at a group of 2,000 protestors in the south-western rural district of Aksy on 17-18 March 2002. Six people died and 62 were injured.[4] The demonstrators were protesting the imprisonment of the parliamentary deputy representing Aksy, Azimbek Beknazarov, who had been an outspoken critic of President Askar Akaev. Following Beknazarov's imprisonment in January 2002, tensions were high in Aksy and parents kept their children home from school in protest. After rumours that Beknazarov was being beaten in jail, angry protesters briefly took visiting government officials hostage.[5]
>
> The shootings occurred on a quiet country road leading into the regional centre, Kerben, as the police tried to stop the demonstrators.[6] All five demonstrators shot during the initial encounter were men, although eyewitness accounts claim women were at the forefront of the demonstration.[7] Special provisions in the Kyrgyz legal framework prohibit firing at women.[8] The deaths of male demonstrators suggest that the police aimed at the demonstrators, despite press statements asserting that initial warning shots had been fired into the air.[9] Five of the six demonstrators who died were hit by gunshots, while at least ten of the injured had bullet wounds. Others suffered beatings and head injuries. On the night 17-18 March, villagers gathered outside the regional police station in Kerben to protest the shootings. During that night, another person was shot from a police car.[10]
>
>
>
> Protesters pray at the six-month anniversary in September 2002 of an opposition demonstration in Aksy at which police shot and killed at five people.
>
> The shooting triggered a wave of protests, all of which were peaceful. At present, the Beknazarov opposition remains active, though fewer in number than in spring 2002, when as many as 10,000 were expressing their dissatisfaction with the government.[11]
>
> The disturbances in Aksy, and the subsequent political crisis, fostered a number of significant changes in policy. The government of Kyrgyzstan resigned in May 2002 and was replaced. In September 2002, the government established a commission to develop constitutional amendments to strengthen the legislative branch. The next month, President Akaev announced that he would not seek re-election in 2005. Additional resources were ploughed into infrastructural improvements in the south.
>
> In the wake of the Aksy events the Kyrgyz government invited the OSCE to initiate a programme on police reform. One of the eight components in the EUR 3.8 million (USD 4.1 million) project is introducing Kyrgyz police to 'less-than-lethal-force' methods in crowd control. The aim is to prevent future bloodshed of this type. Local human rights organizations in Kyrgyzstan, however, see the programme as directed at the suppression of civic initiatives in Kyrgyzstan and have voiced strong criticism of the OSCE.[12]

LEGAL SMALL ARMS POSSESSION

The Kyrgyz government has retained a strict legal regulatory system of small arms that mirrors the legal framework of Soviet legislation.[13] The Law on Arms divides weapon types into three categories: battle, service, and civil arms.

State holdings: Battle and service arms

There are no public figures on Kyrgyzstan's official stockpile of arms. Based on the number of armed servicemen, the government is estimated to possess a total of 50,000 weapons. The army has 10,900 active servicemen and the border guards 5,000 (IISS, 2002). On the assumption that the formula for calculating the number of guns in national armies—

2.25 arms per soldier—holds for Kyrgyzstan, there are 24,525 weapons in the Kyrgyz army. Each border guard is likely to have at least one gun, which raises the overall figure for military possession close to 30,000. The main law-enforcement agency is the Ministry of Internal Affairs (MVD), which has 17,000 staff.[14] It is complemented by 1,200 members of the National Security Service (formerly KGB). MVD officials claim that there is at least one gun per individual in law enforcement.

The Kyrgyz army uses weapons which, transferred from the Soviet forces in May 1992,[15] resemble those of other former Soviet army units. The most common weapons are Kalashnikovs—AK-47, AK–74, AKM Kalashnikov (modernized assault rifle—Makarov pistols, and Dragunov sniper rifles (SVD). Army officers claim that there have been no new supplies of arms since independence, although some press reports note Russian arms supplies to Kyrgyzstan in 1999.[16] Statistics on declared imports/exports for Kyrgyzstan show no military imports (Table 10.1). The financial constraint on the Kyrgyz forces ensures that the arms inventory has remained modest. Soviet troops, which were relocated to Russia after 1991, took much of the equipment with them as they left.

Table 10.1 Imports of small arms by Kyrgyzstan (reported by exporting state)

Commodity	Time period	Total value (USD)	Exporters and % of total trade value to Kyrgyzstan	
Shotguns, shotgun-rifles for hunting	1993-2000	237,685	Canada	29.5
			Germany	22.7
			Russian Federation	47.7
Rifles for hunting	1996-2001	170,406	Austria	2.3
			Germany	3.5
			Russian Federation	94.2
Small arms ammunition and parts	1994-96	46,067	Germany	80.3
			Russian Federation	19.7
Revolvers and pistols	1995-98	14,187	Spain	26.9
			Switzerland	73.1
Cartridges, shotguns	1995-98	4,624	Switzerland	40.2
			United Kingdom	59.8

Note: The tables may considerably underestimate Kyrgyz arms trade.

Source: Comtrade database, NISAT database

Civilian holdings

There are strict legal rules governing civilian possession, and the legal framework resembles the stringent Soviet system of gun control. Despite an extensive regulatory framework on the registration of weapons and the issuing of appropriate documents to gun owners, no official figures on legal civilian possession are available.[17] However, the MVD and the Hunters' Association[18] agree on their estimate of approximately 15,000 registered arms in Kyrgyzstan.[19]

Eighty per cent of all registered hunting guns in Kyrgyzstan are held in the Chui Oblast, the area surrounding the capital Bishkek.[20] In other regions, such as Batken and Osh Oblasts, possession of registered hunting guns is found predominately in urban centres.[21] Kyrgyzstan differs from most other countries in having fewer rather than more hunting weapons registered for rural areas. This is explained by the still disproportionate share of Russian hunters, most of whom live in urban centres, and possibly also by less complete registration in rural areas.

> There are strict legal rules governing civilian possession, and the legal framework resembles the stringent Soviet system of gun control.

The Kyrgyz law on civil arms subdivides arms into four groups: (i) arms for self-defence; (ii) gas pistols; (iii) sport arms; and (iv) hunting arms (Kyrgyzstan, 1999, paras. 2–7). Citizens have to be of appropriate mental and physical health to be granted the right to bear a weapon (Kyrgyzstan, 1999, para. 15). The law allows for the use of arms against other persons in a situation of self-defence. In practice, however, it appears that permission to own weapons is given only to members of the Hunters' Association, which in 2002 had 7,410 registered hunters. Each hunter can have up to four guns (two smooth bore shotguns and two rifles). Most members, however, have only one or two weapons.[22] Overall membership of the hunting association decreased during the 1990s, falling from 25,900 (fishermen included) in 1990 to 8,617 in 2002. This is explained by Russian emigration from Kyrgyzstan: most members in the Hunters' Association were ethnic Russians at the time of independence.[23] A relative increase in prices might also be a factor.

The great majority of hunting guns are produced in Russia, with Izhevskii Mekhanicheskii Zavod and Tulskii Oruzheinyi Zavod dominating the market (PRODUCERS). The most common hunting guns are the double-barrel shotgun TOZ-34 and the BAIKAL IZH-27 Over and Under Shotgun. Russian imported shotguns cost USD 232–348.[24] The average monthly salary in Kyrgyzstan is approximately USD 35, making purchases of new hunting guns a major investment for the average consumer in Kyrgyzstan. The luxury of a hunting gun is therefore likely to be limited to the country's small economic elite. There has been a steep increase in prices since independence.

In addition to hunters, there are 'legal persons with special authorized tasks' who are licensed to own guns. This category only represents a small percentage of overall gun possession,[25] and includes individual security providers, such as government and private security guards (that is, security for property and money transportation, and protection of nature and natural resources).[26] The most common weapons used within this category are Makarov pistols and gas pistols.

UNREGISTERED AND ILLEGAL POSSESSION

Illegal possession of weapons is difficult to quantify, but a number of indicators suggest that it is low and does not constitute a major security issue. This assumption is based on the opinion of law enforcement officials, supported by a small household survey, moderate gun injury and murder rates, security perceptions, and cultural attitudes to guns. However, there are signs that leakages from government stockpiles occur and that gun injuries appear to have slightly increased.

> Illegal possession of weapons is difficult to quantify, but a number of indicators suggest that it is low and does not constitute a major security issue.

Leakages from government stockpiles

Leakage from army stockpiles has been common in post-Soviet societies, and Kyrgyzstan has been no exception. It is impossible to quantify the extent of the problem. Representatives of the Kyrgyz army claim that a commission checks the weapons inventory of armed forces every third month.[27] In 1996 one such commission found that 26 sub-machine guns, 138 pistols, 5 machine guns, and 17,500 bullets were missing from two regiments and one artillery division (FTI, 2002).

It is unlikely that control commission investigations take place regularly or are able to tackle the problem of arms leakage effectively. The low level of military spending has left the Kyrgyz army in a demoralized state. Low salaries and poor material conditions create an environment conducive to crime. In the period 1993–2002, the Military Prosecutors Office assessed a total of 1,100 cases. More than 30 officers and 500 soldiers were faced with criminal charges. There were seven registered incidents of large-scale theft of firearms by military personnel in the period 2000–2 (Foundation for Tolerance International, 2002). Given the high overall corruption levels in the Kyrgyz government structure, the actual crime rate among army personnel could be substantially higher than that revealed in the Military Prosecutor's statistics.

> **Box 10.3 Ministry of Internal Affairs: Weapons stock control**
>
> According to MVD officials, weapons in MVD facilities are held in locked facilities with one door for the duty officer and a window for issuing weapons to other officers, who are not allowed into the store. Weapons in storage are checked at the beginning of each shift.
>
> Weapons loss resulting from negligence is severely punished. At a minimum, the officer is dismissed and has to repay two to three times the cost of the weapon, whether or not it is later found. In cases of possible criminal intent, the MVD's special investigation service intervenes and reports to the minister.
>
> A weapons theft in 2003 at the Jalalabad OVD station raises questions about the implementation of these procedures. On 15 May, 2003, ten people entered the Jalalabad OVD offices, assaulted the security guards, and stole some 35 weapons (around 20 Kalashnikov automatic rifles, more than ten Makarov and Stetchkin pistols, a Dragunov sniper rifle, and a machine gun) (*Vechernii Bishkek*, 2003). They then left Jalalabad for the Aksy region. Eventually, most members of the group were arrested and the bulk of the weapons recovered, although the sniper rifle remains unaccounted for. An investigation attributed the success of the attack to lax procedures. The head of the Jalalabad interior administration was dismissed, along with a number of his deputies. A subsequent ministerial decree ordered the installation of CCTV monitors both in weapons stores and in the corridors outside them. Owing to lack of funds, this measure has not been fully implemented.

Kyrgyz soldiers guard their headquarters in Batken in September 1999. For several weeks, armed radical Islamists, allegedly from Uzbekistan's Muslim opposition, held hostages in this mountainous region.

However, as noted above, Kyrgyzstan's overall stockpile is likely to be relatively small as the Soviet troops that were relocated to Russia after 1991 took much of the equipment with them when they left. In addition, it is possible that many of the stockpile leakages did not remain in the county, and were transferred to Tajikistan. (See the section below on trafficking.)

Gun possession according to officials and the population

Kyrgyz law-enforcement agencies, although reluctant to make specific estimates, stress that illegal gun possession is likely to be low.[28] From 1996 to 2004, the MVD confiscated 5,000 guns. This is a low figure in comparison with Tajikistan, where 22, 831 guns were confiscated in the same period (Tajikistan, 2003). There are some reports of the (illegal) possession of home-made guns in rural areas (that is, converted gas pistols). It is unlikely, however, that this is a widespread phenomenon.[29]

The household survey, carried out in villages close to the borders with Uzbekistan and Tajikistan, which are considered the troubled areas of the country, supported the view that overall private gun ownership is low. Half of the respondents claimed that 'almost no households' had guns, while 24 per cent noted that 'a few households' have guns. Seventy-eight per cent said they had never heard a gun, while 76 per cent claimed that they had never seen a firearm.[30] The respondents tended to cite hunting rifles as the most common weapon (40 per cent), but other weapons, such as Kalashnikovs (20 per cent) and pistols (13 per cent), were also mentioned. Fifty per cent of the respondents observed that criminals were the group in society most likely to have guns, while as many as 25 per cent reserved that role for businessmen.

Gun crime

The perception that illegal guns and general possession among the population are low is supported by very moderate gun injury and gun murder rates in Kyrgyzstan. Official statistics indicate a relatively low reported crime rate in

Kyrgyz society that appears to have decreased since the first years of independence. The total number of crimes in 1993 was 42,495; in 2001 the figure fell to 39,986.[31] However, the overall murder rate shows a slight increase over time. Officially reported gun deaths remain at a low level with no obvious upward trend: 6 in 2000, 11 in 2001, 9 in 2002 (0.2 per 100,000).[32] The proportion of murders committed by use of a gun is relatively small, which is a further indicator that guns are not so widely available (see Table 10.2).

Figure 10.1   Public opinion on firearm possession

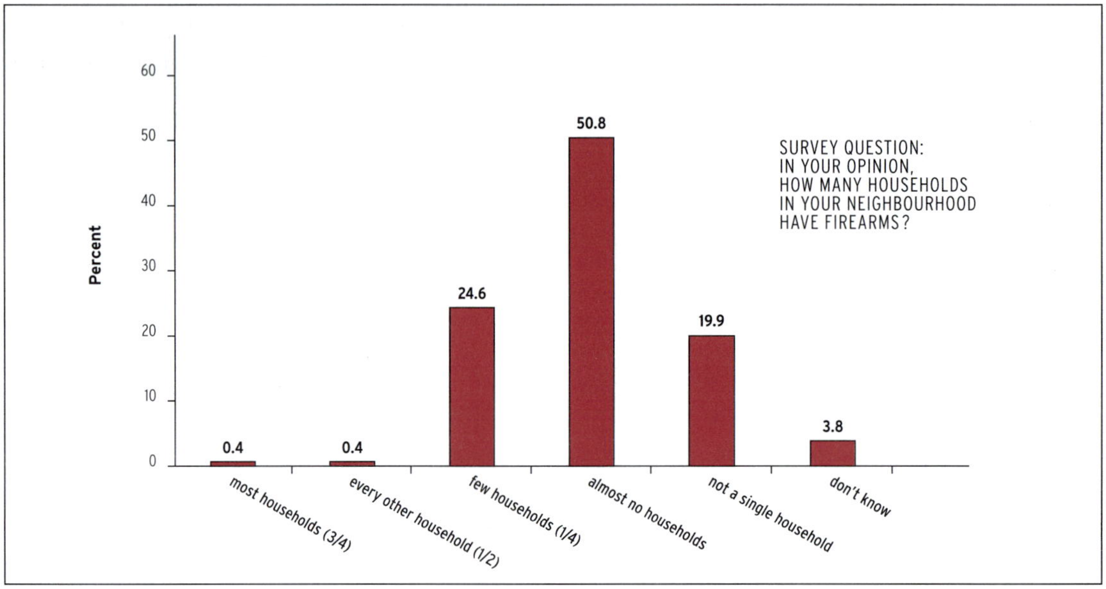

SURVEY QUESTION: IN YOUR OPINION, HOW MANY HOUSEHOLDS IN YOUR NEIGHBOURHOOD HAVE FIREARMS?

Category	Percent
most households (3/4)	0.4
every other household (1/2)	0.4
few households (1/4)	24.6
almost no households	50.8
not a single household	19.9
don't know	3.8

Moreover, in the household survey conducted in Batken and Osh Oblast only 2.5 per cent ticked 'armed robbery' when asked to identify the most common types of crime. 'Theft' and 'drunken disorder', by contrast, received high scores.

The crime statistics confirm the trend of higher urban than rural gun possession. In the period 2001–3, 65 per cent of the 325 reported gun offences took place in urban centres. MVD analysts estimate that there are between two and three gun-related offences in Bishkek per month (Kyrgyzstan, 2003).

The perception that illegal guns and general possession among the population are low is supported by very moderate gun injury and gun murder rates in Kyrgyzstan.

Table 10.2   Percentage of murders committed with firearms

Country	%
Argentina	58.47
England and Wales	7.80
Hungary	21.46
Kyrgyzstan	**10.65**
Tajikistan	83.30
United States	63.39

Source: WHO (2003)

Gun Injury

The available national health statistics show a slight increase in gun-related violence and injuries. There were 17 accidental injuries from guns in 1989, 21 in 1996, and 26 in 1999. The figures for 1989, which are the only available statistics broken down by gender, reveal that no women received accidental injuries from guns. In addition, interviews with medical officials in Bishkek suggest that they rarely encounter gun trauma cases in female patients. They also note, more generally, that knives are more frequently used in domestic disputes than guns.[33] Representatives from women's crisis centres and injury statistics from these centres confirm that guns are rarely used in violence against women in Kyrgyzstan.[34] Gun injuries among the male population tend to be concentrated in the age group 15–39. The injury figures for Kyrgyzstan are substantially lower than for Tajikistan, where in just one of the city hospitals in Dushanbe between two and three patients are admitted every month with gun injuries.[35]

Figure 10.2   Number of gun injuries, 1989-99

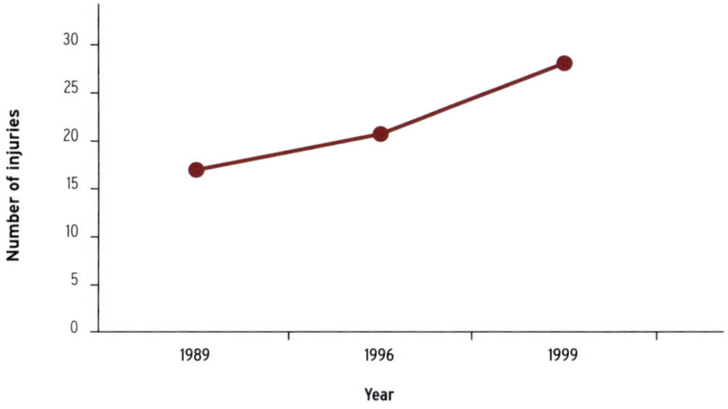

Source: Unpublished mortality statistics from National Statistics Committee of the Kyrgyz Republic

SECURITY PERCEPTIONS

Perceptions of personal security have improved since 1991. Local analysts note that the early period after independence was a time of upheaval and insecurity, during which citizens might have been more inclined to possess guns for their personal safety.[36] Thirteen years after the break-up of the Soviet Union, trends within the Kyrgyz state and society have become more predictable. There is still ambiguity in relations between the police and civilians (such as over expectations of bribes), but basic law and order, and hence personal security, seem to be guaranteed by law-enforcement structures.[37] Interview material and statistics point to better personal security in rural areas than in urban ones.[38] In both settings, however, due to low levels of gun possession, small arms are not a major factor influencing crime patterns and perceptions.

In describing perceptions of security, almost all respondents (98.7 per cent) said that no one in their household had been threatened or intimidated by the use of guns in the last three months. Half of the respondents (53 per cent) felt that their personal safety had not changed over the past decade, while 37 per cent claimed that it had got worse. Most of the respondents thought their safety was the same (52 per cent) or better (33 per cent) than in other parts of the country.

> **Box 10.4 Ethnic violence in southern Kyrgyzstan[39]**
>
> During the week of 4 June 1990, violence between ethnic Uzbeks and ethnic Kyrgyz broke out in the southern city of Osh and the surrounding villages, sparked by disagreement over land. The Kyrgyz nationalist organization Osh Aymaghi demanded that land belonging to an Uzbek collective farm be distributed to the Kyrgyz for housing projects. As the authorities started reallocating small parts of the land, clashes broke out on the outskirts of Osh city. The violence continued in Uzgen and other nearby areas the following day. Fear of attack and pledges of revenge from both sides fuelled the escalation in fighting. The riots ended when a state of emergency was imposed and Soviet troops were brought in, preventing mobs of Uzbeks from Andijan in neighbouring Uzbekistan from joining the riot.[40] Official sources claim 120 Uzbeks, 50 Kyrgyz, and one Russian were killed. The investigating commission registered more than 5,000 crimes, including murder, rape, and pillage. Most commentators believe that the death toll is likely to have exceeded 171.[41]
>
> Kyrgyz authorities and law enforcement officials stress that there was no widespread use of small arms during the riots. Instead, the protestors used knives, axes, and agricultural tools. Transcriptions from court proceedings against perpetrators indicate that many crimes, including murder, were committed without the use of firearms; however, small arms (in particular pistols and hunting rifles) were also used in a number of recorded instances.
>
> The law enforcement bodies and local authorities neither predicted nor reacted efficiently to the uprisings. However, Kyrgyzstan is the only former Soviet state that initiated a major juridical process following the mass ethnic unrest. This development indicates that the Kyrgyz law enforcement structures continued to function relatively well in the period immediately after the transition from Soviet republic to independent nation.
>
> The Osh and Uzgen events of 1990 constitute the most serious ethnic conflict to date in Kyrgyzstan: however, there have been smaller incidents in south Kyrgyzstan, such as clashes between Tajiks and Kyrgyz in the Batken area in 1989. In January 2003, tensions mounted between Tajiks and Kyrgyz in Batken Oblast over new border check posts, but fighting was prevented. Frustrations over the alleged political advantages of the titular ethnic group and the struggle over scarce resources, such as water and land, run along ethnic lines. There is no indication that any of these underlying causes of hostility will disappear in the near future.
>
> Interview data suggest continuing animosity between the two communities in this region. The phenomenon is exacerbated by the clear under-representation of Uzbeks both in local administrations and at the national level, and by continuing tensions between the two governments over border demarcation and border closure. In short, there has been and there remains a potential for conflict along ethnic lines in this region of Kyrgyzstan.

CULTURAL ATTITUDES TO GUNS

Kyrgyzstan has a non-permissive gun culture. As the proverb 'Even an uncharged gun shoots once a year' testifies, Kyrgyz society is aware of the dangers associated with gun proliferation, and discourages misuse of arms. The household survey confirms these attitudes. A large majority of respondents said that buying a gun was a not a legitimate use of household resources and considered that guns place households at greater risk instead of providing protection. Representatives of women's organizations and crisis centres claim that gun possession is only weakly associated with masculinity. To judge from the interview material, it seems fair to conclude that gun possession is not an essential ingredient in the construction of male identity in Kyrgyz culture, and that considerations of masculine image and self-esteem do not give rise to gun demand.

The survey showed that slightly more women than men (81 per cent versus 69) held that it was not legitimate to spend household resources on buying firearms. Other questions designed to reveal gender perspectives elicited surprisingly similar responses from men and women.

There seems to be some evidence that attitudes towards gun ownership and use would be different in a conflict situation. When asked whether they would defend the village against attack (as it had been during the period of ethnic conflict in the early 1990s), 69 per cent said they would do so. Forty-six percent claimed they would use a gun if under attack. The responses displayed a pattern of ethnic conformity, making the issue of gun availability particularly important.

Figure 10.3 Public opinion on the legitimacy of firearm purchase by households

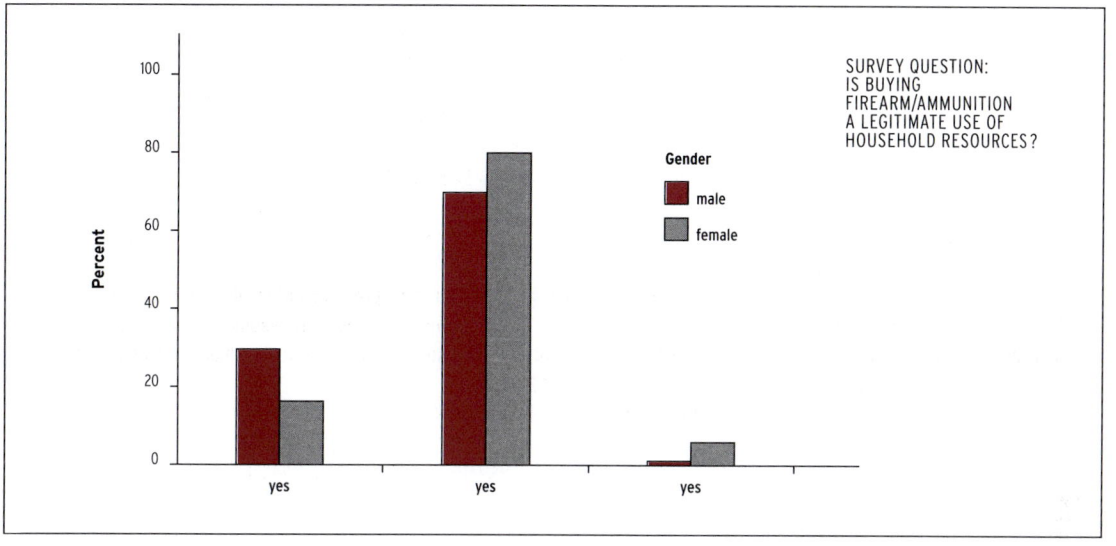

Gun possession is not an essential ingredient in the construction of male identity in Kyrgyz culture.

GUN AVAILABILITY

The household survey asked respondents how guns could be obtained in a situation where 'a person from your neighbourhood, for whatever reason, would need a gun'. A larger number (30.5 per cent) replied that a person would need to 'ask around', while 21 per cent noted that guns would be available 'from the black market'. Both answers indicate that people believe that informal channels for gun purchases exist in southern Kyrgyzstan. However, it needs to be borne in mind that, even when respondents assume the existence of these informal channels, they might not themselves have been connected with or have access to black market arms trading.

By contrast, only 13 per cent responded that a person could 'get a licence and buy one'. The low score of official channels is no surprise, given that there is only one store in the region (Osh city) selling legal weapons. Only 5 per cent indicated that a person could get guns if he 'knew of a hidden cache'. Curiously, more people in Osh Oblast selected this possibility than in Batken, even though most of the caches are thought to be hidden in Batken Oblast. This points to a significant degree of separation between the Islamic rebels and the local population. When asked to indicate neighbouring regions where arms might be available, the majority indicated oblasts in Tajikistan: Gorno Badakhshan Autonomous Oblast (36 per cent) and Sogd Oblast (17 per cent).

BLACK MARKET

The main items circulating on the black market in Kyrgyzstan are, according to interviews with informed observers, Makarov pistols and Kalashnikovs.[50] Price estimates for a Kalashnikov vary within the range from USD 500–1500.[51] These are very high prices compared with other countries. The steep prices are explained primarily by the relatively moderate supply and circulation of guns. The price of weapons has increased in black markets in Bishkek and Osh. In Dushanbe in Tajikistan, by contrast, prices rose prior to 1994/95 but fell from 1997 onwards when the civil war ended and the government consolidated its position. The early increase in prices in Dushanbe was caused by increasing demand. The drop in prices is likely to have been caused by a fall in demand since it occurred in conjunction with a government crack-down on illegal gun possession. Supply may be limited by the relative absence of arms traders and the existence of heavy punishments for arms smuggling. It is worth mentioning that prices are lower in the southern city of Osh, which is located close to the Tajik border. While law-enforcement officials stress that the black market in Kyrgyzstan is very modest, they estimate that 20–25 per cent of the few illegal guns in Kyrgyzstan come from border smuggling, 30–35 per cent from leakage in the army, and the remainder from old hunting rifles and home-made guns.[52]

Box 10.5 Incursions of Islamic rebels on Kyrgyz territory

In 1999-2000 there were several incursions from Tajikistan into Kyrgyzstan by activists from the Islamic Movement of Uzbekistan. The IMU had emerged in the Ferghana valley and some of its members had fought with the United Tajik Opposition (UTO) in the Tajik civil war. The IMU later based itself in Afghanistan, where members received training and financial support from al Qaeda. During the incursions, the IMU demanded that the Uzbek government release all religious activists imprisoned in Uzbekistan, reopen mosques previously shut down, permit Muslim dress in Uzbekistan, and introduce sharia law (ICG, 2000b). Estimates of the size of IMU vary greatly. International observers who lived near IMU bases in Tajikistan claim that the IMU never consisted of more than 50-60 fighters.[42] By contrast, newspaper reports, usually citing Russian military sources, estimate up to 5,000 fighters (ICG, 2000b, p. 5).

Kyrgyz soldiers practice aiming rocket-propelled grenade launchers at the military base in Osh City, Krgyzstan, during the hostage crisis in mountainous villages in August 1999.

The first incursion was on 6 August 1999. The group initially took four hostages, who were later released. On 22 August, the group seized another 13 hostages near Kan village in the Batken area. Fighting broke out between the Kyrgyz army and militants as the rebels approached the Uzbek Sokh enclave, which is surrounded by Kyrgyz territory. Uzbek fighter planes bombed Kyrgyz areas where the rebels were located without Kyrgyz authorization. The rebels released the hostages on 25 October 1999 and retreated to Tajikistan (ICG, 2000a).

A further, large-scale incursion took place the following year. IMU fighters entered both Uzbekistan and Kyrgyzstan in separate groups on a number of occasions in the period August to September 2000. A key area of IMU activity in Kyrgyzstan was the Karavshi valley leading down to the Tajik Vorokh enclave on Kyrgyz territory.[43] Government officials claim that 50 Kyrgyz soldiers and border guards died in the events of 1999 and 2000, while the counted IMU death toll is at least 120.[44]

The Kyrgyz National Security Service has found ten weapon caches in the mountains near Batken.[45] The biggest cache was discovered in June 2000. The majority of the arms were of Soviet production, though there were some items of Chinese and Belgian origin. A few American-produced grenades were also recorded.[46] The recent discoveries have been more modest, the latest discovery (in July 2003) containing only a small reserve of 200 Chinese produced rifle bullets.[47]

The Kyrgyz government was unprepared for the incursions in 1999. Following the first incursion, however, new border posts were erected and troops were relocated to the south.[48] All the Central Asian countries have tightened control at border crossings. This has impeded movement by the local population. Most cross-border traders are forced to pay bribes to the border guards and some civilians have been shot while trying to cross the borders illegally. Uzbekistan has unilaterally mined its border with Kyrgyzstan.

Many of the soldiers who served in the Batken operations were veterans of the Afghan war. Soldiers who served in the Kyrgyz army note that the equipment they used to fight the IMU was old: the firearms, machine guns, and grenade launchers dated from 1974. They also claim they were paid only a small percentage of the salary promised (USD 50 a day in 1999), some say as little as USD 28 in total (IWPR 2000). Local analysts note that the low and irregular pay encouraged the military personnel to sell equipment, including arms, on the black market.[49]

Table 10.3 Black market prices in 2003 (USD)

	AK-47	Makarov pistols
Bishkek (Kyrgyzstan)	800–1,000	300–500
Dushanbe (Tajikistan)	400	500–600
Osh (Kyrgyzstan)	250–1,200	50–80

Note: The prices are approximate and were listed in the following confidential interviews: Representative of the National Security Service of the Kyrgyz Republic, 17 July 2003; informed observer and former drug trafficker in Osh and Batken Oblast, 7 August 2003; and Former Tajik MVD officer, 20 August 2003. Makarov Pistols are higher-priced than Kalashnikovs in Dushanbe after 1996 because of the government crack-down on gun possession, Makarovs are easier to hide and hence in higher demand.

PRODUCTION AND TRADE IN WEAPONS

Kyrgyzstan has no weapons production, but in Soviet times the republic was a major producer of ammunition for the Soviet armed forces, providing as much as 30 per cent of Soviet force requirements.[53] There is still ammunition production at the Bishkek Machine Tool Factory (Bishkekskii Mashinostroitel'nyi Zavod). Kyrgyzstan was the 13th largest exporter of ammunition in 1996 by value, with the bulk of exports going to former Communist countries.[54] There is one recorded incident of military small arms export from Kyrgyzstan: 199kg of military weapons to Slovakia in 2000. There has also been one recorded episode of illegal ammunition transfers: Kyrgyzstan sold three million 5.45 calibre assault rifle rounds for USD 180,000 in 2000 to Armenia (Moscovskiy Konsomolets, 2001).[55] Some of these exports may have been officially sanctioned. Armenia, for example, is one of Kyrgyzstan's defence partners in the Collective Security Treaty.[56] Others, however, point to corruption and the lack of effective export controls. The absence of a domestic military-industrial complex, with the exception of ammunition production, obviously restricts Kyrgyzstan's potential as a legal or illegal exporter of weapons.

Table 10.4 Exports from Kyrgyzstan (reported by Kyrgyzstan): Small arms ammunition and parts

Destination	Trade value in USD/year	
	1995	1996
Bulgaria	2,004,399	225,000
China	225,000	264,000
India	n/a	453,500
Kazakhstan	93,800	402,199
Russian Federation	542,000	257,699
Tajikistan	n/a	156,000
Uzbekistan	4,941,000	2,785,100
Total	7,806,199	4,543,498

Note: The tables are likely to considerably underestimate Kyrgyzstan's trade in small arms.

Source: Comtrade database, NISAT database

SMALL ARMS SURVEY 2004

Map 10.1   Largest reported exporters of small arms ammunition and parts in 1996

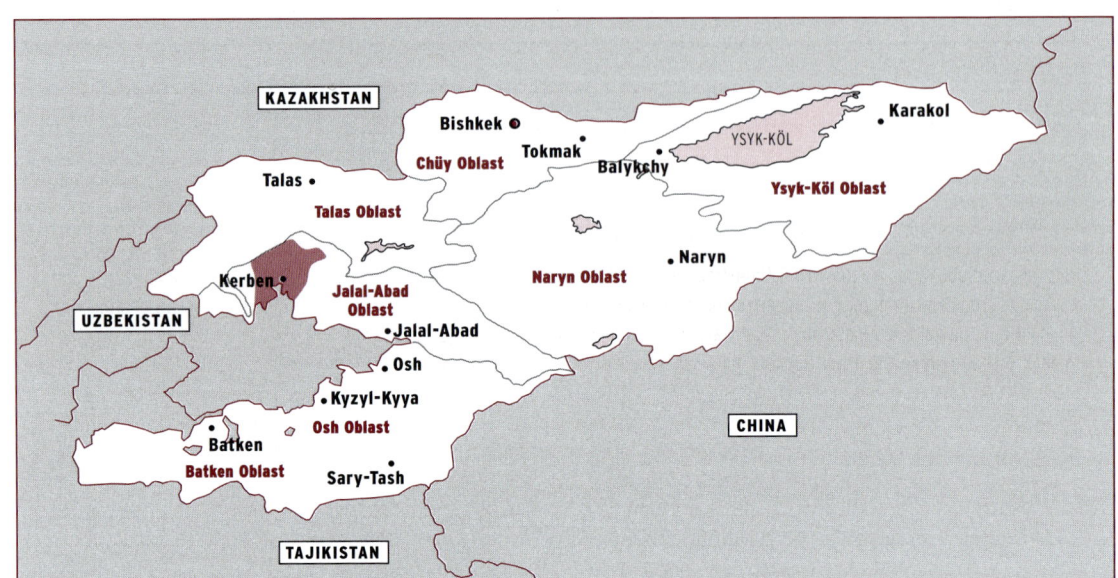

TRAFFICKING

There have been three main categories of arms flows through Central Asia. First was the retreat of Soviet forces and equipment from Afghanistan in 1989 and subsequent supplies of guns from Russia and other countries to their Afghan allies. The second flow was the arming of different factions in the Tajik civil war from 1992 to 1997. These weapons came mainly from Russia, Uzbekistan, Iran, and Afghanistan. The third flow pertains to the intensification of arms shipments to the Northern Alliance following 11 September 2001 and the rearming of the Kabul government.

The majority of shipments associated with the Russian withdrawal from Afghanistan were sent via the Uzbek–Afghan border rather than through Kyrgyzstan and Tajikistan, since transportation infrastructure in southern Uzbekistan was more developed.[57] Supplies to warring factions in Tajikistan during 1992–97 came from a range of sources. The Russians supplied government forces with arms during the civil war.[58] Russian supplies to the government came, most likely, through airports in government-controlled areas such as Kuljab, as well as through the long-established Russian supply chain from Osh to Murgab.[59] Although Russian military supplies flowed principally to Russian forces and to those of the Tajik government, interviews with ex-fighters reveal that leakage from Russian stockpiles to all factions in the civil war was endemic.[60]

The Russian supplies to the Northern Alliance in Afghanistan following the Taliban seizure of power in 1996 and then particularly after 2001 probably did not transit through Uzbekistan direct to Afghanistan, given the Uzbek decision to seal the Uzbek–Afghan border. It is likely, therefore, that Russia shipped weapons to the Northern Alliance by air or via the above-mentioned Murgab–Osh road. The Northern Alliance also received weapons from Iran and other states. That Kyrgyz territory was used as a conduit for some of this assistance is illustrated by the Osh rail wagon incident of 1998 (see Box 10.6).

Kyrgyzstan itself may have acted as a supply country during the Tajik civil war. To judge from supply and demand logics, it is likely that guns from Kyrgyzstan entered Tajikistan. In 1996–97 a Makarov pistol cost USD 900–1,000 in Dushanbe while in Osh it sold for USD 120. For this reason, it is probable that much of the leakage from army stockpiles in Kyrgyzstan described above did not remain in the country but exited to Tajikistan. Until 1999, the border between Tajikistan and Kyrgyzstan was unguarded with the exception of a few border crossings on main roads.[63] There are, however, no records of official Kyrgyz arms shipments to Tajikistan. Moreover, interviews with former combatants in Tajikistan showed no indication of major arms deliveries from Kyrgyzstan.[64] This suggests that arms shipments from Kyrgyzstan involved small quantities and were probably conducted by individual sellers and buyers.

> **Box 10.6   Weapons transit through Kyrgyzstan bound for Afghanistan[61]**
>
> Between 4 October and 13 October 1998, three trains arrived in the southern Kyrgyz city of Osh filled with 700 tonnes of weapons (though few small arms) and ammunition, hidden under 300 tonnes of food supplies. The cargo was listed as 'humanitarian aid' destined for Afghanistan. The trains originated in Mashad (Iran) and the Iranian embassy in Kyrgyzstan was named as the owner of the cargo. The shipment crossed Turkmen and Uzbek territory before arriving in Osh. The third train reportedly stopped in Bekabad, Uzbekistan, where four wagons were seized by local Uzbek authorities. The arms and food were intended for the United Front (Northern Alliance) in Afghanistan.
>
> Several countries were implicated in the arms transfer. Iran was the initiator but cooperated closely with Russia. The role of the Turkmen, Uzbek, and indeed Kyrgyz governments remains an open question. Some investigations stress the complicity of the Kyrgyz government. However, in an interview with the Small Arms Survey, Muratbek Imanaliev, who was Foreign Minister at the time, claimed that the Foreign Ministry knew nothing of the arrangements but that there had been an agreement among top military representatives from all countries in the region.[62]
>
> The Osh incident sheds interesting light on arms-related issues in Central Asia. It confirms the persistence of Russian involvement in the region and highlights the continued use of the old Soviet military infrastructure. More importantly, it illustrates the lack of coordination, control, and oversight both among and between national ministries and local authorities. The local authorities that opened the cargo and exposed it to the media were allegedly uninformed about the content of the wagons. The head of Osh Customs department, I. Masaliev, and chief of the Osh Security Service, Colonel O Suvanaliev, were both dismissed after the incident. Despite official assurances from the Kyrgyz government that the cargo was returned to Iran, the United Front later claimed that the weapons had reached them.

Is there currently any arms trade or trafficking through Kyrgyz territory? Members of the anti-terrorist coalition continue to resupply certain groups in Afghanistan, particularly with ammunition. Much of the weaponry used in Afghanistan is of Soviet and Russian origin. Spare parts and ammunition from mainly Russian producers would therefore also be in demand. These producers might ship goods through Kyrgyz territory.[65] Contrary to what some European analysts argue, there is no available evidence suggesting large-scale northward shipments of small arms from Afghanistan through Central Asia. Analysts arguing otherwise assume that arms flows accompany drug flows (Pirseyedi, 2002). However, most local analysts and law-enforcement personnel in Kyrgyzstan insist that there is no northbound trafficking in arms. Russia is a major producer of guns, which in turn suggests that the demand for guns originating from outside Russia itself is low.[66]

Drug traffickers use guns for protection, but there is no available evidence of major arms shipments accompanying drugs shipments. Intelligence sources from one Western country suggest that guns might be one commodity in the recently established barter exchange of psychotropic drugs.[67] However, these individual intelligence reports on northbound arms trafficking are not confirmed by statistics of seizures at the border by the Kyrgyz border guards or by the annual reports by the State Commission on Drugs Control under the President of the Kyrgyz Republic.[68] By contrast, on the Afghan–Tajik border drug traffickers are heavily armed and there are almost daily instances of serious skirmishes between Russian or Tajik border troops and well-armed drug dealers. The groups transporting drugs further through Tajikistan into Kyrgyzstan or Uzbekistan are not so heavily armed.

While there appear to be no substantial flows,[69] a number of arms caches are distributed throughout Tajikistan and Kyrgyzstan and are a cause for concern. Some caches along the Afghan–Tajik border seem to be mainly intended for the

> Contrary to what some European analysts argue, there is no available evidence suggesting large-scale northward shipment of small arms from Afghanistan through Central Asia.

protection of drug dealers caught in skirmishes with border guards. Others have been left in Tajikistan after the civil war by opposition fighters belonging to groups that are by now mainly inactive. Yet others are IMU stores in Tajikistan and Kyrgyzstan. Approximately ten caches of weapons have been uncovered in the Kyrgyz mountains (see Box 10.5). These guns were probably carried into Kyrgyzstan prior to the first major IMU incursion in 1999. The IMU continues to operate in Central Asia, though in a much reduced form. In August 2003, there were reports of a group of 20–25 unarmed IMU fighters making its way into Ishkashim region and then infiltrating Kyrgyz and Uzbek territory.[70] The fact that these fighters were unarmed as they crossed suggests the continued presence of hidden caches in Central Asia. However, to judge from the inventory of recent caches found by the authorities, these mountain weapon storages seem relatively modest.

There is significant illegal trafficking in women in Kyrgyzstan. The International Organization for Migration (IOM) estimates 4,000 women are trafficked each year, many of whom are flown out of Osh airport.[71] There is no available evidence that groups organizing trafficking in women are also involved in illegal arms sales. Given the absence of a link between drugs and arms, it is reasonable to believe, for similar reasons, that there is also no substantial link between trafficking in women and in arms.

CONCLUSION

Most of the literature recycles the common belief that Central Asia as a whole is awash with arms. In the discussion about small arms in Kyrgyzstan, it was suggested that many of the factors that frequently contribute to small arms problems were evident in the region: economic decay, weak and illegitimate government, fragile law-enforcement structures, widespread corruption, regional inequities, and substantial social frustration, including an important component of ethnic tension. However, despite the serious economic, social, and political challenges Kyrgyzstan faces, small arms are not a crucial security issue in Kyrgyzstan. Legal possession is low and consists mostly of hunting guns. Illegal possession is difficult to quantify, but appears to have little impact. Leakage has occurred, but it appears to have been sporadic, declining over time, and relatively insubstantial to begin with. Gun use and associated death and injury are quite low, and do not appear to be increasing. The population does not perceive a significant threat from small arms. There is little evidence to substantiate claims that Kyrgyzstan is a significant transit country for the small arms trade. The evidence that Kyrgyzstan is an important transit country for drugs is reasonably compelling, Kyrgyzstan also plays a role as both a source and a conduit for human trafficking. Direct evidence that the people involved in these activities also smuggle substantial amounts of small arms is almost impossible to obtain, in Kyrgyzstan as elsewhere. However, pricing data and the lack of significant gun confiscation from traffickers suggest that the link between the trafficking of guns and that of drugs and people is not a serious problem in the country. In short, with respect to small arms, Kyrgyzstan seems to be a rather benign environment.

The explanation for this finding has historical, economic, social, and cultural components. In the first place, Kyrgyzstan was not a substantial weapons site during Soviet times and therefore leakage from Soviet military stores and movements was smaller than it was in many other Soviet republics (such as Tajikistan, Georgia, and Moldova). In addition, the simple fact that Kyrgyzstan did not experience large-scale civil conflict meant that governmental structures did not disintegrate. According to interview data, they retained much of their Soviet-era culture of strict weapons control.

Hunting weapons are expensive and were in the past disproportionately held by the Russian minority, many of whom emigrated in the early years after independence.

The study of Kyrgyzstan revealed that the degree and seriousness of small arms possession is less alarming than previously thought. This finding is perhaps at first surprising given economic decline and social fragmentation in Kyrgyzstan and armed conflict in neighbouring countries, as well as high levels of organized crime, phenomena often thought to be associated with gun crime. However, Kyrgyzstan does not fit our expectations and thus highlights the necessity of unpacking regional generalizations and understanding the processes that lead to small arms possession and misuse.

10. LIST OF ABBREVIATIONS

BOMCA	Border Management Central Asia
EU	European Union
EXBS	Export Control and Related Border Security Assistance
FTI	Foundation for Tolerance International
ICG	International Crisis Group
IMU	Islamic Movement of Uzbekistan
IOM	International Organization for Migration
IWPR	Institute for War and Peace Reporting
MVD	Ministry of Internal Affairs
NGO	Non-governmental organization
OSCE	Organization for Security and Co-operation in Europe
OVD	Oblast (county) Internal Administration
UN	United Nations
UNDP	UN Development Programme
UNODC	UN Office of Drug Control
UNODCCP	UN Office of Drug Control and Crime Prevention
USSR	Union of Soviet Socialist Republics

10. ENDNOTES

[1] For a discussion of the origins and growth of the IMU, see Rashid (2002, in particular pp. 137–86).

[2] For a useful account of post-Aksy political changes, see Freedom House (2003, p. 332).

[3] The quote is from the inscription on the memorial for the Aksy victims, placed along the Kara Suu-Kerben road in Aksy region.

[4] There is confusion as to how many people were injured and whether police forces suffered injuries. Government officials claimed on 18 March 2002 that 47 police officers were wounded. RFE/RL (2002). A list compiled by the neutral NGO Foundation for Tolerance International lists six people dead and 27 injured.

[5] Interview, NGO leader in Aksy, 25 August 2003, and local opposition representatives in Kara Suu, Aksy region village, 26 August 2003.

[6] After viewing the MVD's video recording of the events, informed observers said they were able to identify the voice of the regional MVD head ordering troops to open fire. Confidential interview, Aksy, 26 August 2003.

[7] Eyewitness account obtained by the Small Arms Survey from villagers in Karagygach, Aksy region. The eyewitness account is one of several forwarded by IWPR to the government commission in charge of investigating the Aksy events.

[8] Kyrgyzstan (1994, Section 3, paragraph 4).

[9] RFE/RL (2002).

[10] Interview with NGO leader in Aksy, 25 August 2003.

[11] Estimates by NGO representative in Aksy, 25 August 2003.

[12] *Central Asia–Caucasus Analyst* (2003); RFE/RL (2003).

[13] The key provisions are found in the Law on Arms of June 1999.

[14] Interview, Asanaliev, Karavai Colonel Deputy Director for Academic Affairs, MVD Academy of the Kyrgyz Republic, Bishkek.

[15] Interview, Kenjesariev, Mr., Head of the Department of Military-Technical Cooperation Ministry of Defence of the Kyrgyz Republic, 28 August 2003.

[16] Interview Kenjesariev, Mr., Head of the Department of Military-Technical Cooperation, Ministry of Defence of the Kyrgyz Republic, 28 August 2003. The Small Arms Survey study on Russia notes that

heavy machine guns, grenade launchers, and ammunition were exported to Kyrgyzstan in 1999 (Pyadushkin, 2003).

17. Neither the archives on guns in the Ministry of Internal Affairs' county (oblast) departments nor the membership records of the Hunters' Association are computerized. All permits for hunting weapons are given on the basis of membership of the Hunters' Association. However, records for Batken Oblast in 2002 indicate ten members, while the Ministry of Internal Affairs Batken department's records for 2002 indicated 472 hunters with 484 registered hunting weapons. It is unclear how this discrepancy has come about and indeed whether the local law enforcement bodies are aware of it. Likewise, the recent theft of weapons in Jalalabad suggests problems in implementing MVD procedures for control of weapons stocks (see Box 10.4). In short, while Kyrgyzstan's legal framework is extensive on paper it is unlikely that the full control mechanisms envisaged have actually been implemented.

18. The Union of Societies of Hunters and Fishermen in the Kyrgyz Republic is referred to as the Hunters' Association throughout this chapter.

19. Interview, Ivanovich, Ivan, Head of the Chui Oblast section of the Union of Societies of Hunters and Fishermen in the Kyrgyz Republic, 16 July 2003, and Nazarov, Mr., Deputy Director, Criminalistic Center, MVD, Bishkek, 27 August 2003.

20. As per the Hunters Association's membership statistics, there is a growing trend towards concentration of legally registered guns in Chui Oblast. In 1990, 11,200 of the 25,900 members were from Chui Oblast, while in 2002 6,234 of the 8,617 members were from Chui Oblast. National membership records made available to the Small Arms Survey by the Hunters Association.

21. Oblast membership records made available to the Small Arms Survey by Osh Hunting Association

22. Interview, Ivanovich, Ivan, Head of the Chui Oblast section of the Union of Societies of Hunters and Fishermen in the Kyrgyz Republic, 16 July 2003.

23. Oblast membership records made available to the Small Arms Survey by Osh Hunting Association and Interview Ivanovich, Ivan, Head of the Chui Oblast section of the Union of Societies of Hunters and Fishermen in the Kyrgyz Republic, 16 July 2003.

24. The prices are for new, legally imported hunting rifles available in Kyrgyz hunting and arms stores. The importer needs to obtain permission from Kyrgyz and Russian authorities as well as from the Kyrgyz embassy in Moscow. Transportation, customs, and registration costs inflate the prices. Hunting rifles are cheaper in Kazakhstan and Russia but the purchaser has to obtain relevant import permits independently. Interview, Ivanovich, Ivan. Head of the Chui Oblast section of the Union of Societies of Hunters and Fishermen in the Kyrgyz Republic, 16 July 2003.

25. Nazarov, Mr., Deputy Director, Criminalistic Center, MVD, Bishkek, 27 August 2003.

26. Law of the Kyrgyz Republic on Arms no. 49, 9 June 1999, para. 4. The law on arms also allows for collection of guns and for arms to be awarded by government agencies to officials as appreciation for service. Law of the Kyrgyz Republic on Arms no. 49, 9 June 1999, paras. 6, 7.

27. Interview, Kenjesariev. Mr., Head of the Department of Military-Technical Cooperation, Ministry of Defence of the Kyrgyz Republic, 28 August 2003.

28. Interviews, representative of the National Security Service of the Kyrgyz Republic, 17 July 2003, Nazarov, Mr. Deputy Director, Criminalistic Center, MVD, Bishkek, 27 August 2003

29. Interviews, Tugelbaeva Bermeta Galievna, President of Women's Association DIAMOND, 15 July 2003, representative of the National Security Service of the Kyrgyz Republic, 17 July 2003.

30. This finding might be questionable. It may reflect reticence in answering questions about the presence of weapons in regions that have been tense in the past. In addition, it may reflect the use of the phrase 'strelkovoe' (shooting) as opposed to 'obychnoe' (common) 'oruzhie' (weapon) in the survey. Strelkovoe oruzhie is often associated with a military weapon.

31. It is uncertain how many crimes are unreported in Kyrgyzstan; in the EU an estimated one-third to one-half of all crimes are reported.

32. National Statistical Committee Kyrgyz Republic. Unpublished data.

33. Interview, Sopuev, Andrei A. Dr. Deputy Director (Scientific Research), National Surgical Center of the Kyrgyz Republic.

34. Interview, Tugelbaeva Bermeta Galievna, President of Women's Association DIAMOND, 15 July 2003.

35. Interview, Polatovich, Artikon Karim, Head of Science National Medical Reconstruction Unit Dushanbe, 20 August 2003.

36. Interview, independent journalist, Bishkek, 17 July 2003.

37. Interview, independent journalist, Bishkek, 17 July 2003.

38. Interview, Ismailov, Bahadir, OSCE legal expert, 5 December 2003.

39. This section draws extensively on Lubin and Nunn (1999) and Tishkov (1995, pp. 133–49).

40. Interview with Abdimunon Joldoshov, expert, Secretariat of the Special Representative of the President of the Kyrgyz Republic on Foreign Investment, 24 July 2003.

41. Lubin and Nunn (1999) claim Kyrgyz authorities have admitted to at least 300 dead, but that the number could be significantly higher. The ICG alleges, on the basis of UNDP sources, that as many as 1,000 people were killed in the fighting (ICG, 2001, p. 6).

42. Confidential interview with the Head of Mission of an international organization, Dushanbe, 15 August 2003.

43. Interview, Sahdimonov, Abdilbek, Foundation for Tolerance International Program Officer, former head of staff in Batken Oblast Administration, 29 July 2003.

44. Estimates of number of dead soldiers given in confidential interview with Batken Oblast Administration Official, 30 July 2003. Figure of 120 dead IMU fighters from ICG (2000b, p. 5).

45. Representative of the National Security Service of the Kyrgyz Republic, 17 July 2003.

46. Interview, representative of the National Security Service of the Kyrgyz Republic, 17 July 2003.

47. Interview, representative of the National Security Service of the Kyrgyz Republic, Batken Oblast, 30 July 2003.

48. Interviews, Sarikevich, Amankulov Taluntbek, Commander of Kyrgyz Border Guard Service in Batken Oblast, 31 July 2003; Kenjesariev, Head of the Department of Military Technical Cooperation Ministry of Defence of the Kyrgyz Republic, 28 August 2003; Baisakov, Sheishenbek, Head of Oblast Internal Affairs (OVD) Batken Oblast, 31 July 2003.

49. Interview, independent journalist, Osh, 22 July 2003.

50. Interview, representative of the National Security Service of the Kyrgyz Republic, 17 July 2003.

51. Kyrgyzstan (2003). Interview with representative of the National Security Service of the Kyrgyz Republic, 17 July 2003, and with informed observer and former drug trafficker in Osh and Batken Oblast, 7 August 2003.

52. Interview, representative of the National Security Service of the Kyrgyz Republic, 17 July 2003.

53. Interview, Kenjesariev. Mr., Head of the Department of Military-Technical Cooperation, Ministry of Defence of the Kyrgyz Republic, 28 August 2003.

54. The value of exports was USD 4.5 million. See Nisat database.

55. See also SAFERNET's Krgyzstan report, Canadian Centre for Foreign Policy <http://www.ryerson.ca/SAFER-Net/>

56. The Collective Security Treaty Organization, whose aim is to enhance military and political integration between its members, currently includes Armenia, Belarus, Kazakhstan, Kyrgyzstan, Russia, and Tajikistan.

57. Interview, Bondarets, Leonid M., Senior Expert, International Institute for Strategic Studies under President of the Kyrgyz Republic, Bishkek, 25 August, 2003.

58. Interview, former Tajik MVD officer, 20 August 2003.

59. At present 50–60 trucks leave every week from southern Kyrgyzstan with supplies for the Russian 201 Motorized Rifle Division and for the Russian Border guards stationed in Tajikistan.

60. Interview, Former Tajik MVD officer, 20 August 2003.

61. This box draws extensively on the excellent research undertaken by Human Rights Watch (2001), particularly Appendix 1, Case Study: Supplying the United Front: Iranian and CIS Cooperation.

62. Interview, Imanaliev, Muratbek, Academic Dean, American University in Central Asia, 29 August 2003. In principle, this movement of weapons raises significant questions about the involvement

of border guards in the trafficking of weapons. However, at the time (1998), there was no organized Kyrgyz border service and the frontier to Tajikistan was essentially unmonitored.

[63] Interviews, Baisakov, Sheishenbek, Head of Oblast Internal Affairs (OVD), Batken Oblast, 31 July 2003, Sarikevich, Amankulov Taluntbek, Commander of Kyrgyz Border Guard Service in Batken Oblast, 31 July 2003, and Hudayberdiev, Zarif, Lt. Col., Head, MITBC Department, Boundary Service of the Kyrgyz Republic, 28 August 2003.

[64] Interview, journalist, Kulab region, Tajikistan, 16 August 2003, and Former Tajik MVD officer, 20 August 2003.

[65] Interview, Knjasev, Alexander Alexeivich, lecturer in international journalism, Kyrgyz–Russian Slavic University, 13 August 2003.

[66] The one likely exception is specialty weapons used by professional killers. In these instances, weapons from outside the jurisdiction in which the crime takes place are preferred.

[67] Confidential interview, intelligence officer from a Western country, Bishkek, 5 August 2003.

[68] Interviews, Gairfulin, Almas, Deputy Head of State Commission on Drugs Control under the Government of the Kyrgyz Republic, 11 July 2003, and Hudayberdiev, Zarif, Lt. Col., Head, MITBC Department, Boundary Service of the Kyrgyz Republic, 28 August 2003.

[69] This raises the intriguing question of whether Kyrgyzstan is in this respect typical of or unique among the countries of the region. Answering this question, however, would require substantial further work in neighbouring countries.

[70] Confidential source material and *Eurasia Insight* (2003).

[71] Interviews, Chenais, Fredric, Associate Expert, IOM Bishkek, 18 July 2003, and US intelligence officer, Bishkek, 5 August 2003.

10. BIBLIOGRAPHY

Central Asia and the Caucasus Analyst. 2003. 'The OSCE Will Help the Law Enforcement Bodies of Kyrgyzstan.' 30 July.

Eurasianet. 2003. *Eurasia Insight*. 'Sightings of IMU Militants Reported in Remote Area of Uzbekistan.' 7 September.

Freedom House. 2003. *Nations in Transit—2003*. New York: Freedom House.

FTI (Foundation for Tolerance International). 2002. *Small Arms*. Report. Bishkek: FTI.

Human Rights Watch. 2001. 'Afghanistan: Crisis of Impunity—The Role of Pakistan, Russia, and Iran in Fuelling the Civil War.' *Report*, Vol. 13, No. 3 (C). July.

ICG (International Crisis Group). 2000a. *Central Asia: Crisis Conditions in Three States*. ICG Asia Report No. 7. 7 August.

—. 2000b. *Recent Violence: Causes and Consequences*. Central Asia Briefing. 18 October.

—. 2001. *Incubators of Conflict: Central Asia's Localised Conflict and Social Unrest*, ICG Asia Report No. 18. 8 June.

Interfax (Moscow). 2000. 'Kyrgyzstan: Border Guards Discover Large Arms Cache in Batken Region.' 20 June.

IWPR (Institute for War and Peace Reporting). 2000. 'Kyrgyz Private Relives Batken Nightmare.' *Reporting Central Asia*, No. 18. 1 September.

Kyrgyzstan. 1999. *Law on Arms of the Kyrgyz Republic*. No. 49. Bishkek. 9 June.

—. 2003. *Report on Small Arms and Light Weapons*. Bishkek: Ministry of Foreign Affairs.

Lubin, Nancy and Sam Nunn, 1999. *Calming the Ferghana Valley: Development and Dialogue in the Heart of Central Asia*. Report of the Ferghana Valley Working Group of the Center for Preventive Action, Senator Sam Nunn working group. New York: Century Foundation Press.

MacFarlane, S. Neil and Stina Torjesen. 2004. *Kyrgyzstan: A Small Arms Anomaly in Central Asia?* Occasional Paper No. 12. Geneva: Small Arms Survey. <http://www.smallarmssurvey.org/OPs/OP12%20kyrgyzstan.pdf>

Moskovskiy Komsomolets (Moscow). 2001 'Buddy, Can You Spare a Bullet! Kyrgyzstan Secretly Arming Armenia.' 3 May, p. 2. <http://www.nisat.org>

Norwegian Initiative on Small Arms Transfers (NISAT). 2003. NISAT Database <http://www.nisat.org/database >

Pirseyedi, Bobi. 2002. *The Small Arms Problem in Central Asia: Features and Implications*. Geneva: United Nations Institute for Disarmament Research (UNIDIR).

Pyadushkin, Maxim with Maria Haug and Anna Matveeva. 2003. *Beyond the Kalashnikov: Small Arms Production, Export, and Stockpiling in the Russian Federation*. Occasional Paper No. 10. Geneva: Small Arms Survey.

Rashid, Ahmed. 2002, *Jihad: The Rise of Militant Islam in Central Asia*. New Haven: Yale University Press.

RFE/RL. 2002. 'Bloodshed and Rioting as Police Fires into Crowd of Beknazarov Supporters.' *RFE/RL Central Asia Report*. Vol. 2, No. 11. 21 March.

—. 2003. 'OSCE Announces Modernization Programme for Kyrgyz Police.' *RFE/RL Central Asia Report*. Vol. 3, No. 24. 11 July.

Tajikistan. 2003. *Report of the Government of the Republic of Tajikistan on the Implementation of the Programme of Action to Prevent, Combat and Eradicate the Illicit Trade in Small Arms and Light Weapons in All Its Aspects*. Dushanbe: Presidential Administration.

Tishkov, Valery. 1995. '"Don't Kill Me, I'm a Kyrgyz!": An Anthropological Analysis of Violence in the Osh Ethnic Conflict.' *Journal of Peace Research*, Vol. 32, No. 2.

United Nations. Statistics Division. 2003. COMTRADE (UN Commodity Trade Statistics Database) <http://unstats.un.org/unsd/comtrade/>

UNODC (United Nations Office of Drug Control). 2003. *The Opium Economy in Afghanistan: An International Problem*. Vienna: UNODC.

UNODCCP (United Nations Office for Drug Control and Crime Prevention). 2002. *Illicit Drugs Situation in the Regions Neighbouring Afghanistan and the Response of ODCCP*. Vienna: UNODCCP.

Vechernii Bishkek. 2003. 'Bezpredel.' 16 May.

WHO (World Health Organization). 2003. *Mortality Database*. <http://www.who.int>

Index

A9 Group 107
accessibility thesis 182–6
Accuracy International 27, 30
Aceh, Indonesia 191
Afghanistan
   disarmament programme 58
   imports 128
   Kyrgyzstan 310
   MANPADS 84, 85–6, 88, 89, 92
   trafficking 322–3
   US production 11, 28–9
Africa
   crime and violence 175, 176, 178, 179, 192–200
   see also individual countries; sub-Saharan Africa
age, victims of violence 180, 183
air guns 107–8, 189
aircraft
   illicit brokering 145
   MANPADS attacks 90–1, 93, 94
AK-47 assault rifles
   crime in Africa 194, 195
   destruction of surpluses 60
   Iraq 47–8, 49
   Kalashnikov series 15, 28, 34, 319
   Kosovo 197
   Kyrgyzstan 319, 321
   Saudi National Guard 55
al Qaeda 55, 88, 102, 310, 320
Albania 44, 54, 133
Albright, Madeleine 92
Algeria 102, 108, 109, 123, 128, 134, 152
Amadeo Rossi 22, 123
American Samoa 283, 284, 302
ammunition 27
   Brazil 21, 22
   global trade 100
   Kyrgyzstan 321
   non-lethal force 221–3
   Pacific 280–1, 302
   United States 11–12
amnesties 57
   Pacific 303
   Solomon Islands 298–300
   Sri Lanka 59
   Thailand 71
   United Kingdom 188
Amnesty International 1, 126, 127, 133
Angola
   arms embargo 265, 269
   brokering 152, 165
   disarmament of civilians 57
   imports 108
      Brazil 123
      human rights 128, 129

   illicit trade 88, 112, 165
   MANPADS 88
anti-aircraft weapons 33
   see also man-portable air defence systems
anti-materiél rifles 27, 30
Anti-Social Behaviour Act (2003) (UK) 189
anti-tank guided weapons (ATGW) 27, 33
anti-tank weapons 27, 33, 34
   see also rocket-propelled grenade launchers
anti-terrorism laws, policing 220
APEC *see* Asia-Pacific Economic Cooperation
Arab League 152
Argentina
   production 17, 18–21
   stockpiles 51, 53, 61
   transfers 52, 109, 123, 130
Armenia 54, 152
Arms Trade Treaty 133
Asia *see* Asia-Pacific; South-East Asia
Asia-Pacific
   firearms deaths 175, 176, 177, 178, 200
   producers 9, 10
   violence and crime 179
   see also Pacific
Asia-Pacific Economic Cooperation (APEC) 93
assault rifles 11, 28–9, 30
   crime in Africa 194
   producers 8, 27, 34
   see also AK-47; FN-FAL
ATF *see* Bureau of Alcohol, Tobacco, Firearms and Explosives
AUC *see* Autodefensas Unidas de Colombia
Australia
   Bougainville 295
   civilian ownership 184–6, 283
   disposal programme 57, 58
   exports 103, 129, 132
   gun control 67, 184–6, 192, 301, 302, 303
   imports 109, 280–1, 282
   policing 218
   production 11
   smuggling 285, 286
   state-owned firearms 57, 284
   stolen firearms 61, 62, 63, 286
   transparency of transfers 117
   violence and crime 179, 295
Austria
   brokering 156, 157, 161
   exports 101, 103, 107
      human rights 128, 129, 130, 131, 132
      producer dependence on 124
   imports 109
   transparency of transfers 117
Autodefensas Unidas de Colombia (AUC) 130, 141, 164
Azerbaijan 54

B2 Group 107
Bangladesh 191
Barrett Firearms Manufacturing 11, 27, 30
Bayart, Jean-François 193
bayonets 107–8
Belarus 108, 129, 132
Belgium
   brokering 156, 157, 159, 161, 164
   exports 100, 101, 103, 107
      human rights 125, 129, 130, 132
      producer dependence 124
   imports 109, 120–1, 123
   MANPADS 81
   transparency of transfers 117
Belize 234
Benin 113, 152
Beretta 22, 27, 31
Bersa S.A. 20, 123
Biting the Bullet (BtB) project 2, 252, 259–62
Bloomfield, Lincoln 58
Blowpipe 82, 84, 85
BMS *see* United Nations, First Biennial Meeting of States
Bolivia 18, 21, 51, 52
Bonn–Berlin process 270
Bosnia and Herzegovina 133
Botswana 123, 193
Bougainville 5, 293–7
   disposal programmes 277, 296–7
   leakage 287, 288, 289
Boutros-Ghali, Boutros 270
Brazil
   exports 100, 101, 102, 103, 107, 134
      human rights 128, 129, 130, 131
      producer dependence on 122–3
   gun control 43, 69–71, 72
   imports 109
   policing 232, 233
   production 7, 11, 17, 18, 21–2, 122–3
   stockpiles 51, 52, 53, 54
   transparency of transfers 116, 117
Bremer, Paul 44
brokering 4, 141–71
   Brazil 70
   definitions of 143
   licensing 147, 149, 153–7, 161, 166
   monitoring 252–3, 256, 259
   national regulations 151–66
   regional control initiatives 148–51
   stockpile security 56
Browning Hi-Power 34
Browning M2 heavy machine gun 32, 34
BtB *see* Biting the Bullet
Bulgaria
   arms embargo on UNITA 265, 269

INDEX

brokering
    extraterritorial jurisdiction 159, 160
    licensing 153, 154, 155, 156, 157
    penalties 161
  destruction programmes 58, 60
  exports 103, 129, 132
  MANPADS 82, 88
  RPG-7 manufacture 36
  transparency of transfers 117
Bureau of Alcohol, Tobacco, Firearms
  and Explosives (ATF) 12, 119
Burkina Faso 113, 132, 193
Burundi 109, 129

C2 Group 107–8
Cambodia 56, 88, 89, 131
Cameroon 193, 194–5, 196
Canada
  crime and violence 62, 179, 187
  disposal programmes 57, 58
  exports 101, 104, 129
  gun control 43, 68–9, 192
  homicides 62, 68
  imports 100, 108, 109, 120, 121
  stockpile lethality 53
  stolen firearms 61, 62, 63
  transparency of transfers 117
Cape Verde 113
carbines 29–30
Caribbean
  firearms deaths 175, 176, 177, 178, 199–200
  stockpiles 50
Carl Gustaf recoilless rifle 33, 35
Cassese, Antonio 181
categories of weapons 118
Cenrex 163
Central African Republic 194, 195
Central America, producers 9, 10
Central Europe, violence and crime 176, 178, 179, 200
Centre for Humanitarian Dialogue 259
Chabal, Patrick 193
Chad 194
Chechnya 90, 92, 109, 132
children, policing 236
Chile
  imports 123
  production 17, 18, 22–3
  stockpiles 51, 52, 53
China
  destruction programmes 58, 60
  exports 100, 101, 104
    C2 Group 108
    human rights 126, 128, 130, 131, 133
  imports 108, 128, 129
  MANPADS 81, 82, 83, 84, 88, 93, 94
  policing 220
  producers 10, 82
  RPG-7 manufacture 36
  transparency of transfers 117
Civil Reserve Air Fleet (CRAF) (US) 91
civil society, monitoring 257, 258–62, 271
civilian firearms
  brokering 155
  disposal programmes 57
  Iraqi stockpiles 47
  Kyrgyzstan 313–14
  Latin America 17, 50, 51–4

Pacific 277, 286–7
  producers 13–14, 16, 17, 18–19, 22
  sidearms 28
  Sri Lanka 59
civilian ownership
  Africa 198
  Australia 184–6, 283
  deterrence 182–6
  Kyrgyzstan 312–14, 316
  Pacific 277, 282–3, 300–1
  self-defence 174, 181, 198
  stockpiles 3, 43–75
  violence and crime 173, 174
Colombia
  imports 108, 109, 123, 134
    Brazilian 123
    human rights 128, 129–30
    United States 120
  MANPADS 88
  production 18, 23–4
  stockpiles 51, 52, 53
Colt's Manufacturing 11, 27
Common List of Military Equipment (EU) 155
community links, policing 227–9
Companhia Brasileira de Cartuchos (CBC) 21, 22, 123
conflict weapons
  crime in Africa 194–6
  Iraq 3, 43, 44–50, 54, 71–2
  Kosovo 197
  Pacific 289, 290–6
  Sri Lanka 59
conflicts
  deaths 175
  Iraq 44–50
  Pacific 290–6
  post-conflict police reforms 240–1
  role of brokers in 142
Congo, Democratic Republic of 109, 126, 130
Consolidated Appropriations Act (2004) (US) 12
control
  accessibility thesis 182–6
  Argentina 18–19
  Australia 67, 184–6, 192, 301, 302, 303
  Canada 43, 68–9, 192
  effectiveness of legislation 182, 186
  exports 144, 155, 158
  illicit brokering 141–66
  MANPADS 90–4
  Pacific 300–3
  United Kingdom 67, 188–9, 192
  United States 66–7
  violence and crime 182–6
Control Arms campaign 1
Conventional Armed Forces in Europe (CFE) Treaty 78
Cook Islands 283, 285, 302
corruption, policing 233
Costa Rica 130
costs of gun crime 191, 199, 290–6
craft production 8, 10, 24, 277, 288
crime 2, 4, 173–211
  accessibility thesis 182–6
  Africa 192–9
  Brazil 69–70
  brokering penalties 160–2
  Canada 62, 68
  economic costs 190

  Iraq 44, 50
  Kyrgyzstan 315–16
  Latin America and the Caribbean 50, 52
  monitoring 255
  Pacific 295
  police criminality 233
  prevention programmes 190
  South Africa 63
  Sri Lanka 59
  stolen firearms 60–5
  sub-machine guns 30
  Thailand 71
  United Kingdom 67
  see also policing
Croatia 129, 133
crowd control 233–5, 312
CS (tear) gas, policing 223, 235
Cunningham, Charles 70–1
customs 101, 108, 116, 120–1, 146
Cyprus 100, 108, 109, 132
Czech Republic
  brokering 153, 156, 157, 158, 160, 161
  C2 Group exports 108
  exports 101, 102, 104, 134
    human rights 129, 130, 131, 132
  imports 101
  transparency of transfers 117

Dade County, Florida 57
Dakar, Senegal 193, 194
Davis Industries 119
DDR see disarmament, demobilization, and reintegration
deactivated guns 189
death squads, policing 233
deaths
  Kyrgyzstan 315–17
  non-conflict 174–204
  see also homicides; suicides
demonstrations, policing 233–5, 312
Denmark 109, 124
detainees, police executions 230–2
deterrence 182–6, 190
development programmes, monitoring 251–2
differentiated use of force 220–4
disarmament 56–60
  Brazil 69–71, 72
  Iraq 49–50
  Pacific 294, 295–300
disarmament, demobilization, and reintegration (DDR) 196, 256
disposal programmes
  Australia gun control 184–6
  national reporting 256
  obsolescent and surplus weapons 56–60
  old police weapons 57
  Pacific 277, 295–300, 303
diversions, brokering 154, 155, 163
DNI see Dutch–Norwegian Initiative
documentation, brokering 144, 146, 163–4
double-licensing 153, 156
drugs, Kyrgyzstan 323
DShK-38/46 heavy machine gun 32, 34
Dutch–Norwegian Initiative (DNI) 150

EAPCCO see Eastern Africa Police Chiefs Cooperation Organisation
East Timor 126, 240–1

329

Eastern Africa Police Chiefs Cooperation
    Organisation (EAPCCO) 253
Eastern Europe, violence and crime 176, 178,
    179, 200
Economic Community of West African States
    (ECOWAS) 100, 112–14, 150, 152
economic costs 190–2, 290–6
ECOWAS see Economic Community of West
    African States
Ecuador
    exports and human rights 130, 132
    production 18, 24
    stockpile 51, 52, 53
Egypt 36, 81, 82, 89, 133, 152
El Salvador 130, 240
embargoes
    brokering 142, 144, 145
    human rights 128
    monitoring 249–50, 263–71
emergency, states of, policing 220
end-user certificates (EUCs) 144, 163–4
Eritrea 87–8
Estonia 154, 155, 156, 157, 158, 160, 161
Ethiopia 128, 130
ethnic issues
    Kyrgyzstan 318
    policing 228, 236
EU see European Union
EUCs see end-user certificates
Euromissile 27
Europe
    producers 9, 10
    see also Central Europe; Eastern Europe;
        European Union; Western Europe
European Convention on Human Rights 218
European Union (EU)
    brokering 147–8, 150, 152, 155–7, 166
    embargoes 128
    exports 108, 124, 125
executions, extrajudicial 230–2, 236
exports 99–134
    Kyrgyzstan 321–2
    national reports 101
    necessity for producers 118–25
    Pacific 277, 280, 282, 303
    transparency 114–18
    see also brokering
extrajudicial execution 230–2, 236
extraterritorial jurisdiction 158–9, 161

Fábrica Boliviana de Municiones (FBM) 21
Fábrica de Armas y Municiones del Ejército
    (FAME) 25
Fábricas y Maestranzas del Ejército (FAMAE)
    22–3
Falcone, Pierre Joseph 165, 166
FAMAE see *Fábricas y Maestranzas
    del Ejército*
FAME see *Fábrica de Armas y Municiones
    del Ejército*
FARC see *Fuerzas Armadas Revolucionarias
    de Colombia*
FBM see *Fábrica Boliviana de Municiones*
Fiji Islands
    conflict 290–2
    gun ownership laws 283, 302, 303
    imports 281
    leakage 287, 288

state-owned firearms 284
stockpile security 55
FIM-43 Redeye 80, 82, 84
FIM-92 Stinger 82, 83, 84, 88
financing, illicit brokering 144
Finland
    brokering 156, 158, 159, 161
    exports 104, 124, 129, 132
    imports 109
    militia 46
    stolen firearms 63
    transparency of transfers 117, 126
fire-and-forget missiles 79
*Firearms Commerce in the United States
    (ATF)* 12
*Firearms Manufacturing and Export Report
    (ATF)* 12
Fisher, Ian 46
flags of convenience 146
'fleeing felon' 218–19
Fleishman, Jeffrey 44
FN Herstal 11, 22, 27, 28, 29, 31
FN-FAL assault rifle 22, 28, 34, 195
FN-MAG light machine gun 22, 34
Forjas Taurus 11, 22, 23, 123
Framework Convention on International Arms
    Transfers 133
France
    brokering 154, 156, 157, 160, 161, 165
    destruction programme 58
    exports 104, 107
        human rights 128, 129, 130, 131, 132
    imports 110
    MANPADS 82, 84, 93
    policing 218, 225
    producers 82, 124
    transparency of transfers 4, 116, 117
Fray Luis Beltrán (FLB) 19–20
French Polynesia 281, 282, 283, 302
Fuerzas Armadas Revolucionarias de Colombia
    (FARC) 24, 88, 108, 130

G-3 assault rifles 23, 25, 28, 29, 60
Galil rifle 23
Gambia, The 113
gender
    Bougainville conflict 295
    Krygyzstan 317
    policing 227, 235
    victims of violence 178, 179, 183–4, 194
General Dynamics 7, 27, 82
general-purpose machine guns (GPMG) 31
Geneva Process 259, 262–3
Georgia 54, 130, 132, 309
Germany
    Brazilian imports 123
    brokering 150, 157, 159, 160, 161
        licensing of 154, 155, 156
    C2 Group exports 108
    destruction programmes 58, 60
    exports 100, 101, 104, 107
        human rights 128, 129, 130, 131, 132, 133
        producer dependence on 123, 124, 125
    imports 100, 108, 110, 120
    MANPADS 81, 82
    policing 236–7
    RPG-7 manufacture 36
    Small Arms Trade Transparency Barometer 4

stockpiles 53, 54, 56, 60
transparency of transfers 116, 117
Ghana 113, 194, 196
global small arms trade, annual update 100–14
Global Witness 112
Glock 26, 27, 49, 57
governments
    firearms theft 65
    Russian Federation 15, 16
    stockpile security 54–60
    transparency in the United States 12
GPMG see general-purpose machine guns
Greece 81, 87, 110, 124, 236
grenade launchers 27, 32, 34
    see also rocket-propelled grenade launchers
Guinea 113, 131, 193, 196
Guinea-Bissau 113

Heckler & Koch (H&K) 7, 27, 28, 29, 31, 126
Hezbollah 37, 89, 93
High-Precision Weapons Corporation 15
highway bandits, Cameroon 193, 194–5, 196
HN-5 82, 84, 88
homicides 174–202
    accessibility thesis 182–6
    Africa 192–3
    Australia 184–6
    Canada 62, 68
    Iraq 44
    Kyrgyzstan 315–16
    Latin America and the Caribbean 50, 52–4, 69
    Pacific 295
    substitution effect 186–90
    Thailand 71
    United Kingdom 189
Honduras 110, 130, 236
Hong Kong 129, 131
human rights 1–2
    Algeria 102
    brokering 161
    Indonesia 99
    policing 4, 213–43
    transfers 99, 125–33
    violence and crime 173
Human Rights Watch 1, 112, 127, 235, 271
human security movement 173
Hungary 131, 153, 156, 157, 160, 161

IACP see International Association of Chiefs
    of Police
IANSA see International Action Network
    on Small Arms
ICCPR see *International Covenant
    on Civil and Political Rights*
ICVS see *International Crime Victim
    Surveys*
IFM see Isatabu Freedom Movement
illicit firearms
    Africa 194, 198
    amnesties 57, 59, 71, 188, 298–300, 303
    Australia 185
    Canada 68
    Kyrgyzstan 314–17
    Latin America 24, 51, 52
    Pacific 298–300, 303
    Pakistan 195
    Thailand 71
    United Kingdom 188

INDEX

illicit trade
  Brazil 70
  brokering 141–66
  Canada 68
  ECOWAS 112
  Kyrgyzstan 311, 322–4
  MANPADS 88–9, 90, 92–3
  Mexico 52
  monitoring 249–72
  Pacific 277, 285–90
  Serbian exports 103
  stolen firearms 60–1
  through Saudi Arabia 102
  through Yemen 102
Imbel 21, 22
IMI *see* Israeli Military Industries
imports 99–134
  Kyrgyzstan 313
  Pacific 280–2, 303
  United States 13
IMU *see* Islamic Movement of Uzbekistan
IMZ *see* Ishevsky Mekhanichesky Zavod
India 87, 101, 128, 235
Indonesia
  imports 99, 108, 128, 130–1
  policing 225–6, 233, 235
  stockpile security 55, 56
Industria Militar (INDUMIL) 23, 24
Industrias Ruiz Cabañas 25
Industrias Tecnos 25
Ingram 24, 31
injuries
  cost of gun crime 191
  Kyrgyzstan 315, 317
  rubber bullets 222–3
Inoguchi, Kuniko 58
instrumentality theory 186–90
Interlaken process 270
International Action Network on Small Arms (IANSA) 2, 133, 259–62
International Alert 259
International Association of Chiefs of Police (IACP) 223
International Covenant on Civil and Political Rights (ICCPR) 214, 216–17
International Crime Victim Surveys (ICVS) 179
international customs data 101, 108, 116
International Peace Information Service 127
International Peace Monitoring Team (IPMT) 298–9
international tracing instrument 251
intimate partner violence 183–4
IPMT *see* International Peace Monitoring Team
Iran
  exports 102, 103, 104, 134
    C2 Group 108
    human rights 128, 132, 133
    into Iraq 48
    RPG-7 manufacture 36
Iraq
  assault rifles 28–9
  brokering 165
  embargoes 100, 266
  fatalities 50
  human rights 128
  MANPADS 77, 84, 90
  RPG-7 35, 36, 37

  stockpiles 3, 43, 44–50, 54, 71–2
  United States production 11
Iraqi Civil Defence Corps 49
Ireland, Republic of 124
Isatabu Freedom Movement (IFM) 288, 292–3
Ishevsky Mekhanichesky Zavod (IMZ) 14, 15, 16, 122
Islam, Kyrgyzstan 310–11, 320, 324
Islamic Movement of Uzbekistan (IMU) 310, 320, 324
Israel
  brokering 161
  exports 104, 129, 130, 131
  imports 101, 108, 110, 120, 121, 134
  MANPADS 93
  mortars 33
  policing 220, 222
  production 11, 30, 36
  stockpile security 56
  transparency of transfers 117
Israeli Military Industries (IMI) 11, 27, 29, 31, 36
Italy
  brokering 161
    jurisdiction 163–4
    licensing 153, 154, 155, 156, 157
    penalties 160
  exports 100, 101, 104, 107
    human rights 128, 129, 130, 131, 132
    producer dependence 124
    to Cyprus 108
  imports 110
  MANPADS 81, 87
  transparency of transfers 117
Ivory Coast 109, 131
Izhmash (Izhevsk Arms Factory) 11, 14, 15, 16, 27, 29, 122

Jamaica 53, 54, 191, 238
Japan
  brokering 161
  exports 101–2, 105, 107, 131, 132
  imports 100, 108, 110, 120
  MANPADS 82, 84
  suicide 187
  transparency of transfers 117
Javelin ATGW 33, 82, 84
Jordan 47
juvenile prisoners/detainees 231

Kashmir 47
Kazakhstan 132, 311
Kenya 57, 133, 194, 233
kinetic energy weapons 81
Kiribati 283, 284, 302, 303
Kleck, Gary 61
KMP *see* Kovrov Mechanical Plant
knives 107–8
Kosovo 191, 197
Kovrov Mechanical Plant (KMP) 14, 15, 122
KPV heavy machine gun 33
Kuwait 10–11, 110, 120
Kyrgyzstan 5, 309–27

Lakhani, Hemant 162–3
Laos 131
Lasserre S.A. 20, 123
Latin America
  firearms deaths 175, 176, 177, 178, 199–200

  non-fatal crime 179
  production 7, 16–26
  stockpiles 50–4, 60, 71–2
Latvia 132, 153, 161, 163
law enforcement *see* policing
leakages
  Iraq 44–50
  Kyrgyzstan 314–15
  Pacific 285, 286–90
  police stockpiles 230
  stockpiles 43–4, 54–65, 71–2
Lebanon
  civilian gun ownership 47
  MANPADS 89, 93
  transfers 108, 110, 132, 134
legislation
  Australia 184–6
  brokering 147, 162–6
  effectiveness 182, 186
  national 66–71, 255
  Pacific 277, 300–3
  self-defence 181
  transfers and human rights 133
  United Kingdom 188–9, 192
  United States 12, 66–7
Lesotho 193
Liberation Tigers of Tamil Eelam (LTTE) 37, 89
Liberia
  conflict weapons and crime 196
  disarmament of civilians 57
  embargoes 269
  illicit brokering 144, 145, 164
  imports 103, 109, 112, 127, 128, 131, 132
Libya 130, 268
licensing 66–71
  Brazil 69–71
  brokering 147, 149, 153–7, 161, 166
  exports 116, 117, 118
  Iraq 47
  Latin America 52
  Pacific 301–2
  transfers and human rights 125–6
light weapons 8, 14–16
Lithuania 87, 154, 155, 157, 160, 161
LTTE *see* Liberation Tigers of Tamil Eelam
Luxembourg 107, 124, 129, 132

M-4 carbine 11, 29
M-14 rifles 29
M-16 assault rifles 11, 12, 28
M-40 recoilless rifle 33, 34
M-107 sniper rifle 11
machetes 107–8
machine guns 31–2
  heavy 31–2, 34, 46
  light 31, 34
  producers 13, 27, 119, 120
MAG 31
Makarov pistol 28, 34, 319, 321
Malawi 224, 227
Malaysia
  MANPADS 87
  stockpile security 55, 56
  transfers 120, 123, 130, 131
Mali 113
man-portable air defence systems (MANPADS) 3, 15, 33, 46, 77–97
MANPADS *see* man-portable air defence systems

331

manufacturers *see* producers
marking, national reporting 256, 302
marksmen 29
Marlin Firearms 13–14
Marshall Islands 283, 284
Matra BAe Dynamics 82, 83
Mauritius 234, 240
mentally disabled people, policing 236–7
Mexico
    exports 105, 129
    imports 110
    MANPADS 87
    production 17, 18, 24–5
    stockpiles 51, 52, 53
    transparency of transfers 117
Mezosy, Geza 164
Micronesia, Federated States of 280, 283, 284, 302, 303
Middle East
    firearms deaths 175, 177, 200
    producers 9, 10
military firearms
    inventories 46
    Iraq 44–50
    Kyrgyzstan 312–13
    Latin America 51
    market 38
    Pacific 284, 287–90
    pistols 28
    producers 10–11, 13–14, 16
    stockpile security 54–6
Mine Ban Convention 261
Minimi 31
Minin, Leonid 163–4
MISAC *see* Monitoring the Implementation of Small Arms Controls
missile-launching weapons *see* man-portable air defence systems
Mistral 82, 83, 84
Moldova 103
Molot 14, 15, 16, 122
Mombasa attack (2002), MANPADS 85, 86, 87–8, 90
monitoring 5, 249–71
Monitoring the Implementation of Small Arms Controls (MISAC) 259
Montenegro *see* Serbia and Montenegro
mortars 8, 33–4, 46
Mozambique 193, 230, 240
murders *see* homicides
Myanmar 88, 128, 131

Nadi Framework 301
Namibia 129, 130, 193, 240
National Rifle Association (NRA) 70–1
NATO *see* North Atlantic Treaty Organization
Nauru 280, 281, 283, 284, 285, 302
necessity, policing 218–19
Nepal 109, 120, 121, 125
Netherlands
    brokering 150, 153, 154, 155, 156, 158, 159, 161
    destruction programme 58
    exports 108, 124, 130
    imports 110
    MANPADS 81
New Caledonia 280, 281, 282, 283, 284, 302
New Zealand

Bougainville conflict 294, 295
    civilian ownership 283, 301, 302, 303
    imports 120, 123, 280, 281, 282
    leakage 287, 288
    smuggling 285
    state-owned firearms 284
    violence and crime 179, 295
NGOs *see* non-governmental organizations
Nicaragua 130, 132
Niger 113, 132
Nigeria
    illicit shipments for Liberia 144
    imports 114
    violence and crime 193, 194, 196, 198
Niue 283, 284, 285, 302
non-governmental organizations (NGOs)
    monitoring 257, 258–63, 269, 271
    UN Biennial Meeting of States 2
non-lethal force, policing 221–4
Norinco 27, 29, 31, 32, 36
North America
    producers 9, 10
    violence and crime 173, 176, 177, 178, 180, 199–200
North Atlantic Treaty Organization (NATO) 79, 81, 92, 154
North Korea
    MANPADS 81, 82, 88, 89
    transfers and human rights 126, 128, 131
Northern Alliance 322, 323
Northern Ireland, policing 221–2, 223, 234–5
Norway
    brokering 150, 155, 156, 157, 158, 159, 160, 161
    exports 105
    imports 110, 123
    MANPADS 81
    policing 221
    stolen firearms 63
    transparency of transfers 117
NRA *see* National Rifle Association
NSV heavy machine gun 32, 34

OAS *see* Organization of American States
obsolescent weapons, destruction 57–60
offshore financing, illicit brokering 144
Oleoresin Capsicum (OC) sprays 223
Omega Foundation 11
Organization of American States (OAS), brokering 143, 147–9, 152, 166
Organization for Security and Co-operation in Europe (OSCE)
    brokering 149–50
    Document on Small Arms and Light Weapons 125
    intergovernmental transparency 114
    Kyrgyzstan 312
    MANPADS 93
    monitoring 253
    Principles Governing Conventional Arms Transfers 125
OSCE *see* Organization for Security and Co-operation in Europe

Pacific 5, 277–305
    conflict 290–6
    control legislation 300–3
    disarmament 296–300

    stockpiles 55, 56, 277, 280–5
    trade 280–90
    see also Asia-Pacific
Pacific Islands Forum 252, 278–9
Pakistan
    conflict weapons and crime 195
    exports 102, 103, 105, 128, 130, 131, 134
    imports 101, 123, 131
    MANPADS 81, 82, 87
    RPG-7 manufacture 36
Palau 283, 284, 302
Palestine 47, 56
Palestinian National Authority (PNA) 89, 240
Panama 130, 141
Papua New Guinea
    Bougainville conflict 293–6
    civilian ownership 283, 301, 302
    home-made firearms 288
    imports 280, 281, 282
    leakage 288, 289
    smuggling 277, 285–6
    state-owned firearms 284
    violence and crime 295
Paraguay 18, 25, 51, 52, 123, 130
parliamentary transparency 114
Participatory Rural Appraisal (PRA) 191
Patten Report 223, 234–5
PBRs *see* plastic baton rounds
pepper spray 223
Peru 18, 25, 51, 53, 123, 130
Peshawar District, Pakistan 195
Philippines
    imports 121, 123
    policing 225, 226
    reform measures 67
    stockpile security 55, 56, 63
pistols 8, 27–8, 34
    Argentina 20
    Brazil 22
    Ecuador 24
    United States 13, 14, 119, 120, 121
plastic baton rounds (PBRs) 223, 234–5
PNA *see* Palestinian National Authority
Poland
    brokering 154, 155, 157, 159, 160, 161
    exports 129, 130
    MANPADS 82
    RPG-7 manufacture 36
police 2, 4, 213–47
    crime in Africa 194, 195
    Iraq 49
    Kyrgyzstan 313
    old weapons 57
    Pacific 284, 287–90
    Solomon Islands 298–9
    stockpiles 43
policing 2, 4, 213–47
    community links 227–9
    criminality 196, 233
    crowd control 233–5
    Kyrgyzstan 312
    Latin American production 17
    political manipulation 232–4
    post-conflict reforms 240–1
    training 224–7
    vulnerable persons 235–7
Political Terror Scale 127
politics, police 232–4

INDEX

Portugal
  exports 105, 124, 129, 130, 132
  imports 110
  policing 216–17
  transparency of transfers 117
PRA *see* Participatory Rural Appraisal
prisoners, police executions 230–2
privacy 12
private security companies (PSCs) 196–8
privatization of security 174, 196–8, 199
Pró Legítima Defesa 70–1
producers 3, 7–41
  export dependency 118–25, 134
  Kyrgyzstan 321–2
  Latin America 16–26
  MANPADS 77, 78, 81–3
  Pacific 303
  Russian Federation 14–16
  United States 10–14, 67
Productos Mendoza 25
proportionality, policing 218–19, 225
prosecutions, illicit brokering 162–6
PSCs *see* private security companies
public transparency 114

QW-1/QW-2 82, 84

RAMSI *see* Regional Assistance Mission to Solomon Islands
Raytheon–Lockheed Martin 27, 82
recoilless guns 33
refugees, policing 236
Regional Assistance Mission to Solomon Islands (RAMSI) 299–300
regions
  brokering 147, 148–51
  national reporting 257
registration 66–71
  active-universal or passive-partial 43, 68
  Australia 62
  brokering 147, 149, 159, 161
  Canada 62, 68–9
  Kyrgyzstan 313
  Latin America 52, 69–71
  Pacific 302
  stolen firearms 60, 62
  Thailand 71
  United States 12
regulation *see* control
Remington Arms Co. 13–14
rental markets, Canada 68
replicas 189
reporting
  arms embargoes 267
  brokering 160, 161
  monitoring 249–50, 254–8
  policing 237
responsibility 65, 66–71
Revolutionary United Front (RUF) 132, 164
revolvers 8, 20, 21, 22, 23, 27–8
  United States 13, 14, 119, 120, 121
rifles 29–30
  Brazil 22
  Russia 122
  United Kingdom 189
  US producers 13, 14, 119, 120, 121
Right-to-Carry (RTC) laws 186
rocket-propelled grenade launchers (RPGs) 8, 34,

35–7, 46
Romania
  brokering 153, 155, 156, 158, 161
  destruction programme 58
  exports 101, 105
  RPG-7 36, 37
  transparency of transfers 117, 118
Royal Canadian Mounted Police 57
Royal Ordnance 22
RPD light machine gun 31, 34
RPF-7 rocket-propelled grenade launcher 8, 34, 35–7, 49
RPGs *see* rocket-propelled grenade launchers
RPK-74 31
rubber bullets 221–3
RUF *see* Revolutionary United Front
Russia
  arms trafficking to Afghanistan 322, 323
  assault rifles 28
  destruction programmes 58, 60
  exports 100, 101, 102, 105, 134
    Cyprus 108
    human rights 128, 129, 130, 131, 133
    producer dependence on 121–2
  grenade launchers 32
  imports 109, 128, 132
  machine guns 32
  MANPADS 79, 81
    attacks 90
    authorized transfers 87
    control of 92–3, 94
    illicit transfers 88
    producers 82
    stockpiles 83, 84
  pistols 28
  producers 8, 10–11, 14–16
  RPG-7 35–7
  stockpile security 54–5, 103
  transparency of transfers 117
Rwanda 128, 130, 132, 265

SA-7 79, 80, 82, 83
  information 86
  Mombasa attack (2002) 77, 87–8
  stockpiles 84
  transfers 87–8, 90
SA-14 82, 90
SA-16 Igla 82, 83, 84, 87, 89, 92
SA-18 82, 84, 87, 90, 92–3
Saab Bofors 35, 82
SADC *see* Southern African Development Community
SAF sub-machine gun 23
Salopek, Paul 127
Samoa 281, 283, 284, 285, 302, 303
sanctions 263–71, 291
Santa Barbara Sistemas 7
Saudi Arabia
  exports 105, 128, 133
  imports 100, 102, 108, 111, 123, 128, 134
  MANPADS 90
  stockpile security 55, 102
security
  Kyrgyzstan 317–18
  privatization of 196–8, 199
  see also stockpile security
SEESAC *see* South Eastern Europe Clearinghouse for the Control of Small Arms and Light

Weapons
self-defence
  accessibility thesis 182–6
  crime in Africa 198
  frequency of defensive uses 184
  international law 181
  Kyrgyzstan 314
  Pacific licensing laws 301
  policing 217–18
  violence and crime 173, 174
Sellier & Bellot 27
Senegal
  imports 101, 114
  violence and crime 193, 194, 195, 196, 198
Serbia and Montenegro 58, 103, 129, 131, 133, 144
sexual minorities, policing 236
SG 540 assault rifles 23
shotguns
  Argentina 20, 21
  Brazil producers 22
  United Kingdom 189
  US producers 13, 14, 119, 120
Shrem, Marco 141
Sierra Leone
  arms embargo 112, 268, 269
  brokering 152, 164
  conflict weapons and crime 196
  illicit trade 112, 164
  imports 109, 114, 128, 132
Singapore
  exports 102, 103, 105, 129, 130, 131, 134
  grenade launchers 32
  imports 123
  MANPADS 81, 82
  production 11
Singapore Technologies Kinetics 11, 27, 29
sky marshals 66
Slovak Republic 36
  brokering 154, 155, 156, 157, 160, 161
  exports 129, 131
Slovenia 153, 154, 156, 157, 160, 161
Small Arms and Cartridges Corporation 15
small arms definition 8
small arms and light weapons (SALW), definitions 8, 107–8
Small Arms Trade Transparency Barometer 3–4, 99, 115–18, 134
Smith & Wesson 13–14, 27, 119
smuggling *see* illicit trade
sniper rifles 27, 29
Society for the Defense of Tradition, Family and Property 70–1
Soghanalian, Sarkis 165, 166
Solomon Islands 5
  civilian ownership 283, 302, 303
  conflict weapons 289
  disarmament programme 58, 277, 296, 298–300
  home-made firearms 288
  human costs 292–3
  imports 280
  leakage 287, 288
  police weapons 230
  state-owned firearms 284
  stockpile security 55
Somalia
  arms embargoes 264

333

SMALL ARMS SURVEY 2004

illicit brokering to 163
imports 109, 128
MANPADS 88
RPG-7 35
stockpile security 54
trafficking through Yemen 102
South Africa
   Brazilian imports 123
   brokering
      arrests 164
      definition 143
      extraterritorial jurisdiction 159
      legislation 161
      licensing 154, 155, 156, 157
   crime 63
   destruction programmes 58, 60
   exports 105, 128, 129, 130
   MANPADS 87
   policing 217, 218, 219, 229
   production 11
   reform measures 67
   stockpile lethality 53, 54
   stolen firearms 63, 64
   transparency of transfers 117
   violence and crime 192, 193
South America, producers 9, 10
South Eastern Europe Clearinghouse for the Control of Small Arms and Light Weapons (SEESAC) 252
South Korea
   exports 106, 129, 130, 131, 132
   imports 10–11, 100, 108, 111, 120
   transparency of transfers 117
South-East Asia
   deaths 175, 176, 177, 200
   stockpile security 54–5, 56
Southern African Development Community (SADC) 252
Southern African Regional Police Chiefs Co-operation Organisation (SARPCCO) 217
Soviet Union
   destruction of surpluses 60
   Kyrgyztan 309
   MANPADS 79, 81
   RPG-7 35
   stockpile security 54–5
   see also Russia
Spain
   exports 102, 106
      Cyprus 108
      human rights 128, 129, 130, 131, 132
      producer dependence on 124
   imports 111, 120
   stolen firearms 63
   transparency of transfers 117
specialist munitions, UK police 222
squad fire support weapons 31
Sri Lanka 59, 108, 109, 131
Starburst 82, 84
Starstreak 82, 84, 87
states of emergency, policing 220
Stinger 83, 85, 86, 87, 89, 92
Stinger Project Group (SPG) 81, 82, 92
Stockholm process 270
stockpile security 54–65, 86–90
   brokering 143–4, 145
   Kyrgyzstan 314–15
   Latin America 52–4

MANPADS 78, 84, 90
Pacific 277
stockpiles 3, 43–75
   Iraq 43, 44–50
   Kyrgyzstan 312–13
   Latin America 50–4
   leakage to terrorist groups 102
   MANPADS 77, 83–4
   monitoring 255
   Pacific 277, 280–5
   registration 66–71
   transfers 99
storage
   firearms theft 65
   Kyrgyzstan 315
   Pacific 277
   police firearms 229–30
   stockpiles 43
Sturm, Ruger & Co. 13–14, 119
sub-machine guns 27, 30–1
sub-Saharan Africa
   conflict-related deaths 175
   crime and violence 192–9
   producers 9, 10
substitution effect 186–90
Sudan 109, 132, 133
suicides 174–80, 199–202
   accessibility thesis 182–6
   Africa 192–3
   means 187
   Pacific 295
   substitution effect 186–90
surface-to-air missiles *see* man-portable air defence systems
Suriname 130
Swaziland 193
Sweden
   brokering 156, 158, 159, 160, 161
   exports 106, 124, 130, 132
   imports 111
   MANPADS 81, 82, 84
   policing 221
   stolen firearms 63
   transparency of transfers 117
Switzerland
   brokering 153, 154, 156, 157, 160, 161
   exports 106, 107, 128, 129, 131, 132, 133
   firearms inventories 46
   imports 101, 111
   MANPADS 81, 82
   RPG-7 manufacture 36
   transparency of transfers 117
Syria 48, 93

Taiwan 111
Tajikistan 309, 310, 320, 322–4
Taliban 92, 128, 132, 310
Tamils 37, 59, 89
Tanzania 193
tax havens, illicit brokering 144
Taylor, Charles 269
Temex 144
terrorism
   leakage from Saudi Arabia 102
   MANPADS 77, 78, 89, 90, 92–3
   policing 220
   RPG-7 36–7
   United States 66

Thailand
   crime and violence 71
   exports and human rights 130, 131
   imports 111, 120, 121
   Israeli stockpiles 56
   MANPADS 89, 93
   policing 232
   RPG-7 manufacture 36
   stockpile security 55
thefts of firearms 43, 54–6, 60–5, 66, 185
thermobaric warheads 36
third-party brokering 144, 148, 155–6, 162, 163–4
time-to-crime studies, stolen firearms 60
Togo 114
Tokarev pistol 28, 34
Tonga 280, 281, 283, 284, 302, 303
Torres Strait 286
tourism, Fiji Islands 290–2
TOZ *see* Tulsky Oruzheiny Zavod
tracing 256
trade *see* illicit trade; transfers
training
   MANPADS 85, 89, 94
   policing 224–7
transfers 2, 3–4, 99–139
   exports 99, 100–8
   global trade 100–14
   human rights 125–33
   illicit brokering 141–66
   imports 100–1, 108–14
   Iraq 44
   Kyrgyzstan 321–2
   Latin America and the Caribbean 18, 50
   MANPADS 77, 83, 87–9, 92–4
   Mexico 52
   monitoring 5, 249–71
   Pacific 280–5, 303
   transparency 114–18
   United States 11
transit trade, Cyprus 108
transparency 114–18
   import and export data 100–1
   monitoring 252, 253–4
   Small Arms Trade Transparency Barometer 3–4
   transfers 99
   United States 12
transportation, illicit brokering 144–7
Treaty on Conventional Forces in Europe (1993) 58
truncheons 107–8
Tulsky Oruzheiny Zavod (TOZ) 14, 15, 122
Turkey
   exports 106, 130, 131, 132
   imports 101, 111
   MANPADS 81
   transparency of transfers 117
Turkmenistan 311
Tuvalu 283, 284, 302, 303

Uganda 56, 109, 130, 133, 193
Uighur 310
Ukraine
   brokering 155, 156, 157, 158, 160–1
   destruction of surpluses 60
   exports and human rights 132
   MANPADS 92–3

INDEX

UNDDA *see* United Nations, Department for Disarmament Affairs
UNDP *see* United Nations, Development Programme
União Nacional Para a Independência Total de Angola (UNITA) 129, 265, 269
UNICEF *see* United Nations, Children's Fund
UNICRI *see* United Nations, Interregional Crime and Justice Institute
UNIDIR *see* United Nations, Institute for Disarmament Research
unintentional deaths 174–80, 202, 295
UNITA *see* União Nacional Para a Independência Total de Angola
United Arab Emirates 111, 123, 132
United Kingdom
  exports 106, 107
    arms sales to Indonesia 99
    C2 Group 108
    human rights 128, 129, 130, 131, 132
    producer dependence on 124
  gun control 67, 188–9, 192
  imports 111, 120
  MANPADS 82, 84, 87
  mortars 33
  policing 221–3, 226, 228, 231, 234–5, 239
  stolen firearms 63
  transparency of transfers 117
United Nations (UN)
  Basic Principles on the Use of Force and Firearms by Law Enforcement Officials 214–17, 219–27, 229–31, 234, 237–8
  brokering 148
  Children's Fund (UNICEF) 251
  Code of Conduct for Law Enforcement Officials 214, 215, 216–17, 227, 232, 233, 235
  Commission on Human Rights 1
  Comtrade 103–6
  Conference on the Illicit trade in Small Arms and Light Weapons in All its Aspects 141, 250
  Conference process 249, 250–63
  Declaration on the Elimination of Violence against Women 227, 235
  Department for Disarmament Affairs (UNDDA) 254, 258, 263
  Development Programme (UNDP) 251, 257, 258, 263
  embargoes 5, 128, 249–50, 263–71
  Firearm Regulation Study (1998) 61
  First Biennial Meeting of States (BMS) 2
    brokering 147–8, 152
    destruction of surpluses 58
    monitoring 249, 250–1, 260
    reporting 254
  Human Rights Committee 216–17
  Institute for Disarmament Research (UNIDIR) 251, 258
  International Crime Victim Surveys 179
  Interregional Crime and Justice Institute (UNICRI) 179
  Latin America and the Caribbean 50
  monitoring 249–72
  Principles on the Effective Prevention and Investigation of Extra-legal, Arbitrary and Summary Executions 225, 230
  Programme of Action 2, 50, 147, 151, 249–64, 271–2
  Programme for Coordination and Assistance for Security and Development (PCASED) 112
  Register of Conventional Arms 93, 115, 253
  Report of the Panel of Governmental Experts on Small Arms 8
  Small Arms Conference (2001) 2, 147
  UN Firearms Protocol 252
United States
  Afghanistan 89
  assault rifles 28–9
  brokering 160, 161
    extraterritorial jurisdiction 158
    licensing 154, 156, 157
    regulation 162–3
    trials 165
  Bureau of Alcohol, Tobacco, Firearms and Explosives (ATF) 11
  carbines 29
  civilian firearms 51
  Consolidated Appropriations Bill 66–7
  crime and violence 179, 187, 189–90, 191
  exports 100, 101, 106, 107
    dependence of producers on 119–21
    human rights 128, 129, 130, 131, 132
  frequency of defensive uses 184
  grenade launchers 32
  gun ownership as deterrence 186
  imports 100, 101, 108, 111
    European 124
    Latin American 17, 18, 19, 20, 22, 123
  Iraq 44–5, 49–50
  machine guns 31
  MANPADS 81, 82, 88, 92, 93
    Afghanistan 89
    authorized transfers 87
    stockpiles 84
  Manufacturing Census 11
  missile countermeasures on civilian aircraft 91
  National Strategy for Combating Terrorism 66
  policing 217, 223, 226, 228, 238
  producers 1, 8, 10–14, 38
  reform 66–7
  Russian imports 122
  self-defence 181
  Small Arms Trade Transparency Barometer 3–4
  stockpiles 53, 56, 57
  stolen firearms 60, 61, 62, 63
  transparency of transfers 116, 117
  victims of firearm violence 61, 183
Universal Declaration of Human Rights 181, 213–14
Uruguay 51, 52, 53
Uzbekistan 309, 310–11, 318, 322
Uzi sub-machine guns 30

V.A. Degtyaryov Plant 14, 15, 122
Vanuatu 280, 281, 283, 284, 302, 303
Venezuela
  exports and human rights 130
  imports 103, 108, 111, 120, 123, 134
  production 18, 26
  stockpiles 51, 52, 53
victims, violence, and crime 178, 179–80, 191
Vietnam 81, 82, 87, 89, 131
vigilante groups 196–8
violence 2, 4, 173–211
  accessibility thesis 182–6
  Africa 192–9
  economic costs 190–2
  Iraqi stockpiles 44
  Latin America 52–4
  Pacific 295
  United Kingdom 188–9
vulnerable persons, policing 235–7

WA *see* Wassenaar Arrangement
Wallis and Futuna 283, 284, 302
'War on Terror' 66
warning shots, policing 219
Wassenaar Arrangement (WA)
  brokering 149, 155
  categories of weapons 118
  classification 116
  MANPADS 92, 93
  monitoring 252
  transparency of transfers 114, 115, 253
Western Europe, violence and crime 175, 176, 177, 178, 179, 200
WHO *see* World Health Organization
Winchester Ammunition 11–12
Winchester Olin 27
World Health Organization (WHO) 201, 251

Yelinek, Shimon 141, 164
Yemen 88, 102, 123, 134
Yugoslavia, former
  arms embargo 268
  destruction of surpluses 60
  policing 241
  transfers and human rights 127, 128, 133

Zambia 127, 193, 194, 195, 196
Zastava Arms Company 103, 144
Zimbabwe 130, 193, 232